Pluralism in Africa

**Published under the Auspices of the
African Studies Center
University of California, Los Angeles**

Pluralism in Africa

**Edited by
Leo Kuper and M. G. Smith**

University of California Press
Berkeley, Los Angeles, and London 1971

University of California Press
Berkeley and Los Angeles, California

University of California Press, Ltd.
London, England

First California Paper-bound printing, 1971
ISBN: 0-520-01872-9

Designed by Lynn Marcus
Printed in the United States of America

Preface

The papers in this volume, except for the concluding papers, were presented to an interdisciplinary colloquium arranged by the African Studies Center, University of California, Los Angeles, and held in the spring of 1966. They deal with the nature and social consequences of pluralism, and with problems of social cohesion and change in plural societies. The contributions have been arranged in four parts: Part I is introductory and consists of theoretical papers; Part II presents case studies in precolonial, white settler, colonial, and independent African societies; Part III is a discussion of general perspectives; and Part IV presents our conclusions in regard to theories of pluralism and conceptual approaches. While the case studies deal with pluralism in African societies, the theoretical interest extends beyond the boundaries of Africa to a general concern with the relations between groups under conditions of structural, social, and cultural pluralism.

The contributions made in discussions during the colloquium were most stimulating and have been of the greatest help in developing the main themes. We gratefully acknowledge the contributions of the participants: Marilyn Affleck, Corrine Armstrong, Beryl Bellman, Daniel Biebuyck, Wairimu Bowman, Alfred Brown, John Brown, Philip Burnham, Alifeyo Chilivumbo, Francis Carney, Henry Chipembere, Marge Clark, Peter Clark, Robert Collins, Paul Doody, Harvey M. Feinberg, Walter Goldschmidt, Thomas Gosebrink, Robert Griffeth, Jan Hajda, Sondra Hale, Michael Halliwell, Charles Harper, Richard Harns, Doyle Hatt, Steve Heyneman, Lloyd C. Honore, Martin Legassick, Angelo Loiria, Clifford Lutton, Sally Moore, John Meyer, Richard Moyer, Dickson C. Mwazoli, Anthony Oberschall, Hasu Patel, Merrick Posnansky, George Phillips, John Purcell, Charlotte Quinn, Kristin Ravetz, Theodore Ravetz, Catherine Read, Barry Schutz, John Spence, Charlotte Stolmaker, Nina Terebinski, Betty Thomas, and Robert Zwinoira.

We wish to express our grateful thanks to the African Studies Center for its interest and enthusiasm, and its superb organization of the colloquium. We are especially grateful to Ailene Benson, John Brown, James Coleman, Thomas Gosebrink, Jo Mitchell, and Benjamin Thomas, all of the African Studies Center. We also thank Stephen Coddington, Edward Leddel, and Edna Bonacich for their help in preparing the papers for publication. We wish particularly to thank Grace Stimson for her editorial work on the manuscript.

L. K.
M. G. S.

Contributors

Alexandre, Pierre. Professor of Bantu Languages, École des Langues Orientals. Lecturer in Sociolinguistics, École Pratique des Hautes Études, Paris. Head of African Research Division, Centre d'Études des Relations Internationales, Fondation des Sciences Politiques. Field experience in Cameroun and Senegal. Publications include *Les Populations du Nord-Togo* (with J.-C. Froelich and R. Cornevin); *Le groupe dit Pahouin* (with Jacques Binet); *Manuel élémentaire de langue bulu; Système verbal et prédicatif du Bulu;* and *Langues et langage en Afrique noire.*

Davidson, Basil. Visiting Professor of African History, University of California, Los Angeles, 1965. Field experience in Zambia, Rhodesia, and West Africa. Publications include *Report on Southern Africa; The African Awakening; The Lost Cities of Africa; Black Mother; The African Past; Which Way Africa: The Search for a New Society;* and *A History of West Africa to the Nineteenth Century* (with F. K. Buah).

Gluckman, Max. Professor of Social Anthropology, University of Manchester, England. Field experience in South and Central Africa. Publications include *The Judicial Process among the Barotse of Northern Rhodesia; The Ideas in Barotse Jurisprudence; Custom and Conflict in Africa; Politics, Law and Ritual in Tribal Society;* and *Order and Rebellion in Tribal Africa.*

Kuper, Hilda. Professor of Anthropology, University of California, Los Angeles. Field experience in South and Central Africa and Uganda. Publications include *An African Aristocracy; The Uniform of Colour; Indian People of Natal;* and *The Swazi: A South African Kingdom.*

Kuper, Leo. Professor of Sociology, University of California, Los Angeles. Field experience in South Africa. Publications include *Durban: A Study in Racial Ecology* (with Hilstan Watts and Ronald Davies); *Passive Resistance in South Africa;* and *An African Bourgeoisie.*

Lofchie, Michael. Assistant Professor of Political Science and Associate Director of the African Studies Center, University of California, Los Angeles. Field experience in Zanzibar and East Africa. Publications include *Zanzibar: Background to Revolution.*

Mazrui, Ali A. Professor and Head of Department of Political Science, Makerere University College, University of East Africa, Makerere. Field experience in East Africa. Publications include *The Anglo-African Commonwealth: Political Friction and Cultural Fusion;* and *Towards a Pax Africana: A Study of Ideology and Ambition.*

Smith, M. G. Professor of Anthropology, University of California, Los Angeles. Field experience in West Africa and West Indies. Publications include *Government in Zazzau, 1800–1950; The Plural Society in the British West Indies; Kinship and Community in Carriacou;* and *Stratification in Grenada.*

Thompson, Leonard. Professor of African History, University of California, Los Angeles. Field experience in Southern Africa. Publications include *The Unification of South Africa, 1902–1910; The Cape Coloured Franchise;* and *Politics in the Republic of South Africa.*

Van den Berghe, Pierre L. Professor of Sociology, University of Washington, Seattle. Field experience in South Africa and Central America. Publications include *Caneville: The Social Structure of a South African Town; South Africa: A Study in Conflict; Race and Racism;* and *Africa: Social Problems of Change and Conflict* (editor).

Contents

x Contents

Part I Introduction

Introduction to Part I

There are many societies that do not readily conform to expectations derived from much of contemporary sociological theory. They are societies possessed of a minimum of common values. They appear to be maintained more by coercion than by consent. They are divided by sharp and persistent cleavages, which threaten their dissolution. Changes in their structure are often accompanied by violence and bloodshed, as in the many internal wars during the past generation, from the time of the Hindu Muslim conflict in India to the conflict between the seceding state of Biafra and the Federal government of Nigeria. The analysis of the plural structure of these societies is an important and challenging task. It is with this analysis, and its implications for social theory, that we are here concerned.

The volume opens with a general introduction to the theory of pluralism and the plural society, conceived in the tradition of J. S. Furnivall, who applied the concept of the "plural society" to tropical societies under colonial domination. The terms refer to societies with sharp cleavages between different population groups brought together within the same political unit. The characteristic expressions of pluralism, in this context, take the form of dissensus, and of conflict between racial, tribal, religious, and regional groups; and the system is maintained by domination, regulation, and force.

There is an older tradition in which pluralism refers to a dispersion of power between groups which are bound together by crosscutting loyalties, and by common values or a competitive balance of power. This is conceived to be conducive to democratic government and to the avoidance of extreme conflict in the adjustment of group interests.

The two traditions are often distinguished at the societal level by reserving the term "plural society" for conceptions in the first tradition, that of Furnivall, and the term "pluralistic society" for conceptions in the second tradition. At the structural level, they are sometimes distinguished on the basis of assumed differences in the character of the plural units: in analyses of "plural societies" the plural units are generally racial, ethnic, religious, or regional groups, while in analyses of "pluralistic societies," they are generally functionally differentiated groups. But the problem is not simply that of avoiding terminological confusion in references to the two traditions; and the two traditions do not in fact deal with analytically distinct phenomena. Racial, ethnic, regional, and religious groups in "plural societies" may be functionally differentiated, and functionally differentiated groups in "pluralistic societies" may have an ethnic, racial, regional, or religious social base. Moreover, the structure of relationships between the plural units in the two types of society may be quite similar.

Both traditions are in fact concerned with social and cultural pluralism. However, they derive quite different expectations, and develop quite different theoretical models, of the characteristic political forms of pluralism, and of the characteristic social relations between the plural sections of the society. An important question, then, is whether a more general theory can be developed, specifying the conditions that affect the political and other manifestations of pluralism and influence the relations of the plural sections toward conflict or harmonious adjustment of interests, and toward sectional domination or democratic participation. This is of special interest in relation to many of the newly independent states which comprise a diversity of peoples, since the process of national integration in these states is often conceived as a process of change from a communally differentiated society to a functionally differentiated society, in which crosscutting relationships and loyalties transcend the initial racial, ethnic, religious, and regional divisions.

These are the themes in the opening paper by Leo Kuper, entitled "Plural Societies: Perspectives and Problems." He comments on the two traditions and on an earlier paper by M. G. Smith, "Social and Cultural Pluralism," in which Smith develops a general theory of the "plural society" in the Furnivall tradition. There is discussion of the problem of effecting a synthesis of approaches in a broad theory of social change, in which pluralism is viewed as a dimension of all societies; and comment is offered on the need for inquiry into the conditions under which there may be nonviolent evolutionary change from societies characterized by divisive conflict and sectional domination to societies with adjustive relationships between the plural sections and democratic participation. The suggestion is made that the problem of peaceful transformation may be rendered less intractable if analysis proceeds in terms of a general theory of pluralism as a dimension of all societies, rather than in terms of such polar types as "conflict" and "equilibrium" (or consensual) models of society.

The second paper, "Institutional and Political Conditions of Pluralism," by M. G. Smith, extends the Furnivall tradition. Pluralism is defined, in terms of both structure and culture, as connoting simultaneously "a social structure characterized by fundamental discontinuities and cleavages, and a cultural complex based on systematic institutional diversity." M. G. Smith discusses the minimum conditions of cultural diversity and structural discontinuity which constitute pluralism, and distinguishes homogeneous, heterogeneous, and plural societies. The plural society is described as characterized by political inequality in the incorporation of the plural sections, and by the domination of a culturally distinct minority. Great importance is attached to the mode of incorporation of the plural sections as a significant and persistent influence on the structure of their relations. The paper concludes with an analysis of the modes and conditions by which plural societies may be stabilized, or by which they may be transformed into heterogeneous nation-states by abolition of the inequalities of differential incorporation.

Since these two papers were circulated in advance to members of the colloquium, who reacted to them in their own contributions, they have been retained largely in their original form, almost entirely so, in the case of M. G. Smith's paper. In the paper, "Plural Societies: Perspectives and Problems," Leo Kuper has made minor changes in the text, and adds a discussion of controversial formulations in footnotes. The paper by Pierre van den Berghe, "Pluralism and the Polity," though presented later in the colloquium, has also been included in the introduction since it is concerned with the theoretical exploration of issues raised in the first two papers. At the conceptual level, van den Berghe concentrates on pluralism in preference to the concept of the "plural society," the utility of which he questions. He treats pluralism as a variable, exploring its different dimensions, and he seeks to specify the conditions affecting the political expression of pluralism. Under what conditions is pluralism associated with despotism, and under what conditions with democracy?

During the course of the colloquium, and under the stimulus of different theoretical perspectives and of the case studies of African societies, there were continuous interchanges and movements of ideas concerning pluralism. This is already present in the introductory papers, in a changing approach by M. G. Smith from an emphasis on cultural pluralism, which is analyzed in Leo Kuper's paper, to an emphasis on the structural aspects of pluralism, which Smith develops in his own papers, and which is also stressed by Pierre van den Berghe. It is indeed present in the whole conception of the colloquium, which was originally designed for a study of plural societies, but changed, in its focus of analytic interest, under the stimulus of discussion, to the analysis of pluralism. The contributions in this colloquium may thus be read, in a sense, as documenting a continuous discourse on pluralism, which we temporarily conclude in Part IV by drawing together some of the diverse approaches here presented.

Chapter 1 Plural Societies: Perspectives and Problems*

Leo Kuper

The plural society, in the context of this colloquium, includes the colonial societies that subjected most of the peoples of the world to the domination of rulers of different race and culture. It includes the many new states that achieved independence after World War II and now seek to transform from state to nation the medley of peoples inherited in arbitrary combinations from the colonial powers. But the term is not simply a synonym for colonial societies and some of their successor states, though pluralism may find extreme expression in these societies. Rather, it denotes societies characterized by certain conditions of cultural diversity and social cleavage, in whatever way these conditions of social and cultural pluralism arise from the contact of different peoples and cultures within a single society.

There are two quite antithetical traditions in regard to the nature of societies characterized by pluralism.[1] The first tradition, which I am following, is relatively recent. It is expressed in the theory of the plural society. In this tradition, the stability of plural societies is seen as precarious and threatened by sharp cleavages between different plural sections, whose relations to each other are generally characterized by inequality. The second tradition is much older, and offers a conception (or ideal type) of the pluralistic society, in which the pluralism of the varied constituent groups and interests is integrated in a balanced adjustment, which provides conditions favorable to stable democratic government. The second tradition is well established in the United States, and I refer below to some contemporary examples of this tradition. The adoption of, or affinity for, one tradition or the other is no doubt shaped by different experiences of social life, in the colonies or in the United States, but it

* I should like to thank Doyle Hatt, John Purcell, and Nina Terrebinski for their criticisms of this paper, when it was originally presented.

seems also to derive from the opposition between two basic social philosophies expressed in the antithesis between equilibrium models of society (particularly consensual) and conflict models of society. The difficulties that arise in the attempted synthesis of these models also affect attempts to relate the different conceptions of the plural society and the pluralistic society in a broader framework.

"EQUILIBRIUM" MODEL OF PLURALISM [*]

The "equilibrium" model tends to associate democracy with pluralism.[2] Shils indeed emphasizes his view that pluralism is consistent with diverse political positions—conservatism and liberalism, laissez-faire and socialism, traditionalism and rationalism, hierarchy and egalitarianism. But he does not regard these differences in political position as crucial; he argues instead that the really crucial dividing line in politics lies between pluralistic moderation and monomaniac extremism;[3] and much of his discussion of pluralistic society concerns liberal democracy, which presumably exemplifies for him the ideal realization of the principles of pluralism.[4] Kornhauser also finds in pluralism a basis for liberal democracy. He writes that a pluralist society supports liberal democracy;[5] that liberty and democracy tend to be strong where social pluralism is strong;[6] and that where the introduction of democracy is not based on a pluralist society, democracy may readily lose out to new forms of autocracy.[7]

The political structure of the society, in the "equilibrium" model, is itself plural. A system of constitutional checks and balances is designed to effect a separation of powers among the legislature, the executive, the administrative sector, and the judiciary, and in this way to ensure pluralism in the structure of authority. The struggle for power by political

---

[*] Both terms, *equilibrium* and *model*, call for explanation. *Equilibrium* is too suggestive of harmonious relationships and static balance between groups, and is hence misleading in reference to the theories discussed. *Dynamic equilibrium* and *competitive balance* would be more satisfactory terms to convey that struggle, and that distribution of strength, between groups which are perceived as providing conditions restraining a monopoly of power, and favorable to the exercise of individual rights. Because of the use made of this paper during the colloquium and in the contributions, I have retained the term *equilibrium*. By *model*, I intend to convey that I am discussing abstract constructs and not empirical descriptions of group relations. Kornhauser specifically describes his conception as an abstract type, and as a model: Shils' approach in *The Torment of Secrecy* is largely normative—how a pluralistic society *should* work. I have abstracted from their views so as to present a model of the plural society in terms of its political form, social basis, mode of integration, and main determinants. For critical discussions of pluralist theories, see *inter alia*, Joseph R. Gusfield, "Mass Society and Extremist Politics," *American Sociological Review*, 27 (Feb. 1962), 19–30, and Charles Perrow, "The Sociological Perspective and Political Pluralism," *Social Research*, 31 (Winter 1964), 411–422.

parties and leaders is seen as the plural political counterpart of the social pluralism of competing interest groups, and as the basis for democratic rule (in the sense of popular choice among competing candidates).[8] If analysis of political process is directed to the role of elites, then political pluralism is represented by a divided elite.[9]

As the preceding references indicate, the social basis for political pluralism is to be found in social pluralism.[10] This may be conceived as a balance, and a relative autonomy, between institutional spheres. Shils, in his discussion of the pluralistic society, describes this aspect:

Every society is constructed of a set of spheres and systems: the domestic and kinship system, the political system, the economic system, the religious sphere, the cultural sphere, and the like. Different types of societies are characterized by the preponderance of one of the systems or spheres over the others. . . . The system of individualistic democracy or liberalism is characterized by an approximate balance among the spheres. Liberalism is a system of pluralism.[11]

In addition to the separation of spheres, Kornhauser emphasizes the presence of a strong structure of stable and independent groups, intermediate between the individual and the state. This provides the basis for a system of social checks and balances, a dispersion of power contributing to the maintenance of political pluralism.[12]

Integration is seen as effected in part by a system of crosscutting loyalties or multiple affiliations. Thus Kornhauser argues that a multiplicity of associations is not in itself a sufficient basis for the pluralist society. The different associations, such as ethnic associations, may be highly inclusive, encompassing many aspects of their members' lives, and thus encouraging social cleavage, divisive loyalties, and submission to authoritarian control. Hence Kornhauser insists on multiple affiliation as a further condition of pluralism.[13] This extends the concept of pluralism to the level of individual pluralism, in the sense of individual participation in a variety of plural structures. The pluralist dispersion of the individual's different roles is expected to foster diversity of interests, to restrain exclusive loyalties, and to link the plural structures together by innumerable ties of personal relationship.[14] It may also be expected to contribute to integration by promoting the diffusion of common values.

The commitment to common values is, of course, the main basis for integration in the consensual form of the "equilibrium" model. Shils, in his discussion of pluralistic societies, refers to some of these common values—sentiments of communal affinity among the elites, respect for the rule of law and belief in its sanctity, moderation in political involvement, commitment to gradual change, and recognition of the dignity of other values and activities within the society.[15] But the "equilibrium" model of the pluralistic society does not necessarily postulate consensus. Kornhauser describes it as exhibiting a fluidity and diversity of value standards which make difficult the achievement of consensus; [16] and he finds the basis for integration in the competitive balance of independent groups and in the multiple affiliation of their members.[17]

The model of the society is thus one of political pluralism, with a corresponding social pluralism in which the units are bound together by crosscutting loyalties and by common values or a competitive balance of power. It is a model that appeals to an optimistic view of society and of the relationships between social groups. The wide acceptance in the United States of models of this type as fairly descriptive of the society is encouraged by the experience in the acculturation and absorption of white immigrants from many different nations.[18] From this point of view, optimism is easy to understand. It is more difficult to understand in the context of the relationship between American whites and American Negroes. Here there is much that recalls the more pessimistic view of the plural society of conflict theory.

"CONFLICT" MODEL OF PLURAL SOCIETIES *

The "conflict" model of the plural society derives from Furnivall,[19] who applied the concept to tropical societies. For Furnivall, the political form of the plural society is one of colonial domination, which imposes a Western superstructure of business and administration on the native world, and a forced union on the different sections of the population.[20]

The social basis is a medley of peoples living side by side, but separately, within the same political unit. It is in the strictest sense a medley of peoples, "for they mix but do not combine. Each group holds by its own religion, its own culture and language, its own ideas and ways. As

---

* M. G. Smith disagrees with my description of his approach in the essay, "Social and Cultural Pluralism," as presenting a "conflict" model of the plural society. He comments that homogeneity cannot be equated with harmony, nor pluralism with conflict, and draws attention to relations of group conflict in such homogeneous societies as the Nuer, and to relations of quiescence sometimes observed in plural societies. However, I think personally that the term "conflict" is not inappropriate for the type of antagonistic relations he portrays. They are of such a nature, and so characterized by dissensus and cultural incompatibility, that their incorporation within a single society necessitates sectional domination based on coercion by force and regulation; change in these relations is usually violent, and quiescence may belie the turbulence beneath the surface (presumably as in volcanoes). This seems to me a picture of group conflict, overt or covert, manifest or latent, which distinguishes M. G. Smith's concept of the plural society, with its tendency to group violence and social disintegration, from the competitive balance and ordered adjustments of the first model. Quite apart from terminology, however, there is a major substantive problem. The type of society described by M. G. Smith and analyzed in many of the colloquium papers, has, in fact, often been characterized by sharp conflicts and violent processes of change; and one of the main themes of the colloquium concerns the modes of transformation or "depluralization" of these societies to more stable entities, less threatened by societally disruptive conflicts.

individuals they meet, but only in the market place, in buying and selling." [21] Economic symbiosis and mutual avoidance,[22] cultural diversity and social cleavage, characterize the social basis of the plural society.

In the functioning of the society, there is a primacy of economic forces, relatively freed from social restraint. Furnivall argues that the plural society, arising where economic forces are exempt from control by social will, is a specifically modern invention, because only in modern times have economic forces been set free to remold the social order; [23] and he quotes with approval, as applicable to plural societies, the following description of colonial Java by Dr. Boeke:

> There is materialism, rationalism, individualism, and a concentration on economic ends far more complete and absolute than in homogeneous western lands; a total absorption in the exchange and market; a capitalist structure with the business concern as subject, far more typical of capitalism than one can imagine in the so-called "capitalist" countries, which have grown up slowly out of the past and are still bound to it by a hundred roots.[24]

The economic forces act as determinants, creating and maintaining the plural society in situations of cultural and social diversity under colonial domination.

Integration is not voluntary, but imposed by the colonial power and the force of economic circumstances. Furnivall [25] emphasizes the prevalence of dissensus: there is a failure of the common or social will not only in the plural society as a whole, but also within each of the plural sections, which are atomized from communities with corporate life to crowds of aggregated individuals. Lacking a common social life, men in a plural society become decivilized, and share in common only those wants that they share with animal creation. Even the worship of Mammon, the sole common deity, does not create consensus, for the typical plural society is a business partnership in which bankruptcy signifies, for many partners, release rather than disaster. At many points, economic forces tend to create friction, "and the plural society is in fact held together only by pressure exerted from outside by the colonial power; it has no common will." [26] The failure of the common will is a crucial element in Furnivall's discussion of the plural society; and the institutions he discusses under the heading "Resolutions of Plural Economy," namely, caste, the rule of law, nationalism, and federalism,[27] may each be viewed as a possible mechanism for attaining some measure of consensus.

The most extensive analysis of the "conflict" model of the plural society is given by M. G. Smith in his essay, "Social and Cultural Pluralism," *

---

* As this essay is readily available, it is not reprinted here. In the course of the colloquium there was substantial revision of the conceptualization of the plural society. My comments here relate to M. G. Smith's views as they were formulated at the time the colloquium began.

first published in 1960 in the *Annals of the New York Academy of Sciences*. In the tradition of Furnivall, he sees plural societies as characterized by cultural diversity, social cleavage, and dissensus, but he organizes these characteristics within a different theoretical framework.

The political form of the plural society, in Smith's concept, is domination by one of the units, or more precisely, domination by a unit that is a cultural minority. This is in part a matter of definition. Smith argues that if the different units of the plural society were to carry on their different institutional practices, including the political, they would constitute separate societies. Since they are bound together within a single polity, however, it must follow that the formal political institutions of subordinate sections have been repressed as a condition of the political unity of the total society under control of the dominant group: "plurality of form in political institutions cannot obtain."[28] The further specification of the form of government as domination by a cultural minority is again a matter of definition, suggested perhaps by the observation that under these circumstances pluralism attains its most characteristic expression. Smith writes that when the dominant section is also a minority, the structural implications of cultural pluralism have their most extreme expression, and the dependence on regulation by force is greatest.[29] Pluralism under a dominant minority corresponds to an extreme type.

The specification of domination by one section as characteristic of plural societies is not, however, simply a matter of definition. The necessity for it arises also from theoretical consideration of the nature and consequences of cultural pluralism. Smith defines cultural pluralism as the practice of different forms of compulsory institutions, such as kinship, education, religion, and economy, these different forms being incompatible in the sense that roles are not interchangeable.[30] Since institutions combine social and cultural aspects, the culturally differentiated sections will also differ in their internal social organization.[31] There is therefore a social pluralism corresponding to the cultural pluralism, but the boundaries of the culturally differentiated units and the structurally differentiated units may not fully coincide, since there may be a marginal association between adherents of different cultural traditions, and conversely there may be social division between adherents of the same cultural tradition.[32]

Cultural pluralism is the major determinant of the structure of the plural society. It plays much the same role of primacy as economic forces in Furnivall's analysis. It is cultural pluralism that imposes the necessity for domination by a cultural section. Smith writes that "where culturally divergent groups together form a common society, the structural imperative for maintenance of this inclusive unit involves a type of political order in which one of these cultural sections is subordinated to the other. Such a condition derives from the structural requisites of society on the one hand, and the condition of wide cultural differences within some populations on the other." [33] Elsewhere, he describes the monopoly of power by one cultural section as the essential precondition for maintenance of the total society in its current form.[34]

Other factors are secondary to cultural pluralism. Thus racial differences derive social significance from cultural diversity. They are stressed in contexts of social and cultural pluralism. Culturally distinct groups of the same racial stock may even express their cultural differences in racial terms.[35] In culturally homogeneous units, on the other hand, racial differences lack social significance.[36] Hierarchic race relations in a society reflect conditions of cultural heterogeneity and tend to lapse or lose their hierarchic character as cultural uniformity increases.[37]

Plural societies are held together by regulation and not by integration. Smith appears to restrict the term "integration" to a social cohesion which derives from consensus. He writes that "social quiescence and cohesion differ sharply, and so do regulation and integration." [38] There is no predominance of common values and of common motivations in the plural society, and in consequence the society must be held together by regulation. This regulation consists in the rigid and hierarchical ordering of the relations between the different sections. Since the various sections are culturally differentiated, consensus is a remote possibility. Further, the subordinate sections are unlikely to accord equal value and legitimacy to the preservation of the hierarchic pattern. Thus authority, power, and regulation are of crucial significance in maintaining, controlling, and coordinating the plural society. Changes in the social structure presuppose political changes, and these usually take a violent form.[39]

Comparing the approaches of Furnivall and Smith, there is basic agreement on domination by a cultural minority as characteristic of the plural society. This is a matter of historical fact for Furnivall, and a matter of definition and theoretical necessity for Smith. Again, both writers emphasize social cleavage and cultural diversity as qualities of the plural society. For Furnivall, this cultural diversity is again historical fact, tropical colonial societies having brought into contact two contrary principles of social life: a tropical system resting on religion, personal custom, and duties, and a Western system resting on reason, impersonal law, and rights.[40] For Smith, cultural diversity is implicit, as a theoretical necessity, in the concept of the plural society: it is the necessary and sufficient condition of pluralism.

Major differences between the two models are first in the range of societies conceived as plural. Furnivall is primarily concerned with colonial tropical societies under the impact of Western economic expansion. Smith includes societies other than colonial pluralities, whether originating in conquest and consolidation or by migration, and whether attributable to Western economic activity or to other forces. They differ also in the approach to causal factors. Furnivall stresses the role of colonial capitalism in the formation of the plural society; cultural diversity is the context within which the primacy of economic forces disintegrates the common will and transforms groups into mass aggregates. Smith, on the other hand, imputes causal significance to cultural incompatibility or wide cultural differences, regardless of the specific content of the cultural differences.

The model proposed by Smith has the advantage of extending the perceptions of Furnivall within a general theoretical framework. But it has serious social implications and a number of critical questions must be raised. Smith distinguishes two basic mechanisms, one of integration and the other of regulation, by which' groups may be held together within the same society. Integration rests on common values and common motivations at the individual level, and on the functional relations of common institutions at the societal level. It presupposes cultural homogeneity (or cultural heterogeneity, but only in the form of variations around a common basic institutional system).[41] Cultural diversity or pluralism automatically imposes the structural necessity for domination by one of the cultural sections. It excludes the possibility of consensus, or of institutional integration, or of structural balance between the different sections, and necessitates nondemocratic regulation of group relationships.

This implies a distinction between two basic types of society, integrated societies characterized by consensus and cultural homogeneity (or cultural heterogeneity, as described above), and regulated societies characterized by dissensus and cultural pluralism. It implies that cultural homogeneity (or heterogeneity) is a requisite for democratic forms of government; [42] and it suggests the prediction, in concrete terms, that many of the newly independent states may either dissolve into separate cultural sections, or maintain their identity, but only under conditions of domination and subordination in the relationships between groups.

Since cultural diversity is assigned a crucial role in political structure, it becomes necessary to define the nature and extent of the diversity, which necessitates political domination.[43] Smith recognizes that there are differences in the degree of cultural pluralism,[44] and presumably also in the degree of incompatibility between institutions. While it is no doubt true, as he remarks, that these differences do not affect the analytical status of the social phenomena as expressions of cultural pluralism,[45] they may be highly relevant for the political consequences. This relevance seems also to be accepted by Smith in his reference to "wide cultural differences" as imposing the need for domination.[46] No doubt a certain measure of cultural pluralism may be entirely consistent with democratic participation in government by the different sections.

There are also distinctions to be made in the texture or patterns of cultural pluralism. Thus cultural pluralism between sections may be expected to vary in different institutional contexts. There may be a greater incompatibility in familial institutions, for example, than in religious; and presumably some institutions have greater salience for the political constitution of a society. Thus in many plural societies which seek to unify their peoples through a uniform system of law, institutional diversity in family law is nevertheless often given explicit recognition, the customary regulation of family relationships in the different sections being accorded legal status. This cultural pluralism in family institutions may have little relevance for political structure; or it may have political significance under certain social conditions, but not others. In order to assess the political consequences of cultural pluralism, it is therefore necessary to distinguish different patterns of cultural pluralism and to relate them to the varied social conditions under which they appear.

The problem is further complicated by the inevitable coexistence of common institutions and plural institutions. The model of cultural pluralism represents an extreme type which would be most nearly approximated immediately after the establishment of a plural society by conquest. Even then, certain shared activities are likely to have preceded conquest. Once the plural society is constituted, some growth of common institutions, in addition to common governmental institutions, and some association between members of different cultural groups, are inevitable. Intersectional association and common institutions may be expected to modify the political consequences of cultural pluralism, and the relationship between what is common and shared and what is divisive and incompatible must therefore be analyzed as part of the social context of cultural pluralism, affecting its political expression.

Social conditions may also influence the perception of cultural pluralism. To some extent, objective measures of cultural pluralism can be devised without regard to particular social contexts or the perceptions of members of the society. Thus it is possible to make paired comparisons between different family institutions, and to assert that one set of differences exceeds the other.[47] But there is also a relative and subjective element in the measurement of cultural pluralism. Cultural differences may be magnified or minimized. Members of the society may seek out and emphasize elements of cultural similarity as a basis of association, or they may stress cultural differences as absolute impediments to association. The political significance of pluralism is likely to fluctuate with the changing conditions of domination. Rather than accord primacy to cultural pluralism, it may contribute to understanding to analyze its significance in a plural society as in part a derivative of domination. Smith sees racist ideology as derivative, as symbolizing and legitimizing intersectional relations.[48] In much the same way it may be argued that cultural pluralism is, in some measure, an ideology of domination or of conflict in a struggle for power between different groups, the significance that the parties attach to cultural difference varying with changes in the structure of their relationships, and more particularly, with changes in relative power.

Cultural pluralism may also be seen as relative to the systems of government in the plural societies and to their dominant legal and political philosophies. Some systems of government may be more tolerant of cultural differences than others. Political philosophies influence the extent to which cultural sections are the basis of administration, as in systems of indirect rule, or are denied recognition and replaced by other categories of administration. In a paper dealing with "The Sociological Framework of Law," [49] Smith assigns a significant role to the theory of law of the dominant power. He argues that the common law tradition in the British system and the acceptance of the ruler's discretion as a legitimate source of law in Islam contributed to a flexible recognition of African traditional systems of authority and law, whereas the French emphasis on the imperium of the French state as the source of law impeded the administrative and legal acceptance of African cultural pluralism. If there is validity to these comments, then cultural pluralism may be seen not only as a cause but also as a consequence of political domination.

POSSIBLE SYNTHESIS OF APPROACHES: [50] PROBLEMS OF SOCIAL CHANGE

Comparison of the "conflict" and "equilibrium" models raises further problems for research. The two types of society appear to be so antithetical as seemingly to exclude the possibility of evolutionary change from cultural pluralism and divisive conflict to political pluralism and equilibrium. So sharp are the contrasts between them that it is difficult to see how actual societies approximating the plural society of the "conflict" model might transform by relatively peaceful progression into societies corresponding to the pluralistic society of the "equilibrium" model.

There is the antithesis in political form between liberal democracy and sectional domination. In the culturally plural society, there may indeed be such democratic institutions as constitutional checks and balances against concentration of power and competition between politically organized elites for the votes of the electorate. But these institutions may regulate and diversify political action mainly within the dominant section, which however operates as a relatively unitary political force in relation to subordinate sections.

In both societies, the social basis is a plurality of groups. In the "equilibrium" model, autonomy of institutions and independence of intermediate organizations promote dispersion of power and diversity of interest: the competition between interest groups results in a balanced adjustment.

By contrast, in the "conflict" model, independence of the cultural sections implies dissolution of the society; intersectional conflict threatens the very existence of the society. The independence of organizations even within the dominant section may be controlled by insistence on the maintenance of intersectional differences; or these organizations may present a relatively united front toward subordinate cultural sections even in the absence of such control. In the case of subordinate cultural sections, there is likely to be extensive limitation of the autonomy of institutions and of the independence of intermediate organizations. The very right to organize may be carefully restricted, since organizational capacity is an important resource in the struggle for power between cultural sections. The dominant group may promote, within a subordinate section, organizations that diversify interest and fragment solidarity, such as traditional structures in counterpoise to modernizing elites; and it may establish, as instruments of domination and segregation, special organizational structures within the subordinate group.[51] In the context of cultural pluralism and domination, intermediate organizations are often the targets and the instruments of a conflict that threatens the stability and continuity of the society.

Again, quite different mechanisms sustain the two types of society. In the "equilibrium" model, integration rests on functional relations between institutions and on common values, or on the competitive and dynamic balance among a plurality of independent groups with limited functions and multiple affiliations of members. In the "conflict" model, the binding mechanism is governmental regulation, and ultimately, force. The contrast between these models may be expressed in terms of antithetical theories of the state. In the "equilibrium" model, the bonds between the plural sections are primary, and the state, as a political entity, expresses this basic social integration. In the "conflict" model, the state precedes and constitutes society; it is the state that is primary and

imposes some measure of ordered relations on otherwise hostile or dissociated groups.

The contrast between the two types of society is such that the same
forms or processes may serve antithetical functions; or they may serve
similar functions for some groups and antithetical functions for others.
Thus Kornhauser, in discussing the pluralist theory of liberal democracy,
argues that the leaders of independent intermediate organizations help to
support the larger system of authority with which their own authority is
inextricably bound.[52] This is likely to be true also for intermediate organizations within the dominant group in a culturally plural society. Indeed
its members may be expected to stress the general duty of respect for the
authority, law, and order which are the basis of their dominant position
in the society. Conversely, precisely because of the role of authority in
the system of domination, there is pressure on subordinate cultural
sections to deny legitimacy to the imposed order and to reject not only
specific laws and authority, but law, order, and authority as such. If
intermediate organizations within the subordinate sections serve instrumental functions for the dominant group, then this may further discredit
authority, both governmental authority and the authority of the leaders
of the organization. If intermediate organizations within subordinate
sections are independent, then the leaders may themselves mobilize their
following for an attack on the social order.

Characteristics that distinguish the pluralist society, in the "equilibrium" model, from other forms of society may be combined within the
plural society of the "conflict" model. Kornhauser, for example, distinguishes mass society from pluralist society by a relative absence of
intermediate relations, which exposes elites to direct action by the masses
and at the same time renders the masses available for mobilization by
elites. He distinguishes mass man from autonomous (pluralist) man by
his alienation both from self and from others. And he finds in discontinuities arising from such circumstances as abrupt changes in authority,
rapid urbanization, and industrialization, conditions conducive to mass
movements.[53] Yet, in Furnivall's concept, mass tendencies are characteristic of plural societies. He writes of the collapse of corporate tribal or
village life, the atomization of society, and the isolation of the individual,
each section in the plural society being a crowd, not a community.[54]

Indeed, many circumstances encourage mass movements in the plural
societies of the "conflict" model. There is discontinuity between the old
and the new. It is specially marked in many of the colonial and white
settler societies of Africa, as a result of the sudden imposition of alien
forms of government, and it is expressed in the sharp contrast between
urban, industrial, and contractual relationships among arbitrary aggrega-

tions of population and the status relationships of kinship-based rural communities. Widespread sentiments of hostility and prejudice, engendered by conflict between cultural sections, offer an extended invitation to mobilize the masses which the political elite cannot be expected persistently to decline. Intermediate organizations in the dominant section provide structures and mechanisms that assist, rather than hinder, mass mobilization by political elites. In the subordinate sections, the very weakness of intermediate organizations and the often ineffectual role of leaders in changing the structure of domination may alienate the masses and drive them to direct action against the authority of the dominant section. Both situations, of domination and of subordination, encourage mobilization of the masses, whether organized in the dominant section or tending to anarchy in the subordinate sections. It is to be expected that in these circumstances, and under conditions of heightened conflict, the essentially authoritarian government of the plural society may seek to extend its power by totalitarian forms of control.

If these two types of society are as antithetical, as qualitatively different, as the above comments suggest, then presumably, empirically, the process of change from cultural pluralism and political domination to political pluralism and "equilibrium" is likely to be abrupt, revolutionary, and violent.

The white settler societies of Africa, for example, approximate a plural society of the "conflict" type in which the basic cleavages are between racial groups. Change to social forms corresponding to the "equilibrium" model would mean movement from domination by a racial and cultural minority to democratic government based on the participation of groups, which are defined by various criteria transcending the racial divisions, such as institutional membership, function, and economic role. Now from the perspective of sharply contrasted and abruptly discontinuous models, it seems almost inevitable that the process of change should be revolutionary and violent. But this prediction may be a consequence of the use of antithetical models, or of extreme types, which leads to a polarization of observation and expectation.

Prediction and research procedures may take a very different form, however, when they proceed from the assumption that common processes and social phenomena underlie both these types of society. If pluralism is seen as a dimension of all societies, and if wide differences in degree do not necessarily imply qualitative differences, then the possibility and expectation of evolutionary change are greatly increased. From this point of view, cultural pluralism is congruent with political pluralism, equilibrium, consensus, and integration, as well as with sectional domination, conflict, dissensus, and regulation. The research problem is to define the conditions of culture, structure, and economy which influence differences in the social context and consequences of cultural pluralism, and in the processes of social change.

The relevant cultural conditions include the patterns and extent of cultural pluralism discussed in the preceding section. They include also political philosophies, though these may be secondary and derivative from other factors, as is perhaps often the case in the period of African independence, when there is great flexibility in ideological choice and commitment. The contrasted ideologies of East and West are available, with financial and other inducements; and concepts of the African Personality, the "Third World," and nonalignment permit an easy adjustment of ideology to local conditions and elite interests. Similarly, the political traditions in the history of the society are relevant, but again, these traditions are greatly varied, as, for example, in the sharply contrasted British colonial traditions of autocratic rule and of democratic precept (and final constitution), to which must be added the political traditions of the colonized peoples themselves. Hence, the commitment to a particular tradition cannot be explained by reference to an orientation toward tradition, but must be sought in the circumstances and interests that influence the selection among traditions.

Among the relevant structural conditions is the demographic basis of cultural pluralism. Thus a demographic context of many small cultural sections may be conducive to political pluralism and consensus, whereas the preponderance of one cultural section encourages a monopoly of power and sectional domination. The relationship between the boundaries of structural and cultural divisions is relevant. Where these coincide, and in the absence of consensus on ultimate values, there is likely to be intense group conflict and forceful regulation of group relationships. Where the boundaries diverge in such manner that there is some association between members of different cultural sections and some cultural homogeneity between members of exclusive social groups, then the situation would seem more favorable to the harmonious adjustment of interests. This is comparable to a situation of multiple affiliation which provides a basis for crosscutting loyalties. At the same time, the divergence between cultural and social boundaries can be a source of acute conflict, and indeed a stimulus to revolution, as in the exclusion of a westernized African elite from admission to the circles of power.[55]

The convergence and divergence of structural and cultural sections are aspects of more general structural phenomena, which Dahrendorf terms monism or superimposition, and pluralism or dissociation.[56] Superimposition refers to a convergence of lines of group conflict (in state, industry, church, and so on) and to an accumulation of causes or issues of conflict. Dissociation refers to a separation of both lines and causes of conflict. At one extreme is a society in which all patterns, issues, and contexts of political conflict are superimposed and combined, dividing the society into large hostile camps. At the other extreme, the intensity of political conflict is reduced to a minimum in a society in which issues of conflict are dissociated, and different conflicts mobilize different sections of the population. Superimposition and dissociation are clearly significant elements in the tendency to disruptive conflict or balanced adjustment.

These same elements are significant also in the relationship between the economic system and cultural pluralism. The superimposition of political inequality on economic inequality, which Marxist theory postulates, seems to be a universal feature of the societies that serve as a model for the pluralism of conflict theory. It is a condition conducive to revolutionary change. From the optimistic perspective of capitalist society, with its idealization of economic growth, the revolutionary potential may be diverted by the sustained and progressive development of the economy. This is expected to temper extremism and to promote a balanced and democratic adjustment of interests by an increased interdependence of different sections consequent upon urbanization and industrialization, a dispersion of centers of power, a growing liberalism under the influence of rising standards of living and of education, and a proliferation of middle classes rewarding political moderation. From a Marxist point of view, economic growth proceeding within the framework of sectional domination in a plural society can only hasten revolutionary change. From both capitalist and Marxist perspectives, progressive economic growth acts as a solvent of the conflicts of cultural pluralism, either by evolutionary or revolutionary means.

Perhaps the system of domination is the crucial factor affecting the possibility of evolutionary change. Different types of domination may have their own somewhat specific laws of change, with varying potentialities for evolutionary transformation.

The comparative study of plural societies in Africa may offer some answers to these questions about the relationship between cultural pluralism, social cleavage, economic exploitation, and political domination. The colonial societies established by Western industrial powers in Africa and the white settler societies of Africa present extreme forms of cultural pluralism. They may be compared with the plural societies of precolonial Africa, presumably less culturally diverse, and with African conquest states founded among culturally homogeneous peoples. The same range of societies offers wide contrasts in political and economic institutions.

There are despotisms, colonies, white settler states, constitutional monarchies, feudal systems, and acephalous societies. Economic institutions include symbiotic relationships between agriculturalists and pastoralists; they include slavery, serfdom, migrant labor, primary industry, mainly agricultural but also extractive, and modern industrial systems.

Comparisons may be made over a period of time within individual societies as well as between different societies. Changes toward common institutions and associations, or toward increasing cleavage and cultural estrangement, may be related to the changed social circumstances that favor these different consequences. There may be a changing significance of cultural pluralism consequent upon structural and economic changes in the society, as, for example, from a paternalist to a competitive system of race relations, or from an agricultural to an industrial economy, or from colonial domination through national liberation to independence. By comparative study it should be possible to determine what regularities and variations are associated with cultural pluralism, and what are the social conditions that shape and diversify the political and other manifestations of cultural pluralism. It may be possible to specify more precisely some of the conditions that influence the relations of the plural sections toward conflict or harmonious adjustment, or the conditions that govern the possibility of evolutionary change from cultural pluralism, divisive conflict, and sectional domination to political pluralism, adjustive relationships, and democratic participation. Perhaps some contribution may be made to a theoretical synthesis of "equilibrium" and "conflict" models of society.

NOTES

[1] See, for example, W. Kornhauser, *The Politics of Mass Society* (London: Routledge and Kegan Paul, 1960), and Edward A. Shils, *The Torment of Secrecy* (London: Heinemann, 1956), on the one hand; and J. S. Furnivall, *Colonial Policy and Practice* (London: Cambridge University Press, 1948), and M. G. Smith, *The Plural Society in the British West Indies* (Berkeley and Los Angeles: University of California Press, 1965), on the other. In both conceptions, the term "pluralism" is used to characterize the general structure of the society. At the societal level, there is a tendency to use the term "pluralist" or "pluralistic" society in what I have described as the "equilibrium" model, and the term "plural" society in the "conflict" model. This would be a way of distinguishing the different conceptions, though the terms are too similar to dispel confusion.

[2] The same association between democracy and pluralism is made by the French sociologist R. Aron in "Social Structure and the Ruling Class," *British Journal of Sociology*, I (March 1950), 1–16. He writes that "democratic societies, which I would rather call pluralistic societies, are full of the noise of public strife between the owners of the means of production, trade union leaders and politicians" (pp. 10–11).

[3] Shils, *op. cit.*, pp. 225–227.

[4] *Ibid.*, Part III.

[5] Kornhauser, *op. cit.*, p. 131.

[6] *Ibid.*, pp. 230–231.

[7] *Ibid.*, p. 141.

[8] *Ibid.*, p. 130.

[9] "The fundamental difference between a society of the Soviet type and one of the Western type is that the former has a unified elite and the latter a divided elite" (Aron, *op. cit.*, p. 10).

[10] It should be noted that political pluralism may give rise to social pluralism. For example, the introduction of a two-party system in the local government of an urban neighborhood may encourage social divisions in a homogeneous and relatively undifferentiated population.

[11] Shils, *op. cit.*, pp. 153–154.

[12] Kornhauser, *op. cit.*, pp. 76–90.

[13] *Ibid.*, pp. 79–81.

[14] Compare this with Shils' description of the pluralistic society as a largely "open" society (*op. cit.*, p. 208). Presumably, in certain circumstances, social mobility may have similar consequences to the pluralist dispersion of roles.

[15] Shils, *op. cit.*, pp. 155 ff., 227. Aron comments that, if freedom is to survive, there is need for autonomy of elites, but also for cooperation between them (which implies the tolerant recognition of other values and a sense of communal affinity): "A unified élite means the end of freedom. But when the groups of the élite are not only distinct but become a disunity, it means the end of the State. Freedom survives in those intermediate regions, which are continually threatened when there is moral unity of the élite, where men and groups preserve the secret of single and eternal wisdom and have learnt how to combine autonomy with cooperation" (*op. cit.*, p. 143).

[16] Kornhauser, *op. cit.*, p. 104.

[17] Some theorists of political pluralism find the basis for democratic order and integration in the equality of power between groups, and the consequent mutual restraint. This seems an insufficient basis. Indeed, relative equality may be a source of conflict and a stimulus to sectional domination. Thus David Easton writes that, in view of the indecisive evidence supporting the hypothesis that equality in power generates restraint, "it might be suggested that equality in power leads rather to fear, semiparalysis in the resolution of important intergroup differences and ultimately the appeal to violence to settle an impossible situation" (*The Political System* [New York: Knopf, 1953], p. 303). Kornhauser comments that "there is no simple relationship between the extent to which power is equally distributed and the stability of democratic order" (" 'Power Elite' or 'Veto Groups,' " in S. M. Lipset and Leo Lowenthal, eds., *Culture and Social Character* [New York: Free Press of Glencoe, 1961], p. 267).

[18] In the context of North American ethnic relations, pluralism is often used to signify toleration of cultural differences in a social context which may vary from society to society. Thus Simpson and Yinger write that "in some societies it implies toleration among cultural groups, but little active cooperation; political and economic unity, but little exchange and common participation in other matters. . . . Cultural pluralism may imply, however, a more active kind of unity among diverse groups, a reaching out toward common goals, a sharing of their different heritages" (G. E. Simpson and J. M. Yinger, *Racial and*

Cultural Minorities [New York: Harper, 1953], p. 23). Brewton Berry describes pluralism "as not merely an ideal, a theory, or a goal toward which its advocates hope that race relations might move; it has been a matter of public policy on numerous occasions." The public policy of pluralism is conceived as cultural freedom or diversity in a context of considerable agreement as to basic ideals, goals, values, mores, folkways, and beliefs (*Race Relations* [New York: Houghton Mifflin, 1951], pp. 332–333).

[19] Furnivall, *op. cit.*, and "Some Problems of Tropical Economy," in Rita Hinden, ed., *Fabian Colonial Essays* (London: George Allen and Unwin, 1945), pp. 161–184. In Furnivall's book, *Netherlands India* (Cambridge: The University Press, 1939), the conflict between groups is brought out in the observation that "finally, the reaction against these abnormal conditions [of pluralism], taking in each section the form of Nationalism, sets one community against the other so as to emphasize the plural character of the society and aggravate its instability, thereby enhancing the need for it to be held together by some force exerted from outside" (p. 459); and "in some ways the position resembles that of Europe during the early days of the Reformation, when men of different creeds lived side by side within the same region but in different spiritual worlds, and it contains elements of conflict no less bitter and prolonged. Probably that conflict will be settled by will rather than by reason" (p. 464).

[20] *Colonial Policy and Practice*, pp. 304–307. Furnivall's earlier conception of the plural society was not limited to tropical or colonial societies.

[21] *Ibid.*, p. 304.

[22] Smith, *The Plural Society in the British West Indies*, p. vii.

[23] *Colonial Policy and Practice*, p. 306.

[24] *Ibid.*, p. 312.

[25] *Ibid.*, p. 307 ff.

[26] Furnivall, "Some Problems of Tropical Economy," p. 168. Furnivall moved from his earlier fears of nationalism in plural societies, as in fact internationalism and divisive (see *Netherlands India*, p. 468, and extract in n. 19, above), to the belief that there was no practical alternative to the principle of nationalism "if we are to find some principle that all may accept as of superior validity to economic interest" (*Colonial Policy and Practice*, p. 547; see also p. 506).

[27] See *Netherlands India*, pp. 464–469; J. Rex, "The Plural Society in Sociological Theory," *British Journal of Sociology*, 10 (June 1959), 116. In discussing policies to cure the defects of the plural society, Furnivall writes that "the *first* problem is to find some principle transcending material ends, some moral principle, that *all* can accept as valid" ("Some Problems of Tropical Economy," p. 171).

[28] Smith, *op. cit.*, p. 67 *et seq.* The question arises whether the participation of culturally diverse units within a single polity necessarily implies domination by one of the units.

[29] *Ibid.*, p. 88.

[30] *Ibid.*, pp. 14, 15, 82, 84, 88. Smith also uses the phrase "wide cultural differences" (p. 62).

[31] *Ibid.*, p. 14.

[32] *Ibid.*, pp. 68–71.

[33] *Ibid.*, p. 62.

[34] *Ibid.*, p. 86.

[35] *Ibid.*, p. 89. Max Weber seems to have made a similar observation in his comment that "incidentally, the development of status groups from ethnic segregation is by no means the normal phenomenon. On the contrary, since objective 'racial differences' are by no means basic to every subjective sentiment of an ethnic community, the ultimately racial foundation of status structure is rightly and absolutely a question of the concrete individual case" (H. H. Gerth and C. Wright Mills, eds., *From Max Weber* [New York: Oxford University Press, 1958], p. 190).

[36] Smith, *op. cit.*, p. 89.

[37] *Ibid.*, p. 63.

[38] *Ibid.*, p. 90. Later (pp. 157–158), Smith comments that plural societies may or may not be highly integrated. Here he appears to be drawing a distinction between the different sections, each of which may be integrated by the functional relationship of its institutions, in contrast with the plural society as a whole. Or he may be referring to the "remote probability" that a plural society may be integrated by consensus.

[39] *Ibid.*, p. 91. This statement needs to be qualified. Independence was achieved by many African states with little or no violence. Different types of plural society, such as colonial or white settler, should be distinguished, and different processes of change, as, for example, change in the pattern of racial recruitment to positions in the society, or change in the actual structure of those positions.

[40] "Some Problems of Tropical Economy," p. 162.

[41] Smith, *op. cit.*, pp. 86–88, 157.

[42] Somewhat the same thesis has been advanced by dominant minorities in plural societies to justify nondemocratic government.

[43] H. I. McKenzie, "The Plural Society Debate: Some Comments on a Recent Contribution," *Social and Economic Studies*, 15 (March 1966), 53–60, and Leo A. Despres, "The Implications of Nationalist Policies in British Guiana for the Development of a Cultural Theory," *American Anthropologist*, 66 (Oct. 1964), 1051–1077, deal with many of the issues raised in my own paper. See also Vera Rubin, ed., *Social and Cultural Pluralism in the Caribbean*, Annals of the New York Academy of Sciences (Jan. 1960), 761–916; J. C. Mitchell, *Tribalism and the Plural Society* (London: Oxford University Press, 1960).

[44] *Op. cit.*, pp. 85–86.

[45] *Ibid.*

[46] *Ibid.*, p. 62.

[47] *Ibid.*, pp. 85–86.

[48] *Ibid.*, p. 90.

[49] See Hilda Kuper and Leo Kuper, eds., *African Law: Adaptation and Development* (Berkeley and Los Angeles: University of California Press, 1965), pp. 24–48.

[50] An analogous problem is raised by Pierre L. van den Berghe, "Dialectic and Functionalism: Toward a Theoretical Synthesis," *American Sociological Review*, 28 (Oct. 1963), 695–705. See also, on the general subject of pluralism, his "Toward a Sociology of Africa," *Social Forces*, 43 (Oct. 1964), 11–18.

[51] For a discussion of these mechanisms, see Leo Kuper, "Structural Discontinuities in African Towns: Some Aspects of Racial Pluralism," in H. Miner, ed., *The City in Modern Africa* (New York: Praeger, 1967).

[52] *The Politics of Mass Society*, p. 77.

[53] *Ibid.*, pp. 111, 115, and Part II.

[54] *Colonial Policy and Practice,* p. 307.

[55] For a discussion of this point, see Kuper, "Structural Discontinuities in African Towns."

[56] R. Dahrendorf, *Class and Class Conflict in Industrial Society* (London: Routledge and Kegan Paul, 1959), pp. 214 ff., 316–317. Dahrendorf's use of pluralism is quite antithetical to the usage in the "conflict" model. Indeed, the plural societies in the "conflict" model are likely to be characterized by "monism" in Dahrendorf's formulation.

Chapter 2   Institutional and Political Conditions of Pluralism

M. G. Smith

Pluralism is a condition in which members of a common society are internally distinguished by fundamental differences in their institutional practice. Where present, such differences are not distributed at random; they normally cluster, and by their clusters they simultaneously identify institutionally distinct aggregates or groups, and establish deep social divisions between them. The prevalence of such systematic disassociation between the members of institutionally distinct collectivities within a single society constitutes pluralism. Thus pluralism simultaneously connotes a social structure characterized by fundamental discontinuities and cleavages, and a cultural complex based on systematic institutional diversity. In this paper I try to isolate the minimal conditions essential and sufficient to constitute pluralism. I try also to show how such conditions generate and sustain social cleavages that distinguish pluralities, while other combinations of institutional and social differences differ in their structural expression. Having summarily indicated some of the principal forms that social pluralism may take, I review briefly the modes and conditions by which it may be stabilized or transformed.

Pluralism may be defined with equal cogency and precision in institutional or in political terms. Politically these features have very distinctive forms and conditions, and in their most extreme state, the plural society, they constitute a polity of peculiar though variable type. Specific political features of social pluralism center in the corporate constitution of the total society. Under these conditions the basic corporate divisions within the society usually coincide with the lines of institutional cleavage, reinforcing and generally converting them into deep and rigid inequalities in social and political life. The enforcement and maintenance of these corporate divisions and inequalities are then normally identified with the preservation of social order and stability. Any modification in the political and social relations between these corporate divisions involves corresponding changes in the conditions of social structure. To seek out the conditions essential for this coincidence of corporate boundaries and institutional discontinuity, we have therefore to discover the minimal degrees and forms of institutional divergence which are required to facilitate, promote, or enjoin the sectional closures that plural polity incorporates; and conversely, we need to inquire how various alternative forms of corporate organization may establish, preserve, or foster institutional differentiation, or reduce or deny its public significance, while permitting its persistence or dissolution equally. In effect, we need first to determine the circumstances and ways in which these modes of corporate organization and institutional differentiation interact to support, reinforce, dislocate, or modify one another, and then to identify the conditions requisite for their stabilization or transformation.

I

To analyze the institutional and political conditions of pluralism, it is first necessary to distinguish pluralism from its principal alternatives, and to indicate how its variable range governs its structural significance.

Since institutions are collective modes of action, organization, and orientation, both normative and cognitive, institutional differentiation correspondingly distinguishes collectivities that differ in organization, standardized procedures, norms, beliefs, ideals, and expectations. Quite commonly, all the members of a distinct society share an identical system of institutions. The boundaries of such societies are defined by the maximum span of the institutional system on which their social organization and cohesion are based. Such conditions of institutional homogeneity, which are characteristic of simple societies, represent the polar opposite of the systematic institutional diversity that constitutes pluralism.

Many societies, including the most highly developed industrial societies, seem to stand midway between these extremes. In these societies the entire population, or at least the overwhelming majority, share a common system of basic institutions, while being systematically differentiated at the secondary level of institutional organization in which alternative occupational, political, and religious or ethnic structures predominate. Societies with this combination of common and exclusive institutional affiliations are properly distinguished by their pervasive heterogeneity from the conditions of homogeneity and pluralism already described. These types of societies differ significantly in structure, complexity, modes of integration, and in their capacities for self-generated development. Though institutional homogeneity and high levels of organizational complexity are mutually exclusive, and no industrial society is ever institutionally homogeneous, social heterogeneity or pluralism is equally consistent with industrial or preindustrial levels of economic and technological organization. Thus the institutional classification is independent of economic or technological criteria.

The most extreme and politically significant expression of pluralism is to be found in the "plural society," as J. S. Furnivall appropriately labeled internally autonomous and inclusive political units ruled by institutionally distinct numerical minorities.[1] The subjugated majority of the population in a plural society may or may not share a single common system of institutions; often the people are internally subdivided by their differing institutional allegiances; but in all cases they simultaneously differ in their political status and in their institutional practice and organization from the discrete minority who rule them. In their colonial phase, all recently independent African states were plural societies;[2] and despite independence, most of these ex-colonies retain their plural character with marginal alteration. Thus pluralism and colonialism are not homologous. Colonialism is merely one mode of pluralism, characteristically instituted in the form of a plural society. However, pluralism is by no means confined to plural societies, although it is in those units that it has its purest expression and most profound effects.

One of the major problems that faces emergent nations with a recent colonial past consists in effecting the transition from pluralism to the heterogeneity requisite for their transformation into cohesive national units. Such transformations have not yet occurred in several Latin-American societies, despite relatively long histories of independence. Of European states that faced a similar predicament at an earlier date, we need merely mention Spain, Portugal, Russia, Germany, and France to indicate the various difficulties, processes, and outcomes involved. One of our concerns in this paper is to detect as best we can the most general conditions requisite for those processes of societal transformation and enhanced political integration on which "modernization" directly depends.

II

A society is a self-sufficient, self-perpetuating, and internally autonomous system of social relations. Such a system distinguishes a population occupying a specific territory; but as a system of social relations, the society is clearly distinct from territory or population. The society is the structure of relations through which the population of members is internally organized as joint occupants of a given area. Changes in population mass or composition, or more obviously in territory, do not themselves directly constitute changes in the social system, although they undoubtedly affect it in many ways. It is with differences in the systems of social relations which constitute societies that the distinctions between pluralism, homogeneity, and heterogeneity are directly concerned.

Social relations are either institutionalized or optional in their base, individual or collective in their form. The range and conditions that govern optional relations at both the individual and collective levels are themselves institutionally prescribed and regulated. Thus the inclusive autonomous system of social relations which constitutes a society is directly or indirectly institutionalized. If the members of the society share a common system of institutions, then they will also share a common framework and pattern of social relations; and their internal differentiation by corporate and personal status will be governed by uniform criteria and principles. If the aggregate is institutionally heterogeneous in its base, then the system of institutionalized relations in which its society consists will be correspondingly heterogeneous in character and form. In consequence, members will differ in the significance they attach to those criteria and principles that regulate their corporate and personal identity and status placement. If the society consists of collectivities divided by fundamental institutional differences, then, within the corresponding corporate divisions whose interrelations constitute the societal level of organization and integration, there will be corresponding diversity of institutionalized relations. In such conditions, members of differing social sections occupy significantly differing positions in relations with one another. In consequence, societies with homogeneous, heterogeneous, and plural institutional systems differ correspondingly in character and structure.

III

Following Malinowski, Radcliffe-Brown, Nadel, and others, we may define institutions as "standardised modes of co-activity,"[3] characteristic of social collectivities. Individual habits are subject to institutional regulation but, being personal and optional, even when common among a given primary group, they differ sharply from institutions which are essentially normative, standardized, and sanctioned modes of collective procedure. It is by virtue of sharing common institutions that an aggregate becomes an organized collectivity; and it is precisely because they are neither the only nor the majority of the collectivity that shares common institutions that local communities are not discrete societies but merely subgroups thereof. In short, its institutional foundation transforms an aggregate into a distinct collectivity even in the absence of any inclusive common organization. Only in consequence of the structural uniformity and functional coherence that a single system of shared and coextensive institutions provides are the acephalous societies familiar to anthropologists analytically or in their members' eyes identified as distinct societal units. Lacking inclusive organization for the collective regulation of their common affairs, these acephalous societies are constituted as institutionally distinct and closed perpetual categories in consequence of their uniform institutional base. Such internal cohesion and external distinctness as they possess, these acephalous societies owe directly to the distinctiveness and homogeneity of their institutional fabric. However, as we shall see, not all homogeneous societies are acephalous; nor are all acephalous societies institutionally homogeneous. While acephalous societies retain their constitution as functionally coherent corporate *categories,* other societies having a representative central organization for the direction of common collective affairs, including external relations, are accordingly constituted as corporate *groups.*

The decisive characteristics of all corporations, categorical and other, are their presumed perpetuity, closure, determinate identity, and membership. A category lacks the coextensive organization that is requisite for its constitution as a group. The corporate group, in addition to the features already listed, possesses this inclusive organization, a set of distinctive common affairs, and the procedures and autonomy necessary to regulate them. Societies unified as corporate groups have common political institutions and regulative organs, thereby enhancing the functional integration derived from shared institutions by specializing a single collective structure authorized to administer certain common internal affairs and to represent the unit externally. This structure is itself corporate in basis and form, being presumptively perpetual, closed, with determinate identity, membership, and form, and possessing the authority, organization, and procedures to discharge its collective regulatory functions.[4]

The authority, responsibility, and resources required for this collective regulation may be vested in a corporate office or structure of offices, or in corporate colleges such as councils, parliaments, or senates. Members of these colleges and official structures exercise political functions over the collectivity and on its behalf since these regulatory corporations are institutionalized as the appropriate agencies for political regulation and integration of the whole. If the "centralized" society shares a common system of basic institutions, and continues to derive its primary underlying cohesion and unity from this condition, the central political agencies serve merely to coordinate, mobilize, and direct collective actions and resources as various exigencies require, and to preserve the institutionally requisite conditions for an orderly collective life. Such modes of political organization and activity presuppose the integration of the society concerned by virtue of the symmetrical or complementary inter-dependences of its corporate elements derived from their shared institutional foundations and modes of action.

Per contra, in a plural society where the rulers form a culturally distinct numerical minority, the aggregate depends for its formation, unity, order, and form primarily on the concentration and active employment of regulative powers by the ruling section through the political framework, in consequence of the institutional cleavages within it, and the exclusive, asymmetrical relations that such cleavages entail. In addition to this primary institutional bifurcation between rulers and ruled, there may be several secondary cultural divisions among the subjugated; but in either case, in the plural society the rulers typically maintain their organization as an exclusive corporate group in order that they may collectively secure and control the political institutions on which the internal order and unity of the aggregate depend, together with their own privileges of status and opportunity. Further, to minimize threats to their regime, the dominant section, through its political organization, actively discourages or suppresses extensive organizations by which the subject population could convert itself from an acephalous, institutionally disprivileged category into a coherent corporate group capable of effective political and social action. Thus the institutional and regulative responsibilities and powers of the central political agencies differ sharply in aggregates of differing institutional base and composition.

The contrast may be summarized most cogently by comparing plural societies and nation-states, the political forms and contexts of modernization. As Broom says, a "nation is the antithesis of plural order. A nation implies common ancestry and cultural homogeneity; a state refers to a dominant political unit, regardless of the variability of its components. A state may contain a plural society." [5]

Analytically we may express the contrast as follows: (1) A nation is usually a single inclusive corporate group whose members—or the majority of them—share common traditions, institutions, history, and ethnic identity. (2) In the nation-state, the state is the derivative political expression of the nation's cohesion and unity. The members of the nation are citizens of the state, which provides all with equal representation, protection, and regulation. Equality of access and obligation to the political organization, and equality of opportunity for participation in the political process, are essentials of national identity and citizenship. [6] Democratic, totalitarian, or dictatorial philosophies of the nation-state all assume these basic relations, although construing them very differently.

(3) Regulatory corporations of the nation-state are equally representative of, binding on, and accessible to all members of the nation as a corporate group.

In the plural society the state is the representative political organ of the ruling section organized as a corporate group, its exclusive and ultimate instrument for the internal domination and corporate control of the institutionally distinct subject populations, who are simultaneously denied political rights, citizenship, and opportunities for their own organization by prescriptions of state, and are accordingly paralyzed as disunited corporate categories. Thus in the plural society the mass of the people are not citizens but subjects; and the state, instead of being the collective political expression of the inclusive aggregate, is merely the external political form of the dominant corporate group, the instrumental framework of its domination, and the ultimate source and expression of prevailing sectional inequalities. Indeed, the political institutions and ideology of the plural society are almost complete antitheses to those of the nation-state, whether democratic or totalitarian. In place of the systematic congruence of representation, access, and accountability which characterizes the nation-state, within the plural society, centralized or acephalous, accessibility, representation, accountability, and power are systematically restricted; and the foundation and primary feature of the polity is its basic division between the rulers, organized as a corporate group, and the ruled, constituted as a leaderless, disorganized residual corporate category, often segmented by its own deep institutional divisions.

Political and social inequalities are as pervasive and fundamental in the plural society as they are ideologically inconsistent with the organization of a modern nation-state, whether democratic or totalitarian. Whereas the citizens of the nation-state, or at least the majority of them, normally share many other common institutions besides the government, in the plural society differential subjugation to the government is often the sole common condition that delimits the aggregate as a unit; and since such a society is established by specifically political action, its boundaries, composition, form, order, continuity, and developmental capacities are all politically codeterminate.

IV

As collectively standardized modes of coactivity, institutions have several interconnected dimensions: activity, social groupings and relations, norms, ideas, values, and orientations. Each institutional system also requires a material base, a social locus, and appropriate resources.

Analytically, the major institutional systems common to all societies, whatever their developmental level, consist of marriage, family and kinship, education, religion, economy, law, and government. Each of these systems may distinguish and integrate several specific institutional patterns, such as inheritance, property, marketing, bureaucracy, military organization, courts, divorce, adoption, contract, and the like. The form and content of these institutional systems vary widely among societies; and so do their differentiation and interconnections. In the simplest societies, kinship institutions virtually embrace the economy, cult, governmental agencies, modes of social control, education, and law; indeed, in the extreme case there may be no separate agency other than the kinship group which is specialized to discharge these functions. At the other extreme, kinship, marriage, and family are segregated from formal economic, political, and religious planes of action, and, to an increasing degree, from education also. Whereas in the simple undifferentiated society, kinship subsumes these latter institutional relations and activities, in the highly differentiated society, each institutional sphere has its own characteristic modes of organization, procedures of action, resources, aims, rules, values, membership, and ideology; and the higher the level of institutional differentiation and specialization, the greater the complexity of these specific structures and thus of the total social order.

All institutions have two analytically distinct, intimately connected aspects: the cultural and the social. Whether culture is restrictively defined as the symbols, norms, values, and ideational systems of a given population, or more inclusively as their standardized and transmitted patterns of thought and action, all institutional organization has a cultural coefficient, since each institution involves collective norms, ideas, and symbols as well as standardized modes of procedure. But since institutions prescribe norms of social grouping and relation, as for example in law, government, cult, or family, all institutions have prominent sociological aspects in the groups they constitute, and in the structures of status and role which they enjoin.

In consequence of this duality, culture and society are equally rooted in the institutional system on which each human aggregate depends for its inner cohesion, distinctive identity, membership, and boundaries. It follows that an institutionally homogeneous aggregate is also socially and culturally homogeneous; institutional heterogeneity likewise involves social and cultural heterogeneity; and social and cultural pluralism are equally rooted in institutional pluralism.

However, these social and cultural dimensions of heterogeneity and pluralism neither necessarily nor always correspond. This is so for two major reasons. Besides ideational and procedural correlates of social relations, culture includes such systems as language, aesthetic styles, philosophies, and expressive forms which may be transferred across social boundaries easily and with little social effect. Conversely, systems of social relations may perdure despite substantial shifts in their cultural content or explicit orientations. Thus, despite their common institutional basis and tendencies to congruence, culture and society may vary independently; indeed, their divergent alignments have special importance in contexts of pluralism, as indicated below.[7]

V

Those institutional systems that are common to all societies whatever their developmental level are evidently basic conditions or requisites of any societal organization. These systems include law, cult, economy, socialization, kinship, and government. Even in the most extreme context of pluralism, each aggregate is identified as a unit by its subjugation to a single common government. Beyond this, their institutional divergence may be almost total. In a heterogeneous society the majority of the members share all or most of the common basic institutions, namely, kinship, education, economy, government, law, and cult, despite institutional differences of a secondary level in the economic, educational, occupational, and even religious spheres. Such secondary differentiations are implicit in the functional specializations with which the complexity and development of these societies are inseparably linked; but as Durkheim and others point out, these institutional specializations are functionally interdependent, with the result that, given a shared institutional base, the aggregate derives cohesion from its internal differentiation at the secondary level of institutional development.

Perhaps Holland and the Scandinavian countries best represent this simple model of the heterogeneous society; such countries as Britain or Belgium contain added ethnic differentiations in consequence of their histories. Other heterogeneous societies such as the United States, the Soviet Union, Mexico, or Brazil embrace many plural features which further complicate their organization but do not alter their basic character since these differences only involve demographic minorities of the wider society.

In this context we should distinguish two modes of pluralism which may be combined with predominant societal heterogeneity. In the first and simpler case, the institutionally distinct minority or segments thereof constitute territorially discrete enclaves, as for example do the various tribal remnants on reservations in the United States or the Indians of Chiapas and other areas in Mexico. In such cases the heterogeneous society merely contains a number of plural enclaves whose members form dependent minorities.

Alternatively, a heterogeneous society may contain several plural communities, as notably in the southern United States. In their internal organization, these plural communities satisfy all the conditions necessary to distinguish plural societies except that, lacking political and cultural distinctness and autonomy, they remain dependent and subordinate local segments of a wider society; and, lacking the corporate closure with which institutional distinctness provides societies, they are continuously subject to the various pressures and influences developed within the society that surrounds them. In short, as United States political history shows, these plural communities of the South are structurally peculiar local segments of the heterogeneous American society that incorporates them, but neither separate nor independent societies.

We should therefore distinguish heterogeneous societies with plural features from those without, and in the first category, those with plural enclaves from those with plural communities, or from others with both.

The essential criterion of the heterogeneous society is that the majority of its members share a common system of basic institutions, together with systematic differentiation at the secondary level of institutional and organizational specialization. In the plural society, a politically autonomous unit ruled by a culturally distinct and politically privileged minority, the sole institutional framework that incorporates the aggregate is government, which normally has the form of a state. Whether it is redistributive or market-based, the economy of such a unit includes the population differentially.

Plural societies vary in the institutional heterogeneity or homogeneity of their ruling sections. The dominant whites in the Republic of South Africa are institutionally and socially heterogeneous, while the Tutsi of traditional Ruanda [8] or the Muslim Paktuns who ruled Hindus in the Swat Valley [9] were rather the reverse. Only if the ruling section of a plural society is institutionally homogeneous, as in Swat, will the unit remain uncentralized—a polity unified by a common structure of corporate domination, but lacking the forms and integration of a state. Wherever the ruling section in the plural society is institutionally heterogeneous, as in Latin America and the Caribbean colonies, in feudal Europe or the colonial Far East, the plural society is always incorporated within the framework of a state.

VI

In addition to the distinction between centralized and acephalous societies, we should also distinguish societies with reference to their ideological basis and majority orientation as sacred (theocratic) or secular.

In the sacred centralized society, typical for example of Islam, differences of cult and belief divide believers and nonbelievers into two distinct religious and political collectivities. If Jews or Christians are also present in substantial numbers, these *dhimmi* are also segregated as separate collectivities. Islam prescribes the political exclusion of nonbelievers and their subordination to the community of the Faithful; and in this respect it merely systematizes the orientation that characterizes all theocratic regimes, including Hinduism, Buddhism, and Christianity. Islam further prescribes the organization of the Faithful into a political community with the form of a state under a ruler and a hierarchy of officials. Thus, where devout Muslims constitute the dominant minority, as in many parts of traditional India, Northern Nigeria, and the Niger Bend at various historical periods, the result is a theocratic plural society in which religion provides the basic legitimation and principle of corporate cleavage, irrespective of other shared institutions, such as kinship or economy.

In all theocratic polities the religious bases and conceptions of society as a divinely prescribed order enjoin pluralism solely on religious grounds wherever the dominant congregation is a minority, irrespective of racial, linguistic, or institutional communities across religious boundaries. Normally each ritually ordained social organization is so distinctive in its form and content that differences in religion usually entail corresponding differences in other institutional spheres. However, this was not always true of Protestants and Catholics, whose religious conflicts during the sixteenth and seventeenth centuries promoted the secularization of European society. Nor have religious differences within the Buddhist or Muslim communities always involved parallel differences in secular institutions. Often rather minor differences of ritual or belief serve to set coreligionists against one another; but unless contraposed groups are also differentiated institutionally, pluralism has no place in their conflict.

VII

We can now begin to examine the relations between institutional divergences of differing degree and type and pluralism or heterogeneity. Our basic question concerns the minimal combinations of institutional or political difference which are necessary and sufficient to incorporate collectivities as separate sections of a wider society. More precisely, we must also try to show how these differing combinations of institutional or political differentiations come to take such effect. These questions are equally central to our understanding of the social processes and structures of plural and heterogeneous societies.

It is true that differences in the basic institutional systems of two collectivities constitute pluralism and establish plural societies where the minority, by reason of its superior resources and organization, dominates the majority, whose institutional organization and resources reduce their capacity for resistance. The ensuing domination may be based on conquest, negotiation, enslavement, indenture, or ideological ascendancy, separately or together. It may be instituted as serfdom, helotage, peonage, slavery, or colonialism, or through restrictive political franchise. In some cases the structure of domination takes the form of caste, although, as we shall see, such "caste" differs profoundly from the Indian institution. In all contexts of pluralism, the dominant section distinguishes itself from the dominated, both politically and by means of their institutional differentiae; and where these social and cultural differences coincide with differences of "race," corporate exclusions and oppositions are frequently expressed in racial terms. Indeed, "racial" coefficients of institutional and political division are often invoked as stereotypes despite their objective absence or their marginal biological significance. The social validity of these racialist classifications and interpretations of social cleavage is obviously unaffected by their scientific status. Where institutionalized, such racial categories are generally local developments of modes of thought that formed part of the traditional culture of the dominant ethnic group.

A strictly demographic typology of pluralism is unsatisfactory because it predicates that which it should explain; explicitly, it makes no attempt to identify the particular types, degrees, or combinations of institutional difference which distinguish conditions of pluralism from heterogeneity. Empirical materials cannot directly resolve this problem. It is therefore necessary to proceed to a theoretical analysis of the implications of institutional differences and continuities of various types for the integration of the social systems in which they appear. In this analysis simple demographic ratios are initially irrelevant.

Meyer Fortes' distinction between the kinship and politico-jural domains of social organization is especially useful in this inquiry.[10] We may generalize this to distinguish the familial or *private* domain and the collective or *public* domain. Fortes, who applies this distinction to the analysis of descent, kinship, and affinity in segmentary lineage societies, shows clearly that in these relatively undifferentiated systems, the same institution may figure prominently in both domains of social life, though typically in different ways. Thus, to cite his own example, in tribal societies with a lineage base, marriage is simultaneously a relation between exogamous corporate lineages and the institutional basis of family life.[11] It thus falls equally in both domains, and in either its position and implications are qualified by its role and place in the other. In centralized societies, marriage is likewise regulated by laws of the state, while retaining its pivotal place in the private domain. As regards divorce, inheritance, paternity, family law, adoption, and the obligations of maintenance, all preeminently centered in the private domain, the position is essentially similar. These relations form part of the law by which the inner organization of the collectivity is regulated. In effect, the elements and organization of the private domain are common to all members of the collectivity that observes uniform institutions of marriage, kinship, family, and domestic organization. Likewise the institutionally homogeneous collectivity owes its integration and distinctness to the communities of procedure and organization which constitute its distinctive and common public domain. Among these elements of the public domain, collective organizations, forms, and modes of action are generally institutionalized in corporate form, whether in law, government, or economy. In addition, such institutions as property, markets, occupational associations, education, labor organizations, and cults are all explicitly collective phenomena which simultaneously serve to regulate relations within the collectivity and to organize and integrate its members as a structurally distinct and bounded aggregate.

Most of the basic institutional systems are represented in either domain, though unequally so, and variably, as societies differ in their modes and levels of institutional development and specialization. For example, in simple societies, routine economic action, education, and basic patterns of ritual action may be almost exclusively centered in the private domain. Commonly, in simple systems, the collective government is also based on kinship groupings. In heterogeneous differentiated societies the position differs sharply; there it is normally possible to consider collective organization and institutional structure with minimal attention to the level of family organization. Nonetheless, all societies, even the simplest, depend for their boundaries, organization, and internal order on the scope and character of their corporate structure, which is explicitly centered in the public domain. Together the corporate forms that the system includes constitute the collective frameworks of social organization for the people concerned. Thus, for example, if the unit's corporate structure includes appropriate modes of grouping for leadership, it will enjoy an explicit political unity under a representative central organization; otherwise, the prevailing corporate organization constitutes the aggregate as an acephalous body whose unity is implicit in its common institutional framework at both the private and the public levels, though without expression in a single corporate form.

VIII

Another feature of institutional systems which requires explicit recognition is their variable interconnection and autonomy. Alternative modes of relations within and between the several institutional sectors of a common system include compatibility, inconsistency, and incompatibility of structure; divergence, complementarity, or equivalence at the formal and functional levels; asymmetrical dependence of one institution on another; interdependence or indifference and autonomy; symmetrical or asymmetrical reinforcements; feedback, congruence, coherence, codetermination, and integration; and conflict or contradiction. These are only some of the more familiar modes in which the institutions of a given system may be interlinked.

Some institutions such as family or cult may have several diverse types of relationships with other institutions in the common social system; but clearly, unless there is a tolerable margin of consistency or coherence among these institutions, they can scarcely combine into a self-perpetuating system capable of supporting an orderly collective life.

To illustrate the variability of institutional interconnections, we may briefly compare certain processes in American and Soviet society. As evidenced by their space programs, these countries have attained similar levels of technological and scientific development. Such equivalence implies substantial convergences in the Soviet and American structures of science and education. Nonetheless, the Soviet Union and the United States differ sharply in the political and economic institutions on which the technological capacities and educational organizations of their several space programs depend, equally though in differing ways. Interestingly, both the Soviet and the American economic systems, despite frequent assertions to the contrary, likewise depend, historically and structurally, for their institutionalization, development, maintenance, and regulation on political institutions that date from creative revolutions. Although substantially similar modes and levels of scientific, technological, and educational organization are equally compatible with the differing Soviet and American economic and political frameworks, Soviet economic collectivism is no more compatible with the American form of political organization than is individualist capitalism with the Soviet political regime. It would seem here, despite Marx, whose practice supports our interpretation against his theory, that instead of the "economic system" or, more specifically, the mode of production, determining the forms and levels of social organization, a specific political structure is prerequisite for the particular economic form, since in this comparison each mode of political organization excludes the alternative form of economy. Thus, although similar scientific and educational institutions may prevail under these radically different social regimes, and though their technological and economic systems may have comparable capacities, these economies, being structurally dependent on the political organization, differ correspondingly in form. Comparable variations characterize the relations between religion and polity in these two industrial states.

This example illustrates the point that while each institutional complex such as kinship or cult tends to form a reasonably coherent and autonomous subsystem, the integration of these several subsystems with one another is normally more variable and indirect than the integration of elements in each. For example, the connections between marriage, family, and domestic organization are more direct and pervasive than those that link familial organization to cult or government, especially in highly differentiated heterogeneous societies. As a corollary, institutions of the same kind drawn from societies with differing cultural traditions are likely to differ in their structural requisites and in their implications, wherever they differ in their elements and inner organization.

If the elements of two societies were hypothetically shuffled together like two decks of cards, the institutional correspondences and interdependencies on which either system initially relied for its inner coherence and efficient sequences of action could scarcely be reproduced by transference to other sectors of the alternative system. The connections between institutions within a system are far too specific and complex for such substitutability, equivalence, or transfer of connections to be generally possible for institutions drawn from historically differing systems. In two societies, specific relations between family, economy, and cult can rarely be the same, given structural differences in either of these sectors. For such transferability to be generally feasible without institutional dislocation and disjunction, the interconnections within and between the different sectors of either system must perfectly replicate and correspond with one another. This is a remote probability on analytic and statistical grounds alike.

A simple imaginary experiment demonstrates that, besides the specific elements that appear to constitute each institutional subsystem, we must also give special attention to their essential interconnections and structural requirements in order to determine their relative autonomy or interdependence within the system as presently constituted or under specific but variable conditions. This condition indicates that when two or more peoples having differing institutional systems are "shuffled together" by historical circumstances into a common inclusive aggregate, the probabilities that an immediate functional correspondence can be established between their several institutional systems is rather low, unless indeed these collectivities, falling at the same level of social development, also belong to a common wider tradition, as did the European immigrants to the United States, and thus already share a sufficiently broad frame of institutional correspondences in substance and form to permit relatively simple assimilation and intersystemic accommodations of their several distinct patterns.

Systemic tendencies toward institutional integration themselves preclude or obstruct facile substitutions and accommodations of the same or complementary institutions drawn from structurally different systems. Further, while some consistency and symmetrical reinforcement between institutions in the private and public domains of any collectivity are essential for the effective and orderly operation of its social system, institutions in either of these spheres require adequate levels of internal autonomy in order that their adjustments to developments in other institutional sectors of the social system may be effected smoothly. The higher the level of institutional differentiation and specialization within the system, the greater the specialization of each institutional sector and the greater the autonomy and flexibility requisite in each sphere to accommodate change generated elsewhere.

IX

Societies vary in the institutional differences that characterize the collectivities they incorporate. These lesser collectivities may share similar institutions of kinship, marriage, and family, while differing in their several public domains; or they may differ in both domains; or, while sharing a common mode of public organization, they may differ in other institutions of the public domain and also in their private domains. Alternatively, the collectivities may initially differ in particular public structures, such as government or cult, while sharing common patterns of organization in other areas. We must now try to determine analytically how such variable combinations of institutional continuity and discontinuity affect the organization and character of the inclusive society.

All politically unified societies possess common governments that exercise jurisdictions within them and on their behalf. This is equally true of colonies and of metropolitan states; but an autonomous exclusive jurisdiction is inconsistent with membership in an effective federation. Thus, insofar as an institutionally diverse aggregate forms a distinct and autonomous polity, whether acephalous as in the Swat Valley or Kachin Hills,[12] or centralized, as is more usual, all its components will be subject to a common government, although often differentially so. In consequence we may exclude the common political system from initial consideration in seeking those specific combinations of institutional divergence and community which distinguish pluralism and heterogeneity.

Employing Fortes' distinction between private and public domains, and recalling the important but variable connections among institutions in these spheres, let us consider certain specific alternatives: for example, situations in which two or more ethnic groups incorporated in a common polity do or do not share common or similar organizations of their private domains in the institutions of kinship, family, and marriage. If continuities in kinship and marriage prevail, then intermarriage and consequent social assimilation are facilitated to the degree that the associated private institutions such as domestic organization, divorce, inheritance, and the like are also common or symmetrically congruent, and insofar as such connubium is not obstructed by geographical separation or by collective regulations in either group, or proscribed in the public domain of the inclusive unit.

European immigrants to America, sharing sufficiently common institutions of kinship and marriage and recognizing American common law as the appropriate standard to regulate these relations, are subject to no national proscriptions against intermarriage. Such groups are, however, influenced by their own collective regulations and by accidents of circumstance, location, and the order in which they entered American society. Religious barriers to intermarriage with outsiders are institutionalized in the public domains of various religious collectivities. Further, strictly ethnic considerations limit the incidence of outgroup marriage. It seems unlikely that, despite the national ideology of assimilation and the absence of any legal proscriptions on this matter, outgroup marriage ratios exceed ingroup ratios, even in the third generation of immigrants among American Catholics of differing ethnic collectivities or among American Jews.

In America, marriage between whites and Negroes or Indians is also restricted, and collective proscriptions are often present. However, in these cases initial differences in the kinship institutions of white, Negro, and Indian Americans are not in themselves wholly sufficient to account for these collective restrictions. Native Indians were originally excluded from American colonial society as enemies or as allies; societal segregation was then mutual; but, as the Indians were overrun, the status of the Indian declined until connubium between the two groups came to be disapproved. The Negro, imported as a slave, was by status initially precluded from marriage with a free person, though not from concubinage.

Among the Tutsi and the Hutu of traditional Ruanda and Burundi, kinship institutions were sufficiently similar for fictional assimilations of

Hutu and Tutsi patrilineages to develop. However, Hutu and Tutsi may
not intermarry. Tutsi, the ruling section of these plural societies, proscribed such unions and thereby constituted themselves and the subject
Hutu as closed perpetual endogamous castes. By these proscriptions the
Tutsi maintained their sectional disassociation from the Hutu around
them, and avoided compromising their relations of dominance by ties of
kinship and affinity. Caste-endogamous marriage served also to reinforce
the closure and the internal cohesion of the Tutsi as a corporate group
controlling the administrative and political structure; for the Hutu, constituted as a corporate category under Tutsi regulation, caste endogamy
merely perpetuated conditions of servitude.[13]

The Fulani of Northern Nigeria fall into two distinct categories: pastoral nomads, who are nominally Muslim, and their settled cousins, who
provide the Muslim intelligentsia and ruling aristocracy of most Central
Sudanic emirates. The nomads and their sedentary cousins share identical kinship institutions; and settled Fulani aristocrats often marry girls of
pastoral stock, though the reverse rarely occurs. However, the two Fulani
communities remain quite distinct by virtue of differences in their respective public domains. Their separation persists despite long traditions of
military and political symbiosis and the formal overrule by settled Fulani
of the nomad communities. Special institutional arrangements were
maintained by ruling Fulani to accommodate the pastoralists to their
regimes without alienation or forced assimilation. In this case, divergences in their public domains served to segregate two branches of a
common ethnic stock despite shared familial institutions and formal
freedoms of connubium.[14]

Evidently, while shared familial institutions permit the assimilation of
separate groups by facilitating connubium, they do not necessarily promote or entail this result; and where the aggregates concerned are
systematically differentiated in the political sphere, as by dominance and
subordination in Ruanda, or by institutional differentiation among the
Fulani, collective boundaries persist even without formal proscriptions of
intermarriage.

On the other hand, where there are initial divergences of content,
form, basis, and scope in the familial institutions of two collectivities,
intermarriage is virtually precluded; and in such conditions intergroup
mating typically proceeds by illicit affairs with ambiguous paternity
obligations, by enforced concubinage in slavery or other forms of servitude, or by institutionalized or illegitimate hypergamy.[15] Given divergent
familial institutions, these appear to be the sole alternatives to collective
endogamy, which perpetuates corporate divisions and is easily transformed into "caste," especially if the separate collectivities are ranked

hierarchically as corporate units and maintain separate and unequal public domains. In such cases, an asymmetrical connubium may be institutionalized as hypergamy or concubinage; but either alternative merely serves to underline the corporate division and inequality. In either case, collective differences in the private domain seal off each aggregate as a separate self-reproducing unit having its own familial and cultural traditions, a segregated collective organization in its public domain, and distinctive contexts of socialization.

The factors that underlie patterns of collective endogamy in such conditions are reasonably clear. Given divergent norms of marriage and family, symmetrical intergroup marriage generates numerous problems of personal and collective status and rights which exacerbate and often mobilize collective hostilities and actively contrapose the two groups. Whenever such unions are legitimized, these conflicts of collective norms and organization are directly evident. In consequence, juxtaposed collectivities that differ in the structure and scope of their familial institutions are generally segregated as biological and social units whose separate cultural traditions are thus preserved and entrenched in the separate contexts of socialization that each maintains.

X

Such corporate closures are basic to the Indian system of caste. Nonetheless, as Hutton remarks, caste in India differs from pluralism.[16] First, caste is an essential dimension and organizational framework of the religion and culture all Hindus share. It identifies and unites these Hindu communities by dividing them on sacred bases. This differentiation is prescribed by a religious framework common to all castes. Second, as an effect of their occupational stereotyping, all local caste groups (*jati*) are directly and indirectly interdependent in the economic and ritual spheres; the various castes accordingly share several common institutions in their common public domain.

Familial institutions of the several castes in any region are also generally identical in form. Intercaste relations are contractual, individual, and of various kinds. These relations simultaneously differentiate the members of any given caste, and link men of different castes in elaborate contractual networks that cut across collective boundaries, dispersing personal loyalties and interests by individuating members of each caste. Such institutional arrangements all belong, like caste itself, in the common public domain. Besides *jajmani* relations, they include tenancy, wage labor, political alliances and factionalism, clientage, representative village councils (*panchayats*), and certain common village rituals, as well as common scales of ritual pollution, marriage and family ceremonies of similar form, and common dependence on Brahminical rites. Further, in most rural areas the dominant caste is also the most numerous, and generally employs its numerical preponderance in the village panchayat to preserve its local dominance and control of local land. Thus in neighboring areas, local dominance is often exercised by differing castes; and frequently these locally dominant groups are ranked low in the ritual hierarchy.

Such elasticities in the structure of secular status are quite consistent with the theoretically immutable ritual stratification of the various castes, since the ritual and secular status scales are only loosely connected and remain relatively independent of each other. As an effect of these conditions, Indian caste institutionalizes communities of action, norms, and social relations based on primary divisions of the people into a series of ranked endogamous categories whose separate autonomy is limited by their prescribed interdependence in the common public domain. In any caste, socialization to Hinduism and to the social order proceeds simultaneously with the inculcation of caste-specific norms and roles.[17]

Indian caste shows that, although continuities of institutional organization in the private domain permit the easy association and assimilation of collective groups by eliminating intrinsic obstacles to common connubium, these continuities are not in themselves sufficient to assure symmetrical intermarriage or the dissolution of collective boundaries; they are indeed unlikely to have such effects wherever the two collectivities are differentiated formally by their differing status and relations in the public domain of the inclusive aggregate. Conversely, as in the United States, ethnic groups and religious congregations may remain relatively endogamous despite similar familial institutions, and despite the absence of any formal proscriptions against connubium, while their members enjoy equivalent status in the inclusive public domain. However, if either collectivity is segregated spatially, its own public domain tends to become specialized, together with its relation to the inclusive society. Under such conditions, and especially if one collectivity is subordinate to the other as in Ruanda, or subsumed by its neighbor as among the Fulani, pluralism prevails through preemption of the societally regulative institutions by one unit to the exclusion of the other, with consequential differentiation of their collective domains and relations.

XI

We can learn most about the specific combinations of conditions which constitute or prevail under pluralism by examining further the varying combinations of institutional and structural diversity in American society. Among American whites, Jews, distinguished by religion and descent, form an internally divided, relatively endogamous group. Adherents of the Orthodox and Catholic faiths are likewise religiously differentiated and internally divided into a number of relatively closed ethnic groups, each distinguished also by its own specific religious organizations, by deep-set tendencies toward endogamy, by ethnic traditions, and sometimes by alternate languages. Protestants, subdivided by denomination and sect and also by ethnic group, probably have the lowest general tendencies toward ethnic and religious endogamy of all major divisions in the white American population. We have to ask in what ways do these parallel Jewish, Orthodox, Protestant, and Catholic differentiations differ, if at all, from the conditions of pluralism.

White Americans of Jewish, Orthodox, Catholic, or Protestant faith may participate freely and equally in common economic, educational, and political institutions; they are legally free to marry or to worship as they please; and in consequence, such closures as these ethnic and religious collectivities separately exhibit are optional and not societally prescribed. Given the institutional continuities in religious and familial institutions shared among these collectivities, individual mobility and assimilation are greatly facilitated so that uniform disassociations are restricted to such specific spheres as ethnicity or cult, where individual affiliations are also optional. Thus, neither the Orthodox nor the Jews nor the Catholics nor any of the various ethnic segments in "White America" are permanently or effectively closed. Indeed, within each group the members are extensively differentiated by various and often contraposed alignments with individuals and groups of differing kinds outside the collectivity concerned. In effect the secular organization of United States society treats religion as one of several institutional spheres in which personal affiliations are optional, expectably diverse, and formally indifferent to the central organization of the common public domain. In consequence, intra- or interethnic and denominational marriages or associations have limited significance in themselves for the wider society, or for the placement of individuals within it. The social identities and capacities of white Americans are not determined by their religious or ethnic affiliations; and, despite their undeniable significance to the individuals and religious or ethnic collectivities concerned, institutional identifications as Catholic, Orthodox, Jewish, or Protestant, or as Irish, Swedish, or Italian, are formally and substantively equivalent alternatives accommodated indifferently to the secular organization of the inclusive aggregate. By themselves, such ethnic and religious affiliations entail no direct or systematic differentiations or inequalities in the public sphere, in the educational, economic, social, and political systems, although they provide effective bases for the organization of corporate groups in pursuit of common interests.

These patterns of social heterogeneity among white Americans presuppose equally effective and uniform segregations of the several institutional spheres—kinship, cult, polity, economy, and education—so that differentiations among the population in kinship or cult do not necessarily entail corresponding differentiations or incapacities in other spheres. Thus, given the formal equivalence in familial institutions and the uniform segregation of religious organizations required by law as a necessary condition of secular equality, collective or individual differences in family and/or cult neither entail, presume, nor systematically correspond with parallel differences in other fields of individual or collective activity. Only by rigorous prescriptive closure such as Amish or Hutterites maintain can religious enclaves achieve a truly autarchic corporate differentiation in this society. In consequence, the structural significance of these ethnic or religious divergences and corporate affiliations for the total society and for the placement of individuals within it remains limited, conditional, and variable. In effect, such differentiated collectivities are equally consistent with the free participation of their members in the common heterogeneous society and can neither disqualify nor differentiate individuals by status or by capacity in the public sector, being themselves by the law and conditions of the secular society together incapable of subsuming and prescriptively regulating the major institutional interests and needs of their members. Thus, these institutional differentiations and collectivities are segregated as equivalent alternatives at the structurally secondary levels of national organization and personal affiliation. They fall primarily within the private domain of the wider collectivity.

XII

It is revealing to compare these white American patterns with others found among Negroes in the United States. Such a comparison shows how corporate divisions, once instituted as structural and institutional disjunctions in the public domain, are internally and externally reinforced and may perpetuate primary cleavages, irrespective of later institutional continuities across their boundaries and discontinuities within them.

Franklin Frazier shows how the Negro's social situation in the United States has tended to institutionalize deformities in all sectors of its private domain,[18] kinship, mating, family, paternity, and domestic organization alike. He shows also that, especially in northern cities, where conditions permit limited Negro professionalization and property accumulations, although Negro family and other social forms have tended to approximate the models institutionalized among American whites, the public domain of Negro society remains equally separate and distinctive.[19] Comparable contrasts in the religious, social, and family life of whites and Negroes in the Deep South are familiar to all.[20] In the North, Negroes and whites are segregated residentially, occupationally, and socially by informal caste or color-caste. The two racial divisions operate parallel but separate and distinctive organizations, and the Negro community characteristically remains economically depressed and dependent on the wealthier, more numerous, and more powerful whites. Thus, economic differentials and spatial and social boundaries interact to reinforce one another.

In the Deep South, despite recent tokenism in churches, courts, registration booths, and schools, caste divisions are basic, formal, and deeply entrenched as the fundamental conditions of Southern corporate structure. The requisite Negro subjugation is facilitated and maintained by their corporate exclusion as a residual category from the public domain of Southern white society. White control is pursued by various devices such as differential justice, denial of political rights, land control, tenancy, sharecropping, occupational and educational inequalities and insecurities, segregation of public facilities and residence, and the like. The recent rise of corporate organizations and public movements against this racial structure of inequality has evoked widespread hostile reactions in the South. Nonetheless, in the northern United States, where these movements won most initial support, parallel racial barriers persist with corresponding inequalities and tensions.

Negro acculturation in America has varied in degree and scope with differences of social circumstance. Negro and white professionals or bourgeoisie share many common institutional patterns; but these classes vary proportionately in both racial categories as a function of the prevailing inequalities of educational, economic, and political opportunity; further, the bourgeoisie and professionals in both races are structurally segregated and, with marginal exceptions, they are occupationally and socially restricted to their own racial categories. Thus, despite extensive institutional continuities across racial frontiers, Negro and white American professionals or bourgeoisie are not socially equivalent; rather, each group is isolated from the other within unequal, closed, and perpetual corporate categories which are racially defined and structurally contraposed. In consequence of this primary cleavage, Negro American professionals are defined first as Negroes, then as Americans, and only finally by occupation, in contrast with their white colleagues. How do the

contexts and correlates of such phenomena illuminate the salient differences between pluralism and heterogeneity?

On their introduction to America, Negroes were racially, culturally,
and socially distinct. Slavery categorized them as the property of their
owners and systematically denied them civil, economic, political, and
other social rights.[21] Following the abolition of slavery after deep strife,
effective substitute controls were developed by the dominant whites in
the Deep South to perpetuate the categorical exclusions on which Negro
subjugation and social inequality were based.[22] All persons of Negro
descent were identified as members of the category excluded from participation in the public domains of Southern white society. In the North, to
which many Southern Negroes emigrated, residential and social segregation produced broadly similar effects by simultaneously excluding them
from white society and by constituting them in urban ghettos as a
residual corporate category, irrespective of their internal institutional
and social differentiations. Given these structural contexts, institutional
continuities across racial boundaries, or institutional discontinuities
within either racial category, have limited relevance, in the wider society,
in either corporation, or to the individuals concerned.[23]

Similar divergences between institutional and corporate boundaries
are observed among the East Indians and Creole Negroes of Trinidad
and British Guiana.[24] In Trinidad, East Indians may identify many local
Creole Negro dishes and other cultural items as elements of "ancestral
Indian culture." Conversely, Negroid Creoles, having forgotten their
cultural debts to East Indians for numerous items, including cuisine,
ornaments, and so on, identify these as traditional Creole patterns. Such
"plural acculturation," cultural exchange, or assimilation merely high-
lights the distinction between strictly cultural and strictly social categorizations within this community. However incorrect these attributions may
be in fact, the primary identification for any individual or cultural item
as East Indian or as Creole Negro is prescribed by this corporate contra-
position. Hybrids, distinguished as *doglas* (bastards), are excluded by
East Indians from their collectivity. Though many middle-class East
Indians and Negroes share common institutional forms and skills, they
remain contraposed by their corporate identities.

Similarly, no American of either race fails to identify an American
Catholic Negro bishop or bureaucrat as first and foremost a Negro—that
is, by his primary corporate identity. In the United States, as in Guiana
and Trinidad, the racial division is institutionalized as a specifically
social boundary between two closed categories, irrespective of institutional continuities across boundaries or differences within either cate-

gory. On either side of these corporate boundaries, each collectivity maintains its distinct "public" organizations, for internal and external collective action in matters of common interest. In all three societies, the contraposed collectivities participate unequally and differently, but primarily as units in the public sector that includes them. As in Guiana or Trinidad, so in the United States, following an initial situation of marked differences between two structurally segregated collectivities, institutional modifications and assimilations have left intact their social boundaries, and social pluralism prevails, regardless of strictly cultural continuities between or differences within either category. In Trinidad and Guiana it is probable that a majority in either category remains unfamiliar with the other's institutional system, and perhaps also in the United States. However, exclusive categorical incorporations are clearly independent of cultural asssimilation or internal differences. Likewise, in Senegal, despite official French doctrines of assimilation and association, similar categorical exclusions contraposed European and *évolué*, despite their common institutional allegiances.[25]

The principal conditions that ensure such persistence of social pluralism despite the prevalence of institutional continuities across social boundaries are inherent in the corporate organization itself. If a social boundary rigidly separates two corporate categories, as in the northern United States, both collectivities will then lack inclusive corporate organizations in which they participate as equals and to whose coordinated actions alone they can look for peaceful changes in the corporate structure. On the other hand, if one of the collectivities has categorical form, while the other is organized as a corporate group, as in the South, the latter is generally dominant, and by virtue of its organizational and other resources, can effectively contain pressures for the dissolution of the corporate boundaries on which its power, status, and privilege are based. Individual actions and alignments cannot demolish or transform these social divisions and corporate units; nor can the representative national government initiate such radical action without assurances of overwhelming support from both collectivities, and especially from the majority of the dominant one.

When two corporations are defined by virtue of a common boundary, this can be abolished only by their separate but joint determination, or by the radical action of one of them. Tokenism is the logical corporate response to external pressures by a national government for the elimination of inequalities by which corporate sections are mutually defined and segregated, as in the Southern states. Cultural continuities or variations can neither erode nor transform these corporate structures directly for the simple reason that sectional divisions and relations are based on other principles, such as power, race, or other criteria of exclusive corporate solidarity and autonomy.

All collectivities that are segregated as or within societies require special procedures and organization to coordinate and regulate their internal action and to guide their relations with external corporations. In consequence, the public domains of segregated collectivities develop specific modes of organization and action to handle their collective interests and problems. The more rigorous and institutionally extensive the segregation of the collectivity, the deeper and wider is its associational boundary, and the more exhaustively are its members socially identified with and dependent upon it. In the structural context of a plural society, each corporate section develops sectionally specific institutions, organizations, and procedures that constitute its distinctive public domain; and if the plurality contains two or more collectivities of equivalent or differing status, their segregation is further reinforced by these mutually distinctive collective organizations. If these social sections are also segregated spatially, as is often the case, then the public domain of either unit enjoys corresponding freedom from external competition or immediate internal challenge. In effect, any institutional development or systematic organization in the collective domains of either section in a context of pluralism tends to reinforce the already existing divisions and separatism of the sections as mutually exclusive, internally autonomous, contraposed corporations. Such structural developments proceed independently of cultural continuities or assimilation across sectional boundaries.

Thus in the Republic of South Africa, as in the United States, the "black bourgeoisie" remain subject to the categorical identities and disabilities of their social sections.[26] In Trinidad, Guiana, and Mauritius,[27] Indians and Creole Negroes have each developed and retained specific sectional structures; and when these social sections were simultaneously enfranchised, their distinctive organizations were quickly converted into political parties, as also in Surinam [28] and Nigeria.[29]

In sum, it seems that the decisive conditions that constitute and perpetuate social pluralism consist primarily in differences of institutional organization in the public domains of segregated collectivities identified as the basic corporate units of social structure, and contraposed in consequence of sharp initial differences in their political status and in their several public domains.

Under such conditions, it is irrelevant whether the inclusive social order emphasizes the functional differentiation and autonomy of institutional spheres within either section. If collectivities are rigorously segregated, spatially and associationally, although the institutional structure may be highly differentiated within either collectivity, their separate public domains will each represent a sectionally specific and structurally distinctive organization. Under such conditions, the societally integrative effects of institutional differentiations and interdependences are restricted by and within the primary demarcation of collectivities as separate associational fields. Similarly, the opportunities for and implications of institutional assimilations or isomorphism are subject to the structural conditions and requirements of the prevailing corporate organization.

XIII

Inclusion of subordinate sections in the representative political institutions of the wider society on terms of formal equality is quite consistent with the maintenance of social pluralism, provided that this plural structure antedates the introduction of "democratic reforms." In such cases, formal democratization of the political process may be merely the means for preservation and stabilization of the plural regime.[30] This implies structurally profound divergences between formal equivalence and substantial reality.

Normally, however, the political regime of the plural society is identified by an exclusive concentration of political and juridical resources and functions in a ruling minority organized as a corporate group. In consequence, all other sections of the population are excluded from these political spheres as local aggregates or categories lacking extensive independent political organizations and capacities. Only where popular legislatures or tribunals prevail, or where offices are filled by direct or indirect election, can the scope of the franchise formally indicate the range of these differential statuses as citizen or subject. In most historic societies, such electoral institutions are lacking, and the ruling group is identified by its monopoly of the central political and administrative offices to which recruitment is primarily by descent or patronage. In either of these regimes, intermarriage and the equal association of the elite with the politically ineligible are normally proscribed. Generally, such structures of domination are centralized under a supreme office or corporation, identified exclusively with the dominant section.

In acephalous plural societies such as Pathan Swat, two further conditions are essential: the collective domination of the ruling group must be secure beyond local challenge; and the dominant section must have special institutional procedures to mediate its internal disputes and to mobilize its dispersed segments for joint action whenever necessary.[31] In centralized pluralities that lack popular electoral institutions, the ruler, identified socially and institutionally with the dominant section, is often ideologically represented as a personification of the polity, a divine king, or other quasi-sacred societal symbol. In themselves, these ideologies are clearly insufficient bases for the sectional dominions they seek to legitimate and rationalize.[32]

The political structure of a plural society is always dependent on a systematic organization of political, administrative, and military means and inequalities for its establishment and maintenance alike. In traditional contexts, sectional monopolies of regulative public structures normally presuppose and entail hereditary recruitments to office, sectional endogamy, and sharply differentiated contexts of socialization. As a result, the dominant section is identified as a self-perpetuating biological and social group by its closure, by its unique organization, by the societal authority of its public domain, and by the imposition of its own institutional order on the aggregate that it rules. The result is a characteristically oligarchic regime based on systematic political and social inequality and designed to preserve and perpetuate the institutional conditions essential for the sectional dominance with which it is identified. Ideologies of differing kind and quality may be elaborated to rationalize such plural regimes; but beyond such antecedent religious prescriptions as Islam enjoins, these ideologies generally misrepresent or sublimate the motivations, interests, and relations involved.

The structural stability of such a plural society has several important requisites. (1) There must be substantial continuity of the economic and ecological conditions in which the structure was first stabilized, involving either an appropriate population policy or a resource base capable of accommodating population increases over substantial periods. (2) There must be relative isolation of the aggregate from other societies of comparable scale and differing type. (3) By design or otherwise, the demographic ratios of the ruling and the ruled should be maintained or improved gradually in favor of the rulers. (4) Sectional identities and boundaries have to be maintained by generalizing the requisite inequalities and differences to all spheres—religious, familial, educational, occupational, economic, and other—with consequent restrictions on intersectional acculturation and exclusion of intersectional mobility. (5) Symbiotic relations, which provide primary compensations for the subordinate section and increase the stability of the regime, and religions that offer deferred compensations—for example, Christianity—should be encouraged in appropriate forms. (6) The cohesion, esprit de corps, and superior organization and resources to which the rulers owe their initial dominance should be maintained or enhanced through collective action that preserves and develops their corporate exclusiveness. Internal dissensions in the ruling group are functional only if they can be institutionalized in forms that subdivide and mobilize the subordinate sections to support elite protagonists, as in two-party systems firmly controlled by the dominant group. (7) Ideally the regime should be legitimized by an inclusive cult that sacralizes the structure and leadership, as in Inca or Ruanda society, by one that offers basic compensation in another life, or by one that advocates withdrawal from the world.

XIV

It is to be expected that in a plural society the dominant section will employ all the political and social resources in its control to stabilize and preserve its power and regime. To this end its members must simultaneously monopolize positions of power and immobilize the subject categories by suppressing or proscribing their collective political organization. To remedy this situation, the subordinate section needs first to develop an effective and inclusive corporate group, as, for example, the consilium plebis at Rome in 439 B.C.,[33] the Hussite congregation in fourteenth-century Europe,[34] the Parmehutu Aprosoma in Ruanda,[35] the Congress Party in India, and so forth. Often the collective protest of a subordinate acephalous section takes the form of social movements, such as Lollardy or Chartism in Britain, Cargo Cults in Melanesia,[36] or the revolutionary movements in France and Haiti at the close of the eighteenth century.[37] In other cases a charismatic leader may direct this sectional revolt through a loosely structured corporate group or body of disciples, as Gandhi did in India, Toussaint and Dessalines in Haiti, John Ball in feudal England, Shehu dan Fodio in the Central Sudan,[38] Miguel Hidalgo in Mexico, or the Mahdi and Bolívar.[39] At all events, as corporate categories, subordinate sections in plural societies lack the inclusive organization requisite for effective political action to challenge the organized and entrenched minorities that rule them; unless they can create and support such units, they remain immobilized by their internal divisions and common situation as residual subject categories.

If religious differences imposed the primary cleavage on which the plural structure rests, as in India, the Sudan, and elsewhere, then conversion and assimilation are necessary to eliminate it. Like Marxism, Islam for example has spread by enforcing the conversion and assimilation of conquered communities. Notably it has encountered sharpest resistance in India, where the ramified categorical organization of caste fragments its pressure and appeals.

Another peaceful process by which the institutional and corporate conditions of pluralism may be dissolved requires the absorption or assimilation of the dominant group into the culture and society of the dominated majority. This course is feasible only where the mass of the

people bear a common culture which is appropriate to the maintenance
of the political regime and which is more elaborately developed than that
of their rulers. Such assimilations occurred among the Liao, Mongols, and
Manchu in China,[40] the Seljuk and Ottoman Turks in Islam,[41] the Bulgars
under Byzantium,[42] and the Fulani in Hausaland.

Symbiosis may preserve a plural structure with minimal modification
by institutionalizing mutually satisfactory accommodations of the rulers
and the ruled.[43] This presumes the maintenance of favorable internal and
external conditions, together with adequate balances between population
and resources. Institutionalized symbiosis excludes structural change by
stabilizing relations of reciprocal interdependence on the basis of institutional and status differences between component sections of the plural
society. It simultaneously represents the ideal resolution of structural
tensions and a condition of stationary equilibrium in such societies.

Clientage, the institutionalized association of men of sharply different
status in contexts of political competition, has often served to integrate
the members of differing social sections in plural societies, such as the
plebs and patricians in early Rome and Athens, the Hutu and Tutsi in
Ruanda, the Fulani and Hausa in Northern Nigeria, and free men of
every station in the feudal systems of medieval Europe and Japan.[44] Such
clientage may only erode corporate divisions if it is sufficiently widespread and general, in consequence of basic cleavages within the ruling
stratum or insecurities in their external context, which require mobilization of intersectional support. Further, to promote structural transformation, the institution should also legitimate and encourage intermarriage
across sectional boundaries, and should facilitate or entail structurally
significant changes in individual status and political identity. Clientage is
institutionalized political symbiosis between individuals and/or reasonably small groups. It may accordingly enhance the internal stability of a
plural order by establishing valuable intersectional affiliations oriented to
factional competitions within the ruling group. By itself, clientage is
unlikely to dissolve sectional boundaries wherever differences of culture,
religion, or race are prominent. In feudal polities which rested heavily on
such relations, the servile majority remained beyond the range of institutional clientage, which was restricted to men of free or noble birth.

XV

Domination by the ruling minority in a plural society may be exercised
collectively through its political institutions, as at Sparta,[45] in Ruanda,[46]
among the Inca,[47] or in Pathan Swat,[48] or by *repartimiento*[49] or the
territorial segregation of the dominated on "tribal" reserves under the
supervision of the dominant groups, as was general in settler societies in

colonial Africa. Alternatively, segments of the subordinate population may be placed directly under the control of individuals drawn from the dominant group. In the latter instance, servitude is personalized; in the former it is collective. Personal servitude has many forms: serfdom, slavery, peonage, indenture, bondage, and so on. It is normally ascribed by allocation, birth, capture, debt, purchase, or lease. Personal proprietorship may be acquired by descent and inheritance, by vassalage, purchase, or official allocations, separately or together.

It is evident that these two alternative modes of instituting sectional dominance, the individual and the collective, establish patterns of intersectional relation among individuals which differ notably in immediacy, intensity, continuity, variability, and scope, and in the opportunities for cultural and social assimilation they provide. Any collective organization of sectional dominance segregates the dominated in local collectivities that foster their cultural distinctness and solidarity. Communally segregated Spartan helots, like the Russian serfs, maintained a spirited collective life apart from their masters, and repeatedly revolted, in vain, as did Negro slaves on New World plantations. In Europe and Japan serfs were subject to far more rigorous and personal supervision of their social life and lacked equivalent incentives and opportunities for revolt. In Ruanda, subject Hutu were simultaneously supervised by at least two hierarchies of officials; [50] and the Inca also institutionalized a dual system of collective administration.[51] In Grenada (West Indies), after emancipation, ex-slaves were habituated to servitude by symbiotic relations and by dispersal in discrete estate communities.[52] In nearby Barbados, sectional legislation explicitly forbade the ex-slaves to move about within the island, thereby tying them to the plantations as a dependent, immobile, landless proletariat, where they remain to this day.[53] In Mexico and other Hispanic New World territories, Indian communities were subjected to individual domination by Creole Spaniards and mestizos as field labor under various forms of peonage; and although violence was common, given the specific personal structure of control, in this context it was rarely generalized at this level of the society, except during wider struggles among superior social sections.

The structure of categorical subordination, organized and exercised collectively through locally discrete autonomous corporate groups, invites frequent revolt to the extent that its conditions are onerous and its supervision lax. This structure insulates the several social sections, and accordingly preserves their institutional differentiations by restricting opportunities for intersectional assimilation. In its most extreme form, it prescribes tributary relations between two politically distinct societies, the explicit antithesis of pluralism, which requires a common corporate organization of disparate elements in one society. By contrast, personal administration of discrete segments of the subordinate section brings corresponding increases in the range, intensity, and frequency of inter-personal contacts across sectional boundaries. Such increases of intersectional personal associations institute corresponding opportunities for cultural and social assimilations consistent with the corporate requirements of the inclusive regime. Under structures of either type, maintenance or modification of intersectional boundaries and relations depends primarily on collective social action rather than on cultural assimilations as such. In consequence, acculturated members of the subordinate section are situationally condemned to frustration, dissidence, or revolt, or to alignment with their superiors as trusted but expendable servitors and aides. This is so because in plural regimes individual qualities are irrelevant for the determination of social identity, which is ascriptive and corporate in base and significance. In effect, intersectional social mobility is kept at a minimum.[54]

Unless the politically excluded category is systematically subjugated by these collective or personal structures of domination, sectional control of the total society remains ambiguous and uncertain, despite sectional monopoly of the political regime; such a situation generates tension and invites revolt. Notably, this is the modal form of social pluralism which prevailed in western Europe from the dissolution of feudalism to the recent establishment of popularly elected representative governments. Characteristically, in this area until the mid-nineteenth century, peasants and emerging proletariats were denied political and civil rights under systems of legal immunity and privilege, sectional administration, and restrictive political franchise.[55] Besides their monopoly of government, commerce, land, law, church, and the officer corps, the dominant sections of these divided societies sought to enhance and preserve their institutional differentiation from the dominated majority by exclusive educational provisions for socialization of their young, and by restrictive control of occupational opportunities. In their heyday, as Disraeli, Mayhew, Marx, and others observed, such societies consisted of two broad categories, the masters and the servants; but under the prevailing frame of organization, servitude was a contractual alternative to unemployment, brigandage, emigration, or forced recruitment to the army, the mines, or the fleet.

Marx and Engels, observing these societies, interpreted their political structures as consequences of the economic inequalities inherent in their capitalist organization;[56] in this they systematically inverted the relations that held between the structures of political and economic inequality.

Analytically and historically alike, the economic inequalities these writers observed were based upon antecedent conditions of political and jural domination and presupposed them. With subsequent enfranchisement of the previously unrepresented section, economic inequalities have steadily reduced as the implications of political equality were realized. Anticipating such effects of political and industrial reform, Marx, whose dialectic led him to look for radical transformation of European society by working-class revolution, condemned gradualism and advocated political polarization. In this he clearly reveals his recognition of the primacy of political relations and action in determining the forms and degrees of social inequality and the conditions of social and economic organization.

In western Europe, during the nineteenth century, disenfranchised categories—Marx's peasants and proletariats—were institutionally differentiated and sectionally segregated from the ruling minority but were not prescriptively subordinated by organized collective or personal systems of domination. They were accordingly identified as masterless subjects, a residual category beyond the polity but subject to the state, which here as elsewhere was the corporate organization of the ruling group. In this context of sectional isolation, trade unions, workers' political associations, revolutionary movements, and ideologies of varying type flourished apace, repeatedly shaking the foundations of these plural societies and successively demonstrating the urgency of incorporating the mass as citizens and providing them with the essential resources of education and organizational access necessary to translate formal citizenship into active capacity. Established political parties representing the elite and its interests occasionally sought to incorporate some of the disenfranchised within their ranks to achieve party advantage, and also to frustrate the emergence of rival structures devoted to sectional interests of the subordinate class. These aims were variably realized; but, as the hitherto disenfranchised acquired citizenship, education, and effective industrial and political organizations, they simultaneously reduced the institutional gulfs that had formerly separated them from their rulers, until, after World War II, the distinctive institutions, organizations, and differences of political status which had once contraposed the social sections of these European nations lost their initial significance; and, with some notable exceptions, the plural societies of eighteenth-century Europe were transformed into heterogeneous nation-states. We can summarize these processes of national development and integration as the progressive elimination of corporate categorizations in the social structure through the extension of citizenship from the oligarchy to all members of the corporate group.

XVI

Colonialism in Africa repeats these European developments with much greater clarity and speed. Once enfranchised in consequence of military disasters and/or changes of political orientation experienced by the imperial states, the African colonial populations could not long be denied autonomy. Having obtained it, the ex-colonial states pursue economic development and social modernization in different ways, by single or multiparty regimes and under ideologies of varying provenience or coherence.

The essential conditions that currently diversify the organization and orientations of these new African states seem to flow in approximately equal measure from their history and from their social constitutions, but their histories and social constitutions both identify these emergent states as pluralities of varying complexity and form. In some states the major political divisions are between regionally segregated ethnic collectivities. In others the primary cleavages are between the westernized elite and the traditional mass, organized in several tribal societies and/or traditional states. In yet others these two modes of cleavage are variously and fluidly combined; and in both the older independent African states, Ethiopia and Liberia, despite striking differences in history and form, social pluralism is basic to the political regime and shows no sign of immediate disappearance.[57] When to these alternatives we add the variable presence of European settler communities, the wide variety in the constitution of plural societies in modern Africa is clear, and a corresponding variety in their political and constitutional forms and developments seems inevitable.

Clearly, to transform these plural societies into institutionally heterogeneous nation-states is no easy task, however desirable or essential it may seem to nationalists committed to ideals of corporate unity, identity, and consensus. Yet, if our analysis of the structural and institutional conditions of pluralism is correct, its transformation into the social heterogeneity that is prerequisite for "modernization" involves the following conditions together: (1) Effective institutionalization of uniform conditions of civil and political equality throughout the country; this especially involves the elimination of elite, sectional, or ethnic privileges in the public sphere. (2) Provision of equal, appropriate, and uniform educational, occupational, and economic opportunities to all cultural sections of the society, and the principled recruitment of active participation in approximately equivalent ratios from all major ethnic groups. (3) Public enforcement of the fundamental freedoms of worship, speech, movement, association, and work. Such measures seem to be equally expedient and necessary for any ex-colonial government, African or other, which is intent on pursuing social modernization by initiating the structural conditions requisite for the progressive but gradual transformation of their rigid plural societies into labile heterogeneous ones.

In this context it is most essential to distinguish substance and form, function and ideology, reality and fiction. Statute books may contain numerous liberal laws which, if implemented systematically, would dissolve the exclusive and unequal corporations in which pluralism consists. However, unless these laws are scrupulously enforced, they merely signalize that pluralism persists in the public sphere under covert or overt pressure. There are also many subtler ways in which an appearance of political and social equality may disguise and perpetuate pluralisms founded on basic social and institutional differences, disabilities, and inequalities. For example, in the Jamaican two-party system based on universal suffrage, each party with its industrial wing may demand internal stability as a condition of economic viability or development. Where such systems entrench historically privileged social sections in control of national organizations, public or voluntary, they stabilize the plural structure under apparently liberal political regimes by restricting the scope for social mobility and intersectional change through their institutionalized corporate factionalism.[58] However, one-party regimes based on mass suffrage may differ very little, if they also place ideological purity, solidarity, internal stability, and economic development ahead of social equality, mobility, and assimilation, and on these platforms institutionalize elite or ethnic domination.

Our survey shows that public regulative structures are the central agencies for the preservation or modification of corporate divisions and relations in plural societies. This is equally true under independence or colonialism, one-party or multiparty regimes. Unless equal and adequate public facilities are provided in representation, administration, education, justice, industrial organization, and occupational mobility, those inequalities and sectional divisions with which the old structure was identified will certainly persist, irrespective of the leadership, organization, and ideology of the state.

NOTES

[1] J. S. Furnivall, "Some Problems of Tropical Economy," in Rita Hinden, ed., *Fabian Colonial Essays* (London: George Allen and Unwin, 1945), pp. 161–184; and J. S. Furnivall, *Colonial Policy and Practice* (London: Cambridge University Press, 1948), pp. 304–312.

[2] Georges Balandier, "The Colonial Situation," in Pierre L. van den Berghe, ed., *Africa: Social Problems of Change and Conflict* (San Francisco: Chandler

Publishing Co., 1965), pp. 36–57; Adriano Moreira, "Rapport général: Aspect juridique et politique," in *Ethnic and Cultural Pluralism in Intertropical Countries* (Brussels: INCIDI, 1957).

[3] B. Malinowski, *A Scientific Theory of Culture and Other Essays* (Chapel Hill: University of North Carolina Press, 1944), pp. 52–74; S. F. Nadel, *The Foundations of Social Anthropology* (London: Cohen and West, 1951), pp. 108–144; A. R. Radcliffe-Brown, *Structure and Function in Primitive Society* (London: Cohen and West, 1952), pp. 197–203.

[4] M. G. Smith, "A Structural Approach to Comparative Politics," in David Easton, ed., *Varieties of Political Theory* (Englewood Cliffs, N.J.: Prentice-Hall, 1966), pp. 113–128.

[5] Leonard Broom, "Discussion," in Vera Rubin, ed., *Social and Cultural Pluralism in the Caribbean,* Annals of the New York Academy of Sciences, 83 (Jan. 1960), 889.

[6] T. H. Marshall, *Class, Citizenship and Social Development* (New York: Anchor Books, 1965), pp. 71–134; Aristotle, *Politics,* trans. Benjamin Jowett, Bk. III, chap. 6 (New York: Modern Library, 1943), pp. 136–138.

[7] M. G. Smith, *The Plural Society in the British West Indies* (Berkeley and Los Angeles: University of California Press, 1965), pp. 68–73, 81, 84–85, 175.

[8] J. J. Maquet, *The Premise of Inequality in Ruanda* (London: Oxford University Press, 1961); Marcel d'Hertefelt, "The Rwanda of Rwanda," in James L. Gibbs, Jr., ed., *Peoples of Africa* (New York: Holt, Rinehart and Winston, 1965), pp. 403–440.

[9] Fredrik Barth, *Political Leadership among Swat Pathans* (London: Athlone Press of the University of London, 1959), pp. 7–30.

[10] Meyer Fortes, "Descent, Filiation and Affinity: A Rejoinder to Dr. Leach," *Man,* LIX (Nov. 1959), 193–197; (Dec. 1959), 206–212.

[11] *Ibid.,* pp. 194–197, 206–208.

[12] E. R. Leach, *Political Systems of Highland Burma* (London: G. Bell and Sons, 1954).

[13] Maquet, *op. cit.,* pp. 46, 64–67; d'Hertefelt, *op. cit.,* pp. 414–419.

[14] Derrick J. Stenning, *Savannah Nomads: A Study of the Wodaabe Pastoral Fulani of Western Bornu Province, Northern Region, Nigeria* (London: Oxford University Press, 1959); Derrick J. Stenning, "The Pastoral Fulani of Northern Nigeria," in Gibbs, *op. cit.,* pp. 361–402. See also M. G. Smith, "The Hausa of Northern Nigeria," in *ibid.,* pp. 119–156.

[15] M. G. Smith, *Stratification in Granada* (Berkeley and Los Angeles: University of California Press, 1965), pp. 175–177, 182–188.

[16] J. H. Hutton, *Caste in India* (London: Cambridge University Press, 1946), p. 117.

[17] Adrian C. Mayer, *Caste and Kinship in Central India: A Village and Its Region* (London: Routledge and Kegan Paul, 1955); Hutton, *op. cit.;* E. R. Leach, ed., *Aspects of Caste in South India, Ceylon and North-West Pakistan* (Cambridge: The University Press, 1960); McKim Marriott, ed., *Village India: Studies in the Little Community,* American Anthropologist Memoir no. 83, vol. 57, no. 3, pt. 2 (June 1955); Thomas O. Beidelman, *A Comparative Analysis of the Jajmani System* (Locust Valley, N.Y.: J. J. Augustin, 1959); Pauline Mahar Kalenda, "Toward a Model of the Hindu Jajmani System," *Human Organization,* 22, no. 1 (March 1963), 11–31; M. N. Srinivas, Y. B.

Damie, S. Shahani, and André Beteille, "Caste: A Trend Report and Bibliography," *Current Sociology*, XIII, no. 3 (1959).

[18] E. Franklin Frazier, *The Negro Family in the United States* (Chicago: University of Chicago Press, 1940).

[19] E. Franklin Frazier, *The Negro in the United States* (New York: Macmillan, 1949), and *Black Bourgeoisie: The Rise of a New Middle Class in the United States* (New York: Collier Books, 1962).

[20] John Dollard, *Caste and Class in a Southern Town* (Garden City: Doubleday Anchor Books, 1957); Hortense Powdermaker, *After Freedom: A Cultural Study of the Deep South* (New York: Viking Press, 1939).

[21] Frederick Law Olmsted, *The Slave States before the Civil War* (New York: Capricorn Books, 1959); Stanley M. Elkins, *Slavery: A Problem in American Institutional and Intellectual Life* (New York: Grosset and Dunlap, 1963); Ulrich B. Phillips, *Life and Labor in the Old South* (Boston: Little, Brown, 1963); Kenneth M. Stampp, *The Peculiar Institution: Slavery in the Ante-Bellum South* (New York: Vintage Books, 1964).

[22] Charles S. Johnson, *Shadow of the Plantation* (Chicago: University of Chicago Press, 1934); Allison Davis, Burleigh B. Gardner, and Mary R. Gardner, *Deep South: A Social Anthropological Study of Caste and Class* (Chicago: University of Chicago Press, 1941).

[23] Gunnar Myrdal, *An American Dilemma: The Negro Problem and Modern Democracy* (New York: Harper, 1944).

[24] Daniel J. Crowley, "Plural and Differential Acculturation in Trinidad," *American Anthropologist*, 59 (1957), 817–824; Daniel J. Crowley, "Cultural Assimilation in a Multiracial Society," in Rubin, *op. cit.*, pp. 850–854; Morton Klass, "East and West Indian: Cultural Complexity in Trinidad," in *ibid.*, pp. 855–861; Elliott P. Skinner, "Group Dynamics and Social Stratification in British Guiana," in *ibid.*, pp. 904–916; Raymond T. Smith, *British Guiana* (London: Oxford University Press, 1962), pp. 98–143; Leo A. Despres, "The Implications of Nationalist Policies in British Guiana for the Development of Cultural Theory," *American Anthropologist*, 66 (Oct. 1964), 1051–1077; *New World* (Georgetown, British Guiana), I (March 1963); Leo A. Despres, *Cultural Pluralism and Nationalist Politics in British Guiana* (Chicago: Rand McNally, 1967).

[25] Paul Mercier, "Evolution of Senegalese Elites," in van den Berghe, *op. cit.*, pp. 163–178; Paul Mercier, "The European Community of Dakar," in *ibid.*, pp. 283–300; Michael Crowder, *Senegal: A Study in French Assimilation Policy* (London: Oxford University Press, 1962).

[26] Leo Kuper, *An African Bourgeoisie: Race, Class and Politics in South Africa* (New Haven: Yale University Press, 1965); J. C. Mitchell, *Tribalism and the Plural Society* (London: Oxford University Press, 1960).

[27] B. Benedict, "Stratification in Plural Societies," *American Anthropologist*, 64, no. 6 (1962), 1235–1246; B. Benedict, *Indians in a Plural Society: A Report on Mauritius* (London: H.M.S.O., 1961).

[28] R. A. J. van Lier, *The Development and Nature of Society in the West Indies* (Amsterdam: Royal Institute for the Indies, 1950).

[29] James S. Coleman, *Nigeria: Background to Nationalism* (Berkeley and Los Angeles: University of California Press, 1958); K. W. J. Post, *The Nigerian Federal Election of 1959: Politics and Administration in a Develop-*

ing Political System (London: Oxford University Press, 1963); Thomas L. Hodgkin, *African Political Parties* (Harmondsworth: Penguin Books, 1961).

[30] In this context, for the reforms of Appius Claudius at Rome, of Solon and Cleisthenes in Athens, and the Carthaginian constitution, see H. Warde Fowler, *The City State of the Greeks and Romans* (London: Macmillan, 1952); Victor Ehrenberg, *The Greek State* (New York: Norton, 1964); M. Cary, *A History of Rome* (London: Macmillan, 1945). For two rather different modern views, see Kenneth A. Heard, *Political Systems in Multiracial Societies* (Johannesburg: South African Institute of Race Relations, 1961); W. Arthur Lewis, "Beyond African Dictatorship: The Crisis of the One-Party State," *Encounter*, 25, no. 2 (Aug. 1965), 3–18.

[31] Barth, *op. cit.*

[32] Marcel d'Hertefelt, "Mythes et Idéologies dans le Rwanda ancien et contemporain," in Jan Vansina, Raymond Mauny, and L. V. Thomas, eds., *The Historian in Tropical Africa* (London: Oxford University Press, 1964), pp. 219–238; M. d'Hertefelt, A. Troubworst, and J. Scherer, *Les anciens royaumes de la Zone Interlacustrine Meridionale* (London: International African Institute, 1962); Maquet, *op. cit.* See also A. M. Hocart, *Kingship* (London: Watts, 1941), pp. 1–11.

[33] Cary, *op. cit.*, pp. 72–83.

[34] Norman R. C. Cohn, *The Pursuit of the Millennium* (London: Secker and Warburg, 1957), pp. 217–236; Howard Kaminsky, "The Free Spirit in the Hussite Revolution," in Sylvia L. Thrupp, ed., *Millennial Dreams in Action: Essays in Comparative Study* (The Hague: Mouton, 1962), pp. 166–186.

[35] Marcel d'Hertefelt, "Les Elections communales et le consensus politique au Rwanda," *Zaïre*, XIV, no. 5–6 (1960), 403–438; see also d'Hertefelt, Troubworst, and Scherer, *op. cit.*, pp. 227–246.

[36] See Cohn, *op. cit.*, pp. 209–217; Thrupp, *op. cit.*; Peter M. Worsley, *The Trumpet Shall Sound: A Study of "Cargo" Cults in Melanesia* (London: MacGibbon and Kee, 1957).

[37] Alexis de Tocqueville, *The Old Regime and the French Revolution*, trans. Stuart Gilbert (Garden City: Doubleday Anchor Books, 1955); Georges Le Febvre, *The Coming of the French Revolution, 1789*, trans. R. R. Palmer (New York: Vintage Books, 1957); James G. Leyburn, *The Haitian People* (New Haven: Yale University Press, 1941); C. L. R. James, *The Black Jacobins: Toussaint L'Ouverture and the San Domingo Revolution* (New York: Random House, 1963).

[38] E. J. Arnett, *The Rise of the Sokoto Fulani, Being a Paraphrase and in Some Parts a Translation of the Infaqu'l Maisuri of Sultan Mohammed Bellow* (Lagos: C.M.S. Bookshop, 1922).

[39] J. Patrick McHenry, *A Short History of Mexico* (New York: Doubleday, 1962), pp. 75–85.

[40] Karl A. Wittfogel and Feng Chia-Sheng, *History of Chinese Society: Liao (907–1125)*, Transactions of the American Philosophical Society, n.s., vol. 36 (Philadelphia, 1949), pp. 1–32; René Grousset, *The Rise and Splendour of the Chinese Empire*, trans. Anthony Watson-Gandy and Terence Gordon (London: Geoffrey Bles, 1952), pp. 231–247, 272–302; Sybille van der Sprenkel, *Legal Institutions in Manchu China* (London: Athlone Press of the University of London, 1962).

[41] Carl Brockelmann, *History of the Islamic Peoples*, trans. Joel Carmichael

and Mosle Perlmann (New York: Capricorn Books, 1962), pp. 163–180, 256–343; H. A. R. Gibb and Harold Bowen, *Islamic Society and the West* (London: Oxford University Press, 1950), vol. 1.

[42] Stephen Runciman, *Byzantine Civilization* (New York: Meridian Books, 1961), pp. 222–229; A. A. Vasiliev, *History of the Byzantine Empire* (2 vols.; 2d English ed., rev.; Madison: University of Wisconsin Press, 1958), I, 281–283, 315–320, 331.

[43] S. F. Nadel, "Social Symbiosis and Tribal Organization," *Man*, 38 (1938), 85–90; M. G. Smith, *Stratification in Granada*, pp. 11–13, 255.

[44] Marc L. B. Bloch, *Feudal Society*, trans. L. A. Manyon (London: Routledge and Kegan Paul, 1961), pp. 145–238; F. L. Ganshof, *Feudalism*, trans. Philip Grierson (London: Longmans, Green, 1952); G. B. Sansom, *Japan: A Short Cultural History* (rev. ed.; New York: Appleton-Century-Crofts, 1962), pp. 270–296, 426–431.

[45] Aristotle, *Politics*, Book II, chap. 9, pp. 107–114; Ehrenberg, *op. cit.*, pp. 33–39, 54, 96–97.

[46] Maquet, *op. cit.*, pp. 96–124; d'Hertefelt, "The Rwanda of Rwanda," pp. 406–407, 420–430.

[47] Sally Falk Moore, *Power and Property in Inca Peru* (New York: Columbia University Press, 1954).

[48] Barth, *op. cit.*

[49] François Chevalier, *Land and Society in Colonial Mexico*, trans. Alvin Eustis (Berkeley and Los Angeles: University of California Press, 1963), pp. 66–69, 277–296; Allan R. Holmberg, "Changing Community Attitudes and Values in Peru: A Case Study in Guided Change," in Richard N. Adams, John P. Gillin, Allan R. Holmberg, Oscar Lewis, Richard Patch, and Charles Wagley, *Social Change in Latin America Today* (New York: Vintage Books, 1960), pp. 67–84.

[50] Maquet, *op. cit.*, pp. 100–124, 129–131, 140.

[51] Moore, *op. cit.*

[52] M. G. Smith, *The Plural Society in the British West Indies*, pp. 262–303; M. G. Smith, *Dark Puritan* (Kingston, Jamaica: University of the West Indies, 1963), pp. 9–11, 22–29, 36–38.

[53] W. M. Macmillan, *Warning from the West Indies* (Harmondsworth: Penguin Books, 1938), pp. 90–91.

[54] M. G. Smith, *Stratification in Grenada*, pp. 205–227, 258.

[55] G. D. H. Cole and Raymond Postgate, *The Common People, 1746–1946* (London: Methuen, 1946); Marshall, *op. cit.*, pp. 71–134; George F. E. Rudé, *The Crowd in History* (New York: Wiley, 1964).

[56] Karl Marx and F. Engels, *The Communist Manifesto* (London: The Communist Party, 1948).

[57] Merran Fraenkel, *Tribe and Class in Monrovia* (London: Oxford University Press, 1964); Edward Ullendorf, *The Ethiopians: An Introduction to Country and People* (London: Oxford University Press, 1965).

[58] M. G. Smith, *The Plural Society in the British West Indies*, pp. 314–319.

Chapter 3 Pluralism and the Polity: A Theoretical Exploration*

Pierre L. van den Berghe

In his introductory statement to this colloquium, "Plural Societies: Perspectives and Problems," Leo Kuper outlines the major characteristics of two widely different approaches to pluralism, which he calls the "conflict model" and the "equilibrium model." The older "equilibrium" tradition has been associated with de Tocqueville and through him with the bulk of North American political and social science;[1] that tradition has asserted that "pluralism" is one of the important conditions making for democracy. The "conflict" school traces its more recent pedigree to Furnivall and includes mostly British or British-trained anthropologists who have worked in colonial societies of Africa and the Caribbean;[2] it associates pluralism with despotism, frequently by a culturally dominant minority. The opening statement by M. G. Smith clearly falls in the second "school." The main task of the present paper is to explore this seeming contradiction.

Since the problem revolves, at least in part, around the definition of "pluralism," I shall first try to specify what I mean by that term. Societies are pluralistic insofar as they exhibit, to a greater or lesser degree, two basic features: (1) segmentation into corporate groups that frequently, though not necessarily, have different cultures or subcultures; and (2) a social structure compartmentalized into analogous, parallel, noncomplementary but distinguishable sets of institutions.

These two defining criteria of pluralism distinguish plural societies both from societies with segmentary kinship units (such as lineages,

---

* I wish to express my appreciation to the colleagues and students who reacted to the oral presentation of this paper at the symposium on pluralism. Subsequent conversations with Leo Kuper, Hilda Kuper, M. G. Smith, and Sally Moore proved to be particularly stimulating.

moieties, or clans) and from societies with a high degree of functional differentiation or specialization in their institutional structure. The segmentary, undifferentiated society is divided into clearly defined corporate groups (typically unilineal descent groups), but it has a unitary, homogeneous institutional structure. On the other hand, the functionally differentiated society has multiple, but complementary and interrelated, institutions. Additional characteristics frequently associated with pluralism are the following: (1) relative absence of value consensus; (2) relative presence of cultural heterogeneity; (3) relative presence of conflict between the significant corporate groups; (4) relative autonomy between parts of the social system; (5) relative importance of coercion and economic interdependence as basis of social integration; (6) political domination by one of the corporate groups over the others; and (7) primacy of segmental, utilitarian, nonaffective, and functionally specific relationships *between* corporate groups and of total, nonutilitarian, affective, diffuse ties *within* such groups.

From the above, it is clear that my usage of the concept of pluralism is more inclusive than, but broadly congruent with, that of M. G. Smith. Unlike Smith, I do not think that incompatibility of institutions based on unrelated cultural traditions is a necessary condition of pluralism.[3] Nor do I believe that much is gained by distinguishing plural societies (characterized by political domination of a cultural minority) from societies with plural features and from heterogeneous societies (e.g., those based on class stratification). I prefer to regard pluralism as a variable, and to include cases of stratification based on "race," caste, estate, or class (in the corporate sense as distinct from strata) as instances of pluralism, even though the constituent groups share the same general culture. To the extent that classes are corporate groups, they will develop subcultural differences and some class-specific institutional structures (e.g., labor unions and political parties).

Interestingly, in his introductory statement to this volume, Smith retreats from his criterion of institutional incompatibility, and speaks of "institutional cleavages" and "institutionally distinct collectivities." He substitutes political domination by an institutionally distinct minority for institutional incompatibility resulting from diverse cultural traditions as the primary basis of plural societies. This new formulation is still unsatisfactory, in my estimation, because then the distinction between a "plural society" like South Africa and a "heterogeneous society" with "plural enclaves" and "plural communities" like the United States boils down to one of demography. Surely, whether the dominant is a majority or a minority does not so profoundly affect the structure of a society as to justify the use of a typology that implies important qualitative discontinuities.[4]

Of course, in extending the meaning of pluralism, and in failing to distinguish between "pluralism" and "plural societies," there is a risk of stripping the concept of all of its analytical power. I have already suggested that two classes of very common phenomena fall outside the scope of my definition of pluralism, namely, corporate group segmentation into institutionally identical units and institutional differentiation or specialization. But how can we further refine the analysis of plural societies (in the broad sense)? Two complementary approaches suggest themselves. The first one consists of distinguishing between cultural and structural or social pluralism as both Smith and Kuper have done, and analyzing the complex relationship between the two.

Lacking the space to expand on this important topic, let me simply emphasize here two dimensions of this relationship.[5] At one level, structural or social pluralism can be regarded simply as the other side of cultural pluralism; for example, an institution such as a rule of descent shared by a specific group in a larger society can be looked at as an element of the total social structure or as a "trait" in the given group's cultural tradition. But at another level, social and cultural pluralism are partially independent variables. Thus, while the two forms of pluralism tend to go together, groups may remain structurally pluralistic even though contact has greatly reduced cultural pluralism. This is the case, for example, with the distinction between Negro and white Americans. Similarly, the lack of correspondence between social and cultural lines of cleavage in South Africa is an important contributory factor to conflict, and an essential factor in understanding pluralism in that country. We shall later return to the crucial importance for the analysis of pluralism of whether the lines of cleavage between groups are parallel or orthogonal to each other.

The second suggestion in the further analysis of pluralism is that the latter be regarded as a question of degree, and that the major dimensions of variability be identified as precisely as possible. Among the main such dimensions are the following:

1) The demographic factor is of some, though not overwhelming, relevance in at least two major ways. First, the number of corporate groups can range from two to several thousand (e.g., in the Hindu caste system). Second, the relative size of the groups, particularly of the dominant group, vis-à-vis the subordinate group or groups can also vary widely. Ruling ethnic or "racial" groups have often constituted only a fraction of 1 percent of the total. At the other extreme are societies like

the United States where the dominant ethnic group constitutes an over-whelming majority: less than 1 percent belong to non-Western cultures and only slightly more than 11 percent are nonwhites. Demographically, pluralism is a direct function of both the number of corporate groups and the size of the subordinate groups in relation to the dominant group.

2) There is a complex interplay between ideology, subjective percep-tion of differences, and pluralism. The subjective perception of "objec-tive" cultural differences may vary widely from one society to another and between groups within the same society. Thus closely related groups frequently magnify differences that appear trivial or nonexistent to a third party. Such is the case, for example, with Nazis vis-à-vis German Jews, or South African whites who claim cultural distinctiveness from South African Coloreds. The reverse may also happen. Thus, most South African Coloreds, who have long sought assimilation to the whites, have tended to deny cultural differences between themselves and the whites. The degree to which differences are subjectively perceived is, of course, one of the factors enhancing social and cultural pluralism, insofar as this perception almost inevitably affects group definition and patterns of interaction.

Beyond the subjective perception of pluralism, the ideological accept-ance or rejection of pluralism also affects social reality. Whether the dominant and the subordinate groups have adopted policies of assimila-tion or separation has influenced reality, at least to the extent that the ideology has been translated into action. (The French and Portuguese assimilation policy in Africa had minimal impact, largely because it remained a dead letter for all but a tiny minority of Africans.) In situations where pluralism is accompanied by the political domination of one group over the others (i.e., in what Smith calls "differential incorpora-tion"), ideological polarization frequently results; this, in turn, results in the breaking of links between groups and the accentuation of pluralism, as Kuper cogently argues in the South African case.[6]

3) Culturally, societies range from maximally pluralistic when the ethnic groups belong to unrelated cultural traditions to minimally plural-istic when only subcultural differences, based on age, sex, class, "race," or caste, are present. An intermediate situation is one in which several historically related ethnic groups belong to the same society (e.g., in Switzerland, Belgium, or Yugoslavia). Within a given society, all of these three main levels of cultural pluralism can coexist. For example, in South Africa, the distinction between an Afrikaner and a Zulu is one of maximal pluralism, between an Afrikaner and an English-speaking white an in-termediate one, and between an Afrikaans-speaking white and an Afri-kaans-speaking Colored a minimal one.

4) At the group level, social pluralism is a direct function of the extent to which mechanisms of social or spatial distance or avoidance exist between corporate groups, or an inverse function of the density of the network of intergroup ties, or, to use a different measure yet, a direct function of the ratio of *intra*group ties to *inter*group ties. Of course, sheer frequency of interaction is not so important as certain qualitative properties of that interaction, such as symmetry, reciprocity, affectivity, diffuseness, intimacy, and segmentarity. Quantitative analysis of a sociometric nature is only a gross first approximation to a far more complex reality. Beyond sheer frequency of interaction within and between groups, the degree of social pluralism is directly related to the degree of role polarization or differentiation between intragroup and intergroup relations. Social pluralism is present to the degree that intergroup relations are confined to affectively neutral, asymmetrical, hierarchical, functionally specific, nonreciprocal ties, and, vice versa, to the degree that ties stressing the opposite of these qualities are restricted within the group. In extreme cases of pluralism, endogamy and commensality restrictions clearly stress this role polarization and severely punish breaches thereof.

For example, intergroup relations may stress asymmetry, hierarchy, and lack of reciprocity, in contrast with intragroup ties which emphasize the opposite of these properties. This was the case in paternalistic slave-plantation regimes, even though intergroup ties were frequent, functionally diffuse, and affectively laden. In more egalitarian or competitive situations of pluralism, role polarization between inter- and intragroup relations is also present, albeit along different dimensions: intergroup ties tend to be more affectively neutral and functionally specific than intragroup ties. Ethnic and racial ghettos in contemporary industrial societies would be cases in point.

5) Another dimension of social pluralism can be found at the level of institutions. There is a wide range in the number and types of institutions shared by members of different corporate groups within a society. Closely related to this notion of scope and nature of shared institutions is that of institutional autonomy. At one extreme, societies characterized by a high degree of social pluralism are integrated only through a set of central political institutions controlled by the dominant group, and of economic institutions in which members of different groups interact asymmetrically. At the other extreme would be cases of minimal pluralism, for example, between white Christians and Jews in the United States where only one major set of institutions, namely the religious, is not shared. An intermediate case could be that of mestizos and Indians in Mexico and Guatemala, where there is, in addition to common political and economic institutions, a common membership in the Catholic church

(however syncretistic Indian Catholicism is) and the resulting set of ritual kinship ties.

6) Finally, at the individual level of analysis, the ease with which persons can move from one group or from one institutional structure to another is inversely related to pluralism. Such cultural and social mobility is obviously one of the mechanisms for the reduction of both cultural and social pluralism. This type of mobility is frequently not unidirectional. In a number of situations, individuals oscillate or "commute" between cultural and social systems.[7]

This somewhat lengthy specification of the concept of pluralism is essential to our central problem, namely, the relationship between pluralism and the polity. Indeed, the seeming contradiction between the two traditions appears to arise partly from different definitions of pluralism and partly from substantive differences in the degree of pluralism found in the societies which provided the empirical basis for the respective theoretical developments. Briefly stated, the "equilibrium" model of pluralism adopts a more inclusive definition of the term and is empirically based on societies that are only moderately pluralistic. The "conflict" model defines pluralism more narrowly, and seeks empirical anchorage in highly pluralistic colonial or slave societies.

Let us turn first to the equilibrium model as developed in the United States. Four striking considerations are relevant here. First, the concept of pluralism used by this school is so broad as to include all phenomena of functional differentiation. For example, the notion of separation of powers which is so central to this school of political theory is an almost pure case of functional specialization or differentiation. Similarly, most of the competing interest groups which seek to influence the polity or capture a share of power are not institutionally autonomous collectivities, but highly segmental and specialized organizations, such as trade unions, professional and business groups, and religious lobbies.

Second, the United States, compared with many other of the world's societies such as the Soviet Union, India, Nigeria, and a great many of the smaller countries, is only moderately pluralistic. Culturally, its pluralism, compared with that of several of its neighbors (Canada, Mexico, Guatemala), is residual and minimal. To generalize about pluralism on the basis of an empirical example which, in several respects, is almost a limiting case is certainly unsound.

Third—and this is the most astonishing aspect of the "equilibrium school"—that school has conveniently disregarded or treated as unimportant the deepest and most enduring cleavage in the American social structure, namely, that between whites and nonwhites. If there is one glaring way in which the United States is a socially pluralistic society, it is in respect to "race," and this is also the way in which it has been most glaringly undemocratic. Indeed, the ability to describe the American polity as democratic without any major qualification is itself an indication of the extent to which racism pervaded, however latently, the thinking of nearly all Americans until recently. Clearly, the United States, together with South Africa, Rhodesia, Australia, and other white settler countries, belonged until World War II in that interesting class of polities which could best be described as "*Herrenvolk* democracies."

Last, the equilibrium model postulates two principal bases of social integration in a pluralistic polity. One consists of the intricate web of multiple affiliations, intersecting lines of group cleavage, and shifting alignments depending on specific issues.[8] The other is a broad measure of consensus about values and about the rules of the political game.

The "conflict model" of pluralism, on the other hand, was developed largely by students of colonial societies which, in a number of instances, once had slavery as well. (Similar conditions were of course also found in less extreme form in the United States, but equilibrium theorists have largely disregarded these facts.) Conflict theorists came to the conclusion that pluralism is associated with despotic minority rule and with relative lack of consensus on both values legitimizing the existing polity and norms regulating political behavior. Plural societies, they have argued, are primarily held together by coercion, and the latter largely results from the superiority of the dominant group in the technology of violence.

In addition to political coercion, which hardly ever exists in pure form, some conflict theorists have argued that plural societies are also held together through common economic institutions. Nevertheless, this factor of economic integration has probably been underestimated by conflict theorists. Certainly, coercion by itself is not sufficient to account for the relative stability of colonial and slave regimes. Most regimes of this type have reduced preexisting "subsistence economies" to asymmetrical dependence on a money economy controlled by the dominant group. To be sure, these ties of economic interdependence were often introduced by land expropriation, forced labor, taxation, and other forms of coercion, but, once established, this nexus of economic ties becomes partly self-perpetuating, independently of the direct use of coercion, and powerfully reinforces the latter. South Africa provides a good illustration: the whites are of course dependent on the nonwhites for prosperity, but the nonwhites cannot withdraw their labor without facing nearly immediate starvation. The African peasantry has long been reduced to *sub*subsistence, and the nonwhite proletariat is completely dependent on economic resources, the control of which is monopolized by the whites. This is one of the main reasons for the lack of effectiveness of nonviolent methods of opposition.

It should be clear from the above treatment that my own position inclines toward the "conflict" view of pluralism. Nevertheless, I do not believe that pluralism is inevitably associated with either democracy or despotism.[9] The relationship is much more complex. Some moderately pluralistic societies have been relatively democratic, but so have many highly homogeneous ones (e.g., a number of politically acephalous African societies). Conversely, many pluralistic societies have been quite despotic, but so have a number of homogeneous countries (e.g., Nazi Germany, Fascist Italy, or Falangist Spain). Thus we apparently have to conceive of the two dimensions as independently variable. Let us try, however, to specify the relationship somewhat further. As a starting point, we may represent the relationship roughly in terms of a two by two table, by reducing two complex sets of variables to two simple dichotomies yielding four ideal types of societies: [10]

	Pluralistic societies	*Homogeneous societies*
Democratic societies	Type I E.g., Switzerland Belgium Canada India Israel	Type II E.g., Post-Fascist Italy Third Republic of France Republican Spain Scandinavian countries Numerous non-literate societies (e.g., Ibo, Nuer)
Despotic societies	Type III E.g., Colonial and slave regimes of Asia, Africa, and the Americas, Tsarist and Stalinist Russia, Napoleonic Empire, Sudanic Empires, Ethiopia	Type IV E.g., Totalitarian countries (Nazi Germany, Fascist Italy, Falangist Spain, Kuomintang and Communist China, Haiti)

For the equilibrium approach, the problematic societies are those of Type III. (Type II societies would be defined as "pluralistic" according to the broader definition of the term used by equilibrium theorists.) For the conflict approach, the most problematic cell is that which comprises Type I societies. The main question then becomes: How are Type I societies different from Type III societies? Or, more specifically, under what conditions is pluralism associated with democracy and under what conditions with despotism?

TYPE I SOCIETIES

Let us briefly mention a few specific cases as a rough empirical reference for our tentative generalizations. Switzerland is perhaps the most "successful" example of an enduring democratic polity in a country characterized by considerable cultural and social pluralism. Four related language groups (German, French, Italian, and Romansch) of greatly unequal size have achieved a stable and relatively amicable confederation of autonomous cantons. Belgium with its three ethnic groups (a Flemish majority, a large Walloon minority, and a small German minority) has also achieved some measure of both stability and democracy; however, throughout the nineteenth century, the French-speaking minority was clearly dominant, and, since then, the "language question" has been a perennial source of conflict over which violence has frequently flared.

The case of Canada shows some similarity to that of Belgium. Two main related ethnic groups (not to mention immigrant groups in a process of assimilation) contend for power at both the federal and provincial levels. The English were long dominant, but over time a greater parity of power and status was developed, and democratic federalism grew uneasily out of continuing conflict and delicate compromises. In respect to the deepest cultural cleavage, however, Canada has been quite undemocratic. The indigenous Indian and Eskimo populations were treated as conquered and voiceless peoples, and administered through a colonial-type system. (In this respect, Canada resembles more closely the United States, Australia, and South Africa.)

Israel also shows a considerable measure of both democracy and pluralism, but, as in the case of Canada, an important minority (the Palestine Arabs) was displaced or subordinated in what became essentially defined as a Jewish nation. But wide cultural differences between the Sabra and the immigrant groups of Asian, African, European, and American origin have proven compatible with fairly democratic institutions. India is by far the largest of the world's more pluralistic societies, but, much as in the case of Israel, the birth of the nation was accompanied by a major attempt at greatly reducing the ethnic and religious pluralism through geographic partition. India, since achieving independence, has been plagued by violent conflict between Muslims and Hindus, by regionalism, by caste rifts, by political cleavages, and by powerful centrifugal forces opposing the use of Hindi as a national language.

The brief sketch of the five countries just mentioned suggests some limiting conditions for the presence of democracy in stably pluralistic societies: [11]

1) The prospects for democratic pluralism appear directly proportional to the degree of consensus about basic values and, hence, inversely proportional to the degree of cultural pluralism. The chances of a democratic polity are reduced in the case of maximal cultural pluralism. Two of the five cases mentioned have only intermediate cultural pluralism (i.e., related ethnic groups), and, in the other three cases, the price of democracy was the exclusion or the considerable reduction and subordination of the culturally most divergent minorities. In the United States, this happened in relation to both cultural pluralism (Indians) and social pluralism (Negroes).

2) In addition to value consensus, democratic pluralism seems to be a direct function of the degree of consensus about the procedural norms of government. In situations where ethnic groups persist indefinitely side by side in a democratic country (as distinguished from cases of rapid assimilation of immigrant groups), there almost invariably exists a precise *modus vivendi* and *modus operandi* ensuring that the distribution of power in the society is roughly proportional to the size of the groups. Thus there will be formal or informal quotas in the staffing of the army and civil service, in the composition of the cabinet, and so on. This is sometimes the case even where pluralism is only minimal (e.g., between Protestants and Catholics in the German Federal Republic). The use of official languages in government and public places is also an important aspect of this *modus vivendi*. The latter will often tend to perpetuate pluralism and even to accentuate it, yet the actual situation is rarely static. Demographic factors (such as immigration and differential birth rates) or the dynamics of acculturation continuously modify the balance of forces, and each group typically seeks to strengthen its position at the expense of others. Relative size of groups in the country at large is of some, but not overwhelming, importance. Regional concentration is often of greater weight. Thus, even a relatively small minority (like the Italian Swiss) clustered in a given area can be more influential than a numerically stronger but more widely scattered minority (e.g., Catholics in the United States).

3) Democratic pluralism also seems to be a direct function of the extent to which norms concerning pluralism itself are shared. These include both more general norms accepting the legitimacy of pluralism and more specific counteracculturative norms ensuring the continued integrity of the groups. The most important issues here are those of cultural and regional autonomy, and more specifically the use and status

of the various languages, and the control and nature of formal education, frequently centering in linguistic and/or religious questions.[12]

4) The prospects for democratic pluralism seem to be inversely proportional to the discrepancy in the levels of technological and scientific development of the constituent groups; that is, democracy is unlikely to arise out of a situation where one group by virtue of its superior technology can easily achieve a monopoly over the means of violence. Conversely, in cases of democratic pluralism, the ethnic balance in the distribution of means of violence (army and police) is frequently a sensitive issue, as recent events in Nigeria and other African countries have shown.

5) Finally, democratic pluralism seems to be a direct function of the degree to which the main lines of cleavage in the society are orthogonal to one another. Four of the most common and most fundamental such lines of cleavage are language, religion, political party, and social class. To the extent that membership in one type of group does not significantly affect the probability of belonging to other types of groups, integration will prevail and conflict will be minimized. At least, such conflict as exists will be unlikely to lead to the disintegration of the polity, unless one type of cleavage assumes overwhelming salience vis-à-vis the others. One of the sensitive areas of overlap concerns that between social class and ethnicity. The correlation between these two factors in Belgium, Canada, and between English and Afrikaners in South Africa has been a major source of conflict. On the other hand, common ties of religion between ethnic groups (as between various Hindu language groups in India) or the lack of complete overlap between religious and language communities as between English-speaking and French Catholics in Canada) has tended to mitigate centrifugal forces. The political lines of cleavage are also very crucial. To the extent that ethnicity is politicized in the form of nationalist parties, pluralistic societies are undermined. Conversely, pluralistic democracies wherein all major political parties cut across ethnic lines (e.g., Belgium and Canada) gain in stability.

There seems to be at least one case where the crisscrossing of lines of cleavage contributes to conflict rather than integration. In situations such as exist in South Africa and the United States, where rigid quasi-caste lines based on "race" are maintained by a dominant group so as to deny equal rights and opportunities to a subordinate group which has been completely or partially assimilated culturally, the lack of empirical overlap between "race" and culture probably results in greater conflict than would be the case if "racial" lines were identical with cultural lines.

In conclusion, Type I societies seem to be characterized by a fairly high degree of consensus about both values and norms regulating political and intergroup behavior, by "technological equality" between the constituent groups, and by at least partially crisscrossing lines of cleavage in their major dimensions of cultural and social pluralism. Furthermore, most of these societies are only moderately pluralistic.

TYPE III SOCIETIES

The elements just mentioned as characteristic of Type I societies are either absent or at least de-emphasized in Type III societies. Consensus about values and norms is seldom an important source of integration. Often the dominant group has established its power through a technological advantage translated into coercive instrumentation. Demographic factors, by themselves, are relatively secondary in both Type I and Type III societies; culturally and politically dominant groups are frequently minorities, and, indeed, very small minorities—sometimes less than 1 percent. The most extreme forms of cultural and social pluralism (i.e., those cases where cultural differences are greatest, where institutional structures are most discrete, where group cleavages are deepest, and where individual contacts between groups are most restricted) tend to be Type III societies.

In both types, conflict may be present in greater or lesser degree. It seems arbitrary to associate conflict exclusively or even primarily with one of the two types. In pre- or nonindustrial Type III societies with a well-entrenched ruling group (such as a hereditary slave-owning aristocracy), overt expressions of conflict may be more effectively suppressed than in Type I countries. The range of empirical variation in conflict is quite wide in both types of societies, although pluralism tends to facilitate conflict by providing ready lines of cleavage which do not exist in more homogeneous societies. The same applies to the dimension of stability. Some democratic plural societies have been quite unstable and some cases of pluralistic tyranny have been relatively stable; however, pluralism in itself provides sources of change (e.g., through contact between culturally different groups) which are not present in homogeneous countries.

While pluralistic societies tend to be more complex, dynamic, unstable, and conflict-ridden than homogeneous ones, these qualities do not serve to differentiate democratic plural societies from despotic ones, except perhaps insofar as the latter tend to be more pluralistic than the former. I believe that the main difference between Type I and Type III societies lies in the bases for social integration. As already suggested, Type III societies, lacking for the most part value and normative consensus, are held together mostly by a combination of political coercion and economic interdependence. In particular, the salience of economic institutions and relationships as foci of integration between dominant and subordinate groups cannot be overstressed. The fact that these economic ties are asymmetrical and exploitative does not detract from the interdependence of groups.

To be sure, without the use of political coercion, the economic yoke would easily be overthrown; but, conversely, without economic symbiosis, coercion by itself would not be sufficient to maintain the despotic rule of a minority. Debt peonage, slavery, contract labor, indenture, and other forms of economic dependence serve at once to reinforce political subjection, to make the latter profitable, and to sustain the ruling group and its repressive apparatus. This apparatus, in turn, has frequently been used to establish and entrench systems of exploitation which transformed self-sufficient peasant populations into dependent, landless serfs or slaves.

Of course, some degree of value consensus may sometimes further reinforce the integration of Type III societies, for example, through the imposition by the ruling group and acceptance by the subject groups of a religious or secular ideology which rationalizes the status quo. Illustrations would be the internalization of feelings of racial inferiority on the part of some Negro Americans or the adoption of Catholicism by Mexican Indians. Some Type III societies, in particular paternalistic slave regimes, have been fairly well integrated while others, like contemporary South Africa, show a high degree of malintegration. The same range of integration could be found among Type I societies, even though the relative salience in the main bases of integration is different. It is characteristic of pluralistic societies, however, that their social structure is less closely integrated than that of homogeneous societies.

To summarize a rather tortuous argument in which I have tried to account for a perversely complex reality, I would lean toward the "conflict school" of pluralism; that is, I believe that pluralism is intrinsically associated with conflict and relative lack of consensus and integration. There is also an empirical correlation between pluralism and despotic minority rule, as can be expected from the fact that most highly pluralistic societies are the product of military conquest, and that the latter in turn is often based on a superior mastery of either the technology or the organization of means of violence. Given, however, certain conditions specified earlier, moderately pluralistic societies have been fairly democratic. To postulate a direct relationship between pluralism and democracy as the "equilibrium school" has done appears unwarranted. Such a viewpoint is based on a loose definition of pluralism, on an examination of only a small part of the empirical spectrum, and on a selective perception of that limited body of data.

NOTES

[1] Among the more recent works that have applied this traditional concept of pluralism to the United States and other societies are William McCord, *The Springtime of Freedom* (New York: Oxford University Press, 1965); W. Kornhauser, *The Politics of Mass Society* (London: Routledge and Kegan Paul, 1960); Edward A. Shils, *The Torment of Secrecy* (London: Heinemann, 1956); and S. M. Lipset, *The First New Nation* (New York: Basic Books, 1963).

[2] Cf. J. S. Furnivall, *Colonial Policy and Practice* (London: Cambridge University Press, 1948); J. C. Mitchell, *Tribalism and the Plural Society* (London: Oxford University Press, 1960); Leo Kuper, *An African Bourgeoisie* (New Haven: Yale University Press, 1965); M. G. Smith, *The Plural Society in the British West Indies* (Berkeley and Los Angeles: University of California Press, 1965); and Pierre L. van den Berghe, *South Africa: A Study in Conflict* (Middletown: Wesleyan University Press, 1965). For other works that do not give a prominent place to the concept of pluralism but nevertheless show close similarities in approach to the "conflict school" of pluralism, see Georges Balandier, *Sociologie actuelle de l'Afrique Noire* (Paris: Presses Universitaires de France, 1955); Max Gluckman, *An Analysis of a Social Situation in Modern Zululand* (Manchester: Manchester University Press, 1958); and Gonzalo Aguirre Beltrán, *El Proceso de Aculturación* (Mexico: Universidad Nacional, 1957).

[3] Cf. M. G. Smith, "Social and Cultural Pluralism," in *op. cit.*, pp. 75–91.

[4] In the last pages of "Pluralism in Precolonial African Societies," in this volume, M. G. Smith de-emphasizes demographic ratio as a determining factor in pluralism and reverts in part to his earlier formulation in "Social and Cultural Pluralism." After reviewing a considerable number of traditional African societies, he concludes that "cultural diversity and the structures of 'interethnic' accommodation" are the main conditions that are "linked closely and consistently among all the societies discussed here. They vary together, directly and equally." Smith thus seems to alternate in his emphasis on cultural heterogeneity on the one hand, and on political domination as affected by demographic ratio on the other. According to Smith's new typology in "Pluralism in Precolonial African Societies," both South Africa and the United States are examples of differential incorporation, in spite of a wide discrepancy in demographic ratios of dominant versus subordinate groups.

[5] I have expanded on this point in the context of South Africa in "Toward a Sociology of Africa," *Social Forces*, 43 (Oct. 1964), 11–18.

[6] See Leo Kuper, "Some Aspects of Violent and Nonviolent Political Change in Plural Societies," in this volume. Kuper is especially concerned with the self-fulfilling aspects of the ideology of conflict, of polarization, and of the inevitability of violence. Political ideology in South Africa is clearly both a product and a determinant of conflict in a plural society. By the same token, the sociological analysis of South African society as a conflict-ridden plural society may itself become a contributing factor to the further development of conflict and pluralism. Indeed, this very criticism has been leveled by a reviewer at my book, *South Africa: A Study in Conflict*.

[7] On this point, see Philip Mayer, *Townsmen or Tribesmen* (Cape Town:

Oxford University Press, 1961), and "Migrancy and the Study of Africans in Towns," *American Anthropologist*, 64 (June 1962), 576–592.

[8] The integrative functions of conflict have been stressed by Lewis A. Coser, *The Functions of Social Conflict* (Glencoe, Ill.: The Free Press, 1956). See also in this connection my article, "Dialectic and Functionalism: Toward a Theoretical Synthesis," *American Sociological Review*, 28 (Oct. 1963), 695–705.

[9] Democracy and despotism are not conceived as all-or-none absolutes, but rather as convenient labels to describe extremes on a continuum, which are at best approximated in practice. The dimension under consideration is the degree of diffuseness and equality in the distribution of power. To the extent that power is disproportionately exercised by the few, the polity is described as despotic; conversely, where power is more equally and widely distributed, we speak of democracy. Since all political systems have excluded some categories of persons from a share of power (the most common being women and children), democracy has always been qualified by the category of persons who are regarded as active citizens. What I have called *"Herrenvolk democracies"* are polities wherein power is relatively diffusely and equally distributed among the members of an ascriptively defined group which, in turn, rules despotically over other such groups.

[10] M. G. Smith explores the same problem in "Pluralism in Precolonial African Societies," using a somewhat more inclusive typology based on the degree to which culturally distinct groups interact, and on whether the interaction is symmetrical or hierarchical. Type I societies in the two-by-two table correspond to what Smith calls "consociations," whereas Type III societies are based on what he calls "differential incorporation."

[11] By *stable* pluralism is meant a situation in which groups, especially ethnic groups, preserve their separate identity and resist assimilation for many generations (e.g., the French in Quebec). The situation of stable pluralism is contrasted with situations of transitory pluralism where immigrant groups, though they may be sizable, self-conscious, and organized, become assimilated within two or three generations (e.g., the Irish in the United States).

[12] The case of Israel does not fit here, but that country does not represent stable pluralism. The ideology of Zionism, the introduction of Hebrew as a national language, and strong pressures on immigrants to assimilate into the emerging national culture—all make Israel more akin to the situation of transitory pluralism of European immigrants in the United States.

Part II Case Studies in African Pluralism

Introduction to Part II

In planning the colloquium on which this volume is based, we made no attempt to canvass the entire range of African colonial experience under Arab, Belgian, British, Dutch, French, Portuguese, or Spanish rule. We did arrange for two studies of French Colonial Africa, including a study of the Algerian revolution, and for studies of Nigeria and Kenya also. Unfortunately, these arrangements could not be carried out, and the volume lacks a formal study of the Algerian society and its revolution. Our case studies deal primarily with African territories formerly under British rule, including certain settler societies, European and Arab.

In considering suitable subjects and topics for study, we selected certain dimensions within the range of variation of African pluralism. These include the historical epochs and constitutional status that distinguish precolonial, colonial, settler, and independent societies; differences in racial composition and policy, by which the societies based on relations between different African stocks are distinguished from those based on divisions between Africans and Arabs, Africans and Europeans, or Africans, Europeans, and Asians (mainly Pakistanis and Indians). We also sought to include studies of divergent processes of development in these plural societies, as illustrated by the violent revolutionary transformation of Zanzibar, the peaceful depluralization of Zambia, and the increasingly rigorous domination in South Africa.

In considering possible contributors to the colloquium, we were guided by the wish to secure a balanced representation of the relevant social sciences—history, political science, sociology, and anthropology. In this respect we were fortunate in gaining the participation of two African historians, Basil Davidson and Leonard Thompson; two political scientists, Michael Lofchie and Ali Mazrui; two sociologists, Pierre van den Berghe and Leo Kuper; three anthropologists, Hilda Kuper, Max Gluckman, and M. G. Smith; and Pierre Alexandre, a linguist with wide administrative experience of French West Africa (A.O.F.).

It could be expected that scholars drawn from different disciplines and having diverse experiences of African situations would bring a variety of approaches, perspectives, and data to bear on our general theme. Thus, in approaching contributors, we thought it best to indicate our major concerns as outlined in the two opening papers by Leo Kuper and M. G. Smith, and, while suggesting a set of topics, to leave our contributors free to organize their materials and comments as they felt best, confident that in this way we would secure abundant data and stimulating reactions from them. While treating substantive issues, some contributors elected to direct their analyses primarily toward general problems of process or conceptualization. We have grouped essays of this character together in Part III. However, even those essays that remain most closely anchored in case data bristle with questions, conceptions, and materials of comparative import.

In reviewing the ethnography on indigenous African societies to identify traditional patterns of interethnic accommodation, M. G. Smith attempts to isolate the structural correlates of collective differences of ethnicity, culture, and race in traditional societies of differing structural type, scale, and complexity. In isolating such variables as differences of race, ethnicity, economy, language, or numbers for distributional study, he illustrates an approach suggested by Leo Kuper and Pierre van den Berghe, while organizing his data around one question: namely, what are the relations between conditions of collective incorporation and commonalty and differences of culture and institutions? Though incomplete, this review reveals the great variety and number of plural situations to be found in the polyethnic indigenous societies of Africa.

In two closely linked essays that analyze ideologies of polarization in Algeria and South Africa, and possibilities of peaceful depluralization in South Africa particularly, Leo Kuper develops his opening contrast between theories of social pluralism which stress its consensual or conflict-laden features. He shows how ideologies that assert the prevalence and necessity of polarization may serve to promote the violence they postulate. It is apparent also that sustained polarization and collective conflict require appropriate ideologies and may generate them. Marxism is not always suited to promote polarization in multiracial plural societies. Having examined the role of ideology in fostering conflict despite numerous and varied intersectional bonds, Leo Kuper considers the opposite case, asking under what circumstances and policies is a relatively peaceful process of racial depluralization possible or likely in (Southern) Rhodesia or the South African Republic. Violent revolution is only one of several courses by which the structure of plural societies may be transformed, and it is not inevitable in such transformation. These two essays, despite their Algerian and South African reference, seek a base for integrating the opposing sociological theories of pluralism by identifying conditions that promote transformations of societies into systems of the opposite type.

Pierre Alexandre, in summarizing the administrative arrangements in French West Africa (A.O.F.) and in interpreting its development, reconsiders the antithetical conceptions of pluralism set out by Leo Kuper and concludes that while these models of social systems seem "irreconcilable at the synchronic level, they may well be reconciled in a diachronic approach," especially in colonial territories like French West Africa where "there never was any *legal* segregation of races *qua* races" (his italics), and the prevailing ideology of assimilation was manifest in vertical and horizontal mobility of administrative officials. Only for a brief spell, between 1906 and 1918, when the handful of scattered administrators accommodated to their local milieu under formidable pressures, did French West Africa simultaneously exhibit features associated with the two contrasted modes of pluralism. But this unstable state changed with increases in the populations of white residents and of occupationally mobile, educated Africans. Surveying these developments, Alexandre sketches a paradigm of societal developments in modern Africa from a precolonial phase of mutually independent, small-scale societies, through colonization under foreign rule, to independence under local elites of predominantly foreign culture, an evolution that resembles and supplements Ali Mazrui's model of depluralization.

Despite many important differences with the A.O.F., Basil Davidson traces a broadly parallel course of development in Northern Rhodesia/Zambia. There, racial exclusiveness was quite as central to the settler polity as it was abhorrent to the official ideology of assimilation in French West Africa. Like Alexandre also, Davidson asks whether it is accurate or useful to consider Northern Rhodesia as a single society, plural or other, before the middle 1940's, when African pressures on the settler regime first made some impact. Implicitly, for Davidson, some active political participation is essential for membership in a common society; and he contrasts society, conceived as an organic system of reciprocal (though not necessarily symmetrical) relationships, however discontinuous or limited, with the phase of unqualified European domination in Northern Rhodesia. This, despite its colonial status, he regards as a "despotism," which continued until the emergence of competitive racial politics following the early Copperbelt strikes and the introduction of color-bar unionism.

This Rhodesian study illustrates the ambiguous nature of metropolitan influence, a relation Leo Kuper emphasizes. As Davidson shows, this ambiguity is especially marked when the metropolitan state is undecided on such matters as racial policy, constitutional status, or democracy in the colonies. However, the *metropole* is not always the sole source of external influence, and the white settlers of Northern Rhodesia drew inspiration, support, and immigrants from the racially exclusive European communities of South Africa and Southern Rhodesia. Nonetheless, despite their differing economies and stresses on racial or cultural criteria of civic and social exclusion, the broad parallelism in patterns and processes of societal development between Northern Rhodesia/Zambia and the A.O.F. extends even to the timing of their critical phase, linked, as Leo Kuper suggests, with the unities of the colonial field in Africa and with major changes in the political situations of European imperial states following World War II.

Basil Davidson concludes his account of the development of Zambia by comparing the capacities of single-party and multiparty regimes based on adult suffrage and common rolls to facilitate processes of depluralization by effective incorporation of its various ethnic groups within the polity on conditions that may foster the growth of "organic" relations between them. For the new states of former French West Africa, Alexandre indicates that the dissolution of ethnic and regional exclusiveness is quite as important for depluralization as the redefinition of relations with the *metropole* and its nationals. In both regions, however, the record shows that depluralization may be initiated peacefully, if the rulers are willing or constrained to accommodate to the surrender of their political privileges. Thereafter, the most critical issues that face peaceful depluralization center on relations within the African majorities themselves.

Hilda Kuper's comparative analysis of the East Indian communities in Natal and Uganda introduces a further complicating feature of plural regimes, excluded from Northern Rhodesia by deliberate policy and represented in the A.O.F. marginally by West Indian members of the French bureaucracy. In South Africa and Uganda, Indian communities were recruited and constituted as enclaves by the ruling group in pursuit of its own interests. Proceeding comparatively, Hilda Kuper reviews the historical experiences and changing social contexts of these Indians enclaved in the white settler society of South Africa and in the "exploitation colony" of Uganda as indentured workers, resident aliens, protected subjects, and citizens with uncertain status and rights. Differences in the situations of these Indian enclaves are clearly related to the differences of constitutional status and social structure of these host societies, and it seems that relations with such third, intermediate, or "stranger" groups provide a valuable index to the nature and direction of the societies of which they are part.

Characterizing pluralism as "a series of confrontations between people perceived (and perceiving themselves) as strangers," Hilda Kuper demonstrates how the accommodations and internal divisions or coalitions of these intermediary aliens illuminate the structure and tendencies of their host societies. In relating the impact of Mahatma Gandhi and the Aga Khan among the Indians of South Africa and Uganda, she also shows how the influence of these two distinct types of charismatic leadership was canalized and restricted by these milieux. Despite its early preparation, this essay furnishes an excellent background for understanding recent developments in Kenya affecting Asian residents.

In Uganda and in South Africa, Indians were classified as Asians, along with local Arabs or Javanese. In Zanzibar, Arabs formed a category distinct from "Asians," as local Pakistanis and Indians were called. That the racial or ethnic categories which figure so prominently in plural societies are generated and altered by structural relations among collectivities is also shown by the complex and changing ethnic classifications in colonial Zanzibar, particularly by the disassociation of Shirazi from "Mainland" Africans, by the dispersal of Swahili among Shirazi and Arabs, and by racial and cultural differences within the Arab bloc. Perhaps the criteria of collective differentiation are always structurally contingent.

Like Hilda Kuper, Michael Lofchie combines a historical account of the social development of Zanzibar with a systematic comparison of differences in structure and development between the island communities of Pemba and Zanzibar. In this study, he demonstrates the difference between objective history and folk interpretations, as revealed in the systems of social classification and structural relations between those categories that furnished the major units of the plural society. By analyzing the influence of these folk conceptions on the collective alignments to which political strategies and ideologies were addressed, Lofchie shows their critical role in the political development of Zanzibar.

The Arab minority that ruled Zanzibar under British protection sought to preserve its position by initiating and leading a local movement for political independence, thereby stirring the fears of disprivileged subjects, Hadimu and Mainland Africans, who dreaded in prospect the restoration of the pre-British regime. Since successive elections destabilized Arab control without improving the prospects of the disprivileged, the Arab elite, on obtaining independence, sought to strengthen itself by sectional policies which stimulated its militant opponents to an early revolt. By his detailed analysis of Zanzibar politics between 1954 and 1964, Lofchie shows how party competitions and the parliamentary system promoted a process of polarization around the issue of Arab or African rule which manifested its range and intensity in the revolutionary aftermath.

These case studies are neither comprehensive nor uniform in their coverage or organization; but they do furnish excellent material for the comparative analysis of pluralism, its components, varieties, emergence, and transformation, and they also enable us to assess the utility of this conception, in its opposing formulations, by application to a wide variety of characteristic African situations. In addition, the case studies illustrate the variable associations of such factors as race, ethnicity, ecology, historical experience, demographic balance, constitutional status, religion, language, and administrative pattern with forms and degrees of pluralism and with their persistence or transformation. They expose the structural bases and impacts of alternative ideologies of assimilation and disassociation, the latter represented here in two forms as revolution and apartheid.

The essays also illustrate how plural societies may differ in their structural complexity and political prerequisites, as shown by the numbers and relations of their differentially incorporated social sections, by their internal divisions, by the changing situations of intermediate groups, and the differing criteria of race, religion, culture, or assumed history on which these collective categories are based. Evidently, as several studies show, the strictly synchronic study of a plural society viewed as a single system is likely to be less rewarding than one that also analyzes its development; but when it is possible to combine such developmental studies with systematic and controlled comparison of clearly defined collectivities, such as those in Pemba and Zanzibar, or the Indian enclaves in Uganda and Natal, the implications and interconnections of relevant variables, such as ecology, history, demography, and collective organization, are most clearly exposed. Within the limits of our inquiry, these substantive essays indicate the range of variables, contexts, structures, and processes that are of central significance for the analysis of pluralism, while illustrating the analytic procedures and problems on which their study rests.

Chapter 4   Pluralism in Precolonial African Societies[*]

M. G. Smith

Pluralism has been identified in my preceding paper [1] by the differential incorporation of two or more collectivities within the same society. It has been argued that such differential incorporation generally presumes significant antecedent differences of institutions, culture, and ethnicity between the collectivities concerned; and further, that it restricts assimilation by preserving or promoting the institutional distinctness of these structurally segregated collectivities. It is possible and useful to test these general ideas by reviewing the ethnographic materials on precolonial Africa. Ideally, even a limited test of these hypotheses would seem to require a comprehensive survey of the continental ethnography; but nothing so ambitious is attempted here; and indeed it is doubtful whether such inquiries would be fruitful without preliminary development of the appropriate concepts, typologies, hypotheses, and procedures. This paper is thus in part designed to illustrate a conceptual framework and method for such comparative analyses.

I

SOCIETY AND CORPORATIONS

In studying social pluralism we are directly and continuously concerned with the conditions, problems, and modes of social cohesion, structure, and development. Following Radcliffe-Brown, Nadel, and others, we can distinguish societies as the widest continuing collectivities bound by common and distinctive forms of social structure.[2] As Fortes says,

Social structure is not an aspect of culture, but the entire culture of a given people handled in a special frame of theory . . . culture certainly in most of

---

[*] I should like to thank Theodore Ravetz for his comments on this paper.

Africa . . . has no clear-cut boundaries. But a group of people bound together within a social structure have a boundary, though not necessarily one that coincides with a physical boundary or is impenetrable. . . . Culture is a unity insofar as it is tied to a bounded social structure. In this sense . . . the social structure is the foundation of the whole social life of any *continuing* society.[3]

Particularly instructive and discriminating analyses of these issues in African tribal societies are given by Nadel and Goody for the Nuba and the LoDagaa, respectively. In both areas of great cultural and social intermixture, these writers independently find collectivities distinguished as societies by reference to structural differentiae, namely, relations of kinship, marriage, and descent.[4] Notably, the critical units that serve to differentiate these geographically intermingled peoples, both analytically and in their own eyes, are mutually exclusive frameworks of corporate organization. Nuba clans may be "symbiotic" or "simple"; and among LoDagaa and Nuba alike, differences in the incidence and form of patriliny or matriliny distinguish societies based on corporate kinship groups of differing constitution.

As Evans-Pritchard says, "By social structure we mean relations between groups which have a high degree of consistency, and constancy. The groups remain the same irrespective of their specific content of individuals at any particular moment, so that generation after generation of people pass through them."[5] Such enduring, closed, and interlocking groups are always corporate units; but corporate groups are only one species of corporation, and, in specifying and analyzing the social structure of any given aggregate, it is equally essential to treat alternative forms such as corporate categories (e.g., the Nuer age-set), commissions (e.g., the Nuer leopard-skin chief), or offices and colleges where these exist.[6]

Evidently corporate constitutions vary with the type, bases, and articulation of their components, and these units and their relations define the social structure and set its boundaries. This being so, if pluralism involves the differential incorporation of collectivities within a common inclusive society, it should always distinguish such structures from systems of uniform or equivalent incorporation in which all units have identical or equivalent modes of articulation in the wider system. It is such differences in the modes of corporate organization and articulation within an inclusive collectivity which generate problems of social integration, cohesion, and solidarity, and serve to distinguish pluralities from other societies, whether the latter are institutionally homogeneous or heterogeneous in kind.

Clearly, in studying the modes, conditions, and correlates of differential association, we are dealing with features and problems that characterize many human societies, traditional and modern alike. It was in part the generality and variety of these conditions which led Herbert Spencer to declare that social evolution proceeded through the progressive compounding of collectivities, in whole or in part.[7] Comparative analysis of pluralism and its alternatives consists very largely in the study of these societal compounds, their varying composition and form, properties, requisites, and modes of development.[8] Such inquiries merit serious study by social scientists of differing disciplines, separately and in cooperation; but to pursue these problems fruitfully in precolonial African societies, we have first to distinguish varieties of collective accommodation and societal structure.

MODES OF COLLECTIVE ACCOMMODATION

Proceeding typologically, we can identify several significantly different levels and modes of collective association between the polar extremes of total societal segregation and social assimilation. Total segregation denotes a condition in which societies have no direct relations with one another; total assimilation involves socialization under uniform or equivalent corporate conditions and structures. Between these poles we can distinguish several intermediate structures of association. For convenience these are presented below in approximate order of increasing assimilation.

Societal *segregations* may be intermittent or continuous, total or segmental, as societies or their segments engage in intermittent external relations of war, diplomacy, trade, or the like, with one another. Such intersocietal relations presume societal boundaries and normally reinforce their mutual exclusions. Individual associations across such boundaries are structurally significant only insofar as they presuppose, establish, or modify corporate structures or links, whether societal or segmental. For example, Azande blood brotherhood imposed corporate obligations on the clansmen of blood brothers.[9]

In the old days, because of the legal nature of the bond, and because the rest of a man's kin were involved, no man would exchange blood without the permission of his father or the head of his homestead, and without consulting the oracles. . . . A Zande is not restricted to making the pact only with other Zande. . . . Blood brotherhood was the only means by which private trade between distant parts could be carried on before European administration.[10]

Funeral friendship, marriage, and joking relations are other standardized modes of collective action which link men of different corporate groups or categories; and though in most cases such relations held between descent groups of the same society, this was not always so.

Intermittent segmental interaction of collectivities incorporated in different societies is common in decentralized or acephalous politics, but it is by no means restricted to such situations. When two societies engage as units in collective relations, whether of war, alliance, negotiation, or trade, their political centralization is presumed. In such cases societal interaction merely reinforces collective boundaries and accentuates the representative roles of regulative corporations in either collectivity. Here also corporate differentiations are enhanced rather than reduced by such intersocietal transactions.

Symbiosis, a complementary association of interdependent elements which presupposes their difference, permits the intermittent or continuous accommodation of societally segregated groups, in whole or in part.[11] Symbiotic relations are often also encapsulated within the boundaries of a single society.[12] Indeed, Indian and other forms of caste institutionalize and exploit this principle in differing ways. Between societies or segments thereof, stable symbiotic relations generally presuppose marked differences of ecology and geographical mobility, as for example between the nomadic Fulani, Shuwa, and other pastoral groups of Northern Nigeria and the sedentary Kanuri or Hausa cultivators around them,[13] or between Bambuti Pygmies and Bira or Amba Bantu speakers of the Ituri forest.[14] Since symbiosis presumes complementarity, it is often unstable as well as unequal. To preserve its autonomy the weaker party must often withdraw physically and terminate one unsatisfactory relation by substituting another. Perhaps the most important instance of societally segmental symbiosis in African history is the slave trade by which Europeans established their economic domination of the West African coast and thus the bases for later penetration.[15] Though these intercontinental relations should be considered in any comprehensive study of precolonial Africa, they are mentioned here only to illustrate the varied forms, conditions, and outcomes of societal symbiosis. Some African units engaged in this trade are mentioned briefly below.

When two societies or segments thereof join together as equal and autonomous collectivities in a distinctive common polity that surpasses alliance in its scope, content, and intensity, while preserving their internal distinctness, we may describe their union as a *consociation,* reserving this generic term for associations of separately constituted corporate collectivites as equal and internally autonomous partners in a common society. *Confederation* is a mode of consociation which characteristically establishes a common college to regulate the common civil affairs of the confederate segments; in Europe, Switzerland, and, in Africa, the Ga townships, the Egba and Fanti, Old Calabar, and other Efik commercial states represent confederacies of differing heterogeneity, complexity, and form.[16] *Federations,* another consociational form characterized by transfer of autonomous jurisdiction over certain collective interests to the central organ, are perhaps best represented in Africa by the Ashanti Union in its later phase.[17]

Though reserving various rights of veto or disassociation to their members, confederations normally regulate a wider range of common affairs than do such acephalous consociations as the Terik-Tiriki [18] or the Bulibuli-Bwezi of Bwamba.[19] As indicated below, both these unions remained acephalous, secular, and restricted in content and scope. Like the Ga and Egba townships, the Terik-Tiriki union emerged as a conscious response to external threats; but the more complex and segmental Bulibuli-Bwezi consociation was directed primarily toward societal coexistence. However, neither combination manifests any general scheme of ritual unification. We should therefore distinguish these secular acephalous consociations from others that are ritualized, such as the Tallensi and Kagoro,[20] and from other unions with symbolic or executive centers, whether secular or ritualistic, such as the confederations and federations mentioned above. The essential characteristics of all types of consociation are the preservation of their corporate components as structurally distinct, internally autonomous, and politically equal members of the societal unit. Often these corporate segments remain culturally distinct in different ways as, for example, in Bwamba or among the Ga, Egba, and Terik-Tiriki. However segmental equality is not restricted entirely to jural verisimilitude. Symmetrical complementarity at the ritual level, or equivalence at the secular, assures substantive parity by institutionalizing complementary interdependence.

Such consociations as Kagoro and Tallensi represent *amalgams* produced by the union of two or more ethnically distinct collectivities. Such *amalgamations* may be usefully distinguished from other forms of consociation by the identical inner organization of their corporate components as well as the uniformities, complementarity, or equivalence of their articulation with one another in the wider society. Consociations may thus be usefully classified by the internal differences of their component parts. For example, after two centuries of close association, Terik and Tiriki still differ sharply in language, social organization, ecologies, and cults. Bulibuli and Bwezi, having amalgamated, now appear to differ solely in language. In Kagoro and Tallensi societies the associated parts still differ in certain ritual and secular qualities. Ga segments differ primarily in cult, Egba in organization and speech.[21]

Assimilation denotes that condition in which uniformities of internal organization and external articulation are sufficiently general and intense for a single corpus of law and custom to have equal validity for all types of social relation in all groups. In this condition individual freedoms of association and contract are uniform, and social integration at the normative or ecological level is in theory high.

Differential incorporation obtains when the structure of the inclusive collectivity prescribes differences in the modes of articulation of particular corporate components. Generally, systems of differential incorporation segregate some units by jural, political, and/or ritual disabilities, while reserving control of public resources and policy for other units. Being explicitly corporate in their base, form, and reference, structures of differential incorporation proscribe individual and collective changes of status and relation in affairs of critical interest. Their order and continuity accordingly require the maintenance of a uniform and rigid scheme of relations between corporate collectivities distinguished as units of differing status, rights, and autonomy. Such regimes minimize individual mobility and collective assimilations by harnessing their resources, material, ideological, and social, to block or suppress conditions or tendencies that seem to threaten their structure. Under such conditions individuals derive their personal and public rights exclusively from their status identification with one or another of the differentially articulated corporate units. Normally such societies owe their maintenance to a central regulative organization which is prescriptively reserved for the dominant corporate group; but in Africa, as elsewhere, political centralization is not always present.

Collectivities differentially incorporated in a given society may or may not differ sharply in their constitutions, cultures, provenience, or languages. Where differentially articulated collectivities differ antecedently in social organization, language, and culture, the plural characteristics of the ensemble are most obvious and its cohesion is correspondingly weak; but, under differential incorporation, even institutionally similar collectivities will develop differences of organization and procedure in consequence of their differing structural situations, resources, autonomies, societal responsibilities, status, and rights. The collectivity that exercises corporate responsibility for societal order and policy must then specialize procedures and arrangements to administer these societal affairs as well as its own. Other collectivities, denied participation in the inclusive public domain, will lack the corresponding political and jural structures; and, unless directly administered by members of the ruling group, they must therefore develop distinctive procedures and arrangements to handle their own internal affairs. In such differing contexts, collectivities that were once similar in institutional and corporate organization develop important structural differences over time. Nonetheless, where the structurally differentiated collectivities share such common institutions as kinship, property, or cult, the prospects are probably better for increased assimilation and social cohesion.

This typology indicates the principal modes of interethnic accommodation and societalization of immediate interest. However, these alternatives represent states and processes of accommodation rather than mutually exclusive structural types. Consociations and amalgamations are often hard to distinguish; and any mode of collective accommodation from segregation to amalgamation can be converted into a system of differential incorporation by the subordination of some components to the domination of others. Further, in many societies, such as the Ngwato, Tawana, or Lozi, differential incorporation and amalgamation are employed together to accommodate differing collectivities.[22] In Bonny and Old Calabar, the commercial oligarchy resembled a confederation of autonomous and rival "houses" that cooperated to dominate a larger slave population and to exploit the hinterland and the European trade.[23] In these cases oligarchic unity was prerequisite for collective domination.

By concentrating on alternative corporate forms of collective accommodation, we give structural priority to collectivities and their corporate relations. The mere presence of culturally distinct individuals within a social unit does not establish pluralism unless they are corporately identified and segregated as distinct units, whether categorical or group. This is so because institutional communities or differences are collective facts. Metics or resident aliens are merely a residual category of nonsocietalized persons whose local residence is optional and structurally indifferent. In short, to analyze and compare the corporate organization of different societies, the appropriate units are corporations whose members are organized as distinct aggregates. At the present level of analysis, individuals are separately significant only as members or representatives of corporate units, unless by their acts and relations they initiate structural change or modifications in the corporate organization.

TYPES OF SOCIETY

Inevitably in the preceding discussion we have dichotomized African societies as acephalous and centralized, following general practice. This dichotomy is neither so self-evident nor so simple as it appears. Such societies as the Hausa, Nyakyusa, or Tswana remain acephalous or uncentralized despite their internal organization in a number of centralized and mutually independent states. Other societies such as the Ngonde or Shilluk, though having titular chiefs, were hardly less "anarchic" than the Nuer or Tiv who had none, and considerably more so than the Yakö or Kipsigi who relied on associations of differing base and type for internal order and cohesion. Perhaps the traditional dichotomy between states and stateless societies confounds two different meanings of the term "polity"; nonetheless we can still employ it to classify African societies, so as to study the distribution of pluralism and its alternatives among them.

Following Fortes and Evans-Pritchard, Paula Brown, Barnes, Southall, Bernardi, and others,[24] we may first distinguish certain pure forms of acephalous society by differences in the type of corporate units on which they are based. As relatively pure types, societies differ structurally as they are based on corporate *bands,* on corporate *descent groups* of varying type, on an inclusive series of *age-sets,* or on inclusive or exclusive corporate *associations* whose members are heterogeneous as regards age and descent. These four modes of corporate organization represent alternative bases for certain pure forms of acephalous society. In most empirical cases, however, we do not deal with pure types. Normally the society is distinguished by its specific combination of some of these corporate forms, often with chieftainship also. Excluding band organization, these varieties of corporate grouping are equally compatible with centralized direction by a chief or by a regulative college; indeed, in many African societies, descent groups, age-groups, or corporate associations furnish the highest regulative units and the machinery for administration. Following Weber, we should also distinguish self-regulating corporate groups from units of similar form which are subject to the direction of a higher external authority, whether chiefly or collegial.[25]

To develop this corporate taxonomy, we must reexamine the notion of band organization, since this term has several meanings. A "band" is a mobile residential group, regarded by its members and others as a distinct continuing unit. Thus, structurally, band organization distinguishes a societal type in which bands are the sole or largest corporate groupings, linked through their members by individual ties of friendship, kinship, or affinity, but without any wider collective framework. Ecologically, the term is generally reserved for the residential organization of mobile societies, and its application is thus often restricted to peoples who depend solely or primarily on hunting and gathering for subsistence. For ecological reasons collectors are generally mobile, and most mobile peoples do move about in small groups most of their lives. Thus for some anthropologists, band organization is synonymous with the residential groupings of all mobile peoples, while for others it describes the structural level of hunters and gatherers.

These equations are misleading because they assimilate two distinct sets of criteria, the ecological and the structural. Despite their collecting ecologies, neither the Eskimo nor the Indians of northwestern America (Nootka, Kwakiutl, Bella Bella, etc.) were residentially organized in bands; nor apparently were the Australian aborigines, since another term, "horde," was used to distinguish their local groups. Australian aboriginal societies were integrated on various corporate principles that aligned the members of different hordes together for certain purposes, while differentiating the members of each horde. In these societies, bands or hordes were neither the only nor the most important collective unit; and even their corporate status remains ambiguous. Even so, despite their common dependence on collecting economies, the native societies of Australia and the American Northwest differ structurally from one another and from such societies as the Shoshone or Nambikuara which lacked any collective organization beyond their bands. Many other mobile societies, such as the pastoral Fulani of Northern Nigeria [26] or the militaristic Ngoni of Fort Jameson in Northern Rhodesia (Zambia),[27] also have social organizations that differ radically from band organization, though their residential groupings take that form. Moreover, if mere mobility of residential units is sufficient to distinguish band organization, then we must recognize it also among the plateau Tonga [28] and other swidden cultivators of Central Africa, grouped in small shifting villages. However, neither among Kwakiutl, Australians, Fulani, Fort Jameson Ngoni, or Tonga are "bands" the maximal units of collective organization, nor are their local groups independent of wider and crosscutting corporate alignments. Fort Jameson Ngoni owed their unity to an inclusive age-regimental organization and central chiefship. Fulani and Tonga societies are organized around clanship and lineage which crosscut and align local groups. While Cheyenne and Australian aborigines are collectors, Fulani are cattle herders, Tonga are cultivators, and Ngoni were primarily raiders. In sum, while most mobile societies share similar modes of residential grouping, many, and especially those of pastoral nomads, are incorporated on bases quite different from simple "band organization." One has merely to consider the Bedouin, Kazak, Mongols, Cheyenne, Crow, Somali, Tuareg, and Turkana to appreciate this point. It is necessary then to accommodate our taxonomy to these conditions by distinguishing mobile societies that are organized in bands merely for residential purposes from others in which bands are the sole or major units of corporate organization. As our examples indicate, since the ecological coefficients of these structural categories vary widely, our distinctions should center on their differences of corporate organization.

To summarize, besides acephalous and centralized societies, we must distinguish mobile and sedentary ones; and within the mobile category we should distinguish those that are residentially organized in bands from others in which band organization is virtually synonymous with the collective form and level of social organization. Clearly, mobile societies may be either centralized or acephalous; but all mobile peoples organized solely in bands lack centralization.

With such problematic exceptions as the Ga, Efik, and Yakö, centralization in sub-Saharan Africa has been generally identified with the chiefly regulation of public affairs through differentiated and specialized administrative staff. By such structures, Fortes and Evans-Pritchard initially distinguished societies having government from those without; [29] but clearly these writers did not assume that the mere presence of a titular headman or chief, as for instance in Anuak or Ndembu villages or in pastoral Fulani or Bushman bands, constitutes "a government" or a "centralized authority." The administrative staff is at least of equal importance; and among Kipsigi, Kikuyu, and Yoruba, or in Old Calabar, its structural priority is suggested by the absence or executive nullity of the chief.[30] On the other hand, the mere presence of an administrative staff, however effectively organized, does not guarantee the stability of the political aggregate as a continuing unit of central administration. Among Azande, Nyakyusa, Alur, Shambala, Tswana, Fort Jameson Ngoni, and other peoples having centralized authority, chiefdoms split frequently and in certain cases almost ritually at each generation.[31] In yet other societies of varying stability, the central chiefship was predominantly ritual and symbolic. To classify African chiefdoms by reference to their durability and by the secular or ritual symbolic character of their regimes would ignore several important dimensions such as the character, functions, and differentiation of the administrative staff, the scale of the political unit, its number of organizational levels, its ecological and demographic situation, ethnic heterogeneity, and the constitutional character and composition of its ruling councils.

Further, though this gross classification of African chiefdoms may serve us well, we should distinguish lesser chiefdoms from such imperial states as Mali, Songhay and Dahomey, Benin, Ethiopia, Kanem-Bornu, Sokoto, the old Wolof state, Ashanti and the Zulu under Shaka and Dingane. In terms of the common contrast between centralized and uncentralized polities, effective imperial systems seem to be overcentralized, since their effective administration presumes unusual concentration of administrative and political power at the center by appropriation of decisive autonomy from the administered units. With few exceptions, empires are always pluralities of varying degree, composition, and structure. The imperial order presupposes central control of greater resources, including force and intelligence, than can be marshaled against it by any single subjugated component. However, emperors, like others, depend on their administrative staff for loyal and efficient enforcement of their orders; in consequence imperial systems are constantly subject to secessions by territorial officials, to palace coups and usurpations, to foreign invasion and popular revolt. However spectacular their careers or spread, they are accordingly rather less stable than lesser chiefdoms that include more intensively societalized populations.

We emerge then with an operational scheme based on dimensions of acephaly and centralization and mobility and sedentarization. Societies in each of these categories are structurally distinguished by the type of corporation on which they depend for their boundaries and integration. As alternative bases for pure forms of corporate structure, we have distinguished bands, descent, age, association, and chiefship, classifying chiefdoms by their stability and ethnic character. However, neither are all mobile societies structurally based on bands, nor is age-organization restricted to acephalous societies, nor are all chiefdoms equally sedentary or centralized. In general we shall have to deal with mixed conditions and with combinations of corporate models rather than with societal examples of pure forms.

Some typology of African precolonial societies based on criteria of corporate structure is essential to any comparative review of interethnic accommodations within or among them. This is especially so because societies and ethnic accommodations of differing type are distinguished by their corporate organization, as was shown in the two preceding typologies. In short, our attempts to distinguish societal types, boundaries, and structures of ethnic accommodation emphasize the corporate nature and bases of these units, as well as their differences.

This feature of the conceptual framework has important values for our comparative review. Lacking the resources necessary for an exhaustive survey of African ethnology, we can still undertake a systematic comparative analysis of the differing forms of interethnic accommodation in traditional African societies by combining these typologies of societal forms and of accommodative structures. Since they share a common corporate framework, they have many close and direct connections. Being separately comprehensive, together they may also furnish an adequate framework for a discriminating comparative analysis of traditional societies selected for their typological relevance.

Differences of ecology might seem to offer a superior basis for classification of precolonial African societies. However, as we have seen in discussing band organization, an ecological taxonomy is relatively indiscriminate in its categories and problematic in its relevance to societal boundaries, structures, and institutions for the accommodation of differing units. By gross ecological criteria, besides "nomadic" and sedentary societies, we can distinguish only those that derive their subsistence from hunting, gathering, or fishing, from pastoralism, from agriculture or mixed husbandry, from commerce, manufactures, or war. It is evident that no direct correspondences between differing forms of social structure or interethnic accommodation and such gross differences of ecological or economic system can be adduced or inferred. Some consociations combine collectivities of differing ecological adaptation; others combine units of identical ecological type; and in both cases the corporate structures are influenced by many nonecological factors. Bearing in mind these alternative modes of livelihood, we need also to examine the demographic, historical, and structural contexts of these collective accommodations to isolate the significance of the ecological factor in any individual case.

One central problem of sociological theory concerns the various possible bases of social order and correlative conditions of social cohesion. In treating pluralism and its alternatives we are explicitly concerned with this question; but since societies vary in their composition and type, to seek a general answer we must undertake a systematic comparative analysis of differing patterns of interethnic accommodation which appear in societies of differing type. By employing corporate criteria to typologize societies and patterns of consociation, we simplify the problems of comparative analysis in this inquiry.

The typology of interethnic accommodations presented above represents a series of feasible alternatives to and structures of social and cultural pluralism. To determine their relative congruence with societies differentiated by structural type, we need, however cursorily, to examine representative cases drawn from the ethnographic materials on each societal category. In this way we may perhaps perceive relations of necessity, exclusion, or relative consistency between differing types of interethnic accommodations and differing types of corporate structure. Alternatively we may see how social systems of similar type can develop and sustain differing modes of inter-ethnic accommodation. For such comparative inquiries the structural framework adopted here has obvious values.

INDICES OF DIVERSITY

We need further to distinguish within the collectivities we shall survey those differences of race, ethnicity, provenience, language, ecology, social organization, cult, and other institutional patterns that may facilitate or promote pluralism. Only in this way can we refine and develop the study of societal responses to cultural diversity beyond the position reached by Fortes and Evans-Pritchard more than twenty-five years ago.

Having distinguished acephalous segmentary societies with a lineage base from centralized units, Fortes and Evans-Pritchard noted that all the centralized societies described in their volume "appear to be an amalgam of different peoples, each aware of its unique origin and history." They accordingly inquired "to what extent cultural heterogeneity in a society is correlated with an administrative system and central authority." On the data available, they remarked that

centralised authority and an administrative organisation seem to be necessary to accommodate culturally diverse groups within a single political system, especially if they have different modes of livelihood. A class or caste system may result if there are great cultural, and especially, great economic divergences. But centralised forms of government are found also with people of homogeneous culture and little economic differentiation, like the Zulu. It is possible that groups of diverse culture are the more easily welded into a unitary political system without the emergence of classes, the closer they are to one another in culture. A centralised form of government is not necessary to enable different groups of closely related culture and pursuing the same mode of livelihood, to amalgamate, nor does it necessarily arise out of the amalgamation. Nuer have absorbed large numbers of conquered Dinka, who are pastoral people like themselves with a very similar culture. They have incorporated them by adoption and other ways into their lineage systems; but this has not resulted in a class or caste structure, or in a centralised form of government. Marked divergencies in culture and economic pursuits are probably incompatible with segmentary political systems such as that of the Nuer or the Tallensi. We have not the data to check this.[32]

Despite numerous monographs and comparative studies of African polities published since 1940, I know of no general attempt to investigate and to develop these important suggestions of Fortes and Evans-Pritchard. To advance their analysis, besides discriminating typologies of societies and interethnic accommodations, we also need to discriminate conditions and degrees of cultural and ecological diversity within and between collectivities. To this end we should distinguish consociations of differing content and form by objective and by folk differences of language, ethnicity, race, culture, history, economy, cult, kinship, and other social institutions, thereby enabling us to assess the relative significance of differing cultural and racial conditions in promoting institutional accommodations of differing basis and type in societies distinguished by differing modes of corporate organization. In this paper we cannot undertake to detail all the institutional and cultural correspondences or divergences among the various peoples whose accommodations are mentioned below. Rather the reader is asked to assume that unless specific differentiae are mentioned, the collectivities concerned are of similar culture, language, and ethnic stock.

"Ethnicity" here denotes common provenience and distinctness as a unit of social and biological reproduction; it accordingly connotes internal uniformities and external distinctness of biological stock, perhaps of language, kinship, culture, cult, and other institutions. Collectivities entering into the institutional accommodations listed below are typically distinct ethnic units or segments thereof. Thus social units formed by combinations of elements from the same ethnic group—for example, the Kikuyu *rugongo* (community, ridge), the Ibo village group, or the Ashanti confederacy [33]—do not directly concern us, since no interethnic unions are directly involved. In studying social and cultural pluralism, ethnic combinations are clearly strategic.

Often ethnicity simultaneously connotes distinctions of descent and race; however, biologically closed communities of the same cultural, linguistic, and racial group are ethnically undifferentiated, though segregated as units of marriage and descent. In short, ethnic, racial, and communal units differ, though all are based on descent. In the African ethnographies from which our data are drawn, differences of tribal name, origin, and identity are generally taken as evidence of "ethnic" difference; yet even here, as Nadel and Goody show, caution is advisable in translating tribal designations into ethnic, cultural, and social units or boundaries. As a working rule, we can ignore those situations in which the historical and cultural correlates of tribal differentiations are indeterminate, as, for example, among the various Yoruba, Ibo, or Kikuyu collectivities. Unless the data indicate otherwise, it seems wiser to treat such peoples as distinct ethnic stocks whose internal differentiation, though worthy of note, does not obscure their unity or difference from adjacent groups.

In a society that contains a plurality of ethnic stocks, as defined here, perhaps the most significant index of ethnic closure is extent and form of common connubium. Even under structures of corporate amalgamation, ethnic groups of identical racial and linguistic stock may perpetuate their distinctness indefinitely, provided that each restricts connubium to its own members. Conversely, symmetrical connubium between ethnic groups facilitates their mutual assimilation in proportion to its relative frequency. Some examples are cited below. These considerations apply equally to groups differentiated by objective criteria of race.

Adjacent ethnic groups, though objectively and historically of common stock, often represent their differences in racial terms. Such folk ideologies must be distinguished from objective distinctions of racial type, as defined by genetic characteristics, in order that we may isolate the racial factor for direct analysis.

For various reasons, both historical and analytic, relatively few monographic studies of African societies give equal attention to the internal organization and cultural distinctness of the various tribally or ethnically differentiated segments of composite societies. Perhaps Nadel's study of the Nupe remains the outstanding attempt to provide the ethnographic data necessary for detailed analysis of the conditions of social cohesion within an African society of this composition and complexity.[34] Faced with such situations, anthropologists have generally restricted their intensive investigations to specific local units having high degrees of internal homogeneity and corresponding external distinctness. Thus Fortes described the Tallensi society as a separate, self-contained system, though historically it seems to have been subject to the Mamprussi chiefdom of Nalaragu.[35] Alternatively, anthropologists concerned to study ethnically and culturally heterogeneous chiefdoms have concentrated their attention almost exclusively on the culture and organization of the ruling group and on its system of administration. Schapera's studies among the Tswana, Gluckman's among the Lozi, and mine on Zaria may be cited as illustrations. For methodological reasons, such restrictions and concentrations of field investigation are often unavoidable. The anthropologist who undertakes to study several cultures in equal detail during one or two years of fieldwork often fails to study any unit adequately at all.

Facing such problems among the Nuba of Kordofan, Nadel selected ten tribes as representative units by certain strategic criteria. Of these ten, he devoted one year to three adjacent groups—Heiban, Otoro, and Tira—and two months apiece on average to the others.[36] This example indicates why detailed anthropological studies of all the culturally differentiated groups within a common aggregate remain rather rare; but, in consequence, we are often ill-informed about the specific nature and extent of the institutional and other differences that distinguish the various segments of a heterogeneous group.

Where the accommodation of culturally dissimilar peoples within a common society forms the principal object of study, as in Nadel's work on Nupe, Southall's on the Alur, or Maquet's on Ruanda,[37] the relevant ethnography is generally presented with variable completeness and stress. Alternatively we can sometimes combine ethnographic studies from two or more sources to furnish a reasonably detailed picture of cultural and social differences within the wider aggregate. Thus we can supplement Maquet's account of the Hutu in Ruanda by Edel's work on the independent Chiga belonging to the same ethnic and cultural stock.[38] Likewise we may employ C. K. Meek's ethnographic surveys of certain subject tribes in Zaria Province to fill out my picture of the Hausa emirate.[39] For the Terik and Tiriki mentioned below, we can draw on the ethnographies of Wagner and Huntingford which describe the two parental stocks.[40] Yet even with such extrapolations, our information on the concrete cultural and social differences of ethnically segregated units within a common inclusive society remains uneven and often sketchy. Under such conditions, we have often to use the grossest differentiae—population figures, local distributions, tribal designations, differences of language, connubium, economy, and kinship or cult—to illuminate reported differences or equivalences of political status and organization. In effect, anthropological concentration on the inner cohesion of relatively homogeneous and distinct collectivities deprives us of much needed data on the differences and relations of ethnic divisions in a wider society.

With these qualifications and typological categories we can nevertheless review interethnic associations reported in African societies of differing type, beginning with the simplest units and, where the material permits, undertaking limited comparisons of differing structures and situations among societies of identical type. Our review is organized by the preceding societal typology. It deals only with sub-Saharan Africa and is far from complete. It consists simply in reporting the differing formations found in societies of each category with summaries of their central features. However, these societal types are not all mutually exclusive. They do serve to organize the data and to facilitate comparative analysis in structurally consistent terms, but, where appropriate, I have not hesitated to cite cases out of this order; for example, it is convenient to discuss different types of mobile society together. Lineages and age-sets are found as well with chiefship as without. It is neither necessary nor possible to set up a system of mutually exclusive societal types; we need merely note the important particulars of corporate organization in each instance.

In conclusion, we may try to summarize the data from three points of view: first, we may try to determine what situational factors and ranges of cultural or "ethnic" diversity seem to be linked with institutionalized differences of incorporation or other types of interethnic association; second, we may inquire into the relationships between differences in the structures of interethnic accommodations and in the structures of the societies concerned; third, we may try to determine how far, and under what conditions, differential incorporation presupposes, preserves, or generates the institutional and social differences that constitute pluralism.

II

Mobile Societies

In Africa the pure form of band organization is found among Bushmen, Pygmies, Twa, Bergdama, Hottentots, and Wandorobo. Despite

Jeffries, it seems that at least some of the people loosely described as Twa or Batwa are pygmoids encapsulated in other societies.[41] It is also possible that some Twa are of Bushmanoid (Khoisan) stock, others of Pygmoid stock, and still others, such as the Swamp Twa, of "Bantu" stock.[42] By all criteria the best examples of band-organized African societies are the Kalahari Bushmen and the Pygmies of the Ituri forest; and for these we have fine data.

Few Bushmen in Bechuanaland or Southwest Africa retain their communal independence from adjacent tribes, Bantu or Hottentot. Schapera estimates that among the Ngwato, a Tswana tribe of approximately 100,000 (in 1946?) there were approximately 10,000 (Sarwa) Bushmen; and among the nearby Tawana another 4,000.[43] By contrast, the !Kung, one of the few Bushmen tribes to retain independence by withdrawal to the desert, are estimated at about 1,000.[44] Among the Tswana, Bushmen (Sarwa) formerly lived as serfs (*malata*),

parcelled out in local groups among the [Tswana] chiefs and other leading tribesmen. They and their descendants were permanently attached to the families of their masters, to whom they paid special tribute, and whom they served in various menial capacities; such property as they acquired was at their masters' disposal; if oppressed, as they often were, they had no access to the tribal court; and they lacked many other civic rights, including participation in the political assemblies [of Tswana communities and tribes].[45]

Evidently Sarwa still remain in substantive serfdom despite its formal abolition under European rule; and having no connubium with their Bantu superiors they form an endogamous caste in Tswana society. So do the Pygmoid Twa in such lacustrine polities as Ruanda, where, being politically useful to the traditional Tutsi rulers, they enjoyed certain privileges.[46] Nowhere outside the Kalahari are Bushmanoids entirely autonomous. Wherever found, they are always subjugated as a caste of endogamous serfs. By contrast, the Wandorobo, surrounded by Masai, though segregated as dependent and endogamous communities despite their adoption of Masai language and Masai age-set organization,[47] were neither incorporated in Masai society nor reduced to serfdom.

Bambuti Pygmies of the Ituri forest, probably the largest and least affected Pygmy group that remains, preserve their cultural and social autonomy from forest-dwelling Bira, Lese, Mangbetu, and other Bantu-speaking peoples by withdrawal to the forest, by symbiotic accommodations which the Bantu regard as subordination, by periodic relocation, and by other means. Though, like the Wandorobo, they have adopted the languages of the people around them, these Bambuti preserve their cultural and social distinctness and integrity by segmental symbiosis with differing Bantu groups, receiving bananas, metal tools, weapons, and other Bantu products in return for meat and forest wares. To illustrate the current situation, among the Bantu-speaking Amba, "the Pygmies are also drawn into this political system. Pygmy bands are tied to specific maximal lineages and here again the system of alliance is stated in terms of exogamy . . . even though in actual fact there is but little intermarriage." [48] As among !Kung bushmen, so among the Bambuti, individuals can easily shift their band affiliations; and bands, being mobile, can disengage from unsatisfactory collective relations. Thus associations between Bantu and Pygmies are segmental and symbiotic, these accommodations serving to demarcate societal boundaries. No single acephalous society includes both groups. [49]

South of the Sahara, nomadic pastoralists organized in migratory bands predominate in the Horn, in Ethiopia, throughout the Sudan, and along the Rift Valley as well as in Southwest Africa. Many of these peoples maintain societal segregation, for example, the Somali, Galla, Karimojong, Turkana, Nuer, Pokot, Samburu, and most Masai. Such groups do not immediately concern us. Other pastoralists, who have subjugated local cultivators, as in Ankole, Toro, Ruanda, Sukuma, or Northern Nigeria and Niger, are discussed below. Still other pastoral populations have nomadic routines that entail their continuing symbiotic accommodations with sedentary peoples in whose territory they graze their stock. In these conditions many pastoral groups have been formally incorporated as distinct segments in such traditional states as Ethiopia or Kanem-Bornu. [50] These pastoral units normally retain their internal autonomy, though recognizing the suzerainty of the local chief and his rights of supervision. In the central Sudan, the pastoral Fulani studied by Stenning, Hopen, and Dupire [51] provide nice examples of these intersocietal accommodations.

Numbering several millions, Fulani pastoralists are now scattered across the Sudan and Sahil from Futa Toro in Senegal to Sennar in the Sudan. Their society is complex and stratified in a hierarchy of castelike divisions, some of which are occupationally specialized, [52] while all are segmented into agamous patriclans and lineages in which descent lines are differentiated by seniority and rank. Local bands consist mainly of agnates, their wives and dependents, under the direction of an active man, the *ardo* or *ruga*, belonging to the senior generation and descent line. Each band operates as a separate social and pastoral unit under its headman, moving in seasonal cycles from wet- to dry-season pastures. While stressing their social separateness, these pastoralists maintain mutually rewarding relations of economic symbiosis with the farming communities around them. Often these seasonal migrations recurrently crossed the boundaries of territorial states.

In Hausaland pastoralists resident in a given state during the wet season were required to render allegiance and cattle tithe (*zakka*) as ordained by Muslim law to its ruler through their headman, his superior, the Fulani chief, and the supervising official (*hakimi*) who administered the unit on behalf of the chief. During dry seasons the nomads could move freely within and between adjacent chiefdoms, such as Katsina, Zamfara, or Kano, whose rulers had agreed to recognize one another's extraterritorial rights over migrating bands normally resident in their chiefdom. This administrative pattern, known as *bin kanu* (following heads) or *bin Filani* (following Fulani), prevailed from the eighteenth century, when the Hausa states were mutually autonomous, and was probably developed from the older model of the Bornu *chima jeribe*, the Sultan's officer placed in charge of a particular pastoral "clan" wherever they moved.[53] This flexible administrative arrangement, which was evidently devised to accommodate pastoral transhumance while ensuring continued official control of the nomads, presumed and preserved those differences of language, ethnicity, cult, internal government, stratification, ecology, connubium, and kinship which distinguished the pastoralists from the agricultural peoples. The administrative arrangement provided a framework for continuing the economic symbiosis of these groups, subject to political regulation by the state. Thus though formally incorporated in territorial states under their own headman, the pastoralists were structurally segregated from the agricultural population; and, to facilitate official control, they were systematically subdivided under differing official jurisdictions. These arrangements combined elements of symbiosis, segmental attachment, and subordination.

Evidently during the eighteenth century these pastoralists had reason for dissatisfaction with their lot; and after one or two abortive revolts, between 1804 and 1810 they rallied to the jihad proclaimed by Usman dan Fodio, an outstanding Muslim leader of the settled Fulani, and overthrew their former rulers, except in Bornu. However, this conquest did not eliminate or transform the earlier societal segregation and symbiosis of pastoralists and farmers; and although the pastoralists thereafter enjoyed improved political and administrative conditions, their segmental subordination under *bin kanu* jurisdiction persisted even in those states with a settled Fulani ruling class.

In certain respects unstable local groups of shifting cultivators such as the plateau Tonga and Ndembu of Northern Rhodesia or the mobile "residential segments" of militaristic Ngoni approximate an organization based on bands. In consequence of their fragile and miniscule organization, these Tonga peoples were unable to offer effective defense to slave raiders or to expanding chiefdoms nearby, for example, the Lozi or the Ngoni. Even the Ila, who developed communes numbering up to 3,000,

weakened by divisions and feud, were incapable of resisting Lozi dominion or raids by slavers.[54]

In its pure form, band organization, whatever its ecological basis,
appears to have a limited capacity for incorporating segments of other
collectivities as units. In Africa only those mobile peoples who subsist
solely by hunting and gathering lack wider frameworks of corporate
organization. Stratification enables some pastoralists to incorporate individuals into their bands as slaves or serfs. Without it, lineage adoptions,
clientage, and social and cultural assimilation are likely alternatives, as
among the Nuer, Mandari, and Arusha Masai. At Arusha, local Masai,
having forcibly absorbed large numbers of Bantu-speaking Meru cultivators, through interbreeding, association, and mutual acculturation, by
assimilation developed a unique amalgam of Meru and Masai customs
which marks them off as a genuine hybrid group, equally distinct from
other Masai and Meru.[55] Other pastoralists, notably Tuareg, settle their
slaves and serfs in discrete communities, visiting them periodically to
levy tribute and administer their affairs; Tuareg also maintain comparable relations with vassal Tuareg clans who render service and tribute in
kind.[56] Thus pastoralists may adopt agriculture upon assimilation, as at
Arusha, or they may incorporate individuals or family groups of the same
or alien stock as slaves, clients, allies, or serfs. Larger subordinate collectivities are generally set apart as dependent communities, whether or not
they belong to a common ethnic stock, as, for instance, the Masai Dorobo
or the Tuareg *imghad*. Alternatively a pastoral society may incorporate
one or more servile endogamous castes of occupational specialists who
move from band to band, as do the smiths and barber-doctors among the
Tuareg,[57] or these servile castes may be attached to particular lineages
and bands, as are the Yibir, Midgaan, and Tumaal bondsmen (*sab*)
among the Somali.[58]

Excluding such complex developments beyond the level of band organization among pastoralists, band-organized collectors face alternatives of decimation by external assaults as among Bushmen; encapsula-
tion and subordination by surrounding societies as among the Masai
Dorobo and the Ruanda Twa; serfdom as among Sarwa; or withdrawal
to freedom in such refuge areas as the Kalahari or the Ituri Forest.
Where the band persists as an internally autonomous and institutionally
distinct unit after formal incorporation in a wider society, its subordination by caste or serfdom is general. Alternatively, it may remain distinct
through residential segregation and specialized symbiotic relations, as
Wandorobo do among Masai. Evidently band organization can rarely
accommodate an institutionally distinct group without changes of struc-

tural type as in Arusha, or without explicit stratification and a political hierarchy, as among Tuareg.

DESCENT SYSTEMS

Corporate groups based on descent are widespread in Africa. They vary greatly in constitutive principles and in form. Besides patriliny and matriliny we find some systems of cognatic descent, for example, among Mambila (and perhaps Mende), and others of double unilineal descent such as the Yakö, Mbembe, Lodagaba, Herrero, Nyaro, and Tullishi.[59] It is necessary also to distinguish categorical clans from corporate descent groups, segmentary from rank-differentiated lineages, dispersed from localized groups, and exogamous from endogamous and agamous units.

Many African societies formerly depended for their inner coherence and external boundaries wholly or primarily on their organizations as closed systems of interdependent descent groups of specific form, interrelations, and span; this is especially clear in such acephalous or stateless societies as the Somali, Tonga, Nuer, Tallensi, and Tiv.

It is often assumed that societies organized wholly or primarily on the basis of corporate descent groups cannot easily accommodate large numbers of aliens. To discuss this question clearly we need first to distinguish between the degree and condition of "statelessness" and the structure of corporate kinship groups. It is not immediately evident that the Shilluk, for example, achieved a higher degree of internal "centralization" than the nearby Nuer or Dinka; likewise the Tuareg, while recognizing drum chiefs (*Amenokal*), remained without effective central organization. Nonetheless, their society incorporated Negro slaves (*iklan*), hybrid serfs (*haratin*), vassal clans (*imghad*), and servile castes (*ineden*), all differentiated by specific lineage attachments as well as by occupation and by biological, jural, and political status.

Materials published since 1940 on lineages in acephalous and centralized societies of different kinds show that acephalous societies based on unilineal descent may incorporate aliens of similar or different culture with varying thoroughness and by various means. These mechanisms of accommodation may also prevail among lineages in state-organized societies. Here we can only consider some modes of incorporation current in acephalous societies with unilineal bases.

Among the Gusii of Kenya "stranger groups which are not strong enough to rank as clans seem to be faced with the same alternative as confronts individual strangers; if they do not go 'home' they must (outside Getutu) somehow achieve assimilation." This is generally done "by means of genealogical fictions, and a deliberate disregard of totemic and other anomalies; or, in Getutu, by means of a purely political relationship." Unlike other Gusii tribes, all of whom claim common agnatic descent from MoGusii—as Tiv and Lugbara claim descent from their tribal ancestors—the "Getutu tribe does not pretend to be a lineage. . . . It is a political grouping (of stranger groups) arranged around one dominant lineage—the clan of Nyakundi." [60] In this respect Getutu is structurally similar to the typical Nuer tribe in which the dominant clan (*diel*) has aristocratic status, other lineages being attached to it, with or without genealogical fictions, and at various levels of segmentary organization.[61] Dinka modes of affiliating newcomers through their lineage structure differ mainly in lack of single lineages that serve as tribal spines.[62]

Among the acephalous Amba of western Uganda, the consociation is more complex. Amba are organized in exogamous agnatic lineages, each occupying a separate village. Their country, Bwamba, contains four distinct speech communities: Bulibuli or "Amba proper" whose Bantu dialect is similar to that of the Ituri Bira; Bwezi whose speech is cognate with Toro; Vonoma, a smaller Bantu-speaking group; and Mvuba who speak a Sudanic tongue.[63] Winter says that "beyond this linguistic differentiation" he "was never able to discover the slightest cultural trait which might be used as a criterion for separating these . . . groups." [64] As we have seen, even the forest Pygmies are attached to particular maximal lineages.

Since each maximal lineage occupies a distinct village, and the society contains four separate speech communities, the Amba have developed a system of lineage linkages by alliance and by exogamy which systematically attaches specific Bwezi and Bulibuli groups as allies, these two accounting for four-fifths of the population. "The system of linked lineages is related to the major linguistic division in the society, that between the Bulibuli and the Bwezi. . . . Each Bwezi lineage is linked to a Bulibuli lineage." [65] Linked lineages are obliged to support one another at rituals, by marriage, and by mediatory action or fighting in the frequent feuds that distinguished Bwamba as a separate social system. Needless to say, this population, committed by its corporate organization to perpetual divisions and internal struggle, was incapable of mobilizing an effective defense against the expanding Toro to the east; and when the British pacified Uganda, its incorporation by Toro was well advanced.

Among the Kagoro of Northern Nigeria and the Tallensi of northern Ghana we find consociations of different quality and form. The original Kagoro, organized patrilineally and by mutually exclusive modes of marriage relation—exogamy (*bin*), wife stealing (*nendwang*), and intermarriage (*niendi*)—called themselves Ankwei. These Ankwei owed their independence from Muslim conquest to their location on the Kagoro rock, after which they were generally known. During the past century nearby peoples of similar linguistic and cultural stock, but of different tribal groups, fled from the Muslim Hausa-Fulani armies to the rock. Probably the earliest of these refugees were ancestors of the present Kadau clan who came from Katab. As the refugees increased in number and heterogeneity, Ankwei clan heads classified them together as Munzaram, Kadau retaining precedence. For a while Kagoro contained two incipient moieties, Ankwei and Munzaram. When further immigrants appeared, following new raids, they were initially segregated in a third section known as Kpashan; but, probably because Ankwei society, founded on a system of two mutually exclusive types of marriage relations between corporate lineages, could more easily accommodate a moiety organization than a trichotomy, Munzaram and Kpashan were assimilated into an immigrant moiety within which intermarriage was forbidden, though intercommunity wife stealing among them was legitimate. Meanwhile Ankwei maintained their old relations of exogamy, wife stealing, and intermarriage, but, under Kpashan exogamy, the moieties intermarried systematically. Nonetheless, except for Kadau, their oldest local elements, these Kpashan-Munzaram were excluded from direct participation in the earth ritual (ci) through which Ankwei priests and lineage heads traditionally pursued community well-being. Ankwei had no ancestral cult; and by 1950 neither had Kpashan. Consequently, being defined by their exclusion from ritual as a secular exogamous moiety, Kpashan specialized institutions of secular chiefship, thus establishing social complementarity with the ritually dominant Ankwei. Today slightly the larger moiety, Kpashan hold almost all Kagoro chiefships, including the tribal office, and Christianity has further undermined Ankwei ritual dominance. Long before this, however, tribal unity was established by Kpashan and Ankwei intermarriage under the Kpashan exogamy rule.[66]

Among Tallensi similar patterns of complementary consociation were established between the indigenous Talis of the Tong hills in northern Ghana and immigrant Mamprussi whose chiefs at Mamparugu evidently exercised dominion over Taleland before the Anglo-French occupations.[67] Descendants of these Mamprussi immigrants now form the large section known locally as Namoos, among whom the Mosuorbiis are the senior clan in which the ritualized local "chiefship" vests. Mosuorbiis are divided into four large localized lineages, each having separate linkages and alliances with particular Tale lineages and clans.[68] Indeed, "Namoos and non-Namoos frequently form constituent lineages of the same clan, holding complementary ritual offices, divided by the same structural cleavages as separate Talis and the Tongo Namoos, but inseparably joined by equally strong structural ties and common interests." [69]

As among Kagoro, besides their ritual interdependence, Namoos and non-Namoos in Taleland are integrated through intermarriage, local community ties, and other common interests. Segments of these two contraposed categories are bound together by particular alliances and ties of clanship which enjoin mutual support as mediators or participants in feud, ritual, and secular affairs. Though initial cultural differences between the ancestral Talis and immigrant Mamprussi remain obscure, they certainly include chiefship, language, and perhaps other social institutions as well. Though some social and cultural differences persist, these now serve as symbols of corporate identity, complementarity, and membership in the common inclusive society. By selective conversion of certain cultural differences into ritualized symbols of corporate identity and complementarity, Namoos and "real Talis" have used them to create a wider society and a more complex integration.

Among the Nuba of Kordofan, another area settled by refugees of differing linguistic and cultural stock, Nadel reports a situation that "precludes a sharp division admitting of no overlapping in groups whose cultural makeup would differ in every detail." [70] Though the average Nuba tribe asserts its cultural homogeneity, several tribes, such as Otoro and Moro, are internally quite diverse. However, employing local self-identifications, Nadel distinguished these tribes "by the system of reckoning descent," by the "nature of the clan organisation," and by the "presence or absence of a certain shamanistic spirit-possession cult" [71]—that is, by three "pivotal features," two of which identify forms of corporate grouping which organize and segregate each tribal society. As in Taleland, so too in Nuba, Nadel identified complementarity as a pervasive and important feature of the amalgamations and coalescence of differing groups as tribal units. "The clans hang together, as it were, by two hinges, one is biological necessity—clans depend on each other for marriage . . . ; another is spiritual necessity—the knowledge that the welfare of each clan depends on supernatural help in the possession of the other. Segments are indispensable to each other and thus to the existence of the society as a whole." [72]

Persisting differences of ethnicity, culture, and cult were thus institutionalized in these amalgams as social complementarity and ritual symbiosis, perhaps most clearly among the Dilling Nuba.[73] Such mechanisms and conversions enabled various refugee communities in these hills to organize themselves as symbiotic unions into bounded tribal societies characterized by jural equivalence, internal solidarity, and common external distinctness. As tribes differ in their cultural and social composition, they differ also in structure and inner cohesion.

Among the Nilotic Mandari, client lineages were attached to leading members of localized landowning clans, organized under petty headmen or "chiefs" who administered the common affairs of their local communities in consultation with clan elders. Here the explicitly secular relation of clientage provided a uniform basis for the social and political attachment of hosts and immigrants, whether drawn from similar or differing ethnic and linguistic groups. These immigrants were separately linked to local lineages, which, by preserving their genealogical distinctness, emerged as the "aristocratic" elements of these weakly structured segmentary chiefdoms.[74] As among the Tallensi, Nuba, Kagoro, Amba, and Nuer, these Mandari clients, though diverse, were neither culturally nor ethnically too remote to prevent assimilation or amalgamation. Among the Tuareg, Somali, and pastoral Fulani, certain differences of ecology, culture, language, and race may underlie the differential incorporation of particular ethnic groups; but most *imghad* or vassal clans in Tuareg society are simply Tuareg groups reduced by force; and at Arusha, sharp differences of race, language, ecology, and culture between Meru and Masai were no barrier to their total coalescence.

The most thorough social incorporation that unilineal descent permits involves adoption of outsiders into the host lineage as members with full rights. This is more easily done for individuals than for groups. Among Mandari, accessory lineages were perpetually segregated by attachment to landowning lines as clients, though enjoying favorable situations in return for special services.

The absorption of individuals into unilineal descent groups may proceed by genealogical fictions, by adoption, or by complementary, usually uterine, filiation. The latter at best permits an incomplete and conditional attachment under systems of agnatic descent, and is excluded by matriliny; in contrast, genuine adoption ensures full jural equivalence of the adopted member, as among the Yakö, a Cross River people in southeastern Nigeria who practice a system of double unilineal descent. Yakö patrilineages and matrilineages alike regularly recruit members by purchasing children from nearby tribes, these children being brought up as full members of the purchasing lineages.[75] In this area Yakö are not unique in pursuing lineage expansion by such means.

The Ibo institution of *ohu* slavery shows that acephalous unilineal organization is quite consistent with differential incorporation of culturally similar or alien groups. Under this system, corporate patrilineages purchased or captured slaves whom they settled in discrete communities, as among Tuareg, and held as corporate property. *Ohu* slaves were defined as chattels by their lack of jural and political rights.[76] As shown below, the Efik and Ijaw practiced similar institutions.[77]

In the Congo the matrilineal Lele also recruited captives and transferred free persons by contract as "pawns" for personal or collective ends.[78] Lele society seems to have revolved around the institution of pawnship by which non-Lele were often assimilated; Douglas suggests that such pawnship is a characteristic institution of other Central Bantu with a matrilineal organization.[79] Certainly the modes of "slavery" reported among Luvale and Suku correspond closely to the pawnship Douglas describes.[80] Notably, despite its collective bases, forms, and contexts, this institution of pawnship generally attached invividuals to one another as lord and pawn, whereas the *ohu* system of slavery was a relation between corporate groups similar to helotage. However, Lele corporate groups could also hold pawns, while individual Ibo could own slaves.

Simple correspondence of kinship organization neither guarantees assimilation and symmetrical incorporation nor precludes differentiation by caste, as can be seen among the Ndebele, Ruanda, Tuareg, Wolof, Fulani, or Somali.[81] On the other hand, differences in kinship organization and practice either demarcate societal boundaries, as among the Nuba or the Lowiili-LoDagaba, or reinforce collective segregations in structurally heterogeneous units, as among Terik-Tiriki or between the Bahima and Ba'iru in Ankole.[82]

AGE ORGANIZATION

In its most developed form, age organization consists in a series of corporate sets instituted at regular intervals, each of which enrolls all men of the same social unit and age. Sets are thus ranked as senior and junior in a timeless order, and, being societal in span, define the societal boundaries by their limits. This mode of social organization, which is characteristic of many acephalous societies in East Africa, seems to be structurally inconsistent with matrilineal organization, especially in its dispersed form. Age-sets may form an autocephalous or self-regulating series, in which case one or more senior sets generally exercise directive functions over the others on behalf of the total collectivity or its local divisions, as, for example, among the Galla, Kipsigi, or Masai. Alternatively the structure may be heterocephalous and subject to external direction, whether by such colleges as the Yakö Yabot and Yakambam, the Kikuyu Kyama, and the Yoruba Ologboni, or by a local chief as in the age-regimental organizations of centralized southern Bantu, such as the Tswana, Zulu, Swazi, Ndebele, or among the northern Ngoni.

In patrilineally organized acephalous societies, age organization is either restricted by lineage boundaries, as among the Gusii, or by personal and local factors, as among the Tiv, or it may be rendered totally ineffective by the lineage organization, as among the Nuer. Rarely do we find age organization and segmentary lineages flourishing together as equally significant structures without some distinct supervisory body, whether this is collegial as among the Ibo, Yakö, and Kikuyu, or chiefly as among the southern Bantu.

Where age organization is both the dominant corporate form and the basis of societal integration, as in many acephalous East African societies, aggregates that differ in the structure of their age systems constitute distinct societies, irrespective of continuities in other institutional spheres such as kinship, language, cult, or economy. This is illustrated by tribal differentiations within the Karimojong cluster and among the Nandi-speaking peoples.[83] It is evident also among Galla, Ibo, Meru, and Masai.[84] Differing in formal details and in the ceremonial organization by which they institute their age-sets, such ethnic clusters divide into distinct tribes, many of which are further broken down into smaller aggregates which average approximately 40,000 persons, apparently the widest units within which age-ceremonials are celebrated and age-sets are routinely instituted together.

Although necessary wherever this type of organization prevails, formal identities of age organization, including the synchronization of the age-sets in parallel series, are not in themselves sufficient to create a society out of people who differ in other institutional spheres, unless expressly agreed upon by the collectivities. The Siuei Dorobo, though adopting Samburu language and age-set organization, remain beyond the limits of Samburu society, having differing patterns of marriage, kinship, and ecology.[85] Likewise the irrigation-based Sonjo, though replicating the age organization of the Masai around them, are segregated as a distinct group by kinship, economy, language, and cult. Indeed, Sonjo copied Masai age organization as an essential instrument for their own defense.[86]

An illuminating example of consociation based on deliberate adoption of a common system of age organization is provided by the Tiriki, a branch of the Bantu Kavirondo, and the Terik, a small tribe of Nandi-speaking Nilo-Hamites.[87] Tiriki, an agricultural people organized in exogamous segmentary patrilineages, are now distinguished from other Abaluyia, their parental tribe, by consociation with the Nandi-speaking Terik who lack segmentary lineages and remain predominantly pastoral in their ecology and orientation.[88] Though forming a common society, the two collectivities are separated by sharp differences of culture, ecology, and social structure.

The Terik-Tiriki association probably began around 1750, when Terik, having recently split from the Nandi with whom they were then at feud, came under intense military pressure from the Nilotic Luo due south and, lacking the Nandi support they had previously enjoyed, were in urgent need of allies.

According to tradition, about eight generations ago the need for numerical reinforcements led the Terik to offer asylum to wandering or refugee segments of Abaluyia lineages, on condition that the menfolk would become incorporated into the Terik warrior group; that is, become initiated into Terik age-groups. . . . These groups provided the organisational structure for Terik military regiments; thus every Abaluyia immigrant was obliged to undergo initiation into an age-group of military age. . . . Initiation converted the Abaluyia immigrants into full-fledged members of the Terik tribe. . . . Differences of opinion and belief concerning female initiation proved to be an effective deterrent to intermarriage between Terik and Teriki, and probably in large measure have been responsible for the Terik and Teriki maintaining discrete linguistic and cultural identities through the generations, in spite of their intense military, political and ritual interaction.[89]

Tiriki still retain their distinctive language, agricultural economy, ancestor cult, segmentary lineage system, and multilineal community organization. They also observe clanship prohibitions with their Abaluyia kin nearby: "The Tiriki-Terik alliance is a case of a bicultural society where both groups have over a considerable period of time continued to interact with and view each other on a basis of social equality." [90] At Arusha the union of Masai and Meru, though not initially consensual, produced a thorough social and biological hybrid, a structurally distinct "tribe"; but Kipsigi, another Nandi-speaking tribe, also incorporated and assimilated a Gusii group who had been cut off from its stock without any changes in their own organization.

The use of heterocephalous age divisions to incorporate and control large aggregates is best illustrated from the southern Bantu, where its various forms among the Tswana, Zulu, Swazi, Ndebele, and other groups illustrate vividly the flexibility and accommodative capacities of this structural form. By means of their inclusive age-regimental organizations, Zulu and Swazi achieved high degrees of chiefly centralization and tribal amalgamation.[91] In nearby Tswana chiefdoms, such as the Ngwato, control over local regimental segments was dispersed throughout a hierarchy of hereditary headsmen of local communities, many of which were distinct in language, customs, and civic status from their Ngwato rulers.[92] The Ndebele state, formed by a Nguni group that broke away from Shaka, illustrates yet another pattern.

These Ndebele (Matabele) Nguni increased their numbers by receiving Sotho immigrants and allies whom they renamed Enhla. The Ndebele enrolled the Enhla within their age-regiments under Ngoni commanders. Together the two groups overthrew the large chiefdom of Mambo north of the Limpopo and made that territory their own. The "people of Mambo," already a heterogeneous lot, were categorized as Lozwi or Holi in contradistinction to the Zansi or ruling Ngoni and their Enhla or Sotho affiliates. Like Enhla and Zansi, Lozwi were enrolled in the Ndebele age-regiments, which were organized as separate towns under Zansi commanders.[93] Despite this common participation in the age-regimental system, Ndebele society was organized as a hierarchy of three endogamous castes, in which the Zansi or "Ngoni proper" represented about 15 percent; the Enhla, mainly Sotho and Tawana, about 25 percent; and the subjugated indigenous people, Lozwi or Holi, about 60 percent. "Intermarriage was forbidden and . . . political power lay in the hands of Zansi." [94] Both the Zansi and Lozwi castes were segmented by older tribal, linguistic, and cultural divisions, Zansi being either Shangana or Swazi Nguni, while the Lozwi included Venda, Kalanga, Nyai, Shankwe, and other tribes. By contrast, the Enhla lacked internal tribal divisions.

Though one age-regiment contained only Lozwi, all others were caste-heterogeneous and under direct command of resident Zansi princes or nobles: "Virtually all the important officials and regimental chiefs were drawn from that [Zansi] caste." [95] Enhla, whose ancestors were originally "used for all manual work, and were treated as a separate group," [96] came to occupy an intermediate status after Ndebele conquest of the Mambo chiefdom.

Within the Ndebele area proper, the Lozwi seem to have had no direct political power. . . . In the central area, no Lozwi could be placed in authority over any group containing a single mmber of either of the immigrant castes. Many seem to have "belonged" to some Zansi or Enhla in the sense that these could claim their services, and it was Lozwi who did all the manual work except in the case of the poorest upper-caste households." [97] "Intermarriage between members of different castes . . . was completely forbidden. In the last decades of the kingdom extramarital intercourse was equally unlawful." [98]

Zansi employed the term "Holi" to denote inferior or servile groups within or beyond the Ndebele chiefdom. To insult Enhla, Zansi frequently addressed them as Holi. These differences of corporate status persisted despite enculturation within the age organization. In the regiments Lozwi and Enhla were trained in Ndebele customs, organization, and language; nonetheless, the Lozwi maintained their Shona customs and language for internal intercourse throughout much of the Ndebele chiefdom until and after 1893, when the state was overthrown.[99] Though dependent on farming, the ruling Ngoni (Zansi) identified themselves as warriors, cattle herders, and rulers, while Lozwi were classified as hunters, farmers, laborers, and craftsmen. Even in 1950, Lozwi differed from Zansi in certain features of language, kinship, and ritual, as well as in social and political status.

By combining monopoly of office with caste prescription and compulsory enrollment in common age-regiments, the Ndebele instituted a structure of social and political inequality based on the systematic differential incorporations of affiliated Sotho and conquered Shona. As shown below, other caste-stratified conquest states in the Great Lakes region, lacking age-regimental organization, subjugated their servile castes equivalently by differing means.

The Ndebele state differs in structure, stability, and scale from nearby conquest states founded by other Nguni segments which, like the original Zansi, had broken out of Shaka's kingdom. It is instructive to compare briefly the Ngoni societies of Nyasaland (Malawi) and Zambia with the Ndebele of (Southern) Rhodesia, paying special attention to differences in the structure and roles of their age organizations.

In Malawi, the Ngoni founded nine separate chiefdoms, two of which were moderately large. These Ngoni devoted themselves here, as elsewhere, to cattle herding, to cultivation—primarily a woman's task—and to extensive raiding for loot, land, and captives, most of whom the Nyasa Ngoni exported as slaves, retaining a few to serve in royal courts and households.[100] These latter were numerically and structurally unimportant, being jurally excluded as chattels from free Ngoni society, despite their enculturation. The Nyasa Ngoni evidently made no attempt to incorporate captive or conquered peoples in their age-regiments; and, having no alternative structures capable of accommodating and socializing large numbers of non-Ngoni to their society, these Ngoni slaughtered or sold defeated groups into slavery, without even seeking to occupy their lands.

In Zambia (Northern Rhodesia) the Fort Jameson Ngoni, another roving militaristic group, organized first in societally extensive age-regiments and then in regimentally heterogeneous "residential segments" or bands, under nonhereditary lieutenants, systematically incorporated all captives in their age-regiments, thereby continually expanding their numbers and strength by successful raiding.

The Ngoni depended largely on the efficiency of their army for the continual inflow of captives, on which the strength and continued existence of the state depended. The age-set system provided them with an efficient army, and in addition was a means whereby the centrifugal tendency in the segmentary system was partly checked. Each major [residential] segment had members in each regiment, and each regiment was drawn from every major segment.[101]

This unifying effect of the age-set system applied particularly to the recent captives. It appears to have been through the regimental system that recent captives, both men and women, were indoctrinated into Ngoni ways and made to feel that they, too, were Ngoni. In the residential system, recent captives were dependents rather than lords. In the age-set system there was no such distinction. Men captives were drafted into the regiment appropriate to their apparent age, and boys were enrolled with their coevals. They were called upon to fight in the same way as their aristocratic comrades, and were offered the same prospects of promotion, both within the age-set system and in the segmentary organisation, as the result of successful fighting. Many of the well-remembered segment heads who achieved rapid promotion after capture, are described as being successful warriors.[102]

Barnes estimates that at various times the paramount chief of the Fort Jameson Ngoni probably commanded about 10,000 warriors.

Thus, while the Ndebele employed their age-regimental organization to subordinate their affiliates and subjects and to constitute a plural society based on differential incorporation by caste, the Fort Jameson Ngoni employed the same institution to expand their society by assimilating defeated and captive peoples, thereby creating a perpetually fissile and expanding "snowball state" based on intensive assimilation and universalistic achievement orientations. By contrast, the Nyasa Ngoni excluded all free outsiders from their society; as conquerors and raiders, they left themselves little alternative to wholesale slaughter and slave trading. Since these three Ngoni peoples all shared common origins, social organization, and ethos, their contrasting structural developments provide a nice study of the relationships between differing modes of societal exclusion or incorporations and changes in societal structure.

ASSOCIATIONS

Besides bands, lineages, and age systems, we can distinguish two categories of corporate associations, both of which are heterogeneous, at least as regards age and descent, and often residence as well. Some associations are both compulsory and societally comprehensive, as, for example, the Poro in Liberia and Sierra Leone, the Ogboni or Oshugbo among the Yoruba, Egbo or Ekpe among the Efik of Calabar, Ekine in Bonny, and so on.[103] Such inclusive associations that incorporate all adult male members of the community are internally stratified in several grades, the senior of which forms an inner college that regulates the association's affairs, and often those of the community also.

Associational polities vary widely in structure. Where chiefship is found with these graded inclusive associations, as among the Yoruba, Mende, Kpelle, or Temne, whether secular or sacred, the chief generally depends on the association for political support;[104] and sometimes, as in

Old Calabar or among the Western Ibo, the senior grade of these communal associations directed civic life in chiefless societies.[105]

Alternatively, a community may contain one or more corporate associations with restricted memberships recruited on the basis of differing combinations of principles such as seniority, descent, occupational and economic status, and cooption by current members. Where a community contains several associations, these are usually differentiated by function, jurisdiction, membership, and relative status; and either one unit, the most senior, then regulates the community's affairs independently or through the other associations, or a loose hierarchic structure of overlapping memberships enables the most senior and exclusive association to enforce its decisions indirectly through others. These different patterns are found without chiefs among the Ibo,[106] Yakö, and Mbembe,[107] and with chiefs in Liberia, Sierra Leone, the Central Cameroons, and among the Sukuma of Tanganyika.[108] In some Central Cameroons societies, these variably specialized and exclusive associations provide rulers with flexible and effective instruments for routine government and for control of incorporated communities.

Here we are concerned only with corporate associations under conditions of interethnic accommodation. It is clear that these structures may promote or obstruct the assimilation of alien individuals or groups. Where such associations are central to societal regulation, then, whether exclusive, or inclusive and graded, the degree and conditions of assimilation of alien individuals or groups correspond with their opportunities for active membership in the senior associations or grades thereof. Thus, though the Efik of Calabar enrolled their slaves in the inclusive Egbo, these slaves rarely if ever advanced beyond the lowest grade.[109] By contrast, among the nearby Yakö, men adopted into a lineage were eligible, on achieving appropriate status, to represent it on those associations in which it had corporate membership.[110]

In associationally regulated societies, social pluralism presumes effective exclusion from these organizations as, for instance, the exclusion of *ohu* slaves among the Ibo, or slaves among Efik. Notably, in these cases the jurally excluded category consists of aliens drawn from different ethnic and linguistic groups.

Another distinct associational pattern involves the confederation of distinct and internally autonomous collectivities, as, for instance, the Egba confederations at Ibadan (1829) and at Abeokuta (1830).[111] Prior to their settlement at Abeokuta as mutually distinct, internally autonomous groups, each under its own hereditary chief and officials, the three Egba collectivities differed somewhat in language, organization, and culture.[112] They were in fact forced to confederate, however loosely, by common external threats; but their association was marked by divisions and rivalries.[113] To this day, at Abeokuta, "each of the three Egba sections and Owu has its distinct dialect, and intermarriage between persons of different sections is not common—though certainly not unusual. Each township endeavours to retain its own individuality and importance." [114]

Setting aside this Egba confederation and certain others, such as the Ashanti or Fanti, which brought together collectivities of common ethnic and linguistic stock, we find similar consociations in Ga townships, formed by the amalgamation of immigrant and indigenous peoples of differing language, culture, and ethnic stock. Each Ga town includes Adangme-speaking immigrants and aborigines whose language was Kpesi, a dialect of Twi. These Ga municipal confederations developed in the late seventeenth century on Fanti and Akwamu models, under military pressure from slave raiders. As the earliest local occupants, and thus "landowners," the aborigines retained ritual leadership in each confederation; but each component group retained internal autonomy under its own head or council of elders.

Each of the Ga "towns" was a confederation of a varying number of Houses or patrilineages—whose members traced their descent back to the founder of the House. . . . Membership of a patrilineage may be acquired by adoption as well as by birth. . . . When numbers become too great the Houses break up into sub-Houses—but no new set of names are created. Public offices, both religious and secular, are vested in the lineages: each Ga "town" is managed and run by its "big people" who are all representatives of lineages and sublineages. . . . The lineage is collectively responsible for the behaviour of its members.[115]

There has never been any political confederation of the "towns." . . . Each "town" today consists of several so-called "quarters" (akutso), each representing a separate party of colonists which attached itself to the original group of settlers, preserving many of its own customs and the worship of its own gods, but acknowledging the supremacy of the senior god of the "town" and its priest, who was head of the "town." The "quarter" was essentially a military unit, the "town" itself being a military confederation which would never have united except for military ends.[116]

To symbolize its unity, each town appointed a Mantse as ritual figurehead. A college of senior priests (wulomei) drawn from its various quarters adjudicated complaints arising between them. The principal organization involving all townsmen was the asafo or militia under officials in each quarter, chosen for their abilities. The asafo was responsible for maintaining internal law and order as well as external defense. Since at each level of Ga township organization, corporate units of the same order and type had equal representation, despite ethnic and cultural differences, all elements had an equal voice in the common government and responsibility for it. Although this uniform distribution of collective rights and duties was restricted to such matters of common interest as communal rituals, defense, and internal peace, by instituting these egalitarian conditions, and by preserving the integrity of each component unit, the communes created favorable circumstances for cultural and social assimilations which, though incomplete, have steadily increased through ritual and social interactions, until today the aboriginal Kpesi dialect has all but disappeared in favor of Ga. Here the constitutional framework of "federation" created a structure of amalgamation which, given the economic similarities and relatively compact settlement pattern of the component groups, facilitated and perhaps ensured their mutual assimilation. These Ga consociations had many parallels with the Egba unions at Abeokuta and with the various Akan confederacies, despite their lack of executive chiefship and their greater initial heterogeneity.

Among the Efik and nearby Ijaw, townships were also formed by confederate associations of "houses," which were internally stratified corporations based on prominent patrilineages. Though some Efik states had hereditary "monarchs," their weak authority was subject to councils of senior oligarchs, the heads of leading "Canoe Houses." [117] At Calabar the senior Yampai grade of the Egbo Society "constituted the actual executive government of the Efik. It enforced its laws by capital punishment or fines, . . . and by trade boycotts against European traders or other Efik towns." [118] Like Abeokuta and the Ga communities, these Efik and Ijaw commercial ports of southwestern Nigeria were heterogeneous units composed of immigrant groups and local settlers.

Each Canoe House was an internally autonomous corporate unit, simultaneously a trading firm, a military unit for slave raiding by canoe, and an economic and social unit, holding exclusive corporate properties and political rights. However, unlike the Ga townships, these coastal Nigerian trading states were highly stratified, explicitly oligarchic, culturally mixed, and structurally pluralistic.

Being actively engaged in slave raiding and trading, Canoe Houses recruited and retained militarily effective slaves drawn from nearby communities, mainly Ibo, Ibibio, Ekoi, and other Cross River "Semi-Bantu." Many of these lineage slaves were permanently located in farming settlements outside the town under the exclusive direction of their "Canoe House." Others resided with the house group in town.

At nearby Bonny these town slaves were fully assimilated into the lineage structure, and between 1836 and 1852 more than half the new heads of houses were slaves "adopted" as sons.[119] Bonny lacked an inclusive stratified association like the Calabar Egbo, through which the oligarchs directed community affairs. At Calabar masters treated their slaves as chattels, and slaves and widows were slaughtered at their funerals. Though enrolled in Egbo, these Calabar slaves were always restricted to its lowest grade; and though by 1840 outnumbering the free men of Calabar, under this regime they had no individual alternative to submission.

However, in 1850–51 slaves settled on lineage farms outside the town constituted themselves into a corporate group known as the Blood Men through a collective oath "to resist the encroachment and oppressions of the Duke Town gentry and to preserve themselves from being killed on all occasions according to the old customs." [120] This movement "was not organised by slaves to secure their freedom, but was an assertion of their rights." [121] It succeeded in abolishing human sacrifice, although the oligarchs directed Egbo against them; having extorted this major concession, in 1861 the Blood Men withdrew their pressure, leaving Egbo as the "centralising legislative, political, and executive body, but with gradually diminishing authority" as European control of the area increased.[122]

At Calabar and other Efik trading towns, these oligarchies had emerged from heterogeneous immigrant aggregates through competition in a favorable economic context. The Egbo and Ekine societies provided powerful men with effective instruments for joint communal control; and the peculiar military and economic specialization of these townsfolk encouraged their acquisition of slaves for cultivation, trade, war, and, if surplus, for sacrifice. As trade and wealth increased, so did the number of alien slaves localized on lineage estates outside the republican ports. By 1850 these culturally and socially alien slaves outnumbered their masters, whose ritual exercises in conspicuous consumption had increased steadily as export markets for slaves declined. Finally, as their personal risks of ritual slaughter mounted, the slaves were constrained to unite in protest.

CHIEFDOMS AND CHIEFTAINCIES

To avoid problems of distinguishing chiefship from such priestly or symbolic offices as the Ga Mantse, Tallensi "chiefs," Meru Agwe, Masai Laibonak, or Anuak "nobles," it is convenient to isolate chiefdoms as politically discrete aggregates of varying complexity, composition, scale, and duration, distinguished also by the ritual, symbolic, or secular character of their headship, and by its effectiveness and stability. Our present purpose being merely to isolate alternative conditions and modes of ethnic incorporation in African chiefdoms, we need only employ two crosscutting classifications. First, we should distinguish segmentary, segmenting, and other weak or labile polities such as the Mandari, Jukun, Azande, Mende, Shilluk, Sukuma, Ngonde, Northern Ngoni, Shambala, or Alur from durable, relatively centralized aggregates such as Nupe, Ankole, Buganda, Lozi, Ruanda, Dahomey, Zulu, Swazi, Benin, or Yoruba. Though overlapping somewhat, these categories differ importantly. Our second classification distinguishes plural from relatively homogeneous states. In these terms, Ruanda, Ankole, the Barotse, Toro, Alur, Zande, Ngonde, Ndebele, Nupe, and some Hausa and Tswana units differ from Ashanti, Shilluk, Jukun, Mende, Buganda, Bunyoro, nuclear Benin, Nyakyusa, and Yoruba, which were predominantly homogeneous in ethnic and cultural composition. Perhaps such societies as the Swazi, Sukuma, Zulu, Ganda, or Fort Jameson Ngoni which assimilated alien elements rather extensively represent a distinct group or a subclass of the "homogeneous." By special institutions of perpetual kinship and positional succession the southeastern Lunda were also able to incorporate aliens as internally autonomous units linked through their own headmen to the Lunda chief by unique perpetual relations.[123] Such amalgams also belong in our "homogeneous" group. Finally, the historic empires— Ethiopia, Bornu, Songhay, Mali, Macina, Dahomey, Sokoto, and others— being pluralities of greater or less degree, form a subclass of plural polities. This dual classification of African chiefdoms or states should satisfy our present interests.

The traditional anthropological contrast between ritual and secular chiefship has limited value in this inquiry, given the variable combinations that we encounter. Though the Shilluk Reth, the Jukun Aku, the Yoruba Obas, and the rulers of Benin, Buganda, Ruanda, Ngonde, and Nyakyusa were emphatically ritual figures, while the Mende, Temne, Lozi, Mambwe, Shambala, Tswana, Swazi, Nyoro, Tuareg, and Nupe chiefs were primarily secular, ritual and secular features are combined so variously in Alur, Zulu, Ankole, Ashanti, Bornu, Ruanda, Mossi, and Buganda that these mixtures defy casual treatment.

We need here note only one direct implication of a strictly ritual chiefship. Where this defines the basis and scope of political authority, the polity necessarily excludes all persons of differing culture until they have been socialized to the ideology by indoctrination. Such polities as the Shilluk, Jukun, Benin, or Yoruba, identified by sacred kingships, are inherently exclusive, and can accommodate or affiliate culturally distinct collectivities only by tributary relations, enslavements, serfdom, or other modes of differential incorporation. In Ngonde, Nyakyusa immigrants, already familiar with divine chiefship, readily accepted the divinity of the Ngonde Kyungu as a sacred chief, after which they were locally segregated under their own headmen.[124] Among Nyakyusa, being status equals, divine chiefs opposed one another by secular means, notably war, and where successful, incorporated the defeated within their own units.[125]

Ritualized chiefships in pluralistic states of the segmentary and centralized types may be illustrated by Shambala, Alur, and Ruanda. In these societies the ruling group first established itself in the area by infiltration. Following this, in Ruanda, Tutsi domination was based on conquest, but not so in Shambala, Sukuma, or among the Alur, where Luo-speaking Nilotes imposed their rule on acephalous collectivities of different language and stock.[126] Though Alur now form rather more of the society they dominate than do the Kilindi clan whose Shambala chiefdom is strikingly similar in growth and type, the latter have achieved greater assimilation and executive control over the local people; [127] but in both societies chiefship proliferates by dispersion of segments of the royal clan. Evidently, both Alur and Shambala chiefdoms were established peacefully by immigrant groups over larger aboriginal populations, primarily, it seems, because, as strangers, the immigrants could provide a relatively unbiased mediation and settlement of disputes among the local feuding lineages. In nearby Sukuma, immigrant "Hamites" also established similar chiefship over Bantu-speaking cultivators without any evidence of conquest.[128] In these segmentary states, chiefly power is weak, stratification restricted, and jural equivalence general within and between the associated ethnic stocks. While these societies retain this general form, their structures of chiefly authority and political integration are labile and fragile. Ngonde represents another variant of this type.[129]

In Ruanda, by contrast, the Tutsi rulers established a regime of caste, reduced Bantu-speaking Hutu to serfdom, virtually forbade intermarriage, denied Hutu political office and rights, organized Tutsi armies for conquest, taxation, and internal police, and concentrated antecedent Hutu religious conceptions of "divine chiefship" in the Tutsi Mwami (king) who normally delegated his ritual functions to official priests. Hutu acceptance of Tutsi domination evidently varied regionally within Ruanda. In 1959 the state contained 2.6 million, of whom 16 percent were Tutsi, 83 percent Hutu, and 1 percent Pygmoid, Twa, retained by Tutsi as spies and informants.[130] Various writers have asserted that Hutu regarded Tutsi as innate superiors, and thus accepted their subjugation. Political developments in Ruanda following on the introduction of universal suffrage effectively discredit this view.[131]

In nearby Burundi, which has a similar racial and cultural constitution and history, the dominant Tutsi, representing about 12 percent of 2 million people, had further stratified themselves into two ranked endogamous castes, the noble Tutsi-Banyaruguru and the inferior Tutsi-Hima.[132] As in Ruanda, so in Burundi, the Mwami, or king, was represented as a divine figure; and by these means the ruling Tutsi sought to sacralize their regime and legitimate its inequalities.[133] In nearby Ankole, another caste-stratified society composed of agricultural "Bantu" serfs under immigrant pastoral "Nilotes," the Mugabe (king), though not explicitly sacralized, was invested with magical objects and qualities.[134] Given recent developments in Ruanda and Burundi, it is reasonable to doubt whether the Mugabe of Ankole, the Mukama of Toro, and their peers in Zinza, Haya, and similar adjacent states, however heavily ritualized their persons, positions, or regimes, are any more acceptable to their "Bantu" serfs.[135]

In adjacent Bunyoro and Buganda, where immigrant "Hamitic" pastoralists intermarried extensively with the Bantu cultivators, though differences of civil and political status are prominent and pervasive, these no longer distinguish recognizable racial or cultural divisions.[136] Whereas differential incorporation of ethnic sections was basic to the social structures of Ruanda, Burundi, Ankole, Toro, Zinza, and Haya, in Bunyoro and more so in Buganda and Busoga, social and cultural assimilation proceeded through the progressive amalgamation of the differing ethnic stocks; and in Buganda, on the eve of its colonization by the British, centralizing despots, having rooted out hereditary lineage claimants to territorial office, instituted an open monocratic officialdom recruited primarily by merit and by royal favor.[137] In this respect assimilation and universalism in Buganda offer instructive parallels with Fort Jameson Ngoni patterns.

Rigid stratifications marked by jural and social exclusions of various types are widespread in traditional polities established and maintained by the forcible domination of one ethnic stock over others. Besides the racially complex interlacustrine kingdoms we may cite the Ndebele, the Lozi before and since Lewanika, Nupe, Zande, Tswana, Dahomey, Wolof, Tuareg, and most Hausa-Fulani emirates.[138] Imperial states inevitably magnify these structural and cultural differences and segregations of rulers and ruled, and are typically administered through systems of multiple domination.

Several of these ethnically stratified traditional polities are highly fissile, for example, Azande, Tswana, and Fort Jameson Ngoni.[139] Despite intensive assimilation of alien elements, the Ngoni state split repeatedly under stresses generated by its own militarized political organization. On the other hand, such plural states as Barotse, Hausa-Fulani, Nupe, Ruanda-Urundi, and Ndebele show considerable stamina and resilience; even more so do those heterogeneous societies that instituted the gradual progressive amalgamation of their diverse ethnic elements, for example, Swazi, Buganda, Bunyoro, Yoruba, Mende, and Lunda. Empires being notoriously fragile and superficial structures, their dissolution or overthrow need not detain us.

Anthropological studies of African conquest states and native pluralities rarely examine the situation, experience, attitudes, and institutions of subject peoples in adequate detail. Faced with such complex structures of cultural and social divergence, anthropologists tend either to plead lack of historical data or, on grounds of varying validity, to argue that the subjugated are adequately socialized to their situation and accept the regime as necessary or beneficent. Sometimes the anthropologist asserts that the subjugated accept their subordination as normatively valid; on other occasions the symbolic features of chiefship and state are invoked as sufficient unifying or legitimating factors. Sheer lack of feasible alternatives, and routine habituation to subordinate status, may thus be translated as evidence of institutional assimilation or structural indifference.

In studying centralized states, anthropologists are generally obliged to rely on the rulers' support; in consequence they are often excellent apologists for the stability and justice of the traditional regime. Also guided by Durkheimian notions of sacred chiefship, collective representations, and social solidarity, they often interpret political strife or its absence as equal proof of normative consensus. Perhaps for Africa, Nadel provides the most sensitive and sustained analysis of the conditions and reactions of a subjugated people in his account of the Fulani conquest state of Nupe. Unfortunately Nadel chose to rest his analysis on Toennies' inappropriate contrast between community and state. Having defined "the state" as "inter-tribal or inter-racial," he concludes that its "political co-ordination calls into being a co-ordination of interest—actual interest-units—which in certain respects overcomes heterogeneity of tribe, or culture, and even class, and includes the whole people." As integrative factors, Nadel lists "self-enhancement that . . . sublimates the humiliating experience of political dependence and inferiority, . . . the appeal of [the] mystic and supernatural, . . . [and] the appeal to an historical (or quasi-historical) turn of mind." [140] The significance of these impressionistic and inspecific psychological states for the integration of the plural society of Fulani Nupe remains problematic; and though Nadel was himself a highly trained psychologist, he made no attempt to measure the strength or integrative effects of the sentiments he invoked to support his metaphysical finding of a "new proud consciousness of unity which embraces the whole kingdom" in Nupe.[141] Neither do his appeals to the values of Islam nor to the symbolic collective character of the local kingship carry conviction, since in this state, Islam and the Fulani kingship are both identified by history and doctrine with the Fulani conquest and domination of Nupe. Indeed, despite his initial stress on the Islamic acculturation of the Nupe, in his monograph, *Nupe Religion,* Nadel shows that its Islamic proselytization is at best imperfect and casual.[142]

Ruanda, Ankole, Toro, Ndebele, and Zande were conquest states, and in each the rigid stratifications consisted in the uniform subjugation of conquered peoples by collective exclusions from political and administrative rights. Among Lozi, Tswana, Kanuri of Bornu, Mossi, Baganda, and Banyoro, as in Dahomey, we are confronted with centralized polities which vary most significantly in the extent to which their particular distributions of jural and political rights coincided with cleavages of ethnic and cultural identity. In some of these archaic states, differential incorporation took the form of occupationally distinguished endogamous castes, notably among the Wolof, Ndebele, Burundi, and Tswana; of vassalage, as in Tuareg, Ankole, and Hausa; of slavery and quasi-caste, as in Hausa, Dahomey, and Nupe; or of amalgamation and assimilation in varying degrees, as among Basuto, Swazi, Baganda, Zulu, Mossi, and Mende. In each case the rigor, uniformity, and span of the social stratification indicate the measure, form, and scope of the prevailing differential incorporation of initially distinct ethnic and cultural groups; and in each case it appears that the modes and degrees of cultural and social assimilation or exclusions correspond closely with the structure of incorporation, differential or other. Where access to political office and jural institutions is differentially distributed, whether by age-sets, clientage, serfdom, or by corporate associations of either type, sectional barriers segregate the associated units correspondingly; and this structure of ascriptive collective exclusion impedes enculturation and assimilation alike, insofar as it divides the collectivity into a series of closed perpetual categories, whose members are by birth or personal condition immutably identified with particular units. Some Swazi, Tswana, Lunda, and others have incorporated immigrant or conquered peoples as local communities directly under their own headmen, or under representatives of the ruling group. In the former case, segmental autonomies and tribal allegiances were simultaneously assured; in the latter, the domination of the acceding group was achieved by its conquerors or hosts. Since structural disassociations were instituted variably, institutional assimilations varied also. Where, however, as in Bornu, the Sokoto Empire, or Ethiopia, large segments of acephalous tribes or conquered chiefdoms were attached as subordinate but self-administering units owing tribute and allegiance to the ruling group, the perpetuation of social boundaries and cultural differences was simultaneously prescribed. In general, such societal attachments do not extend beyond the norms of external relations between two political groups. At most they represent consociations characterized by the symbiosis incidental to indirect subordination. Where the dominant peoples are acephalous they can rarely maintain such accommodations without specializing institutions such as Tuareg caste, Somali bondage, or the Ibo system of corporate *ohu* slavery. Evidently, as the Sukuma, Shambala, and Alur cases show, not all polyethnic units that depend on a common hereditary chiefship need be centralized or explicitly inegalitarian.

By virtue of its history as a major center of trade, communications, learning, and government, the city of Timbuktu presents unusual patterns of social and cultural pluralism, which Horace Miner has elegantly described. During the sixteenth century, Timbuktu was perhaps the leading city of the western Sudan. On the fall of Songhay in 1592, it was overrun by Moors, and never recovered its former prosperity or influence. Subject variously to Tuareg, Bambara, and to the Arma, its hybrid elite, descended from Moroccan soldiers and local women, in 1940 the township contained some 3,500 Arma and their Songhay (Gabibi) serfs, approximately 1,500 Arabs and their slaves, and some 1,000 Tuareg slaves known as Bela, each group distinguished by language, status, occupation, kinship, local distribution, age organization, ritual practice, and by separate connubium.

Each of these social sections ranks as a unit uniformly in the city structure, Bela having the lowest status and the Arabs the highest, while Arma and their Gabibi serfs dominate the town.

For centuries these collectivities have lived in the city without social assimilation, despite considerable illicit interbreeding. Sectional boundaries are presumed and reinforced by institutionalized patterns of collective dissociation, conflict, and interaction. As in Furnivall's model, the market provides the major meeting place for the city's plural stocks, the mosque, the minor. As in our other examples, pluralism at Timbuktu antedated European colonialism by generations, and under chronic if unstable Arma domination, other ethnic groups within the city suffered enough for them to invite or welcome Bambara and Tuareg attackers.[143]

Mere differences in the number, population, language, and culture of the associated groups evidently do not directly account for the particular form and stability of their common society. Under Moshesh and his successors, the Koena Sotho developed the Basuto chiefdom unchallenged by local aborigines, Phetla and Phuthi, or by immigrant Natal Nguni. In 1934 these non-Sotho elements represented only 13.5 percent of the chiefdom's population, while Koena were less than 30 percent.[144]

Though Bemba and Bisa share common culture, language, and traditions of origin, Bisa, who numbered 42,000 in 1933, had long since split off from the Bemba, their former rulers, who were then about 114,000 strong.[145] Among the Swazi, "one-fifth were 'true Swazis,' one-seventh were 'prior' inhabitants, and the remainder were migrants," or defeated peoples.[146] The ruling Swazi "did not seek to impose their customs and tolerated the cultural peculiarities of others." [147] The Swazi aristocracy integrated this heterogeneous population through hereditary local chiefships, many (75 of 169) held by Swazi princes, the majority by leading commoner lineages of Swazi or of localized ethnic groups, linked to the dynasty by uterine and affinal ties. In addition, the Swazi employed their age-regimental organization to incorporate and assimilate these aboriginal and immigrant aliens to their society and political order.[148]

In various Tswana "tribes" or chiefdoms, the nuclear or ruling group forms less than one-fifth of the total population, for example, among the Tawana and in Ngwato.[149] In the territorial hierarchy, the basic units are local wards, "outlying villages," and sections or districts in the larger tribes. Traditionally the headmen of wards and sections alike were leading members of dispersed branches of the tribal ruling clan. In addition,

where . . . outlying villages were made up mainly of foreigners of the same stock who have come into the tribe, their hereditary ruler would be recognised by the Chief . . . as the headman of the village where they settle. The headmen of these outlying villages, if they and their people belong to a foreign community, often have the privilege of receiving *sehuba* (hunting tribute) from their followers, and of having a *lesotla* (official farm) ploughed for them. They cannot however, although they sometimes attempted to, claim *dik-gafela* (grain) tribute, or organise their own initiation ceremonies, summon a *letsholo* (council meeting) or keep stray cattle. These are the prerogatives of the tribal chief.[150]

Thus, although aliens of approved stock were allowed to administer their internal affairs, their subordination and amalgamation were pursued by an administrative organization that fragmented them. Such political institutions preserved and enhanced differences of ethnic identity, custom, language, connubium, and collective status. Moreover, besides amalgamated aliens, other peoples "of inferior stock or defeated in war were reduced to collective serfdom in subject communities . . . under the care of special district headmen. . . . Any property owned by these people could be taken at any time by their overlords." [151] In short, political institutions in the larger Tswana tribes combined structures of amalgamation and of differential incorporation alike, each applied to discrete collectivities. The Lozi organization of their commoners, subjects, and tributary peoples was rather similar.[152] In Barotse, as in Ruanda, the kingship and government were identified as organs of the ruling group; in Barotse only the Aluyi conquerors were "true Lozi." [153] Likewise in Norman and Angevin England, the monarchy and political institutions, though territorially effective, remained the distinctive organization and property of the Norman and Angevin nobles.

History and Structure: A Brief Comparison

In closing this survey it is useful to compare briefly certain Hausa and Fulani emirates of Northern Nigeria and Niger which, in consequence of their differing corporate organizations, differed correspondingly in their cohesion and development. These polities—Zaria, Kano, Katsina, and the independent state of Maradi—might also be compared with Nupe, as described by Nadel, and Adamawa, as described by Kirk-Greene,[154] all units of the same region and cultural bloc. This comparison may also illustrate the complex historical processes through which divergent or similar social structures emerge.

Until 1807, Maradi, an area peopled mainly by patrilineally organized pagans (azna), formed the northernmost district of the Muslim Hausa chiefdom of Katsina. Between 1804 and 1807 the Hausa states of Katsina, Kano, and Zaria were all overrun by Fulani followers of the Sheikh Usman dan Fodio, who launched a general jihad against the Hausa chiefdoms in 1804. Fulani emirs and conquering aristocracies replaced the old Hausa ruling strata in all three states; and, having defined the conquered as heathen (kahirai), and thus beyond the pale of Islamic law, Fulani imposed severe burdens of labor, taxation, and arbitrary levies upon them, especially in Katsina and Kano, where the struggle had been harsh and long. At Maradi, the local pagans, resenting oppression, revolted in 1815–1817, surprising the Fulani and summoning the Hausa chief of Katsina, Dan Kasawa, then settled near Zinder, to return to rule and lead their resistance. Supported by many Muslim Hausa, Dan Kasawa drove back the Katsina Fulani, liberated Maradi and a wide surrounding area, and established there the successor state of Hausa Katsina, leaving his heirs an effective base from which to pursue reconquest of their ancestral chiefdom. For the rest of the nineteenth century Maradi waged continuous war on Fulani Katsina, with substantial success.

Kano was conquered in 1805–1807 by a combination of leading local Fulani clans which, having partitioned the territory, administered it collegially for two years until the Shehu appointed an emir to represent him. During their conquest the Kano Fulani had been helped by certain dissident Hausa, including some members of the old Kutumbawa Hausa dynasty. In return, besides rewarding these Hausa allies with fiefs and offices, the ruling Fulani distinguished them as Hausawa from other

Hausa who had either resisted or remained aloof from the struggle. The latter were classified as Habe, a generic Fulani term for serfs, free subjects without political rights, or outsiders of "inferior stock." At Kano, to this day, these *Hausawa* have retained many privileges as minor partners in the Fulani regime. Habe, classified as heathen in consequence of their initial opposition or indifference to the Fulani jihad, were denied benefit of Muslim law and subjected to punitive taxation (*jizya*), to corvée, and to other forms of subordination. As in Katsina, the Fulani appropriated for themselves all territorial and political offices, thereby reconstituting the defeated people as a subject category excluded from political and jural institutions in equal measure.

At Zaria also the Fulani conquest was achieved by a combination of clans and factions, some local, others immigrant, each under its own leader and pursuing its own ends; but whereas at Kano the Shehu did not appoint anyone to command his supporters until the country was won, in Zaria the Fulani jihad was waged under the Shehu's delegate, Musa, a Fulani from Mali. On Musa's death, his chief assistant, Yamusa, of different lineage, succeeded; and over the next fifty years Zaria developed four competing Fulani dynasties. At Kano also the second Fulani emir, Dabo, founded a second dynasty, but thereafter all subsequent emirs were Dabo's issue. Only at Zaria were the Hausa divided in their response to the Shehu's summons for strict observance of Islam. The Fulani were thus the more easily able to overthrow them. Musa, the new ruler, appointed several local and immigrant Hausa to high offices in his state; and though Musa's successors, driven by dynastic rivalries, appropriated most of these positions for their Fulani clients and kin, in Zaria, Hausa continued to share in the government as territorial officials (*hakimai*), village chiefs (*dagatai*), courtiers (*fadawa*), executive agents (*jekadu*), and also as clients (*barori*). On occasion, Hausa were appointed even to such senior positions of state as Galadima, for example, in 1883–1904.

By 1843 the rulers of Maradi were sufficiently strong to organize a general revolt of Hausa within Katsina against the Fulani dominion. This was harshly suppressed by the Fulani emir Sidiku with assistance from Kano and nearby Fulani states. Shortly afterward, in 1848–49, at Kano, certain Hausa clerics protested strongly against Fulani oppression. When summoned by the emir they fled southward among the Ningi pagans, whom they organized into a powerful force and directed against Kano with marked success over the next forty years. Faced with Habe (Hausa) revolt and threats of revolt, in Katsina and Kano, the local Fulani increased their pressure on the conquered people, systematically excluding them from political office and due process and rights under Muslim law. In Katsina, Sidiku, having suppressed the great revolt of

1842–43, first concentrated an enormous slave force around the throne; thereafter his successors made increasing use of slave staff and forces in their administration and campaigns. At Kano, where the ruler also relied on slaves, by firmly identifying the Fulani aristocracy with his regime, he sought to secure his power against slave subversion and Habe threats together. At Zaria slaves lacked power as a function of the multidynastic political structure; and occupational offices, which carried substantial income and prestige, were allocated to Hausa by 1850, thereby explicitly associating them with the Fulani regime. At Katsina these occupational offices, vested with powers of taxation and special jurisdictions, were allocated by the ruler to his slave staff. At Maradi, as at Zaria, the occupational offices were predominantly allocated to freemen. In Kano they had little place, territorial taxes being increased instead.

Maradi was a plural society composed of the ruling Muslim Hausa minority and a pagan majority administered under their own local headmen, whom the chief formally appointed and protected against his Hausa supporters. The Katsina successor state at Maradi had been founded by pagan initiative and revolt on their invitation to Dan Kasawa. It was thus explicitly consensual in its base and character, and its cohesion was continuously reinforced by military opposition to nearby Fulani. Besides their long historical connection, the Muslim and pagan collectivities at Maradi were united by military and political symbiosis in their common struggle against the Fulani of Katsina, Zamfara, and Sokoto. Thus, despite pluralism, explicit in the cultural and social segregation and institutional divergence of these two collectivities, the Muslim Hausa and pagans of Maradi were bound together by common history, territory, leadership, opposition to Fulani, and by a carefully devised political structure which fostered consensus, segregation, and mutual loyalties. Despite its hierarchic form and asymmetrical complementarity, the plural society of Maradi was clearly consensual in its character, origin, and base.

Plural structures that differed sharply from Maradi in type developed at Katsina and Kano. There the Hausa (Habe) majority were systematically denied jural and political rights, or relations of clientage and protection. They were never formally and categorically accepted or treated as Muslims. Differential taxation, corvée, and Fulani monopoly of military, political, and jural resources were pervasive and uniform. Habe were identified by corporate disabilities in political, civil, religious, and economic spheres as a leaderless category, the subject people, likely to revolt, and thus to be suppressed. Nonetheless Fulani males, while reserving their kinswomen in marriage for themselves, recruited harems of Hausa concubines whose offspring, under Fulani patriliny and Islamic law, had their father's status. Thus the Fulani aristocracy increased rapidly in number in proportion to the total population.

At Zaria, in consequence of the continuing association of local Hausa with Fulani in the government of the state, a condition that increasing dynastic rivalry for supporters sustained, Fulani and Hausa, though distinguished by descent, were increasingly assimilated by interest, intermarriage, and institutions. Neither was there any serious threat of Hausa revolt at Zaria, nor were its Hausa subject to the differential justice, taxation, and military exclusions that characterized Katsina and Kano. Nonetheless, the Zaria emirate was also clearly a plural society, its major division falling between the Muslim Hausa-Fulani settled in the north and the large pagan population of southern Zaria which included some thirty-three tribes divided by language, culture, and territory into units, few of which could resist Hausa pressure effectively. At Zaria, then, the Muslim Fulani and Hausa amalgamated to exploit and dominate this human reservoir, and with it, the territory. These differing histories and modes of corporate organization together account for the significant differences in social cohesion and cultural assimilation which distinguish these four states today as in the past.[155]

III

CONCLUSIONS

To reduce to order these comparative materials on indigenous African societies, we need to consider the incidence and cultural or structural correlates of each relevant variable—race, ethnicity, demographic ratios, language, ecology, and territorial organization. In doing so, we need only ask whether units sharing identical or equivalent conditions exhibit corresponding cultural and structural similarities, and whether units that differ in each of these conditions differ also in their social organization and cultural diversity.

First, we should note that with the sole exception of band organization in its pure form, each societal type provides examples of all modes of interethnic accommodation, namely, segmental segregation, symbiosis, symmetrical or complementary consociation, amalgamation, assimilation, and differential incorporation. If the category of band organization is extended to all mobile societies such as the Tuareg, Fulani, Somali, Masai, and Fort Jameson Ngoni, we would find all alternative forms of interethnic accommodation among people organized in nomadic bands. This extension has little to recommend it on analytic and structural grounds; however, it shows that neither nomadism nor ecological type precludes interethnic accommodations of differing character and form, including those variable modes of symbiotic attachment and subordination which often link band-organized and sedentary peoples. Thus, our societal typology neither excludes nor prescribes particular modes of consociation in any structural category.

Proceeding then to seek uniformities of covariation, we may consider racial factors first.

Race evidently has no invariant implications in societal accommodation. Masai and Meru, Kipsigi and Gusii, Hamites and Bantu in Buganda, Bunyoro and Busoga, Arma, Arab, and Negro in Timbuktu, and, perhaps most instructively, Tuareg, Arabs, and Negroids in the Central Sudan, though objectively of differing race, have hybridized by marriage and concubinage, and at Timbuktu without them, and with differing results. Typically, men of the dominant stock beget children on subject women; and wherever agnation prevails, the children are then directly affiliated to their father's lineage and stratum, though socialized to their mother's culture and often to her language. In consequence, Hamites have adopted Bantu language and culture in Buganda, Sukuma, and Arusha; Fulani have adopted Hausa; Mamprussi, the Mole-Dagbane speech of Talis; Kpesi, the language of Ga, and so on. However, among the matrilineal Tuareg, a man's offspring by his slave concubine are excluded from his lineage by the rule of uterine descent; and, since their mothers had no place in the Tuareg lineage structure, such hybrids were segregated as *buzaye* apart from their father's kin in autonomous communities of their own as privileged serfs. Thus besides Tuareg, divided into noble and vassal clans, the society incorporated Negro slaves and hybrid serfs. Tuareg serfdom derives in part from the structure of Tuareg lineage groups.

We have already cited several instances of endogamous caste instituted within racially homogeneous groups, for example, the Ndebele, the matrilineal Wolof, the Tutsi in Burundi, and some Ibo. Thus connubial closures may be instituted irrespective of racial community. Conversely, connubium may prevail despite racial difference. The dissimilar responses to similar situations of Ndebele, Nyasa, and Fort Jameson Ngoni on the one hand, and of the Hamitic and Nilotic rulers of Ruanda, Buganda, Burundi, Bunyoro, Ankole, Sukuma, and Busoga on the other, show that racial and ethnic amalgams of equivalent diversity may develop in diametrically opposed ways, biologically, culturally, and structurally. Evidently, mere identities or differences of race have no uniform implications for the modes of consociation in such mixed societies.

The same conclusion emerges when these materials are analyzed to isolate uniform patterns of consociation linked with particular conditions of ethnic composition. We need merely mention here the persisting division between Egba groups at Abeokuta; between the affiliated Enhla and Zansi castes; in the Tswana, Swazi, and Lozi societies; in Bwamba, Zande, and Alur; or among the Karimojong tribes. Clearly, where institutional or spatial factors obstruct connubium, an ethnically homogeneous population becomes progressively segregated into distinct groups, as, for example, among Karimojong. Conversely, where symmetrical connubium prevails, racially or ethnically heterogeneous populations become correspondingly assimilated at biological, cultural, and structural levels. The presence, mode, and conditions of connubium are evidently structural and cultural facts.

Essentially the same negative conclusion emerges when linguistic communities or differences are isolated for comparative study. Linguistic differences prevail in Timbuktu, Bwamba, and the Terik-Tiriki communities, and among the Egba, the Lozi, Tswana, and Ndebele, despite diverse interethnic structures and the use of local lingua francas. In the interlacustrine kingdoms, the Hausa-Fulani emirates, Azande, Ga, Kagoro, Tallensi, among the Samburu and Masai-Dorobo, Tuareg, Wolof, Arusha, Mandari, Shambala, Alur, at Calabar, Bonny, and in the Pygmy-Bantu symbiosis of the Ituri Forest, initial differences of language have disappeared in very different structures of continuing association.

As Fortes and Evans-Pritchard have emphasized, ecological communities or differences are clearly important in ethnic accommodations; but these also do not have any invariant connotations for the resulting societal structures or their development. Thus Terik and Teriki have retained their differing ecologies within a common wider society, while at Arusha and among the Kipsigi, accommodations of dominant pastoralists and subjugated cultivators have produced very different results. At Arusha pastoral Masai sedentarized as hoe farmers. Among Kipsigis the agricultural Gusii became converted to pastoralism.

Tuareg and Fulani ecological patterns are of interest here. Fulani themselves are divided into a sedentary population and nomadic pastoralists; the "noble" Tuareg based their economy on pastoral services of vassal Tuareg clans, on agricultural income from serf and slave settlements, on services from servile castes, and on the returns of desert transport, commerce, and raiding. Vassal Tuareg herd beasts, nobles, men; and Tuareg society includes all.

The remarkable difference found among interlacustrine communities of Hamitic or Nilotic pastoralists and Bantu cultivators also show the flexibility of these ethnic ecological frontiers; clearly such variations and changes both proceed structurally.

At Timbuktu also the ecological specializations that distinguish its major "ethnic" segments, or "castes," as Miner calls them, are clearly effects rather than antecedents of their specific accommodations. Likewise at Calabar and Bonny, ecological specializations in slave raiding and commerce emerged in response to a specific historical situation, thereby differentiating some tribesmen as mercantile communities from others on whom they preyed. The differing local situations of Pygmoid and Bushmen groups as serfs in Tswana, political spies in Ruanda, symbiotic associates in Masai and the Ituri areas, or as independent refugees in the forest and desert also reveal the influence of differing structural contexts on ecological adaptation. Perhaps this is most pronounced among the Ndebele and Fort Jameson Ngoni, who specialized institutions to train their captives in the social ecology of war.

It goes without saying that mere similarities of ecology do not in themselves entail specific patterns of association. Among the Barotse, Tswana, Basuto, Ndebele, Zande, Mende, Ga, Egba, and the various Hausa-Fulani or Ngoni units we find considerable divergence in the forms of societal organization and interethnic accommodation despite relatively uniform ecological conditions in each aggregate. Mandari attach immigrants as clients, while Nuer affiliate them by genealogical fictions. Yakö purchase and socialize outsiders as lineage members, while northeastern Ibo place them in *ohu* slavery. Evidently mere similarity or difference of strictly ecological adaptations has no direct or uniform implications for societal structures of interethnic accommodation.

Demographic differences in the ethnic composition of these precolonial societies do not correspond uniformly either with differences in their degrees of cultural diversity or with their forms of social structure. Indeed, these ethnic proportions are themselves often effects of structural conditions. Thus, the Efik merchants, the northeastern Ibo, Tuareg, Fulani, and others increased the populations of their societies by the capture or purchase of adults or, in Umor, of children. Whether these aliens were enslaved and segregated as at Calabar, or assimilated by the age organization as among some Ngoni or in Canoe Houses at Bonny, or socialized to serfdom as in Timbuktu, is clearly a function of the social and cultural organization, context, and history of the dominant group. Likewise, whether and how the relative numbers of institutionally distinguished strata persist or change over time under constant external conditions depends indirectly on conditions of social structure. So does the social significance of these ethnic or stratum ratios. Samburu outnumber Dorobo but do not subordinate them. At Timbuktu the dominant Arma and their Gabibi serfs outnumber other townsmen; at Calabar slaves outnumbered freemen only after 1840; at Arusha, where mutual assimilation was most complete, in due course the Meru outnumbered their Masai captors.

Among Ndebele, the Zansi ruling caste represent 15 percent; in Burundi and Ruanda, Tutsi castes represent between 12 and 16 percent. Inevitably caste minimizes the capacities of ruling groups for disproportionate demographic increases by restricting polygamy among them. Even hypergamy hardly affects this position. In like fashion the system of matrilineal descent has denied Tuareg the capacity for disproportionate demographic expansion by excluding children of Tuareg men and their concubines from the matrilineages essential for individual incorporation in free Tuareg society. By contrast, since 1807 the adjacent Fulani have steadily increased their numbers and proportions relative to their Hausa subjects. Fulani demographic expansion derives in part from their privileged political position which assured them an almost unlimited supply of concubines by purchase or capture, from slave estates and by other means; but Fulani demographic expansion also depended on their own patrilineal descent system reinforced by prescriptions in Islam. In consequence, unlike Tuareg, who are also Muslims, Fulani have increased disproportionately through reproduction by slave concubines. In the interlacustrine region, Hamitic rulers, following similar patterns, increased progressively in numbers and demographic ratios, and in assimilation with the subject Bantu in Sukuma, Bunyoro, and Buganda, unlike the Nilotes in Ankole, Toro, Ruanda, or Burundi. Evidently, demographic ratios are more likely to reflect specific conditions of social structure within the dominant group than to determine independently the patterns of interethnic accommodation.

We are thus left with two interdependent but analytically separate categories: cultural diversity and the structures of "interethnic" accommodation. It is clear that these conditions are linked closely and consistently among all the societies discussed here. They vary together, directly and equally. Further, on our evidence the decisive factor in this covariance appears to be structural. Cultural differences among societalized collectivities depend for preservation or dissolution on the structure of interethnic accommodation itself. Where accommodative structures prescribe or encourage assimilation, as in Buganda, among the Fort Jameson Ngoni, Ga, Yakö, Kipsigi, Mandari, Nuer, Arusha, Samburu at Bonny, or in Zaria, cultural and institutional differences are correspondingly transformed into institutional, biological, linguistic, and structural community. Insofar as the structure establishes symmetrical or complementary associations, as for example among Terik and Tiriki, Namoos and "real Talis," Ankwei and Kpashan in Kagoro, Egba, Bwamba, Ga, at Maradi, or within the various Nuba tribes, institutional and cognate differences, biological, linguistic, and other, persist insofar as the context permits or enjoins. Even such symbiotic structures as *bin kanu* or the various Bantu-Pygmy, Masai-Dorobo, or Tutsi-Twa relations illustrate this primacy of accommodative mode in promoting collective segregation or its converse, assimilation. So do the various institutions of slavery, caste, regimental socialization, clientage, adoption, and the like illustrated here. So far as our data extend, the only variable that correlates uniformly with these distributions of cultural and ethnic difference is the structure of accommodation; and clearly, as these examples show, it is this accommodative structure that sets the conditions, limits, forms, and rate of enculturation and interaction across corporate boundaries. It appears then that differential incorporation preserves or promotes cultural pluralism in spheres and degrees that reflect its particular form and scope. Conversely, the extent to which institutionally diverse ethnic groups are uniformly incorporated within an inclusive society sets the conditions and scope of their assimilation, at least by the corresponding removal of collective differences from the public to the private domain where individual and group affiliations and practice are optional and labile. Likewise, collectivities consociated as equivalent or complementary units within a common society are correspondingly free to modify, develop, or maintain their distinctive institutional structures within limits set by the specific conditions and contexts of their union. Whether these relations between the levels of cultural divergence and the modes of incorporation are illusory or tautological requires attention. If they are neither, then our conclusion opens the field for further study. It also illustrates the merits of the comparative method in social anthropology.

NOTES

[1] M. G. Smith, "Institutional and Political Conditions of Pluralism."

[2] A. R. Radcliffe-Brown, *Structure and Function in Primitive Society* (London: Cohen and West, 1952), pp. 188–204; S. F. Nadel, *The Foundations of Social Anthropology* (London: Cohen and West, 1951), pp. 183–188; Marion J. Levy, *The Structure of Society* (Princeton: Princeton University Press, 1952), pp. 111–148.

[3] Meyer Fortes, "The Structure of Unilineal Descent Groups," *American Anthropologist*, 55, no. 1 (Jan.–March 1953), 22–23.

[4] S. F. Nadel, *The Nuba: An Anthropological Study of the Hill Tribes of Kordofan* (London: Oxford University Press, 1947), pp. 9–10; John R. Goody, *The Social Organization of the LoWiili* (London: H.M.S.O., 1956), pp. 18–26; John R. Goody, *Death, Property and the Ancestors* (London: Tavistock Publications, 1962), chaps. i, xix.

[5] E. E. Evans-Pritchard, *The Nuer: A Description of the Modes of Livelihood and Political Institutions of a Nilotic People* (London: Oxford University Press, 1949), p. 262.

[6] M. G. Smith, "A Structural Approach to Comparative Politics," in David Easton, ed., *Varieties of Political Theory* (Englewood Cliffs, N.J.: Prentice-

Hall, 1966), pp. 113–128; M. G. Smith, "Political Anthropology," *International Encyclopedia of the Social Sciences* (New York: Macmillan, 1968), XII, 193–202.

[7] Herbert Spencer, *The Principles of Sociology* (3 vols.; New York: Appleton-Century, 1902), vol. 2, pt. 5.

[8] Radcliffe-Brown, *op. cit.*, pp. 201–202; M. Fortes and E. E. Evans-Pritchard, "Introduction," in M. Fortes and E. E. Evans-Pritchard, eds., *African Political Systems* (London: Oxford University Press, 1940), pp. 9–10; Emile Durkheim, *The Division of Labor in Society*, trans. George Simpson (Glencoe, Ill.: The Free Press, 1947), pp. 175–199.

[9] E. E. Evans-Pritchard, "Zande Blood-Brotherhood," *Africa*, 6 (1933), 369–401, repr. in E. E. Evans-Pritchard, *Essays in Social Anthropology* (London: Faber and Faber, 1962), pp. 131–161.

[10] P. T. W. Baxter and Audrey Butt, *The Azande and Related Peoples of the Anglo-Egyptian Sudan and Belgian Congo* (London: International African Institute, 1953), p. 75.

[11] Nadel, *The Nuba*, p. 207.

[12] S. F. Nadel, "Social Symbiosis and Tribal Organization," *Man*, 38 (1938), 85–90; Nadel, *Foundations of Social Anthropology*, pp. 168, 179–183.

[13] Derrick J. Stenning, *Savannah Nomads: A Study of the Wodaable Pastoral Fulani of Western Bornu Province, Northern Region, Nigeria* (London: Oxford University Press, 1959); C. E. Hopen, *The Pastoral Fulbe Family in Gwandu* (London: Oxford University Press, 1958); Marguerite Dupire, *Peuls Nomades: Etude descriptive des Wodaabe du Sahel Nigérien* (Paris: Institut d'Ethnologie, 1962).

[14] Colin M. Turnbull, *The Forest People* (New York: Simon and Schuster, 1961); Colin M. Turnbull, "The Mbuti Pygmies of the Congo," in James L. Gibbs, Jr., ed., *Peoples of Africa* (New York: Holt, Rinehart and Winston, 1965), pp. 281–317.

[15] K. Onwuka Dike, *Trade and Politics in the Niger Delta, 1830–1885* (Oxford: Clarendon Press, 1956); C. W. Newbury, *The Western Slave Coast and Its Rulers: European Trade and Administration among the Yoruba and Adja-speaking Peoples of South-Western Nigeria, Southern Dahomey and Togo* (Oxford: Clarendon Press, 1961); Robert Cornèvin, *Histoire du Dahomey* (Paris: Editions Berger-Levrault, 1962), pp. 241–284.

[16] G. I. Jones, *The Trading States of the Oil Rivers: A Study of Political Development in Eastern Nigeria* (2d ed.; London: Oxford University Press, 1963); Daryll Forde, ed., *Efik Traders of Old Calabar* (London: Oxford University Press, 1956); M. J. Field, *Social Organization of the Ga People* (London: Crown Agent for the Colonies, 1940); K. A. Busia, *The Position of the Chief in the Modern Political System of Ashanti* (London: Oxford University Press, 1951); William Tordoff, "The Ashanti Confederacy," *Journal of African History*, 3, no. 3 (1962), 399–417; Madeline Manoukian, *Akan and Ga-Adangme Peoples* (London: International African Institute, 1950); Saburi O. Biobaku, *The Egba and Their Neighbours, 1842–1872* (Oxford: Clarendon Press, 1957); P. C. Lloyd, *Yoruba Land Law* (London: Oxford University Press, 1962), pp. 225–240.

[17] R. S. Rattray, *Ashanti Law and Constitution* (Oxford: Clarendon Press, 1929); Busia, *op. cit.*; Tordoff, *op. cit.*

[18] Walter H. Sangree, "The Bantu Tiriki of Western Kenya," in Gibbs, *op.*

cit., pp. 43–79; Robert A. LeVine and Walter H. Sangree, "The Diffusion of Age-Group Organization in East Africa: A Controlled Comparison," *Africa*, 32, no. 2 (1962), 97–110.

[19] E. H. Winter, *"Bwamba: A Structural-Functional Analysis of a Patrilineal Society* (Cambridge: Heffer, 1956); E. H. Winter, "The Aboriginal Political Structure of Bwamba," in John Middleton and David Tait, eds., *Tribes without Rulers: Studies in African Segmentary Societies* (London: Routledge and Kegal Paul, 1958), pp. 136–166.

[20] M. G. Smith, "The Social Organization and Economy of Kagoro" (unpublished MS, 1951); M. G. Smith, "Kagoro Political Development," *Human Organization*, 19, no. 3 (1960), 137–149; Meyer Fortes, "The Political System of the Tallensi of the Northern Territories of the Gold Coast," in Fortes and Evans-Pritchard, *op. cit.*, pp. 238–271; Meyer Fortes, *The Dynamics of Clanship among the Tallensi* (London: Oxford University Press, 1945).

[21] Winter, "Aboriginal Political Structure of Bwamba," p. 155; Lloyd, *op. cit.*, pp. 224–238; Smith, "Kagoro Political Development"; Fortes, "Political System of the Tallensi"; Meyer Fortes, "Ritual and Office in Tribal Society," in Max Gluckman, ed., *Essays on the Rituals of Social Relations* (Manchester: Manchester University Press, 1962); Manoukian, *op. cit.*, pp. 94–104; LeVine and Sangree, *op. cit.*, pp. 102, 105.

[22] Isaac Schapera, *A Handbook of Tswana Law and Custom* (2d ed.; London: Oxford University Press, 1955), pp. xi–xiii, 1–12, 18–28, 31–32, 88–103; Isaac Schapera, *The Tswana* (London: International African Institute, 1953), pp. 9–16, 34–38, 46–56; Isaac Schapera, "The Political Organization of the Ngwato of Bechuanaland Protectorate," in Fortes and Evans-Pritchard, *op. cit.*, pp. 56–62; Max Gluckman, *Economy of the Central Barotse Plain* (Northern Rhodesia: Rhodes-Livingstone Institute, 1941), pp. 4–9, 11–16, 89–101; Max Gluckman, "The Lozi of Barotseland in North-Western Rhodesia," in Elizabeth Colson and Max Gluckman, eds., *Seven Tribes of British Central Africa* (Manchester: Manchester University Press, 1951), pp. 1–8, 13–27, 56–58, 87–89.

[23] Jones, *op. cit.*; D. Simmons, "An Ethnographic Sketch of the Efik People," in Forde, *op. cit.* (2d ed., 1963), pp. 1–26; G. I. Jones, "The Political Organization of Old Calabar," in Forde, *op. cit.* (1956 ed.), pp. 116–160.

[24] Fortes and Evans-Pritchard, "Introduction," in Fortes and Evans-Pritchard, *op. cit.*, pp. 1–23; Paula Brown, "Patterns of Authority in West Africa," *Africa*, 2 (1957), 261–278; J. A. Barnes, *Politics in a Changing Society* (Manchester: Manchester University Press, 1954), pp. 41–63; Aidan W. Southall, *Alur Society* (Cambridge: Heffer, n.d. [1956]), pp. 229–263; B. Bernardi, "The Age-Set System of the Nilo-Hamites," *Africa*, 22 (1952), 316–322; Daryll Forde, "Governmental Roles of Associations among the Yakö," *Africa*, 31 (1961), 309–323.

[25] Max Weber, *The Theory of Social and Economic Organisation*, trans. A. M. Henderson and Talcott Parsons (Edinburgh: William Hodge, 1947), p. 135.

[26] Derrick J. Stenning, "The Pastoral Fulani of Northern Nigeria," in Gibbs, *op. cit.*, pp. 363–401; F. W. de St. Croix, *The Fulani of Northern Nigeria* (Lagos: Government Printer, 1944).

[27] Barnes, *op. cit.*

[28] Elizabeth Colson, "The Plateau Tonga of Northern Rhodesia," in Colson

and Gluckman, *op. cit.*, pp. 110–121, 151 ff.; W. Allan, Max Gluckman, D. U. Peters, and C. G. Trapwell, *Land Holding and Land Usage among the Plateau Tonga of Mazabuka District: A Reconnaissance Survey, 1945* (London: Oxford University Press, 1948), pp. 33–70.

²⁹ Fortes and Evans-Pritchard, *op. cit.*, pp. 5–7.

³⁰ J. G. Peristiany, *The Social Institutions of the Kipsigis* (London: Routledge and Kegan Paul, 1939); H. E. Lambert, *Kikuyu Social and Political Institutions* (London: Oxford University Press, 1956); A. H. J. Prins, *East African Age-Class Systems* (Groningen: J. B. Wolters, 1953); P. C. Lloyd, "Sacred Kingship and Government among the Yoruba," *Africa*, 30 (1960), 221–223; P. Morton-Williams, "The Yoruba Ogboni Cult in Oyo," *Africa*, 30 (1960), 363–374; Simmons, *op. cit.*; Jones, "Political Organization of Old Calabar."

³¹ E. E. Evans-Pritchard, "The Zande State," *Journal of the Royal Anthropological Institute*, 93, pt. I (June 1963), 134–154; Godfrey Wilson, "The Nyakyusa of South-Western Tanganyika," in Colson and Gluckman, *op. cit.*, pp. 253–291; Southall, *op. cit.*; Edgar V. Winans, *Shambala: The Constitution of a Traditional State* (Berkeley and Los Angeles: University of California Press, 1962); Isaac Schapera, *Government and Politics in Tribal Societies* (London: Watts, 1956), pp. 175–187; Barnes, *op. cit.*, pp. 41–63.

³² Fortes and Evans-Pritchard, *op. cit.*, pp. 9–10.

³³ L. S. B. Leakey, *Mau Mau and the Kikuyu* (London: Methuen, 1952), pp. 34–36; C. K. Meek, *Law and Authority in a Nigerian Tribe* (London: Oxford University Press, 1937); M. M. Green, *Ibo Village Affairs* (London: Sidgwick and Jackson, 1947); Busia, *op. cit.*

³⁴ S. F. Nadel, *A Black Byzantium: The Kingdom of Nupe in Nigeria* (London: Oxford University Press, 1942); S. F. Nadel, "Nupe State and Community," *Africa*, 8, no. 3 (1935), 257–303; S. F. Nadel, *Nupe Religion* (London: Routledge and Kegan Paul, 1954).

³⁵ Fortes, "Political System of the Tallensi," pp. 239–240, 255–258; Fortes, *Dynamics of Clanship among the Tallensi*, pp. 1–29, 39; Elliott P. Skinner, *The Mossi of the Upper Volta* (Stanford: Stanford University Press, 1964), pp. 5–7.

³⁶ Nadel, *The Nuba*, p. 7.

³⁷ Nadel, *Black Byzantium*; Nadel, *Nupe Religion*; Southall, *op. cit.*; J. J. Maquet, *The Premise of Inequality in Ruanda* (London: Oxford University Press, 1961).

³⁸ May M. Edel, *The Chiga of Western Uganda* (London: Oxford University Press, 1957).

³⁹ C. K. Meek, *Tribal Studies in Northern Nigeria* (2 vols.; London: Kegan Paul, Trench, Trubner, 1931), II, 1–219.

⁴⁰ Gunter Wagner, *The Bantu of North Kavirondo* (2 vols.; London: Oxford University Press, 1949–1956); G. W. B. Huntingford, *Nandi Work and Culture* (London: H.M.S.O., 1950); G. W. B. Huntingford, *The Nandi of Kenya: Tribal Control in a Pastoral Society* (London: Routledge and Kegan Paul, 1953).

⁴¹ M. D. W. Jeffries, "The Batwa: Who Are They?" *Africa*, 23, no. 1 (1953), 45–54; Marcel d'Hertefelt, "The Rwanda of Rwanda," in Gibbs, *op. cit.*, pp. 406–407.

⁴² M. V. Brelsford, *The Tribes of Northern Rhodesia* (Lusaka: Government

Printer, 1956), pp. 96–99; G. P. Murdock, *Africa: Its Peoples and Their Culture History* (New York: McGraw-Hill, 1959), pp. 8–12.

[43] Schapera, *Government and Politics in Tribal Societies*, p. 19.

[44] Lorna Marshall, "The !Kung Bushmen of the Kalahari Desert," in Gibbs, *op. cit.*, pp. 247, 274.

[45] Schapera, *The Tswana*, p. 37.

[46] D'Hertefelt, *op. cit.*, pp. 411–425.

[47] G. W. B. Huntingford, *The Southern Nilo-Hamites* (London: International African Institute, 1953), pp. 54–70 (Dorobo), 102–120 (Masai); Paul Spencer, *The Samburu: A Study of Gerontocracy in a Nomadic Tribe* (London: Routledge and Kegan Paul, 1965), pp. xxii, 281–291.

[48] Winter, "Aboriginal Political Structure of Bwamba," p. 155. Edel, *op. cit.*, pp. 3–4, 102, reports devastating Pygmy attacks on Chiga villagers at an earlier date.

[49] Turnbull, *The Forest People;* Turnbull, "The Mbuti Pygmies," pp. 283–287, 301–302.

[50] Ernesta V. Cerulli, *Peoples of South-West Ethiopia and Its Borderland* (London: International African Institute, 1956); A. Schultze, *The Sultanate of Bornu*, trans. P. A. Benton (London: Oxford University Press, 1913); H. R. Palmer, *Gazetteer of Bornu Province* (Lagos: Government Printer, 1929).

[51] Stenning, *Savannah Nomads;* Stenning, "The Pastoral Fulani"; Hopen, *op. cit.;* Dupire, *op. cit.;* Marguerite Dupire, "The Place of Markets in the Economy of the Bororo (Fulbe)," in Paul Bohannan and George Dalton, eds., *Markets in Africa* (Evanston: Northwestern University Press, 1962).

[52] Heinrich Barth, *Travels and Discoveries in North and Central Africa* (2 vols.; London: Ward Lock, 1902), II, 168–169.

[53] J. R. Patterson, "Report on Borsari District, Bornu" (Provincial Office, Bornu; unpublished MS, 1918), p. 16, §46; M. G. Smith, "The Two Katsinas" (unpublished MS).

[54] M. A. Jaspan, *The Ila-Tonga Peoples of North-Western Rhodesia* (London: International African Institute, 1953), pp. 16–18, 35–36, 44–45, 50. See also Allan *et al.*, *op. cit.;* Brelsford, *op. cit.*, pp. 51–64.

[55] Evans-Pritchard, *The Nuer*, pp. 221–228; Jean Buxton, *Chiefs and Strangers: A Study of Political Assimilation among the Mandari* (Oxford: Clarendon Press, 1963); Jean Buxton, "The Mandari of the Southern Sudan," in Middleton and Tait, *op. cit.*, pp. 67–96; P. H. Gulliver, *Social Control in an African Society: A Study of the Arusha, Agricultural Masai of Northern Tanganyika* (London: Routledge and Kegan Paul, 1963), pp. 5–14.

[56] Barth, *op. cit.*, I, 282–283 and *passim;* Horace Miner, *The Primitive City of Timbuctoo* (Princeton: Princeton University Press, 1953), pp. 19–23 and *passim;* Johannes Nicolaisen, "Political Systems of Pastoral Tuareg in Air and Ahaggar," *Folk*, I (1959), 95–104; Johannes Nicolaisen, *Ecology and Culture of the Pastoral Tuareg* (Copenhagen: National Museum, 1963), pp. 393–446; Henri Lhote, *Les Touaregs de Hoggar* (Paris: Payot, 1955).

[57] Lloyd Cabot Briggs, *Tribes of the Sahara* (Cambridge: Harvard University Press, 1960), pp. 138, 157–160; Nicolaisen, *Ecology and Culture of Pastoral Tuareg*, pp. 10–24.

[58] I. M. Lewis, *A Pastoral Democracy: A Study of Pastoralism and Politics among the Northern Somali of the Horn of Africa* (London: Oxford University Press, 1961), pp. 14, 187 f., 263 f.

[59] F. Rehfisch, "The Dynamics of Multilineality on the Mambila Plateau," *Africa*, 30, no. 3 (1960), 246–261; Daryll Forde, *Yakö Studies* (London: Oxford University Press, 1964), pp. 85–134; Rosemary Harris, *The Political Organization of Mbembe* (London: H.M.S.O., 1965); Goody, *Social Organization of the LoWiili*, pp. 38–90; John R. Goody, "Fields of Social Control among the Lodagaba," *Journal of the Royal Anthropological Institute*, 87, pt. 1 (June 1957), 75–104; Kenneth L. Little, *The Mende of Sierra Leone* (London: Routledge and Kegan Paul, 1951), pp. 96–112; Gordon D. Gibson, "Double Descent and Its Correlates among the Herero of Ngamiland," *American Anthropologist*, 58 (1956), 109–139; S. F. Nadel, "Dual Descent in the Nuba Hills," in A. R. Radcliffe-Brown and Daryll Forde, eds., *African Systems of Kinship and Marriage* (London: Oxford University Press, 1950), pp. 333–359; Nadel, *The Nuba*, pp. 327–341.

[60] Philip Mayer, *The Lineage Principle in Gusii Society* (London: Oxford University Press, 1949), pp. 29–30, 27 ff.; see also p. 14.

[61] Evans-Pritchard, *The Nuer*, pp. 212–217; E. E. Evans-Pritchard, "Kinship and the Local Community among the Nuer," in Radcliffe-Brown and Forde, *op. cit.*, pp. 360–391.

[62] Godfrey Lienhardt, "The Western Dinka," in Middleton and Tait, *op. cit.*, pp. 97–135.

[63] Winter, "Aboriginal Political Structure of Bwamba," pp. 136–138; Brian K. Taylor, *The Western Lacustrine Bantu* (London: International African Institute, 1962), pp. 72–74.

[64] Winter, "Aboriginal Political Structure of Bwamba," p. 137.

[65] *Ibid.*, p. 155.

[66] Smith, "Social Organization and Economy of Kagoro"; Smith, "Kagoro Political Development"; M. G. Smith, "Secondary Marriage in Northern Nigeria," *Africa*, 23, no. 4 (1953), 304–312; Meek, *Tribal Studies in Northern Nigeria*, II, 90–100.

[67] Skinner, *op. cit.*, pp. 6–7; Fortes, "Political System of the Tallensi," pp. 239–240.

[68] Fortes, "Political System of the Tallensi," pp. 240, 245–247, 258–260.

[69] *Ibid.*, p. 246. See also Fortes, "Ritual and Office in Tribal Society."

[70] Nadel, *The Nuba*, p. 9.

[71] *Ibid.*, p. 9; see also p. 13.

[72] *Ibid.*, p. 207.

[73] *Ibid.*, p. 423. For more intensive analysis of institutional diversity among adjacent populations, see Goody, *Social Organization of the LoWiili*; Goody, *Death, Property and Ancestors*.

[74] Buxton, "The Mandari"; Buxton, *Chiefs and Strangers*.

[75] Forde, *Yakö Studies*, pp. 71–80, 103 ff.; Daryll Forde, "Unilineal Fact or Fiction: An Analysis of the Composition of Kinship Groups among the Yakö," in Isaac Schapera, ed., *Studies in Kinship and Marriage* (London: Royal Anthropological Institute, 1963), pp. 38–57.

[76] W. R. G. Horton, "The *Ohu* System of Slavery in a Northern Ibo Village Group," *Africa*, 24, no. 4 (1954), 311–336.

[77] Jones, "Political Organization of Old Calabar"; Jones, *Trading States of the Oil Rivers*, pp. 53–62.

[78] Mary Douglas, *The Lele of the Kasai* (London: Oxford University Press, 1963), pp. 141–173 and *passim*.

[79] Mary Douglas, "Matriliny and Pawnship in Central Africa," *Africa*, 34, no. 4 (1964), 301–313.

[80] C. N. M. White, "Clan, Chieftainship and Slavery in Luvale Political Organization," *Africa*, 27, no. 1 (1957), 59–74; Igor Kopytoff, "The Suku of Southwestern Congo," in Gibbs, *op. cit.*, pp. 458–459.

[81] A. J. B. Hughes, *Kin, Caste and Nation among the Rhodesian Ndebele* (Manchester: Manchester University Press, 1956); G. P. Gamble, *The Wolof of Senegambia* (London: International African Institute, 1957), pp. 44–65; Maquet, *op. cit.*; d'Hertefelt, *op. cit.*, pp. 406–411, 433; Briggs, *op. cit.*, pp. 157–163; Miner, *op. cit.*, pp. 19 ff.; Lhote, *op. cit.*; Nicolaisen, *Ecology and Culture of Pastoral Tuareg*; Barth, *op. cit.*, II, 281–284; K. Oberg, "The Kingdom of Ankole in Uganda," in Fortes and Evans-Pritchard, *op. cit.*, pp. 128–136.

[82] Taylor, *op. cit.*, pp. 101–103; Goody, *Death, Property and Ancestors*; Nadel, *The Nuba*; LeVine and Sangree, *op. cit.*

[83] P. H. Gulliver, "The Karamojong Cluster," *Africa*, 22, no. 1 (1952), 1–21; P. H. Gulliver, *The Family Herds: A Study of Two Pastoral Peoples in East Africa, the Jie and Turkana* (London: Routledge and Kegan Paul, 1955); Huntingford, *The Nandi of Kenya*, pp. 12–53; LeVine and Sangree, *op. cit.*, pp. 99–102; Bernardi, *op. cit.*

[84] G. W. B. Huntingford, *The Galla of Ethiopia* (London: International African Institute, 1955); H. A. Fosbrooke, "An Administrative Survey of the Masai Social System," *Tanganyika Notes and Records*, no. 26 (1948), 1–50; Huntingford, *The Nandi of Kenya*; B. Bernardi, *The Mugwe: A Failing Prophet—A Study of a Religious and Public Dignitary of the Meru of Kenya* (London: Oxford University Press, 1959); G. I. Jones, "Ibo Age Organization," *Journal of the Royal Anthropological Institute*, 92 (1962), 191–211.

[85] Paul Spencer (*op. cit.*, pp. 281–299) contrasts their position with that of the Masula phratry and Rendille tribe.

[86] Robert F. Gray, *The Sonjo of Tanganyika: An Anthropological Study of an Irrigation-based Society* (London: Oxford University Press, 1963), pp. 9–19, 83–96.

[87] LeVine and Sangree, *op. cit.*; Sangree, "The Bantu Tiriki."

[88] Gunter Wagner, "The Political Organization of the Bantu of North Kavirondo," in Fortes and Evans-Pritchard, *op. cit.*, pp. 197–236; Wagner, *The Bantu of North Kavirondo*; Huntingford, *Nandi Work and Culture*; Huntingford, *The Nandi of Kenya*.

[89] LeVine and Sangree, *op. cit.*, pp. 101–102.

[90] *Ibid.*, p. 105.

[91] Max Gluckman, "The Kingdom of the Zulu of South Africa," in Fortes and Evans-Pritchard, *op. cit.*, pp. 25–55; Hilda Kuper, *An African Aristocracy: Rank among the Swazi* (London: Oxford University Press, 1947), pp. 117–136; Hilda Kuper, *The Swazi* (London: International African Institute, 1952), pp. 22–24.

[92] Schapera, *Handbook of Tswana Law and Custom*, 104–117; Schapera, "Political Organization of the Ngwato," pp. 56–82; Schapera, *The Tswana*, pp. 28–29, 37–39.

[93] Hilda Kuper, A. J. B. Hughes, and J. Van Velsen, *The Shona and Ndebele of Southern Rhodesia* (London: International African Institute, 1954), pp. 45, 72 ff.; Hughes, *Kin, Caste and Nation*, pp. 52–56.

[94] Hughes, *Kin, Caste and Nation,* p. 56. These alternative spellings of Ngoni (Nguni) are established north and south of the Limpopo, respectively. I follow the spelling of my sources.

[95] Kuper, Hughes, and Van Velsen, *op. cit.,* p. 73.

[96] *Ibid.,* p. 73.

[97] *Ibid.,* p. 73; see also p. 92; and Hughes, *Kin, Caste and Nation,* p. 56.

[98] Kuper, Hughes, and Van Velsen, *op. cit.,* p. 74.

[99] *Ibid.,* pp. 93–94.

[100] Margaret Read, *The Ngoni of Nyasaland* (London: Oxford University Press, 1956), pp. 41, 81–84, 88, and *passim.*

[101] Barnes, *op. cit.,* p. 39.

[102] *Ibid.,* p. 40.

[103] Kenneth L. Little, "The Role of the Secret Society in Cultural Specialization," *American Anthropologist,* 51 (1949), 199–212; Kenneth L. Little, "The Political Function of the Poro," *Africa,* 35, no. 4 (1965), 349–365; 36, no. 1 (1966), 62–72; Little, *The Mende of Sierra Leone,* pp. 240–253; G. W. Harley, "Notes on the Poro of Liberia," *Peabody Museum Papers,* 19, no. 2 (1941); Morton-Williams, *op. cit.;* P. Morton-Williams, "An Outline of the Cosmology and Cult Organization of the Oyo Yoruba," *Africa,* 36, no. 3 (1966), 243–261; Daryll Forde, *The Yoruba-Speaking Peoples* (London: International African Institute, 1951), pp. 17–21; Lloyd, *Yoruba Land Law,* pp. 18–20, 38–42, 146–149, and *passim;* Simmons, *op. cit.,* pp. 3–26; Jones, "Political Organization of Old Calabar"; Jones, *Trading States of Oil Rivers,* pp. 18, 65–69, 80, 87, and *passim;* Robin Horton, "The Kalabari Ekine Society: A Borderland of Religion and Art," *Africa,* 33, no. 2 (1963), 94–114.

[104] James L. Gibbs, Jr., "The Kpelle of Liberia," in Gibbs, *op. cit.,* pp. 214–223; Morton-Williams, "Yoruba Ogboni Cult"; Morton-Williams, "Cosmology and Cult Organization of Oyo Yoruba"; Lloyd, "Sacred Kingship among the Yoruba," pp. 221–237; P. C. Lloyd, "The Traditional Political System of the Yoruba," *Southwestern Journal of Anthropology,* 10 (1954), 366–384; V. R. Dorjahn, "The Organization and Functions of the Ragbenle Society among the Temne," *Africa,* 29 (1959), 156–170.

[105] Jones, "Political Organization of Old Calabar"; Simmons, *op. cit.;* Meek, *Law and Authority in a Nigerian Tribe,* pp. 66–69.

[106] Meek, *Law and Authority in a Nigerian Tribe,* pp. 132, 148–184; Daryll Forde and G. I. Jones, *The Ibo and Ibibio-Speaking Peoples of South-Eastern Nigeria* (London: International African Institute, 1950), pp. 18–21, 26, 73–75, 89–93, and *passim.*

[107] Forde, "Governmental Roles of Associations among the Yakö"; Forde, *Yakö Studies,* pp. 135–209; Rosemary Harris, "The Political Significance of Double Unilineal Descent," *Journal of the Royal Anthropological Institute,* 92, pt. 1 (1962), 86–101.

[108] Harley, *op. cit.;* Lloyd, "Traditional Political System of the Yoruba"; Little, "Political Function of the Poro"; Gibbs, "Kpelle of Liberia"; Phyllis M. Kaberry, "Traditional Politics in Nsaw," *Africa,* 29 (1959), 366–383; P. M. Kaberry and E. M. Chilver, "An Outline of the Traditional Political System of Bali-Nyonga, Southern Cameroons," *Africa,* 31, no. 4 (1961), 355–371; E. M. Chilver and P. M. Kaberry, "Traditional Government in Bafut, West Cameroon," *Nigerian Field,* 28, no. 1 (1963), 4–30; R. Delarozière, *Les Institutions politiques et sociales des Populations dites Bamileke,* Institut Français

d'Afrique Noire, Centre du Kameroon, Memo 3 (1950), pp. 66–98; Hans Cory, *The Indigenous Political System of the Sukuma and Proposals for Political Reform* (Dar es Salaam: Eagle Press, 1954), pp. 63–91; D. W. Malcolm, *Sukumaland: An African People and Their Country* (London: Oxford University Press, 1953), pp. 33–43.

[109] Simmons, *op. cit.*, p. 16; Jones, "Political Organization of Old Calabar," pp. 136–148.

[110] Daryll Forde, "Death and Succession: An Analysis of Yakö Mortuary Ritual," in Max Gluckman, ed., *Essays on the Rituals of Social Relations* (Manchester: Manchester University Press, 1962), pp. 89–123; Forde, *Yakö Studies*, pp. 135–209; Harris, "Political Significance of Double Unilineal Descent."

[111] Biobaku, *op. cit.*, pp. 1–26; Lloyd, *Yoruba Land Law*, pp. 225–238.

[112] Biobaku, *op. cit.*, pp. 5–7; Lloyd, *Yoruba Land Law*, pp. 227–231.

[113] Lloyd, *Yoruba Land Law*, pp. 229–230.

[114] *Ibid.*, p. 231.

[115] Manoukian, *op. cit.*, pp. 73, 81.

[116] *Ibid.*, pp. 81–83.

[117] Jones, *Trading States of the Oil Rivers*, pp. 51–71.

[118] Simmons, *op. cit.*, p. 16.

[119] Jones, *Trading States of the Oil Rivers*, pp. 172–173.

[120] Hope Waddell, cited in Jones, "Political Organization of Old Calabar," p. 149.

[121] Jones, *loc. cit.*

[122] *Ibid.*, p. 157.

[123] Ian G. Cunnison, "Perpetual Kinship: A Political Institution of the Luapula" *Human Problems in British Central Africa*, no. 20 (1956), pp. 28–48; Ian G. Cunnison, *History of the Luapula* (Cape Town: Oxford University Press, 1951).

[124] Godfrey Wilson, *The Constitution of Ngonde* (Livingstone, Northern Rhodesia: Rhodes-Livingstone Institute, 1939), pp. 12 ff.

[125] Wilson, "Nyakyusa of South-Western Tanganyika," pp. 278–289; Monica Wilson, *Good Company: A Study of Nyakyusa Age-Villages* (London: Oxford University Press, 1951), pp. 19–38.

[126] Southall, *op. cit.*, pp. 3–8, 152–227, 348–351; Cory, *op. cit.*, pp. 1–4.

[127] Winans, *op. cit.*

[128] Cory, *op. cit.*, pp. 1–3; Malcolm, *op. cit.*, pp. 20–21.

[129] Godfrey Wilson, *Constitution of Ngonde*.

[130] D'Hertefelt, *op. cit.*, pp. 406–407, 416–417, 421–423; Maquet, *op. cit.*; Alexis Kagame, "Le Pluralisme ethnique et culturel dans le Rwanda-Urundi," in *Ethnic and Cultural Pluralism in Intertropical Countries* (Brussels: INCIDI, 1957), pp. 268–293; Helen Codere, "Power in Ruanda," *Anthropologica*, n.s., 4, no. 1 (1962), 45–85.

[131] Codere, *op. cit.*; Marcel d'Hertefelt, "Les Elections communales et le consensus politique au Rwanda," *Zaïre*, XIV, no. 5–6 (1960), 403–438; Marcel d'Hertefelt, "Stratification sociale et structure politique au Rwanda," *Revue Nouvelle*, XXI (1960), 449–462; Marcel d'Hertefelt, "Développements Recents," in M. d'Hertefelt, A. Troubworst, and J. Scherer, *Les anciens royaumes de la Zone Interlacustre Meridionale* (London: International African Institute, 1962), pp. 227–236.

[132] Albert Troubworst, "Le Burundi," in d'Hertefelt, Troubworst and Scherer, *op. cit.*, p. 120. See also Albert Troubworst, "L'Accord de clientele et l'Organisation politique au Burundi," *Anthropologica*, n.s., 4, no. 1 (1962), 9–44; Kagame, *op. cit.*

[133] Troubworst, "Le Burundi," pp. 143–155. See also M. Luwel, "Développements recents: Burundi," in d'Hertefelt, Troubworst, and Scherer, *op. cit.*, pp. 237–246.

[134] Oberg, *op. cit.*, pp. 121–163.

[135] *Ibid.*, pp. 1–40; Margaret Chave Fallers, *The Eastern Lacustrine Bantu* (London: International African Institute, 1960).

[136] John Beattie, *Bunyoro: An African Kingdom* (New York: Holt, Rinehart and Winston, 1960); Martin Southwold, "The Ganda of Uganda," in Gibbs, *op. cit.*, pp. 85–86.

[137] Martin Southwold, *Bureaucracy and Chiefship in Buganda* (Kampala: East African Institute of Social Reserach, 1960); Audrey Richards, ed., *East African Chiefs* (London: Faber and Faber, 1960), pp. 41–77; for Soga, Nyoro, Toro, Ankole, Haya, Zinza, and Ha, see *ibid.*, pp. 78–228.

[138] Brelsford, *op. cit.*, pp. 6–19; Gluckman, *Economy of the Central Barotse Plain*, pp. 11–15; Gluckman, "Lozi of Barotseland," pp. 4–5, 87–88; Cornèvin, *op. cit.*, pp. 197–215; Gamble, *op. cit.*; Baxter and Butt, *op. cit.*, pp. 1–22, 26–40, 48–64, 72; Nadel, *Black Byzantium*, pp. 12–26, 405–406, and endpaper map.

[139] Evans-Pritchard, "The Zande State," pp. 134–154 (see bibliography on pp. 153–154); Barnes, *op. cit.*, pp. 43–63; Schapera, *Government and Politics in Tribal Societies*, pp. 157–178; Isaac Schapera, "Kinship and Politics in Tswana History," *Journal of the Royal Anthropological Institute*, 93, pt. 1 (June 1963), 134–154 (see bibliography on pp. 153–154); 93, pt. 2 (Dec. 1963), 159–173; Barnes, *op. cit.*, pp. 43–63.

[140] Nadel, *Black Byzantium*, pp. 69, 138; see also pp. 12–26; and Nadel, "Nupe State and Community."

[141] Nadel, *Black Byzantium*, p. 139.

[142] Nadel, *Nupe Religion*.

[143] Miner, *op. cit.*, pp. 3–47 (esp. 17–23), 175–202, 240–266, 271–274.

[144] Y. G. J. Sheddick, *The Southern Sotho* (London: International African Institue, 1953), p. 15; Ian Hammett, "Koena Chieftainship in Basutoland," *Africa*, 35, no. 3 (July 1965), 241–250.

[145] Brelsford, *op. cit.*, pp. 32–34; Wilfred Whitely, *Bemba and Related Peoples of Northern Rhodesia* (London: International African Institute, 1951), p. 7.

[146] Kuper, *African Aristocracy*, p. 18.

[147] *Ibid.*, pp. 54–71, esp. 57–58.

[148] *Ibid.*, pp. 117–133.

[149] Schapera, *Handbook of Tswana Law and Custom*, pp. 4–11, 19–28, 91–103, 118–124.

[150] *Ibid.*, p. 95; see also p. 63.

[151] *Ibid.*, p. 121; see also pp. 118–121.

[152] Gluckman, "Lozi of Barotseland," pp. 4–8, 14–18; Brelsford, *op. cit.*, pp. 8–12; Jan Vansina, *Kingdoms of the Savanna* (Madison: University of Wisconsin Press, 1966), pp. 174–179, 212–216.

[153] Gluckman, "Lozi of Barotseland," pp. 19–21.

[154] A. H. M. Kirk-Greene, *Adamawa Past and Present* (London: Oxford University Press, 1958).

[155] Barth, *op. cit.*, I, II; S. J. Hogben, *The Muhammadan Emirates of Northern Nigeria* (Oxford: Clarendon Press); M. G. Smith, *Government in Zazzau, 1800–1950* (London: Oxford University Press, 1960); M. G. Smith, "Historical and Cultural Conditions of Political Corruption among the Hausa," *Comparative Studies in Society and History*, 6, no. 2 (1964), 164–194; Smith, "Social Organization and Economy of Kagoro," and "The Two Katsinas (unpublished MSS); M. G. Smith, "The Jihad of Shehu dan Fodio: Some Problems," in I. M. Lewis, ed., *Islam in Tropical Africa* (London: Oxford University Press, 1966), pp. 408–424; *Documents scientifiques de la Mission Tilho (1906–1909)*, Ministère des Colonies (Paris: Imprimerie Nationale, 1911), II, 461–468, 510–537.

Chapter 5   Some Aspects of Violent and Nonviolent Political Change in Plural Societies

A. Conflict and the Plural Society: Ideologies of Violence among Subordinate Groups [*]

Leo Kuper

This paper deals with an aspect of political change in plural societies. These I define in the present context as societies characterized by cultural diversity and social cleavage arising from the contact of different peoples within a single political unit.[1] The process of political change in plural societies often takes the form of violent conflict, as in Algeria, Zanzibar, and Rwanda, and some students believe that this is its general, if not inevitable, form.[2] The movement toward violence is likely to generate appropriate ideologies; and I want here to examine some of the elements and functions of an ideology of violence for subordinate groups in a plural society. In constructing this ideology, I draw ideas mainly from Frantz Fanon's book, *Les damnés de la terre*,[3] where the ideology is formulated with great force and clarity in the context of the extreme violence of political change in Algeria. I rely also on statements by

[*] Paper presented to the Sixth World Congress of Sociology, Évian, September 1966, and reprinted by permission of The International Sociological Association. I have made a few changes.

African political leaders in South Africa, a plural society in which the consummation of political change may be equally violent.[4]

I

Common elements in an ideology of violence are the declaration of the necessity for violence as the only efficient means of change, the justification of violence on moral grounds, and the rejection of nonviolent techniques; there may or may not be an idealization of violence as creative rebirth for those who use it. Inevitably the elaboration of this ideology calls for assertions as to the nature of the society that is to become the battleground of violent conflict, and as to the qualities of the dominant group which make this conflict inevitable. These assertions describe the society as polarized into the two radically conflicting groups of oppressors and oppressed; and they establish (or seek to establish) the collective destiny of the oppressed and the unyielding domination of the oppressors, thereby guarding against what are conceived to be the erosions of individualism and the illusions of concessions and evolutionary change.

The argument as to the necessity for violence rests in part on repetitive declaration: "From birth it is clear to him [the colonized] that this narrow world, strewn with prohibitions, can only be called in question by absolute violence";[5] "The starving peasant, outside the class system, is the first among the exploited to discover that only violence pays";[6] or "We have seen that it is the intuition of the colonised masses that their liberation must, and can only, be achieved by force."[7] The argument also rests, more or less persuasively, on such empirical generalizations as that the history of freedom is written in blood,[8] or on generalizations derived from the many examples of violent political change in plural societies, or on such more specific generalizations as that offered by Fanon when he describes the process of decolonization:

National liberation, national renaissance, the restoration of nationhood to the people, commonwealth: whatever may be the headings used or the new formulas introduced, decolonisation is always a violent phenomenon. At whatever level we study it . . . decolonisation is quite simply the replacing of a certain "species" of men by another "species" of men. . . . The naked truth of decolonisation evokes for us the searing bullets and bloodstained knives which emanate from it. For if the last shall be first, this will only come to pass after a murderous and decisive struggle between the two protagonists.[9]

The moral justification for violence derives from oppression and humiliation, from the transparency of the connection between the good fortune of those who rule and the misery of those who are ruled, and from concepts of human dignity and the rights of man. But these conditions and beliefs justify radical political change, and not necessarily violence, as the instrument of that change. Violence, at any rate from the standpoint of civic order and the rule of law, must rather find its legitimation in the qualities ascribed to the plural society and its ruling group, as in Fanon's denunciation of colonialism, which he declares is not a thinking machine or a body endowed with reasoning faculties: it is born in violence, it is maintained by violence, it speaks the language of violence, and in the final stages of the movement toward national consciousness, it transforms the atmosphere of violence among the colonized into violence in action; it is violence in its natural state, and it will yield only when confronted with greater violence.[10]

The rejection of nonviolence, which is the counterpart of the commitment to violence, also finds its legitimation in the structure of the society and the qualities of its rulers. The rejection may be defensive, implying the higher moral worth of nonviolence, and justifying the anguished choice of violence as compelled by the imperviousness of the rulers to supplication, petition, reason, argument, demonstration, and civil disobedience. It is in these terms of disillusionment with the government of South Africa, and with nonviolence in the face of its obdurate inhumanity, that leaders of the African National Congress explain the organization of *Umkhonto we Sizwe* (Spear of the Nation) [11] for violent action. Yet even in this movement toward revolutionary struggle, there was a deliberate selection of sabotage as the initial means of violence in preference to terrorism or guerrilla warfare, which would more fiercely inflame racial hatred.[12]

In contrast with the unhappy denunciation of nonviolence in the particular circumstances of the plural society, the rejection of nonviolence may be expressed in terms of cynicism or contempt for its futility. Thus the Non-European Unity Movement ridiculed the civil disobedience campaign of 1952 for its naïve conception of racial domination in South Africa:

The Herrenvolk has made up its mind over 300 years not to climb off the backs of the Non-Europeans of its own accord and free will. . . . There is no possibility of any of these laws being modified or repealed because the ruling class have had it brought to their notice that the non-Whites hate these laws. They are fascists, and they know that we hate them and their laws. There is only deception and self-deception in dealing with "Malanazis" as though they were "democrats" and "Christians" who will suffer pangs of conscience because certain non-white "leaders" are in gaol. The function of leaders is to lead; the gaols are there to hinder and not help the cause of freedom.[13]

So, too, Fanon reacts to the nonviolent reformist techniques with contempt. He describes them as a practice of therapy by hibernation, a sleep cure used on the people.[14] He sees nonviolence as the creation of the colonial situation,[15] functioning like the inevitable religion to calm down the natives: "All those saints who have turned the other cheek, who have forgiven trespasses against them, and who have been spat on and insulted without shrinking are studied and held up as examples." [16] Indeed, far from a defensive and reluctant choice of violence, Fanon positively affirms violence. He writes that it is in and through violence that the colonized man finds his freedom: [17] only out of the rotting corpse of the settler can life spring up again for the native.[18] Where Gandhi sees the realization of truth in *satyagraha* (soul-force), Fanon finds it, for the colonized, in violence:

Violence alone, violence committed by the people, violence organised and educated by its leaders, makes it possible for the masses to understand social truths and gives the key to them. Without that struggle, without that knowledge of the practice of action, there's nothing but a fancy-dress parade and the blare of the trumpets. There's nothing save a minimum of readaptation, a few reforms at the top, a flag waving: and down there at the bottom an undivided mass, still living in the middle ages, endlessly marking time.[19]

And Sartre, in interpreting and endorsing Fanon's ideology of violence for the colonized, declares that

he shows clearly that this irrepressible violence . . . is man re-creating himself. I think we understood this truth at one time, but we have forgotten it —that no gentleness can efface the marks of violence; only violence itself can destroy them. The native cures himself of colonial neurosis by thrusting out the settler through force of arms. When his rage boils over, he rediscovers his lost innocence and he comes to know himself in that he himself creates his self.[20]

The ideology of violence, as I have shown, includes a characterization of the plural society. The main component of this characterization is a polarized conception, which directs violence unambiguously against the enemy.[21] The complex patterns of pluralism are reduced to the simple dichotomy of a dialectical opposition. For Fanon, it is a dialectic without possibility of synthesis, without possibility of a higher unity. The colonial world is a world of two species, a world divided into two reciprocally exclusive divisions. Between them, no conciliation is possible, for of the two divisions, one is superfluous.[22] Their roles may change: the quarry may become the hunter, the oppressed the persecutor.[23] But there can be no sharing of power. An irreconcilable conflict, an absolute opposition of interests, separates the parties. Decolonization is total, complete and absolute substitution, without transition: it is the abolition of one zone, its burial in the depths of the earth or its expulsion from the country.[24] In a world of radically opposed and irreconcilable interests, there can be no evolutionary change toward a shared society. Individualism cannot bridge the collective destiny of the parties in the struggle for freedom; [25] and concessions may merely be the cloak for a less blatant but more complete servitude.[26]

There may be, in plural societies, a necessary association, an ideological fusion, between the call to violence and the conception of polarized groups. Certainly, ideologies of revolutionary violence in South Africa increasingly show this tendency, with dogmatic assumptions as to the unity of the oppressed and the unity of the oppressors, and the reduction of the great diversity in structure, values, and function within each of these categories to a crude dichotomy of violence.[27]

II

I have described the call to violence and the associated characterization of the society as ideology, thereby assuming that the ideas are to be interpreted as expressing the needs and desires of those who proclaim them, rather than as offering an analysis of the objective structure of the plural society and its potentiality for peaceful change. But the ideas may nevertheless quite accurately portray dominant tendencies within the society while at the same time serving sectional interests in a revolutionary challenge to the structure of rule. There may be an extreme polarization between the ruling and subject groups, and violence may indeed offer the only possibility of political change. Instead of assuming the ideological function of the ideas in question, it becomes necessary to examine them in the social context to which they refer.

The empirical evidence hardly sustains the generalization that decolonization is always a violent phenomenon. In the recent struggles for independence in Africa, there has certainly been extreme violence in some territories, as in Algeria and Kenya, or presently in Angola and Mozambique; but in most African territories, decolonization, as distinct from the aftermath of decolonization, has been attended by relatively little violence. The violent phenomenon was colonization rather than decolonization, and even then, not all colonial rule in Africa was imposed by violence.

A Marxist might argue that there has been little or no decolonization in Africa; that the contemporary independence of African states is appearance, not reality; that the reality is the persistence of colonialism in the masked form of neocolonialism; and that westernized African elites, the new incumbents of the old colonial posts, fulfill functions analogous to those of their colonial predecessors. But this shifts the basis of the argument and finds the necessity for violence in Communist revolution, while conceding that important changes in the relations of the races within the plural society and in the whole structure of the plural society may be effected without violence.

A more cogent argument as to the generality of violence in the process of decolonization is that decolonization must be seen as a global process. From this perspective, the colonial power occupies a field with colonial possessions on the perimeter and engages in a struggle with other powers for position in a changing world situation. The violence that acts as the catalyst of change is not violence within a particular colonial territory, but violence directed from any point on the colonial perimeter, and the violence, or threatened violence, of international conflict. Viewed in this way, as in Fanon's *Pour la révolution africaine*,[28] there can be little doubt of the violence of decolonization, though differences in its incidence between the French and British empires show that violence is not simply a function of the process of decolonization.

The empirical evidence for the inevitability of violence is more convincing in the case of settler societies than in colonial societies. There are many differences between them which have relevance for the probability and intensity of violence, such as the very permanence of the settler population and its determination to persist in the enjoyment of numerous vested interests. There is the intense involvement of the settlers in their relations with the subject groups, since privilege and indeed survival may be precarious in the close immediacy of their living together. Fanon asserts a direct relationship between the size of the settler group and the extent of violence, arguing that the violence of the colonial regime and the counterviolence of the native balance each other and respond to each other in an extraordinary reciprocal homogeneity, and that "this reign of violence will be the more terrible in proportion to the size of the implantation from the mother country." [29] The relationship is probably more complex. A larger number of settlers would be associated with greater economic development and greater interdependence between the groups. This interdependence is likely to inhibit the outbreak of violence; but if violence does break out, then it may be all the more intense, destructive, and intersuicidal by reason of the dependence of the groups on each other.

Perhaps of greatest significance is the contrast in constitutional status. The line between settler and colonial societies is not easily drawn, since colonial status may be associated with a substantial settler class as in Algeria and colonial societies may have many of the characteristics of settler societies (the so-called "settler colonies" as distinct from the "exploitation colonies"). Yet even in these "settler colonies," the different constitutional status of the colony has the significant consequence that it immediately involves a third party, the colonial power itself. To be sure, the colonial power is a main protagonist, and it may in fact heighten destructive violence by engaging its relatively great military resources in the conflict. But its role in an era of decolonization may be very different, and may include elements of mediation. In the metropolitan center, a measure of detachment from deep emotional involvement in the conflict is possible, or at any rate groups in the metropolitan center may achieve this detachment and function in much the same way as a third party to encourage a nonviolent adjustment of interests. Certainly this third-party role was a significant factor in the resolution of conflict in Kenya, and may still prove so in Rhodesia, though this becomes increasingly unlikely.

In the conflicts of settler societies, however, no third party with a possible mediating role is automatically involved. The United Nations might so function, but for the cold war which wages international peace through local dichotomies of violence, as in Korea and Vietnam. As Fanon observes, "today, peaceful co-existence between the two *blocs* provokes and feeds violence in the colonial countries. . . . Between the violence of the colonies and that peaceful violence that the world is steeped in, there is a kind of complicit agreement, a sort of homogeneity." [30] If this observation has any validity for colonial countries, in which the colonial power has the opportunity and responsibility to resolve conflict, it will be all the more valid for settler societies, in which independent status offers a freer field for the masked play of international war. In the context of the cold war, the intervention of third parties in the conflicts of a settler society seems likely to foster a polarization of the society into two hostile camps, corresponding to the strategic needs of the great powers. [31]

The theoretical argument for the necessity of violence as the instrument of change rests on assumptions as to the nature of man and society. I will accept, for purposes of this discussion, the assumption that men have to be forced from positions of dominance, that they will not voluntarily relinquish or share the power they have once enjoyed. I will accept and indeed make the case that there are many special circumstances in plural societies which render ruling strata extraordinarily tenacious of power and exclusive in their exercise of power. These societies often take the form of domination by a minority of different race and culture with more highly developed technology. [32] The domination is deeply embedded in the political and other institutions of the society and supports elaborate and strongly fortified structures of privilege. Rationalizations that dehumanize the subject peoples and glorify the civilizing mission of their overlords justify ready recourse to repression and force. The use of force is encouraged also by greater development of political institutions, the generation of disproportionate political power as compared with economic and other institutional power. Particularly in white settler societies, the monopoly of power, the appropriation of scarce resources, and the contrasts in life situations suggest a dialectical opposition of interest between the groups. But even accepting all this, these assumptions and generalizations would only establish the need for great pressure to bring about political change; they do not prove that violence is the only efficient means for that change.

At this point, the argument for violence may move to the assertion, as by African leaders in South Africa, that nonviolence has proved ineffective. It does not follow that violence will therefore be effective, though this is always assumed. Nor is it easy to determine whether the possibilities of nonviolent action were fully explored, let alone exhausted. There are questions of cost, of the threshold of nonviolence, and of the structure of power. Men vary in their tolerance of suffering and readiness for self-sacrifice. Hence a subjective element enters into the assessment of the extent to which such techniques as civil disobedience have been fully tried out; the answer is relative to the leaders' perception of tolerable cost. Then too, among the mass of followers, the threshold of nonviolence may be low in the sense that culture inclines them toward impatience with nonviolence.

Other circumstances, in the conditions of the plural society, may contribute to the same result and indeed foster an easy recourse to violence. These conditions would be such as contribute to the formation of mass society,[33] as, for example, abrupt discontinuities in culture and authority, and between rural and urban centers; the agglomeration and insecurity of many new townsmen in slum and shanty; and the incitement of hardship, humiliation, and brutality. In consequence, the leaders may find that they have little latitude for experimenting with nonviolence, and the repressive and violent exercise of government authority may offer them even less. It is to be understood then that they might conclude that they had exhausted the possibilities of nonviolent political change when, from the perspective of Gandhian *satyagraha*, they had merely initiated preliminary campaigns.

If the society is polarized, then it may be reasonable to infer that political change will be abrupt, revolutionary, and presumably violent. Polarization implies a division into two camps—the oppressors and the oppressed—with few relationships that transcend group barriers and restrain conflict by the ties of crosscutting loyalties.[34] Interests are in dialectical opposition [35] and values antithetical; the subject peoples deny legitimacy to the social order and the rulers respond with increasing repression. Social cleavages are superimposed [36] so that domination in political structures coincides with domination in other institutional structures. The dichotomy of values is pervasive, unresolved conflicts cumulate, and minor, seemingly isolated, issues quickly escalate to the level of the total society. There is no neutral ground of detachment from the struggle, which drives all strata into opposing camps; there is no appreciable intermediate area of living which might serve as the foundation for a more inclusive system of relationship.

Clearly, most plural societies do not conform to this pure type of polarization: it represents revolutionary ideology rather than sociological analysis. Perhaps the closest approximation is to be found in the early stages of conquest and consolidation of power. Later, as the plural sections coexist within the same society, relations of interdependence and of common interest begin to mitigate the extreme enmity and to modify the sharp division. These integrative relationships, varying with the nature of the society and its mode of production, may be fairly negligible in an "exploitation colony" and more extensive in an industrialized "settler society," as in South Africa. Here, the stark simplicity of a model of polarized relationships quite distorts the complex reality of racial hatreds, which vary in intensity, expression, and direction among different racial groups and social strata. In its exclusive concern for cultural conflict and racial cleavage, it ignores the effects of shared knowledge and understandings, of common religious beliefs, of interdependent participation in an exchange economy, and of social relationships across racial barriers; and it projects as present reality social perceptions that derive from an operational blueprint for revolution.

III

These ideologies and the social perceptions they crystallize may serve as an index of the probability of violence. They mark a qualitative change in relations which seems to precede the outbreak of violence; they may of course be the agent of that change. This is not to say that violence necessarily follows the dissemination and wide adoption of revolutionary ideologies within a plural society. And conversely, violence may erupt quite spontaneously, without ideological overture. Indeed, the relationship between ideology and violence may be reversed, the ideology emerging from the violence, not the violence from the ideology.

The rulers may contribute to the probability of violence by their ideological reactions to the threat of violence. They may declare that these people understand only the moral persuasion of force, which must be firmly used for preservation of law and order.[37] They may refuse concessions, since these would seem to reward violence; they may also believe that concessions are a delusion, leading not to an adjustment of interests but to the eventual subordination of the rulers themselves. Being convinced of the absolute incompatibility of different sections of the plural society, and therefore of the impossibility of social synthesis, they perceive the alternatives as either to rule or to be ruled. There is thus an almost exact correspondence between the ideologies of revolution and of counterrevolution, expressing dialectical opposition and reflecting a long history of ideological exchange. For theorists who believe that by the inescapable pragmatism of all action, force and the threat of force unavoidably breed more force,[38] the reproduction of ideologies of violence is merely a particular expression of this more general process.

A quite different response to the threat of violence is by way of "concessions," and these may in fact reduce the probability of violence; much of the movement to independence in the British African colonies has been in this form, that is to say, in the form of evolutionary change. There are certainly many contrary examples of "concessions" that proved to be quite illusory and served simply as devices for maintaining domination. But these historic events (such as manipulations of a qualified franchise) cannot be translated directly into universal laws. It is necessary to specify the conditions that exclude the possibility of evolutionary change by means of concessions. No doubt, these conditions are most likely to be found in settler societies.

Since the violence threatens the very existence of the plural society, the response may be a series of measures designed to knit the society more closely together. This has been the response of the South African government, regardless of its much advertised policy of apartheid (separation) which professes quite the contrary. The government has in fact used a mixed strategy of violence, "concessions" and "integration." Violence is long established in South Africa as an appropriate traditional technique for the governance of people of different race; and I think it probable that, but for the hostile reaction of outside powers to the Sharpeville massacre, the government would have sought a solution by holocausts of violence. As to "concessions," the most important are the Bantustans, in which Africans are promised self-rule. These concessions seem to be the very epitome of the concessions ridiculed in the revolutionary ideologies: their promises appear to be illusory, merely a decoy to fragmentation and continued domination. But this is not certain. Underlying the belief in the illusory nature of concessions is the assumption that the initiative rests entirely with the dominant group. Where subordinate groups have some possibility of initiative, as in the Bantustans, the consequences of concessions are indeterminate, depending on the way Africans use them, and not only on the plans of the government. The Bantustans may or may not offer a base for a challenge to white domination.

More immediately significant than these "concessions," if they can possibly be described as such, are the means by which the government seeks to bind the society more firmly together. Gluckman, in *Custom and Conflict*,[39] demonstrates from Nuer society the principle that the greater the interdependence between groups, the greater the likelihood of institutional mechanisms for resolving conflict. There is certainly great interdependence between the races in South Africa, resulting from long years of contact and from high levels of economic growth and industrial development, which draw increasing numbers of all races into a common exchange economy. This economy rests largely on nonwhite labor and is therefore particularly vulnerable to racial conflict. In these circumstances, the government has not met the threat of violence by the creation of institutional mechanisms for resolution of conflict, and few of these mechanisms have developed spontaneously outside the framework of government. Instead of resolving conflict, the government's policy is to contain conflict and to "integrate" the plural sections or, more specifically, to coerce them into togetherness.[40] The government generates more political power and greater capacity for violence; it elaborates authority structures for more total control; and it creates special structures for ordering the parts within the preordained whole.

I have argued that few plural societies show the polar structure ascribed to them in ideologies of violence. There is generally tension between the ideological image and the social reality. For this reason, violence is often directed initially within the group itself. A whole vocabulary emerges to stigmatize those who do not conform to the brutal dichotomy of violence. In terms of graphic abuse, it distinguishes different categories of nonconformist; at the same time it exposes them almost equally, the altruist and the nonracist as well as the spy and the informer, to indiscriminate retribution.

A like process engages the rulers. Though at all times they direct aggression outward, they also pillory their own dissenters. They may rely more on due process and resort less to summary procedure, but as the conflict escalates, they too ultimately silence their nonconformists. There is nonconformity within each of the groups and interrelationship between members of different groups. It is not the society that is polarized, it is the ideology; indeed it is one of the functions of the ideology to polarize the society. Where the plural divisions are of different race, then the ideology of polarization becomes racism.[41]

If the goal is a polarized society, then violence would seem to be an efficient means to that end. It easily multiplies in a plural society, where the intermingling of peoples affords lavish occasion for violence; it deeply engages the personalities of the parties; it spreads sentiments of exclusive solidarity and silences moderation; it recalls ancient wrongs and heightens present anguish; it inflames hatred and inspires sacrifice.

For these reasons too, violence may be an efficient means for awakening an apathetic populace, for heightening political awareness, and for fostering political action. Plural societies often, perhaps generally, take the political form of minority domination, and sometimes these minorities are very small. In these circumstances, the subject population, if resolute, might readily effect social change by nonviolent means. This is probably true for Rhodesia, and perhaps even for South Africa, though this is much more doubtful. It is not so much that the nonviolent techniques are ineffective in themselves, as that the subordinate groups are not ready for effective political action of any kind, violent or nonviolent. Given much quietude, apathy, and confusion among the people, the leaders are likely to despair of building an effective organization for nonviolent action, particularly under continuous harassment by the authorities. Understandably they may turn to violence, which then becomes also a method of political campaigning and organization.

Where the commitment is in any event toward violence, and where nonviolence is felt to be repugnant, the problem becomes one of military strategy, which, under the present conditions of the cold war, will include the assistance or intervention of a third party. Where, however, the commitment is to peaceful resolution of conflict, and racial or other internal war is perceived as incitement to atrocity and by no means ennobling, then there is a real dilemma in relation to such countries as South Africa. Perhaps it is not true, or only partly true, that the society is so polarized and so devoid of middle or bridging structures as to exclude the possibility of nonviolent, evolutionary change. Perhaps it is not true, or only partly true, that given the character of the rulers and their imperviousness to morality and reason, only violence can prevail. Perhaps it is not true that the possibilities of nonviolence have been fully explored, and perhaps the ineffectiveness of the nonviolent campaigns stems in part from political unpreparedness.

Suppose all this is granted (and it would be questioned by many observers), there is still the agonizing problem of immediate and intense suffering under a rigidly maintained system of domination. Violence does seem to offer some better prospect of relief. In any event, the parties are moving toward the atrocity of violence. But it seems unlikely that violence will be effective in bringing about political change, unless outside powers assist the revolutionary parties. So too, it seems unlikely that peaceful political change can be brought about by forces internal to the society: in this case also, there will be need for outside intervention. If it is indeed true that effective violent and nonviolent action both presuppose active intervention from without, then presumably the final arbiter of South Africa's fate will be the great powers themselves, and the choice between violence and nonviolence will be largely determined by their international relations.

NOTES

[1] For discussion of plural societies, see J. S. Furnivall, *Colonial Policy and Practice* (London: Cambridge University Press, 1948); J. C. Mitchell, *Tribalism and the Plural Society* (London: Oxford University Press, 1960); John Rex, "The Plural Society in Sociological Theory," *British Journal of Sociology*, 10 (June 1959), 114–124; M. G. Smith, *The Plural Society in the British West Indies* (Berkeley and Los Angeles: University of California Press, 1965); Pierre L. van den Berghe, "Toward a Sociology of Africa," *Social Forces*, 43 (Oct. 1964), 11–18; and Leo Kuper, "Sociology: Some Aspects of Urban Plural Societies," in Robert A. Lystad, ed., *The African World* (New York: Praeger, 1965), pp. 107–130.

[2] See, for example, Smith, *op. cit.*, p. 91.

[3] Quotations in the text are from Frantz Fanon, *The Wretched of the Earth*, trans. Constance Farrington (New York: Grove Press, 1963).

[4] I have omitted, for the most part, discussions of the ideologies of the dominant groups and the policies they pursue which provoke subordinate groups to violence. For analysis of these aspects in South African society, see my *Passive Resistance in South Africa* (New Haven: Yale University Press, 1960), and *An African Bourgeoisie* (New Haven: Yale University Press, 1965).

[5] Fanon, *op. cit.*, p. 31.

[6] *Ibid.*, p. 48.

[7] *Ibid.*, p. 57.

[8] There is much corroboration from the shelters of the academic world. See, for example, Rupert Emerson, *From Empire to Nation* (Boston: Beacon Press, 1960), p. 331: "The great issues of nationalism and self-determination have been settled not by the genteel processes of votes and majorities but by the revolutionary rising of peoples and the successful waging of wars, which have carried history with them."

[9] Fanon, *op. cit.*, pp. 29–30.

[10] *Ibid.*, pp. 31, 48, 56, and *passim*.

[11] See Kuper, *An African Bourgeoisie*, p. 384.

[12] Nelson Mandela, *No Easy Walk to Freedom* (London: Heinemann, 1965), pp. 168–174.

[13] Kuper, *Passive Resistance in South Africa*, pp. 152–153.

[14] Fanon, *op. cit.*, p. 52. He qualifies his comment with an ironic illustration of success attendant on nationalist reform in Gabon.

[15] Karl A. Wittfogel, in *Oriental Despotism* (New Haven: Yale University Press, 1957), p. 331, mentions passive resistance as a response to Oriental despotism.

[16] Fanon, *op. cit.*, p. 53.

[17] *Ibid.*, p. 67.

[18] *Ibid.*, p. 72.

[19] *Ibid.*, p. 117.

[20] *Ibid.*, p. 18.

[21] In "Zoot-suiters and Mexicans: Symbols in Crowd Behavior" (*American Journal of Sociology*, LXII [1956], 14–20), Turner and Surace demonstrate a similar process in violent crowd behavior, where a clearly unfavorable symbol was required as the rallying point for violence against the Mexicans.

[22] Fanon, *op. cit.*, pp. 31–32.

[23] *Ibid.*, p. 42.

[24] *Ibid.*, pp. 29, 33.

[25] *Ibid.*, pp. 37–38.

[26] *Ibid.*, p. 113.

[27] See my discussion of ideological change in *An African Bourgeoisie*, chap. 23.

[28] In Frantz Fanon, *Pour la révolution africaine* (Paris: François Maspero, 1964), see "Décolonisation et indépendance" (pp. 119–125), "Lettre à la jeunesse Africaine" (pp. 135–140), "La guerre d'Algérie et la libération des hommes" (pp. 167–172), "L'Afrique affirm son unité et définit sa stratégie" (pp. 177–181), and esp. pp. 124, 135, and 171.

[29] Fanon, *The Wretched of the Earth*, p. 69.

[30] *Ibid.*, pp. 62–63.

[31] Diversification of international structure, consequent on Chinese international intervention, seems likely to affect the external pressures for polarization.

[32] For a characterization of colonial society, see Georges Balandier, *Sociologie actuelle de l'Afrique Noire* (Paris: Presses Universitaires de France, 1955), chap. i. M. G. Smith specifies domination by a cultural minority as one of the characteristics of plural society.

[33] See discussion by W. Kornhauser, *The Politics of Mass Society* (London: Routledge and Kegan Paul, 1960), particularly Pt. II.

[34] See Max Gluckman, *Custom and Conflict in Africa* (Oxford: Basil Blackwell, 1963), chap. i, and S. M. Lipset, *Political Man* (Garden City: Doubleday, 1960), chaps. vi, vii, for discussion of consequences of crosscutting loyalties and cross-pressures.

[35] See Fanon's discussion, *The Wretched of the Earth*, p. 66.

[36] R. Dahrendorf, in *Class and Class Conflict in Industrial Society* (London: Routledge and Kegan Paul, 1959), pp. 213–218, deals with the relationship between the intensity of conflict, and the superimposition of group conflicts and issues of conflict.

[37] This is presumably a rationalization by the rulers for their inability to legitimate their authority.

[38] See, for example, H. H. Gerth and C. Wright Mills, eds., *From Max Weber: Essays in Sociology* (New York: Oxford University Press, 1946), p. 334.

[39] Chap. i, esp. p. 15 *et seq.*

[40] There is a problem in the use of the word "integrate" to describe such societies as the apartheid society of South Africa. "Integration" suggests to many sociologists a unity based on consensus and not a unity that rests largely on regulation and force. Perhaps "integration" might be used where cohesion rests largely on a consensual basis, and "regulation" where its basis is mainly coercive.

[41] Fanon attacks racism in many of his writings (see, for example, *The Wretched of the Earth,* pp. 115–116, 126–127). See also his paper, "Algeria's European Minority," in F. Fanon, *Studies in a Dying Colonialism,* trans. Haakon Chevalier (New York: Monthly Review Press, 1965), pp. 147–178, in which he counters group stereotypes by showing the active collaboration of European and other non-Arab Algerians in the revolutionary struggle. But it is difficult to avoid the racism where dominant and subordinate groups are of different race, and the tenor and the emotional thrust of the general argument in his essay, "Concerning Violence," in *The Wretched of the Earth,* are in fact a powerful call to racism. For a brief discussion of Fanon's work and reactions to it, see David C. Gordon, *The Passing of French Algeria* (London: Oxford University Press, 1966), pp. 121–132. See also A. and V. Zolberg, "The Americanization of Frantz Fanon" (*Public Interest* [Fall 1967], pp. 49–63), for a different interpretation of Fanon's political ideology.

Chapter 5   B. Political Change in White Settler Societies: The Possibility of Peaceful Democratization *

White settler societies are notoriously repressive and undemocratic; indeed, among systems of race relations, they are the very embodiment of racial domination and discrimination. We often assume that transformation of their political structures must be violent, and in revolutionary perspectives, the Algerian war represents the prototype of liberation from white domination. It seems impossible to conceive of *internal* social processes in white settler societies which might *contribute* to evolutionary change from racial conflict and oppression toward consensus and democratic participation. Yet, it is precisely this impossible conception that I examine in my paper, and with particular reference to that most extreme of white settler societies, South Africa. If my conclusions are not encouraging, they may nevertheless invite thought beyond the platitudes of violence.[1] I say "platitudes of violence," since there is an exhaustive literature demonstrating the inevitability of and necessity for a violent resolution of conflict in white settler societies, and resting on a few axiomatic propositions, such as that the history of freedom is written in blood, which may perhaps be a little misleading both in general, and in the particular case.

* I should like to thank Martin Legassick and John Purcell for the prepared discussion they presented when this paper was given to the colloquium. I should emphasize the use of the word "contribute" in the statement of my problem, namely, whether internal social processes in white settler societies might *contribute* to peaceful democratization. In posing the problem in this form, I am assuming that, in such societies as South Africa and under such conditions as presently obtain there, internal social processes *in and of themselves* would be ineffective means to evolutionary democratic change, and that, in any event, in the contemporary world there is inevitable external involvement in the politics of white settler societies.

My purpose then is to comment on some processes of change in white settler societies as they bear on the possibility of peaceful democratization. I shall take two processes of change. The first is a process of individuation. In terms of social structure, it is a process by which individuals, in certain of their roles, become detached from the original racial matrix and enter into new relationships across racial lines, creating new interracial social structures, formal and informal. In terms of culture, it is a process by which individuals come to share many of the same basic institutions as well as a common language. In political terms, individuation may take a form in which members of the subordinate group are progressively incorporated into the political system on the same basis as the white settlers themselves. The means to this fuller political participation may be a qualified franchise, acquisition of elements of the culture of the dominant group qualifying for citizenship, and democracy extending through incorporation of acculturated individuals. Or the stimulus to extension of rights and to progressive incorporation may derive from common participation in religious, economic, and other institutional structures, and from interracial association and shared interests transcending, at certain levels, the racial cleavages.

The second process, at the collective level, is a process of group confrontation and accommodation, in which there is initially an increasing reliance on the collective organization of racially defined groups, a heightened awareness of racial identity, and a more intense hostility. Politically, it is a process by which the organized power of the subject racial group exacts the right to equal participation. The right to participate may be expressed at an individual level through such means, for example, as universal adult franchise, the distribution of power between the different groups guaranteeing individual participation in representative government; or participation may rest on some communal or consociational basis. But before turning to these processes of change, I must define the main characteristics of white settler societies and describe some of the mechanisms that sustain them.

I

The term "white settler society" places the major emphasis on racial difference, on the racial identity of the dominant group, and on the permanence of its settlement. In fact, racial difference (or the imputation of racial difference) is not a prerequisite to the establishment of plural societies, nor are plural societies the exclusive creation of white settlers. Conditions of social cleavage, cultural diversity, and ethnic hostility may be found where the plural sections are of the same race (as in Cyprus) or where the dominant minority is of other than the white race, as in the black settler societies of Liberia and, until recently, of Rwanda.[2] M. G. Smith, in "Pluralism in Precolonial African Societies," offers much evidence to support his conclusion that "mere identities or differences of race have no uniform implications for the modes of consociation in such mixed societies."

Clearly, racial difference has no intrinsic significance. The social consequences derive from the associated cultural meanings and not from the fact of racial difference. There are no doubt unique features in the white settler societies of Africa, but their source is to be found in the conditions of European colonization, in the political philosophies or ideologies of the colonial powers, and in the manner in which structural use was made of racial identity in the constitution and government of colonial and white settler societies. It is by reason of cultural emphasis and structural elaboration that racial difference now appears to assume independent significance as a major determinant of social relations in white settler societies.

Permanent settlement is, of course, a crucial aspect of white settler societies. Maunier[3] distinguishes between colonies for exploitation, where climate does not permit permanent European settlements, and habitable colonies whose temperate sky is favorable to a European population. A more useful criterion is the intensity of settlement, to which he also refers. In terms of intensity of settlement, we may distinguish colonies of exploitation with a sprinkling of relatively transient administrators, traders, missionaries, and so on, from settler societies with an appreciable settler population.

It is difficult, however, to define what constitutes an appreciable settler population, and perhaps not useful to make the attempt. On the one hand, absolute numbers are relevant.[4] Thus, in Kenya, there were scarcely enough white settlers to sustain claims for dominion status on the South African model, though no doubt the presence of many Indian settlers contributed to the frustration of their ambitions. On the other hand, relative numbers are important, relative, that is to say, to such factors as size of indigenous population, mode of production, level of economic development, and means of control and of warfare. Mercier refers to the appearance of racial competition as indicating that the European group has reached a numerical threshold beyond which opposition to the African group will rapidly become more and more violent.[5] Perhaps this numerical threshold might serve to distinguish white settler societies from societies with white settlers.

In any event, however this problem of definition is resolved, it seems clear that settler numbers have significant consequences for the structure of the societies they dominate. Large numbers are likely to be associated with greater economic development, diversification of occupational and class structure, increasing competition between members of different plural sections, the aggressive protection and promotion by settlers of their many vested interests, and extensive occasion for interpersonal contacts and relations. Very small numbers may effect little penetration of the society and constitute an almost irrelevant superstructure.

Settlement implies the expropriation or other acquisition of land from the indigenous population, or at any rate the enclosure of land by the settlers. One thinks immediately of the Southern Rhodesian Land Apportionment Act of 1931, which reserved less than half the colony's land for Africans and declared a roughly equal area open to European settlement; [6] the reduction of African landholdings in South Africa to 12 percent of the total area, or 13.7 percent if the Native Land and Trust Act of 1936 is fully implemented; [7] the reservation for European settlement of the fine agricultural lands in the White Highlands of Kenya; [8] the large holdings of good land by French settlers in Algeria in contrast with the meager holdings and the many landless peasants of the Muslim population; [9] or, to cite a parallel from Arab colonization, the acquisition by Arab settlers on Zanzibar Island (in contrast with Pemba Island) of practically all the arable soil, African settlement being confined to remote areas of poor agricultural land.[10]

It is in relation to land that dialectical opposition between native and settler populations is particularly marked. As a direct consequence of white settlement, local peasants are more narrowly confined in their areas, and subjected to a continuously increasing pressure of population on land. The affluence of the white farmlands and the abundance of their produce stand in sharp contrast to the erosion and infertility of the peasant holdings. It must seem to the peasants that settler wealth is the cause of their own poverty. If peasants are indeed the only revolutionary class in colonial countries, as Fanon asserts,[11] then presumably they are conditioned by this dialectical relationship with the settlers and by their isolation from the interdependence of industrial and urban life.

Constitutional status is certainly relevant to the characterization of white settler societies. In "The Colonial Situation in Southern Africa," Hilda Kuper follows Moreira in defining the colonial situation broadly as arising "whenever one and the same territory is inhabited by ethnic groups of different civilizations, the political power being usually exercised entirely by one group under the sign of superiority, and of the restraining influence of its own particular civilization." [12] Accordingly, she uses the word "colony" for the genus and distinguishes within it "countries where white settlers monopolize power (the Republic and Southern Rhodesia), countries under authoritarian metropolitan control (the Portuguese provinces), countries in which white settlers act on advisory bodies and are jockeying for greater power (Swaziland), and countries where whites have been more restricted in their ownership of land and where metropolitan control is modified by recognition of African interests (Basutoland and Bechuanaland)." This broad approach emphasizes what is common to situations of white domination, while insistence on independent status as a criterion of white settler societies would limit the applicability of the term in Africa to the single case of South African society.

At the same time, independent status is a significant variable with extensive consequences for the political structure of the society and its processes of political change. Both colonial (dependent) societies and white settler (independent) societies may be described as political societies by reason of the very great dominance of the political over other institutions. Perhaps it would be more precise to describe them as characterized by statism, in the sense that the state is dominant in all (or most) sectors of the society.[13] They are in fact constituted by their political institutions and to an appreciable extent they are held together by political regulation. Moreover, the close association between political institutions and settler interests stimulates the settlers to a more intense political involvement in the independent societies. This is true also in the dependent societies as settlers strive for independent status and exercise appreciable de facto political control. In the dependent societies, however, the political institutions are an extension of the political institutions of the metropolitan power and derive their strength from this source; outside of self-governing colonies, there is less need for internal elaboration of political institutions. By contrast, in the independent society there is extensive elaboration of the political institutions which sustain settler domination and regulate a great diversity of plural structures and relationships in the interests of that domination. The independent settler society is heavily weighted with political structures generating abundant political process and power.

It is particularly in times of political change that the presence or absence of a colonial power is likely to be a crucial factor. Where there is conflict between white settlers and the indigenous population in a dependent society, the colonial power may add to the destruction by engaging its own military forces in the struggle, as in Algeria, but it may also act in some measure as a mediating third party, as attempted recently in Southern Rhodesia. In independent white settler societies the lack of this mediating role of a third party may increase the probability of civil war and the intensity of exposure to the conflicts of the cold war.[14] Since I attach so much significance to constitutional status, I will

define white settler societies in a pure sense as characterized by independent status; but since I do not wish to be confined to the single case
of South Africa on the African continent, I will include in the concept,
though in a marginal way and for purposes of analysis, colonial societies
with "appreciable" white settler populations.

White settler societies are further characterized by extreme cultural
pluralism. In contrast with racial pluralism, cultural pluralism has intrinsic significance in the sense that objective consequences flow from the
fact of cultural difference, regardless of the meanings attached by the
actors. At the same time, these meanings are of great social significance.
They are particularly responsive to changes in the structure of power, as
can be seen in African movements from denigration of traditional culture
to apotheosis of African personality; and they have played an important
ideological role in the political struggles of white settlers. We need to
separate the ideological uses of cultural pluralism from its necessary
consequences.

Interpretations of cultural difference have been quite central in the
philosophies and ideologies of colonization. They sustained the belief in
the civilizing mission of the colonial powers, who saw themselves as
carriers of the higher values of white civilization to the culturally inferior
peoples of Africa, and therefore as justified in exercising domination.
They entered into the conception of mandated territories and of trusteeship over subject peoples. They influenced theoretical differences between the French policy of assimilation, with its overriding emphasis on
French culture, and the British policy of differentiation, with its greater
recognition of traditional African cultures.[15] They provided the rationale
in white settler societies for a qualified franchise under such formulas as
the vote to all civilized persons, or for total exclusion from democratic
rights, on the ground of incompatibility between democratic process and
cultural heterogeneity.[16] Indeed, the rationalizations of cultural differences extend over the whole field of social relations: in labor relations, to
justify taxation or low wages under a civilized labor policy or forced
labor;[17] in commerce, to restrict competition and to control and
expropriate;[18] in residence, to segregate, to discriminate in provision of
amenity, and to exclude from desirable localities; in religion, to segregate
and to discriminate in ministerial stipends and ecclesiastical amenity;
and so on, ad infinitum.

This pervasive ideological use, however, in no way affects the validity
of inquiry into the necessary consequences of cultural pluralism, though
it is difficult to isolate these consequences or even to specify accurately
the nature of the cultural differences. Social scientists have often equated
the cultural differences in Africa with evolutionary models, again an

ideological intrusion, European cultures being represented by the evolved forms of *gesellschaft* and African cultures by the more primary forms of *gemeinschaft*. This comparison, while misleading in many ways,[19] correctly emphasizes the significant aspect of differences in institutional specialization as characteristic, for the most part, of the contact between European and African societies. Balandier, in his analysis of the colonial situation, draws attention to the contrast between "a rapid-pace, mechanized, Christian culture with a powerful economy imposed on slow-moving and radically non-Christian cultures devoid of complex technology, and with a backward economy."[20] The contrasts can readily be elaborated further. They refer, however, to a system level of analysis, the unit being the cultural system or the institution, and it is important to relate this mode of analysis to the social situation in which contact takes place, as Balandier emphasizes.[21]

On the ground, as it were, and in the context of individuals relating to one another, the cultural incompatibilities may seem very different. Granted that individuals are representative of their cultures, they may practice very selected aspects. The mode of life of the Trekboers in South Africa was more like that of the pastoral Bantu peoples they met than one would suppose from analysis of their respective cultural systems. Moreover, individuals may have a relatively flexible approach to diversity of cultures. To some extent, they may shuttle between cultural sections or they may adopt many elements of a strange culture as a whole, as in mission stations where Africans acquired within a single generation a European language, Christianity, monogamy, Western education, brick homes, a professional occupation, and new forms of community life. At one level there is contact between cultural systems as affected by institutional incompatibility, reciprocal modification, and the growth of new institutions. At another level there are the varied reactions of individuals, conservative or eclectic or mobile, and the redistribution of populations in some measure between cultures, by processes of individuation. In any analysis of cultural pluralism it is necessary to relate these different manifestations.

Cultural pluralism in white settler societies is associated with differential incorporation, to use the term by which M. G. Smith distinguishes interethnic accommodations in plural societies (in "Pluralism in Precolonial African Societies," above). He describes this as obtaining when the structure of the inclusive collectivity prescribes differences in the modes of articulation of particular corporate components. It is quite characteristic of both white settler and colonial domination that there should be a movement of other groups into the societies, by slavery or indenture or free migration. Hence the component sections often include groups other than white settlers and African peoples as, for example, Indians in Kenya or South Africa; and to these must be added sections of mixed parentage. Corresponding to the overriding dominance of political institutions, the mode of differential hierarchical incorporation is essentially political, and the elaboration of differentiation in other structures rests ultimately on political controls. Some groups may be so loosely related to the main structure that they can best be described as inarticulated.

Between the component sections, and related to their differential incorporation, there are social cleavages or discontinuities; and these I select as a final characteristic of white settler societies. I have commented on them in a paper entitled "Structural Discontinuities in African Towns: Some Aspects of Racial Pluralism." In particular, I emphasize extreme social distance arising from the convergence of many sources of power in the dominant group; race as a primary basis for stratification, pervading the general structure of the society and all special differentiated structures; and the interaction between the general and special systems of stratification as a further source of extreme social distance, expressed in discontinuities in the wage and employment structure of industry, in stipends and amenity in religion, and in extensive segregation of social relationships. Nevertheless, there are social continuities in white settler societies and many social relationships that cross racial boundaries. They are less marked, however, than continuities of culture, which easily diffuses between groups. In effect, racial, cultural, and social pluralisms have different boundaries, and this nonalignment is a major source of tension in white settler societies.

II

If I ask what sustains systems of white settler domination, the plain answer seems to be that in Africa they are not sustained. Outside of Algeria and South Africa, there were too few white settlers, either absolutely or relatively, to constitute an effective force. Among the former British territories in Africa, the only independent state with a substantial white settler population (more than 3 million in a population of over 16 million) is South Africa. In Southern Rhodesia, at the end of World War II, there were 82,386 whites, in Northern Rhodesia/Zambia 21,907, and in Kenya 24,900; by 1960 these populations had grown to some 223,000 in Southern Rhodesia, 76,000 in Northern Rhodesia/Zambia, and 67,700 in Kenya.[22] That is to say, at the beginning of an era of decolonization and militant African nationalism, the white settlers of these countries were about numerous enough to people small country towns, and in the period of constitutional change, many of them were in fact recent migrants. The decisive roles in the political transformation of the British colonies to independent African states were those of the metropolitan power and of African political movements. I assume this will be true also for Southern Rhodesia, and that the attempt to achieve and maintain independence under white settler domination will prove abortive. In the Portuguese territories of Angola and Mozambique, the domination of the small white settler populations [23] seems equally tenuous; in the postwar period, metropolitan power is no guarantee of white settler domination. Independence under settler rule appears to be a necessary, if not sufficient, condition for the persistence of white settler societies.

South Africa is the only example of a relatively enduring white settler society in the British (and Dutch) colonial world. To some extent, we may view South African society, for purposes of analysis, as representing a point in a process of change through initial occupation, followed by intensive settlement and exploitation, to constitutional independence and the development of a seemingly petrified structure of white domination. There were many similarities, for example, in race relations in colonial Kenya, Southern Rhodesia, and South Africa. The diffusion of patterns of white settler domination between the territories, particularly between South Africa and Southern Rhodesia, contributed to these similarities, but they were mainly a consequence of the structure of the situation. This becomes clear from any comparison of white settlers in territories formerly under English dominion with those under French. Though accounts are given in very general terms and may not deal with significant differences in detail, there are many obvious correspondences in white settler structures, attitudes, and relationships as they emerge in, say, Mercier's account of Dakar,[24] or Bourdieu's discussion of Algeria,[25] or studies of English and Dutch settlers in the south. At the same time, care is needed in analyzing these different settler situations as if they constituted a series. South African settlers had attained independence many years before the growth of strong African nationalist movements, and the difference in constitutional status is quite fundamental.

There is no mystery about the means by which white settlers in South Africa have maintained their domination. They have a preponderance of strength and a monopoly of political power which they have used to build a system of domination resting on the manipulation of social cleavages and cultural diversity. But before examining this system, I want to comment briefly on relations within the white group itself: that is, between the Afrikaans- and English-speaking sections in South Africa.

These sections were of very different culture. Leonard Thompson describes the Afrikaner and British sections as two successive fragments from preindustrial and industrial societies, respectively, and shows how the Afrikaner fragment suffered a cultural mutation in its isolation from Western thought while the British, though adapting to South Africa, remained loyal also to Great Britain and its culture.[26] Whether the institutions of these two fragments were absolutely incompatible in any objective sense, I do not know. Certainly, many members of both groups saw themselves as representatives of widely different cultural traditions and indeed of different racial stocks, and there was much mutual repugnance and disdain, and much contempt for, and humiliation of, the Afrikaners by the English. Their different roles in the development of South Africa added to these contrasts and antagonisms. The Afrikaners remained embedded in farming and large sections became greatly impoverished, while the English pioneered in industry and commerce, and prospered.

From this, marked structural discontinuities resulted between English and Afrikaner in most aspects of life, whether measured by distributions between town and country, or in the ecology of the towns, or in income or occupational structure, or by education or prestige. But the discontinuities were not absolute in the sense of excluding individual mobility or social community between the groups, and there were always sections that intermingled, acculturated, and intermarried. Moreover, there was no differential incorporation in the constitutional domain, the Act of Union providing common political institutions for whites.

Political party divisions were primarily between parties of exclusive Afrikaner nationalism, asserting a divisive pluralism of conflict within the white group, and parties of English and Afrikaner integration; but lines of political cleavage have never coincided precisely with ethnic differences. In a very real sense, Afrikaners constitute the political class in the Union (now Republic) of South Africa, and throughout its history they have provided leaders and rank-and-file support for both government and opposition, for exclusive Afrikaner nationalism as well as for white integration.

Now one would probably have predicted a general trend of increasing support for the party of white integration, and a progressive merger of English and Afrikaner by a process of individual mobility. Certainly there were continuing differences in class structure between them, expressed in new forms as large numbers of Afrikaners entered the lower levels of urban employment in competition with African workers; and these differences provided a social basis for distinctive ethnic and racial policies. But on the other hand, there were many circumstances to encourage integration. There were common political institutions affording effective means for evolutionary political change. There was rapid industrialization of the country and opportunity for occupational mobility. There was urbanization, an increasing mutual acculturation, a rising standard of education, and a narrowing of the discontinuities between English and Afrikaner.

On balance, there seems to have been a conjunction of circumstances favorable to integration. This is, of course, difficult to assess with confidence. In any event, it was precisely at this stage that the plural divisions between English and Afrikaner, and the collective principle of ethnic organization, were vigorously reasserted in the systematic fostering by many Afrikaners of social cleavage and cultural diversity, and in the establishment of a wide range of parallel ethnic organizations. For more than two decades, from the celebration in 1936 of the centenary of the Great Trek, Afrikaner nationalism fostered a passionate ethnic sentiment of ingroup idolatry and of outgroup rejection. Relations between English and Afrikaners became fiercely hostile, though always mitigated by many counterpressures of persisting interethnic association and loyalty. In the period immediately prior to and during the early years of World War II, the organization of storm troopers among Afrikaners and the general mood of Afrikaner nationalism threatened a violent resolution of conflict. Indeed, the threat of violence between sections of English and Afrikaners finally abated only in 1961, when South Africa became a republic under Afrikaner hegemony.

Whether English and Afrikaner now draw together, it is difficult to say. Certainly, the English accommodate to Afrikaner power and become increasingly committed to the Afrikaner political ideology of apartheid. There appears to be a growing measure of white integration, reflected in political beliefs, the acknowledgment of Afrikaner prestige, and the continuous restratification of Afrikaners into entrepreneurial and managerial positions. But no precise answer is possible without detailed research to determine whether impressions of integration are well grounded and whether integration extends to a wide range of situations. There may be increasing identification in the public domain giving rise to what outside observers like to describe as the monolithic structure of white domination, while cleavage nevertheless persists in the private domain. At the level of English-Afrikaner relations, there may be a continuing and perhaps intense hostility, but at the level of African-European relationships, there may be a relatively high unity of purpose and effort between English and Afrikaners. If, however, the two groups are indeed progressively integrating at the present time, then the process has been a strange dialectic between increasing fission and growing fusion. No doubt, a common life situation in relation to nonwhites served to restrain too great a polarization between the white sections (though this hardly seemed to be true in the 1930's and 1940's), and common political institutions provided the means for substantial change in the structure of power and of interethnic accommodation, with little violence.

By contrast, there never were effective common political institutions for white and nonwhite. The qualified franchise exercised by Africans and Coloreds in the Cape Colony was not without political significance and might have been a means for evolutionary change to a democratic society by a process of individual mobility. But though retained in the Union constitution, the Cape franchise was not extended to the country as a whole. In consequence, it immediately declined in political significance for evolutionary change. After having been exercised for many years and after protracted political struggle, the franchise was finally rendered totally ineffective when constitutional guarantees proved inadequate to prevent its abolition for the African, and its emasculation for the Colored. In effect, at the level of the constitution or of the public domain, nonwhite affairs were moved from politics to administration.

Nonwhites are now increasingly governed by state departments of African, Colored, and Indian affairs which insulate them from direct political involvement. They are separated by this system of separate incorporation, which in fact relates them in different ways to the total society. For Africans, there are further systems, both of separate incorporation as ethnic subgroups under Bantu authorities or in Bantustans, and of differential incorporation, in urban areas, white rural areas, and African ethnic areas. In urban areas, the mode of incorporation of Africans into industry may perhaps be likened to the compulsory enrollment of Lozwi into the age-regiments of their Ndebele conquerors, accompanied by political and social inequality and proscription of intermarriage.[27] In the white rural areas, though the position of African farm workers cannot be described as serfdom, there are bonds to land and master, and the system is perhaps not so remote from the domination of the Tutsi over the Hutu in Rwanda. In the African ethnic areas, Africans are incorporated as collective units, under collective domination through appointed representatives, in contrast with the many personal structures of authority on white farms and in urban areas; the system is perhaps comparable to the domination by Tswana over peoples defeated in war.[28] If there is a close relationship between cohesion and mode of incorporation, then Africans must indeed be greatly fragmented.

The history of the South African franchise, including as it does some manipulation of the African franchise even in the days of the Cape Colony, is often taken as proof of the illusory nature of a qualified franchise in white settler societies, and of the impossibility of evolutionary change by this means. This conclusion, though very plausible, nevertheless goes beyond the evidence. It must be qualified by reference to the special conditions of the South African franchise: that it was not fully institutionalized in South African society and that the constitutional guarantees for its circumscribed role were not backed by effective power, presumably the organized power of Africans and Coloreds.

Indeed, if there had been a more adequate franchise, albeit qualified, and if Africans and Coloreds had been more politically organized, the changes taking place within South African society and promoting new interracial structures might well have contributed to democratic growth by evolutionary means. I refer to (1) the extensive industrialization of the country, continuously drawing population into the towns and into a common exchange economy, until almost one-third of the African population is urbanized; (2) the increasing economic interdependence of the races and the increasing dependence on nonwhite labor, which constitutes the great majority of the industrial labor force; (3) the emergence of a small but growing class of African professionals, university graduates, and businessmen; (4) the affiliation of a majority of the total population to common religious denominations; and (5) the growing practice by large numbers of all races of many elements of a common culture. The potential significance of these changes for individual mobility and racial integration may be measured by the large number of laws passed since 1948 which seek to prevent the evolution of a common society by the counterassertion of the collective principle of racial or ethnic identity as the basis of all social organization and the determinant of life chances.

Abolition of the African franchise effectively removed a common institution by which individual mobility might have contributed to collective restratification on a nonracial basis. It established an absolute monopoly of power and raised the collective principle of organization as a barrier to individual mobility across racial lines. Through control of the public domain, separation is now systematically imposed not only on racial contacts in public life, but on almost all contacts in the private domain accessible to regulation. By the same means, the government seeks to maintain structural discontinuities through regulation of the system of stratification, attempting to ensure that in no circumstances should nonwhites exercise authority over whites, providing for wide discrepancies in wage levels and life chances, and generally reinforcing structural separation by pervasive racial discrimination. So too, through control of the public domain, and under conditions in which the populations were continuously moving toward greater cultural uniformity, the government seeks to re-create cultural diversity. For this purpose, it relies on segregation of racial and ethnic groups, on local and regional racial and ethnic organization, and above all on a plural system of education to foster ethnocentric sentiment and cultural diversity. Its policy is to fragment nonwhite groups and to align social cleavage and cultural pluralism in a self-sustaining system. But the system is far from self-sustaining; on the contrary, it is increasingly sustained by force and repression.

The result is seemingly paradoxical. As the races grow more and more interdependent in the urban and industrial economy, and as increasing contact offers greater opportunity for association, in almost the same measure, the government passes and implements laws against interracial association and enforces separation in an ever-extending range of relationships. But the paradox is only a seeming one. There is too much interdependence to sustain the threat of severance or divisive conflict. In fact, apartheid restructures the society by an elaboration of intercalary institutions and structures, which bind together, as with hoops of steel, the units-in-separation.[29] Whether the process is likely to be a continuous and increasing binding together until the groups suddenly explode in violence, a revolution through integration, or whether this binding together may generate more gradual processes of change, I do not know.

III

I now return to the main problem and inquire what processes might contribute to a relatively peaceful democratization of white settler society, as I have sketched it—*in extremis,* as it were. I examine first the individuating processes, such as acquisition of the culture of the dominant group by members of the subordinate group or mutual acculturation of individuals of different race, and association between them across racial divisions, creating new interracial structures in the economic, political, religious, educational, and recreational spheres. These are the individuating interracial processes by which sharp distinctiveness between groups becomes blurred, initially at the margins and later more pervasively: lines of structural cleavage and cultural pluralism increasingly diverge; individual status and group status no longer precisely coincide; and interracial solidarities begin to modify and fragment the initial racial solidarities. These are the processes by which roles become diversified; and individuals are released from their original collective affiliation in certain of their roles and affiliate with members of other collectivities. These are the processes that liberals value in the belief that men may transcend the material and group conditions of their lives and that their actions are not simply functions of their social situations. These are the processes valued also by many churchmen, concerned as they are with individual salvation and change of heart. And I should add that these are the individuating processes so contemptuously dismissed as of negligible significance for change in white settler societies by such a weight of authoritative opinion, and with such a weight of seemingly supportive evidence, that it is almost embarrassing to mention them. Yet naïveté is perhaps as valid a basis for inquiry as the absolute conviction of certainty; and it is all the more necessary to raise questions about convictions of this type, since they may have grave consequences for the probability of violence in plural societies, actually contributing to the events they predict, and thereby demonstrating, not the inevitability of violence or the necessity for it, but quite the contrary, that men have a capacity for self-determination.

Revolutionary leaders often portray the society in terms of an absolute polarity between white settlers and native peoples. They describe the groups as virtually two orders of humanity ranged in absolute dialectical opposition; between the collective destiny of the oppressed and the unyielding collective domination of the oppressors, they find no middle ground for individuating interracial processes; and they see evolutionary change as an illusory device for more complete, if less blatant, servitude.[30] These descriptions may have some validity, but their function is not to contribute toward academic discourse and analysis. They are ideologies, like Marxist ideologies of the polarization of society into bourgeoisie and proletariat, and they create or seek to create in the future that which they portray as immediately present. The relevance of these revolutionary ideologies for my argument lies, not in their characterizations of white settler society, but in the fact that their emergence counteracts the individuating processes, which indeed become a special target for attack.

The scholarly argument for denying significance to association and cultural assimilation of individuals of different race rests on conceptions of the structure of white settler society, and on assumptions about human nature and group nature in general, or white settler nature in particular. As to the structure, two aspects are stressed: first, the relation between collective categorization or organization and interpersonal interaction, and second, the relation between the type of change, such as assimilation of culture or occupational mobility, and the basic principle of differential incorporation, such as racial or ethnic identity. Some references to the literature will clarify the argument. M. G. Smith in an earlier paper writes that cultural uniformities, or intersectional personal association, cannot directly erode or transform the corporate structures for the reason that sectional divisions and relations are based on other principles, such as race or exclusive corporate solidarity; in a plural regime, he argues, individual qualities are irrelevant for the determination of social identity, which is ascriptive and corporate in base and significance.[31] So too, Pierre Bourdieu in *The Algerians* stresses the structural aspects when he comments that the colonial situation is the context in which all actions must be judged, and that in this context it would appear that even the most generous actions, including harmonious interpersonal relations between individuals of different groups, have harmful consequences.[32]

Herbert Blumer is presumably arguing to much the same effect when he concludes that industrialization, far from changing the patterns of racial discrimination prevalent in the society, actually adapts to them, nestling inside the established order, and that political pressures and change are necessary to transform racial discrimination in industry.[33] At a somewhat different level and in a different context, Ezekiel Mphahlele proceeds from similar assumptions when he declares that the Church in South Africa, "with its emphasis on the value of the individual personality, has continued stubbornly to bring outmoded standards to the situation; a situation where a powerful *herrenvolk* has for three centuries done everything in the interests of the *volk*. Where persons have been oppressed as a race group, the Church has sought safeguards and concessions for the individual, evading the necessity and responsibility of group action." [34]

The argument that the structure of the situation divests the individuating processes of significance for evolutionary change needs to be supplemented. It is not logically complete in itself; it does not explain why these individuating processes cannot result in action to restructure the situation. It is at this level that the argument may be supplemented by assumptions as to the nature of man and of human groups. Perhaps I can make some of these assumptions explicit. To explain the motivation of man, I shall take a quotation from Michels' discussion of leaders: "The consciousness of power always produces vanity, and undue belief in personal greatness. The desire to dominate, for good or for evil, is universal. These are elementary psychological facts." [35] For explanation of the nature of human groups, I shall turn to the Austrian sociologist Ludwig Gumplowicz, who viewed the state as characterized by the domination of one social group over another and by the incessant struggle for power between social groups: "In its political actions each social group is a perfect unit. It opposes other social groups in behalf of its own interest solely and knows no standard of conduct but success. The struggle between social groups, the component parts of the State, is as inexorable as that between hordes or States. The only motive is self-interest." Moreover, since each social group in its political actions is a perfect unit, the individual is again without significance: "Though there are always individuals who deviate first one way and then the other, they, like meteoric stones which are loosened from their orbit and fly off in all directions, are abnormal, and do not influence the behavior of the group as a whole." [36]

Perhaps most social scientists would deny the universality of these motivations to power and strife. Some may accept them only as characteristic of societies other than their own, or more particularly of white settler groups. They may discern, as does Mannoni,[37] a specific settler mentality, a "Prospero complex" of pride, neurotic impatience, and the desire to dominate, deriving only in part from the colonial situation itself. Or they may derive the settler qualities from the social situation, from the nature of interracial interaction within the society, and from the mutual incitement of prejudice and discrimination,[38] and find the psychological roots predominantly in structural determinants. Pierre Bourdieu, for example, argues that the rationale of the colonial system renders conversion of the dominant group impossible:

The destruction of the colonial system cannot be the result of a conversion of minds which would induce the members of the dominant society solemnly and collectively to give up the privileges they hold in order, by a conscious choice, to "integrate themselves" willingly into the dominated caste or to "integrate it" into their caste, which would mean the same thing if we ascribe to the words their full meaning. This conversion can only be the act of a few "traitors to their caste." The whole rationale of the colonial system tends, on the contrary, to make this sort of collective suicide impossible.[39]

But whatever the derivation of the social and psychological attributes, they are seen as a reinforcement to the collective barriers against the individuating processes of change.

My comments on these theories can only be impressionistic. I see the individuating processes as potentially significant in bridging the plural divisions. It is for this reason that they are often denounced in white settler societies. They create new interracial structures and solidarities and they undermine the sense of color, of racial exclusiveness, on which domination depends. Now, by significance I do not mean to imply that the individuating processes in and of themselves can resolve racial pluralism in white settler societies. It is not enough that the original racial cleavages should be overlaid with numerous interracial relationships and functional differentiations. Though the new relationships effect continuous change in the structure of the society in many different spheres, these changes must still be transposed to the collective or public domain. This follows from the mode of differential incorporation of the ethnic and racial groups. Where ethnic differentiation is purely de facto, it is presumably directly transformed by a de facto coming together. But in white settler societies there is de jure incorporation of racial and ethnic differentiation in the constitution of the state, and in its elaborate, centralized, political and administrative structures. If the individuating processes are to contribute effectively to the transformation of divisive pluralism, then they must act directly on the central political system. And it is precisely at this level that the obstacles are most formidable, since the central political system is the basis of settler domination. Certainly, Marx's concept of the state as the executive of the ruling class exactly describes its role in independent white settler societies.

Characteristically, the franchise becomes the battleground, as settlers seek to exclude other groups from its exercise. Of Algeria, Barbour writes that "in 1936, the proposed Blum-Violette reforms which would have given French citizenship to 30,000 Muslims were brought to nought by the resignation of the Algerian Mayors; meanwhile the project had, it seems, raised real enthusiasm among the Muslims for acquiring French citizenship. Its rejection was the final death-blow to assimilation." He comments that the Statute of 1947, providing *inter alia* for the creation of an Algerian assembly, did offer hope of a peaceful solution, but was never sincerely or completely applied, the elections of 1948 being "managed" by the administration with the apparent intention of excluding "extremists," while other provisions remained a dead letter, in consequence of which "the Muslims rebelled in desperation." [40] In Rhodesia, the elaborate complexities of the constitution and the unilateral declaration of independence from the metropolitan power reduce to the simple formula of a white settler struggle to control electoral and legislative power. In South Africa, opposition by the northern provinces limited the nonwhite franchise from the very inception of union, and thus prepared the way for its virtual abolition. But it is important to note that much of the struggle over the franchise in South Africa was between different sections of the white electorate, which at no time formed a "perfect unit"; and it is interesting to speculate what the course of race relations might have been if Afrikaner-English tensions had sharpened to the point at which the English would have sought a political alliance with Africans, or if the metropolitan power had still retained the right to intervene during the recent constitutional struggles.

The difficulty goes beyond the fact that interracial solidarities must be transposed to the central political system if they are to be effective means for change in the differential incorporation of the races. Control over the political system gives the dominant group the power to maintain racial cleavages, at least initially, notwithstanding the social pressures toward "deracialization." The government responds to conditions that generate interracial solidarity by increasing the rigidity of racial differentiation in the political sphere, and it opposes the individuating processes in other spheres by reasserting the collective principle of racial identity, in the extreme case through systematic legislation and penal sanctions.

The dialectic between the individuating interracial processes and the collective racial processes is clearly charted in the many South African apartheid laws that seek to reverse trends toward nonracial integration. This is of special interest because South Africa is the most highly industrialized of the African territories, and it is often assumed that industrialization will encourage change toward democracy. It raises the standard of living of white settlers and provides them with more abundant and secure opportunity for rewarding employment. This greater prosperity for whites does not entail deeper misery for nonwhites, since the relationship of the races in the industrial process is not dialectical. Nonwhites also advance in living standards, albeit unequally, and begin to move to higher occupational levels, thus reducing the discontinuity in white and nonwhite occupational structures and providing some basis for shared interests, transcending race. These are changes that might perhaps be viewed as conducive to a diminution in racial extremism.

At the same time, industrialization heightens the competition between the races. The South African government's policy of racial job reservation is evidence of the competitive pressure caused by the increasing movement of nonwhites into occupations calling for higher levels of skill, not only manual but also entrepreneurial and professional. This competitive pressure may be expected to grow with continued industrialization. Now it is experienced in a situation in which white settlers control the political system. If the white sector of employment in the economic system is abstracted and represented as a hierarchical structure, I assume that it will be broadly based, comprising that majority of white settlers which follows manual, minor clerical, and administrative occupations or engages in small retail trade. It is this majority that feels the increasing pressure of nonwhite competition and the need for protective racist policies. But since white working class and petite bourgeoisie constitute a powerful force in the political system, including a majority of voters, they are certain to attract political leaders and supporters from other strata to their racist ideologies, which in any event have a wide independent appeal.

This then is the basis for the dynamic movement in South Africa toward more extreme racism. As the economic process generates competitive pressures, so counteracting political processes are released in an attempt to restore equilibrium by increasing the racial repression of the system.[41] As I see the position in South Africa, industrialization gives rise to tension between the political and economic systems, and this tension is resolved by an increasingly rigid emphasis on racial differentiation.

These may well be only the early consequences of industrialization, and continued industrial growth may release democratizing tendencies, but the extensive discrimination against Negroes in the highly industrialized society of the United States should temper too easy an optimism.

Given white settler domination with independent status and the numerical predominance of Africans, the system of parliamentary representative government seems highly resistant to democratization and calculated to inflame ethnic and racial antagonism. There may be more flexibility and a greater potential for evolutionary change in structures of domination based on tributary relations or on serfdom.

At this stage, the introduction of a qualified franchise in South Africa would hardly resolve any of the major conflicts in the society. It might serve to incorporate more fully a small section of nonwhite bourgeoisie, but it would not effect a redistribution of land or of wealth and the masses would continue in their exclusion and impoverishment. Yet, even the reintroduction of a political mechanism, quite traditional in the constitutional history of South Africa, would constitute revolutionary change. There is a fundamental difference between the structures of the economic and political systems. The economic system, under the process of industrialization, tends increasingly toward continuity in structure. The political system, on the other hand, is quite discontinuous, in the sense that it consists of two absolutely distinct orders: there are white voters who are subjects of political and administrative action, and, with token exceptions, nonwhite nonvoters who are objects of political and administrative action. Change in the economic sector can proceed gradually, almost imperceptibly. Political change in the principle of racial exclusion, even if it should take the seemingly evolutionary form of progressive admission to the franchise, would constitute revolutionary change, more particularly since many white settlers would immediately project the qualified franchise, and the demographic ratio of the races, into a plural society under African domination, and no doubt many African political leaders would do the same. The parliamentary system in racially divided societies is calculated to intensify the politics of race.

There is the same disjunction between the individuating processes of structural change and the political processes; indeed, the relations between economic and political change, discussed above, are a particular expression of this disjunction. Under present constitutional arrangements, it is difficult to discern a political basis for action which might relate the individuating processes to constitutional change. Political parties based on white voters with nonwhite participation are not in themselves likely to be effective agents of political change, though they may contribute support. Political parties of nonwhites with some participation by white voters may be more effective, but they are, of course, pro-scribed. It would seem that only large-scale movements of racial collectiv-ities could offer the possibility of mustering sufficient power to change the conditions of political incorporation. Nonwhite collective action rest-ing on the unity of the oppressed is improbable because the oppressed are not united, and such minority groups as Indians and to a lesser extent Coloreds are as vulnerable to the power of Africans as to the power of whites.

In these circumstances, it is inevitable that there should develop, in response to exclusive Afrikaner nationalism, a movement of exclusive African nationalism. This may hold some promise for a more democratic interracial accommodation, though initially sharpening the racial con-flict; but Africans are so fragmented by their different life situations and their different modes of incorporation that they may not be able to mobilize effectively even by means of racial violence. In any event, in the absence of common political institutions, such as English and Afrikaners shared, and in the absence of a mediating third power, the direct con-frontation of organized racial groups with a long history of conflict and oppression between them seems likely to complete the transformation of South Africa into a garrison state or to precipitate holocausts of violence and destruction.

IV

My conclusions, then, are that the collective processes of racial organi-zation and confrontation may very well be ineffective; also, they increase the probability of extreme violence, whereas I am here inquiring into the possibility of a peaceful transformation of white settler societies. Of course, this puts the problem in too stark a form. It might be approached more realistically in terms of the degree of violence or in terms of policies that might diminish the violence of political change. There are likely to be most complex relations between violence and nonviolence, between revolutionary challenge and reactionary response, and between parties of racial radicalism, emphasizing the collective processes, and parties of integrative moderation, concerned with the individuating processes. Democratic changes may progressively emerge from these complex inter-actions.

Regarding the possibly liberalizing consequences of the individuating processes, a crucial difficulty lies in the discontinuity between these ongoing social processes, promoting new interracial solidarities, and a political system under racially exclusive domination, promoting repres-sive, racist counteraction. Formidable barriers insulate the political insti-tutions against liberal interracial influences. By these conclusions, I do

not mean to imply that the individuating processes are without significance, even in the racially extreme Republic of South Africa, or that the
racial groups are polarized. On the contrary, I tend to assume that the
total polarization of groups in a society is a rare phenomenon. Groups
appear to be polarized in revolutionary ideology, which sweeps aside the
mediating structures and the individuating processes. They appear to be
polarized, at times, in academic analysis, since we seem inclined toward
dualisms and dichotomies. Probably extreme polarization is most nearly
attained in the course of, and through the process of, the struggle itself.
Where the struggle has finally taken the form of racial or ethnic civil war,
in our preoccupation with the predominant and overriding forces we
tend to overlook harmonious relations that might have been the basis for
other developments. Yet these interethnic and interracial relations may
be appreciable, even in societies where there is extreme ethnic and racial
discord. I am sure that they are also appreciable and significant in South
Africa, in consequence of a long history of contact and of interaction in
schools and churches and in industry and commerce.

I have examined the individuating processes in terms of the obstacles
to their being politically effective, arising in particular from the constitutional structure of the society. It may be more constructive to approach
these processes from a different point of view and to consider the means
by which they may be rendered politically effective for change from
racial domination to democratic participation. I assumed from the outset
—and this assumption should certainly be qualified by reference to a
relatively immediate period of time—that internal social processes would
not be sufficient in and of themselves to transform the political structure
of South African society. In distinguishing processes of change in colonial and white settler societies, I emphasized the role of the metropolitan
power in the colonies and the absence of a mediating third party in the
independent white settler societies.

Now it is inconceivable in the contemporary world that third powers
should not be involved in the internal conflicts of other societies, particularly where these conflicts are between racial groups; and they are
already so involved in South African society. England and the United
States have large and growing investments in the country, and therefore
an interest in orderly processes of change. Independent African states
have declared their determination to liberate fellow Africans in South
Africa and their intention to use violence for that end. The United
Nations has denounced South African racism for almost two decades and
explores the possibility of applying sanctions. On the one hand, there is a
massive involvement of third parties opposed to racism and, on the other
hand, there are internal processes stimulating interracial association,

with increasing pressure under the influence of industrial growth. Perhaps under certain creative constitutional arrangements and in association with such a mediating power as the United Nations, acting in a role analogous to that of the metropolitan power in colonial society, the individuating interracial processes may provide a basis for relatively peaceful democratic change.

NOTES

[1] In *An African Bourgeoisie* (New Haven: Yale University Press, 1965), I analyze the increasing commitment to violence and the social pressures toward a race war in South Africa; in the preceding paper, "Conflict and the Plural Society," I have commented on some functions of ideologies of violence.

[2] See J. J. Maquet, *The Premise of Inequality in Ruanda* (London: Oxford University Press, 1961); Merran Fraenkel, *Tribe and Class in Monrovia* (London: Oxford University Press, 1964); and J. Gus Liebenow, "Liberia," in James S. Coleman and Carl G. Rosberg, Jr., eds., *Political Parties and National Integration in Tropical Africa* (Berkeley and Los Angeles: University of California Press, 1964), pp. 448–481.

[3] René Maunier, *The Sociology of Colonies*, trans. E. O. Lorimer (London: Routledge and Kegan Paul, 1949), p. 8.

[4] See Georg Simmel's discussion of absolute and relative numbers in "On the Significance of Numbers for Social Life," in Kurt H. Wolff, trans. and ed., *The Sociology of Georg Simmel* (Glencoe, Ill.: Free Press, 1950), pp. 97–98.

[5] Paul Mercier, "The European Community of Dakar," in Pierre L. van den Berghe, ed., *Africa: Social Problems of Change and Conflict* (San Francisco: Chandler Publishing Co., 1965), p. 291.

[6] Herbert J. Spiro, "The Rhodesias and Nyasaland," in Gwendolen M. Carter, ed., *Five African States* (Ithaca: Cornell University Press, 1963), p. 369. There was a small revision of this allocation of land in 1961. See Patrick Kealey, *The Politics of Partnership* (Baltimore: Penguin Books, 1963), pp. 341–342.

[7] Leonard M. Thompson, *The Republic of South Africa* (Boston: Little, Brown, 1966), p. 40.

[8] Roland Oliver and J. D. Fage comment that small proportions of the populations were affected by settlement or land concessions in areas north of the Zambezi. As to Kenya, they write that among the Kikuyu "it is likely that those directly affected constituted less than one per cent. Most of the land alienated in Kenya was taken from the pastoral tribes—the Masai, the Nandi, and the Kipsigis. All that white settlement did to the agricultural peoples was to block their natural expansion into land previously held at the spear's point by the pastoralists" (*A Short History of Africa* [Baltimore: Penguin Books, 1962], pp. 201–202).

[9] Nevill Barbour, ed., *A Survey of North West Africa (The Maghrib)* (London: Oxford University Press, 1959), pp. 217–218, 241–245. Basil Davidson writes: "The situation on the eve of the great insurrection of 1954 was that fewer than one thousand European landowners possessed about one-seventh of all cultivable land outside the barren southern regions, while more than half

a million peasant *families* had no land at all" (*Which Way Africa?* [Baltimore: Penguin Books, 1964], p. 39).

[10] Michael Lofchie, "The Plural Society in Zanzibar," below.

[11] Frantz Fanon, *The Wretched of the Earth,* trans. Constance Farrington (New York: Grove Press, 1963), p. 48.

[12] Hilda Kuper, "The Colonial Situation in Southern Africa," *Journal of Modern African Studies,* 2 (July 1964), 149–150.

[13] See the discussion of statism in colonial societies in Coleman and Rosberg, *op. cit.,* p. 662.

[14] This greater exposure to the cold war is perhaps exaggerated, since presumably the countries in whose sphere of influence the white settler society falls would immediately assert a prior right to intervene, in much the same way as the colonial power.

[15] Current scholarship increasingly shows the varied and overlapping policies and practices of these colonial powers.

[16] See my discussion of "White Ideologies," in *Passive Resistance in South Africa* (New Haven: Yale University Press, 1960).

[17] C. W. de Kiewiet, *A History of South Africa, Social and Economic* (London: Oxford University Press, 1942), chap. ix; James Duffy, *Portugal in Africa* (Baltimore: Penguin Books, 1963), pp. 131–132.

[18] See L. Kuper, H. Watts, and R. Davies, *Durban: A Study in Racial Ecology* (New York: Columbia University Press, 1958), chap. i.

[19] Leo Kuper, "Structural Discontinuities in African Towns: Some Aspects of Racial Pluralism," in H. Miner, ed., *The City in Modern Africa* (New York: Praeger, 1967).

[20] Georges Balandier, "The Colonial Situation," in van den Berghe, *op. cit.,* p. 54.

[21] *Ibid.,* pp. 46 ff.

[22] Figures are from L. H. Gann and Peter Duignan, *White Settlers in Tropical Africa* (Harmondsworth: Penguin Books, 1962), App.

[23] According to *ibid.,* pp. 168–169, there were about 160,000 white settlers in Angola in 1959, and about 80,200 in Mozambique in 1957.

[24] Paul Mercier, "Evolution of Senegalese Elites," in van den Berghe, *op. cit.,* pp. 163–178.

[25] Pierre Bourdieu, *The Algerians,* trans. Alan C. M. Ross (Boston: Beacon Press, 1962), esp. chap. 6.

[26] Leonard M. Thompson, "The South African Dilemma," in Louis Hartz, ed., *The Founding of New Societies* (New York: Harcourt, Brace and World, 1964), pp. 178–218.

[27] See M. G. Smith, "Pluralism in Precolonial African Societies," above.

[28] *Ibid.*

[29] I have analyzed a variety of structures for the maintenance and bridging of structural discontinuities in "Structural Discontinuities in African Towns." I describe intercalary structures as structures inserted, or forming, between the dominant and subordinate racial groups, which serve both to separate and to coordinate their activities.

[30] See my preceding paper in this volume, "Conflict and the Plural Society: Ideologies of Violence among Subordinate Groups."

[31] "Institutional and Political Conditions of Pluralism," above.

[32] Pp. 148–149.

[33] Herbert Blumer, "Industrialisation and Race Relations," in Guy Hunter, ed., *Industrialisation and Race Relations* (London: Oxford University Press, 1965), pp. 220–253.

[34] Quoted in Leo Kuper, *An African Bourgeoisie*, p. 207.

[35] Robert Michels, *Political Parties*, trans. Eden and Cedar Paul (New York: Collier Books, 1962), p. 206.

[36] Ludwig Gumplowicz, *Outlines of Sociology* (2d English ed.; New York: Paine-Whitman, 1963), p. 227.

[37] O. Mannoni, *Prospero and Caliban* (London: Methuen, 1956).

[38] See my paper, "The Heightening of Racial Tension," in van den Berghe, *op. cit.*, pp. 237–247.

[39] *Op. cit.*, p. 150.

[40] *Op. cit.*, pp. 222–224.

[41] See Pierre L. van den Berghe, "The Economic System and Its Dysfunctions," in his *South Africa: A Study in Conflict* (Middletown: Wesleyan University Press, 1965), pp. 183–216.

Chapter 6 Social Pluralism in French African Colonies and in States Issuing Therefrom: An Impressionistic Approach

Pierre Alexandre

This paper is an attempt to correlate France's official and legal policy about social relations in her former African colonies with the actual attitudes and behavior of those Frenchmen who were, in varying respects, supposed to put that policy into effect. Its intent is factual rather than theoretical, despite the fact that it is devoted, to a degree, to showing that, in my opinion, the concept of "plural society" is not a very convenient one, chiefly for semantic reasons. The narrower and more specific concept of "colonial situation," as introduced and defined by such writers as O. Mannoni and G. Balandier (*Psychologie de la colonisation*, 1950; *Sociologie actuelle de l'Afrique Noire*, 1955), seems to offer a more useful and fruitful approach to, and a better explanation of, the self-defeating nature of colonization or colonialism, even, or especially, enlightened colonialism.

AN OUTLINE OF GENERAL EVOLUTION

1) There is a surprising scarcity of French materials on plural societies, especially as regards the former French colonies in West Africa. In fact the phrase "plural society" is difficult to translate into French. Insofar as *société plurale* is used at all [1]—and it seldom is—it is with a rather marginal meaning, somewhat like the English term in Gann's *The Birth of a Plural Society: The Development of Northern Rhodesia under the British South Africa Company, 1894–1914*; that is, it is used to describe, with an optimistic connotation, a society patterned on the "equilibrium" model. A colony would then be, *ex definitione*, a nonplural society, the

achievement of plurality or pluralism (often qualified as "working" or "harmonious") becoming a consummation devoutly to be wished.

Pluralism, in Furnivall's, or Kuper's, or M. G. Smith's concept, was, during the colonial period, one of those unpleasant facts of life better left unmentioned as long as they lasted. In this case it was not officially intended to last, because the whole history of French politics is one of attempts toward social integration and unification. Not that those attempts have always been successful, especially in the colonies. Yet the fact remains that on the whole and despite many shortcomings and deviations, French colonial doctrines tended to nonracialism rather than to multiracialism. That also meant, if I may coin the term, monoculturalism rather than pluriculturalism, at least in theory. In point of fact, the actual necessities of colonial administration combined with those of continued economic exploitation to bring about a more or less reluctant admission of cultural diversity, which was legally embodied for the first time in the 1946 constitution. This was the constitution of the Fourth Republic, whose downfall was caused chiefly by a colonial conflict and resulted in the end of French colonial domination in Africa.

Here I am not primarily concerned with the situation in North Africa, but rather with that in Negro Africa, which is, or was, probably less typical and is certainly less documented. I shall rely on my own experience, on published literature, and on unpublished and sometimes classified administrative documents to which I had access as a former colonial administrator. It is perhaps worthwhile at this point to recall the fact that, up to the thirties, anthropology was taught only at the Colonial Service cadet school (École Coloniale, later on École Nationale de la France d'Outre-Mer, or ENFOM), and that the Institut d'Ethnologie at Sorbonne was created by the Ministère des Colonies in 1930. ENFOMS's motto was *comprendre pour aimer*, but the official view on anthropology was certainly orientated toward efficiency rather than toward love, and well expressed in the official instructions of that governor who told his district officers (I quote from memory): "You can really destroy only what you are able to replace. You shall, therefore, try to penetrate native society and understand it from the inside so as to be able to discover the *points faibles* among its institutions, such points being those on which our civilizing efforts must be brought to bear *en priorité.*" This was the period in which R. Maunier, professor of colonial sociology at the Faculté de Droit [2] in Paris, warned his students against the danger of cultural contagion from the native milieu.

There have been, in fact, many good ethnographers and some good anthropologists among French administrators.[3] In most cases, however (probably including mine), their approach was bound to remain somewhat biased by the very nature of their administrative duties, and this often led to vociferous conflicts with some of the first professional anthropologists who did fieldwork in Africa ("You are stealing my Pongo-Pongos"). In any event the rules of the Colonial Service theoretically compelled administrators to request permission from the ministry before publishing any book or article. This, not unnaturally, led most of them to concentrate on politically innocuous matters and to steer clear of delicate subjects such as race relations or the dysphoric effects of culture contact on African societies. Some resorted to fiction written under a nom de plume to voice their criticisms or just to air more candid views of their actual experiences in the field. It must be confessed that most novels of this kind were quite bad literature, but they still stand as useful sources for the sociologist,[4] more by the implications that can be drawn from them than by their factual contents.

Recent novels by African writers offer a symmetric source (through a mirror, darkly) more significant for the sociologist than for the literary critic. On the other hand, most novels written by casual visitors are like the shallow, cheap sensationalism of the popular press reports. There has been nothing in recent years on a level with Gide's *Voyage au Congo* (1928) or even Londres' *Terre d'ébène* (1929); good journalism has been more concerned with politics than with strictly sociological issues.

2) Is it necessary from the start to make a choice between the "optimistic" or consensus, and the "pessimistic" or conflict, models of plural societies? Or, in other terms, are the two models completely unreconcilable, or can they be envisaged as likely to obtain at different moments in the history of a given society?

I should say that the latter was, on the whole, the view of the French government under Republics III and IV, this kind of official philosophy being supported by arguments drawn from the history of metropolitan France. It was argued (not in these terms) that this history was that of a progression from a plural society of the conflict type to a consensual-plural and then on to a united, nonplural society. This history-book process was to be extended overseas to lead eventually to an ironing out of cultural differences within the framework of *la plus grande France*. I am not sure that this opinion is no longer held in some circles: in August 1965 a letter to the editor in *Le Monde* accused several of my colleagues (and me) of being neocolonialists trying to foster forcibly anachronistic customs and languages upon African states whose sole ambition was to assimilate French culture in the shortest possible time (this last point being partly true). Even the French Communist Party does not completely reject this picture; rather, they complete it by saying that this process of depluralization results in new cleavages along other lines, national cultures being replaced by class cultures. It is significant that the Communist Party opposed bills tending to authorize the use of African languages in primary education, in direct contradiction to the Soviet Union's policy in this field.

One must not believe that this official attitude, divorced from the facts though it may have been, was irrelevant in the context of local situations. Insofar as it was embodied in effective policy, it did have results in Africa, as can be demonstrated to some extent by a number of significant differences between today's so-called French- and English-speaking African states. It is an amusing, or, for a Frenchman, melancholy, game of political and sociological science fiction to try to imagine what could have happened had France implemented assimilation as strenuously as she proclaimed it.

Before entering into some details of the basic principles of French colonial policies, it is not amiss to mention that an all too frequent fault of the American and British political scientists writing on this subject (and most if not all good recent studies have been written by Anglo-Saxons) is an insufficient knowledge of the legal and administrative institutions in what many independent Africans persist in calling *la Métropole*. This lack of information has led many writers to consider certain practices as colonialist which, as abhorrent as they may seem to them, are considered quite ordinary and routine in France. To take but a couple of examples, we have neither habeas corpus nor a real system of local government.

The basic constitutional principle was and still is that *la République est une et indivisible*. This was at first a reaction against the provincial and communal franchises and privileges of the ancien régime, which explains why the Revolution led to a centralization of power in the capital which endures to this day. Despite his official title a French colonial governor did not govern the colony; he was only an administrator and his powers of legislation were scarcely wider than those of a prefect. Regional or district administrators had the powers of a mayor. Neither they nor the governor could enact more than bylaws, subject to a control from Paris far greater than that to which their British or even Belgian counterparts were subjected.

A corollary from this basic principle was the even more important principle of the supremacy and uniqueness of French law, considered as the formal expression of French culture or, as more usually expressed, French civilization. This was the supreme legal criterion, which, in theory, could never be set aside in case of conflict.[5] For conflicts there were bound to be, as a natural result of culture contacts brought about by the colonial expansion. Despite several well-meant attempts to ignore the local facts of life and apply French law in the colonies as in France, for the sake of education,[6] hard necessity compelled the men on the spot to take account of local cultures and institutions. This was sanctioned by colonial regulations, but it was explicitly stated that it was only on sufferance, tolerated rather than officially authorized. Even after the preamble of the 1946 constitution had expressly affirmed the rights of colonial peoples to keep and preserve those of their institutions which were not *contraires à l'ordre public et au respect de la personne humaine,* it was decided, in application of the same constitution, to make the French penal code (promulgated in 1810) applicable to all Africans without distinction of customs.

The most important consequence of this second principle was, up to 1946, the distinction between citizens and subjects. All natives did possess French nationality but most of them were not citizens; that is, they did not have full political rights even in their own country. A subject could become a citizen by giving proof that he had become acculturated into French civilization, which meant, first, that he renounced his customary status and agreed to come under secularized civil law.[7] The system was first applied in Algeria by a decree of 1870. The Jewish community acquired citizenship en bloc, talmudic courts being suppressed. A large majority of Moslems refused to renounce *sharia* and remained subjects. In Black Africa, there were many volunteers for citizenship, especially among Christian converts, but few of the applicants had the financial means to lead a *genre de vie européanisé,* all the more so since the administration was often overly severe in applying the test. The fact remains, nevertheless, that the criteria for citizenship were cultural, not racial.

This nonracial attitude was partly set aside by a 1931 decree allowing a mulatto to become a citizen by proving that one of his parents (in fact his father) was white. The courts, however, extended this privilege to the illegitimate children of West Indians living in Africa, so that a full-blooded Negro could in some cases acquire citizenship by claiming the status of a mulatto. The 1931 decree did not, anyway, turn all mulattos into citizens; it only made things easier for them, and, once they had become citizens, they were subjected to French law, which was not always to their advantage (e.g., as regards inheritance laws in matrilineal societies).

In 1946 the distinction between subjects and citizens was abolished; all colonial natives became citizens without renouncing their personal legal status. The French penal code was, however, as mentioned before, rendered applicable to all citizens. This reform was self-contradicting insofar as penal legislation is primarily a means of protecting and enforcing both private rights (e.g., family, inheritance, property) and ethical, or so-called ethical, taboos closely bound to a particular culture. The courts were confronted with ludicrous situations, since, for instance, Napoleon and his legal advisers had never thought of forbidding cannibalism, but *had* forbidden polygamy.

As far as political rights were concerned, a distinction was made between *citoyens de statut civil de droit commun* (the former citizens) and *citoyens de statut civil musulman ou coutumier* (the former subjects). They voted on separate rolls at first (except in French West Africa), and the latter had to prove they had risen to a certain degree of civilization to be enrolled for voting.[8] (The criteria were slightly surrealistic at times; in fact, what was demanded of prospective voters was that they prove their age and identity; hence the inclusion of "mothers of two children," "holders of hunting or driving licenses," "fetish priests," etc.)

Another important corollary of the "one and undivisible" principle was the practice of direct rule, often opposed to Lugardean indirect rule. In fact this opposition was often less drastic than it sounds: there were no very big differences between the *subdivisions* of Haute Volta and the districts of the Northern Territories of the Gold Coast. The French administrators had to rely to some extent on traditional chiefs, exactly as their British counterparts had in many cases, to take decision out of the hands of Native Authorities. What is important is that the very notion of "Native Authority" was repugnant to French high officialdom. Thus, in 1917 Joost van Vollenhoven, the very able governor-general of A.O.F., wrote in a general instruction to his *commandants* that "authority cannot be divided or sliced down like a cake. You and only you are its sole possessors. Native chiefs have not, cannot have any authority of their own, whatsoever. We have not thrown down kingdoms to build up a new feudality."

After the conquest many African states (Macina, Dahomey, etc.) were broken down into *cantons* (counties) whose chiefs were, according to van Vollenhoven, "civil servants of a peculiar nature." Conversely, *chefs de canton* were appointed in segmentary societies where the precolonial territorial organization did not go higher than village level.[9] Even in the states where the king was kept on his throne or stool and appointed *chef supérieur* (e.g., the *Mogho naba* of the Mossi, the *Uro eso* of the Kotokoli, the *Jermakoy*, etc.), his relationships with subordinate chiefs were completely changed and he lost most of his powers which were, in effect, confiscated by the *commandant*. The pyramidal hierarchy was exactly the same in all territories: it consisted of the territorial governor; a number of big circumscriptions (*cercles* or *régions*), subdivided into smaller ones (*districts* or *subdivisions*), all under the command of European administrators, the *chefs de subdivisions* (district officers) being assisted—repeat: assisted—by a three-tier hierarchy of *chefs supérieurs, chefs de canton,* and *chefs de village* who might or might not belong to the local tribe. The system was, by sheer necessity, more or less tempered, chiefly by the personal action of the *commandants,* with the paradoxical result that it became more and more adapted to the traditional structures while these structures were becoming more and more disintegrated; [10] indirect rule was almost rediscovered just before independence.

The same kind of implacable uniformity obtained in the field of education. If and when there were schools, they were designed on the same pattern. French was the compulsory medium of teaching from the start, and the overall system closely followed that of *la Métropole.* It has been stated that no African students went to French universities before World War II. In fact some did go, several hundred perhaps, and most of them stayed permanently in France after graduation. Only a few, including L. S. Senghor and Sourou Migan Apithy, returned home afterward to seek a political career.

Those Africans who stayed in France—I know at least two who became mayors of the places they settled in—are extreme examples of what I call *vertical* assimilation, a social process whose importance has all too often been exaggerated. There was and still is a certain amount of assimilation of this type, which was the theoretical ideal of French colonization, and all good Frenchmen like to boast about it. But many of the same can easily be led to think there can be too much of a good thing: the late *radical-socialiste* (i.e., left-of-center) politician, Président Edouard Herriot, shortly before his death in 1957, voiced the fear that France would "be colonized by her own colonies." At that time there were some 27 deputies representing 50 million Africans in the French parliament as against 586 for a metropolitan and Algerian population of 52 million.

Far more important for the future of the former French colonies and of Africa as a whole was what I term *horizontal* assimilation, meaning this uniformity in methods of administration and education which resulted in making a politician or civil servant from the Central African Republic almost interchangeable with one from Senegal, and this down to a quite low rung of the political and administrative ladder. This type of assimilation did work in the British colonies too, but, as it seems to me, only to a much lesser extent, even within any given country.

3) The advantage of the pessimistic definition of plural societies is that it simplifies matters: a lone district officer together with a quarter-million tribesmen would constitute a plural society. Conversely, in the

optimistic view, it becomes very hard to tell when a plural society does come into existence—what degree of integration must obtain, at what level, and so on.

Granted the legal assumption implicit in the 1946 constitution that *la République* was a plural society of a kind, things look very different according to the level of observation—the Republic as a whole, *la Métropole*, the A.O.F., a single colony, a district. Even at one level, say the district, there were so many variables that it is nearly impossible to draw a general picture. One thing is certain: there were almost no plural societies among the peoples conquered by the French at the end of the nineteenth century. The two most notable exceptions were the Moslem "empires" or hegemonies of Tekrur and Macina, both dominated by Fulani rulers. A third empire, that of the Malinke conqueror Samori Ture, was broken by the French Marines before its consolidation. Those polyethnic states proved, on the whole, more fragile than the monoethnic ones (such as Dahomey and Mossi). In turn states and protostates were easier to pacify and administer than segmentary societies.

The Colonial territories were certainly plural on two counts: first, because Europeans imposed their rule upon African societies, and second, because these societies were assembled into new political entities, irrespective in most cases of precolonial divisions. Yet, could the population of the Ivory Coast in 1900 or 1910 be regarded as constituting one society, plural or not plural? The answer is perforce ambiguous. There was certainly no Eburnean consciousness at the time, yet the influence of the colonizers was already deep enough to create significant differences with the neighboring Gold Coast.

In fact, integration to a degree first took place at the district (*cercle, subdivision . . .*) level where colonial authority, incarnated as it was in the *commandant*'s person, was more directly felt. Some districts had a homogeneous population, others grouped several tribes or fractions of tribes, boundaries being sometimes modified so as to break up one "difficult" tribe or reunite a "loyal" one; some traditional chiefs were kept with truncated powers, others saw their dominions extended to foreign tribes; nontraditional chiefs were appointed from among *tirailleurs,* former houseboys, or ruling families of other tribes; the *commandants* came and went and were replaced without any regular periodicity. All in all, the very lack of continuity and purpose in French policy had both a disintegrative and an integrative effect on African societies; just because the disruptive effect on tribal life was stronger than under the system of indirect rule, reintegration at a higher level was more of a necessity and probably intervened sooner.

The *commandants* certainly became a part of the social landscape,

some of them assuming heroic proportions in modern African folklore—
not at all on the Sanders-of-the-River model, needless to say, be it only
because, bachelors as they were, they did not remain lonely, some of them
founding prominent dynasties enduring to this day (e.g., the
d'Arboussiers or Delafosses). To be politically successful they had to
Africanize, to go native to a large extent; the difficulty was to avoid
overstepping a fluctuating and ill-defined limit. They tended to become a
new kind of noble savage, earning from travelers and French metropolitan opinion the hostile nickname of *néo-rois nègres*. In fact their authori-
tarianism was limited by the feebleness of their means: they *had* to gain
acceptance rather than to force it. Also, being very short of European
personnel they had to rely more on African assistants with whom they
had closer relations than was the case for the following generation. It can
probably be said on the whole that at this time (i.e., the phase of colonial
organization after the conquest and prior to 1914 or 1918) both definitions of plural societies tended to obtain at the same time, insofar as
political domination by the foreign group coexisted with converging
integration. This seems to hold true as well for the only large colonial
city of the period, Saint-Louis du Sénégal, whose *enfants-du-pays* (Creole) group long stood for a symbol of successful assimilation, both racial
and social.

4) I must confess I have purposely given an overidyllic description of
this period, and that it applied only to French West Africa. In Equatorial
Africa, conquest was immediately followed by ruthless economic exploitation at the hands of chartered companies which lasted to 1940 when
Governor General Eboué, under de Gaulle's authority, finally brought it
to an end. (This is another example of oversimplification for want of
space.) In West Africa, integration in the sense of the optimistic definition of plural societies was slowed down if not actually stopped after
1918, owing to the very success of colonial development. As more and
more white people came to work in the colonies, bringing their families
with them, the racial communities [11] drifted apart, especially in towns,
including the main outstations. There seems to be a critical sex ratio for
white communities, the attainment of which means that the community
becomes inner-directed. No study has been made of actual figures, but,
from the ethnographical angle, I drew the opinion that the limit is
reached when African concubines become unmentionable. It is at this
point that colonial literature begins to concern itself chiefly with stories
about the internal relationships within the white community.

Despite its growth in actual numbers, however, the white community
in French African colonies never became a settler community. There was

only a tiny minority of lifelong residents: a few Roman Catholic missionaries and some *petits blancs* traders, lumbermen, employees, or retired petty officials who had gone native (*bougnoulisés*). From 1914 on, civil servants were essentially nomadic, being transferred from one colony to another in order to prevent them from acquiring too great an influence in any given region. This *système de la plaque tournante,* invented by Governor General William Ponty, was severely criticized by many Africans because one of its results was to deliver colonial officials into the hands of African interpreters, who all too often became the powers behind the *commandants'* desks.

During this period between the two world wars, the growth of the African bureaucracy in public and private employment was even more spectacular than that of the white community. There was no corresponding development of a native entrepreneur group except for coffee and cocoa farmers in Cameroun and the Ivory Coast and petty traders in several tribes (Malinke *dyula,* Bamileke, Hausa). In most cases these African entrepreneurs did not belong in the same group with the bureaucracy. The latter grew up into an integrated group thanks to a monopoly of education, the basis of which was the ability to speak French, which was to become by law a prerequisite to enter politics (and has remained so even after independence). Tribal consciousness was on the decline among this group, whose younger members received little or no traditional education (you cannot attend simultaneously both *école primaire* and *poro* bush). At the same time, they acquired the beginnings of a national consciousness, at the colony level, actuated partly if not chiefly by the differences in development between the richer coastal territories with better educational facilities and a stronger economy and the hinterland colonies which lagged behind (and often happened to have Islam as an integrating factor). This was not nationalism—not as yet. This *évolué* group was still aiming at assimilating, or even at "civilizing," itself. Its members modeled their behavior or at least their manners after those of the white community,[12] which was exactly what the prevalent political philosophy wanted them to do. The measure of their success is given by the ease with which the first politicians, drawn almost exclusively from this group, adapted themselves to life and work in French parliamentary circles after 1946.

I think one of the most important elements to single out at this point is the fact that there never was any *legal* segregation of races qua races. There were all too many actual cases of racial discrimination, unpleasant incidents in public places, unfair treatment of natives, and the like. But discrimination based on race never had any legal sanction and was, in fact, an indictable offense which sometimes led to conviction of white offenders (a strong proportion of the judiciary were West Indians, by the way). This probably explains why racial antagonism was not widely played upon during the political struggle for emancipation after World War II.

5) This struggle was led by members of the *évolué* group. They had been the middlemen of the colonial era, mediating between the colonial rulers and the African population. The political reforms of 1945 which eventually led to independence did not bring about any sharp break, but rather an evolution of this role: the younger generation of the African elite, which has no real experience of the colonial era, is rather prone to accuse the present political leaders, including some of the most radical of them, of still being only middlemen and not revolutionaries. Racial feelings are generally much more bitter in this younger generation than among the older men who grew up under full-fledged colonial domination.

After 1945, the white community became much more numerous than ever before. This meant, in part, that, during the years preceding independence, it was on the whole even more inner-directed than before World War II, and probably less interested in what was happening among the Africans. As a reaction against the Brazzaville conference and the reforms brought about by de Gaulle and the Constituent Assembly, a group of die-hard colonialists, consisting chiefly of a coalition of big *colons*, owners or managers of important firms, and *petits blancs*, employees of private firms and junior European officials, tried to oppose the new trends and to set the clock back, or rather to change the clock. This pre-Poujadist group, called *Etats Généraux de la Colonisation*, wanted to disband the colonial service and to set up local colonial governments of a type reminiscent of the Southern Rhodesian one. They met with total failure and, after 1948, the group disintegrated, *grands colons* and *petits blancs* [13] going their separate ways in trying to come to terms with the new African political bosses. This attempt was quite successful in some states (the Ivory Coast, Gabon, Cameroun) and far less so in others (Guinée, Central African Republic, Mali), the differences stemming from political rather than sociological reasons.

Since independence, what was left of the white community (in some states such as the Ivory Coast comprising *more* people than before) has been functionally integrated within the African dominant group, which is an extension of the former *évolué* group. This does not mean that social relationships are closer than in the colonial era. During this period all the white men were, so to speak, professionals, that is, people whose whole professional career was to be spent in Africa. They had, perforce, an

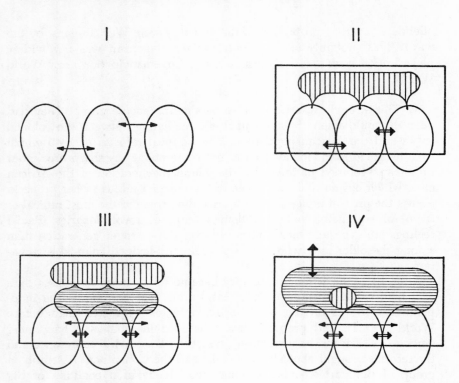

interest in the country which is no longer found among diplomats or technical assistants on short-term assignments. In fact many, if not most, African governments prefer that the foreigners they have to employ be not too much engaged in local problems, for fear of political interference. They are especially wary of the type of well-wishing anticolonialist radicals called *Pieds Rouges* [14] in independent Algeria—and sometimes also of anthropologists (the wise anthropologist calls himself a sociologist).

6) Are the former French colonies then plural societies? Or have they become plural societies or ceased to be plural societies? If the criterion of domination by a foreign group is retained, they certainly cannot be considered as plural after independence. Yet they are not culturally homogeneous. Very sharp tribal differences still obtain in most of them and the political boundaries of independent states still cut across tribal territories. The ruling group is characterized by simultaneous participation in one totally non-African culture and several variegated indigenous ones. The way in which this group exercises its power is highly relevant

here: there would be plurality in the pessimistic sense when and where this group is an oligarchy ruling without participation of the rest of the population, and plurality in the optimistic sense when and where there are efficient means of common popular participation. The trouble is that, despite all propaganda to the contrary, there are reasons to think that all over French-speaking Africa, the elite is an authoritarian, oligarchic group which has to mobilize the masses by methods as harsh as or harsher than those of the former colonial power. In fact, the situation seems on the whole quite comparable to that in the precolonial Islamized "empires" where the ruling group was also polyethnic and united by a common foreign culture—in this case Islam. History shows that all these "empires" eventually fell apart, the pieces recovering sociocultural autonomy as separate polities. We know little of the methods of the Islamized rulers. It can reasonably be advanced that they combined a strong hand in politics with a rather tolerant attitude in the cultural field, Islam being in many cases a privilege and/or a status symbol of the ruling group.[15] Conversion was, as education is today, an opening toward social mobility, and this probably ensured a degree of acceptance of the regime by the subjugated tribes.[16] Yet those "pulsatile hegemonies" (Richard-Molard) proved fragile in the long run. It would be interesting to study the circumstances of their fall and to see whether they still apply in our days of easier communications and state monopoly of superior weapons.

7) The two conceptions of plural society seem quite irreconcilable at the synchronic level. They may well be reconciled in a diachronic approach: nation building does appear in many cases to start with conquest and domination by a culturally foreign group (pessimistic definition), to be followed by integration when power is shared despite cultural differentiations, and then, possibly, by disintegration if new cultural antagonisms are created within the formerly integrated society. Of course, in a Marxian approach, cultural differences within a nation are only superstructures, indexes of economic and political oppositions. This explanation, like most Marxist explanations, is true to a point, but does not cover all cases. What, for instance, of the differences between Switzerland and Belgium, with very similar understructures?

The main fault with the phrase "plural society" is its ambiguity. There *is* an opposition between a consensual and a conflict model of societies, and there can be historical changes from one type to the other and back. Why then try to cover both types by the same term?[17] Plurality, or pluralism—this term is also open to discussion—is the mark of all complex societies; it can even be accepted as the differential criterion between simple and complex societies. Then, at this level of complex society, it can generate either a conflictual or a consensual situation (and I should prefer to reserve "pluralism" to describe the latter case, i.e., when plurality is accepted as a basis for social relations). By dropping the phrase "plural society" altogether one can avoid the risk of nominalism which is in most cases a consequence of equivocal terminology in the social sciences.

NOTES

[1] The term "pluralisme social," being considered a *sine qua non* trait of Western democracy, is used rather more extensively than "société plurale." Of course, the latter term does not translate exactly as "plural society."

[2] All cadets at ENFOM were required to hold a degree in law.

[3] For a recent collection of raw ethnographic reports from this source, see M. Chailley *et al., Notes et études sur l'Islam en Afrique Noire,* Recherches et Documents du CHEAM (Paris: J. Peyronnet, 1962), reviewed by I. M. Lewis in *Africa,* 35, no. 4 (Oct. 1965), 444–445.

[4] There is no French equivalent of the British pukka sahib's "thirty years behind rifle and moustache" school of reminiscences. The best French colonial writers on African subjects stand at a level somewhere between Joyce Cary and Elspeth Huxley. Many novels written by administrators in recent years show strong traces of an attempt at personal vindication vis-à-vis French intellectual circles from which the authors feel they have been unjustly rejected. An analysis of this trend would make an interesting chapter in the study of French anticolonialism, which is still to be undertaken.

[5] In fact, the criterion was set aside for the first time in 1921 by a judgment of the A.O.F. Court of Appeals which recognized the existence of collective landrights, in direct contradiction to the French *code civil.*

[6] This was the philosophy behind the instructions of a *procureur de la République* (director of public prosecutions) directing a magistrate, in 1951, to ignore a case of cannibalism (a crime not provided for in the Code Napoléon) "as the findings of modern child psychology indicate that, if we pretend not to notice, they will renounce it in due time."

[7] I leave aside, on purpose, the case of the Senegalese *citoyens des quatre communes* (Saint-Louis, Dakar, Rufisque, and Gorée) who retained their personal status under koranic law, instead of being made subject to the *statut de droit commun.*

[8] Universal common roll adult suffrage was achieved after the 1956 Front Républicain election.

[9] Compare with the situation of Ganda "chiefs" among the Nilotic people of northern Uganda.

[10] Compare Eboué's 1941 circular on native administration with van Vollenhoven's instructions quoted above; Eboué was a rather good anthropologist, van Vollenhoven a great administrator.

[11] The word "communities" is used here in a very loose sense, for these "communities" never legally had corporate existence.

[12] Frequently a polygynous Togolese had a *femme de salon,* literate and French-speaking, whom he brought to official receptions, and other functions. The *femme de salon,* was not, in most instances, the head wife.

[13] The *petits blancs* officials did not belong to the Colonial Service (*cadre général*), but to the local services (*services locaux*) where they were in direct competition with the *évolué* group.

[14] *Pieds Noirs* was the nickname of the so-called Algerian settler community, including native Jews.

[15] The Fulani *lamibe* in North Cameroun did not encourage mass conversion of pagan tribesmen because it would have meant that the converts were no longer subject to enslavement or to *dhimma* taxation.

[16] On the contrary, the so-called paleonigritic refugee tribes resisted both Islamic and colonial conquest (see J. C. Froelich, "Les problèmes posés par les réfugiés montagnards de culture paleonigritique," *Cahiers d'Etudes Africaines,* 4, no. 15 [1964], 383–399).

[17] Professor Leo Kuper, while kindly trying to put some English into my sociology, notes that "unfortunately these two usages developed quite independently." It is indeed unfortunate.

Chapter 7 Pluralism in Colonial African Societies: Northern Rhodesia /Zambia

Basil Davidson

I

There are few countries in colonial and ex-colonial Africa, or at any rate within Africa south of the Sahara, where the concepts of pluralism may be more helpful to analytical understanding than the British Protectorate of Northern Rhodesia (including Barotseland) which has since become the independent Republic of Zambia. For it is here that a process of pluralism—a movement through several types of pluralist society or pluralist structures, as these are defined in the frameworks set up by Kuper and Smith in their introductory papers to this colloquium [1]—can be more fully and, as it were, neatly seen than in most other territories of the same type. Northern Rhodesia/Zambia seems repeatedly to offer a stimulating field for reflection on the whole regulation-integration pattern of pressure which underlies the dynamic of pluralism, and whose varying configuration motivates the direction of any pluralist society, toward more conflict or less conflict, at any given time.

There would appear to be three reasons why Northern Rhodesia/ Zambia is particularly helpful in this respect. In the first place, this is a country where a good deal is known about at least two precolonial societies which were pluralist in a sense that was fairly characteristic of many precolonial structures in central-southern Africa, and to much the same extent in western Africa as well. Second, this was a colony (a term which may be taken to include the imperial-administrative sense of "protectorate") where European settlement developed a pluralism of conflict, in the sense proposed by Furnivall,[2] and further developed by Smith, which lay somewhere between the "extremes" represented in Central Africa by Southern Rhodesia at one end of the "White settlement spectrum" and Tanganyika at the other. Here it was not taken for

granted from the earliest moment of European arrival, in contrast with
Kenya and Southern Rhodesia,[3] that this was to be a "White man's
country" where the newcomers would install themselves as permanent
and exclusive rulers, and where the scene was accordingly set, almost
from the outset, for a racial separatism so acute and inflexible as practically to deny the existence of any organic community of Europeans and
Africans. Such tendencies developed with the improvement of antimalarial
medicine, and were afterward enlarged to a point at which they could be
dominant for many years; yet even during those years the relatively low
degree of settler density made an important differential between Northern Rhodesia and Southern Rhodesia or Kenya. On the other hand,
European settler power in Northern Rhodesia was generally stronger, as
well as less confined by theoretical safeguards on the eventual rights of
Africans, than in the Mandated (later Trusteeship) Territory of Tanganyika.

Evolving somewhere between these two, Northern Rhodesia was always a country where the drive for entrenched white supremacy had
powerful but never completely effective influence, and where, because of
this and other factors, the concept of a Northern Rhodesian society as
possibly including all the inhabitants remained at least admissible
(though very seldom admitted) within the practical framework of public
(that is to say, of European) debate. Even through what may be regarded as the most sterile years of the colonial epoch—the period between the respective ends of the two world wars, but especially for
Northern Rhodesia, up to the middle 1930's—this racially separatist
society generally held within itself at least a few of the seeds of pluralism
by consensus, by equilibrium, and by democratization. And this relative
mobility (a very limited mobility, as will be seen, and yet one that was
never quite reduced to a standstill) may not be the least reason why
Northern Rhodesia seems attractive to inquiry.

Third, with Northern Rhodesia becoming Zambia, there is the possibility of examining in fairly good detail how a pluralism of embittered
conflict can become, even at the early stages of resolution, a pluralism of
less acute conflict, and can even move toward that kind of pluralism of
equilibrium which supposes the growth of a consensus. It may be that
Nyasaland/Malawi next door would provide as good an example of this
structural series, yet the pattern has been simpler there (if only because
of the absence of a Copperbelt with its provision of urbanized industrial
employment for Africans), and to the extent that it has been simpler, it
may be less instructive. Then, in terms of studying "transition from
pluralism to heterogeneity,"[4] Zambia has very clear advantages over
Kenya, a good deal less resolved today in terms of its basic problems, and

even more over Southern Rhodesia, where the resolution of acute conflict has yet to begin. Moreover, it appears to me, as I shall try to show, that forms of resolution in Zambia have interesting parallels in other parts of Africa where the white settler problem has been unimportant or altogether absent.

This paper accordingly looks at several main configurations through which the pluralist process has passed in recent historical times—since, that is, the eighteenth century—and offers a few tentative conclusions in comparison with some other African territories. One should perhaps begin by noting that the sources are of very unequal value. Up to the middle of the nineteenth century, written accounts are limited to the reports of a handful of Portuguese travelers. Some of these, notably Dos Santos [5] at the end of the sixteenth and Gamitto [6] in the first half of the nineteenth, were remarkably good observers, but their travels seldom took them far from the Zambezi, although Gamitto traveled to the lands of Kazembe (approximately eastern Katanga) through what afterward became the northeastern segment of our territory. Oral traditions are in somewhat better case for a few of the peoples concerned, yet still leave much to be desired. The archaeology of this whole region remains at an early stage of research, though the last few years have brought important advances in the understanding of early Iron Age systems here.[7]

Written sources for Northern Rhodesia are good, even very good, for the Europeans, thanks partly to the lively settlers' newspaper founded by Leopold Moore at Livingstone in 1906,[8] and partly to the well-recorded debates of a Legislative Council formed in 1924. After the end of World War II these sources become still more copious with the launching of more newspapers and a great deal of political, social, and cultural argument recorded outside the scope of the Legislative Council. An additional advantage here is that the settlers' struggle for Federation, and the wider interest stimulated by Federation itself (1953–1963), set going a movement to write books about the country. When I first went there in 1951 there was only one book of any analytical value on the politics of Northern Rhodesia;[9] today there are at least twelve or fourteen, and two or three of these are likely to be of lasting value.

Against all this on the European side, there is practically nothing before the 1940's to record the opinions of Africans. Northern Rhodesia produced neither a Chilembwe [10] nor a Clements Kadalie [11] in the period prior to the rise of Congress and trade union politics at the end of the 1940's; and the little we know of African opinion comes mainly, though very sparsely even at that, through the mouth of one or other of the more liberal spokesmen in the all-white Legislative Council, notably Sir Stewart Gore-Browne. To these, stray allusions the rise of separatist Christian-

ity, especially in its local form of Watch Tower, adds a useful, if somewhat indirect, addendum, while missionary records [12] can sometimes be a
valuable, though also secondary, source. Seldom does one find an opinion
spoken by an African himself.

This alters wonderfully in the late 1940's. At least from 1948 there is a
growing volume of African publications which bear directly on many
aspects of daily life. And with the later stages of the campaign against
Federation, with rapid political advance after 1959, and with independence itself, the African voice is continuously and ever more widely heard.

II

When Europeans first crossed the Zambezi in any numbers during the
last years of the nineteenth century,[13] they found peoples of the Bantu
language group. Many of them had been here for the better part of two
thousand years, had developed considerable immunity against the malar-
ial mosquito which infested the greater part of the country, and had
evolved an indigenous agriculture and a premechanical mining industry,
the latter from about 300 A.D. Theirs was a subsistence economy modified
marginally by a small amount of internal trade. They had the use of
various kinds of primitive money but knew no cash economy. They were
entirely nonliterate.

Europeans unhesitatingly called them "tribes" in a sense that was
explicitly pejorative and meant everything opposed to any development
of the means of material progress or even, with the more extreme interpretations, opposed to any form of juridical and moral order. This term
"tribe" has stayed with us because it is convenient; yet even without its
subjective overtones it may at best be misleading. These peoples were
not nations in the sense of possessing hard-and-fast frontiers, customs
posts, or other attributes of what is usually understood by nationalism. If
they had not formed nations, however, they had certainly formed states.
Some of these states, like those of the Ila and the Tonga, were of a type
that allowed little or no central government. Others, like those of the
Bemba and the Lozi, were of a type that allowed much. Within these
states, simple or complex, they possessed distinctive cultures, whether
sociopolitical, religious, or linguistic; and their respective jural communities were undoubtedly framed by approximate territorial limits—frontiers
of a sort—which were customarily recognized by their neighbors as well
as by themselves.

The larger of these states were plural societies: in varying ways, that
is, they displayed a "political pluralism, with a corresponding social
pluralism, in which the units [were] bound together by crosscutting loyalties and by common values or a competitive balance of power." [14] While

long-indigenous peoples such as the Tonga had achieved since ancient times a high degree of homogeneity, others, such as the Bemba and the Lozi, looked back to incoming ancestors who had arrived in the country during the eighteenth century, established local dominance, and ruled over many different elements more or less imperfectly welded together. Being little stratified in the horizontal sense of caste (and even less in that of class), these peoples with incoming ancestors were organized on a pluralist model which made for the growth of consensus rather than of conflict. Initially, no doubt, these incoming groups had imposed their authority on local peoples by war and repression, but it would seem that the kinship structure of their societies, having a highly absorptive mechanism, made this conflict period a relatively brief one. By the nineteenth century, if not before, Bemba-speaking people had become a homogeneous group. Between themselves and their outlying vassals to the north and south, however, the process was still at a relatively early stage; it is this that helps to explain how the Bemba empire could and did collapse so rapidly on the appearance of European overlordship. It collapsed, that is to say, not from inner conflict, from a failure of its consensus mechanism, but from the pressure of outside strains.[15]

The Kololo settlement in Barotseland during the 1820's offers another example of precolonial pluralism. These Kololo were formidable Sotho migrants from the great military upheavals south of the Limpopo which had begun with the rise of the Mtetwa under Dingiswayo and exploded with the Zulu under Shaka. They moved into the country of the Lozi, whose local political system was at that time rather more than a century old, and imposed their own rule. This imposition was violent, but Sebetwane, who carried it through, tried almost at once for a consensus. He "discouraged the Kololo from adopting the attitudes of a dominant aristocracy, and consciously strove to fuse the two groups into a single people. . . . His policy of fusion was embodied in the decree that 'all are children of the chief.' " This policy was successful during his lifetime to a point where "the Lozi and even the river peoples [over whom the Lozi had ruled] adopted the name Kololo and took pride in the daring military exploits with which it was associated." [16] When his successor rejected fusion, the results proved disastrous for Kololo overlordship.

It would not be hard to make comparisons with other large African societies in the precolonial period. Some, like Ashanti, were able to achieve a marked degree of consensus among peoples of different traditional loyalties, moving toward this by various routes and maintaining it for more or less long periods. Others, like Songhay in its great imperial period of the sixteenth century, were never able to become more than "a characteristically oligarchic regime based on systematic political and social inequality and designed to preserve and perpetuate the institutional conditions essential for . . . sectional dominance." [17] One is reminded in this context of the famous rejoinder of Askia Dawud, one of Songhay's most illustrious rulers, when criticized by a Muslim dignitary for allowing pagan customs at his court. "I am not a fool for doing this," the emperor is said to have replied with a laugh, "but I rule over fools who are both arrogant and impious, and that is why I must pretend to be a fool myself." [18] In fact the emperor's tolerance of pagan customs at his Muslim court reflected the greatest of his problems, which was how to reconcile the Muslim people of his trading cities with the pagan people of his countryside; never resolved by more than partial compromise, this was the conflict that rapidly undermined the Songhay empire once its main cities were captured by the invaders of 1591.

Acute conflicts such as these were absent among the precolonial peoples of Northern Rhodesia. If they accepted European government with little protest or with none, this was not because their societies could easily be split along the grain of inner conflict as the Moroccans were able to split the Songhay system, but because they needed allies and protectors and saw these in European shape. The so-called stateless peoples like the Tonga were simply incorporated into a European-dominated system without their having so much as understood, perhaps, what was really going on. But the Lozi and Bemba rulers had felt the edge of danger from strong African neighbors, and not unreasonably believed that future risks they might incur from a powerful ally whose homeland was evidently very distant must be preferable to the immediate risks they ran from enemies nearby. Only the Nguni in the eastern part of the country resisted the European take-over, and they were soon defeated.

III

If concepts of pluralism seem useful over a long perspective, there remain periods in Northern Rhodesia history, and especially up to the middle 1940's when, by seeming to imply some form of consensus, such concepts may risk obscuring more than they reveal. There was, indeed, a pluralist system of acute conflict at work here. But in order to describe it I myself prefer, as I shall indicate, a sharper and more brutal term, if only to emphasize, in Smith's terminology, that "modes of subjugation" are by no means necessarily tantamount (and certainly were not here) to modes of "willing submission." Here there existed no normative consensual basis, no "common value system," so that authority derived its strength, right up till the middle 1940's, only from an increasingly dense "regulation by force." [19]

In contrast with the Kololo, who had preceded them by about seventy years, the incoming Europeans within ten years or so had so completely embraced the attitudes of domination that to speak of "a Northern Rhodesian society," even acutely divided, is really to speak of what did not exist; then, and for some time afterward, the Africans were no more members of Northern Rhodesian society, as recognized and constituted by duly enshrined authority, than the cattle and the game for whom "reserves" were also soon marked out. This apart, the Europeans were extremely scarce. Here the fond old tag about Southern Rhodesia—*Fair and fine, fair and fine, fifty farms and a railway line*—had even better application. Apart from a few hundred settlers living along a narrow strip northward from Livingstone on the Zambezi, and another small group around Fort Jameson, there were no Europeans in Northern Rhodesia except for a handful of missionaries and administrators, and one or two individual settlers who lived far out in the bush, until well on into the 1930's. Few though they were, however, these Europeans constituted "Northern Rhodesia," and they constituted it separately from the Africans.

The actual process of installation was completed by the last years of the nineteenth century and needs little description here. Armed with his letters patent of 1889, Rhodes had at once dispatched agents across the Zambezi into country then believed to contain great mineral wealth, though not in copper but in gold. Lochner went to Barotseland and secured from the Lozi king, Lewanika, a concession of far-reaching commercial and mining rights across a vast territory between the Zambezi-Congo watershed and the Kafue River. While it must be clear that Lewanika would not have grasped the fuller implications of this, it is also clear that Lochner was perfectly ready to mislead him as to the status of the treaty he was proffering. One of its clauses stated that "this agreement shall be considered in the light of a treaty between my said Barotse nation and the government of Her Britannic Majesty Queen Victoria," [20] whereas, in truth, it was nothing of the kind. Lewanika thought that he was dealing with another sovereign power of status comparable in kind, if not in degree, with his own; in fact, he was dealing with Rhodes's Chartered Company, a very different kettle of fish. Thus trickery and contempt for African opinion prevailed from the outset.

It prevailed elsewhere as well, and notably in the similar concession treaties obtained in the northeastern part of the country by Joseph Thompson.[21] With or without deliberate misrepresentation, the Chartered Company, in any case, possessed itself of scraps of paper which it could present in London as good titles to "effective occupation" of the lands in question. Having such titles, it proceeded to act upon them. But it acted with the most slender means. The whole country was divided, at any rate nominally, into two separate administrations, one in the north-

west and comprising the Barotse concession, and the other in the northeast, based on the Sharpe, Buchanan, and Thompson treaties. Yet for
some time there were no administrative stations of any kind in northwestern Rhodesia, while control remained only partially effective elsewhere.
At the same time the principles of installation were now perfectly valid
in British eyes and were seen as giving full right to government. This
right was to be exercised by the company subject in its main lines to
British governmental approval (exercised either through the High Commissioner for British Central Africa stationed in Nyasaland or through
the British High Commissioner in Cape Town); and here the effective
instrument was the Northeastern Rhodesia Order in Council of 1899,
modeled on the precedent for Southern Rhodesia of the year before. This
gave the company administrative power to make regulations for "the
administration of justice, the raising of revenue, and generally for . . .
peace and order and good government." [22]

These were somewhat greater powers than were granted to the company in Northwestern Rhodesia, "where the imperial Government was
more anxious to have a greater say by reason of the unresolved Portuguese boundary dispute and the existence of a relatively strong native
kingdom with recognized treaty rights." [23] Out of this, in later years,
came the limited separatism of the Barotseland Protectorate. The rest of
the country, however, went the way of the Northeastern Order in Council; and it was not long before the concession treaties were made into a
foundation for complete dominance over all Africans except within the
"home territory" of Barotseland. With the latter exception, the two territories were fully amalgamated after 1911; an all-European Advisory
Council was formed in 1918; and in 1924, after the European community
had voted (in 1922) by 1,417 to 317 against amalgamation with Southern
Rhodesia [24] (an ironical verdict in view of what was to happen thirty
years later), company rule came to an end and the Colonial Office took
over.

Yet the Colonial Office was distant, local revenues were extremely
meager, and it was the settlers who continued to stamp their attitudes on
daily life. Nothing so organic even as a society of "conflict pluralism"
now appeared. Except in occasional policy documents issued in faraway
London, all of which remained at this stage without the slightest practical effect, no intention can be discerned of any wish to build a single
society consisting of different communities. What the settlers had in
mind was to impose a fully integrated but entirely separate European
society upon a congeries of African societies. What mattered in their eyes
was the speed and completeness with which this European society could
be crystallized, made conscious of itself as an entity, and pointed firmly

toward permanent rule over the rest of the inhabitants. Against this the Colonial Office had little but empty words and a few local but very partial administrative palliatives.

One may note, however, that this evolving European community was itself a pluralism. If the earliest arrivals were mostly Englishmen, others soon came from elsewhere. Of a European population totalling 1,484 according to the census of 1911, 16.7 percent were members of the Dutch Reformed Churches (were Afrikaans-speaking people, that is, from South Africa), while 4.6 percent were practicing Jews. There were also 39 Indians—and soon there would be more—to complicate the non-African pattern, while the number of Coloreds (fruit of irregular unions between European men and African women) grew rapidly from the handful signaled in the 1911 census, which also helpfully explained that the territory held only 376 European women to its 1,118 European men.[25]

What passed for political life right up until the 1940's was the strife and rivalry between these segments of the non-African community, but especially between the majority of the settlers and the company (or later the Colonial Office), as well as between the settlers north and south of the Zambezi. Of African politics there was none at all, or none that was recognized as more than an occasion for calling out the police. The notion of settlers' self-rule was present almost from the beginning, yet not at all, as it would be half a century later, as a means of "keeping the Africans out." Only one or two settlers at this time seem to have thought that a time could come when the Africans might threaten to be "in." The enemy was first the company and then the Colonial Office, each of which was successively condemned as somehow depriving the settlers of their birthright or the fruits of their labor.

This feeling among men who had gone to "build a new home for themselves" may have existed among a few individuals from the earliest pioneering days, but it first became vocal in 1908 when the proprietor and editor of the *Livingstone Mail* put in the earliest of many claims to settler independence north of the Zambezi [26]—at a time, one may wryly note, when the Europeans in the territory still numbered fewer than a thousand. Yet the claim, however derisory it may seem today, nonetheless made its mark and became the theme song for nearly half a century of settler politics.

One reason why it came so early was an accident of personality. The founder of the *Livingstone Mail*, Leopold Moore, happened to be a rare bird among his fellows in possessing no mean share of intellectual capacity, political talent, and dry abrasive wit. Moore had originally come from England as a settler in Southern Rhodesia where he opened a pharmacy in the little town of Bulawayo. His ideology is revealed in many editorials and speeches as being a very simple one even in those days of simplified racialism; regarding the Africans as a necessary evil, but not as a danger because they were well kept under, he was mainly concerned at the beginning of his colonial career with what he called the Asiatic menace. He made himself a nuisance to the Chartered Company in Southern Rhodesia, then casting round for means of importing Chinese labor in the hope that it would be more efficient, or at any rate more willing, than African labor; and the company, it is said, placed a boycott on his shop by way of reprisal. "He was unable to hold out and in the end he left Bulawayo, defeated and penniless, filled with hatred against the Chartered Company." [27] He moved to Livingstone north of the Zambezi where he started his little newssheet, first as an editorial scourge of the company's agents in Northern Rhodesia and afterward of those of Whitehall.

Yet Moore and his readers and friends initially welcomed Whitehall: better the distant devil, they thought, than the one next door. They voted in 1922 against amalgamation with Southern Rhodesia not, as we have seen, because they disagreed with the objectives of the Southern Rhodesian settlers, but because they hoped that a period of Colonial Office rule could win them time to acquire their own separate independence. The southern settlers were more numerous, after all, and likely to remain so; amalgamated with the north, sooner or later they would put their own "southern" interests first. Arguments such as these were to crop up time and again as the years went by, often disturbing the unity of the "settlers' front" in the British Central African territories, and especially during the campaign for Federation which was eventually crowned with a ten-year victory in 1953. But by then the rivalry of their southern neighbors had generally come to seem far less dangerous than a much more alarming alternative, the incredible but nonetheless real possibility of African enfranchisement. In the early years of Colonial Office rule, however, the settlers were well enough content with their lot. They had every reason to believe they were the heirs apparent.

IV

By 1924, when the Colonial Office took over, there were all told about 4,000 settlers; and it is from this time that a system that deserves to be called a system rather than a fragmentary political experience comes into being. The notion of imperial trusteeship of African communities is officially enshrined by the protectorate concept of colonial rule; and there are the beginnings of an effective local administration through British district commissioners with a hierarchy mounting to an all-powerful governor at Livingstone, and afterward at Lusaka.

From the outset this system was rigidly segregationist. Years later a hopeful young African waited on the District Commissioner of Broken Hill with a small request. He recalls in his memoirs that when he got inside the DC's office, he said "good morning" in English. "The DC turned to the head clerk and said: 'tell this man in Bemba to say good morning, sir.' Throughout that interview the DC insisted on his head clerk interpreting everything he said into Bemba while I spoke in English." [28] The language of the master race—just, remote, and altogether of a different clay—was not for their inferiors.

Segregation and "trusteeship"—and therefore pluralism? Perhaps. The cultures of the Africans were recognized at an official level; it was vaguely understood that they were parts of the system. Yet recognition at the official level, one may repeat, had little more than theoretical impact on the realities of life. Pursuing their aim of self-rule in an atmosphere of "high imperialism" both here and in the mother country, the settlers found it easy to increase their weight and standing in the political affairs of the colony. If the members they elected to the Legislative Council remained for long in a minority over against the official members nominated from the administration by the governor, the settlers almost invariably set the tone of debate. African affairs seldom or never appear in the records of the Legislative Council except as distant and secondary matters pertaining to "natives" whose own voice remains entirely silent. Even so, the settlers kept up their steady pressure for full control. In 1929 they were granted seven seats to the governor's nine, and in 1939 they gained equality with the official side. Yet at least from the copper boom of 1929 their support for any crucial measure was in fact a practical necessity.

Until 1948, when four spokesmen for African interests were added (two being Europeans and two Africans), the Legislative Council continued to debate and consider African problems as though these belonged to a subhuman species. The "natives" were "there" in a sense, but in a much more important sense they were also "not there." "Their proper management, it was held, ought to be entrusted to individual European employers." [29] Leopold Moore put the point with his customary frankness when he remarked in 1927 that "the natives do not come into contact with this House. They are governed by the people of this country"—the *people* or the *public* or the *nation* always being taken, one may note, to equal the Europeans—"not governed in the sense that they are legislated for by the people, but they are governed by the people who employ them." [30] It is a somewhat sibylline utterance, but one gets the point: the "'natives" were not to be thought of as worthy of government in any constitutional or organic meaning of the term. Persons of a more liberal trend of thought often referred to them as "minors" or "children" or "wards," with the implication that although Africans might eventually become members of society, they had certainly not done so yet.[31]

And so far was this the prevailing attitude, as the records of what was said and done by the Northern Rhodesian Legislative Council during the first twenty years of its existence amply show, that one may, as I have suggested, reasonably question whether the concepts of pluralism, even when taken at the extremes of the conflict model, have any usefully explanatory application here before the late 1940's. Yet what better qualification can one meaningfully attach to it? I shall try to suggest a term. Meanwhile one may note that it was not a caste system, since that implies the theoretical as well as the practical acceptance of some kind of community between rulers and ruled, and here there was no such acceptance. It was not a slave society of masters and servants even in the early capitalist sense, where both elements combined to a single if internally differentiated cultural whole.

Here, on the contrary, there was in practice an utter domination and an unbounded subordination with no bonds or rights or obligations established between the two except those of the settlers' convenience. Nothing appears to have tied these two groupings together except a mutually hateful contiguity from which neither could escape. The Africans regretted that the Europeans were in the country—we have few samples of their opinion, but the statement risks little chance of being wrong—but could not possibly get rid of them. The Europeans longed for the Africans not to be there, physically not there, yet were unable to do without them. The Africans provided labor and in this they were horribly indispensable. If they had to be recognized it was to the extent of their labor value (estimated at the lowest possible rate), and no further. The sentiment grew with time and habit. Discussing African opposition to settlers' amalgamation across the Zambezi, Moore remarked in 1939 that the "natives have got no grounds for liking it or disliking it; we are running the show." [32]

There were of course exceptions. Relations at the personal level might sometimes be cordial and even warm. But the exceptions only prove the rule, while personal relationships had no political effect. Nothing better illustrates what that rule was, perhaps, than a fairly routine statement by the secretary for native affairs, at that time J. M. Thompson, during a Legislative Council defense debate of March 1932. "Our knowledge of our native inhabitants leads us to believe," he reassured the settler members at a moment when unemployment was heavy on the Copperbelt and along the line of rail, and troubles were feared, "that we need have no anxiety about any internal disturbance on any large scale. There is no cohesion among the important tribes in this Territory, and there is no likelihood of it in the near future. In fact, the most important tribes cannot even speak each other's language or communicate with each other in any way, and it would be very difficult for them to discuss any matter of any importance at all." [33] Somewhere "out there" lay the dark sea of natives, silent and mysterious. Every now and then one sent out little expeditions of reconnaissance in the hope of finding out what was going on. Reassured by finding nothing, these returned; and that was all.

V

We may briefly trace the nature of this system in three crucial fields apart from the machinery of legislation: agriculture, labor, and urbanization. Essentially the pattern here was much the same as in other African colonies of European settlement, and measures previously evolved in South Africa and Southern Rhodesia were duly imported as and when they promised to be convenient and useful. Malaria of a severe and epidemic type proved a major deterrent to European settlement in the early years, and it was not until after 1918 that Northern Rhodesia began to be looked upon as a "white man's country." [34] Yet as early as 1904 the few dozen farming settlers in the northeastern highlands, where the land was better than elsewhere, had been able to induce the company to set up a small "native reserve" for the defeated—and expropriated—Ngoni who had themselves come here as conquerors some sixty years earlier; and in 1911 these and other settlers pressed for the generalization of reserves. They were to have their way. In 1913 the company in Southern Rhodesia had set aside 22 percent of the land of that country as "reserves" for some 45 percent of the African population; and what it had done south of the Zambezi, it now proceeded to do in the north as well. [35]

This achieved three purposes. Land division enforced a measure of physical separation so that Africans in the nonreserved territory could be there only on sufferance, and thus in a servile status; they had to come as supplicants, in other words, or they could not come at all. Second, it opened the way for a more effective effort to "force labor out of the villages" and cause rural Africans, by hut or poll tax, to quit their subsistence economy for the cash economy of their new masters; the reserves being limited (though much less so here than elsewhere), they soon became relatively overcrowded. From this there flowed, as elsewhere, a steady deterioration in the fabric of village life, and, over a period of twenty or thirty years, an uninterrupted decline in rural standards of living. [36] Migrant labor now began to have a devastating effect, although this was for long ignored by administration and settlers alike. At the same time it became steadily more available at very cheap rates, so that the "reserves" became an essential component in the whole system. Third (though this again was of less importance here than in other colonies of White settlement), the alienation of fertile land from Africans and the removal of established African populations made it possible to offer more land to would-be settlers.

By 1936 the land pattern had long since fallen into place. Three main divisions had come into existence. The Crown retained title over 11 million acres of forest and game reserve, as well as over 94 million acres which were unallotted; much of this was useless for settlement through infertility or the tsetse fly. Africans retained title over a total of 71 million acres; of this, about 37 million were in the Barotseland Protectorate, while the remaining 34 million were the "reserves" in which the bulk of the population, now estimated at more than a million (although, in the light of better estimates made later on, it was probably much larger), were obliged to reside whenever they chose or could choose to remain at home.[37] For their part the Europeans had just under 9 million acres; 5.5 million of this block were held by two companies, mainly as *latifondi*, leaving a little more than 3 million acres for private farms. How few the latter were in 1936 may be guessed from the fact that they numbered only about 1,100 as late as 1950.[38]

Judged by the standards of South Africa, this division in favor of Europeans was far from severe for the Africans; the latter had lost a lot of good land, but much remained to them.[39] The Europeans multiplied, yet slowly; moreover, they continued to cluster along the line of rail from the Zambezi to Broken Hill and the Copperbelt in the north, and outside this corridor their presence was little felt except in a few rural centers such as Fort Jameson in the east and Abercorn in the far northeast. Inside the corridor, however, they increased their numbers steadily from 1925, when mining surveys led to major finds of sulphide ores with the relatively rich copper content of 3 to 5 percent. Soon the Copperbelt was booming. By 1929 Northern Rhodesia had become par excellence a copper colony, and from now onward it was to be the fortunes of the copper mines which would provide the final regulator in all large questions of policy. European immigration bounded upward. By 1931 the colony had 13,846 Europeans of whom only 1,291 had been born there, while 4,225 had come from the United Kingdom and 6,824 from South Africa.[40] On the eve of the 1931 depression the mines were also employing no fewer than 29,000 Africans in unskilled or semiskilled laboring jobs.

This availability of African labor had the advantage of aiding low-cost production. Later in the 1930's, when the industry had recovered from the slump and was going ahead again, this copper could be delivered at Beira railhead on the east coast at a cost per long ton that was about half that of United States and Mexican copper, and still considerably less than that of Chilean production. Not surprisingly, the industry prospered. By 1937, with the average London price of copper standing at more than £50 a ton, earnings on the ordinary shares of the copper companies were yielding about 80 percent; later, they would go still higher.[41] As in other colonies, however, local taxation remained extremely low (much lower in Northern Rhodesia, for example, than in South Africa where the white population could ensure that a higher proportion of earnings was kept in the country),[42] while income tax was paid in the United Kingdom. There was therefore a considerable economic expansion without a corresponding flow of wealth into the pockets of the European settlers (the actual miners excepted) or, of course, the local Africans.

High copper earnings could thus do little to ameliorate indigenous life. Administrative funds remained chronically in short supply, even while copper shareholders abroad won high rewards. And this occurred at a time when the use of African labor for industrial purposes had begun to pose a number of acute problems of urbanization. Here, as we shall see, the counterfactors making for pluralism soon came into play. One of them was trade union agitation. Another was education. These were, of course, factors of acculturation; yet it needs to be remarked that they barely made themselves felt on any scale that could influence events until the early 1940's. In 1923, for example, administrative expenditure on African education was exactly nil (when about £7,800 was spent on European education),[43] while missionary education unsupported by government money was always a rare phenomenon. The Legislative Council did indeed debate "native education" now and then, although such debates reveal little but settlers opinions on the unwisdom of any such dubious enterprise. In the fairly characteristic year of 1932, for instance, more pages of Legislative Council records are covered by anxieties over rabies caused by "native dogs" than by thoughts on the subject of "native education."

By 1938 the position had somewhat changed, with the government now spending about £44,000 on African education (and some £55,000 on European education).[44] Yet the advance was snail-slow and could not be otherwise, given the paucity of available funds, and it barely touched the secondary level. As late as 1958 there was only one secondary school in the whole territory capable of taking African pupils through the Cambridge Senior Certificate examination,[45] even though the African population by then was certainly more than 2 million. Of higher education for Africans there was, of course, none at all. To the settlers this appeared perfectly right and proper. "There is not one intelligent native in the country," a former Native Commissioner called Cholmely informed his fellow Legislative Council members in 1939; and they weightily gave him their assent.[46]

Throughout the period between the wars, then, this was a conjunction of communities that could be said to form a single society only in the extreme sense offered by Furnivall, one of utterly disparate sections among whom the highest common factor was economic, "and the only test that all apply in common is the test of cheapness: a process of natural selection by the survival of the cheapest." [47] Even this definition will not really serve, since the Africans were not expected to apply any kind of test or even, as J. M. Thompson had explained, "to discuss any matter of any importance at all." And if European spokesmen ever considered the human beings in Northern Rhodesia as constituting something like a single community, even for economic purposes, they did so only within the ideological framework of a crudely vulgarized Darwinism. "Are not biology, history, anthropology," queried Chad Norris of his Legislative Council colleagues in 1930, "all leading us to an appreciation of the supreme importance of heredity, the supreme value to civilization of superior race stocks?" [48]

If then one has to find a name for this curious system as it existed between 1924 and about 1948, one may perhaps best define it not as a pluralism, but as a despotism, though a despotism of a special kind. It was not a despotism of conquest, for there had been no conquest. It was not a despotism of caste, for the rulers were of different ethnocultural origins and were careful to remember the fact. Nor was it a despotism by an oligarchy, since this would have presumed membership of the ruled in the same community as the rulers, and no such membership was ever admitted. Least of all was it a despotism by an elite, because that would have supposed some training or preparation for the exercise of authority, and these settlers had known nothing of the kind. What then was it? Though a little modified by imperial hesitations in the 1930's,[49] it was a despotism by a haphazardly formed collection of men of whom only the merest handful seem ever to have had any conception of a common future with "their Africans," or of the social responsibilities which might have to accompany such a future; and whose absolute power was for a long time modified only marginally by the imperial factor of Colonial Office control or by the "metropolitan factor" of British public opinion. This was "differential incorporation" through crudest regulation by force, supposing no consensus but only subjugation.

Even so, it was not a static system. It held within itself (and it is here that pluralist concepts may after all justify their application to Northern Rhodesia before about 1948) a number of internal factors of change, hard to perceive in the 1930's but steadily more visible in the 1940's, which worked for resolution of conflict and even for a measure of incorporation. In this the settlers were constantly surprised and disappointed. Their despotism supposed a world that stood still. "We came here and we are here to stay and dominate," [50] as Moore pugnaciously explained in 1939. It turned out not to be so after all. But when the ground began slipping from beneath their feet, they did not revise their convictions. For a long time they preferred to ignore the evidence of their own senses.

VI

In 1935 a number of African mineworkers withdrew their labor in protest against certain of their conditions of work. Any such African action was completely illegal, and nothing like this had happened before. A flurried police was called into action. Six African strikers were shot dead, others wounded, many jailed.[51] Immediately, this achieved nothing for the African mineworkers. Indeed, it set them back. Alarmed at possible African encroachment on their "reserved skills," the European mineworkers (under advice from color-bar unions in South Africa) formed themselves into a trade union two years later and introduced a rigidly formalized industrial color bar where only a customary one had previously existed. Yet the strike had other consequences, concealed at the time, which were eventually to prove more important. For it really marked the first small beginning of modern African politics, or the beginning, rather, of a mass participation in activities which acquired an increasingly political undertone.

This flowed from diverse sources. Not the least of these was the influence of separatist Christianity with its rebellious implications for colonial Africa. If Northern Rhodesia did not have its Chilembwe, as in Nyasaland next door, to speak for the cause of Christians who happened not to be Europeans, it had other men of lesser note who preached to the same general effect. Their message was essentially the same as that of the Mozambique pastor in Nyasaland, Charles Domingo, who asked rhetorically in 1911 what the difference was between a white man and black man, and replied: "Are we not of the same blood and all from Adam? . . . If we had power to communicate ourselves to Europe we would advise them not to call themselves 'Christendom' but 'Europeandom.'" Domingo went on to rub in his point by observing that the life of "the three combined bodies, Missionaries, Government and Companies . . . is altogether too cheaty, too thefty, too mockery. Instead of 'Give' they say 'Take away from.'" [52]

Ethiopist ideas couched in similar vein were present in Northern

Rhodesia from the middle times of company rule, and were reinforced by local variants of Watch Tower doctrine. It would be out of place to discuss these here: I want only to make the point that dissident Christianity had taken an acutely if indirectly political form in Northern Rhodesia by at least 1919, when ninety-nine adherents of Watch Tower were charged with sedition and assault arising from refusal to pay tax or admit colonial authority.[53] This current of dissent continued and expanded. By the middle 1930's Watch Tower had become widespread in its propagation of anticolonial ideas, and may reasonably be seen as a parent of the Congress movement of the late forties and fifties.

Direct political action was long in making itself felt. Its incipient origins may be traced among urbanized Africans of the early thirties who had acquired some education. They came together and thought about themselves. Not averse to the emergence of a "middle class" that could eventually help to bridge the abyss between "the European nation" and "the natives," colonial authority even welcomed this development. "There is," remarked the Secretary for Native Affairs in 1931, "a growing tendency amongst natives of the educated classes to form Welfare Associations and Co-operative Societies, and to establish Reading Rooms and Libraries," and government hoped that such organizations would "in time be a useful means of expression of native public opinion." [54] Later on, when these welfare societies flowered into the Congress movement, official benevolence toward "native public opinion" became rather less emphatic.

As it is, these little groups of literate men—there were as yet very few literate women—do offer some indication of African opinion in these otherwise silent days, though it generally came through European spokesmen.[55] One such indication, worth noticing here, was reported by the liberal-minded Sir Stewart Gore-Browne in May, 1936, when telling his legislative colleagues about a meeting he had lately had at Lusaka with a group of "educated natives." They had questioned him intelligently, he said, on the subject of amalgamation of the two Rhodesias, then a matter much exercising settler opinion. At the end of the meeting, Gore-Browne recalled, "a native got up and said, 'Don't you think, Sir, that a question like Amalgamation ought to be put before the native people, that they ought to be consulted?' I said, 'I certainly do and so do a great many other white people, but how should it be done?' He said, 'Our chiefs will speak for us.' At once about twenty natives in the room said, 'No, they cannot talk for us, they do not know what we are thinking, they do not know anything about it.' " [56] Here already, in 1936, one sees the essential cleavage between traditional loyalty and the new political opinions now being formed under the stress of breakdown of traditional life, and—another factor of increasing significance—under the pressure of example provided by settler politics.

Such political questionings as these, couched in a framework of modern political thought and action, even if still at an incipient phase of emergence, were joined to the mass influence of village protest through religious dissent as well as to the lesser but growing protest of semiurbanized Africans working in the mines. Once these elements fused together, however imperfectly, the politics of "national liberation" could begin. This process of fusion was slow and partial, and was further reduced by the circumstances of World War II; yet it went on quietly beneath the surface, exploding only now and then, so that when the Congress movement finally did appear, late in the forties, it surprised both the settlers and the colonial authorities by the strength of its appeal to natives not previously believed, as Mr. Thompson had said in 1932, to be capable of discussing together "any matter of any importance at all."

Formally grounded in 1948, the Congress movement had its organizational origins somewhat earlier in the Copperbelt townships. These origins took their rise not only out of sentiments of protest against job and wage discrimination, but also--and now it was that the politics of pluralism first began to play their part in the reality, as distinct from the theory, of colonial trusteeship—out of an attempt to borrow and reproduce settler methods of organization. We do not know just how far those little groups of clerks and other literate men of the late thirties and early forties were in the habit of reading the official reports of debates in Legislative Council and drawing political conclusions for themselves. But the case of labor organization on the Copperbelt is highly instructive. In this respect the crucial year was 1940.

In 1935, as we have noted, there had been African disturbances on the Copperbelt arising from various causes; and two years later, prompted by their colleagues in South Africa, European mineworkers had formed themselves into a strictly color-bar trade union. This prospered. Well led, it secured concessions from the owners. Striking for still higher wages at the Nkana and Mufulira mines in March 1940, the European miners were again successful in securing most of their demands. But a day later something new occurred. About 15,000 African mineworkers also (though illegally) declared themselves on strike for higher pay. Not too surprisingly, perhaps: at this point the average European wage was above 800 shillings a month, while the average African wage at Nkana was 12½ shillings a month for surface work, and 22½ shillings for work beneath the surface,[57] a European-African differential of about forty to one. Faced with this large withdrawal of African labor, management attempted a compromise by offering an extra 2½ shillings a month which was rejected by the strike leaders, who challenged the management to allow the Africans to work a competitive shift underground with the Europeans in order to expose who were the real producers of copper. This was understandably refused; everyone knew already that most of the work was really done by the African crews while Europeans underground did little more than supervise. And management duly called for strikebreakers.

One has the impression that a few years earlier there would have been plenty of Africans to answer this call, and that strikers would have attempted nothing against them. But by 1940 things were different. On the sixth day of the strike at Nkana a crowd of about 3,000 strikers tried to stop a queue of about 150 strikebreakers from drawing their pay. Police and troops who were standing nearby moved to protect the strikebreakers, and threw tear gas bombs. This enraged the strikers who thereupon assaulted the mining compound office where all civilian Europeans in the vicinity had meanwhile taken refuge. The troops opened fire, killing seventeen strikers and wounding another sixty-five. This ended the affair, and the strikers went back to work.[58]

But it did not end the evolution of African opinion on the Copperbelt. If trade unions could be useful to Europeans, they could also be useful to Africans. And at this point there again intervened what may be called "the metropolitan factor," but it did so in a new way. If effective British metropolitan opinion during the twenties and thirties had been for the most part emphatically prosettler, there came a steady change with the outbreak of World War II and the formation of a Conservative-Labour coalition government in 1940. Pro-African views began to be heard at the official level in Britain. For several years the spokesmen of Labour opinion had developed a strongly liberal trend of thought in colonial affairs—one may see it in many directions, and most influentially, so far as the Parliamentary Labour Party was concerned, in pressures exercised by groups within the Fabian Society—but these spokesmen had wielded no power. Now the war gave them some. New things began to be said, argued, promised. Here, for example, is a fairly characteristic interchange on March 12, 1941, between a critical Labour member of Parliament (later to become secretary of state for the colonies) and a Labour minister in the Churchill coalition government:

Mr. Creech Jones: Will the Government throw the whole of its weight against the practice of the color bar in the [Northern Rhodesian] Copper Belt?

Mr. George Hall [under-secretary of state for the colonies]:
                    I think it necessary to make it quite clear that the Colonial Office and the Government do not stand for the color bar either in this country or in any of the Colonies.[59]

At least a new note had been struck; and it strengthened as the war went on. Labour ministers pressed for the right of Africans to form themselves into trade unions and carried their point. Nowhere did this have larger local consequences than in Northern Rhodesia. By 1950 there were as many as seven properly registered and organized African trade unions there with a total membership of between 30,000 and 35,000, most of whom were in the African Mineworkers' Union. A year later the unions formed a Trades Union Congress on the British model, while the African mineworkers, with the support of the British National Union of Mineworkers, successfully applied for affiliation to the Miners' International, and thereby opened for themselves another useful window on the world. At home, meanwhile, the African miners' union formed in 1949 had pushed up the average level of African wages by 75 percent, and had won recognition as a responsible organization.[60] Viewed against the backdrop of all those Legislative Council debates when the natives had seemed no more than a lay audience of deaf-mutes standing somewhere in the wings, the change was enormous.

Politics followed: if the settlers could advance their interests by form-ing political parties, so also could the Africans. In 1948 the leaders of the Federation of African Welfare Societies (formed in 1946) decided to reconstitute their organization as the Northern Rhodesia Congress, and once again they were helped by "the metropolitan factor." In 1945 the British electorate had returned the Labour Party with an overwhelming majority, and the government arising from it began to put into effect some of the anticolonial ideas worked out during the 1930's. Contacts multiplied between budding African leaders and members or influential supporters of the government in London; at this point, indeed, the history of independence movements in English-speaking Africa becomes temporarily inseparable from their metropolitan connections.[61] In the wake of such developments, the Northern Rhodesian constitution was altered in 1948 (in line with a policy statement of 1944) to allow the indirect election of two Africans to the Legislative Council. Back in 1930 a member of the Legislative Council, Captain T. H. Murray, had spoken for settler expectations: "I cannot conceive the remotest possibility of Africans being able to sit in the Legislature in twenty, or even fifty years' time."[62] In fact the event had come about in eighteen years.

There were, of course, other outside factors at work. These were the years of early Indian independence. They were the years of African awakening in many lands: of the outset of anticolonial campaigning in most of the English and French territories, of the fruition in separate movements of the constituent elements in the old prewar National Con-gress of West Africa, of the foundation and onward growth of the multiterritory Rassemblement Démocratique Africain in the French West and Equatorial colonies, and of other such developments, all of which, indirectly or even directly, had their growing stimulus and influence on the nascent political elite of Northern Rhodesian Africans. Reflecting a new mood across the world, and taking advantage of it, a different Africa was taking shape.

As it did so, the central and enduring equivocation within British policy became increasingly clear. It had existed almost from the beginning, though obscurely, and must call for comment in any historical survey, however brief, of pluralism in the British tropical colonies. Were these colonies for emigration, for *Lebensraum* in the Hitlerite sense? Or were they brought into existence as a means of "advancing the natives to civilization"? It goes without saying, perhaps, that they were thought of as both, though not necessarily by the same people or at the same time or in the same degree. At the outset, of course, there was really no conflict between the two ideas: philanthropy toward the British laboring classes and philanthropy toward the poor savages of Africa could elevate the same comfortable bosom to a sense of charitable mission without any need for particular priorities. It thus inspired the excellent Mrs. Jellaby, for instance, in the heyday of Victorian paternalism. She was, wrote Dickens in 1852, "devoted to the subject of Africa; with a view to the general cultivation of the coffee berry—and the natives—and the happy settlement, on the banks of the African rivers, of our superabundant home population," and she hoped "by this time next year to have from a hundred and fifty to two hundred healthy families cultivating coffee and educating the native of Borrioboola-Gha, on the left bank of the Niger." [63]

Later, it became more difficult to reconcile these ideas. There were certain colonies in Africa, it appeared, which could well support far more than 200 healthy British families, and really ought to do so. Kenya was one of them, and Kenya now raised problems. After 1918 the Kenya settlers, well led and sometimes well connected with influential folk at home, entered the same demand, but far more forcefully, which Moore had bravely proclaimed in distant Livingstone more than a decade earlier. They pressed for an increasing share in the government of the colony. Matters came to a head in 1923. By now, however, there were also many Indians in Kenya; they "heavily outnumbered the Europeans and it was realized in Whitehall that any attempt to discriminate against them [on behalf of European self-rule] might have serious repercussions in India." [64] The Duke of Devonshire, British colonial secretary in the Conservative government of the day, thereupon thought it well to discourage European hopes. He issued the famous declaration of 1923 which bore his name. It remains a capital document and is worth quoting in this context at some length because what it said was later applied to other settler colonies: "Primarily Kenya is an African country, and His Majesty's Government think it necessary definitely to record their considered opinion that the interests of the African natives must be paramount, and that if, and when, those interests and the interests of the immigrant races should conflict, the former should prevail. . . . His Majesty's Government regard themselves as exercising a trust on behalf of the African population, and they are unable to delegate or share this trust, the object of which may be defined as the protection and advancement of the native races." [65]

This caused angry protests among the Kenya Europeans, though it long remained without any practical effect. Elsewhere, and especially in the Rhodesias, British settlers tended to regard it as very much a Kenya affair, and as no doubt unnecessarily provoked by the well-known arrogance of Kenya's political leaders. Southern Rhodesia, at all events, rapidly became after 1923 a standing denial of everything that the Devonshire Declaration might imply, while Moore and his friends, north of the Zambezi, generally assumed that what had happened with Southern Rhodesia would also in due course happen with them: free of "the Asiatic menace," or at any rate sufficiently so, they would steadily advance to settlers' independence.

Yet the equivocation was still there. The Devonshire Declaration remained on the books. It could be used by colonial governors who came under fire from recalcitrant settlers. It could also be repeated and enlarged. And in 1930, during a brief period of Labour rule in Britain, it was repeated and enlarged by the then colonial secretary, Lord Passfield (Sydney Webb), in a restatement of the doctrine of paramountcy which was now extended to other settler colonies.[66] This deeply shocked Moore and his colleagues. Not only did Lord Passfield gratuitously extend the doctrine of native paramountcy and go on to state that "immediate steps to ensure strict conformity" with it were to be taken, but—*O tempora, o mores!*—African development was to become a "first charge" on the territory's revenues. In the event, Lord Passfield ceased to be colonial secretary the following year, sharing in the general eclipse of Labour's fortunes which came with the great slump of 1931, and no steps, immediate or otherwise, were then taken to bring Northern Rhodesian policy into line with his directives.

Even so, the Devonshire-Passfield line of thought had its profound effect. It influenced settler communities to sink their differences and to press for self-rule more resolutely than before; at home in Britain, meanwhile, and on the other side of the equivocation, it gave the critics of colonialism and of settler politics their "charter" for increased political action. And when the Fabians and other Labour groups composed their anticolonial parliamentary questions and held their anticolonial gatherings and discussions during the 1930's and later, it was on the Passfield Declaration that they took their stand. By the late 1940's, in the wake of all that, the "metropolitan factor" had moved weightily to the "trusteeship" side of the old equivocation, and here it would remain right up until the day when British sanctions were declared against European rebels in Southern Rhodesia, and perhaps beyond. Arising from the very structure of British society, this equivocation lies at the heart of much that the British did and said in and about Africa through more than a century; and it makes repeated nonsense of any simplistic views on the nature of British imperialism in that continent.

VII

By the late 1940's, accordingly, Northern Rhodesia was ceasing to be a system of extreme conflict. There were still two widely separated communities and, subjectively at least, one of them still held a posture of complete dominance over the other. But the objective relationship was changing. In many practical ways, some of which we have noted above, the official arbiter had come to recognize the existence not of one nation, but of two nations—of two nations, that is, which were members of a single society that had previously contained only one; and now, pushed on by the "metropolitan factor" under new management, the official arbiter had also begun to act on this recognition. From now onward it becomes possible to speak of the evolution of a pluralist *society* in Northern Rhodesia, as distinct from a pluralist *system* of extreme conflict, without doing violence to the term. With the steady growth of African representation at various levels, whether industrial, political, cultural, or even social, the internal dynamics of this two-nation society began moving, though slowly, out of a pluralist system of intense conflict toward a pluralist society of the equilibrium model "in which the units are bound together by crosscutting loyalties, and by common values or a competitive balance of power." [67]

It would be possible to relate this statement to a number of important developments which steadily revealed how conflict in one area of extreme tension after another could be and was resolved, at least partially, by the assertion of an organic balance of power between Africans and Europeans, and then, as events took their course, by the steady movement of that balance to the side of Africans who now outnumbered Europeans by perhaps forty to one. More democracy, in short, brought more internal peace. Regulation began to give way, if hesitantly and imperfectly, to integration; out of this, gradually, there emerged a structure capable of supporting a consensus.

Not easily, of course. There were times of acute strain and conflict. But the process visibly continued. In 1963 the Federation of Rhodesia and Nyasaland was broken up under African pressure in Nyasaland and Northern Rhodesia, and the two northern territories were allowed to move rapidly toward independence under majority rule. In January 1964 the United National Independence Party (UNIP), militant and far more effective successor to the earlier Northern Rhodesian African National Congress,[68] won 55 out of 75 seats in a greatly expanded Legislative Council, and the party's shrewd and determined leader, Kenneth Kaunda, became prime minister in all but name. Independence followed less than a year later. Though all but a handful of the country's Europeans retained their white supremacy convictions to the end, refusing to accept any of Mr. Kaunda's many appeals that they should give UNIP their support and voluntarily take part in building a new political system,[69] few of them left the country. Within a year it appeared—though in March 1966, perhaps, it is too early to be sure—that most of them had lost their worst fears of what must happen under "native rule," and were fairly content with their situation. They had accepted it with a bad grace, but they had accepted it.

This is not to say that the conflict pluralism of Northern Rhodesia's last fifteen years or so has as yet given way to a Zambian pluralism of equilibrium. Organic integration is still no more than partial. This applies not only as between Africans and Europeans, but also among Africans themselves. There remain serious conflicts on the African side, conflicts essentially of the transition of a traditional society to a modern society, which range from the Lenshina separatist church with its painful sequel in violence and confusion, to a number of troubles between constituent peoples which are still imperfectly resolved. Cultural differences are so many and occasionally so acute that a more or less long period of organizational integration must be required before these can all be made to fit smoothly within a single society, or, one may perhaps say, within an effective modern restatement of the traditional pattern of checks and balances.

The leaders of UNIP were aware of this, and would argue that they conducted their political action and propaganda toward the building of a pluralist consensus even at moments when preindependence tension was at its height. Here are two examples—by no means exceptional, so far as I know the literature—from a provincial UNIP journal, *Zambia Patriot* of Abercorn far in the northeast, whose articles were printed in Bemba as well as in English. The first dates from April 1963 when UNIP was under fairly heavy repression by the authorities. A. J. Mulenga warns that determined enemies may suffer after independence but goes on to make an appeal for reconciliation: "It has been our sacrifice to suffer so great and liberate our Father Land Zambia. And if we would continue having our ill-feeling towards our supposed to be enemies because of the problems they laid ahead of our struggle we would be making a mistake. . . . Friends-come-we-unite. Enemies come and let us unite, but you stand as enemies if you wish to." Three months later, in June, the paper opens with an attack on Kenya regionalism (then being conducted by the Kenya African Democratic Union under Ronald Ngala) which was called Majimboism from its Swahili translation: "UNIP stands for the creation of a sovereign Zambia Nation (hence National in UNIP). . . . it is thus important that all Majimboist tendencies be eliminated be they tribal, economic, racial or political. They must be eliminated voluntarily. If the people will it, let there by as many parties as they like. It is the people who must decide." In the event, as we know, UNIP was to remain the only African party of great significance, but again its protagonists would argue that this was so because only a single all-embracing party could at this stage satisfy the dynamics of consensus.

On a Zambian political view, then, things have come full circle. The traditional consensus of old is reproduced, or at least is on the way toward being reproduced, by a new consensus which reflects the needs and possibilities of modern nation-state existence, and has a wider democratic base. Before concluding this paper, and while rather keenly aware of the risks attendant on trying to isolate any constants in a pattern of events so persistently fluid, I should like to offer a few comments on this Zambian view. Though necessarily telescoped they may serve to promote discussion.

Like many other African nationalists, Zambian politicians and writers have tended to draw a parallel between the "old consensus" of traditional times, precolonial times, and the all-embracing single party or movement of today. In this, no doubt, there is a degree of idealization—or of a necessary and saving belief, shall we say, in the possibility that good may overcome evil—which may be inseparable from all action-urging political doctrines. Very small or even medium-sized societies could indeed achieve a communal consensus in the old days, but wherever large systems emerged the apparent consensus was in fact more likely to "institutionalize elite or ethnic domination." [70] Many "one-party states" in Africa today manifestly do precisely that; and the inverted commas are needed here because this is also the case with states where many parties have been constitutionally free (as in Nigeria) to compete for governmental power. But others, it can be argued, are of a different type: they do not institutionalize elite or ethnic domination but really operate on broadening foundations of consent and participation, and therefore work for the maximizing of consensus rather than conflict.

Nobody has argued this particular view more tellingly, perhaps, than Julius Nyerere, president of Tanzania. Though by no means a materialist in philosophy, he has made it his central point that parties in Africa today can be of national value only insofar as they reflect clear social divisions of interest: "The European and American parties came into being as the result of existing social and economic divisions. . . . Our own parties had a different origin. They were not formed to challenge any ruling group of our own people; they were formed to challenge the foreigners who ruled over us . . . and from the outset they represented the interests and aspirations of the whole nation." To allow the operation of other parties could only be to give a voice to "a few irresponsible individuals who exploit the very privileges of democracy—freedom of the press, freedom of association, freedom to criticize—in order to deflect the government from its responsibilities to the people by creating problems of law and order." [71]

Where such parties have remained national in scope and democratic in structure, they are accordingly claimed by their exponents as being uniquely effective vehicles for a pluralism of equilibrium. In Tanzania, for example, there are many languages and acute contrasts of soil, climate, habitat, or cultural tradition; only a system of "diversity within unity" could hope to prosper. And this is the system of unified diversity which is argued as being inherent in the African one-party approach to pluralism —to a pluralism, that is, which contains within itself a dominant pressure toward the homogeneity postulated, ideally, by the ideology of nationalism, and, looking beyond that, by the ideology of Pan-Africanism.

How then do the ideologists of the "one-party state" meet the point that monopoly must mean corruption: repression and abuse, that is to say, of a kind making for conflict (as in the Western and Northern regions of Nigeria or in Ghana) and hence moving not toward but away from a pluralism of equilibrium? Some do not meet it at all; others brush it impatiently aside. Examples spring easily to mind. These examples, as it happens, do not include Zambia and Tanzania; or perhaps we should say, given the provisional nature of African political structures in the sixties, they do not include them as things stand at present. [72] It soon became clear to Mr. Nyerere and his colleagues in the national executive of the Tanganyika Africa National Union (TANU), Tanganyika's only legal party, that a one-party structure could easily degenerate into repression and abuse. In 1962 and 1963 they were called on to face several explosive cases of both. They accordingly cast around for new forms of "checks and balances," and called for advice from experts, both African and non-African. In the end they evolved a system whereby candidates within TANU could stand for election against each other. Tanganyika elections on this revised model brought several surprises in 1965, not the least of which was the fall of two members of the government.

Here, then, the traditional structure of checks and balances might be said to be coming into force in a new guise. It could be argued persuasively that TANU was not in fact institutionalizing elite or ethnic rule; on the contrary, it could be urged that the system within which it held a central place was institutionalizing a progressively wider measure of democratic participation, whereas a multiparty system would in fact have had the reverse effect, and have tended toward a pluralism limited to the effective presence of a "divided elite" [73]—in the circumstances, necessarily a pluralism of increasing conflict.

Necessarily? It would appear so. For this is exactly what happened with the federal Nigeria which became independent in 1960. Here the true situation was masked by the presence of many parties. Yet the parties in opposition had, in practice, no chance of assuming power except in the very limited sense of a handful of "elites" who were able to share the spoils of office. Increasingly, after the middle fifties, the effective corpus of Nigerian political life was limited to "a divided elite" with little or no opportunity for local candidates, unsupported by party caucuses, ever achieving election. A small number of men in power (each belonging to this or that regionally based party) was opposed in the federal Parliament (and to a lesser degree in the regional parliaments) by a smaller number of men who were not in power. Members of these two groups sometimes acted with each other, and sometimes not, according to the pressures of group or individual opportunism. There was a steady institutionalization of elite rule which no proliferation of parties could in any way reduce; and then, following logically upon this, there were the beginnings of the institutionalization of ethnic rule—in this case of ethnic rule by the emirate officeholders of the north acting through their parliamentary delegates at the center.

This being so, the effective movement in Nigeria was not toward a pluralism of consensus but toward a pluralism of conflict. Not surprisingly, the conflict came, and in no mere verbal form. The eviction from power of the majority party in the Western Region, capped by its leader's removal from political life in 1963, was brought about by the use of federal power in conjunction with a small splinter party in the region itself, but the federal power in question was federal in little more than name, being more and more controlled in reality by the late Sir Ahmadu

Bello, premier of the Northern Region, and his built-in northern majority in the central Parliament. What resulted was extreme conflict: many hundreds of people in the Western Region lost their lives in political strife during the last months of 1965. Seen in this perspective, the destruction of Nigeria's federal regime by army officers on January 15, 1966, could be interpreted as a move to reverse the current, to dethrone the entrenched elites, to prevent an institutionalized domination of all the regions by the largest of them, and to initiate a pluralism of "diversity within unity." Once again, it might be claimed, traditional approaches could receive a new embodiment, but one that could hope to achieve an evolving democratic structure—a structure leading toward consensus —such as the times both required and made possible.[74]

To argue my case beyond this might be merely polemical. Examination of the precolonial Northern Rhodesian/Zambian structural series has shown, perhaps, something of the breaks and linkages that lie between several crucial phrases in the historical experience of these peoples over the past century and more. The value of this demonstration will rest in the degree to which it can illustrate and emphasize the underlying continuity of this experience—its changing content as well as its changing form—from precolonial through colonial to postcolonial times. Further reflection will also show, I think, that the problems of sociopolitical transition posed by decolonization are essentially the same in all African territories, whether or not, for example, they contain white settlers who have exercised local domination.

These problems are concerned above all with a striving for homogeneity, for the achievement of a society of common values by means of the winning of a normative consensus. Ideologically, this striving may be formulated in terms of a nationalism that is nostalgic for the unities, or imagined unities, of the precolonial past. Such formulations need not mislead us; sociologically, the colonial period was far more than an exotic interruption. Its effect was really irreversible. What is now in question, as so many recent tumults and upheavals prove, is the manner in which African authorities will organize, or fail to organize, the socially disruptive consequences of living in a cash economy, of earning wages, of accumulating capital, together with all the sociocultural phenomena associated with these activities. How will their striving for the homogeneity of common values deal with an increasingly acute stratification? Must they suffer this stratification? Can they find their own means of "unified incorporation"? These are questions that can find no answer here. But if the evidence of the 1960's is anything to go by, this striving toward homogeneity (however variously conceived, however differently clothed) is the one great influence that, above all else, will drive the wheels of change. And this, I suggest, is what the whole history of Zambia most clearly if often contradictorily demonstrates, and what gives the Zambian experience, in one guise or another, its close and organic linkage with the experience of every other decolonized territory in Africa, and perhaps elsewhere as well.

NOTES

[1] Leo Kuper, "Plural Societies: Perspectives and Problems," and M. G. Smith, "Institutional and Political Conditions of Pluralism." In discussion of this paper, which I have modified at several points in the light of what was said, there repeatedly emerged a need for further work on (a) the closer definition of various types of pluralism as parts of a wider spectrum of sociopolitical typology, and (b) the possible points of transition and linkage between "conflict" models and "equilibrium" models.

[2] J. S. Furnivall, *Colonial Policy and Practice* (London: Cambridge University Press, 1948), esp. p. 310.

[3] For both, cf. R. Meinertzhagen, *Kenya Diary, 1902–1906* (Edinburgh: Oliver and Boyd, 1957), p. 31: In 1902 the high commissioner, Sir Charles Eliot, "envisaged a thriving colony of thousands of Europeans with their families, the whole of the country from the Aberdares and Mount Kenya to the German border [i.e., of Tanganyika] divided up into farms; the whole of the Rift Valley cultivated or grazed, and the whole country of Mumbwa, Nandi to Elgon and almost to Baringe [i.e., right across into Uganda] under white settlement. He intends to confine the natives to reserves and use them as cheap labor on farms. . . ." This striking testimony comes all the more convincingly in that it was noted at the time by a man whose aunt, Beatrice Webb, was a friend of Eliot's: Eliot was talking within the family circle. *Mutatis mutandis,* the same plans were made, and carried out, for Southern Rhodesia.

[4] Smith, "Institutional and Political Conditions of Pluralism."

[5] There are useful extracts from J. dos Santos, *Ethiopia Oriental* (Convento de S. Domingos de Evora, 1609), in Eric V. Axelson, ed., *South African Explorers* (London: Oxford University Press, 1954), p. 19.

[6] A. C. P. Gamitto, *King Kazembe* (1854), trans. I. Cunnison (2 vols.; Lisbon: Junta de Investigacões do Ultramar, 1960).

[7] B. M. Fagan, *Southern Africa during the Iron Age* (London: Thames and Hudson, 1965), esp. p. 65. For latest summaries, see Fagan, "The Later Iron Age in South Africa," and D. W. Phillipson, "Early Iron-Using Peoples of Southern Africa," papers presented at the Lusaka conference on the history of southern Africa, 1968.

[8] L. H. Gann, *The Birth of a Plural Society* (Manchester: Manchester University Press, 1958), p. 165: "In 1906 he [Moore] was able to start a newspaper of his own, the *Livingstone Mail*, preceded by the *Livingstone Pioneer and Advertiser*, which he subsidized from the profits of his shop. He was able to use this journal as the vehicle of his political views, and since his was the only newspaper in the country it made Moore a prominent person." This is a little ungenerous to Moore: what really made him a prominent

person, newspaper or no, was the intelligence and determination of this unusual man.

⁹ J. W. Davidson, *The Northern Rhodesian Legislative Council* (London: Faber and Faber, 1948).

¹⁰ The best account is in the masterly review by George Shepperson and Thomas Price, *Independent African* (Edinburgh: University Press, 1958).

¹¹ E. Roux, *Time Longer Than Rope* (London: Gollancz, 1948), pp. 161–205.

¹² See R. I. Rotberg, *Christian Missionaries and the Creation of Northern Rhodesia, 1880–1924* (Princeton: Princeton University Press, 1965).

¹³ Résuméd in L. H. Gann, *A History of Northern Rhodesia: Early Days to 1953* (London: Chatto and Windus, 1964), pp. 64, 68.

¹⁴ Kuper, "Plural Societies: Perspectives and Problems."

¹⁵ Audrey I. Richards, "The Political System of the Bemba Tribe," in M. Fortes and E. E. Evans-Pritchard, eds., *African Political Systems* (London: Oxford University Press, 1940), p. 86.

¹⁶ John D. Omer-Cooper, *The Zulu Aftermath* (London: Longmans, Green, 1966), chap. 8.

¹⁷ Smith, "Institutional and Political Conditions of Pluralism."

¹⁸ Mahmoud Kati, *Tarikh el-Fettach,* trans. O. Houdas and M. Delafosse (Paris: E. Leroux, 1913), pp. 209–210.

¹⁹ See the introductory pages to M. G. Smith, *The Plural Society in the British West Indies* (Berkeley and Los Angeles: University of California Press, 1965), esp. pp. vii–xii.

²⁰ Text of concession treaty in Gann, *The Birth of a Plural Society,* p. 215.

²¹ Noted in A. J. Hanna, *The Story of the Rhodesias and Nyasaland* (London: Faber and Faber, 1960), p. 114. Of the part played by missionaries in securing these concession treaties, there is a useful description in Rothberg, *op. cit.,* p. 21. Cf. pp. 25–26: "The Lozi felt that their country had been unfairly seized by a commercial group under the pretext of British protection. They had been prepared to become vassals of a great white queen, but the interposition of the Company had denied them such an opportunity." Not unexpectedly, "Coillard [François Coillard of the Paris Missionary Society, who had reached Lealui, the Lozi capital, in 1885, and played a crucial part in helping Lochner] was regarded as a traitor, and members of his society suffered indignities and occasional physical harm as a result of their role in helping to secure the treaty."

²² Gann, *History of Northern Rhodesia,* p. 92.

²³ *Ibid.,* p. 93.

²⁴ M. Gelfand, *Northern Rhodesia in the Days of the Charter* (Oxford: Basil Blackwell, 1961), p. 140. There is an interesting study to be made on the social composition of these and other settlers. This, too, had its mythology and appropriate attitudes which had their various effect. In the period between the wars it was somewhat unkindly said, in British colonial circles, that the settlement after 1918 was carried out on the principle of "Officers to Kenya, NCO's to the Rhodesias." There was possibly something in it. The Rhodesias had no Lord Delamere.

²⁵ Census figures quoted in Gann, *The Birth of a Plural Society,* p. 175.

²⁶ *Ibid.,* p. 166.

[27] *Ibid.*, pp. 164–165.

[28] Kenneth D. Kaunda, *Zambia Shall Be Free* (London: Heinemann, 1962), p. 17.

[29] Hanna, *op. cit.*, p. 194.

[30] *Debates of the Northern Rhodesian Legislative Council* (hereafter cited as *Legislative Council Debates*), July 20, 1927, col. 143 of appropriate volume (issued annually).

[31] The "childishness" of colonized Africans was a theme rather more favored by the French and the Belgians, though the British were also impressed by it. See, for example, a Belgian Katanga veteran writing in 1946: "The colonizer must never lose sight of the fact that the Negroes have the spirits of children who are molded by the methods of the educator: they watch, listen, feel—and imitate" (L. Mottoulle, *Politique Sociale de l'Union Minière du Haut Katanga pour sa Main d'Œuvre indigène et ses résultats au cours de vingt années d'application* [Brussels: Van Campenhout, 1946], p. 5). *Sous entendu*, invariably, was the implication that the process could be nothing if not exceedingly slow.

[32] *Legislative Council Debates*, June 6, 1939, col. 501.

[33] *Ibid.*, March 7, 1932, col. 437.

[34] Gelfand, *op. cit.*, p. 1: "So great was the loss of [European] life that at the turn of the century men in England believed that Northern Rhodesia was a black man's country only and that it would not be advisable for the European to settle there as he had in South Africa and even Southern Rhodesia. . . . [But] by the time the Colonial Office became responsible for the administration of Northern Rhodesia in 1924, it could be claimed that the European had successfully defeated the environment and that he could survive in this climate."

[35] See Richard Gray, *The Two Nations* (London: Oxford University Press, 1960), and esp. chap. 2 by P. Mason on land policy in the Rhodesias and Nyasaland. The ideology of "reserves"—of removing African homes from the vicinity of African cash employment—had been well defined, in other circumstances, by the British Poor Law Commissioners in the England of 1834, who remarked: "We can do little or nothing to prevent pauperism; the farmers will have it; they prefer that the laborers should be slaves; they object to their having gardens saying: 'the more they work for themselves the less they work for us'" (*ibid.*, p. 47).

[36] A. J. Willis, *An Introduction to the History of Central Africa* (London: Oxford University Press, 1964), p. 290: "In fact the standard of living of Africans in the rural areas was declining during the inter-war period. . . . The publication of Dr. Audrey Richards' *Land, Labour and Diet in Northern Rhodesia* in 1939 revealed the decay of rural life among the Bemba. . . . Frequently more than half of the men would be away from the village at one time, creating an atmosphere of decay and frustration." See also G. St. J. Orde-Browne, *Labour Conditions in Northern Rhodesia* (Col. Office 150, 1938). Such statements can be generalized for the whole of settler Africa, and probably for the whole of colonial Africa, in the interwar period; see my *Which Way Africa?* (Baltimore: Penguin Books, 1967), chaps. 6, 7, for further evidence.

[37] Gray, *op. cit.*, p. 85.

[38] C. H. Thompson and H. W. Woodruff, *Economic Development in Rhode-*

sia and Nyasaland (London: Dobson, 1954), p. 53. I have not been able to find the figures for farms in 1936.

[39] Nor, incidentally, were their farming methods particularly inefficient. Commenting on this shifting subsistence agriculture, known as *chitemene*, the *Economic Survey of the Colonial Territories* for 1951 commented that "research has . . . so far failed to find an alternative for Chitemene methods for poorer soils which is practicable within the extremely limited resources of the cultivators" (quoted in Thompson and Woodruff, *op. cit.*, p. 54). Cf., for forest regions, a comment by soil scientists P. H. Nye and D. H. Greenland, noting that "even now, after a quarter of a century of experiment in the African tropics, we have failed to introduce to the forest regions any method of staple food production superior to the system of natural fallowing used in shifting cultivation" (*The Soil under Shifting Cultivation*, Commonwealth Bureau of Soils, Technical Communications 51 [1960]).

[40] Gray, *op. cit.*, p. 39.

[41] See R. S. Hall, *Zambia* (London: Pall Mall, 1965), p. 259, for a good potted account of copper mining expansion.

[42] As late as 1954, Northern Rhodesian mining companies were still paying local tax at a rate of 25 percent while gold-mining companies in South Africa were paying 50 percent (see B. Davidson, *The African Awakening* [London: Cape, 1955], p. 243).

[43] Gray, *op. cit.*, p. 133.

[44] *Ibid.*

[45] H. Kitchen, ed., *The Educated African* (New York: Praeger, 1962), p. 223.

[46] *Legislative Council Debates*, June 6, 1939, col. 501.

[47] Furnivall, *op. cit.*, p. 310.

[48] *Legislative Council Debates*, Nov. 18, 1930, col. 40.

[49] Cf. the Passfield restatement of the "doctrine of Native paramountcy" dating from 1923, and pp. 233–234, above.

[50] *Legislative Council Debates*, March 21, 1939, col. 332.

[51] Hall, *op. cit.*, p. 131.

[52] Shepperson and Price, *op. cit.*, p. 163.

[53] Gray, *op. cit.*, p. 148.

[54] *Legislative Council Debates*, March 13, 1931, col. 7.

[55] In this context it is worth looking at the *Report* of the Royal Commission of Rhodesia and Nyasaland, under Lord Bledisloe, which inquired into the state of opinion regarding amalgamation, and published its findings in 1939 (Cmd. 5949 of that year).

[56] *Legislative Council Debates*, May 4, 1936, cols. 70–71.

[57] J. Lewin, *The Colour Bar in the Copper Belt* (Johannesburg: South African Institute of Race Relations, 1941), p. 4.

[58] *Ibid.*

[59] *Ibid.*

[60] B. Davidson, *Report on Southern Africa* (London: Cape, 1952), pp. 249–250. Average African underground wages in 1953 had become 130s. 5d., and wages for surface work, 119s. 7d., an enormous increase over figures quoted for 1940 by Lewin, *op. cit.*, and Thompson and Woodruff, *op. cit.*, p. 73.

[61] In discussion of this paper it was argued that the pluralist structure of

Northern Rhodesia, in order to become fully meaningful, would have to include many extraterritorial influences and pressures behind all its communities, whether European, African, Indian, or Colored.

[62] *Legislative Council Debates,* Nov. 18, 1930, col. 30.

[63] Charles Dickens, *Bleak House* (London: Oxford University Press, 1948), pp. 34–37.

[64] Gray, *op. cit.,* p. 5.

[65] *Indians in Kenya,* Cmd. 1922 (1923), p. 10, quoted in Gray, *op. cit.*

[66] *Memorandum on Native Policy in East Africa,* Cmd. 3573 (1930).

[67] Kuper, "Plural Societies: Perspectives and Problems." I make here a distinction between a *system* of differential incorporation and a *society,* supposing the latter to have the organic characteristics of common values, or of evolving common values which the former does not have.

[68] The UNIP was in fact the successor to another movement called the Zambian African National Congress. This had been formed in 1958 by Kaunda and his colleagues as a breakaway movement from the Northern Rhodesian African National Congress (NRANC). The reason for this breakaway was a conviction that the leadership of the NRANC had lost both courage and conviction, which later events were to confirm. By all the evidence the break had not been made without some heart-searchings. In a letter to friends and supporters in London, dated December 2, 1958, Mr. Kaunda remarked: "No one denies the fact that [the ANC leader] has done something to arouse mass consciousness among the African people of Northern Rhodesia, but since the last two years it has been growing clearer every day that the two months he spent with me in Her Majesty's Hostel were more than enough for him, for he has spoken openly that he was not prepared to go to prison. . . . Other people think [he] has looked so despondent politically because he does not see how Africans could get through their present set of problems. Whichever is correct he has brought us all to a standstill . . . ," and hence a clean break was required.

[69] Cf. *Voice of Zambia* for Dec. 1963–Jan. 1964: "It is unfortunate that although UNIP had extended the hand of friendship to the European electorate, in the result it was totally rejected, though the small majority of 121 by which Sir John Moffat [a well-known liberal for the European electorate standing on the UNIP side] was defeated shows that there was in fact considerable support for the UNIP among the Europeans. However, Dr. Kaunda has made it clear that he will not tolerate the perpetuation of a divided nation by these reserved seats [reserved, that is, for Europeans] and has declared that they will be abolished as soon as independence is achieved." There was a good deal of bitterness among UNIP supporters because the European electorate, but for the tiny handful, had vehemently rejected every chance of electoral reconciliation during the run-up period to independence.

[70] Smith, "Institutional and Political Conditions of Pluralism."

[71] J. K. Nyerere, *Democracy and the Party System* (Dar es Salaam, 1963), p. 15.

[72] After the Southern Rhodesian rebellion of November 11, 1965, and its repercussions across the Zambezi, the enhanced recalcitrance of a part of the European minority—mainly on the Copperbelt—began to threaten an as yet fragile structure of crosscutting loyalties between Europeans and Africans; and there began to appear—unwished, it must be said, by UNIP—the old colonial

situation in reverse: the situation in which one community (now the Africans) were "the community" while the rest (now the Europeans) were outside it. It could be expected that a defeat for the rebellion would also be a defeat for this "denationalization" of the Northern Rhodesian Europeans, while the rebellion's success would probably confirm the trend.

[73] Kuper, "Plural Societies: Perspectives and Problems."

[74] With the appalling war that followed, however, any such outcome was clearly to be long delayed.

Chapter 8 "Strangers" in Plural Societies: Asians in South Africa and Uganda[*]

Hilda Kuper

Previous papers in this seminar focused primarily on the opposition between two politically differentiated groups, a dominant minority and a subordinate majority. Other categories of people were recognized, but treated as residual, playing no important part in promoting or possibly deflecting conflict. This paper will introduce a slightly different perspective by concentrating on people described as "strangers" or "foreigners" by other residents (hosts or locals) in two politically demarcated areas that might be regarded as plural societies. More specifically, I will examine in the context of pluralism those diverse categories of people classified as "Asians" (or an equivalent) by Europeans and Africans of Uganda (East Africa) and of the Republic of South Africa.

Describing the position of Asians in South Africa, in 1904 Lord Milner wrote, "The Asiatics are strangers, forcing themselves upon a community reluctant to receive them,"[1] and a program of the present Nationalist Party stated, "The Party holds the view that Indians are a foreign and outlandish element which is unassimilable."[2]

In the political context an "Asian" is not regarded as an isolated individual differentiated by any unique quality of personality, but,

[*] I should like to acknowledge my thanks to Leo Kuper, Corinne Armstrong, Sondra Hale, and Merrick Posnansky, and to the members of the colloquium, for their criticism of an earlier draft of this paper.

The selection of South Africa and Uganda is purely arbitrary, based on the fact that they are the two areas in which I happened to do research. Thus, the only, and rather rare, constant in the comparison is the investigator. Kenya, the area of greatest concentration of Indians in East Africa, had in the preindependence period certain characteristics which superficially resembled those of South Africa more closely (especially the position of white settlers and the government policy toward the land), but analysis at a deeper structural and cultural level would also reveal many important differences.

whether he wishes it or not, as a representative of a collectivity. He has become a symbol, insignificant in himself, but through him Europeans and Africans give a new dimension to their own identity. They are "not Asians" with all that label implies; and they are not concerned with their mirror image.

Much has been written on the "stranger" in fiction, psychology, and sociology, yet "the stranger" in his totality remains, by definition as it were, forever alien and unknown. I will restrict myself to a sociological approach, recognizing that there is not, and cannot be, a definitive interpretation of the "stranger" or of "strangers." [3]

Among the varied, and not necessarily consistent, characteristics attributed to strangers are their mobility (actual or potential); their relative noncommitment, objectivity, or freedom from the conventions of those among whom they are sojourning; the abstract and ambivalent qualities of their relationship with the host founded only on "generally human commonness" so that, as members of the totality, they are both near and far at the same time.[4] Jews have frequently served as the model of the "typical stranger," [5] and their role as traders has given rise to a further cluster of features attributed to strangers as status groups. Thus Weber, using a caste analogy, speaks of people who, because of differences in religious or ethnic background, are relegated to the status of pariahs [6]— distinctive hereditary groups characterized by social and political disprivilege and a significant distinctiveness in economic function, dependent for their existence on the power of some other group whom they followed or accompanied. Moreover, they "live in a 'diaspora' strictly segregated from all personal intercourse except that of an unavoidable sort and their situation is legally precarious. Yet, by virtue of their economic indispensability, they are tolerated, indeed frequently privileged. . . ." [7]

The term "Asian," like the term "stranger," is ambiguous. It has no genetic (racial) validity; the range of physical differences including pigmentation is as wide within the collectivity as between Asians and whites. We will see that its cultural content is equally questionable, and that its reality is relative to situations and arbitrarily defined.

Simmel described the stranger as the individual whose position in the group "is determined essentially by the fact that he has not belonged to it from the beginning, that he imparts qualities into it, which do not and cannot stem from the group itself." [8] Of course, if this criterion were strictly interpreted, very few people would not be strangers. In the colonial period the term would be particularly applicable to Europeans whether administrators or settlers; and they are, in fact, classified as a different species in the language of many African peoples. The position of Europeans as a ruling minority, however, enabled them to assert for themselves identities they considered more favorable. In the new African states they have accepted the classification of "expatriates." Such terms as "foreigners," "strangers," "aliens," and "immigrants" were more frequently reserved for Asians irrespective of their actual period of residence or place of origin, the implication being that *they* were intruders or outsiders.[9]

Pluralism in broadest interpretation is a series of confrontations between people perceived (and perhaps perceiving themselves) as strangers. The confrontations may be hostile or friendly, and the label "strangers" has, in English, a wide range of conceptual refinements with "guests" at one end and "enemies" at the other. The concepts and situations interact and change, and in certain circumstances guests become enemies and enemies become allies. Sociologically, the meaningful position of strangers is affected by such varied factors as numbers, cultural equipment, structural relations, interests, and values, in both space and time.

The socially effective definition of "strangers" is made by an ingroup that has assumed the right to exclude. In a political context the ingroup is the ruling group which regulates classification and incorporation. In both South Africa and East Africa the politically dominant minority has classified the entire population into gross "racial" or "ethnic" categories reflected in the census, a device that serves the same function as self-validating myths of dominant groups in societies that have no system of writing. The census provides a charter of privilege emphasizing distinctions important in the minds of the rulers. In South Africa the gross categories of stratification are whites (Europeans), Africans (natives, Bantu), Asians (mainly Indians), and Coloreds. According to the most recent estimates, the total population in 1965 was 17,832,000, of whom 3,395,000 were whites, 12,162,000 Africans, 533,000 Asians, and 1,742,000 Coloreds.[10] In Uganda under British rule the population was generally classified as European, African, and different categories of Asian (Indo-Pakistani, Goan, and Arab). After independence there were only two main categories—African and non-African—the latter subdivided into European, Indo-Pakistani, Goan, Arab, and other. In 1963 the total population (calculated on the basis of the 1959 census) was 6,536,616, composed of 6,449,558 Africans and 87,058 non-Africans, of whom 10,866 were Europeans, 69,103 Indo-Pakistanis, 2,830 Goans, 1,946 Arabs, and 2,313 others.[11]

Both Uganda and South Africa are political units created by European governments, but their internal structures show few similarities and many differences, and to talk of them as equivalent societies is misleading.

Between 1900 and 1962 Uganda was a protectorate with policy controlled by Britain; in 1962 it was granted independence. Within its boundaries were four African kingdoms, of which Buganda was the most important, and numerous acephalous societies, each with its own internal integration and territorial base. Uganda's geographical and historical position makes it relatively easy for its inhabitants to maintain contact with people in Kenya and Tanzania, the other partners in the (short-lived) East African Federation, and also with the subcontinent of India. Indians were commercially active on the east coast as early as the tenth century A.D.

The Republic, formerly the Union of South Africa, broke from the British Commonwealth in 1961, intensifying the power of local white settlers. The country is divided historically into four provinces, each with specific and differential treatment of both Asians and Africans under a European oligarchy. Europeans, who control the distribution of land, own approximately 87 percent of the total area; Africans are restricted to 13 percent, and Asians have been permitted to purchase less than .01 percent. Asians are geographically, as well as politically, encapsulated; in the Republic more than 80 percent are restricted to the single province of Natal.

Perhaps the most frequent epithet attached by Europeans to Asians is "unassimilable." The extent of Asian nonassimilation is apparent in cultural pluralism, and is most conspicuous in such towns as Kampala (Uganda) and Durban (Natal). Even without a word being spoken there is no mistaking an Indian woman, elegant in sari, sandals, and jewelry, from her European or African peer. Similarly there is a world of contrast between the contents and arrangement of the African market, the Indian market, and the European market, and there is an equally obvious otherworldly gulf separating ancestral shrine, temple, mosque, and church. But cultural differences also cut through and across these categories. In East Africa it is equally easy to distinguish Sikhs, Arabs, and Punjabi by appearance. There are many Asians and Africans, particularly men, who on all occasions wear Western clothes. There are African shops modeled on the Indian *duka* and Asian-owned shops patronized almost exclusively by Europeans because of the relatively low prices and high quality of imported Western goods. Islam and Christianity as proselytizing religions include members of all ethnic groups, and Hinduism is singularly eclectic. In some situations ethnic cleavages are culturally reinforced; but interethnic links are forged by individuals who do not conform. The identification of Asians as unassimilable is thus not necessarily determined by specific visible characteristics but by the orientation and interest of the "host"; physical visibility is a convenient symbol for "strangeness."

It is essentially at the level of political incorporation that racial or ethnic distinctions are most rigidly maintained. Cultural assimilation is largely a reciprocal of political dominance, and those who are supposed to assimilate the culture of others are in fact expected to subordinate the culture that was their own. The deliberate selective retention of difference by a minority, however weak physically, challenges and may even threaten the ethnocentric certainty of the dominant.

The fact that Asians may be regarded as a single ethnic category by both Europeans and Africans does not imply united action or acceptance of a common Asian identity. We will see that in many situations cleavages are sharper within the Asian sector than between Asians, Europeans, or Africans. In a society where power is arbitrarily ascribed, it is convenient for the dominant to treat Asians as if they were a corporate group, and to reinforce this by separate laws, separate schools, and so on; at times it may be convenient for Asians, despite their internal differentiation, to accept this fiction and form Asian organizations to negotiate with the representatives of the dominant group.[12] It is because identification with their own subgroups is so meaningful that the political role of minorities becomes less effective.

I deal with Uganda and South Africa not as comparable units but as areas in which there appear to be comparable and contrasted processes and structured relations. Immigrants to both East and South Africa have been drawn from many parts of the Indian continent, but migration in the two territories followed different principles of selection and the immigrants received different treatment and recognition. Differential rights to land, occupation, cultural freedoms, and participation in government are the resources of domination and the indexes of incorporation which contribute to the pattern of pluralism. The manipulation of these resources has changed over time, which sociologically is not an ordered chronological sequence but a series of structured relationships which may be overlapping, repetitive, or discontinuous. The divisions I have selected are delimited by such significant relationships affecting Asians as slavery, conscription, indenture, resident alien, protected subject, and citizenship.

SLAVERY

ENSLAVING IN EAST AFRICA

In East Africa, where the term "Asian" is applied to Arabs, Goans, and Indo-Pakistanis, the first representatives to enter the territory now known as Uganda were Arabs who came to obtain ivory and to capture slaves. In return, they gave guns, cloth, and other goods. By these cultural innovations, especially the more effective weapons, they altered the balance of power between existing African political communities. Conversely, Arab relationships with Africans were influenced by the African economic and political systems. Where there were already centralized states, the Arabs obtained their economic ends by negotiations with recognized chiefs, causing relatively little destruction, but there was devastation, pillage, and rapine in the acephalous communities of nomadic pastoralists, disinterested in trade and prepared to raid for cattle but not for slaves. As Oliver and Mathew write, "The strong grew stronger and the weaker tended to be annihilated." [13]

Arabs reached the capital of Buganda in 1843, and four years later were aiding the Kabaka with firearms in a war of expansion and were participating in internecine struggles of neighboring kingdoms.[14] The maintenance of the traditional state of Buganda can to a large extent be attributed to Arabs (foreigners) who supplied the Kabaka with weapons and with cloth to pay his soldiers.

By and large, early Arab penetration was "essentially infiltrative and diffuse," and could scarcely be described as colonization. "The number of Arabs in the interior cannot have exceeded a few hundred at the most . . . and at every point this thinly scattered community was interwoven with the indigenous political and social scene. Its members took part in local quarrels; established themselves as local political figures, took African wives and concubines (Arab wives were a rarity in the interior); and dispensed arms by barter or as wages to their African neighbors and employees." [15] Individual Arabs became scribes and skilled craftsmen in the courts of African potentates, who sometimes honored them with land as well as slaves. Thus, Arab slavers and African chiefs collaborated for mutual benefit.

While the first phase of Arab contact was essentially commercial in interest, albeit not in effect, the second was more directly political and religious. The Arab slave trader was not a missionary: to have proselytized his victims "would indeed have precluded him from enslaving them." [16] But he could, and apparently did, expound the principles of Islam to the chiefs, and large-scale conversions began around 1860.[17] For ten years, 1857 to 1867, the Kabaka, Mutesa I, himself observed Ramadhan. In this period, Western "Christian" explorers penetrated the interior and blazed a trail for missionaries, traders, and administrators. Slavery had been prohibited in their own countries and condemned in their colonies. Europeans entering Uganda were primarily interested in controlling the area for the commercial interests of their own governments. The Arabs attempted to destroy the growing number of Africans interested in the teaching of Western missionaries and to seize the political power necessary to stabilize their own commercial interests. In the subsequent conflict between the two sets of foreigners (Arab and European), local Africans were involved as supporters of both sides.

For a time the Kabaka himself supported the Arabs and had a number of Catholics and Protestants executed when they refused to give up their new religions. Then, fearing for his own position, he plotted to wipe out not only Christians but also supporters of Islam. The plot was discovered, the Kabaka fled, and there followed "a brief unnatural alliance between Christians and Muhammadans" [18] who appointed the Kabaka's brother in his stead.

Parallel to the Christian-Muslim schism, a schism that cut across local African loyalties and identification, was the more overt struggle between rival Western powers engaged in the partition of Africa. Within Uganda, Christian missions became known by their countries of origin, "Fransa" (Catholics) and "Inglesa" (Protestants).[19] In 1892 fighting broke out between the Fransa and the Inglesa, and Lugard, then agent of the Imperial British East African Company, intervened decisively on the side of the Inglesa. The Kabaka (Mwanga) who at different periods had supported the Muslims, the English, and the French, recognized the company's supremacy. When the British government finally established the protectorate of Uganda (1894), the importance of Islam as a political power was destroyed. But the division of the population into Muslim, Protestant, Catholic, and "pagan" remained a permanent legacy, and these new identities in some cases united and in other cases reinforced traditional African cleavages.

The British distributed chieftanships and offices of state according to religious affiliations and political role, not according to traditional status. Buganda itself was no longer a united kingdom; and the Kabaka, from being the autocratic symbol of a whole people, became the leader of a faction.

The period of slavery was thus one in which Asians exerted considerable influence, and the conflicts between them and the British, though waged in the name of different religions, were engendered by commercial and power interests that extended beyond the limited boundaries of local African rulers.

ENSLAVEMENT IN SOUTH AFRICA

In South Africa the first Asiatics also arrived in the period of slavery. Slavery, however, can be introduced by foreigners or be used as a technique for incorporating foreigners (and locals) in established societies. This time the slavers were Europeans and the slaves were mainly nonlocal Africans and Asiatics. The Dutch East India Company had initially stopped at the Cape to obtain fresh food for its crews en route to the Far East, and the transformation from a refreshment station for transients to an embryonic white settler society took place unobtrusively when the company allowed some of its members to become free burghers with rights to cultivate land outside the fort. The indigenous Khoisan people (Bushmen and Hottentots) were nomadic hunters and pastoralists, intractable in the face of demands from the burghers. In keeping with the practice of the period, slaves were a recognized resource for domestic and plantation labor. Between 1715 and 1792 the slave population (composed predominantly of people brought from Madagascar, Mozambique, and the Dutch East Indies, but including some indigenes) grew from 2,000 to nearly 15,000.[20]

Constituting an elite stratum of the slaves were political exiles from Java whose leader became the nucleus of a self-conscious Muslim community which remains culturally distinct (endogamous and separated by religion) within the category of Coloreds.[21] Known as the Cape Malays, the exiles numbered over 40,000 in 1958. Afrikaans became the home language of the majority, but a small segment retained an Indian home tongue and formed a link with the majority of Asians in South Africa who came to the province of Natal after the end of slavery.

The abolition of slavery, enforced by the British in 1834, did not mean the incorporation of the Coloreds into European society. Though at that stage they received the right to vote, they were, through the institution of slavery itself, excluded from the full culture of the whites. Only the Muslim core retained a certain religious independence and their own family structure; for the rest, the Coloreds strove to identify with the privileged whites. They isolated themselves from Africans and from the bitter frontier struggles waged between Africans and Boers.

Slavery in South Africa was geographically more limited than in East Africa, and involved no conflict between Asian and African. Paradoxically, it is in the Western Cape, the only province in which slavery was firmly established, that (under the British) a liberal tradition emerged in South African politics, and members of the Cape Colored community (including Muslims) held responsible administrative positions.

Slavery is a blanket term covering both slaver and enslaved. It may appear to represent a single structural mechanism, but, as I have indicated, it has widely different effects, not only according to whether one is at the taking or the receiving end of the exchange, but also according to the nature and complexity of other structured arrangements and ideologies. In both Uganda and South Africa, Asians were perceived as strangers, but in Uganda they inflicted slavery, and in South Africa they were incorporated with slaves.

INDENTURED LABOR AND OTHER FORMS OF RECRUITING AND CONTROLLING STRANGERS

South Africa

Slavery, indenture, and conscription are a few alternative techniques for incorporating foreigners (or locals) and organizing them in the service of a dominant political power. The system of indenturing Indians came about chiefly as a result of the abolition of slavery in the British Empire in 1834, and was part of a planned emigration-*cum*-labor program. The areas and conditions of recruitment and employment were defined both to protect the indentured from the worst abuses of slavery and to provide them on the expiration of their contracts with the choice of a new domicile.[22] Slaves were emancipated in South Africa more than fifty years before slavery was suppressed in East Africa, and indenturing was of longer duration and greater significance in the south.

The whites in South Africa had established their hegemony over the indigenes, but were themselves openly divided into two hostile political camps—Boer and British—differentiated by language, religion, and other cultural attributes. The colony of Natal was already under British rule when a few immigrants, some with experience of Mauritius, introduced cane as a commercial crop for which they required a reliable and continuous supply of cheap labor. The surrounding area was the homeland of the Zulu who had already lost their political autonomy but were not yet prepared to serve the demands of the European labor market. After four years of persistent pressure by the planters, the government of Natal finally negotiated with the governments of Britain and India (itself under the British) to indenture Indians.

Between 1860 and 1911 some 140,000 indentured Indians were shipped to Durban, the port of Natal, initially for labor on the sugar plantations but later, as the system was seen to be profitable, for work on railways, in coal mines, and in domestic service.[23] They became an essential element in almost every sector of the growing economy, but the conditions of their service contracts restricted their freedom of movement and barred them from associating as equals with Europeans. The indentured were bound for three, and later five years, to a particular master; during this time they were segregated in barracks (ghettos) on the premises of their employers. Their pay was slightly higher than that of Africans, but lower than that of European employees. They were excluded from political assemblies and lacked access to the ordinary courts of the country; their main channel of complaint or communication was to the office of the "Protector of Indian Immigrants." The conditions on the estates varied with the character of the owner, but even the most liberal did not go beyond personalizing a few of the "coolies." [24] Sirdars were appointed for their ability to keep order, but the indentured had no organization to express their interests.

To the whites, these Indians had the overriding legal identity of indentured laborers, but they were in fact an unorganized, culturally heterogenous aggregate.[25] Roughly 60 percent were Hindu of different sects; 16 percent Muslim, mainly Sunni; 5 percent Christians, mainly Catholic; and the remainder included Zoroastrians and Jainists. Among the Hindu, the occupations for which they were required led to an emphasis on certain occupational castes and also a deliberate exclusion of others. The majority, estimated at 60 percent, were of the Sudra and Scheduled castes; 25 to 30 percent were Vaisya (merchant); 10 to 15 percent were Kshatriya (military and governmental), with a small scattering of Brahmins (priests and scholars).[26] Recruiters selected or accepted, the indentured by individual qualification, and most came as isolated persons, or with a few kin or friends. Women, preferably not wives, were recruited in the proportion of 30 to 100 and later 50 to 100 men. They were drawn from villages and towns in the south and central provinces and shipped through the ports of Madras and Calcutta. The mother tongues included Tamil, Telugu, Hindi, Urdu, and several minor languages of India.

In South Africa, the indentured had to forge a new identity. From the time of their embarkation many traditional restrictions on social distance and ritual purity could no longer be maintained, and the high ratio of men to women made it impossible to adhere strictly to correct caste endogamy. Many of them realized that because of the South African conditions to which they had to adapt, they would not again be accepted by their kin, and so could never return to India.[27]

At the same time, like other immigrants to foreign lands, they tried to organize many of the new relationships along familiar lines and retain some of the old customs. The religious distinction between Hindu and Muslim remained meaningful and provided the broadest boundary of endogamy. Each plantation owner allocated a site for a temple or a mosque, or for both, and permitted the rituals of village, as well as Sanskritic, Hinduism. Important differences in marriage regulations continued to separate northern from southern Hindus. Local dialectal differences became relatively unimportant, but two major, rather hybridized, versions of Tamil and Hindi (Hindustani) emerged. English developed as the main language of communication with Europeans, and Indians acquired a few words of different African languages.

The institution that showed the greatest persistence as an ideal or normative influence was the extended joint family, an ideal essentially different from the monogamous nuclear family of the Europeans and from the polygynous ideal of the Africans.[28] The Indians remained a distinctive and isolated enclave largely through their particular type of kinship network. New families were started on the estates, but the ideals of arranged marriages, joint households, and strict control over women appear to have been maintained, or inculcated, by the more respected immigrants.

The indentured had been promised that on completion of their period of service they would be allowed to remain in the country as free citizens, or receive a free passage back to India. So valuable did their services prove that landholdings were offered as an inducement to those willing to reindenture, but as the number of reindentured increased, an earlier promise of citizenship was not fulfilled, and after a few years the offer of land was withdrawn.

Indenturing was terminated in 1911 by the British government of India in response to protests by Indians against bad treatment during the period of indenture and the nonfulfillment of promises to the free or ex-indentured. As an interested but external center of power, Britain imposed this economic sanction in the hope of changing the internal policy of South Africa. The sanction did not have the desired effect because by that stage African political and economic independence had been broken, and a supply of African labor, even cheaper than the labor of the indentured Indian, was available and was substituted under different, albeit equally rigorous, controls.

The indentured Indians were brought into competition with Africans as unskilled manual workers. African males were recruited from segregated reservations as temporary migrant laborers, a policy inaugurated on a large scale with the development of the mining industry. The conditions of migrant African workers were in some respects similar to those of the indentured Indians: they too were treated as transients, were restricted in their movement, were not free to choose a particular employer, and were housed in compounds (ghettos). But there were also marked differences of which the most important, for our consideration, were that only African males were recruited, that their wages were lower (on the assumption that the workers were unmarried or that their families were supporting themselves in the reservations), and that their period of service was limited to approximately nine months, after which they were expected to return to their kin and traditional culture on tribal reservations.

Between indentured Indians and migrant Africans, there was little or no communication and considerable latent hostility. Though the majority of Indians were illiterate, they were aware of a great literate tradition. Many were peasants, but they had knowledge through experience of a wide diversity of occupations and of a money economy. Ideologically and ritually, the Africans with their more specific and exclusive ancestral cult presented sharp contrasts to the values of the more universal religions of Hinduism and Islam. Though the caste hierarchy broke down on the estates, the indentured tried to arrange marriages within narrow religious and linguistic boundaries. They were totally opposed to marriage with Africans, not on the basis of color, but on that of culture. Africans in turn despised the indentured as servile and of poor physique. More especially they objected to the rigorous endogamy of Indians and the close supervision they exercised over their women. Antagonism is said by informants to have been intensified by the fact that the few cases of miscegenation which occurred were between Indian (Muslim) men and African women.

When the period of indenture was over, Indian men, unlike migrant African workers, had no land or kin on the reservations, and moved with the wives and children acquired during indenture to establish more permanent roots in peri-urban and urban areas. The Indian family persisted as a closed unit and the ex-indentured became market gardeners, unskilled laborers, or petty traders.[29]

The economic role of the ex-indentured had changed from that of captive (indentured) labor to that of free workers, and Europeans then saw them as potential competitors who had to be brought into a new restrictive relationship. They were given a political status that may be described as "resident aliens," a status already held by "passenger" Indians.

The "passengers" were immigrants who had entered the country at their own expense to trade and serve in commerce. Unlike the indentured who were mainly Hindus from the south, the passengers were predominantly Gujarati- and Urdu-speaking Muslims who embarked, not from Calcutta and Madras, but from Bombay. They were relatively few in number (some 10 percent of all Indian immigrants). They were able to retain basic domestic relations with kin outside Africa, they continued to contract correct marriages in India, and they considered themselves distinct from, and superior to, the indentured. Initially they were accommodated under more flexible administrative arrangements in South Africa, and were allowed to move freely. They opened shops not only near the plantations where the indentured were employed, but also in African tribal areas and in European centers.

Passenger Indians, by entering trade, challenged white privileges and were the first to be affected by anti-Indian legislation. Wealthy mer-

chants responded by organizing legal defense. Europeans wielded different types of coercive control over indentured and passengers until, as
free Indians, the ex-indentured became economically mobile; they were
then identified and treated as undesirable aliens.

The reaction of Europeans to the indentured, and to the passenger and
ex-indentured, Indians depended almost entirely on European economic
interests and reflected contradictory trends in the European community
itself. On the one hand, European employers desired more and more
cheap, efficient labor; on the other, European traders and businessmen
demanded a cessation of immigration to stop Indian competition. Thus
we find legislation to import more laborers accompanied by legislation to
prevent the settlement of Indians in the country.

But the more cohesive self-conscious passengers felt they had nothing
to gain by associating with the ex-indentured, and initially excluded
them from their organizations. This economic cleavage, reinforced by
cultural divisions carried over from the "homeland," was narrowed under
the unique leadership of Mahatma Gandhi (known then only as Mohan-
das Karamchand).[30] Gandhi, himself from Gujarat and of the merchant
caste, first entered South Africa to represent the legal interests of passenger clients.

Much has been written about this great man. In the context of this
colloquium, his presence in South Africa raises a most important question: What is the significance of an outstanding individual in plural
societies? Or, more specifically, what is the significance of a charismatic
stranger in a country unwilling to accept him, his people, or his ideas?
Parodying the role of Pilate, I cannot stay for an answer, but can only
emphasize the obvious. Seen in historical perspective, the immediate and
local influence of a leader may be less significant than the long-term
repercussions of his ideas. In South Africa Gandhi founded the Indian
Congress, inspired and led the first passive resistance movements, and
developed the ideology of *satyagraha*. But the concessions he gained for
his people were limited. Despite the devotion he inspired among the
heterogeneous Indian population and the respect he won even from General Smuts, the South African prime minister, he could not change the
racial structure of South African society. Indians continued to be unwanted foreigners. In 1913, two years after the British withdrew permission to indenture Indians to South Africa, and the year Gandhi himself
went back to India, the South African government introduced legislation
that virtually stopped any further Indian immigration. It then tried by all
means short of direct force to get Indians to return to India, though
Indians in South Africa argued that they were no more alien than the
whites, and that for the majority "repatriation" meant expatriation.[31] But

the significance of Gandhian ideology, developed in the conflict situations of South African pluralism, extends beyond the interactions of a few thousand South African–born Indians (of whom over 70 percent are descended from indentured laborers), and a white settler government: it influenced African political movements; it inspired the interracial resistance movement against unjust laws in 1952; and it formulated for people throughout the world new ideals and modes of action.

UGANDA

In East Africa, indenturing not only began later and lasted for a shorter period than in South Africa, but had less direct effects, culturally and structurally. Other less restrictive techniques, especially voluntary contracts and employment for the several departments of government, enabled the colonial power to recruit and govern Asians as a distinct category in the total population.

Since the time of Arab slaving, Indian merchants had been in contact with the East African coast as financiers of some of the expeditions, though they had not themselves ventured into the interior. With the arrival of the British in East Africa, an entirely new situation developed. The British had already established their ascendancy over India, and were able to use Indian troops to defeat Arabs and Africans. The Arabian Sea, the route of Arab dhows, was a frontier easy to cross, and the East African territories became an extension of the British Indian Empire. India became the main recruiting ground for personnel required by the British administration in East Africa for the lower and middle ranks of the civil service and for skilled and semiskilled crafts.

In 1895 the British sanctioned the building of the Kenya–Uganda railway as essential for the economic development of their new colonies. Indians rather than Africans were preferred as laborers. Some 32,000 Indians were indentured in East Africa, but their position was very different from that of their compatriots in South Africa: the main enterprise itself was specific and limited in time; the country was dangerous and unhealthy; few women were brought over; and living conditions were not such that family attachments could be established or old ties irrevocably broken. The result was that more than 80 percent returned to India at the end of their contracts.[32] Of those who remained after the completion of the railway in 1901, some 2,000 continued to be employed as railroad workers, and the others (approximately 4,000) spread throughout the territories of East Africa. Only a few hundred settled in Uganda, and they did not form a distinctive category of ex-indentured.[33]

In the wake of the indentured, and after the opening up of the interior, came a number of Indian petty traders and skilled artisans, whose immigration was spontaneous and virtually uncontrolled. They were the functional equivalent of the South African passenger class, but whereas in South Africa the passengers evoked the active hostility of the white settlers, in East Africa and especially in Uganda where white settlers were few, they were more privileged and more secure. In South Africa they were a small minority; in Uganda, after the indentured returned, they constituted the majority of the Asian population. Virtually no restrictions were placed on their entry until the Africans themselves were about to be granted independence. Between 1911 and 1963 their number increased, largely through immigration, from 2,216 (0.07 percent of the total population) to 82,100 (1.17 percent).[34] At the same time, and perhaps because of their greater security, the Indian traders and artisans not only maintained their own exclusive subcultures but developed new factions. They were divided along religious lines into Hindus, Muslims, Sikhs, Jains, Christians, and Zoroastrians.

The Hindus were mainly Sanatan (orthodox) of different sects who upheld caste and subcaste endogamy, and returned to India whenever possible to perform important family rituals. The Muslims were divided into Sunni and Shia, and this division, rooted in disputes over the position of the Imam (religious leader), was equaled by the social distance between subdivisions within the Shia (Ithna-Ashari, Ahmediya, and Ismaili). Even the Sikhs, though united by religion, differentiated themselves as Jat (agriculturalists and petty landowners) or Ramgarya (craftsmen). The Goans, all of whom were Catholics, dissociated themselves from other Indians.

Cutting across religious differences were certain common languages. Most Hindus and Muslims spoke Gujarat or Cutch, the Sikhs spoke Punjabi, and the Goans, Konkani. Within these languages were dialectal differences evaluated in terms of locality and of caste. Even occupations were largely linked to caste or commercial associations.

These major differentiations were, and are, intensely meaningful to the East African "Asian";[35] it was by reference to them that the Asian asserted his superiority over the Africans.

The policy of the British government toward Asians in Uganda was guided by its policies (which changed over time) toward the local Africans. Traditional African societies, especially the Baganda, were granted considerable autonomy within their own territories. Sale of land to non-Africans was described as "alienation of land," and non-Africans (whites as well as Asians) were restricted from buying land in "African" territory; hence, most of the Asians were located in the towns. However, they had freedom of movement in carrying out their trade and their commercial activities; and though they lived and worked most of their lives in East Africa, it was not only permissible, but often considered desirable, to retain homes and identity in India.

RESIDENT ALIENS

SOUTH AFRICA

Perhaps the crucial mark of strangers is that they have no guaranteed rights in the land.[36] Of course, in a conquest state they are not alone in this fate; unlike the conquered, however, they cannot claim the right of prior occupation. In South Africa the domination of white settlers is anchored in their policy of territorial segregation, with conquered Africans encapsulated in reservations ("Bantu homelands" and "native townships") and Asians segregated without security of ownership or occupation. As resident aliens who have come from the outside, albeit initially at the request of the "host," the Asiatics are expected to return when they have served his purpose.

By the time Gandhi had left South Africa, each of the four provinces had restricted Asian land rights in different ways. The most stringent residential exclusion was imposed in the Free State as early as 1891. In the Transvaal, Asians could own fixed property but only in limited areas especially assigned for their residence, and they were specifically excluded from mining or from acquiring land in mining areas. In the Cape Colony and in Natal the approach was more permissive, but it always emphasized that ownership or occupation was a privilege and not a right.[37]

Restrictions stamping Asians as resident aliens were forcibly expressed in "ghetto acts" (segregating people in areas often peripheral to those of the whites), "pegging acts" (designed to maintain existing limited distribution of landed property), and "expropriation acts" (benefiting one racial group at the expense of another). The Group Areas Act of 1950, the most extreme example of legalized expropriation, gave the government unlimited power to rearrange areas of established residence, property ownership, and trade.[38] These discriminatory measures, used at different times and with different degrees of subtlety, evoked various forms of protest from Indian leaders, some Europeans, and sympathizers outside South Africa. Thus it was the 1946 "Ghetto Act" (officially the Asiatic Land Tenure and Representation Act) which led the Indian government to withdraw its High Commissioner, apply trade sanctions, and place restrictions on the entrance of white South Africans into India.[39]

The Group Areas Act, which inflicted severe hardship on the weakest groups (Asians, Coloreds, and urbanized Africans), produced a chain of complex reactions. In some situations people who perceived one another as strangers drew together and people of a single "ethnic identity" opposed one another. In Natal the Asians were the main scapegoats of white avarice, but there was neither complete cleavage on racial lines nor unanimous action within them. Indians and Europeans held public meetings (protest and prayer, jointly and separately); ratepayer associations were organized; individual leaders interviewed "city fathers"; and different techniques, ranging from bribery to courting arrest on moral principles, were tried. And while the act brought Indians together on the basis of common suffering, the different efforts to alleviate suffering created other divisions. Moreover, the law had differential effects on the Indians; for the first time the more wealthy were able to set up distinctive suburbs which they could develop on Western middle-class standards. A few outstanding Indian leaders succumbed to the temptation of withdrawing with their families to more congenial environments where they were not constantly confronted with the abject poverty of the majority of their fellow countrymen (with many of whom they had nothing in common except discrimination).

Resident aliens were a political and legal, not an economic or cultural, category. They included members of the lower and middle classes and followed occupations ranging from street sweeper to barrister and doctor. Though all the indentured Indians were poor, and not all the passengers were rich, the dynamic aspect of the economy was the emergence over the years of a relativley wealthy and educated elite from the ex-indentured. Yet, contrary to the European stereotype, the majority of South African Indians remained poor. In Durban, the city with the largest Indian population, the per capita income in 1951 was roughly the same as that of Africans, and less than one-third that of whites.[40]

In the economic structure Asians were pressed between two powerful opposing forces, one represented by Europeans, who monopolized privileges through such restrictive techniques as job reservation and the color bar (backed sometimes by law and sometimes by convention), the other represented by Africans who were considered physically stronger and were prepared to accept a lower scale of pay. When non-Europeans entered into labor disputes with European management, there was a tendency to replace Indians by Africans.

As resident aliens without the strength of numbers and with limited economic resources, the South African Indians could never effectively challenge the white settler government. In the course of time, and despite local and international conferences, they lost political privileges they had previously possessed. The municipal vote and the parliamentary vote had been taken from them and they were politically as well as socially disprivileged. They were at an equal disadvantage in relation to Africans, who were subjected to additional political restrictions. It suited the book of the South African government to use the Indian, as "the outsider," as a buffer and a scapegoat.[41]

The history of South African Indian politics reveals the weak and ambivalent position of strangers without power attempting at different times to negotiate alliances with whites and with Africans. This can perhaps be most clearly illustrated by the differences in organization and objectives of the four passive resistance campaigns. The first (1903) was directed against restrictive and humiliating immigration laws introduced in the Transvaal and affecting the rights of traders in and with that province. The trader was the resister, the leader Gandhi. The second resistance campaign, also under his leadership, was directed against wider issues, directly related to the indentured: first, the poll tax imposed on free Indians who failed to reindenture or to deport themselves back to India, and second, marriage laws that, according to a court judgment, made Indian marriages contracted in accordance with Indian tradition illegal. Passenger and indentured participated in protest, and women from both groups joined in and inspired the resisters. The second passive resistance campaign, ending in 1913, emancipated Indian politics from the personal interests of the traders and paved the way for the rise of a political elite drawn from all sections of South African Indians. But only Indians were involved, and resistance was seen as a last resort. More usual were negotiations and deputations at both the national and international level.

The third passive resistance campaign was primarily a protest demonstration by a group of young educated radicals who, having first organized themselves into a nonracial antisegregation council, took control of the South African Indian Congress. Some 2,000 Indians, mainly workers and clerks but including a number of well-known professional men and women, and led by two young doctors (one a Muslim from the Transvaal, the other a Hindu from Natal), deliberately violated an old trespass law and were jailed for a month. The specific issue on which they organized was the Ghetto Act of 1946, but like all symbols, the act had far wider and more meaningful associations. After their release from prison, the two doctors, followed by a batch of resisters, crossed the border of Natal into the Transvaal, repeating Gandhi's initial act of resistance. But this time it was a symbolic bid for freedom and equality of all subordinated people. Significantly enough, the more conservative Indians, represented by two antagonistic individuals, were at the same time appearing before the United Nations to voice the grievances of the Indians in South Africa.

The fourth and last nonviolent resistance movement (1952), known as the Defiance Campaign against Unjust Laws, expressed a further development of identification between Africans and Indians. The laws selected as rallying symbols affected Africans more directly than Indians. The campaign was organized jointly by the African National Congress and the Indian Congress. The majority of the 8,557 resisters who went to jail were Africans, but in Natal each group of resisters was led by one of the elite of both groups.[42]

The Indians had in fact become organized on ideological grounds—protest and compromise—into two distinct political associations, the South African Indian Congress and the South African Indian Organization. The former was represented by radical educated leaders interested in nonracial development, mass support, and identification with Africans; the latter expressed essentially the interests of traders and merchants, afraid to lose their hard-earned position and acutely aware of the threat of rising African nationalism.

The South African Indian Congress, which entered with Africans and white radicals into the Congress Alliance, produced a "Freedom Charter." The government retaliated and charged the leaders with treason. The South African Indian Congress was declared an illegal organization, the ban including its allies as well.

A new phase was beginning in South Africa: the submissive resident alien was being accommodated as the "third-class citizen."

PROTECTION: "BRITISH SUBJECTS"

In South Africa, Indian traders were treated not only as competitors, but as specific (stranger) competitors; on this basis restrictive legislation was justified or rationalized. In East Africa, Indians were classified as British subjects and were more readily accepted; as traders they received considerable protection. They became relatively privileged middlemen, in relation to whites and Africans, in the marketplace. Trading did not require ownership of land but the privilege of mobility, a privilege denied Indians in South Africa but enjoyed by Indians in East Africa.

Mobility, however, was not approved by the more settled local African populations. On the contrary, it was an obvious hallmark of strangers as "foreigners." It meant they were less bound by local conventions, and perhaps less loyal to local leaders. And it was not only Asians but immigrant Africans who were resented by the locals. Audrey Richards records that in certain districts these foreigners, outnumbering locals in the proportion of three to two, were a major source of economic concern and political friction.[43] Many came from Ruanda-Urundi in Belgian mandated territories and from less properous areas in the Uganda Protec-

torate to search for work in the relatively wealthy agricultural country of
the Baganda. Employment was largely on cotton, coffee, and sugar
plantations, where most of the landowners were Baganda who considered the "foreign" Africans their inferiors.[44] Asians were a different type
of foreigner; they were more wealthy, more powerful, and more disliked.

The Asians who remained in, or migrated to, Uganda after the completion of the railway were predominantly semiskilled and skilled workers.
In the Indian social-caste framework they were above the Sudra
(menial) castes. Africans, however proud, rich, and skilled, were outside
the boundaries of the caste system, and conceptually relegated to positions of inferiority. Europeans were also placed outside the system, but
the British held the reins of power and the Asians recognized that their
own security and advancement depended on British goodwill and protection. Numerically, Asians and Europeans were both minorities in
Uganda, but the Europeans had the stronger influence because the
protectorate was ruled from Britain, whereas the government of India
(also under the British) was prepared to exert only limited economic and
moral sanctions to defend the interests of Indians in Africa.

Thus, prior to World War II, Asians negotiated politically with whites,
and made no efforts to gain African support. British and Asians together
constituted the official central bureaucracy; Africans were left with relative autonomy in their specific districts. On the government-established
Executive and Legislative councils, the problem of proportionate representation was initially expressed, not in terms of Africans against Asians,
but in terms of Asians against Europeans. Not until 1945 were the first
Africans nominated to the Legislative Council; this action marked the
beginning of a steady process of Africanization of the central government.

Throughout the period of British protection, Asians in East Africa
developed a number of separate, and often hostile, associations and
pressure groups. Though frequently treated as a single unit, Asians
seldom reacted with unity. Associations such as the Central Council of
Indian Associations found it difficult to get general support and were not
so well institutionalized as smaller communal organizations. Cultural
differences within the population became symbols for competing segments. Many associations were based on religion and received direction
from India. Events in India created further cleavages in Africa. Thus, on
partition of India, the Moslems of Uganda demanded separate seats on
the Legislative Council, and formed the Central Council of Moslem
Associations as an organization distinct from the former Central Council
of Indian Associations. Fissiparous tendencies were virtually unchecked:

within the Moslem segment, there were five different factions, three Gujarati-speaking, two Punjabi-speaking; within the Hindus, there were orthodox and reform, each with its own discrete castes.

Loyalty to one's own group was expected to be a primary motivation; in societal activities that went beyond communal limits, individuals had little authority. Within the separate communities there was considerable consensus on the interests that should be developed or maintained, especially in the fields of religious, educational, and welfare activities. This consensus, of course, was expressed by individuals chosen from the closed group by its own members. There was no political association comparable to the South African Indian Congress; in East Africa, to a far greater extent than in South Africa, Indian politics were conducted at the personal level between communal representatives and officials of the government. A pattern of patronage developed, expressed in invitations to public functions with a sundown party at the governor's residence as the apex of achievement. Leadership was often deflected into communal rivalries and the ambition for personal recognition.[45]

In a population so divided, it was inevitable that in political situations candidates should emphasize communal, religious, and language differences, thus weakening what little political strength the Asian minority might have had. Voting on a racial basis (described as "communal representation") was considered an essential correlate of colonial policy in extending participation in government to nonwhites. When the period of protection was moving to a close and it became clear that independence would be granted to the Africans, the Asians once again had to face up to the issue of their communal representation. The more conservative were eager for the British to set aside seats for minorities under the new constitution, but they were opposed by a small band of young Western-educated Uganda-born Asians who formed the Uganda Action Group. Its leaders, critically aware of the weaknesses among their own people and sensitive to African reactions, argued that to gain a few protected seats in a national assembly established under the aegis of a colonial power would perpetuate Asian factionalism and further alienate the African majority.

The hostility to Asians from a large section of the African population had become increasingly obvious. The position of Asians was to some extent complicated by the fact that Kampala, the largest town with a majority of Asian traders, fell within the boundaries of Buganda. It was from Baganda chiefs who had been given land in freehold by the British that Asians bought estates on which they grew cotton and sugar. Of 80,000 square miles, roughly 300 were owned by Asians (described as "alienated from Africans"), and antagonism was expressed against them as landowners and landlords as well as merchants, industrialists, and traders.

Mutually derogatory stereotypes developed, but Africans more frequently resorted to direct action. In 1949 the Bataka Party, led by a number of educated African reactionaries and one of the first modern African political movements, had its followers indulge in a spate of rioting and arson. In 1959 the Uganda National Movement organized a boycott of non-African traders in protest against the Wild Commission, which had recommended, in addition to a common roll for the election of all representative members of the Legislative Council, special provision for the adequate representation of minorities. Violence was directed against the Asians, and the Uganda National Movement was declared unlawful. The boycott continued even after its formal organization collapsed. The Uganda Action Group, which had aimed at counteracting ethnic isolation and identifying Asian with African interests, challenged Asian separation, but its own support was too limited and came too late to make a major impact on African leaders, or even to become known to the African masses.

The limited and ambivalent position of Asians under the Protectorate is well illustrated by the development of the Shia Khoja Ismaili community.[46] Shias in general hold that religious and secular leadership are inseparable, and must descend patrilineally through Ali, who had married the Prophet's daughter; but the only sect that holds that the visible living Imam still walks among them is the Shia Khoja Imami Ismaili. Their Imam is the Aga Khan.

The first Aga Khan to take an interest in East Africa visited Uganda in the 1930's and found among his followers many of the poorer and more backward Asians. Thereupon he inaugurated a series of communal financial enterprises (including an insurance company and a building society) and developed a vast educational and welfare program. His plans were executed by personally selected individuals who held their positions in the face of intense competition. Many of the most important tasks were carried out by honorary officers, who received their main rewards in the form of titles, which, with the exception of the European title "count," were traditional Ismaili titles, and carried an order of precedence on Ismaili ceremonial occasions. All power, sacred and secular, was vested ultimately in the Aga Khan. By 1960 the Ismailis were wealthy and influential, owning considerable property and running the most efficient schools, hospitals, and welfare societies. The decisions of the Aga Khan were issued as firmans (canonical injunctions or edicts) which were read from the pulpit in the *jamatkana* (Ismaili name for mosque).

They were accepted without dispute and were expected to receive immediate action. Firmans issued by the late Aga Khan and his successor, his son Ali, were increasingly directed at westernizing the Ismailis of East Africa. As a result, Ismailis spoke more English than Gujarati, girls and women wore Western dress, girls as well as boys received an education, Islamic laws of divorce were modified, and in general there was wider recognition of the value of the individual in the secular world. This was particularly noticeable at the kinship level, where there was a deliberate move toward developing the nuclear monogamous family as a residential unit, on the principle of a house for each family on a cooperative tenant-into-owner basis. At the same time the Ismailis were constantly reminded by the Aga Khan of their Islamic tradition and civic obligations: it was they who contributed money to complete the mosque at Kibuli, the center of Sunni worship, and it was they who first opened their hospitals and their schools to other ethnic groups.

Though no other Asian segment achieved such cohesion and success for its members, the Ismailis were accommodated as strangers both in the total context of Uganda and in the Asian population from which they had in many respects become disassociated and alienated. Under protection, the direction of Ismaili development supported European power as well as culture, and the Aga Khans, themselves sophisticated products of the West, were able to act as competent negotiators with British officials. The advances they achieved for the Ismailis were not necessarily seen as advantages by the larger Indian communities, and their relationship to Africans was paternalist rather than egalitarian. Ismailis did not attempt to proselytize Africans by doctrinal conversion, and intermarriage was virtually nonexistent. There were fewer African Ismailis than African Sunnis or Ahmaddiyas.

The ascriptive leadership of the Aga Khan in East Africa provides interesting contrasts with the position of Gandhi in South Africa. Gandhi, with all his vision and charisma, could claim no divine sanction to back his directives and authorize the continuity of his followers in his absence. Moreover, his goals were more universal and hence more difficult to achieve; those of the Aga Khan were more specific and realistic. The Aga Khan did not attempt to change the structure of colonialism; on the contrary, he instructed his followers to be law-abiding and to cooperate with the rulers as far as possible. He neither courted nor suffered imprisonment, and when he visited his followers in East Africa, he was treated as an honored guest by his British hosts.

The Ismailis of Uganda are only a fragment of the widely dispersed followers of the Aga Khan. As a spiritual leader, and without a fixed territory, he instructed Ismailis to give political loyalty and service, insofar as these did not conflict with the tenets of Islam, to the people among whom they lived. Accordingly, East African Ismailis have invested their money and their faith in East Africa, not in India or Pakistan. Through the leadership of the Aga Khan, the contacts and influence of the Ismailis spread beyond the marketplace; schools, hospitals, welfare centers, apartment houses, and business buildings stand as concrete symbols of Ismaili achievement and social effort. The coming of African independence, however, underscores the ambivalent role of people perceived as "strangers" who have a distinctive, religiously based, corporate identity, even though they have established permanent roots in the country of their domicile, and who must now accommodate to new, and possibly more hostile, hosts.

CITIZENSHIP

UNDER APARTHEID

Citizenship is a status theoretically distinct from that of alien resident in that the government accepts an obligation to grant alien subjects protection and other stipulated privileges. The South African Nationalist government finally decided that it could not expect South African–born Indians to expatriate themselves to India; nor could it exterminate them. Therefore, in 1961, the government formally took note of their existence and granted them a status that could be described as "pariah citizenship": not all subjects are citizens, and some subjects are more subject than others. Structural discontinuity between outright subjection and full citizenship may characterize a plural society, and scaling from lower-grade citizenship to full citizenship may indicate a change to a heterogeneous society. But the change from subjection to citizenship may not take place in all sections uniformly. In South Africa, the subject status of Africans remained when the status of Indians was officially changed. The cleavage between Africans and Asians was reinforced and to some extent widened; that between Asians and other citizens was potentially narrowed. De jure recognition need not imply de facto changes or advantages.

In 1961 the Nationalist government created a separate department of Indian Affairs, whereby the Indians as a distinct "racial" group would receive special attention. This move was in accord with the established procedure of organizing the entire administration by race rather than by function, systematically removing from the structure of the country institutions and practices that might develop a single nonracial society.[47] It offered no hope that Indians would ever be permitted to share in white political power and be recognized as full citizens with the same rights as South African–born whites.

Citizenship as expressed in the right to vote was taken from Indians in Natal as early as 1896, when the white settlers realized the ex-indentured were potential competitors and the number of passengers was increasing; the acceptance of Indians as permanent subject citizens in 1961 did not reinstate their right to vote. As far as possible the government effort has been to maintain Indians as a subordinated, isolated minority, and use them when necessary to increase the distance between African subjects and white masters. Racial zoning under the Group Areas Act has been effected on a national scale, with each different racial group a potential enemy of the whites. The location of Africans in terms of military control is openly acknowledged; in certain parts of the country "Indian areas" are strategic buffers between whites and blacks; Indian traders have been restricted mainly to "Indian areas," preventing them from trading either in African areas or in areas of established European trade. Job reservation (i.e., employment on a racial basis) is being strictly enforced. Indians may still not move from one province to another without special permission. In each province they are educated in separate schools, treated in separate wards of non-European hospitals, and buried in separate cemeteries.

Exclusion coincides with what can be described as the positive ethno-centrism of certain sections of the Indian population. Indians, particularly since India became independent, have placed a high value on their (idealized?) past, and have selected more self-consciously than Africans from the culture of the West. Africans, including the African elite, are in general more conspicuously westernized than Indians despite the fact that traditional Bantu culture has been persistently preserved, particularly in Natal, by a vast network of European directed legislation, whereas Indian culture has received no comparable recognition. Paradoxically, since the Indians have been put into the status of low-grade citizens, their great cultural heritage is receiving more positive official recognition and encouragement than when they were resident aliens. A segregated Indian university has been established by the government, to which many of the more self-conscious and wealthier Indians are contributing, and special courses in Indian languages and Indian history are being developed.

Thus while the distinction between Indians as resident aliens and third-class or pariah citizens is politically minimal, it is ideologically significant: instead of emphasizing the "unassimilability" of Asiatics as a basis for rejection, the latest development of apartheid policy fragments opposition by stressing cultural (especially linguistic and religious) distinctions. Individuals who attempt to counter political isolation by participating in a universal culture and nonracial institutions are penalized, and the South African government has increasingly assumed the power to fine, imprison, ban, banish, and kill individuals who oppose the apartheid system. But the fact that Indians are still politically more privileged, and that proportionately more Asiatics than Africans are educated and wealthy, may alienate Africans further from Indians and hence intensify the dependence of the Indian minority on Europeans. The negative stereotype of Indians held by many Africans of Indians is perpetuated by the contrast between their own low subject status and the Indians' pariah citizenship. Since Indian as well as African opposition leaders have been silenced, Indians fear that there may be a further deterioration of their position if Africans seize control.

UNDER AFRICAN INDEPENDENCE

Unlike the white settler government of South Africa, Britain was prepared to give Uganda independence before the Africans resorted to violence. The transition from the status of protected subject to full citizen was more peaceful in Uganda than in Kenya, where Mau Mau preceded, and precipitated, independence. In preindependent Uganda, violence had been directed primarily against Asians, but recognized hostility and an uneasy truce prevailed between the more privileged Baganda and other Africans, especially in the smaller political communities of the less prosperous north. Throwing off colonial control does not necessarily change a plural society to a heterogeneous society. Pluralism that pre-existed the colonial regime may attempt to reassert itself as the rulers of an erstwhile dominant kingdom try to extend their power over other and generally smaller political communities arbitrarily brought together under the colonial regime into a single new state. Should these other communities ally themselves and successfully resist, they could in turn establish their own alien hegemony. And it is even possible that a nonindigenous group settled in the country, if numerically strong and united, might assume control. In Uganda it probably would not affect the Asians if the Baganda or the Lango or any African coalition controlled their incorporation; it is clear that, unlike those in Fiji and Mauritius, Uganda Asians are a weak and divided minority who cannot exercise, let alone seize, power.

The organization of Africans into modern political parties was considered a prerequisite to independence and democracy. The fragmented Asian minority was placed in the difficult position of choosing among African politicians whose movements were influenced by ethnic regionalism and religious loyalties. The first modern African political party, the Uganda National Congress (UNC), started in 1952, expressed a nonracial policy in its manifesto:

In a happy and harmonious society, we cannot afford to create another South Africa in Uganda, wherein the tyrannizing race will be the African race. Uganda is essentially an African country, and must always remain so. It follows naturally from this that its fate must, and will, be determined by the majority of the people in Uganda, Africans. But this does not mean that the citizens of Uganda from the other races, provided they take on Uganda citizenship, will be denied their rights.[48]

The second political party, the Democratic Party (DP), was recruited mainly from Catholics; it also declared support for all underprivileged groups. In the preindependence election of 1961 the struggle was between the Uganda People's Congress (UPC), an outgrowth from the UNC, and the DP. The UPC was strong in all areas of the country except Buganda, and until 1965 was the major voice of regions and people opposed to the conservative and traditional exclusiveness of the Baganda. Apollo Milton Obote, president-general of the UPC and a Lango from the West Nile (i.e., a northerner), was elected the first prime minister of independent Uganda.

Independence was not simply a change of masters insofar as Indians were concerned. If one looked at structure without people, one might possibly say that an African bureaucracy had taken the place of the British civil service and assumed its manners. But the ideology of the new African bureaucrats was essentially different in that there was a change from racial separatism and stratification to a *theory* of nonracialism.

The Obote government stated its belief that the interests of the country would best be served by forging national unity among the people, whatever their racial origin or tribal background. Representation on racial lines was abolished, and there was no place for the Asian community as a distinct political entity. The basis of citizenship was extended in accordance with the policy of nationalization. Africans automatically ceased to hold British passports and opted for citizenship of their respective countries. Special provision was made in the constitution for granting citizenship to Asians, and most Asians living in East Africa could have obtained East African citizenship.

But the granting of citizenship to an exotic minority is not a guarantee of its security: Asians were well aware of the difference between the theory and the practice of equal citizenship.[49] In their public utterances most Asian leaders had taken a stand in favor of constitutional development toward African self-government and of adult universal suffrage, but they also knew that they were still stereotyped by Africans as Asians and foreigners and were politically and economically vulnerable. Large numbers were therefore not prepared to abandon British citizenship and commit themselves to African citizenship. Ismailis were advised (but not commanded) by the Aga Khan to take up citizenship out of loyalty to the country of domicile. The position was less clear for those who retained close ties, economic and familial, with people in India, or were equipped for work in other countries and feared that African promises were not bona fide. The advantages and disadvantages of African citizenship were carefully weighed, and sometimes it became expedient for one member to "take the papers" and serve as a "hostage" for the benefit of the family business. Asian hesitancy in acquiring African citizenship was cited by a number of Africans as further justification of the stereotype of Asians as selfish opportunists wanting the best of all worlds and the obligations of none. But though the African government of Uganda, unlike the white settler government in South Africa, made no discriminations within the category of citizen, the general security of Asians (whether citizens or not) was directly and adversely affected. The theory of nonracialism was soon translated into an avowed policy of Africanization, justified on grounds of removing the inequalities of the colonial period. Wherever possible new positions in the administration and all public services—hospitals, schools, post offices, police, and the like—were given to Africans in the following order of preferential selection: Uganda Africans, other East Africa Africans, expatriate Europeans, others, and (last and least) Asians. Asians already in government service were retained, but an embargo was put on their promotion.[50] The army, which paid more highly than almost any other government agency, was recruited entirely from Africans. African trade unions, the most effective pressure groups in East Africa, had no Asian members and "would certainly oppose any concession to the non-black citizen."[51] Ugly racist episodes were sufficiently frequent to justify Asians in their fear of Africanization. Aware of their weakness in numbers and their lack of organization, those who could, emigrated; the rest submitted and tried to compromise.

Leading Asians argue that if they integrate at the political level, many of their economic and social problems will be dealt with more sympathetically and successfully; but politics in Uganda are increasingly governed by internal rivalry and hostility among the various African groups, especially those of the southeast (the Bantu-speaking) and the northwest (Nilotic). One of the few areas of agreement between opposed African parties is that the Asians are not Africans. Individual Asians may be accepted—two were even elected as members of the Buganda Lukiko District Council after independence—but they and their supporters know they dare not speak against Africanization.

Africanization is more than a political process. It involves the view Africans have of themselves and their view of others (which is influenced by the view they think others have of them). Most Asians in East Africa had come to accept the hierarchical and racial structure established by the British, which in some respects protected the caste system of India. While aware of their own subordination and internal differences, the Asians treated the Africans as an inferior and undifferentiated collectivity. Many Asian-African relations are still at the shopkeeper-customer or master-servant level. The intricacies of Asian culture remain closed to African outsiders, especially at the intimate, personal level. When Asians are told to Africanize to the extent of giving up their own cultural identity, they face the problem: What is "African culture"? In Uganda the different ethnic units, especially the Baganda, wish to retain their cultural distinction. Asians hope that they can be accepted as a cultural subgroup in an increasingly heterogeneous society.

It is difficult to assess the emotional significance of cultural differences, but it is naïve to assume that greater knowledge would automatically reduce antagonism. The reverse may in fact be true. Indians and Africans have many different values; an area of mutual ignorance may ease public relations.

The majority of Asians are not prepared to give up their distinctive customs in the personal domain, but they are making many attempts to reduce the hostility evoked by their role in commerce. Some are taking Africans as directors or partners, and there is a general effort to train Africans in the wide range of skills in which Asians have proved their competence. As yet, however, very few African firms employ Asians in subordinate roles. Under Africanization, interaction between Asians and Africans has become more extensive and deliberate, but Asians remain conspicuous foreigners, politically, economically, and culturally.

Immigration from India had risen rapidly between 1913 and 1945 (when African independence was first bruited). Thereafter it began to decline: after independence in 1962 immigration was offset almost exactly by permanent emigration. Figures for the first quarter of 1964 for Kenya (we have no figures for Uganda) reveal that permanent Asian emigration was almost double immigration. The permanent emigrants are mainly families who retained contact with India, or Western-educated individuals who have skills or professions by which they can support themselves elsewhere. But 60 to 65 percent of Asian residents are East African–born, and though they may have gone to India or Pakistan to visit kinsmen, they claim East Africa as their home; in the early colonial period, they served as *tertium gaudens* ("the third who enjoys").[52] But the favorable position ended when Britains and Africans united in a common goal—the transfer of authority to Africans. They then became a weak minority of outsiders.

CONCLUSION

In Uganda and South Africa, territories arbitrarily delineated by conquest and negotiations between external powers, foreigners became rulers of traditional local communities. In this context I have analyzed a series of developments relating specifically to the incorporation of one section of the population classified as Asians on a racial basis, and also described as strangers, foreigners, or aliens.

As slavers in East Africa, Arabs (the first wave of Asian foreigners) introduced weapons and other goods which made them acceptable as individuals to African chiefs. When, however, European foreigners challenged Arab trade, Arabs organized as a political unit recruiting on a religious basis. Conflict resulted, and religious labels separated Muslim, Protestant, Catholic, and pagan, but did not obliterate racial cleavages. In South Africa, the first Asians came as slaves, and became involved in the major conflict between Boer and British as objects rather than actors. The liberation of slaves intensified the antagonism of the Boers toward the British, but liberated slaves were not accepted by either group as equals. They became part of the category of Coloreds with their own internal divisions expressed in religious endogamy.

By indenture, Asian immigrants with varied backgrounds and values were recruited by white immigrants for work that local Africans scorned or were unable to perform. In South Africa the indentured were spatially segregated from, but ideationally aware of, both white masters and African tribesmen. The majority of indentured remained in South Africa, where they abandoned, often deliberately, minor differences of religion, language, and custom. Traditional caste barriers were broken down, and endogamy was redefined in local, religious, linguistic, and racial terms. In East Africa, the social changes produced by the indentured were less obvious and direct than the immediate cultural contribution—the building of the railway. Having completed this task, the indentured virtually disappeared as a social as well as a legal category. Traders and craftsmen from India who took advantage of the route opened by the railway were peaceful entrepreneurs, protected subjects of the British Empire which had established itself in East Africa by defeating both Arabs and Africans, with the help of Indian troops.

The ex-indentured became resident aliens in South Africa and, together with a small percentage of passengers, served as the target of specific discrimination by the dominant white minority. In the process of accommodating to a racially stratified society, they developed a complex set of associations. In the political arena, leadership was divided between individuals seeking to compromise with the white government, and individuals prepared to join Africans in protest movements. In either case, the effectiveness of Indians was limited by several factors, especially their small number, their restricted economic resources, and their ideological sectarianism.

In Uganda, Asians, as British subjects with citizen status, were initially supported by, and in turn supported, the Protectorate government. Their extraterritorial contacts with caste and kin in India intensified their pride in a separate cultural identity. Their favorable position at the cultural as well as the political level was possible only so long as the majority of the population (Africans) did not challenge the authority of the colonial power and demand that their own status be changed from that of protected person to that of full citizen. Ironically, the individual most active and successful in identifying a section of Asians (the Ismailis) with their African domicile was, himself, through the essential nature of his office, a symbol of restricted Asian influence.

Asian resident aliens were recognized as permanent residents in South Africa by an administrative formality. Their functional position was not radically changed: their separate identity, codified in a racial population register, continued to be used as the basis of further governmental discriminatory action. However, their existence was positively, rather than negatively, recognized; and those prepared to accept the conditions of apartheid were relatively secure and provided a buffer against demands for full citizenship by Africans.

When Uganda received independence, Asians were permitted to claim African citizenship by birth or naturalization, but in effect this did not provide them with the economic or personal privileges they had held under the British. As a small ethnic minority, they could not retain their position by voting on a common roll, and in the evaluation of applicants for positions and privileges, the classification "Asian" still qualified the category of "citizen." When told to "Africanize," they found Africanization a highly ambiguous and elusive concept, since there was no homogeneous African culture. Within the African population there were cleavages between Bantu and non-Bantu and between leaders of the same linguistic cultural community. The Asians remained strangers to all.

This résumé of the relations of Asians, viewed as strangers, to non-Asians raises a number of general issues relevant to the theory of pluralism and plural societies discussed in earlier papers, particularly the perpetuation of difference, the difficulties of comparison, and the dimensions of process.

In both South Africa and Uganda, cultural pluralism has at times been deliberately maintained by strangers. But even when they decided to assimilate, they could be excluded by the host, who tended to interpret cultural differences as racial differences since political domination rested on a racial ideology.

Rigid restrictions on interaction with strangers, even allegedly total exclusion from political and social intercourse, are, however, a type of involvement, indicating a positive awareness of one another's existence. The direction of interaction is inevitably asymmetrical, with Asian strangers generally responding to contact rather than initiating it. In the racial hierarchy of South Africa, Asians were placed by whites in positions inferior to themselves, superior to Africans, and more or less equal to but separate from Coloreds. But they are not completely passive or neutral; especially in societies where there are several distinctive racial or ethnic categories, strangers may play important roles as intermediaries. This was particularly evident in the development of the Ismailis and in South African Indian political movements.

Strangers who are few in number and have little access to powerful external allies have limited means of changing the structure. They may try to exert influence by nonviolent political pressure, by supporting nonracial associations, and, if wealthy, by buying protection. But these techniques may intensify antagonism and underwrite their political insecurity as foreigners. Individual contacts, though personally significant, are unlikely to change the structure. At the same time, attempts by those in power to coerce foreigners to assimilate (i.e., abandon their own culture) may consolidate them as a racial or ethnic opposition. They may withdraw into an island of positive ethnocentricism, affirming in the private domain their traditional values, expressed in language, food, dress, and kinship and marriage obligations. Endogamy is the most effective technique of withdrawal and is the aspect of Asian culture most strongly criticized by Africans who interpret it as deliberately anti-African. There is no guarantee, however, that wider knowledge will reduce hostility; it is naïve to assume that enmity is rooted in ignorance. On the contrary, hostility and dislike may grow with knowledge, and the knowledge may simply enable opponents to handle situations of conflict more effectively; by predicting the next move, they may be able to counteract it. The boundaries of social distance remain entrenched in mutually derogatory stereotypes.

At certain periods and in limited respects, Asians in Uganda and South Africa correspond to Weber's description of "pariah people," but I am reluctant to apply to them a classification by which in India the status and role of persons were fixed for all time within a total caste structure sanctioned by Brahminic Hinduism. In Africa, the jural status of Asians changed with political developments, the range of occupations included both unskilled manual labor and the professions, and religious affiliations were not restricted. Though Asians may at times have been perceived as pariahs, they did not perceive themselves as such, and only the conceptual classification of them as "strangers" remained paramount and distinctive throughout the processes of differential incorporation. In the structural framework of pluralism, strangers form an elusive category; they need have no corporate identity, and though they may sometimes cooperate, they may also pursue divergent and antagonistic goals. Their position is not fixed; their significance varies; their autonomy is always limited. If they are without access to military force or political security, they must survive by manipulating, and accommodating to, those in power, but they may also try to ally with groups that are more or less oppressed. The response is complex. Their separation as Asians gives an illusion of total isolation, of being as it were easily detachable. But there may be considerable interaction at more covert levels. In the realm of crude power politics, they may be ignored, but their presence and their own awareness are an integral part of the total situation. In South Africa, the elimination of Asian strangers proved to be impossible; had the government succeeded, opposition between whites and Africans would have been more direct and perhaps more intense. In independent East Africa, the return of Asians to India may be expedient as a political platform, but if effected, it would not reduce the cleavages between local African ethnic groups.

Finally, I have dealt with pluralism mainly at a structural and cultural level, but would like to stress the importance of underlying ideological factors. Politico-economic arrangements (slavery, indenture, etc.) are influenced by complex sets of ideas about the sort of people involved in these relationships—the ingroup and the outgroup, those above, beneath, and equal, the values of respective religions, and so on. Structure and culture may moreover appear to be relatively unchanged, but ideas, often introduced by strangers, may be crucial in long-term events. (The effect of Gandhi's ideas was greater after he had left South Africa than while he was in the country.) Some of the Asians in Uganda perceive themselves as belonging to a society that stretches, through caste links, beyond the territorial boundaries of the particular state; and it is this caste identity that they claim as the most meaningful.

Within an arbitrarily delineated political structure we can analyze the observable network of relations connecting different categories of inhabitants in any territory and across its boundaries, but we must beware of the danger of translating relationships that are changing in form, content, and rate into rigidly formulated "analytic units" of autonomous political arrangements, which are then used as "real units" of comparison. The analysis of such plural societies as South Africa and Uganda indicates the relativity of the concept of "society," and the ways in which relationships between hosts, strangers, and locals change with the scale and level of analysis. Asians contributed to cultural and structural pluralism, and, as a distinctive category, tended to diminish or divert conflict between a dominant minority and other sections of a disprivileged majority.

NOTES

[1] Quoted by G. H. Calpin, *Indians in South Africa* (Pietermaritzburg: Shuter and Shooter, 1949), p. 29; see also p. 109.

[2] Quoted by Pierre L. van den Berghe, *South Africa: A Study in Conflict* (Middletown: Wesleyan University Press, 1965), p. 152.

[3] For general sociological discussions of "the stranger," see R. Frankenberg, *Village on the Border* (London: Cohen and West, 1957); and A. Schutz, "The Stranger," *American Journal of Sociology*, XLIX, no. 6 (1944), 449–507. "Strangers" as a category are discussed by Georg Simmel in *Introduction to the Science of Society*, trans. R. Park and E. W. Burgess (Chicago: University of Chicago Press, 1924), pp. 322–327, and in Kurt H. Wolff, ed. and trans., *The Sociology of Georg Simmel* (Glencoe, Ill.: Free Press, 1950). See also Max Weber, *The Sociology of Religion*, trans. E. Fischoff (Boston: Beacon Press, 1963), esp. on "Pariah peoples"; R. M. Williams, Jr., *Strangers Next Door* (Englewood Cliffs, N.J.: Prentice-Hall, 1964); Margaret M. Wood, *The Stranger: A Study in Social Relationships* (New York: Columbia University Press, 1943).

[4] Wolff, *op. cit.*, pp. 402–408.

[5] Louis Wirth, *The Ghetto* (Boston: Beacon Press, 1964), p. 78.

[6] Weber, *op. cit.*, p. 66.

[7] *Ibid.*, p. 189.

[8] Wolff, *op. cit.*, p. 402.

[9] See, for example, in the South African Hansard, the following speeches made by the Minister of the Interior; Senate, 31 January 1956, Hansard, 3 cols., 495/514; Assembly, 9 May 1956, Hansard, 15 cols., 5260/8, printed by Cape Times Ltd., C. P. Parow, Government Printer. In a debate in the House of Lords, July 14, 1920, Lord Emmott said Indians were being treated as "partners" in India and "pariahs" in Kenya (quoted in George Delf, *Asians in East Africa* [London: Oxford University Press, 1963], p. 17).

[10] Muriel Horrell, comp., *A Survey of Race Relations in South Africa, 1965* (Johannesburg: South African Institute of Race Relations, 1966), p. 110.

[11] *Statistics Abstract 1963*, Uganda Ministry of Planning and Community Development, Statistics Division, Office of the Prime Minister, printed by the Government Printer, Entebbe.

[12] H. S. Morris, "Communal Rivalry among Indians in Uganda," *British Journal of Sociology*, VIII, no. 4 (Dec. 1957), 306–317.

[13] R. Oliver and G. Mathew, *History of East Africa*, I (Oxford: Clarendon Press, 1963), 210.

[14] K. Ingham, *The Making of Modern Uganda* (London: Allen and Unwin, 1958), pp. 37–39; Roland A. Oliver, *The Missionary Factor in East Africa* (2d

ed.; London: Longmans, Green, 1965), pp. 108–116; Oliver and Mathew, *op. cit.*, pp. 272–273.

[15] Oliver and Mathew, *op. cit.*, p. 287.

[16] Oliver, *op. cit.*, p. 202.

[17] D. A. Low, *Political Parties in Uganda, 1949–1962* (London: Athlone Press of the University of London, 1962), p. 10.

[18] Ingham, *op. cit.*, p. 38.

[19] A. J. B. Hughes, *East Africa: The Search for Unity* (Harmondsworth: Penguin Books, 1963), p. 148.

[20] J. S. Marais, *The Cape Coloured People, 1652–1937* (London: Longmans, Green, 1939).

[21] Isak D. Du Plessis, *The Cape Malays* (2d ed.; Cape Town: Maskew Miller, 1947), pp. 1–7.

[22] Mabel Palmer, *The History of Indians in Natal* (London: Oxford University Press, 1957), pp. 4–11.

[23] See Calpin, *op. cit., passim;* Hilda Kuper, *Indian People in Natal* (Pietermaritzburg: Natal University Press, 1960), *passim;* Palmer, *op. cit., passim.*

[24] For example, see the description of early conditions in R. G. T. Watson, *Tongaati* (London: Hutchinson, 1960). For a more sociological analysis, see Pierre L. van den Berghe, *Caneville: The Social Structure of a South African Town* (Middletown: Wesleyan University Press, 1964).

[25] An aggregate can be distinguished from a corporate group by its limited structure and by the relative autonomy of its members (see J. H. Fichter, *Sociology* [Chicago: University of Chicago Press, 1957], pp. 87–93, 109–119).

[26] Kuper, *op. cit.*, p. 7.

[27] *Ibid.*, chaps. i, ii.

[28] *Ibid.*, chap. vi.

[29] R. Burrows, *Indian Life and Labour in Natal* (Pietermaritzburg: South African Institute of Race Relations, 1952), pp. 10–20.

[30] Indentured and passenger Indians had certain interests in common, and Gandhi, himself a Gujarati who arrived in South Africa to deal with a business dispute of Gujarati clients, brought the two sections together in the South African Indian Congress which he formed in 1885 (see P. S. Joshi, *The Tyranny of Colour: A Study of the Indian Problem in South Africa* [Durban: E. P. and Commercial Printer, 1942], chaps. 3, 4; also Palmer, *op. cit.*, pp. 48–75).

[31] See Somarsundarum Cooppan, "The Indian Outlook," in Prudence Smith, ed., *Africa in Transition: Some BBC Talks on Changing Conditions in the Union and the Rhodesias* (London: Max Reinhardt, 1958), pp. 159–168; Hilda Kuper, "The Indians of Natal," in *ibid.*, pp. 115–124.

[32] See especially Cyril Ehrlich, "The Uganda Economy, 1903–1945," in V. Harlow, E. M. Chilver, and A. Smith, eds., *History of East Africa*, II (Oxford: Clarendon Press, 1965), 407–408, 441–442; and Ingham, *op. cit.*, pp. 98–99, 103.

[33] H. S. Morris, "Indians in East Africa: A Study in a Plural Society," *British Journal of Sociology*, VII, no. 3 (Oct. 1956), 195. Morris states that more than 90 percent of the indentured returned to India.

[34] R. R. Ramchandi, "Racial Conflict in East Africa with Implications for the People of Indian Origin: A Case Study of Uganda," University of Delhi, 1965 (mimeographed).

[35] A. Bharati, "A Social Survey," in D. P. Ghai, ed., *Portrait of a Minority: Asians in East Africa* (London: Oxford University Press, 1965), pp. 13–63.

[36] Weber writes: "When a tribe loses its foothold in its territory it becomes a guest or pariah people" (H. H. Gerth and C. Wright Mills, eds., *From Max Weber: Essays in Sociology* [New York: Oxford University Press, 1958], p. 399).

[37] Joshi, *op. cit.*, pp. 165–177, 198–213.

[38] L. Kuper, H. Watts, and R. Davies, *Durban: A Study in Racial Ecology* (New York: Columbia University Press, 1958), chaps. vi, vii.

[39] Palmer, *op. cit.*, p. 138.

[40] Kuper, Watts, and Davies, *op. cit.*, p. 66.

[41] The antagonism toward Indians came into the open in the Durban Riots of 1949, when Africans (mainly migrant laborers) attacked Indians and looted Indian shops. The riots, however, brought together African and Indian leaders and nonracist whites. For a report on this see Kenneth Kirkwood, *The Durban Riots* (Johannesburg: South African Institute of Race Relations, 1950).

[42] Leo Kuper, *Passive Resistance in South Africa* (New Haven: Yale University Press, 1960), p. 123.

[43] A. I. Richards, *Economic Development and Tribal Change* (Cambridge: Heffer, 1952), chap. i.

[44] *Ibid.*, p. 39.

[45] R. H. Desai, paper delivered at East African Institute Conference, 1963; Morris, "Communal Rivalry among Indians in Uganda," pp. 313–317; Yash Tandon, "A Political Survey," in Ghai, *op. cit.*, pp. 71–75.

[46] Morris, "Indians in East Africa," p. 200.

[47] T. Karis, "South Africa," in Gwendolen M. Carter, ed., *Five African States* (Ithaca: Cornell University Press, 1963), p. 572.

[48] Hughes, *op. cit.*, p. 173.

[49] Tandon, *op. cit.*, pp. 65–88.

[50] D. P. Ghai, "An Economic Survey," in Ghai, *op. cit.*, p. 9.

[51] Yash Ghai, "The Future Prospects," in D. P. Ghai, ed., *Portrait of a Minority: Asians in East Africa* (London: Oxford University Press, 1965), p. 140.

[52] Wolff, *op. cit.*, pp. 154–162.

Chapter 9   The Plural Society in Zanzibar[*]

Michael Lofchie

Political domination by an ethnically and culturally differentiated minority, and an unmistakable tendency for the broad social division of labor to exhibit a racial configuration, are the central ingredients in one concept of a "plural society." This usage of the concept is closely associated with the writings of the colonial historian, J. S. Furnivall, and the anthropologist, M. G. Smith. In extreme instances, a single racial group is predominant at each level of the plural society's class structure, especially at the elite level. As ethnic, economic, and political group boundaries tend to be identical, group memberships are culturally exclusive. The whole society, therefore, suffers from a high degree of nonintegration.

The concept of pluralism has also been employed by some sociologists to describe a different pattern of social organization. As Leo Kuper has pointed out in "Plural Societies: Perspectives and Problems," a distinctively North American tradition of social science treats pluralism as an integrative mechanism and regards the plural society as characterized by restrained conflict, basic consensus, solidarity, and equilibrium. In the formulations of Lipset and Kornhauser, for example, the most important aspects of pluralism are that group boundaries continually cross and intersect one another and that, as a result, individuals experience multiple countervailing group loyalties. These multiple loyalties tend to prevent individuals from developing a total commitment to any single class or ethnic group. Because of their ties to a large number of social organizations, the members of society have an interest in the peaceful resolution of disputes. Thus, the segmentation of group affiliations tends to produce a political culture marked by attitudes of restraint, and conflict occurs through a political process of bargaining and compromise.

[*] I wish to express gratitude to Professors Leo Kuper and M. G. Smith and to UCLA graduate students Betty Thomas, Michael Halliwell, and Steven Heyneman for their valuable comments on an earlier version of this paper.

The term "plural" society is employed in this essay in the same basic sense formulated by Furnivall and Smith and refers to those social systems characterized by a high degree of ethnic differentiation in the economic realm and by domination of a cultural minority in the political sphere. While the Lipset-Kornhauser model of pluralism is highly useful in dealing with industrially advanced societies, it has limited utility in approaching traditional plural societies or plural societies in the developing nations. These plural societies exhibit a distinctive form of political conflict. Pervasive ideas of human equality and representative democratic government have made the conspicuous political and social inequalities of plural societies appear increasingly illegitimate both to the world community of nations and, more important for our purposes, to their internal majority populations. In domestic politics, this fundamental dissonance between a political culture of equality and prevailing sociopolitical arrangements has generated extreme conflict. This conflict is characterized by the quest of subordinated majorities for a political status reversal.

Until the African revolution of early January 1964,[1] Zanzibar's political and social arrangements corresponded closely to the theoretical model of a plural society. Culturally distinguishable racial and communal groups were differentially incorporated into the society's political system and differentially positioned in its economy. Political power was concentrated in the hands of a small Arab oligarchy which had formed Zanzibar's ruling class since the mid-nineteenth century. This group's position of political domination was based on its historical status as a landed aristocracy, its ownership of the best land, its near monopoly of the highest administrative levels of the Zanzibar government, and its privileged treatment by British colonial authorities. The Arab oligarchy comprised only a small proportion of the entire Arab community, which amounted to about 17 percent of Zanzibar's total population; most Arabs did not have a position of influence or wealth in the society. Despite wide social differentiation among Arabs, the entire community possessed a high degree of political solidarity; the overwhelming majority of Arabs at all levels of the social structure not only identified themselves primarily as Arabs but considered themselves, as Arabs, to be members of a political and economic elite.

Asians (persons of Indo-Pakistani descent), comprising about 6 percent of the population, were primarily a middle-class group and virtually monopolized trade, commerce, and the clerical levels of the civil service. Some Asians were extremely wealthy and those who owned the large import and export firms were by far the richest Zanzibaris. As a community, however, Asians were politically ineffectual, owing to a range of factors including communal fragmentation and a cultural disinclination toward political participation, and were consistently unable to exert political influence commensurate with their economic status. The Asians' unwillingness to undertake concerted political action helped facilitate continuing political domination by a small minority of Arabs.

An African majority, including slightly more than three-fourths of the total population, formed the broad underprivileged mass of Zanzibar society. Of all the racial groups in Zanzibar, Africans were the least incorporated into the political structure and the most economically disadvantaged. By and large the occupational range of the African community was confined to rural fishing, petty agriculture, and unskilled manual labor. As the poorest Zanzibaris, most Africans were unable to afford higher education. This lack, together with a tendency by both the British colonial authorities and the Arab oligarchy to ignore the political interests of Africans, prevented them from gaining access to positions of political or administrative influence. No African was nominated to the Zanzibar Legislative Council or selected for an upper-level administrative assignment until after World War II.

The African community was not politically unified. The basic division was between Africans who regarded themselves as the indigenous inhabitants of Zanzibar and an immigrant African minority of recent mainland origin. The former, accounting for nearly three-fourths of the total African population, preferred to use the term "Shirazi" instead of "African" as a category of communal self-description. Historically, the concept of a Shirazi identity originated in the migration to Zanzibar of a small number of Persians around the thirteenth century, and the term originally referred only to those Zanzibaris claiming a particularly high admixture of Persian descent. Shirazis were thus, at one time, a distinct ethnic group, quite separate from three indigenous African tribes, the Hadimu, the Pemba, and the Tumbatu. In recent times, however, the notion of Shirazi descent became attractive to all indigenous Africans as a method of differentiating themselves in terms of length of residence and genealogical descent from the more recent mainland immigrants. In the twentieth century, the concept of mixed Afro-Persian descent embraces all three indigenous tribal groups, and the term Shirazi is far more commonly used than the separate tribal names. Significantly, Zanzibar's indigenous inhabitants did not view themselves as Africans and sought to distinguish their identity, culturally and historically, from mainland Africa.

The immigrant African community of Zanzibar originated in the nineteenth century when the Arab colonists imported large numbers of African slaves to work as domestic servants and as field laborers on the plantations. Since the Arab slave trade extended throughout eastern Africa, the mainland African community included persons from a wide range of tribes and places. Many mainlanders traced their ancestry to areas as remote from Zanzibar as the Congo, Nyasaland, and Mozambique. The most numerous tribal groups were the Nyasa, Nyamwezi, and Yao, with Sukuma and Makonde also heavily represented. After the abolition of slavery, mainland Africans also migrated to Zanzibar, primarily to seek seasonal employment in the clove plantations. Large numbers of these seasonal migrants remained permanently either as squatter-farmers or to seek employment in Zanzibar Town. Regardless of their widely differing tribal origins or the different reasons for their presence in Zanzibar, the mainland African minority shared a strong sense of communal solidarity, and mainland Africans were highly aware of the historical and ethnic differences between themselves and the Shirazis.

This pattern of communal differentiation determined the basic structure of prerevolutionary Zanzibar politics. Political organizations initiated and led primarily by mainland Africans were determined to reverse the inherited pattern of status relations between their community and the Arab oligarchy. By achieving political power, they hoped to place the entire African community on an equal socioeconomic basis with both Arabs and Asians. These political organizations were able to gain only limited support within the Shirazi community, since most Shirazis were unwilling to associate politically with mainland Africans. Arab-led political groups were basically motivated to prevent the occurrence of a status reversal. They hoped to maintain political power in Arab hands so that governmental authority could not be employed to bring about a change in the social structure. Unlike other immigrant racial oligarchies elsewhere in Africa, the Arab minority of Zanzibar sought to preserve its privileged political position, not by coercion, but by gaining sufficient African support to win a majority of seats in a popularly elected national assembly. Arabs benefited from the communal cleavage between Shirazis and mainlanders, and their political party attracted sufficient Shirazi support to succeed in its objective. Their success in preserving minority political domination through parliamentary means, despite the racially plural pattern of social organization, made Zanzibar unique among Africa's contemporary plural societies. It also directly contributed to the African revolution: Africans opposed to Arab rule seized power by revolutionary means because they had been unable to do so through constitutional methods.

HISTORICAL ORIGINS OF THE PLURAL SOCIETY

Though Arab contact with East Africa is of ancient origin and can be traced to pre-Islamic times, a resident Arab oligarchy did not emerge in

Zanzibar until the early nineteenth century. Before then, Arab travel to East Africa was largely for commerce. Relations with local African communties were almost wholly confined to trade, which was conducted on a seasonal basis and did not require permanent settlement. Some Arabs settled in coastal towns which, functioning purely as trading enclaves, did not seek to establish political domination over the indigenous African peoples. Incipient traces of a plural mode of social organization could be discerned within the towns in the practice of African slavery, in the employment of Africans as servants and manual laborers, and in the arrival of Asian immigrants to perform clerical and managerial functions in Arab businesses, but most Africans were virtually unaffected by this aspect of Arab contact.

Zanzibar's development as a racially plural society began abruptly in the first half of the nineteenth century when it became the administrative capital of the sultanate of Oman, an Arab state that was the principal point of origin of Arab trade and early settlement in East Africa. Oman had found it difficult to exercise effective control over the coastal towns nominally under its sovereignty. Local Arab settlers, especially in Mombasa, the largest and most important Arab trading enclave, were seeking political and economic autonomy from Omani rule. This situation, together with a substantial increase in the volume of the slave trade, made it attractive to Oman to establish a new capital in East Africa. Such a move would not only brighten the prospect of control over the coastal settlements, but would make it easier to regulate and monopolize Indian Ocean commerce. Zanzibar offered several advantages as a site for the new capital. Its small, scattered African population meant that there could be little resistance to large-scale Arab immigration. Its location afforded easy access to most of the coastal towns and a good strategic base from which to intercept competitive shipping. Moreover, it possessed an abundant supply of fresh water, a more temperate climate than the mainland, and a well-protected harbor. For all these reasons, the Sultan of Oman decided, in about 1830, to locate his capital on the western coast of Zanzibar Island.

This decision had immediate and profound consequences. It was followed by a heavy wave of Arab immigrants, consisting not only of traders and businessmen, but of civil servants, administrators, court followers, and military personnel. The social attitudes of these new arrivals were different from those of earlier Arabs in East Africa. Previous Arabs had regarded East Africa as only a temporary domicile, an interruption of life in Oman; even when they lived in the area for many years, they made little effort to re-create Arab culture and social life in the diaspora. Many had come as bachelors, leaving family behind in Oman, and intermarriage and concubinage with African women were frequent. As a result, the early Arab trading settlements were character-ized by a blending of Arab and African cultures, rather than by cultural and social differentiation.

The Omani immigrants to Zanzibar, however, viewed it as a permanent home. They not only came to Zanzibar *en famille*, but attempted to reproduce an Omani style of life on the island. As they constituted a royal and aristocratic element as well as a commercial middle class, they were culturally differentiated and exclusive in relation to the indigenous African communities. As the newcomers encouraged permanent immi-gration of kith and kin from Oman, the first wave of arrivals was followed by a steady stream of colonial immigrants.

Economic necessity forced some immigrants into agriculture and, under pressure to provide for a rapidly expanding population, the Sultan introduced the clove as an export crop. Clove production flourished. World market prices for cloves being high, there was an agricultural boom. The dramatic economic success of cloves created a heavy demand for arable land. At this point, a new idiom entered Arab-African relations —the alienation and occupation of African land. There is serious debate over whether or not the land alienated by Arabs on Zanzibar Island was occupied by Africans before the Arab arrival. Extensive historical and anthropological arguments are raised on both sides. The fact remains, however, that the alienated areas represented by far the best arable land, that Africans regarded these areas as their own, and that land alienation aroused among Africans a sharp resentment of the Arab presence.

Arab land alienation on Zanzibar Island assumed a form that gave it enormous political significance in the decade before the African revolu-tion. The island is roughly bisected by a hilly ridge running irregularly north and south. This ridge divides the western section of the island, an area of rich, highly fertile soil, from the east, where the soil is rocky, of poor quality, and unsuitable for intensive cultivation. Because of this geographic feature, the Arabs' acquisition of arable land imposed a residential pattern segregating them from the local African communities. The Arabs came to enjoy an almost exclusive occupation of the western section where they developed a productive plantation agriculture de-voted to the commercial production of cloves and coconuts. The African community was confined to the eastern areas of the island where only sparse cultivation was possible, and where fishing was a necessary sup-plement to the meager existence afforded by agriculture.

Many Africans traveled frequently between the two areas to seek employment either as agricultural laborers on Arab plantations or as manual workers in the city. They therefore became aware of the stark economic contrast between the affluence of Arab life and the impoverishment of their own villages. Land alienation thus became, for local Africans, the most conspicuous symbol of their political and economic subordination to the immigrant Arab elite.

The establishment of a full-fledged Arab government, together with the expansion of Arab settlement into the interior and massive alienation of African land, created a critical need for methods of social control which would ensure the stability and safety of the Arabs. Departing from the practice of earlier Arab settlements in East Africa, the Sultan's regime initiated measures to bring the indigenous African population under administrative and legal supervision. Initially the Sultan's officials hoped to govern the African communities through a form of indirect rule, employing traditional African institutions as vehicles for control. Although Zanzibar Africans had a centralized chieftancy, the Mwinyi Mkuu, their institutional structures were too fragile to withstand the impact of the Arab intrusion and the incessant Arab demands for agricultural labor and tax payments. Gradually the indigenous African political system broke down, the institution of the Mwinyi Mkuu ceased to function, and the Arab regime established a system of district officers with direct police and judicial powers over Africans. This series of events completed the forcible subordination of the African population of Zanzibar Island to Arab rule.

Arab occupation and settlement of Pemba Island differed substantially from that of Zanzibar. Prior to the establishment of the sultanate on Zanzibar, Pemba had been harshly governed by the Arab settlers of Mombasa. A delegation of Pemba leaders visited the Sultan and enlisted his support in overthrowing Mombasa rule. Thus, when Omani Arabs first arrived in Pemba, they came not as a colonial invading force but at the open invitation of the local population. This meant that Pemba Africans did not regard Arab immigrants as unwanted intruders but instead welcomed them as a sort of liberating force. As a result, the Arab settlement in Pemba never faced a major problem of social control and found it unnecessary to impose the rigorous administrative controls that were employed in Zanzibar.

Land alienation was never so important in Pemba as it was in Zanzibar. Fertile soils abound in Pemba and are found throughout the island. No such conspicuous geographical feature as Zanzibar's central ridge demarcates fertile from infertile soil, and only in a few remote areas of Pemba is the land unsuitable for intensive cultivation. As a result, Arab land alienation in Pemba was not accompanied either by the progressive restriction and segregation of the African community to areas of inferior soil or by any sense among Pemba Africans that the Arab incursion had deprived them of their best land. The Arab settlers introduced the clove to Pemba and, since Africans remained in possession of much fertile land, cloves became an African as well as an Arab crop. The economic success of the clove industry was, to a large extent, shared by Pemba Africans, and Pemba society never developed the marked economic differential between Arabs and Africans which existed in Zanzibar. For all these reasons, Arab colonialism in Pemba was comparatively benign, and personal relations between Pemba Africans and the new Arab immigrants were on the whole cordial and friendly.

Despite the major differences between Zanzibar and Pemba islands, both developed plural societies. There were visible differences in wealth between Arabs and Africans; the average Arab landholding was substantially larger than the African landholding, even in Pemba. Moreover, there was a considerable cultural differential between the two communities. The Arabs came to Zanzibar as representatives of a civilization that was far superior to that of the Africans in its military, technological, and economic capabilities. The cultural differential also extended into the religious realm. The Arabs were members of the Ibadhi denomination of Islam, a liberal and reformist version of the Muslim faith, whereas the Africans were conventional Sunni. The Arab version of the religion was purer than the African version, which combined Islamic beliefs with local African religious rituals and practices. The most important aspect of cultural differentiation, however, was that Arabs had become an undisputed ruling class; even in Pemba, where there was an element of consent, Arabs exercised a monopoly of political power and left no doubt of their ability to maintain control by force if necessary.

The African communities of Zanzibar had been highly vulnerable to this colonial conquest. Their exposed and indefensible insular position made it extremely difficult to prevent seaborne intrusion; in fact, Zanzibar had experienced a series of colonial settlements—Persian, Portuguese, and Arab—long before the establishment of the Omani sultanate. These previous incursions had made a considerable impact on the culture of Zanzibar Africans; they brought about, for example, the conversion of Zanzibaris to Islam and added a rich admixture of Persian religious traditions and practices to Zanzibar culture. The long history of colonial contact made Zanzibar susceptible to the establishment of an Arab state. Zanzibaris had become deeply acculturated in the customs and traditions of the Middle East and, because previous alien settlement had been benign, they were accustomed to accepting it without resistance. But the major factor of vulnerability was the absence of political unity among the local Africans.

Zanzibar Africans were divided into three main tribal groups: the Hadimu, who occupied the central and southern sections of Zanzibar island; the Tumbatu, who had originally occupied Tumbatu Island just off the northwest coast of Zanzibar Island, and who had spread into northern Zanzibar and southern Pemba islands; and the Pemba, who occupied most of Pemba Island. These groups could be said to constitute tribes only in the loosest sense of the term. Each had originated in the migration to Zanzibar of Africans from a wide variety of points in East Africa. The original immigrants had settled in scattered villages on the two islands, and their political organization did not extend above the village level. Each tribe, therefore, consisted basically of a loose network of autonomous village communities. Though the Hadimu and, to an extent, the Tumbatu had begun to evolve more centralized political institutions, effective authority was still confined to the village level when the Omani Arabs arrived. The Hadimu did possess a chief in the person of the Mwinyi Mkuu, but his power was checked by the countervailing powers of largely autonomous village elders. Thus, there was no tradition of concerted unified action among Zanzibar Africans even at the tribal level. When Arabs began to settle in large numbers and to acquire land, the Africans were unable to muster the degree of unity requisite for massive resistance.

The basic reason for the lack of a unified African response to Arab colonialism—and indeed for the absence of unity among Africans in contemporary Zanzibar politics—was that the three indigenous tribal groups had experienced widely varying patterns of contact with the emergent Arab state. Only the Hadimu suffered direct, intense, and immediate deprivation as a result of Arab settlement. As the residents of central and southern Zanzibar Island, they alone were dispossessed by early Arab land alienation and, because this created a major problem of social control, the Hadimu were placed under a system of native administration far more repressive than that imposed on the Tumbatu or the Pemba. The Tumbatu were almost completely unaffected by Arab land alienation; they were largely a fishing community, and their land area, on the northern peninsula of Zanzibar island, was remote and of poor quality. Moreover, since the Tumbatu were a seagoing people, many of them found employment as sailors or captains in the Arab Indian Ocean trade, thus frequently achieving a marked economic improvement over life in traditional Tumbatu villages. Aside from the opportunity for employment, the creation of an Arab state did not alter the day-to-day life of the Tumbatu. Since Arab political dominance had extremely low visibility, the Tumbatu had little reason to resent their subordination to alien rule, or to develop a sense of grievance against it. The Pemba had positive reason for accepting the Omani presence: the Omani arrival meant the end of rule by Mombasa and the development of a lucrative commercial agriculture.

Thus, a strong sense of collective political grievance against the Arab regime developed only among the Hadimu. Their resentment of the Arabs was largely unshared by the Tumbatu or Pemba tribes. During the prerevolutionary era, the Hadimus' political antagonisms toward Arabs made them natural allies of the mainland African community. When mainland Africans decided to form an "African" political party in Zanzibar, the Hadimus were not only the first to join but virtually the only Shirazis ever to join in massive numbers.

A heavy influx of Asian immigrants during the nineteenth century added a third component to the plural aspect of Zanzibar's social structure. In eastern Africa, the Asian community had, since ancient times, performed a middleman role as a managerial class in the Arab Indian Ocean trade. Like the Arabs, the Asians had viewed the coastal trading enclaves as a temporary domicile and were reluctant to establish permanent residence. After the establishment of the sultanate in Zanzibar, however, a more permanent Asian immigration was encouraged by the Arabs, both for commercial purposes and to fill the clerical levels of the Sultan's bureaucracy. Ultimately, Asians came to enjoy a near-monopolistic position in both spheres, dominating wholesale and retail commerce, foreign trade, and most middle-range civil service positions. They gradually established a permanent home in Zanzibar, although a marked feature of Asian life was a strong emotional and cultural attachment to India.

Zanzibar's evolution into a plural society was completed by the end of the nineteenth century. The most important aspect of social organization was that political influence and economic privilege were differentially available to the society's racial and ethnic communities. Outside the marketplace and the sphere of political domination, there was very little contact between members of different racial communities. When such contact did occur, it was usually in the context of superior–subordinate, master–servant, or employer–employee. Racial consciousness thus became an extremely important part in the daily life of the average Zanzibari and, in the period before the revolution, it became the fundamental basis of competitive group politics.

The advent of British colonialism and the establishment of a British protectorate over Zanzibar in 1890 did not alter the racial quality of Zanzibar's class structure. Having negotiated a protectorate agreement with the Sultan's government, Britain gave special recognition to the fact that Zanzibar was, in constitutional terms, an Arab state. Through much of the twentieth century, this recognition was reflected in a variety of colonial practices designed to preserve the Arabs' elite status. Arabs were given special priority for membership in the Legislative Council and for positions on various governmental advisory boards. Members of the Arab community were given preference for top governmental positions, where they also enjoyed differential salary scales over members of other racial communities. Arab children were almost invariably selected for government scholarships for overseas study and, when they returned, were assured of high-level administrative assignment. The Arab Association was frequently consulted in the formulation of government policy, and in numerous informal ways Arabs were able to exert influence on the day-to-day conduct of governmental affairs.

The generally autocratic nature of British colonialism also had much to do with preserving Zanzibar's plural society. Under colonial rule, the major tasks of government were conducted by a disinterested efficient bureaucracy which was largely unanswerable to local opinion, except for its informal contact with Arab leaders. Colonialism did not allow for the free play of opposed political forces; not until the 1950's were Africans able to use the political arena as a vehicle for challenging the Arabs' oligarchic position.

Even the gradual introduction of representative parliamentary institutions did not qualify Britain's assumption that it had a treaty obligation to regard Arab interests as paramount. Constitutional evolution was viewed, somewhat ethnocentrically, as involving a changing relationship between protector and protected (the Arabs) rather than as a process with enormous bearing on the distribution of power within Zanzibar society. Moreover, the creation of democratic governmental structures was regarded as a long-range process involving several generations, and British administrators in the protectorate widely assumed that the Arab community would play an important tutelary role in this process. Not until after World War II did the full meaning of political democracy become clear, and at that time Britain sought to introduce special constitutional devices, such as communal representation, which would enable the Arab community to defend itself politically against the overwhelming African majority.

In sum, the plural society that emerged in Zanzibar in the mid-nineteenth century remained intact throughout the era of the British presence (1890–1963). Racial differentiation in political and economic life became the sole issue around which competitive politics revolved and was the major impetus of the African revolution in early 1964.

DIMENSIONS OF ZANZIBAR PLURALISM

Ethnic consciousness was the most powerful determinant of group solidarity in Zanzibar, and prerevolutionary politics were conducted almost entirely in the idiom of communal conflict. The formation of racial groups did not, however, conform to strict genealogical lines. After the nineteenth century there was a certain amount of racial intermarriage, especially between Arabs and Africans, and many Zanzibaris were, in the purely genealogical sense, of mixed descent. But self-identification, common acceptance, and the general pattern of conduct almost invariably operated to locate such persons unambiguously in one racial group or another. The most accurate method of defining any ethnic or racial community in Zanzibar is to determine whether its members shared a sense of common racial identity. As these corporate units largely correspond to historical and genealogical reality, there are conspicuous cultural and physical differences among them. Thus, the most salient and important features of prerevolutionary Zanzibar were its social organization as a racially plural society and the high visibility of this pluralism to all Zanzibaris.

ARABS

The Arab minority of Zanzibar was, in proportion to the total population, the second-largest dominant alien minority in Africa. Constituting approximately one-sixth (16.9 percent) of the total population, Zanzibar's Arab oligarchy was surpassed in percentage size only by the European community of South Africa. The data in table 1, drawn from the government census of 1948,[2] indicate the numerical and proportional sizes of Zanzibar's principal racial communities.

TABLE 1

DISTRIBUTION OF POPULATION BY ETHNIC COMMUNITY, 1948

Race	Zanzibar Island		Pemba Island		Total	
	Number	Percent	Number	Percent	Number	Percent
African	118,652	79.3	81,208	70.9	199,860	75.7
Arab	13,977	9.3	30,583	26.7	44,560	16.9
Asian	13,107	8.8	2,104	1.8	15,211	5.8
Other [a]	3,839	2.6	692	.6	4,531	1.6
Total	149,575	100.0	114,587	100.0	264,162	100.0

[a] Includes Europeans and Comorians, the latter a small group of approximately 3,000 persons who had migrated to Zanzibar from the Comores Islands.

The Arab oligarchy, a very small segment of the entire Arab community, was composed almost entirely of the descendants of a few hundred well-to-do Omani families. This group had constituted a self-perpetuating elite since the earliest days of Arab colonialism because its decisive advantages in income, style of life, and social contacts enabled successive generations to gain a superior education and thereby to qualify more easily for the highest commercial and administrative positions. With British indulgence, and through a variety of political practices including nepotism, favoritism, and outright corruption, Arabs established virtually monopolistic control over economically strategic sectors of the government. Indeed, Arab control in vital areas of public administration was so complete that the Arabs exercised a decisive influence over the whole social structure of the protectorate. By allowing Asians to monopolize middle levels of the civil service and the economy, and preventing Africans from advancing, the Arab oligarchy was able to safeguard its own dominant position.

The Arab oligarchy enjoyed enormous social prestige. Indeed, the Swahili term *u-arabu*, which literally means "being like an Arab," was a common euphemism in Zanzibar for "cultured." As the true founders of the Faith, a historic landowning aristocracy, and a ruling elite deferred to even by the British, the Arab elite embodied the highest virtues of Zanzibar society. Deference to the Arab community became a major factor in prerevolutionary Zanzibar politics. It helps to explain why large numbers of Africans supported political organizations initiated and led by Arabs, despite the radical economic differences between the two communities.

The landed Arab aristocracy was nevertheless a rapidly declining group in Zanzibar, both in terms of landholdings and overall economic position. The decline was brought about by several factors. Many of the early Arab families had fallen heavily into the debt of Asian bankers and moneylenders during the nineteenth and early twentieth centuries. High rates of interest and falling clove prices made it impossible to repay these debts, and considerable Arab land was passing into Asian hands. The Islamic practice of partitive inheritance also led to a rapid decline in the economic position of many Arabs. After two or three generations, many of the largest Arab plantations had been fragmented into plots no larger than peasant holdings. These factors, combined with the Arab tradition of lavish entertainment, generous hospitality, and a tendency toward conspicuous consumption, siphoned off Arab wealth and significantly reduced the size and income of the landed Arab oligarchy. By the end of World War II, the Arab community was far more dependent upon its position in government administration and the professions than upon land for its position of social and political preeminence.

The overwhelming majority of the Arab community was in the middle and lower classes—petty shopkeepers, peasant farmers, and semiskilled craftsmen. There were several distinct groups among the poorer Arabs.

One group consisted of the descendants of the original Omani families that had suffered declining economic fortunes as a result of indebtedness, partitive inheritance, and high expenditure. This group constituted a sort of ruined aristocracy. Many of these impoverished Arabs intermarried with indigenous Africans, since income and style-of-life differences were removed and African landholdings were an attractive economic incentive. An important result of such intermarriage was that in recent times, the "poor Arab" class was of mixed descent, with skin color noticeably different from that of the remaining Arab elite, which intermarried far less frequently.

Recent arrivals from Oman formed a second group of poorer Arabs. Known as "Manga" Arabs (*Manga* is the Swahili term for the Omani region of Arabia), this group was distinguished from the older Omani settlers not only by its recent arrival but also by the fact that its members had no intention of establishing permanent residence in Zanzibar. By and large, the Manga Arabs stemmed from the lower classes of Arabian society and came to Zanzibar with the intention of earning enough money to improve their position at home. For this reason, they usually entered shopkeeping and urban trades rather than agriculture and lived modestly and frugally during their stay in Zanzibar. The Manga were of the purest Arab descent of all Zanzibar Arabs, because their average length of residence was less than a generation and because they usually did not intermarry with the local Arab or African communities. Before the era of open racial politics in Zanzibar, considerable tension and hostility marked the relations between the Manga Arabs and the older Omani elite, largely because of economic differentials and because the older settlers tended to remain indifferent to the economic hardships suffered by the newcomers.

The most numerous section of the Arab lower class consisted of persons who were not identified as Arabs by government census takers until fairly recent times. As late as the census of 1931, long after the establishment of the sultanate and the period of heavy Arab immigration, Arabs were officially recorded as less than 9 percent of all Zanzibaris. Since the major upsurge in the Arab population occurred within a very brief period of time, from 1924 to 1931, when the Arab population rose from 8.7 percent to 14.2 percent of the total population, it is likely that the figures were affected by different census procedures and criteria. Moreover, many non-Arabs may have decided to identify themselves as Arabs in an effort to qualify for the social and economic privileges that the British government accorded members of the Arab community.

Most of the "new" Arabs came from a single ethnic group, the Swahili. While the Arab community was gaining nearly 15,000 members between

1924 and 1931, the Swahili community declined by more than twice that figure, and nearly disappeared as a separate ethnic identity. Originally the term "Swahili" had simply referred to persons of mixed Arab-African descent and Islamic faith, whose ancestors came from the East African coast. The Swahilis were thus not a tribe in the strict sense of the term, being joined only by common religion, common language (Swahili), and a vague sense of common geographical and historical origins. Ethnic solidarity among Swahilis was not strong enough to pose an obstacle to a change in ethnic self-description. More important, the ethnic term "Swahili" had recently acquired a highly pejorative meaning which signified boorish manner, low pedigree, menial occupational position, and general social inferiority.[3] Being a Swahili thus meant substantial loss in status, and the negative stereotype of the term provided a strong incentive for Swahilis to seek a new and more respected ethnic identity. The dominant motivation behind the Swahilis' exodus from their own community was a search for a more prestigious self-identification; the fact that nearly half of this group chose "Arab" as a category of self-description illustrates the high social esteem in which Zanzibar Arabs were held.

The Swahilis' ability to "become" Arabs illustrates a basic difference between the Arab oligarchy of Zanzibar and other dominant racial minorities in Africa. Unlike the white oligarchies of South Africa and Rhodesia which have erected legal and social barriers to prevent trespass across racial boundaries, in Zanzibar the Arabs were not a completely closed community. One of the most noticeable physical features of Zanzibar society was the substantial number of persons who identified themselves as Arab and who were of darker complexion than many Africans. With few exceptions, however, these darker-skinned Arabs were of much lower economic status than the original Arab elite group. Regardless of differences in skin color or in economic position, persons identifying themselves as Arabs formed a highly solidaristic political unit whose cohesion was based on a sense of shared racial identity.

The openness of the Arab elite to penetration from below was the natural consequence of a situation in which all racial groups contained a certain number of persons of mixed descent. It was not a matter of deliberate Arab policy, but it had enormous political importance: the possibility of racial assimilation operated to preserve the racially plural character of social stratification. Those few Africans or persons of mixed Afro-Arab descent who managed to achieve a degree of upward economic mobility tended to change their self-identification accordingly and to become Arabs. The high status and prestige of the Arab community was a strong incentive for anyone possessing the economic wherewithal to pass as an Arab in his social and communal relations. Because these groups shared a common religion (Islam) and a common language (Swahili), because skin color was not an absolute criterion of racial community, and, most important, because the rising group never amounted to more than a very small number of persons, upwardly mobile individuals were usually able to gain entry into the elite structure of Zanzibar society, culturally and politically. As a result, Zanzibar's political elite tended to remain Arab in terms of self-decription and general pattern of behavior. In this way, the movement across racial boundaries which resulted from individual economic mobility, however minimal in absolute numbers, reinforced rather than undermined the racial aspect of political domination and the social division of labor.

This form of racial passing also added to the overall stability of the society by providing a kind of safety valve. In the twentieth century, Zanzibar did not experience the emergence of a social class comparable to the bourgeoisie of prerevolutionary France or the African middle classes of southern Africa—a class that while rising economically, remained unassimilated culturally and socially into the political ruling group. Such alienation did not become politically significant until after World War II.

Few people were actually able to change their socioeconomic position. Economics, skin color, and social acceptance were, on the whole, immovable obstacles to upward mobility by Africans. While persons of mixed descent and, on a few occasions, Africans as well were able to alter their self-description to suit changing personal circumstances, not enough people were involved to alter the racial character of social stratification. Since very few non-Arabs ever achieved the highest level of Zanzibar society, the Arab oligarchy remained a highly differentiated entity, distinct from the mass of the population, not only economically, but also in being of visible Arab descent.

ASIANS

The Asian community furnished Zanzibar's middle class: Asians filled the clerical and technical levels of the civil service; owned and operated most of the protectorate's wholesale, retail, and import commerce; dominated the export of cloves; and managed and staffed the large international banking and insurance firms. By the mid-twentieth century, Asians had also become a significant landowning group. Asians had initially been unwilling to acquire rural property, largely because ownership of land would imply a more permanent relationship to Zanzibar than most were willing to acknowledge. Eventually, however, through foreclosures on indebted Arabs, they came into possession of many of Zanzibar's productive clove and coconut estates. Thus, though constituting only a

very small minority of the total population, Asians owned a vastly disproportionate share of the nation's wealth; several Asian families had long
since surpassed all Arabs as the wealthiest Zanzibaris. Like the Arabs, the
Asians enjoyed advantages in income and style of life which gave their
class position a self-perpetuating quality. Unlike the Arab community,
however, Asians never became a major political force. Though able on
rare occasions to act successfully as a pressure group, the Asian community was unable to translate its economic strength into corresponding
political power.

The political weakness of the Asian community is traceable principally
to three factors: divisive communalism and religious fragmentation, the
vulnerability of middle-class status, and a pronounced tendency to remain culturally and emotionally oriented toward India.

The Asian community was composed of a myriad of religious and
ethnic subgroups. The basic division was between Hindu and Muslim
Asians, who formed approximately one-fourth and three-fourths of the
Asian community, respectively. They were further divided along religious or caste lines. The Muslim Asian community, for example, included
such diverse denominations as Ismailis, Bohoras, Ithna-Asharis, and Sunnis. Several small Asian groups (Parsees, Sikhs, and Goans) followed
entirely separate and distinct religious practices. Most Asians felt far
deeper loyalty to their particular subgroup than to the Asian community
as a whole. This tendency was especially noticeable in recent years when
the partition of India and Pakistan generated considerable antagonism
between Hindu and Muslim Asians. The result of extreme fragmentation
was that Asians were unable to cooperate with one another and thus
could not function politically as a unified group.

The Asians' middle-class status also made their political position difficult. As a community of businessmen, traders, and shopkeepers, Asians
were dependent on customer and client relations with the Arab and
African communities; as a class of lower civil servants, Asians were
usually under the jurisdiction of Arab superiors. Moreover, Asian civil
servants lacked the economic autonomy that the Arab administrators
derived from occupying a level of unchallengeable bureaucratic power
or from large agricultural landholdings. The pressure of being located in
sectors of the society where intercommunal relations were critical served
to foster a nonpolitical ethos of deference, service, and profit within the
Asian community. Most Asians tended to view political conflicts, not
simply as largely irrelevant to their lives, but as potentially damaging to
their social and economic status in Zanzibar society.

A marked tendency to remain culturally and emotionally attached to
India and, more recently, to Pakistan also helps to account for Asians'

noninvolvement in Zanzibar politics. Asian cultural separatism was reflected in a variety of ways: in a very low rate of intermarriage with local communities; in the maintenance of strong family and economic ties with the Asian subcontinent; in the tendency to speak Indian languages rather than Swahili in the home; and in the preference for segregated living areas which would permit a partial re-creation of Asian life.

Most Asians also looked to India and Pakistan, rather than to Zanzibar, for their ultimate political protection and security. Their homes were far more frequently adorned with photographs of Ghandi, Nehru, or Ayub Khan than with pictures of local leaders. In the past, this attitude had led to a peculiar indirect mode of political participation. Asians sought to exercise influence on the Zanzibar government through diplomatic pressures brought to bear by the government of India. When India announced that it could no longer protect its overseas minorities and told Asians abroad to accept the consequences of life in the diaspora, Zanzibar Asians were deprived of their sole mode of participation in local politics. Because they were unconcerned with local issues, Asians never sought to replace the diplomatic pressure of the Indian government with effective local organization.

AFRICANS

Africans were a politically and socially disprivileged majority: they furnished the protectorate with its peasant farmers, fishermen, and manual workers. The Africans faced several major barriers to upward mobility. The presence of an Asian community culturally acclimated to middle-class status made it extremely difficult for Africans to compete successfully for more lucrative employment, even at the clerical level of the civil service or in commerce. Moreover, Zanzibar's educational system strongly favored the well-to-do at the expense of the poverty-ridden, especially at the secondary school level where school fees were usually beyond the means of the average African family. Overt discrimination also handicapped African mobility. Even qualified Africans had great difficulty in securing positions in government or business, since Arabs or Asians in authority strongly preferred to hire members of their own communities. Thus, the African community's overall position, like that of the Arab and Asian communities, had a self-perpetuating quality. Successive generations were unable to overcome the syndrome of impoverishment and discrimination.

Communal divisions among Zanzibar Africans assumed enormous political importance in the period preceding the African revolution. The African community's overwhelming numerical strength made it potentially the most powerful political group in Zanzibar under an elected form of government, but the chronic and long-standing ethnic tension between Shirazis and mainlanders prevented Africans from becoming a unified electoral force. As a result, they consistently lost elections and thus failed to wrest power from the Arab oligarchy through the electoral process. Failure in the political arena was the immediate cause of the African revolution. A revolutionary army, composed principally of mainland Africans, overthrew Arab rule by force because the lack of overall communal solidarity among Africans had convinced many that Arab paramountcy never could be ended by orderly constitutional procedures.

Table 2 gives approximate population figures for the various African

TABLE 2

AFRICAN POPULATION IN ZANZIBAR, 1948

Community	Number	Percentage of all Africans
Hadimu	41,500	20.7
Tumbatu	44,000	22.0
Pemba	57,500	28.8
Total indigenous Africans (Shirazi)	143,000	71.5
Mainland Africans	57,000	28.5
Total of all Africans	200,000	100.0

ethnic groups in 1948. Socioeconomic differentiation between mainlanders and Shirazis intensified and perpetuated the sense of estrangement between the two communities. The mainland African minority was predominantly an urbanized group, with the vast majority of its members manual workers. Zanzibar's dock workers, household servants, hotel and restaurant help, commercial laborers, and daily paid municipal workers were overwhelmingly of mainland African origin. The few mainlanders who lived in the rural areas were usually squatter-farmers on estates and plantations belonging to Arabs or Asians. In contrast, Shirazis were a predominantly rural group and their basic economic pursuits were agriculture and fishing. As agriculturists, Shirazis cultivated land which they themselves owned, privately or communally.

This pattern of social differentiation gave rise to markedly different attitudes toward Zanzibar on the part of mainlanders and Shirazis. The mainland Africans experienced life in Zanzibar as a combination of economic deprivation and political alienation. As landless manual workers, they were not only in Zanzibar's lowest economic stratum, but their urban residence placed them in proximity to the Arab and Asian elites whose affluence made their own poverty appear more extreme in comparison. Moreover, mainlanders were deeply aware of their historical origins in the slave trade or as migratory labor; their lowly background, together with their menial economic status, made it difficult for them to regard themselves as full-fledged members of Zanzibar society. Several generations removed from their countries of origin, the mainlanders were unable to return home and unable fully to accept life in Zanzibar. Despite being legal citizens of the protectorate, the mainlanders were stateless persons, psychologically and emotionally.

Shirazis, on the other hand, possessed a sense of national pride at being the first Zanzibaris, and their concept of mixed Persian descent created a profound awareness of an ancient cultural and historical heritage. Living in remote villages, they were less exposed to daily contact with Arabs and Asians than the mainlanders and were thus less aware of the economic and political domination of Zanzibar by alien elites. Moreover, as rural landowners and fishermen, Shirazis lived with a dignity denied to the mainlanders, and they viewed themselves as full citizens of Zanzibar society.

A social portrait of Zanzibar's class structure just before the era of competitive racial politics is presented in tables 3, 4, and 5. Three quantitative indexes of social structure—landownership, occupational status, and access to higher education—are used to illustrate the close coincidence between racial community and economic class in Zanzibar. The three tables are based on a social survey of Zanzibar conducted in 1948 by Professor Edward Batson of the University of Capetown, South Africa. Quantitative surveys of any developing country must be treated with considerable skepticism, and Zanzibar is no exception. Batson's survey figures, however, can, with the usual cautions, be regarded as fairly reliable.[4]

The historic preeminence of cloves and coconuts as Zanzibar's basic cash crops has affected the manner in which Zanzibaris calculate the value of land. The only consideration taken into account is the number of trees on a particular plot. Other factors such as farm buildings, proximity to transportation, and even the quality of the soil have practically no influence on land values. As a result, Zanzibaris often measure a person's wealth according to the number of trees he owns. Following this tradition, both government and private surveys of landownership have employed a "number of trees" index to gauge the value of landed property in the hands of the different racial communities.[5]

Table 3, providing an estimate of landownership based on number of trees, shows that in 1948 Arabs owned more than two-thirds of Zanzibar's largest plantations, and that nearly one-third of the largest estates had passed into Asian hands. One of the most striking features of Zanzibar society revealed by the table is the limited size of the Arab landed aristocracy. Even if the top two categories of ownership are taken to constitute landed wealth, Zanzibar society in 1948 contained less than 500 Arab heads of families who enjoyed a position of social preeminence based on land. Given the low rate of profit of clove and coconut cultivation in the twentieth century, it is probably more realistic to employ only the top category of the table to indicate a position of real landed wealth. The total number of wealthy Arab agriculturists in Zanzibar after World

TABLE 3

LANDOWNERSHIP IN ZANZIBAR BY RACIAL COMMUNITY, 1948

Number of trees	Percentage of parcels				Total number of owners
	Arab	Asian	Shirazi	Mainland African	
3,000 or more	68.8	31.2	. .	. .	240
1,000–2,999	56.1	6.1	20.2	17.6 [a]	570
250–999	51.9	5.2	33.8	9.1	3,635
50–249	14.5	0.3	74.2	11.0	13,680
Less than 50	16.0	0.1	66.6	17.3	10,250

[a] This figure, which represents 100 mainland African landowners, was recorded entirely in Pemba.

War II, therefore, probably amounted to no more than 200. Table 3 thus helps to confirm the devastating toll being taken of the Arab elite group by its indebtedness and partitive inheritance practices.

Table 3 also indicates fairly substantial African landholding in the second and third categories of ownership. Though some Shirazis, Pemba Shirazis in particular, had always retained possession of a certain amount of land, the Africans' overall position was significantly improved over the early part of the century. A government survey of landownership taken in 1922 indicated that 96 percent of the owners of all plantations with 1,000 or more trees, and 85 percent of the owners of plantations with between 500 and 1,000 trees, were Arabs.[6] The resurgence of African landownership was directly related to the steady deterioration of the Arabs' position and occurred in two ways. First, land was being leased and sold to Africans by Asian financiers who had foreclosed on Arabs and who preferred African to Arab debtors because the Arabs' reputation had been damaged by the inability of earlier generations to repay loans.

Second, in an effort to prevent further erosion of their position, the Arabs of Pemba had established a special procedure whereby Africans could acquire land. Under this procedure an African who agreed to plant and cultivate a virgin piece of Arab land for five years could, at the end of this period, assume legal possession of half of the area. In this connection it should be noted that the 100 mainland Africans who appear in category 2 of the table lived on Pemba Island. The deterioration of the Arabs' virtual monopoly of Zanzibar's arable land was accompanied by an increase not only in Asian but also in African landownership.

The heavy preponderance of Arabs and Asians in elite Zanzibar society was also reflected in the pattern of occupational differentiation among the races. Table 4 ranks approximately 58,000 Zanzibaris following

TABLE 4

OCCUPATIONAL DISTRIBUTION IN ZANZIBAR BY RACIAL COMMUNITY, 1948

Occupational level	Percentage of workers				Total number of workers
	Arab	Asian	Indigenous African	Mainland African	
Upper	4.2	95.8	..	..	120
Upper middle	26.0	59.2	6.3	8.5	710
Middle (nonmanual)	26.1	33.3	27.3	13.3	5,400
Middle (manual)	6.0	34.9	12.1	47.0	1,735
Lower middle	17.1	4.7	54.1	24.1	35,160
Lower	13.5	0.9	36.9	48.7	14,635

nonagricultural pursuits according to six occupational levels: [7] (1) *upper,* including owners of large commercial firms, top professionals, and ranking administrators (e.g., heads of government departments, high school principals, doctors, lawyers, architects); (2) *upper middle,* comprising auxiliary professional workers (e.g., teachers, newspaper editors, retail shopkeepers); (3) and (4) *middle,* including nonmanual uncertified clerical and administrative personnel and skilled manual workers (e.g., koranic school teachers, clove inspectors, timekeepers, taxi drivers, carpenters, barbers); (5) *lower middle,* including semiskilled workers and itinerant workers (e.g., street vendors, coffee sellers, house servants, boat boys, builders of native huts); and (6) *lower,* composed of laborers (e.g., coconut, clove, and other agricultural workers, street sweepers, coconut huskers, porters). Table 4 reveals that Arabs and Asians monopolized Zanzibar's highest occupational category and constituted more than 85 percent of the second highest. The most striking feature, however, is the extent to which Asians outstripped Arabs at the top professional levels of Zanzibar society. There can be little doubt that, by 1948, the Asian community was the most economically advantaged of all Zanzibar's racial groups.

This conclusion does not, however, qualify the proposition that Arabs formed Zanzibar's preeminent political stratum. Not only were Asians relatively quiescent politically, but the elite of the Asian community (categories 1 and 2) was concentrated overwhelmingly in the private sector of Zanzibar society, in commerce, industry, and finance. The Arab elite was composed primarily of top-ranking government administrators who functioned at the level of permanent secretary and district commissioner. Moreover, the wealthiest Arab landowners were also a part of the

TABLE 5

ACCESS TO HIGHER EDUCATION IN ZANZIBAR BY RACIAL
COMMUNITY, 1948

Educational level	Percentage of students				Total number of students
	Arab	Asian	Indigenous Africans	Mainland Africans	
Standards I–VI	30.4	7.8	40.2	21.6	12,205
Standards VII–IX	29.9	41.3	12.8	16.0	1,440
Standards X–XII	31.4	46.8	3.2	18.6	620

Arab "political class." The heavy Arab representation on the Legislative Council, on local government bodies, and on various governmental advisory committees was drawn from the landowner group. In contrast with the Asians' fragmented and basically apathetic attitudes toward politics, the Arab elite was a cohesive and assertive political force.

Access to higher education is a major determinant of a society's long-range pattern of social stratification. In this respect, as in landownership and occupational distribution, the differential incorporation of racial and communal groups into the institutional structures of Zanzibar society was highly conspicuous. The extent of this differential incorporation is indicated in table 5.[8] Though the Asian community formed less than 6 percent of the total population, almost half of the students at the highest levels of the secondary school system were Asian children. This radical disproportion was a consequence of urban residence, overwhelming preponderance in the clerical, managerial, and commercial sectors of the society, and a pervasive cultural emphasis on education rather than on politics as a vehicle for achieving and maintaining social status. Arab children accounted for nearly a third of the student body in the top three grades of secondary school, a figure almost double the Arab proportion of the total population. The Arabs' relative disadvantage vis-à-vis Asians in no way weakened the political status of the Arab elites. Because of the costs of secondary education, family wealth was a prime determinant of access to the upper grade levels, and nearly all the Arab students in secondary school were children of the oligarchic stratum of the community. Upon matriculation, they formed the intellectual core of the Arab political class, its administrators, journalists, and leaders. Though the number of Arab secondary school graduates was far smaller than the number of Asians, it was always sufficient to make the Arab political class a viable political force.

Though less than one-fourth of the total population, Arab and Asian children constituted well over two-thirds of the student population in the top three grades of Zanzibar's secondary school system. Their proportion was even higher in government secondary schools, since the large number of mainland Africans in Standards X–XII includes children of approximately 2,000 Christians who received a high school education in missionary schools. The real character of the Zanzibar school system is to be seen in the position of the Shirazi community. Though constituting approximately three-fifths of the total population, Shirazis accounted for only about 3 percent of the student body in the highest grades. In sum, Zanzibar's educational system did not function as a vehicle for social mobility through which subordinated racial groups could matriculate to the higher economic levels of the society, but was simply a mechanism by which already overprivileged racial communities were able to reinforce their control of elite socioeconomic status.

Tables 3, 4, and 5 show that Zanzibar's major communal groups were differentiated by economic and social status. Zanzibaris of different races did not share sufficient common occupational or economic interests to create politically meaningful bonds of solidarity across racial lines. The economic estrangement of racial communities extended into most other spheres of life as well. Zanzibar did not possess a network of noncommunal social clubs and voluntary associations. The only voluntary groups in the society which had significant numbers of members were organized along communal, not functional, lines: the Arab Association, the Indian Association, the Shirazi Association, and the African Association. Recreation, sports, and informal social relations were conducted almost wholly within the boundaries of these racial associations and, for this reason, Zanzibaris had little opportunity to establish interpersonal contacts and relationships across communal lines. When modern politics began, race was almost the only meaningful basis on which political organizations could be formed.

FACTORS OF INTEGRATION: LANGUAGE AND RELIGION

Two important aspects of Zanzibar culture, the Swahili language and the Islamic faith, cut across racial boundaries and, to a certain extent, constituted factors of integration among economically differentiated racial communities. Linguistic uniformity was especially characteristic of the Arab and African communities. All Zanzibaris spoke Swahili, and for Arabs and Africans a common version of this language was the first tongue. Although some Arabs spoke Arabic and there were regional dialects of Swahili within the African community, both groups were highly conscious of sharing a single mode of speech. The Asian community, however, was culturally differentiated along linguistic lines. With very few exceptions, members of the Asian community retained Indian languages as their first tongue and used Swahili only as a vehicle of communication with Arabs and Africans. As a result, the Swahili spoken by Asians was inferior and ungrammatical, and Asians could always be distinguished by their mode of speech as well as by their economic and physical characteristics.

The Islamic religion was the most important factor tending toward integration among Zanzibaris, furnishing as it did a powerful impetus toward the formation of political solidarities across racial boundaries. More than 95 percent of Zanzibar's total population was Muslim, and there was a high degree of religious unity even along denominational lines. Sunni Muslims constituted nearly four-fifths of the total population and almost nine-tenths of all Muslims. Religious commonality, like linguistic commonality, was especially characteristic of the African and Arab communities. Nearly all Africans and the vast majority of Arabs were of the Sunni denomination.

Politically significant patterns of religious differentiation did exist in Zanzibar. Although approximately three-fourths of the Asian community were Muslims, the majority of these were Shia rather than Sunni, and the community was further fragmented by the presence of additional Muslim subgroups and a sharp cleavage between Muslim and non-Muslim. The Arab oligarchy was predominantly Ibadhi rather than Sunni, a division somewhat similar to the difference between Episcopalian and Baptist Protestant denominations, namely, "high-culture" and "low-culture" versions of the same faith. Perhaps most important, the mainland African community contained about 2,000 Christians who actually represented only a small percentage of all mainlanders, but whose presence led to a widespread, though inaccurate, stereotype of the community as a Christian group. Arab political leaders were able to exploit this stereotype, stigmatizing the mainlanders as the real aliens to Zanzibar since they did not share the Islamic faith of other Zanzibaris.

The basic feature of Zanzibar's religious system, however, was that practically all Zanzibaris were Muslim and viewed a common religion as an important bond. The ubiquity of Islam meant that Zanzibaris shared not only a common theology but the pervasive religious environment that accompanied it. Shared institutions such as mosques, koranic schools, and Muslim charities, and common practices such as holidays, rituals, and ceremonies, were conspicuous symbols of a mutual religious identity.

The social and political values of Islam also contributed to a religious environment conducive to multiracial solidarity. The Koran treats racial diversity as a divine creation and endows it with sacred status as a means through which peoples of different races may come to share close social bonds. Two scriptural passages, frequently called to the attention of Zanzibaris, stress the Prophet's insistence on the divine imperative of harmonious race relations: "Among his signs is the creation of the heavens and the earth and the diversity of your tongues and complexions" (Koran: 30, 31); and, "Men, we have . . . divided you into nations and tribes so that you might come to know one another" (Koran: 49, 13). Before the African revolution, Arab political leaders employed these passages in an effort to gain acceptance by Africans and to discredit African political organizations that sought to recruit support on the basis of economic antagonisms toward the Arab community.

The political theory of Islam also enabled Arab leadership to canvass for African acceptance and support. One important koranic passage reads: "Obey God and His Apostle and those who have authority over you" (Koran: 4, 62). In terms of this passage, deference to established authority was, like racial harmony, a divinely imposed personal obligation. As a historic ruling elite, Arabs were able to derive therefrom a religious basis of legitimacy and to argue that any effort to reverse communal power relations was a violation of divine imperatives. They also argued that loyalty to the sultan was a religiously ordained obligation stemming from the principle of deference. Many Africans who supported Arab-led political groups did so in the firm conviction that this was a religious duty, believing that to support a politically radical African movement was against the sociopolitical teachings of their faith.

Common religion was therefore both consistent with and supportive of the plural pattern of Zanzibar society. By enjoining against racial conflict, and counseling acceptance and deference, it gave added strength to the Arabs' position as a political and economic elite. As Zanzibaris understood their religion, any effort to alter the pattern of stratification or to challenge Arab authority was a violation of religious obligation.

There were thus two basic and contradictory political tendencies in Zanzibar society: a tendency toward political equilibrium and multiracial harmony based upon common adherence to the Islamic faith; and a tendency toward extreme racial conflict stemming from the severe economic differentiation among the races. Islam operated to mute the racial antagonisms inherent in an economically plural society, and its articulated values caused many Africans to support the Arab elite or to refuse association with radical African movements. The racially plural aspect of the economy generated extreme antagonism, however, and accounts for the African community's bitter determination to overthrow the Arab oligarchy and establish an African government.

THE POLITICS OF PLURALISM, 1954–1964

The unique feature of prerevolutionary politics in Zanzibar was the effort of the Arab oligarchy to preserve its position by gaining the acceptance and political support of the African majority. This method was fundamentally different from the usual technique of dominant racial minorities which have attempted to retain power by coercive means elsewhere in Africa. The racial oligarchies of South Africa and Rhodesia, for example, have persistently refused to allow any liberalization of the political system, for wherever majority rule has been introduced, the chosen leaders of the subordinated majority have been brought to power. In contrast with these alien settler communities, the Arab oligarchy of Zanzibar actively sought to bring about the introduction of a representative parliamentary system based on universal suffrage, and tied its political future to the idea of gaining sufficient African electoral support to win a majority of the constituencies.

The basic reason for this strategy, as opposed to a strategy of coercive domination, was that the Arab community had no real alternative in the face of the British presence in Zanzibar and emerging African nationalism. By the early 1950's, British colonial policy in Africa had become clear. That policy was to introduce representative parliamentary democracy, prior to withdrawal, in all territories that lacked substantial white settler minorities. Although Britain was willing to delay the implementation of this policy in Zanzibar, and to qualify it by such constitutional devices as communal representation and specially reserved seats, there was little doubt that in the long run the African community's overwhelming popular majority would have to be reflected in the constitutional arrangements of the society. Militant African nationalism was already the most conspicuous feature of politics on the continental mainland and would inevitably spread to Zanzibar. Therefore, any political system constitutionally based upon special treatment for an elite non-African minority could, at best, be short-lived. Forward-looking members of the Arab community could not have avoided the conclusion that if an immigrant oligarchy was to survive within a democratic political context, it would have to attract the support of a sufficient number of Africans to win or control a majority of seats in a popularly elected national assembly.

There was an element of desperation in the Arabs' position. As a declining oligarchy, the Arab community faced the prospect of a steady erosion of its political power through the operation of such economic forces as indebtedness, falling clove prices, and land fragmentation. The effectiveness of the Arab political class had always depended on a wealthy landowning group able to devote considerable time to political activity. The disappearance of this group would transform the Arab elite into a class composed solely of civil servants and would drastically diminish the Arab community's ability to maintain political power. In order to gain unchallenged political power, therefore, the Arabs had to bolster, and eventually rebuild, their deteriorating social and economic position.

The problem confronting Arab leadership was how to attract widespread electoral support within the African community. The solution agreed upon—to initiate a Zanzibar nationalist movement—had several advantages related to long-range Arab strategy. By engendering a rupture in Arab-British relations, it would detract from the Arabs' reputation as the most favored racial group under the colonial policy of the protectorate government. Anticolonial nationalism would also focus attention on British rule as the common enemy of all Zanzibaris and thereby not only obscure the fact that the Arab oligarchy was itself a colonial group but would also provide a potential basis for uniting members of all racial communities. If successful, Arab-led nationalism might wrest control of Zanzibar away from Britain before continental African nationalism could spread to the protectorate and arouse the African community into political action on its own. In June 1954, the Arab Association rejected British proposals for a communal roll election and demanded immediate constitutional progress toward independence along fully democratic lines. To dramatize its position, the association boycotted the Legislative Council and appealed for popular support for the cause of Zanzibar's freedom.

From its inception, and for a considerable period thereafter, Zanzibar nationalism was a distinctly Arab movement. The Arabs' motives were not entirely strategic, but stemmed in part from genuine patriotic and religious sentiments. The Arab community had always regarded Zanzibar as its own country, a view reinforced by Britain's repeated declaration that the protectorate was constitutionally an Arab state. Although the British intrusion had in no essential way impaired the Arabs' social or economic status, the Arab community experienced a strong sense of political loss; Arabs deeply resented British rule, which they believed had subordinated a once sovereign and independent Arab nation.

Islamic beliefs also generated nationalistic sentiments among Arabs. The concept of "jihad," an eternal struggle against nonbelievers, imbued Arab nationalism with the quality of a religious crusade against foreign infidels. The heavy Islamic emphasis on multiracialism was also a source of nationalistic motivation. Several Arab leaders were firmly convinced that nationalism would furnish the means whereby they might unite all Zanzibaris in the spirit of multiracial harmony enjoined by the Koran. Moreover, Ibadhi Islam, the religious creed of the Arab political elite, has a strong admixture of liberal democratic tenets, stressing, for example, that the will of God can be expressed only through the free choice of the whole community. The Arabs' effort to end autocratic British rule and to establish a constitutionally democratic policy in Zanzibar may therefore be viewed as an attempt to fulfill basic religious obligations.

The Arab Association abandoned its boycott of the Legislative Council in early 1956, when the British government withdrew its proposal for a communal roll election and announced that a national election based on a common roll procedure would be held in 1957. The most important feature of the boycott was not that it had forced the colonial government to come to terms, but that it had attracted considerable support within the African community. Encouraged by this success, Arab politicians assumed the leadership of a small multiracial party, the Zanzibar Nationalist Party (ZNP), and began to campaign in preparation for the 1957 election.

The ZNP enjoyed several advantages. As the first nationalist party in the protectorate, it was able completely to preempt the symbols of nationalism and to identify itself exclusively with the demand for "Freedom, Now." ZNP leaders and organizers were able to travel throughout the country recruiting African support. Unchallenged by any African electoral rival, they effectively argued that any Zanzibari who wished to support the cause of national freedom would necessarily have to join their party. The popular appeal of the ZNP, which presented itself as a multiracial party loyal to the sultan, was enhanced both by the religious validation it ascribed to its principles and by the widespread affection for the monarch. The ZNP was also strengthened by its ability to command substantial financial and personnel resources. As the party of the Arab elite, it not only attracted large campaign funds but was staffed by Arab intellectuals who possessed considerable organizational and political experience. In fact, throughout its political history, the ZNP was able to muster financial, organizational, and personnel resources unmatched by any other party.

African nationalism in Zanzibar developed almost wholly in reaction to the threat of Arab domination posed by the ZNP. No attempt to form an African political party was made until February 1957, only six months before the election, and even then it had only limited success. The principal impetus to form an African party came from the mainland African community which, for historical and economic reasons, harbored the deepest sense of grievance against Arab rule. Mainland African leaders sought to unite their political organization, the African Association, with the Shirazi Association, but the degree of unification achieved was slight. The African and Shirazi associations of Zanzibar Island agreed to cooperate for the sake of the election and to nominate candidates jointly, but the Shirazis refused to sanction a full merger. The name chosen for the campaign, Afro-Shirazi Union (ASU), was intended as much to symbolize the fact that each association would continue to maintain full autonomy as to dramatize a degree of unity between the two communities. The African and Shirazi associations of Pemba were unable to cooperate even to this extent, each insisting on contesting the election as a separate political group.

The ASU operated under a number of other disadvantages. As a movement of reaction and fear, the ASU was markedly conservative in its campaign. Its leaders asserted that the election ought to be postponed and independence delayed until such time as Africans could compete on an equal social and economic footing with members of other racial communities. They argued that Zanzibar Africans suffered under two colonialisms, British and Arab, and that if the former granted Zanzibar independence, the latter would impose on the African community a far harsher and more autocratic rule. The ASU campaign did not compare favorably with the militant crusading nationalism of the ZNP, and left the ASU open to the charge that it was a racial party and that its views were a fundamental violation of Islamic precepts. Although the ASU officially endorsed the principles of multiracialism and loyalty to the sultan, its gestures in this direction were lukewarm and its anti-Arab theme raised serious doubts in the minds of many religiously inclined voters.

The ASU also had extreme difficulty in obtaining financial support and in attracting able leadership. As a party of impoverished Africans, it could neither command the sizable donations that buoyed the ZNP nor avail itself of an economically independent nucleus of intellectuals. Not only was its leadership politically inexperienced, but it consisted of people who could not afford to donate more than part time to political activity.

The results of the 1957 election foreshadowed difficulties to be faced by African political organizations in Zanzibar. The ASU was unable to win a parliamentary majority, for the pattern of voting revealed no widespread support for parties or candidates espousing anti-Arab views. Such support existed only on Zanzibar Island, where the ASU won three out of four seats and gained 63 percent of the popular vote. The ASU's popular base, however, was almost entirely confined to mainland Africans and Hadimu Shirazis who, owing to their historical experience of land alienation, were receptive to the mainlanders' anti-Arab sentiments. No other ethnic group supported the ASU in significant numbers. Since the party was unable to contest the election on a national basis, it received only 35 percent of the total popular vote.

Campaigns based on anti-Arab appeals were particularly ineffective in Pemba. African Association candidates whose views corresponded closely to those of the ASU were defeated by overwhelming majorities. The two victorious Shirazi candidates had refused to campaign on anti-Arab grounds and had articulated a multiracial ideology not strikingly different from that of the ZNP. Moreover, the ZNP, despite the visibility of Arab leadership at the top of the party, gained 30 percent of the popular vote in Pemba, approximately twice its Zanzibar figure. Although the ZNP did not win any seats, it demonstrated an ability to attract considerable African support, not only on Pemba but to a certain extent on Zanzibar Island as well.

The 1957 election revealed two aspects of Zanzibar politics relevant to the ZNP's long-range electoral success. First, with the exception of the mainland African and Hadimu communities, most African voting was based on communal loyalties rather than on a favorable response to anti-Arab appeals. This was particularly true in Pemba. The two victorious Pemba candidates were highly placed leaders of the Shirazi Association, and their electoral success resulted primarily from their close personal identification with the Pemba Shirazi community. Even on Zanzibar Island, communalism was an important supplement to anti-Arab feeling in producing African support for the ASU. The ASU candidates were established leaders of the African and Shirazi associations, and the Shirazis' reluctance to merge before the election can be explained in terms of their desire to draw upon long-standing communal ties as well as their resentment of Arabs.

The importance of communalism as a determinant of most Africans' voting behavior greatly encouraged the ZNP. It meant that the party's defeat resulted, not from resentment of the Arabs, but from the novelty of a multiracial organization in a society where communal separatism was a long-established and deeply ingrained tradition. This distinction was critical to the formulation of subsequent ZNP election strategy. In the elections that followed, the ZNP did not seek to justify or conceal Arab leadership, nor did it base its propaganda on winning popularity for the Arab community. Instead, it concentrated on discrediting old traditions of communal separatism and used Islamic religious precepts to win acceptance for its own multiracial viewpoint.

The most important aspect of national politics revealed by the election was the fundamental political difference between Pemba and Zanzibar islands. Pemba Shirazis clearly demonstrated an extreme reluctance to associate themselves with an anti-Arab political ideology. The refusal of the Pemba Shirazi Association to align itself with the African Association before the election, the multiracial stance taken by its leadership during the campaign, and the substantial electoral support for the ZNP were dramatic evidence of the Pemba Shirazis' basically cordial attitude toward the Arab oligarchy. After 1957 the ZNP's multiracial campaign style attracted additional support among Pemba Africans, and its final electoral victory was based principally on its popular strength on Pemba Island.

The Hadimu and mainland African communities of Zanzibar Island were highly receptive to anti-Arab views. The ZNP never won a constituency in which either of these communities formed a majority of the electorate. Hadimus and mainlanders preferred, in overwhelming numbers, to give their support to an African party that espoused the overthrow of the Arab oligarchy and the transformation of Zanzibar into an African-ruled state.[*]

THE BACKGROUND OF REVOLUTION

The difference between Zanzibar and Pemba islands stemmed from many social and historical factors. Three of these factors stand out: historical differences in the circumstances of Arab arrival and land alienation; differences in the political efficacy of the mainland African community; and varying degrees of social modernization on the two islands.

---

[*] The Tumbatu Shirazis behaved politically very much like the Pemba Shirazis, and the northern peninsula of Zanzibar Island was therefore similar to Pemba in its voting pattern. On Pemba Island, it made little difference politically whether a constituency was inhabited by Pemba or Tumbatu Shirazis.

THE ARAB ARRIVAL AND LAND ALIENATION

The Arabs established themselves on Zanzibar as an invading colonial force and paid little heed to the wishes of the indigenous African communities. Under the impact of the massive Arab intrusion, traditional African political institutions quickly broke down and were replaced by an autocratic form of colonial administration. The Arab settlers alienated vast areas of African land, assuming possession of practically all the arable soil and restricting African settlement to remote areas of poor agricultural land. Arab colonialism on Zanzibar Island was thus accompanied by residential segregation of the African population, the development of conspicuous economic inequalities between Arabs and Africans, and consequently, the growth of intense African resentment of the Arabs.

Arab settlement of Pemba differed in all these respects. It was initially undertaken at the invitation of the local African population, and this strong element of African consent made it unnecessary for the Arabs to establish strict administrative controls. Arab land alienation also assumed a far milder form. As fertile soils were evenly distributed throughout Pemba Island, Arab land acquisition did not segregate the African population or deprive Africans of fertile areas for cultivation. Since Africans as well as Arabs were able to engage in clove and coconut production, the economic differential between the two communities never assumed the proportions reached on Zanzibar Island. Moreover, as the wealthiest Arabs preferred to live permanently in Zanzibar Town (located on Zanzibar Island), the economic differences that did exist on Pemba Island were fairly inconspicuous. The absence of residential segregation and of extreme economic differentiation also facilitated a far higher rate of intermarriage between Africans and Arabs on Pemba. The overall result was an absence of deeply rooted racial animosities.

DIFFERING MAINLAND AFRICAN INFLUENCES

The political influence of mainland Africans was far stronger on Zanzibar Island than on Pemba. Over two-thirds of the mainland Africans lived on Zanzibar Island, most of them residing in the African section of Zanzibar Town. Their urban concentration, their deprived economic status, and their historic legacy of bitterness against the Arabs caused the mainland community to become a nucleus of radical discontent. Their influence was felt most strongly by the Hadimu. At any given time, approximately 10 percent of the Hadimu Shirazis were residents in Zanzibar Town. Here, they were exposed directly to the anti-Arab sentiments of the mainland Africans. Since the Hadimu were in any case receptive to these views because of Arab land alienation, the presence of mainland Africans served to reinforce existing Hadimu predilections toward anti-Arab feeling. Many Hadimus traveled frequently between their homes and Zanzibar Town, and in this way the political sentiments of the African community became dispersed throughout the central and southern areas of Zanzibar Island.

No such urban nucleus of mainland Africans existed on Pemba Island. Although there were about 15,000 mainlanders residing there, most of them were scattered throughout the rural areas. Since the general environment of Pemba was unreceptive to anti-Arab views, it was impossible for the mainland community to exert any political influence on the indigenous African population. In fact, many Pemba Shirazis harbored strong prejudices against mainland Africans, whom they tended to consider as prone to violent behavior and as a potential source of Christian influence. These stereotypes led many Pemba Shirazis to resent the mainland Africans to a far greater degree than they resented the Arabs, and contributed directly toward the Pemba Shirazis' later preference for political association with Arab rather than mainland African-led political organizations.

DIFFERENTIAL SOCIAL MODERNIZATION

Uneven social modernization also contributed to the vast political difference between Zanzibar and Pemba islands. Zanzibar Island has been a scene of extensive development in the introduction of Western-style educational, economic, and social institutions. The island also possessed a well-developed infrastructure and communications system. Most of these facilities were in Zanzibar Town, the center of the protectorate's administration, commerce, and trade. About one-quarter of the African population of Zanzibar Island was permanently urbanized and thousands of Africans were absorbed into the modern occupational and social sector of the society. These Africans were brought into contact with a new secular political and social environment. Uprooted from traditional ties and affiliations and exposed daily to the gross racial and economic inequalities of the country, the Africans of Zanzibar Island were available for recruitment into agitational mass movements seeking a far-reaching political and economic reconstruction of Zanzibar society.

Pemba lagged far behind Zanzibar in the introduction of novel economic and social institutions. Though the island was the source of three-fourths of the protectorate's clove production, very little commerce was carried on locally, since all sales and export were conducted from Zanzibar Town. As a result, Pemba had little urbanization and the island remained a predominantly rural and agrarian society. Thus, Pemba Africans were largely unaffected by the forces of social change and modernization which mobilized the Africans of Zanzibar. Islamic religious beliefs and a traditional cultural milieu remained the paramount commitment of most Pemba Africans. They were unwilling to join a revolutionary mass movement.

Despite the major differences in racial attitude between the African populations of Zanzibar and Pemba, African leaders did attempt to form a united organization after the 1957 election. The two Shirazis from Pemba joined the ASU, which was then renamed the Afro-Shirazi Party (ASP), and, for a brief time, Zanzibar possessed a single African party united on the general principle that political power must eventually pass into African hands. The strains between the leaders of the two islands proved to be too damaging, however, and at the end of 1959 the ASP split, the Pemba Shirazis withdrawing to form their own political party, the Zanzibar and Pemba People's Party (ZPPP). The split symbolized the irreducible disagreement between Pemba and Zanzibar Africans over the question of race. The ZPPP at once officially adopted a multiracial position similar to that of the ZNP and presented it publicly as the major difference between itself and the ASP.

The split in the ASP did serious damage to the African political cause. It splintered the African community into two bitterly opposed political groups divided along regional, ethnic, and ideological lines. The ZPPP had its strength in Pemba, among Pemba and Tumbatu Shirazis, and was ideologically opposed to the idea of Zanzibar becoming a wholly African-ruled state. The ASP was left with significant strength only on Zanzibar, among mainlanders and Hadimu, and its leaders believed that an African assumption of political power was the only valid purpose of political action. Though the ASP was by far the larger of the two parties, the split had left it in desperate condition, bereft of leadership and organization in Pemba, and demoralized by the slim prospects of unity in the African community.

Zanzibar's second general election was scheduled for January 1961. The basic positions of the two major parties did not differ from those of 1957. The ZNP campaigned as a multiracial party loyal to the Sultan and placed strong emphasis on the point that these principles were sanctioned by the Koran. Its policies were immediate independence, the creation of a constitutional monarchy, and the development of Zanzibar's economy along nonracial lines. The ASP endorsed multiracialism and loyalty to the sultanate, but its heaviest campaign emphasis was on the need for Africans to unite to end Arab rule. The ASP remained troubled by the question of independence and argued that premature termination of British rule would leave Africans exposed to an even harsher Arab colonialism. On economic policy, the ASP stressed the need for special measures to place Africans on an equal economic and social footing with Arabs and Asians.

The ZPPP had difficulty in distinguishing itself from the ZNP. Its warm endorsement of multiracialism made its ideological position identical to that of the Arab-controlled party. ZPPP leaders argued, however, that their party represented a middle ground between the mainland African–dominated ASP and the Arab-led ZNP. The ZPPP's most reliable source of strength was that it represented a political continuation of the Pemba Shirazi Association in its leadership and organizational structure.

The significant electoral differences between the major parties did not lie in their ideological or programmatic positions but in their contrasting emotional appeals to the electorate. The ZNP campaigned as the religious guardian of an Islamic Zanzibar. It represented the ASP as a party of Christian mainland Africans who, if victorious, would forcibly impose Christianity as a national religion. In Arab and Asian areas, the ZNP depicted its rival as a party motivated by racial hatred and asserted that an ASP government would treat non-African minorities with violence and discrimination. The ASP represented the ZNP as the party of a feudal Arab class, and ASP speeches were pervaded with the accusation that a ZNP victory was tantamount to the return of slavery and meant the permanent political and economic subjugation of Africans. Political appeals of this sort added immeasurably to the racial hostility already present in a society where economic stratification followed communal lines, and gave political conflict in Zanzibar a special quality as a process marked by implacable communal animosities.

The election ended in a deadlock. The country had been divided into twenty-two constituencies and no party gained a majority of the seats. The ASP won ten, the ZNP, nine, and the ZPPP, three. Leaders of the ASP and ZNP negotiated with the ZPPP over the formation of a coalition government, but the ZPPP itself split in such a way that a constitutional crisis ensued. One ZPPP leader decided to join the ASP, giving that party eleven seats, and two ZPPP leaders chose to form a coalition with the ZNP, giving these two parties a total of eleven seats. Since no group had a majority, the British government added an additional constituency and called for another election to be held in June.

The important difference between the January and June elections was that in June the ZPPP formally aligned itself with the ZNP in an electoral coalition. This was the natural product of the Pemba Shirazis' close relations with the Arab community and of their strong tendency to prefer association with Arabs over any involvement with the mainland African community. Though the ZNP-ZPPP alliance can, in part, be explained in terms of a deal between the two parties, it really represents the consequence of the vast historical, social, and economic differences between Zanzibar and Pemba islands.

ZNP-ZPPP alliance virtually assured the outcome of the June election. Since popular voting patterns did not change and since the two coalition parties pooled their resources in close constituencies, they were able to carry all the areas that each had previously carried separately. The ZNP-ZPPP gained thirteen of the twenty-three constituencies and assumed control of the Zanzibar government. A prime minister was appointed from the leadership of the ZPPP to symbolize an African presence in the councils of state and to demonstrate the genuineness of the coalition's principle of multiracialism, but the politically significant feature of the postelection government was that Arab leaders of the ZNP assumed control of practically all the important ministries.

Zanzibar's fourth and final general election before independence was held in July 1963. It did not differ from the election of June 1961 in any fundamental respect. The ZNP-ZPPP alliance, fused into a single party dominated by Arab leaders of the ZNP, possessed financial and organizational resources far superior to those of the ASP. The general style of campaigning, the spatial distribution of popular support for all parties, and the final outcome of the election were all basically similar to those of June 1961. The ZNP-ZPPP coalition gained eighteen out of thirty-one constituencies, thereby ensuring that Arab ministers at the head of a disciplined party would be in control of the Zanzibar government when independence was achieved.

Table 6 shows the number of constituencies and the percentage of the popular vote gained by each party in Zanzibar and Pemba in the elections of January and June 1961 and July 1963.[9] The election results dramatically illustrate the political impact of the historical and social differences between Zanzibar and Pemba Islands. Here is a portrait of a society in which Africans were not unified in opposition to Arab rule, but were themselves divided along ethnic lines. The basic line of cleavage was between mainland Africans and Hadimu Shirazis on the one hand, and, on the other, Arabs who were supported by most other Shirazis and practically all Asians. The pattern is clearly reflected in the distribution of electoral support among the contending parties.

The ASP had its greatest strength on Zanzibar, where it consistently won a majority of the constituencies and gained more than three-fifths of the popular vote. Practically all this support came from constituencies inhabited by Hadimu and mainland Africans. The party was never able to do nearly so well on Pemba, where, in each election, it failed to win more than two constituencies. An important aspect of the ASP's position

TABLE 6

RESULTS OF THE ZANZIBAR ELECTIONS OF JANUARY 1961, JUNE 1961, AND JULY 1963

Party	Zanzibar January 1961 N[a]	P[b]	Zanzibar June 1961 N	P	Zanzibar July 1963 N	P	Pemba January 1961 N	P	Pemba June 1961 N	P	Pemba July 1963 N	P	Total January 1961 N	P	Total June 1961 N	P	Total July 1963 N	P
ASP	8	61.1	8	63.6	11	63.1	2	23.0	2	36.6	2	44.4	10	43.2	10	50.6	13	54.2
ZNP	5	34.6	5	32.4	6	31.5	4	43.0	5	38.8	6	28.0	9	38.5	10	35.5	12	29.8
ZPPP	0	4.3	0	4.0	0	5.4	3	34.0	3	24.6	6	27.6	3	18.3	3	13.9	6	16.0
Total	13	100.0	13	100.0	17	100.0	9	100.0	10	100.0	14	100.0	22	100.0	23	100.0	31	100.0

[a] N = number of constituencies.
[b] P = percentage of popular vote.

on Pemba was its rapidly increasing popular support. Between January 1961 and July 1963 the ASP nearly doubled its popular strength there, and, by the final election, it had attracted the allegiance of more than two-fifths of the Pemba electorate.

The ASP's increasing strength on Pemba was a result of several factors. The party had modulated the strident anti-Arab tone of its campaign and gave stronger regional emphasis to multiracial and religious themes designed to attract the support of a conservative Islamic electorate. The ASP had also begun to recover from the disastrous effects of the 1959 split; by 1963 it had developed an ability to campaign intensively through most of the island, reaching areas that had hitherto been only marginally exposed to its views. Another cause of increasing ASP support was a growing tendency among Pemba Shirazis to become disillusioned with the ZPPP. Pemba Shirazis had originally supported the ZPPP as an extension of the Pemba Shirazi Association and as an autonomous third force espousing multiracial views. The ZPPP's expanding relationship with the ZNP and its eventual absorption into the larger party damaged its neutral image, forcing Pemba voters to make a clear choice between the ZNP and the ASP.

The tendency of Pemba voters to prefer the ASP was in part related to the ASP's ability to alter its image and present a more multiracial appearance, but, more important, it resulted from a visible change in the political climate of the island. Seven years of intensely competitive partisan activity had exposed Pemba Shirazis to the secular political concepts of representative democracy. New norms of equality and participation had been introduced into Pemba society and began to call into question the older religiously derived values of deference and multiracial harmony, particularly insofar as the latter implied acquiescence in a system of social and political inequalities. Once this occurred, Islam began to lose commanding influence over the Pemba Shirazis' political behavior; its diminishing power could best be seen in the ASP's growing strength.

The ZNP's greatest popular strength was on Pemba, despite the fact that the percentage figures indicate decreasing ZNP appeal. The apparent ZNP decline on Pemba is really attributable to the deteriorating popular support for the ZPPP. As a matter of election strategy, the ZNP frequently allowed its electoral partner to nominate a coalition candidate in constituencies where the commitment of ZPPP voters was weakening but where the strength of ZNP support could be counted upon to supply the margin of victory. As this tactic caused numerous ZNP members to vote officially for a ZPPP nominee, it produced a decline in the number of votes actually registered for the ZNP, when in fact ZNP supporters were far more loyal than those of the ZPPP.

The ZNP did have a certain amount of strength on Zanzibar Island, where it gained the support of approximately one-third of the electorate. The spatial distribution of this support indicates that the party made its strongest appeal to immigrant minorities, Arabs and Asians in particular, and to Tumbatu Shirazis.

The ZPPP was entirely a Pemba party. Though it gained isolated clusters of support on Zanzibar Island, it never won a constituency there, and maintained only one or two local branches on the island. At best a weak third party, the ZPPP initially enjoyed substantial political influence because of its balance-of-power position. After its organizational absorption into the ZNP, the ZPPP's influence and support declined, and by June 1963 it functioned almost entirely as an electoral adjunct of its senior partner.

The notable feature of the 1963 election was that the ASP won nearly 55 percent of the popular vote and gained some 13,000 more votes than the two coalition parties combined. The ASP's defeat has frequently been attributed to electoral gerrymandering by the Arab government in cooperation with the British colonial administration. That allegation is not true. The ASP was defeated because its popular support was concentrated in a smaller number of constituencies which it won by huge majorities. In the mainland African constituencies, for example, the ASP gained more than 90 percent of the popular vote. In Pemba, on the other hand, the ASP's support was scattered throughout the island. Though the party was supported in 1963 by about 43 percent of the Pemba electorate, it possessed majorities in only two of fourteen constituencies. In many other Pemba constituencies, the ASP was defeated by narrow margins. This combination of concentration and dispersion of the ASP electorate, rather than an unfair arrangement of constituency boundaries, accounts for the ASP's ability to gain a clear majority of the popular vote while failing to win a majority of the seats.

Although the election was impartially conducted and the ASP's defeat could have occurred in any parliamentary system based on single-member constituencies, many ASP members were deeply convinced that their party had been cheated out of a victory. This belief had strong influence on the distribution of power within the ASP in the months following the election. Moderate leaders, who wished the party to function as a loyal parliamentary opposition and to avoid revolutionary activities that might provoke the government into taking repressive measures, found it extremely difficult to gain support for their position. Power passed into the hands of militants. This group, arguing that the ASP had been unfairly deprived of victory, asserted that violence was the only method by which Africans would be able to overthrow Arab rule and assume political power.

After the election the ZNP-ZPPP government initiated a series of policies designed to consolidate its political position and to stabilize the social and economic bases of its power. Its major attention was devoted to transforming Zanzibar from a freely competitive parliamentary system into an authoritarian state. This policy was manifested in the introduction of a series of laws that made it virtually impossible for opposition groups to function openly. The most repressive of these measures was a law for the control of societies which gave the minister of the interior complete power, at his own discretion, to ban any political group he considered a threat to "good government." The law was so broadly written that it could be applied to a peaceful parliamentary opposition as easily as to a revolutionary group. It probably weakened rather than strengthened the viability of the government, for it further undermined the moderate element in the ASP and forced the opposition, in desperation, to adopt a conspiratorial strategy.

The government's economic policy further contributed to a mounting sense of bitterness and frustration within the ASP. Of particular significance was the ZNP-ZPPP coalition's agricultural program, which was marked by a thinly veiled determination to reestablish the economic wealth of the landed Arab aristocracy. The specific issue in question was a substantial loan that the British government had given to Zanzibar to foster economic development in agriculture. The coalition parties introduced legislation to create a land bank that would use the British funds to offer long-term, low-interest loans to farmers who wished to diversify agricultural production. Under the land bank plan, the farmer offered his land in collateral for the loan, the amount of the loan being proportional to the size of the farm.

The ASP opposed the land bank scheme because the loans were scaled to the size of farms. It contended that Arabs, who owned the best land and had much larger farms than Africans, would benefit disproportionately. ASP parliamentary leaders argued that the funds should be used first to accomplish basic land reform, and that this objective should precede efforts at crop diversification. Government spokesmen, however, responding that the ASP argument was based on racial grounds and was designed to undermine the political unity of the society, refused to accept the opposition viewpoint. Since the consequence of the collateral provision of the Land Bank program would clearly have been to exacerbate the differential in landed wealth between the races, the government's refusal to consider land reform further deepened the hostility between itself and the ASP. ASP leaders became convinced that the coalition was committed not only to the maintenance of a racial oligarchy but to the preservation of the economic inequalities that accompanied it.

The ASP's conviction that the ZNP-ZPPP coalition had embarked on an uncompromising racial course designed in the narrow interests of the Arab oligarchy was reinforced by a split within the ZNP. This party had always contained a small group of political radicals, primarily younger Arabs with a scattering of Shirazi ZNP supporters. The radicals had, in the past, sought to force the ZNP to acknowledge publicly the problem of racial inequality and to adopt policies that would lead to more equal economic distribution among the various ethnic communities. The radicals had always favored such policies as land redistribution, the deliberate recruitment of Africans into administration, and major educational reform. Though consistently unsuccessful in persuading the ZNP to adopt these measures, the mere presence of the radicals in the party had given the ZNP's declared multiracialism a certain degree of plausibility. Just before the July 1963 election the radicals broke away from the ZNP and formed a separate party called 'Umma' (the Masses). Their defection left the ZNP in the hands of older and more conservative Arab leaders who were unprepared to accept a compromise with the political demands of Africans. Their defection also ended any possibility that internal pressure in the ZNP would force the party into adopting a more moderate policy. The exodus of the radical element dispelled any lingering doubt within the ASP that revolution was the only feasible course of action.

REVOLUTION

Zanzibar achieved its independence in early December 1963, and the African revolution occurred approximately one month later. A small, secretly organized group of Africans seized control of the two principal government arsenals and the Zanzibar radio station, overcame ineffectual police resistance, and arrested the leaders of the ZNP and the ZPPP. The Revolutionary Council, composed largely of ASP leaders, was established to complete the transfer of power from Arab to African hands.

The ZNP-ZPPP government was highly vulnerable to such a coup. Zanzibar possessed no army, and the small police force had been weakened and demoralized by policies that had been designed to strengthen political loyalty. The rank and file of the Zanzibar police had been composed predominantly of mainland Africans who had been recruited by the British colonial administration in nearby East African countries. Arab political leaders, fearing that these policemen were loyal to the ASP, believed they could not be depended upon to be loyal to the government in the event of a racial crisis. The ZNP therefore began repatriating the mainland police to their countries of origin, replacing them with local Zanzibaris of proven political loyalty. This program stripped the Zanzibar police of its most experienced and skilled members and forced the hasty recruitment of untrained personnel.

Just before the revolution, the government fired a large number of mainland policemen without repatriating them to East Africa. This action created on Zanzibar a large group of disaffected mainlanders who harbored a deep personal grievance against the ZNP-ZPPP regime. Moreover, the discharged men were experienced in the use of arms and familiar with the logistics of the Zanzibar police. The revolutionary army drew heavily on this group for its hard-core membership.

The government's geopolitical position was also very weak. The entire governmental establishment was located on a small triangular peninsula jutting out from Zanzibar Town. The larger section of the town, which was adjacent to the main part of the island, completely enclosed the peninsula and was inhabited almost exclusively by mainland Africans and Hadimu. The rural areas near the town also contained an overwhelming majority of ASP supporters. The closest area of ZNP support was the extreme northern peninsula of the island.

Once the revolutionaries had captured the arsenals and the radio station, located in the African section of the town, the government was geographically isolated, without means of defense or communication, and separated from its own supporters by vast distances occupied by Africans loyal to the ASP. There was simply no way for the ZNP to rally or organize its followers in resistance to the coup.

The immediate consequence of the revolution was physical destruction of the Arab oligarchy. During a protracted period of violence which followed the initial seizure of power, several thousand Arabs on Zanzibar Island lost their lives in a futile and unorganized effort to resist the African revolutionaries. Most Arabs fled the rural areas and subsequently lost their land, either through spontaneous occupation by African squatters or through confiscation by the Revolutionary Council. In the atmosphere of open racial animosity which followed the revolution, Arabs who were able to remain on their farms or in their shops found it impossible to lead a normal economic life. The Arab administrative elite also lost its position in the society. The new government discharged most of the Arab civil servants and replaced them with Africans. The revolution thus not only deprived the Arab minority of political power but reduced most Arabs to a state of economic impoverishment. Today the Arab minority in Zanzibar exists largely on the sufferance of the revolutionary regime.*

The revolutionary government also sought to reduce the historic economic differential between Africans and Asians. Asian civil servants were removed from their government positions in large numbers, to be replaced by Africans. Apart from the loss of jobs and the inevitable violence that accompanied the revolution, the Asian community was not immediately affected by the change of regime. Most Asian business firms have not been interfered with, and little Asian property has been confiscated. The Asian community's economic position has deteriorated markedly, but principally because of the severe disruption of commercial life and the economic depression that followed the revolution, rather than because of direct government action against the Asians.

CONCLUSION

The African revolution dramatizes certain fundamental attributes of the political process in Zanzibar in the decade 1954–1964. First, parliamentary institutions had not acquired intrinsic legitimacy. There was no consensus on the rules of the game; and Zanzibaris viewed the representative system introduced by Great Britain in wholly instrumental terms, accepting the prescribed framework of conflict only so long as it seemed useful or necessary in the struggle for power. Politics occurred in the idiom of parliamentary procedures because the presence of Great Britain required it, but the basic political values of all party members were substantive, and the ultimate determining motivation was a compulsion to achieve and maintain political power by whatever means were necessary.

The lack of any consensus on constitutional or procedural values resulted from the absence of crosscutting and countervailing political affiliations. Zanzibar society had, by 1963, become totally polarized into two opposing forces, the ZNP-ZPPP and the ASP. Although these parties expressed disagreement over foreign and domestic questions, there was really only one political issue between them: Which race would ultimately gain political power? There was no source of political disagreement which cut across racial or party lines and brought together people who were divided on the racial question. Moreover, the feeling on the racial issue was so deep that it obscured every potentially neutral area of social life and fostered among members of the society a total commit-

---

* It is impossible to calculate precisely how many Arabs remain in Zanzibar today. Not only do estimates of those killed in the revolution vary enormously, but the Revolutionary Council forcibly repatriated a large but unknown number of Arabs to Oman. In addition, many Arabs fled to Dar es Salaam. The total decrease in the Arab community attributable to loss of life, repatriation, and emigration probably amounts to about 10,000 persons.

ment to their chosen political group and to its ultimate victory. With the possible exception of the Pemba Shirazis, no ethnic group had crosscutting political ties, and thus there was no effective pressure on the parties to moderate their views on the racial question or to accept the value of compromise.

Even Islam was rapidly losing effectiveness as a factor of racial integration. By January 1964, Zanzibar society had become divided between those for whom Islamic multiracial precepts had broad political meaning and those for whom they did not. Among Africans, this division corresponded to the cleavage between ZNP-ZPPP supporters and supporters of the ASP. During the seven years of competitive party politics, ASP members had become accustomed to resisting the obligation to support Arab leadership which is inherent in Islamic social norms. Either by segregating religion from the sphere of politics, or by rejecting Islam altogether, anti-Arab Africans were able to insulate themselves against religious pressure toward multiracial association. Dramatic evidence of this insulation against religion emerged after the last election: several Pemba villages that had supported the ASP began collectively to repudiate Islam on the grounds that it was an "Arab" religion and that it betrayed the political interests of Africans. Bitter and fundamental disagreement over the political status of religion thus deepened the cleavage among Zanzibaris who supported different political parties.

The polarization of political conflict caused Zanzibaris to misunderstand and misinterpret one another's political parties to a degree that made mutual accommodation impossible. To ASP supporters, the ZNP symbolized the restoration of an Arab feudal society in the form of a modern police state, the return of slavery, and the end of any hope for a better life for Africans. For ZNP members, the ASP symbolized the reckless destruction of a society in which Arabs and Africans had always lived in peace, the wanton disregard of the Islamic faith, and political domination by uncouth and uneducated mainland Africans.

A second aspect of Zanzibar political life dramatized by the revolution was the basic weakness of the Arab oligarchy. The Arab elite had become wholly dependent upon Great Britain for the preservation of its position in society. When Britain left, the Arabs were unable to maintain control on their own. The Arabs' political weakness was the result of an extended process of social transformation which had occurred gradually during the 125 years they had lived in Zanzibar. The Arab colonial class had originally constituted a powerful baronial aristocracy whose control over the local population was based on technological and military supremacy and on an ability to use its superior force to implement a rigid system of local administration. By the middle of the twentieth century, the Arab elite had evolved into a class of civil servants, professionals, and well-to-do farmers. Its political supremacy and its parliamentary victory stemmed from an organizational and administrative superiority and from an ability to manipulate religious symbols to attract African support. Without the ancillary police and military assistance furnished by Great Britain, organizational skill and control of the civil service were insufficient bases for preserving the plural society.

NOTES

[1] In April 1964, Zanzibar merged with Tanganyika to form the United Republic of Tanzania and thereby, in formal terms, ceased to exist as a sovereign independent nation. As a British protectorate and as an autonomous national unit, Zanzibar comprised the two East African offshore islands of Zanzibar and Pemba and a few adjacent islands. The total area is approximately 1,020 square miles: Zanzibar is roughly 640 square miles, and Pemba, about 380. For a full-length study of historical and political developments in Zanzibar, see Michael F. Lofchie, *Zanzibar: Background to Revolution* (Princeton: Princeton University Press, 1965).

[2] Zanzibar Protectorate, *Notes on the Census of the Zanzibar Protectorate, 1948* (Zanzibar: Government Printer, 1953).

[3] A. H. J. Prins, *The Swahili-Speaking Peoples of Zanzibar and the East African Coast* (London: International African Institute, 1961), p. 11.

[4] Professor Batson was commissioned to conduct the survey by the Zanzibar government, and had the cooperation of the colonial administration. He and his staff employed several means of checking the figures that fieldworkers collected. An official census had been taken earlier in the same year, and census figures were available, as were the files of various government departments. An important factor of reliability was that, in 1948, overt communal politics had not yet begun and matters of racial identification were far less sensitive than they later became. The Batson survey has never been published but exists in Verifax form in Zanzibar and in South Africa.

[5] Edward Batson, "Social Survey of Zanzibar," vol. 14, "Land Ownership" (Verifax).

[6] This survey is quoted in Edward Batson, *Report on Proposals for a Social Survey of Zanzibar* (Zanzibar: Government Printer, 1948), p. 36.

[7] Batson, "Social Survey of Zanzibar," vol. 5, "Occupations."

[8] *Ibid.*, vol. 10, "Educational Achievements."

[9] Lofchie, *op. cit.*, chap. viii, "Voting Behavior and Party Organization."

Part III　General Perspectives

Introduction to Part III

The papers in this section are specifically concerned with general problems of pluralism rather than with case studies of particular areas and situations.

Ali Mazrui, in "Pluralism and National Integration," explores the integrative role of conflict. He defines pluralism eclectically in such a manner that it accommodates both divisive conflict between ethnic groups in the Furnivall tradition and competitive pluralistic institutions in the tradition that relates democratic participation to the dispersion of power. He distinguishes four stages of group relations, ranging from bare *coexistence* and distinct identities, which is the minimum degree of integration, through *contact* and *compromise* to *coalescence* of identities, which is the final stage of national integration. Conflict arising from increased contact is seen as a necessary, but not sufficient, condition for integration; it acts indirectly to promote integration by providing the occasion for the cumulative experience of conflict resolution. It is conflict resolution, however, and not conflict, which deepens the degree of integration in a society. Mazrui comments on the paradox that while conflict itself has a propensity to force a dissolution, the resolution of conflict is an essential mechanism of integration. His comments on Nigeria should be of special interest, since they were made prior to the war between the federal government of Nigeria and Biafra.

Leonard Thompson introduces the study of language as a field for the analysis of the relations between structure and process and as a significant dimension and index of pluralism. He argues that the linguistic situation in any society interacts with all other aspects of that society, and that the changing linguistic situation cannot be wholly explained in terms of the structure of accommodation (or of differential incorporation), but may itself be a major determinant of structural change, as in the rise of the nation-state in Europe. He emphasizes the importance of language as the fundamental instrument of human communication, facilitating or impeding interaction between the plural sections, and offers a typology of languages which may be related to the stages of integration described by Mazrui. *Parochial* languages would be prevalent in situations of bare coexistence; the use of a *lingua franca* would be associated with increasing contact, while the possession of a *national* language, spoken by virtually all the citizens of a state, would presumably indicate some movement toward a coalescence of identities. The use of language as an instrument of domination is illustrated by the South African case, but the situation is paradoxical, and Thompson comments that the central contradiction in South African society between a policy of racial domination and a process of racial integration is clearly reflected on the linguistic plane. This complexity of tendencies is the theme of Max Gluckman's paper.

Gluckman, in "The Tribal Area in South and Central Africa," analyzes interaction in a single, sociogeographic field, that of Zululand in the 1930's, deriving from his analysis reflections on plural societies and pluralism. He finds the theories of "consensus" and "conflict" as delineated in the opening essay insufficiently refined to describe the complexity of interaction he observed, and he develops a specialized vocabulary of concepts for different forms of consensus and conflict. Of particular value is the distinction he draws between "consensus" as referring to agreement between persons on a goal or value and structural "cohesion" as defining the extent to which the structure of a field is maintained in something like continuous pattern. A society may have a very high degree of consensus among the actors in a social field while the degree of structural cohesion is very low; Gluckman suggests that this seems to be the case in many newly independent African states.

Gluckman rejects the implication that there are societies of "conflict" and societies of "consensus." On the basis of his own research in Zululand, his work in three rural areas in Zambia, and his observation of common interests between members of different racial groups, he takes issue with Basil Davidson's portrayal of pure hostility in the statement, "Nothing appears to have tied these two groupings [of Africans and whites] together except a mutually hateful contiguity from which neither could escape." He argues that there is no such thing as overall "consensus" in any social field of interaction, and that "conflict" is present in varying degrees in different situations. Drawing from the same body of theory as Mazrui, he comments that cooperation itself is the source of strife, and that certain forms of strife can lead to cooperation: the analytical separation of concepts distorts the empirical complexity of social processes that simultaneously comprise divergent tendencies.

Chapter 10 Pluralism and National Integration

Ali A. Mazrui

Our definition of pluralism is comprehensive. In its diversity of tribal and racial groups, we would regard Uganda as a case of ethnic pluralism. In its variety of systems of life, we would regard it as an instance of cultural pluralism. In the competitive relationship between Catholicism, Protestantism, and Islam in the life of the country, we would attribute religious pluralism to the total society. In its multiparty system, however unstable, the country had for a while maintained competitive pluralistic institutions —a framework for power contests in the polity. In its quasi-federal structure, while it lasted, the country had *constrictive* pluralistic institutions—an attempt to narrow the field of contest in advance by entrenching a certain division of powers prior to the scramble for other areas of political or social control. Pluralism is, in short, a complex of relationships between groups in a wider society.

Having given a rough working definition of pluralism by invoking the Ugandan example, our next task is the no less ambitious enterprise of trying to understand the nature of integration. We shall devote more time to this in the next section. We shall then go on to relate pluralism to nationalism, and analyze the interrelationship with reference to the two "Anglo-Saxon" cases of Britain and the United States. Our next preoccupation in the paper will then be the role of the state in the integrative process. In this regard we shall utilize some of the insights afforded by Marxism. We shall finally examine political activity as an exercise in integration. Our example in this last section will be Nigeria. This is not, of course, because Nigeria is among the areas of the world the author knows most about. On the contrary, the author's knowledge of Nigeria is derived from the general literature of that country and not from direct research experience therein. We choose Nigeria to illustrate the integrative function of politics mainly because of an impression that it may well be the best example in Africa of the phenomenon we have in mind. The picture we draw of Nigeria itself may conceivably be inaccurate. But if a mythical Nigerian "model" nevertheless enables us to explore new hypotheses about the nature of the integrative process, the exercise may still be worth it.

Our conclusion at the end of the paper will be both a summary of the rest of the analysis and an attempt to place our preoccupations here within the context of political development at large.

THE INTEGRATIVE PROCESS

The process of national integration involves four stages of interrelationship between the different groups in the country. The minimum degree of integration is a relationship of bare *coexistence* between distinct identities within the borders. These groups need not even know of each other's existence. There are a number of tribal communities in almost every African country which have no idea where the boundaries of their country end, which tribes are their compatriots and which are not. Their coexistence with a number of other groups in the same national entity is not always a conscious coexistence. But it is there all the same.

The second degree of relationship between groups is a relationship of *contact*. This means that the groups have at least some minimal dealings with each other or communication between each other. The groups need not be on friendly terms. Tribes at war are still in a relationship of contact. And by that very reason they are at a higher stage of integration in spite of the war.

A third degree of integration between groups is a relationship of *compromise*. By this time the dealings between the groups have become sufficiently complex, diverse, and interdependent to require a climate of peaceful reconciliation between the conflicting interests. The groups still have clearly distinct identities of their own, as well as distinct interests. But the process of national integration has now produced a capacity for a constant discovery of areas of compatibility.

The final stage of national integration is the stage of *coalescence*. This is a coalescence of identities, rather than a merger of interests. Diversity of interests would continue. Indeed, should the society get technically complex and functionally differentiated at the same time as it is getting nationally integrated, the diversity of interests would increase as the distinctiveness of group identities gets blurred. Capacity for compromise would still be needed at the stage of coalescence. But the conflict of interests is no longer a conflict between total identities.

But what is a total identity? Illustration is in this instance the best definition. A tribe in a relationship of bare coexistence with other tribes has a total identity of its own. But the Hotel Workers Union in Uganda or the American Political Science Association is only a partial form of identity. The process of national integration is a partialization of group identities—as the tribes or communities lose their coherence as distinct systems of life. But the process of national integration is not only a partialization of older affiliations. It is, of course, also a quest for a new kind of total identity. Success comes when partially eroded group personalities coalesce to form a new national entity.

In practice the process of integration is not even. The same African country might have groups that are in a relationship of bare *coexistence* with the rest of the country, groups that have established *contact* with others on a broad scale, groups that have begun to develop politics of *compromise,* and groups that show a tendency toward *coalescing* with each other.

But by what mechanism does the process of integration move from stage to stage? This is what introduces the place of *conflict* in the integrative process.[1] A relationship of bare coexistence has little conflict potential. Somehow contact has to be established with other groups before conflict situations can seriously arise. The move from coexistence to contact may be caused by a number of different factors. It may be caused by migrant trade, or by movements of population, or by a newly built road. By definition, conflict plays little part in converting a relationship of separate coexistence into a relationship of contact.

Where conflict plays a crucial part is in moving from a relationship of contact to a relationship of compromise, and then from compromise to coalescence. It is the cumulative experience of conflict resolution which deepens the degree of integration in a given society. Conversely, unresolved conflict creates a situation of potential disintegration. The groups within the society could then move backward from a relationship of, say, compromise to a relationship of hostile contact.

One might even argue that internal conflict within a country is inherently disintegrative. Yet, paradoxically, no national integration is possible without internal conflict. The paradox arises because, while conflict itself has a propensity to force a dissolution, the *resolution* of conflict is an essential mechanism of integration. The whole experience of jointly looking for a way out of a crisis, of seeing your own mutual hostility subside to a level of mutual tolerance, of being intensely conscious of each other's positions and yet sensing the need to bridge the gulf—these are experiences which, over a period of time, should help two groups of people move forward into a relationship of deeper integration. Conflict resolution may not be a sufficient condition for national integration, but it is certainly a necessary one.

But what makes conflict resolution itself possible? Sometimes it is the cumulative power of precedent, of having overcome other crises before. Experience of previous clashes sharpens the capacity to discover areas of mutual compatibility on subsequent occasions of tension. Another factor which makes conflict resolution possible is awareness of reciprocal dependence. It may be true that, for purposes of economic development in a given area, it is essential that two particular tribes in the region must get along with each other. But this "truth" would not help the cause of conflict resolution between the two groups unless they realize, first, that economic development is an important common need, and, second, that it is a need which can best be met if the two groups stopped fighting each other.

A third factor which might ease conflict resolution in a given society is a shared ideology. And the most basic ideology for national integration is, of course, the ideology of nationalism itself. It is to this that we must now turn.

PLURALISM AND NATIONALISM

For our purposes here it may be meaningful to distinguish nationalism from national consciousness. We may define "national consciousness" here as a sense of a shared national identity. We may define "nationalism" as a more assertive or more defensive degree of that consciousness. It has been argued that "modern nationalism, as we know it today, has its original seat in England." [2] It is true that England has had her moments of militant nationalism. But on the whole she has come to take her nationhood so much for granted that her philosophers have spent relatively little time on it. Leading British philosophers have seldom concerned themselves in depth with issues like the definition of a "nation," or the reality of "the collective soul," or the concept of "fatherland." And so when Hans Kohn comes round to paying special attention to nineteenth-century nationalism he finds himself choosing John Stuart Mill as the "prophet" of British nationalism.[3] In the company of Mazzini, Treitschke, Michelet, and Dostoevsky, John Stuart Mill is hardly a striking example of a "people's prophet." Kohn might have done better if he had looked for a British politician or statesman to symbolize British patriotism. British political philosophers were simply not adequately preoccupied with the "fatherland."

American political thought has had more of a nationalistic component than is found in British thought. And this is what brings us back to pluralism. It is possible that one important reason why Americans are more nationalistic than Britons is because the United States is more pluralistic than Great Britain. It is easy to see why a country should become extranationalistic if it has a sense of external insecurity. What is apt to be overlooked is that a country can also become extranationalistic if it develops a sense of *internal* insecurity. The United States is significantly more heterogenous than Britain. This might be precisely the factor that has helped to create a greater sense of internal insecurity in the United States than in Britain. Complex heterogeneity multiplies the number of possible conflict situations between groups. The need for devices which would help the resolution of those conflicts becomes greater than ever. National consciousness is indeed there. But the situation is such that the sense of a shared national identity cannot be taken completely for granted as a moderator in intergroup tensions. And so that national consciousness has to take the more militant form of assertive nationalism. The potential for violence between groups has to be "qualified" by a diversionary consideration. Georg Simmel once said: "It is almost inevitable that an element of commonness injects itself into the enmity [between two groups] once the stage of open violence yields to any other relationship, even though this new relation may contain a completely undiminished sum of animosity between the two parties." [4] In the case before us in this paper, we would need to alter Simmel's sequence of causation. For us it is the "element of commonness" itself which makes "the stage of open violence" yield to another relationship. The dangers of American heterogeneity need to be conquered by a highly developed sense of a shared Americanness. This inner sense of internal insecurity in the United States is perhaps what continues to make American national consciousness more *self*-conscious than British patriotism normally is.

In May 1965 the *Observer* of London described the United States and Communist China as "the two most ideologically inspired states of the modern world." [5] This was an exaggeration. But it still has relevance to the question before us. The United States might have looked "most ideologically inspired" to a relatively ideological British newspaper precisely because the British themselves were less militant than Americans in their patriotism.

In a sense, it is ironical that the most powerful country in the world should show signs of insecurity greater than those of her weaker ally. But the irony would be striking only if one thought of insecurity in externalistic dimensions, in terms of danger from outside. [6] Once we think of insecurity in terms both of external danger and of internalized fears of fragmentation, it becomes much less surprising that the more pluralistic of the Anglo-Saxon powers should also be the more assertively nationalistic.

PLURALISM AND THE STATE

On the basis of the stages of integration we have defined, we might now say that the United States has achieved a high degree of *compromise* relationships between total identities within itself. But Great Britain has achieved a greater degree of *coalescence* between its groups. In the meantime, the cumulative experience of conflict resolution in the United States is gradually leading toward less compromise and more coalescence. In terms of political arrangements, a federal structure is an institutionalization of compromise relationships. But the American federal system is perhaps already feeling the strain of the integrative process toward national coalescence. The institutional expression of such coalescence will presumably be a more unitary form of democracy.

The idea of conflict leading ultimately to coalescence shares some assumptions with the Marxist concept of integration. But certain distinctions need to be made. The dialectic in Marxism is sometimes described as a process of "reconciling opposites." In effect, the Marxian synthesis is not a "reconciliation." The idea of reconciling opposites is more implicit in *compromise* relationships than in synthesizing ones. A proletarian dictatorship, for example, is not an exercise in compromise. As Engels put it, "the proletariat uses the state not in the interests of freedom, but in order to hold down its adversaries." [7] Compromise with adversaries can, by the logic of Marxism, be only a tactical move. One compromises with the opposing forces only until such time as one can "synthesize" them altogether. And the synthesis is achieved by the liquidation of the separate identity of the preceding thesis.

There are other differences, too, between the concept of compromise and the concept of synthesis. Compromise tends to be a position *below* the ideal; it is at best a *"second* best" to all concerned. A Hegelian or Marxian synthesis, however, is a step *nearer* perfection than the two opposites from which it emerged. A synthesis combines the best elements from each side. A compromise combines not what is best, but what is least objectionable to the contestants.

Bringing the distinction nearer to our own preoccupations in this paper, we note that while a quest for synthesis is essentially antipluralistic, a quest for compromise is an acceptance of pluralism. If we use Rousseau's terms, the General Will is a synthesis of interests. The will of all is a compromise between conflicting interests. The General Will is supposed to be a collective good that is independent of particular interests. The will of all is an arithmetical exercise, a balancing of particular interests.

Institutionally, a one-party state has a bias for synthesizing, while a multiparty system has a propensity to compromise. The one-party system seeks to embody the General Will. The multiparty system wants to discern the will of all.

But for our purposes the big difference between Marx and Rousseau is that Marx has a theory of integration while Rousseau has not. For Marx, society moves toward closer integration by the mechanism of struggle and contradiction. This is not very far removed from a theory which looks upon the integrative process as a response to a cumulative experience of conflict resolution. One point of difference between the Marxist view of integration and ours here is that while Marx thinks of integration in terms of a coalescence of classes, our own theory here allows for the possibility of there being more important differences between groups than class differences. Indeed, the Marxist concept of the integrative process assumes a high degree of a preexistent ethnic and cultural integration. This is an assumption which cannot be made in analyzing integration in, say, African countries. In fact, tribes and races are more total identities than are economic classes. The process of integrating tribes and races tends therefore to be more complex.

Another difference between the Marxist view of integration and the one we are putting forward here concerns the nature of conflict resolution. Marx thinks of conflict resolution in terms of absolute victories. The conflict between the proletariat and the bourgeoisie can only end in the victory of the proletariat. But conflict resolution can be thought of in terms of *adjustments,* rather than victories. And it is the latter conception of conflict resolution which might perhaps offer the best insights into the process of integrating total identities.

A related point of theoretical divergence concerns the Marxist concept of the "withering away" of the state. This is a concept which is often underestimated by Western commentators. Yet, as part of a theory of integration, the idea of an ultimate withering away of the state has a depth of insight which deserves greater recognition than it has had so far. The process of integration is, after all, a process of reducing the potential for internal violence in a given society. And the concept of the state is intimately connected with the concept of controlling violence and its causes. If social integration therefore reaches a stage when there is only a limited degree of latent violence in intergroup relations, the state loses the most fundamental of all its roles.

An alternative way of approaching the problem is through the Weberian definition of a state. Weber defined the state in terms of its "mo-

nopoly of the legitimate use of physical force within a given territory." [8]
But if a country has deep internal cleavages, the state's monopoly of the
use of force may often be challenged. Even the legitimacy of the state
may itself be in question, let alone its claim to a monopoly of violence.
Mutually hostile groups may feel that they both retain the right to
resolve their differences by a test of physical strength. The paramount
duty of the state might then be to try to stop private resort to violence.

But as the integrative process gets under way, the cleavages in the
society would get less acute. When a highly developed sense of compromise is achieved, latent violence would be much reduced. And when the
stage of actual coalescence begins to take place, private resort to violence
between groups would become even more rare. What then would the
state become? For the first time the state might indeed now have a clear
monopoly of the legitimate use of force. All the groups might at last
agree that only the state should be permitted to invoke forceful sanctions
against offenders in a given dispute. This is the stage when the different
groups have at last been integrated into a suprafactional community. The
integrative process may therefore be almost definable as a process toward
the centralization of social violence. It is national integration which
gradually gives the state a real monopoly of the legitimate use of physical
force.

Yet, because the different groups are now less inclined to resort to
private force in their own disputes, the state's role as an instrument of
suppression is drastically curtailed. Of course, there is still work to be
done in such fields as social welfare, the building of roads, and general
national planning. But a fundamental change takes place when a society
achieves a stage of deep internal coalescence. "State interference in social
relations becomes, in one domain after another, superfluous, and then
dies out of itself; the government of persons is replaced by the administration of things." [9] In saying this, Engels was indeed exaggerating. So
was Lenin in envisaging a time when people would "become accustomed
to observing the necessary rules of social intercourse" and when there
would be "nothing that evokes protest and revolt and creates the need for
suppression." [10] But they were both right in suggesting that ultimate
integration must lead to the redundancy of the state as an instrument of
suppression. Their notion of what divides groups against each other was
too simple. But their grasp of the logic of the integrative process was
profoundly sound.

Involved in all this is the integrative function of suppression itself in
the precoalescent phases of development. For Marxism, sustained oppression creates a class consciousness among the oppressed. But for our purposes in this paper what should be noted is that sustained oppression

helps to create national consciousness itself. A study of the Royal Institute of International Affairs argued in 1939 that

Every government which has ever been set up has done something to increase the amount of homogeneity between its subjects, although it may at the same time have taken other steps which increased the differences of opinion among them and stimulated opposition to itself. . . . the downfall of governments may (with many exceptions) be attributed to the failure to produce cohesion among their subjects. . . . The fact remains that any collection of men which has ever been subjected for any length of time to the same government will continue indefinitely to bear the marks of that subjection, and will possess a common factor making for unity among subsequent generations.[11]

The most dramatic demonstration of this is the effect of colonial governments on their subjects. Africans, for example, will continue to bear indefinitely the mark of their subjection to European colonial rule. But contrary to what the above quotation argues, the downfall of colonial governments was not due to "failure to produce cohesion among their subjects." On the contrary, it was the success of colonial governments in creating such cohesion which led to their own downfall.

PLURALISM AND POLITICS

But the fall of African governments after independence is a more complicated phenomenon. How much did the *ancien régime* of independent Nigeria contribute to the greater unification of Nigeria? It is too early to be sure. But we ought to be on guard against assuming too readily that the Nigerian government before the first coup was a factor for disunity. It is possible that it was precisely the worst excesses of the regime which were the most integrative. Nothing helped the movement for a unitary state in Nigeria more dramatically than the mess in which the previous regime left the federal structure. The unitary movement may not succeed even now. Perhaps Nigeria is too pluralistic a country to be ruled on any basis other than that of quasi federalism. But the very fact that there is now a quest for *tighter* integration is substantially attributable to the errors of the previous regime.

Another possible measurement of how far the first independent regime helped to unify Nigeria lies in the initial reaction of the north to the assassination of two distinguished northerners in January 1966. Did the northerners accept the assassination of Balewa and the Sardauna simply because they were faced with the military might of the south? Or had the excesses of the previous regime disillusioned northerners, too? If the answer at the time was a simple fear of military might, this did not tell us much about the rate of integration in Nigeria. But should by any chance the answer have included northern disenchantment with the era of

Balewa and Ahmadu Bello, this would be more significant. Nigeria had never before been jointly disenchanted by the same government. While the people of other countries might have resented colonialism, the people of Nigeria had not even shared a joint feeling of anticolonialism. The north especially had been too suspicious of the south, and too cautious in her assessment of independence, ever to get worked up into a strong feeling of nationalism. Perhaps there had also developed a basic Anglophilia within the northern elite which refused to be transformed into an anti-British militancy for the sake of independence. Nigeria therefore approached independence without the unifying services of a shared spirit of anticolonialism.[12]

It is possible that disenchantment with the first independent government of Nigeria was the first centrally directed feeling of political opposition that northerners had ever shared with southerners in recent times. This factor would have been of direct integrative significance for the country as a whole. Would northern reaction to the assassination of Balewa and Ahmadu Bello have been less placid had this taken place within the first year of independence? This is not certain. Yet it is conceivable that four years earlier northern reaction would have been stronger. That it should be conceivable is itself of significance.

The northern acceptance of the changed situation was not likely, of course, to last forever. Indeed, there were early reports that the north was getting restive and was beginning to demand the punishment of at least some of the individual assassins of northerners.[13] This does not negate the proposition that the previous regime had, by some of its very excesses, served an integrative function. In terms of our more general theoretical position, the first coup was one momentous kind of conflict resolution in the slow unification of Nigeria. The aftermath of the coup was bound to create sooner or later other types of conflict situations. And some of these latent conflicts had their origins in the manner in which the preceding conflict was resolved.

A third factor about the first independent regime which might have been unifying was the fact that it was a *political* regime. It is tempting to look at the new military regimes as better instruments of national consolidation than the previous band of politicians. The whole idea of military rule implies discipline. And the principle of discipline has perhaps an inner aversion to "factionalism." We might therefore say that demands for unity and demands for discipline are almost logically interconnected. When Lenin wanted to ensure that the Communist Party of the Soviet Union was fully united, he thought of its organization in quasi-militaristic terms. He was convinced that the "Communist Party will be able to perform its duty only if it is organised in the most centralised manner, if iron discipline bordering on military discipline prevails in it, and if its Party centre is a powerful and authoritative organ, wielding wide powers." He was opposed to what he called "factionalism." He believed in "the unity of will of the vanguard of the proletariat as the fundamental condition of the success of the dictatorship of the proletariat." [14] It might therefore seem that the new military regime in Nigeria had, by bringing in the ethos of discipline from the barracks to the polity, started a new and more vigorous phase of national consolidation in the country.

Yet the fact that the Balewa regime was a regime of politicians is not necessarily a point against it in the calculus of integration. A militarized polity today might avert disunity without achieving integration. There is more to the integrative process than militaristic discipline. The discipline of men under arms is ultimately designed to win victories. Integration, however, is a matter of resolving conflict in more diverse, and often more subtle, ways. The concept of conflict animates both the military and the integrative process, but it does not affect them in the same way. It is these considerations which should caution us against dismissing the premilitary regime in Nigeria as altogether countercohesive. It is not always remembered that political activity, as a continual intrigue and search for agreement, has an integrative function in its own right.

Perhaps one factor which, for a while, saved Nigeria from becoming another Congo was the higher degree of politicization that Nigeria had undergone well before independence. The fragmentation of the Congo on attainment of independence was, in part, directly attributable to Belgian prohibition of political activity during the colonial period. By its very nature, nationalistic activity before independence would have had a propensity to involve more and more of the general populace. Experience elsewhere demonstrated that anticolonial sentiments fostered by a few "agitators" in the capital city gradually spread outward and increased a consciousness of the territorial unit in the population as a whole. To that extent political activity in British Africa especially was an important contributory factor toward national integration in each colony. The Congo was kept in a state of depoliticization; the consciousness of territorial identity was retarded for that very reason.

But does politics still serve an integrative function *after* independence? The answer is yes. In the case of the Congo, it has been that country's relative inexperience in the arts of national politics that has kept it in a state of actual or potential civil war. Where political activity seems to be so divisive as to result in a civil war, the reason is usually because there was an inadequate capacity for politics in the population in the first place. The resort to arms comes when politics has *failed*. But one major reason why politics as an exercise in compromise fails in a country like the Congo is precisely because the Congolese capacity for political solutions is as yet underdeveloped.

If a resort to arms is an indication that politics has failed, what about the resort to an army coup? The answer varies with each country. In Ghana political life under Nkrumah had, in the words of Dennis Austin, already been "reduce[d] . . . to a barely discernible level of private conflict among his followers over the distribution of presidential favours." [15] The army coup might therefore be regarded as the first step toward the renationalization of politics in Ghana.

In Nigeria, however, the army coup was essentially a retreat from politics. If the previous regime achieved nothing else, it certainly achieved the nationalization of political activity in Nigeria. The defense of the north against the south previously took the form of isolation away from the south. By the time of the coup the northern strategy had become an *infiltration* of the south. The interest of the north in consolidating its federal power was perhaps the most significant integrative event in Nigeria's history. Tribalism and regionalism in Nigeria had indeed become worse than ever. Yet, by a curious paradox, the nationalization of politics in Nigeria was taking place at the same time. Contrary to most expectations a few years previously, observers were already talking about single-party tendencies in Nigeria.[16] The federal system was indeed in jeopardy. But now the danger was not merely disintegration, though that was still there. There was the new danger of imposed unitarism. That the latter danger should have become conceivable was perhaps the most dramatic feat of integration that the previous regime had accomplished.

Yet, it was in part precisely that feat which precipitated the events that led to the army coup. In an important sense the crisis of Nigeria arose from the fact that politics had been integrating the country too rapidly. The new northern desire for hegemony in the south was, in national terms, a significant improvement over the old northern isolationism. But the nationalization of politics in Nigeria was growing faster than the country's capacity for compromise. To put it in another way, Nigeria was nationalizing her politics before she had perfected her techniques of conflict resolution. After all, to place political activity on a rising scale of nationalization is to increase the areas of possible conflict between groups. It is with these resultant conflicts that the Nigerian system could not cope, in spite of its expansion and, to some extent, because of it.

This was not, of course, all that was wrong with Nigeria. Nigerian politics was getting more national and more nasty at the same time. Yet the nastiness itself was often a bewildered response to the new conflicts that nationalized politics was creating. Occasionally one form of nastiness atoned for another. In a country plagued with nepotism, for example, bribery has sometimes a useful function to serve. A person from the "wrong" tribe might be able to get his particular skill utilized only after paying the necessary "dash." It might be unfortunate that he should have to pay. But it might have been even more unfortunate if that skill had no way of getting itself utilized. To put it in another way, the person from the "wrong" tribe needs a chance to compete for a particular prize. But he has to buy a ticket in order to get into the competing arena, whereas his rivals from the "right" tribe have free access into the arena. To have to buy a ticket for admission might still be better than total exclusion from the arena. It is this consideration which sometimes converts bribery into an antidote to nepotism.

In East Africa bribery is at times an antidote to racialism. Indian traders competing with Africans for licenses or other commercial favors have sometimes to atone with cash for their racial handicap. Racialistic nepotism would give priority to Africans. But bribery from the Indian trader might sometimes tip the scale back into a position of fair competition. To modify our other metaphor, the Indian has to buy a ticket to get into the marketing compound, whereas his African rivals are sometimes given free access. But once the Indian is in the market, he may in any case be sufficiently superior as a businessman to compensate for the ticket he was forced to buy.[17]

There are varied reasons why we might lament the phenomenon of bribery both in East Africa and in Nigeria before the coups. But we should be clear about the reasons. It may be true that tribal and familial nepotism is essentially disintegrative in its exclusive tendencies. But precisely because nepotism is disintegrative, bribery may often perfom a function of reintegration. It may help to break down barriers of nepotistic exclusiveness. It may, in short, ease the process of conflict resolution in a competitive and pluralistic society.[18]

CONCLUSION

On their road toward national coalescence few of the developing areas have got much beyond the stage of *contact* and enforced submissiveness. Indeed, some of the groups are still in a relationship of bare *coexistence* with each other. But in some of the countries, and Nigeria may still be one of them, the politics of *compromise* may have started to take root. The roots may not as yet be deep. Growth in such instances is a slow process. But it is important that the process has begun.

In the meantime students of political development at large should perhaps reexamine more fully some of their assumptions about the wider process. Many of the studies of political development after independence have implied a process which is at least semiconsciously induced. The attention of scholars has tended to be drawn toward the role of political parties, or of the military, or of the bureaucracy at large, or toward the function of education in national integration. These are or can be crucial elements in the process of development. But their relevance for development can be a little too conspicuous and diversionary. They could command so much attention that scholars might overlook the integrative function of factors which are less *obviously* pertinent—but crucially pertinent all the same.

Perhaps there is such a thing as *political development as a laissez-faire process*. Yet the principle of laissez-faire in the political version of development is not an injunction against government intervention in the *economy*. It is merely an assertion that while economic development can, under certain circumstances, be consciously induced, political development is much less responsive to conscious manipulation. The case for government intervention in the economy might still remain very strong. After all, people must not starve even if they are yet to be integrated or have yet to devise a stable political system. What should be remembered is that political development is, in the ultimate analysis, a cumulative accident. It is the accretion of side effects of random factors, some of which may, in fact, be actual social ills. It is possible for unemployment to be a positive contribution to the long-term political development of a country, while some new road built at the wrong time militates against national cohesion. The total effect depends on a total complex of factors.

The scholar should therefore be cautious in categorizing whole processes as being either developmental or counterdevelopmental, integrative or disintegrative. One may discern a propensity in one direction or the other, but still allow for modifying side effects. One may regard corruption as counterproductive and still allow for its functionality in certain key areas.

National integration is, of course, only one aspect of political development. But it is perhaps the most fundamental. The crucial capacity which is to be cultivated in the integrative process is, as we have indicated, efficiency in the art of conflict resolution. To develop that efficiency the experience of conflict is, by definition, itself essential. But the process of integration is a gradual multiplication of areas of conflict, coupled with a gradual diminution of violence in those conflicts. In other words, conflict becomes more *extensive* as areas of competition become more complex, and less *intensive* as resort to violent solutions diminishes in frequency.

Finally, it should be emphasized that a process of integration is, in essence, a process of depluralizing society. Pluralism itself never completely disappears, but a society ceases to be a plural society when the stage of *coalescence* is fully reached. To put it in another way, there is pluralism in every society. For pluralism is often a competitive complex of diverse groups—and virtually every society has its rival groups.

When Harold Laski rebelled against the notion of "Man *versus* the State," what he substituted in its place was a view of society which thought of political life in terms of relations between groups, rather than relations between the government and the individual. The theory that Laski was putting forward was a theory of pluralism.

But a "plural society" is not simply a society with pluralism. All societies have pluralism. What distinguishes plural societies from others is the *kind* of pluralism involved. The extreme case of a plural society is a society of total identities, of self-contained cultural systems or exclusive racial groups. This is perhaps the kind of "plural society" which, as J. C. Mitchell suggests, comes nearest to being "a contradiction in terms." [19] Relationships between the groups are at the level of either bare coexistence or minimal contact. This is perhaps the "pure type" of a plural society.

But as the integrative process gets underway, the total identities are increasingly partialized. By the time coalescence is reached, the society has been substantially depluralized in this special sense. As in England, the society may still have a highly structured *class* pluralism. Yet England has ceased to be a plural society. England is almost a "pure type" of an integrated nation. Complete coalescence with the Scots and the Welsh has not been fully achieved, though it is well advanced. The relationship of the English with the northern Irish is perhaps still basically a compromise relationship, but with substantial areas of coalescence. But the preponderant English themselves have achieved cohesion. The process of national integration among the English has virtually come to an end.

Yet, for as long as certain forms of pluralism persist, there is still room for further depluralization. England has virtually completed national integration, but there is considerable room yet for *social* integration. There is room especially for increased erosion of class distinctions.

Yet, while national integration is *finite*, social integration is *not*. The ultimate error of Marxism is perhaps to assume that there is an end to social integration. Having made that assumption, Marxism was logical in further assuming that there was an end to the need for the state as well. Perfect social integration would indeed make the state redundant. Yet because social integration is an infinite process, the state continues to be necessary for the purpose of giving it direction.

Nevertheless, in its formulation of the role conflict in social change, and in its conception of perfect coalescence, however unrealizable, Marxism still affords useful insights into the nature of the integrative process.

As an ideology Marxism does itself often create conflict. But as a methodology it helps us to understand it. After all, the integrative process is, in the ultimate analysis, the story of conflict and its role in socializing man.

NOTES

[1] I realize that the term "conflict" is sometimes carelessly used. But for our purposes here it is useful for social analysis precisely because it is comprehensive. For us the term ranges from the American Civil War to the contest for the election of Mrs. Wallace as governor of Alabama. For our purposes they are all different degrees of conflict.

[2] See Carlton J. H. Hayes, *Nationalism: A Religion* (New York: Macmillan, 1960), pp. 38–39. Hans Kohn argues in similar terms in *The Idea of Nationalism: A Study of Its Origins and Background* (New York: Macmillan, 1944), pp. 155–183.

[3] Hans Kohn, *Prophets and Peoples: Studies in Nineteenth Century Nationalism* (New York: Macmillan, 1957).

[4] Georg Simmel, *Conflict and the Web of Group-Affiliations,* trans. Kurt H. Wolff and Reinhard Bendix (New York: Free Press of Glencoe, 1964), p. 26.

[5] *Observer* (London), May 9, 1965.

[6] For a stimulating discussion of the proposition that "conflict with outgroups increases internal cohesion," see, for example, Lewis A. Coser, *The Functions of Social Conflict* (Glencoe, Ill.; Free Press, 1956), pp. 87–110. See also Max Gluckman, *Custom and Conflict in Africa* (Oxford: Basil Blackwell, 1963), esp. pp. 11–26.

[7] Letter to Bebel, quoted by V. I. Lenin in *State and Revolution* (1917) (New York: International Publishers, 1932).

[8] See Max Weber, "Politics as a Vocation," in H. H. Gerth and C. Wright Mills, eds., *From Max Weber: Essays in Sociology* (New York: Oxford University Press, 1958), pp. 77–78. Gabriel A. Almond has broadened Weber's definition to include types of political organization other than the state (see his "Introduction," in Gabriel A. Almond and James S. Coleman, eds., *The Politics of the Developing Areas* [Princeton: Princeton University Press, 1960], pp. 6–7).

[9] See F. Engels, *Socialism, Utopian and Scientific* (1877), trans. E. Aveling (Chicago: Kerr, 1914).

[10] Lenin, *op. cit.*

[11] Royal Institute of International Affairs, *Nationalism* (London: Oxford University Press, 1939), p. 4.

[12] James S. Coleman is a little more cautious than this in his assessment (*Nigeria: Background to Nationalism* [Berkeley and Los Angeles: University of California Press, 1958], pp. 353–368). See also Richard L. Sklar, *Nigerian Political Parties* (Princeton: Princeton University Press, 1963). On the attitudes of the old northern elite, consult especially C. S. Whitaker, Jr., "Three Perspectives on Hierarchy: Political Thought and Leadership in Northern Nigeria," *Journal of Commonwealth Political Studies,* III, no. 1 (March 1965), 1–19.

[13] See, for example, Walter Schwartz, "Nigerians Want More Than Bribery Trials," *Observer* (London), May 8, 1966.

[14] Quoted by J. Stalin in *Foundations of Leninism* (1924) (rev. trans.; New York: International Publishers, 1932).

[15] D. Austin, *Politics in Ghana, 1946–1960* (London: Oxford University Press, 1964), p. 48.

[16] See, for example, John P. Mackintosh, "Electoral Trends and the Tendency to a One Party System in Nigeria," *Journal of Commonwealth Political Studies,* I (Nov. 1962), 194–210. See also Nnamdi Azikiwe, "Essentials of Nigerian Survival," *Foreign Affairs,* XLIII, no. 3 (April 1965), 447–461.

[17] This is an exaggeration of what happens in East Africa. The idea of Africanizing commerce at the expense of Asians is an open policy and does not always involve such underhand dealings. For some discussion of corruption in East Africa, see J. David Greenstone, "Corruption and Self-Interest in Kampala and Nairobi," *Comparative Studies in Society and History,* 8 (Jan. 1966), 199–210; and Colin Leys, "What Is the Problem about Corruption?" *Journal of Modern African Studies,* 3, no. 2 (1965), 215–230.

[18] For a stimulating discussion of forms of corruption in Northern Nigeria, see M. G. Smith, "Historical and Cultural Conditions of Political Corruption among the Hausa," *Comparative Studies in Society and History,* 6, no. 2 (Jan. 1964), 164–194. For more general analyses of corruption, see M. McMullan, "A Theory of Corruption," *Sociological Review* (Keele), 9, no. 2 (July 1961), 181–201; Ronald E. Wraith and Edgar Simpkins, *Corruption in Developing Countries* (London: Allen and Unwin, 1963); and Carl J. Friedrich, "Political Pathology," *Political Quarterly,* 37 (Jan.–March 1966), 70–85.

[19] "The term 'plural society' itself is a contradiction since the idea of 'society' in terms of usual sociological definition implies 'unity'—the antithesis of plurality. The problem of plural societies, then, lies in this contradiction—in what way can these societies be both 'plural' and 'societies'—indeed, if they are 'plural' can they be societies?" (see J. C. Mitchell, *Tribalism and the Plural Society* [London: Oxford University Press, 1960], p. 25).

Chapter 11 Historical Perspectives of Pluralism in Africa*

Leonard Thompson

Like other social scientists, the historian is concerned to try to make sense of the appalling complexity of the data of human experience; and one of his techniques is to identify related phenomena, to compare them, and to place them in some universal perspective. But, while some social scientists are inclined to select structural phenomena as the crucial links between particulars, most historians attach greater weight to historical succession. Otherwise, we fear we may end up by comparing units between which the similarities are of secondary importance and the differences are transcendental, or by ignoring vital relationships because they do not emerge from the analytical framework that has been selected. Most historians are inclined to agree with Collingwood when he criticizes Toynbee's monumental edifice on the ground that in selecting Civilizations as his units of historical study, he abstracts data from their sequential context and produces a distorted "scissors-and-paste" version of reality.[1]

The present chapter is intended to develop two points that are relevant to the study of pluralism in Africa: one, by discussing colonialism as the historical link between the traditional societies and the independent states that have emerged upon the world scene since World War II; and the other, by isolating linguistic phenomena, which are rarely given the attention they warrant by analysts of pluralism.

THE ROLE OF COLONIALISM IN AFRICA

Colonial rule was imposed upon a myriad of traditional African societies which differed enormously among themselves. Some were plural and

* I am grateful to Professors Leo Kuper, Martin Legassick, and Eugen Weber for comments on the draft of this paper.

others were not; but in every case the structure of society under colonialism was plural. Indeed, the very concept of pluralism was first developed by J. S. Furnivall in relation to a colony, and more recently Georges Balandier has analyzed colonialism as a distinct type of pluralism.[2]

There are many ways in which all colonial societies differ from all other types of societies. A colony is a dependency of a distant imperial power. Ultimate authority over a colony is exercised by people who are not members of that society and who, for the most part, have never visited that society and know very little about it. Consequently, the colonial policy of the imperial ruler is determined not so much by the realities of the colonial situation as by metropolitan political considerations that are external and irrelevant to the colonial society. Britain lost the Thirteen Colonies as a result of ignorance and apathy rather than malice. In the perspective of a British, French, Belgian, or Portuguese politician, the fate of an African colony was usually a minor consideration. Throughout the colonial period, it was notoriously difficult to get a quorum in the House of Commons when a colonial issue was before it. From the point of view of members of the colonial society, therefore, metropolitan policy was utterly capricious. Hence there was frequent exasperation, not only among the subject peoples, but also among the colonial white minority (transients and settlers alike).

However, the effects of metropolitan supremacy were often offset by an exceptional gap between law and reality, form and substance. A metropolis might issue an order that ran counter to the wishes of the colonial white minority, but the latter would often have effective means of nullifying it. Colonial officials were vulnerable to pressures from the local minority, of which they formed a part. Consequently, metropolitan authorities always had great difficulty when they tried to mitigate the effects of colonial pluralism. In Spanish America, viceroys and other officials used the formula, "I obey but do not execute," when they refrained from promulgating edicts received from Madrid.[3] Governors of African colonies, too, had ample resources for obstructing metropolitan commands. They could argue the case in dispatches full of special pleading, which would be difficult to controvert because of the governors' command of the data, and after months, even years, of delays the metropolitan authorities might yield or let the matter drop. Alternatively, governors could promulgate a law and refrain from enforcing it. British governors used both tactics in the West Indies and the Cape Colony to thwart the British program for the "reform" of the institution of slavery in the 1810's and 1820's.[4] There were similar possibilities for obstruction at the lower levels of colonial administration. A district commissioner, or his equivalent, with or without the connivance of his governor, could thwart orders from headquarters by delaying tactics or by sheer administrative inaction. These methods became more difficult to apply as improvements were made in methods of communication, such as the introduction of the submarine cable, the telegraph, the telephone, and the radio telephone; but it was very late in the colonial epoch before all district commissioners were linked with their colonial headquarters by telegraph or telephone. Thus, there was a built-in mechanism for preserving the plural features of a colonial society, even when the metropolitan authorities wished to reduce them. The history of Rhodesia from 1891 to the present day is very largely the record of the blocking, by white men on the spot (from Cecil Rhodes to Ian Smith), of the spirit and the substance of policies laid down in London.

Whereas colonialism certainly had disruptive effects upon African societies, dividing some at the time of the Partition and creating new cleavages by providing modern education for only a few Africans, it also started a process of integration in Africa. The boundaries of a colony usually incorporated many precolonial African societies (Basutoland and Swaziland were exceptions). Our judgment of when the societies in a particular colony ceased to be distinct and became sufficiently integrated to be labeled a single society depends on our concept of society. Whatever our judgment on that point, at the time of independence the colonial boundaries became the boundaries of the postcolonial states (with comparatively few modifications), and every postcolonial government seems to be committed to the maintenance of the territorial integrity of its state and to the welding of its inhabitants into a nation. Consequently, the number of actual political units and potential nations in postcolonial Africa, though large for optimum efficiency in a world at the present technological level, is far smaller than the number of political units and embryonic nations in precolonial Africa. Whatever the intentions of the imperial powers may have been, colonialism has in fact been an instrument for the amalgamation of African societies. In Asia, similarly, India, Indonesia, and Malaya are striking examples of the amalgamative effects of colonialism.

While all colonies had some attributes in common, and colonialism almost always initiated a process of amalgamation, colonies differed widely among themselves. The crucial difference was described by A. G. Keller as long ago as 1908, when he drew a distinction between what he called "tropical colonies" and "temperate colonies." [5] In the tropical colony (alias "colony of exploitation"), the dominant white minority consisted of administrators, soldiers, managers of plantations and/or commercial houses, and missionaries. Virtually all these whites were transients who pursued careers in the colony but returned to their country of origin on retirement. In the temperate colony (alias "colony of settlement"), besides the transients there was also a community of white settlers. It was not only a difference of numbers: it was a question of permanence, self-perpetuation, identification, commitment, and purpose.

The differences between the two situations were profound. In the tropical colony, the white people were members of institutions (government, business establishments, missionary societies, etc.) with headquarters in the metropolis. They looked upon the metropolis as "home"; and they were in fairly close touch with changes in metropolitan policy. Forming a mere addendum to the colonial society, they could be comparatively painlessly removed from it. On the other hand, the white settlers in the temperate colony became an integral part of the colonial society and their links with the metropolis weakened. When decolonization took place, they either acquired absolute power over the colonial society or they resisted, bitterly and violently, the transfer of power to the African majority.

Temperate Africa includes not only the Mediterranean littoral and South Africa, but also the highland belt running from Kenya to Rhodesia. The rest of the continent is essentially tropical and was unattractive to settlers.[6] Today, the former temperate colonies may themselves be classified in a sequence: from South Africa, where the whites succeeded in eliminating metropolitan control and acquiring absolute power, through Rhodesia where, at the time of writing, the whites have, at least temporarily, achieved the same objective, to Algeria, where the same result was averted only by an eight-year war; Kenya, where white settlers conspired unsuccessfully to seize power between the two world wars and power was transferred to the African majority after a serious African revolt; and Zambia and Malawi, where the white settlers were always less powerful and the transition to majority rule was somewhat less violent. The differences in the two basic types of colonies persist in the postcolonial states. In the former tropical colonies, today, as previously, white people are no more than transients. In the former temperate colonies, the white community remains an integral part of society.

SOCIAL CHANGE: THE LINGUISTIC FACTOR

In studies of pluralism, too little weight has been attached to problems of communication between people who speak different languages. The linguistic situation in a society is more complex and more subtle than is generally realized. It has deep psychological and emotional dimensions. It interacts with all other aspects of society. It varies independently of the "structure of accommodation"[7] between the component parts (if that phrase is to have any clear meaning). And it may itself be a major agent of structural change.[8]

Language is the fundamental instrument of human communication. If two people lack a common language, they can communicate only by noise, gesture, and touch, as do animals. If they both have complete mastery of a common language, they are able to communicate with each other to the limit of their conceptual capacities. Between these two extremes there is a spectrum of intermediate degrees of communication. Typically, two members of the same society with different home languages will be able to communicate with each other in one of those two languages, or in a third, for a specific operational purpose, and no more. A dominant minority wishing to preserve the status quo in a plural society has an interest in creating at least a limited, operational mode of communication with the subject peoples, for effective control and exploitation. It may try to prevent the development of more complete means of communication, lest they should promote mutual understanding, a sense of shared humanity, and cultural assimilation, and thereby threaten the plural structure of the society. On the other hand, a dominant minority may try to transmit a complete mastery of its own language in the hope that it would at the same time implant its value system in its subjects and make them loyal.

Second, at a particular moment in time, the languages of the world may be classified on a spectrum in terms of their range. At the one end are parochial languages, spoken only by small local communities. At the other end are a few universal languages, which are the major international media of commerce, diplomacy, and scholarship. In between there are many intermediate classes, including dominant languages, which are spoken by a majority of the citizens of a state; national languages, which are spoken by virtually all the citizens of a state; and lingua francas, which, though not necessarily dominant or national in any particular state (though they may be), are operational media of communication between inhabitants of different states. In the course of time, the relative status of languages changes. Some parochial languages disappear; others increase their range, becoming dominant languages, national languages, lingua francas, or even eventually universal languages—as with Greek and Latin, which started as parochial languages in the preclassical Mediterranean world, and French and English, which began as parochial languages in early medieval Europe.

The master of a universal language has an open sesame to the achievements and ideas of mankind beyond the borders of his particular society; and at the other end of the spectrum the possessor of only a parochial language cannot communicate beyond the range of his fellow parishioners. Consequently, a dominant minority may consider that it has an interest in confining its subject peoples to knowledge of parochial languages, so that they shall be unable to combine with one another, and shall be immune from the direct impact of the press, the literature, the radio, and the television emanating from the wider world.

The linguistic situation in many societies, especially in societies which comprise two or more collectivities and which fall short of full nationhood, is extremely complex. To understand it, we need to know the answers to a series of questions: What languages are spoken within the society? How are these languages related to one another, to the languages spoken in contiguous societies, and to universal languages? What is the distribution of home languages throughout the society, in terms of the numbers of speakers, the regions where they live, their occupations, their ethnic groups, and their classes or castes? What is the distribution and *what are the degrees of mastery,* of second, third, and additional languages throughout the society, in terms of numbers, regions, occupations, and ethnicity, and classes or castes? What are the discernible factors promoting change in the linguistic situation in the society (e.g., the kinship system, the administrative system, the educational system, the economic system)? What have been the processes of change in the linguistic situation? Only when we are in possession of these data shall we be able to know the extent to which the different social groups within the society are capable of communicating with one another and with the outside world; only then can we project present trends into the future and estimate what the linguistic position is likely to be at a later time, other factors remaining as they are.

The function of linguistic factors in society is often underestimated by American social scientists because they have never been a major impediment to the growth of American nationhood.[9] But the American experience is nevertheless extremely instructive. Forcibly abstracted from Africa and then regrouped on the western side of the Atlantic Ocean without regard to their linguistic origins, the Negro slaves soon adopted a dialect of English as their home language in North America. The successive waves of immigrants from continental Europe and from Asia have also been absorbed into the English-medium milieu, and English-medium domination has been a major factor in the assimilative process in the United States. Today, American society hangs together by virtue of the capacity of American citizens to communicate with one another toward the limits of their conceptual abilities, as much as for any other reason. The position would have been very different if different languages had prevailed in the different states or among the different ethnic groups. Today, the prospects for Negroes in American society would be much grimmer than they are if the Negroes were not able to communicate with other Americans in their own home tongue.

We may also note the function of linguistic factors in the rise of nationalities and nation-states in Europe. In the early Middle Ages, the use of Latin as the language of Church and government emphasized the gulf between rulers and subjects, though recruitment to the Church was fairly open and provided an avenue for upward mobility. Gradually, vernacular languages became the languages of courts and governments, and this was a process crucial to the growth of nationalities. The boundaries of many of the nation-states in the modern era correspond closely with linguistic boundaries. Thus language was a major determinant of social and political development in Europe.

THE LINGUISTIC SITUATION IN PRECOLONIAL AFRICA

We are very poorly informed about the linguistic situation in precolonial Africa. This is partly because the sorts of information we require for a comprehensive account of the linguistic situation are elusive, even in a contemporary society; but this inherent difficulty is compounded by the fact that anthropologists, ethnologists, historians, and even linguists have generally been insufficiently sensitive to the social implications of linguistic situations.[10] One may search the literature without finding any systematic account of the linguistic situation in any pluralistic precolonial African society. The anthropologist J. A. Barnes, in his otherwise admirable study of the Fort Jameson Ngoni, says nothing at all about the linguistic situation in that society, although it was a striking case of the preservation and transmission of a language by a conquering people.[11] Although some studies of African societies by anthropologists contain statements about language, they rarely deal with the critical questions about communication across linguistic barriers.

Precolonial Africa, with more than 800 languages,[12] was a continent of great linguistic diversity. Most languages were territorial in scope: they were spoken by virtually all the inhabitants of a specific area. Often the territorial range of a language was coterminous with the territorial range of a political unit. Sometimes, on the other hand, a language extended far beyond the limits of a single political unit. Thus the several mutually intelligible dialects of Nguni (from Zulu to Xhosa) were spoken by people who, before the time of Dingiswayo and Shaka, were divided among a large number of small chiefdoms; and so were the several mutually intelligible dialects of Sotho (Tswana, Pedi, and southern Sotho). In other cases, different languages were spoken by different groups within the same political unit, when intergroup communication was either in the home language of one of the groups or in a lingua franca which was not necessarily the home language of any of the groups. Several lingua francas spread over comparatively large areas as languages of commerce or administration, such as Maninka-Bambara-Dyula over much of West Africa, Hausa over much of Northern Nigeria and Niger, and Swahili, which spread inland along the Arab trade routes from the east coast ports where it originated.

The linguistic consequences of conquests varied. In many cases the conquerors adopted the language of the conquered, probably, as Smith says, because of the prevalence of unions between male conquerors and female subjects, and the dominant role of the women in transmitting language to their children.[13] But we also have examples of the opposite process. Mzilikazi fled from Shaka to the Transvaal with about two or three hundred Nguni followers (mostly men) in 1819. During the next twenty years he was joined by more Nguni refugees, and the children of Sotho women sired by the Nguni men in the Transvaal were brought up to speak Nguni. This process continued after the Ndebele fled from the Voortrekkers to Rhodesia, and to this day the Ndebele form of Nguni is the language of the Ndebele people of Rhodesia. Other Nguni dialects were taken by refugees from Shaka still farther afield to Malawi and Zambia.[14] Still more striking is the case of the Kololo, who transmitted their Sotho language to their Lozi subjects so effectively that the Lozi continue to speak Sotho to this day, although they destroyed the Kololo monarchy and annihilated the Kololo men as far back as 1865.[15]

But these are only superficial probes of the very complex and varied linguistic situation that existed in precolonial Africa. For most areas we lack the time depth to discern the processes of linguistic change; and where two or more linguistic communities were associated, we know far too little about the degree to which they were able to communicate with one another. Undoubtedly many Africans were bilingual or multilingual. W. E. Welmers reports an interesting example from a small area in Nigeria, where the local home language is Kutep. Many Kutep-speakers also speak Jukun, a regional language; and some speakers of both Kutep and Jukun also speak Hausa, the dominant language in Northern Nigeria.[16] Though these data were obtained in the colonial period, the situation was probably much the same in the nineteenth century. But we still do not know the inner social realities of the situation. How effectively could the Kutep-speakers communicate with the Jukun and the Hausa? To what extent were Kutep-speakers at a disadvantage for their lack, or incomplete mastery, of Jukun or Hausa? Did mastery of Jukun or Hausa promote mobility? Similar questions could be asked of the precolonial situation in most parts of Africa, without getting clear answers. We simply do not know enough; and it is to be hoped that anthropologists and historians who do fieldwork in Africa in the future will obtain as much information as possible about systems of communication in multilingual societies, as well as other types of data.

THE LINGUISTIC SITUATION IN COLONIAL AFRICA

In the colonial period new languages were introduced into African societies.[17] White administrators found it essential to develop systematic means of communication with their African subjects, if only for the effective transmission of orders. This could be done either by training a corps of Africa interpreters, or by conveying a smattering of the European language to the African chiefs and headmen, or by conveying a smattering of an African language to the white administrators, or by some combination of these methods. Which technique prevailed in a particular case varied with the nature of the precolonial linguistic situation, the nationality of the European rulers, and the extent of white settlement. In an area where there was a multiplicity of parochial African languages and no dominant language or lingua franca, communication was usually via local African interpreters; but where an African language was dominant over a wide area (as with Hausa in Northern Nigeria) or there was a widespread lingua franca (Swahili in Kenya and Tanganyika), European administrators were more likely to learn that language. The French and the Portuguese generally despised and ignored African languages, so that in their colonies African education, from the very beginning, was usually in the French or Portuguese medium. This made it very difficult for Africans to acquire basic literacy, and dropout rates in junior elementary classes were very high. But in French Africa, some of those who managed to surmount the literacy and foreign-language hurdle had a good prospect of acquiring a thorough, modern French education. The British and the Belgians were somewhat less arrogant, but more concerned to maintain social distance between themselves and Africans. In British and Belgian colonies, elementary education was formally started in an African language, with a shift to English or French somewhere before the high school level. This system resulted in more widespread elementary education and a less complete identification of literacy with a European language. The presence of white settlers controlling farming or mining enterprises increased the scale of the demand for low-level, operational means of communication, so that in settler areas, debased, oversimplified, operational sublanguages came into being, such as "kitchen kaffir" in South Africa.

In all colonies there was a quantitative limit to the white minority's need for communication with Africans, and subsidies to missionary institutions for educational work, and government-controlled educational programs, were related to this limit. Although the limit rose with economic development, the proportion of the African inhabitants of colonies who obtained any sort of literary education was always small—in French and Portuguese colonies, abysmally small. There was also a qualitative limit. In the colonial situation the capacity for full communication between ruler and subject, transcending the mere operational level, was a rare phenomenon. Among whites, it was normally confined to exceptionally conscientious missionaries and administrators; among Africans, to exceptionally talented, studious, and ambitious individuals. Nevertheless, it was this latter group who, in every colony, by virtue of their mastery of a universal language, had access to the ideologies and technologies of the wider world; and it was they who became the leaders of the liberation movement and (where successful) the heirs of the colonial regime. Now that admirable comprehensive surveys of nationalist movements in most parts of Africa have been made, we need depth studies of the processes of change in specific cultural attributes under colonialism, and especially in the linguistic situations. Such studies will powerfully illuminate the colonial version of pluralism.

THE LINGUISTIC SITUATION IN POSTCOLONIAL AFRICA

In postcolonial Africa, the creation of states preceded the consolidation of nations; so that if nations do develop within the present territorial framework, the European chronological sequence will have been reversed. Many factors contribute to the transformation of pluralistic societies into nations; but one of the most obvious requirements is an effective means of communication. If citizens of the same state cannot communicate with one another on account of language barriers, they can hardly be expected to develop a sense of common nationality. This truism is, I think, recognized by the ruling classes of the postcolonial African states; but, preoccupied as they have been with more urgent problems, they do not seem to have given serious consideration to this question; and in any case there is no cut-and-dried formula for success in linguistic engineering for political ends.

The simplest linguistic objective to work toward, if one is to build a nation, is that one language should eventually become the instrument of communication for all purposes by all citizens of the state. But to say this is not to solve the problem of initiating a successful movement toward that objective. There is the question of deciding which language is to become the national language. In postcolonial sub-Saharan African states at the present time, the members of the ruling class are masters of the language of the former metropolitan power, and in many cases that language is the only one in which all the members of the elite from the diverse regions of the state can communicate with one another. The fact that the same language, being a universal language, is suitable for the conduct of relations with other states, inside and outside Africa, is a further attraction. That is why at this stage French or English is an official language, and often the only language of administration and of secondary and higher education in the postcolonial states in sub-Saharan Africa.

It is doubtful, however, whether a European language is likely to become the most efficient nation-building instrument in many African states. European languages are still foreign to the African masses. They are spoken in the homes of only a minute proportion of the African population. To make one of them the sole official language in an African state is to prolong, perhaps to perpetuate, the horizontal cleavage which colonialism created in African societies, and thereby to impede rather than promote the growth of nationality. It is also to continue the pedagogical error of the French and the Portuguese by confronting children with a double hurdle at the very outset of their education.

The other way to achieve the goal of a single national language is to select a local language for the purpose. In states where one language is the home language of the vast majority of the people, this solution is probably the best. A universal language, such as English or French, can still be taught as a subject in secondary and higher education. But the number of such states is small. Most African states contain more than one home language, and in many states there are numerous home languages, no dominant language, and no lingua franca. Thus the problem is extremely difficult. To upgrade one truly parochial language to national status is to create for the majority of the people the same pedagogical difficulty that the French and the Portuguese created, and at the same time to hinder the growth of nationality by emphasizing vertical divisions within the society, between the community whose home language has been favored and the other communities.

Enough has been said to illustrate the complexities of the problem. The linguistic history of India since independence shows how politically divisive a problem it can be. In the toughest cases, the wisest policy would seem to be to use the different parochial languages for elementary education and local administration, so far as practicable, and to select the dominant language, a lingua franca, or the language of the former metropolitan power as the language of secondary and higher education and central government. Then, with the spread of education, the selected language will ultimately become an instrument for effective communication between all the citizens and may promote a spirit of nationality. If, however, the selected language is not a universal language, people should also be encouraged to learn one as a third language, to enable them to communicate with the greater society beyond the confines of the particular state. There are several possible variations of this policy, such as the one adopted in Switzerland, where at the regional (cantonal) level the language that is dominant in the region is preferred, at the national level three languages rank equally, and the majority of the people are bi- or even trilingual.

In plural societies where the dominant minority is determined to maintain its position, there are ways of manipulating the linguistic situation to this end. This is done in the two tropical African states that lacked an orthodox experience of colonialism. In Liberia, where the dominant minority consists of the descendants of Negro settlers from the United States, knowledge of English is essential for participation in the political system and assimilation into the dominant group. The "aborigines" speak numerous parochial languages at home and still have inferior opportunities for acquiring English, so that linguistic differences are perpetuated to reinforce the ethnic barrier. In Ethiopia the dominant minority speak Amharic and there, too, the majority of the population is divided into numerous parochial linguistic groups. Amharic is the only official language and the only language that is permitted as a medium of instruction in the schools, including the mission schools, before the sixth grade, where English is often used. Once again, the double hurdle, combined with differential educational opportunities, plays a significant part in the perpetuation of pluralism.

It is in postcolonial societies controlled by white minorities that the techniques of linguistic manipulation for the maintenance of pluralism are applied most pervasively, most subtly, and most effectively. The South African case warrants special attention.

THE LINGUISTIC SITUATION IN SOUTH AFRICA

The principal home languages of South Africans are English, Afrikaans, Nguni (including Xhosa, Zulu, Swazi, and Ndebele), and Sotho (including southern Sotho, northern Sotho or Pedi, and Tswana). Of these, English is the only universal language. Afrikaans is not spoken outside South Africa, except by Afrikaners who live in Rhodesia and Zambia; but it is sufficiently close to Dutch for Afrikaners to be able to make themselves understood by Dutchmen, and vice versa. Though Nguni and Sotho are not mutually intelligible, they are related languages of the southern Bantu group.[18] Nguni is also spoken in Swaziland and Rhodesia, and Sotho in Lesotho and Botswana; both are related to the other Bantu languages which are dominant up to the equator. Table 1

TABLE 1

Distribution of Home Languages among Population Groups of South Africa, 1960

(In thousands)

Group	English and Afrikaans	English	Afrikaans	Other European	Nguni	Sotho	Other Bantu	Asian	Total
Whites	45	1,151	1,791	102 [a]	—	—	—	—	3,089
Coloreds	14	154	1,337	5	—	—	—	—	1,510
Asians	1	64	7	—	—	—	—	404 [b]	476
Africans	—	—	—	—	6,540	3,403	985 [c]	—	10,928
Total	60	1,369	3,135	107	6,540	3,403	985	404	16,003

[a] Notably Dutch and German.
[b] Notably Tamil and Hindi.
[c] Notably Tsonga and Venda.

SOURCE: Data for whites, Coloreds, and Asians from Republic of South Africa, *Population Census, 1960, Sample Tabulation* (Pretoria: Government Printer, n.d.), 1. 46, 11. 33, and 11. 63, resp.; for Africans, from Murriel Horrell, comp., *A Survey of Race Relations in South Africa, 1965* (Johannesburg: South African Institute of Race Relations, 1966), p. 110.

shows the distribution of home languages among the four officially designated population groups of South Africa in 1960.

Within the dominant white minority, language is the most obvious distinction between the two communities, who are often referred to as "English-speaking" and "Afrikaans-speaking" white South Africans. When the British conquered the Cape Colony in 1806 the Afrikaners were a distinct, but poor and unorganized, people. Their spoken language was already Afrikaans, but insofar as they read or wrote, they continued to do so in Dutch. During the ensuing century of British supremacy in South Africa, there were times when it seemed likely that English would become the dominant language and that the Afrikaners would eventually be absorbed by the British settlers. Lord Milner, high commissioner from 1897 to 1905, certainly intended that to happen; and many British settlers despised Afrikaans and shared his wish. But since the 1870's a group of predikants had been impressing upon the Afrikaner people the need to preserve their language and their church, in the face of British imperialism and the economic and political ascendancy and cultural arrogance of the British settlers. This spadework bore fruit in the Afrikaans literary movement that began in 1905. This movement played an important part in reviving the morale of the Afrikaner people and maintaining their social cohesion when they were threatened by the defeat of the two republics in the war of 1899–1902. The Afrikaner poets were profoundly aware of the political significance of their work. As Jan Cilliers wrote in 1907, "it is clear to every Afrikaner that only our own literature, steeped in the Afrikaner spirit and intelligible to Afrikaners, through and through in language and content, that only such a literature is really calculated to hit the mark here. Who wants to help us to build up such a literature for our people? We have a people to serve, we have a nation to educate; we cannot wait!" [19] There continued to be some confusion in the Afrikaner ranks, because conservatives preferred to maintain Dutch as the literary medium for the Afrikaners; but both factions maintained a united front in the National Convention of 1908–09, with the result that the South African constitution provided for the equality of Dutch with English as the official languages of the Union. J. B. M. Hertzog, the leader of the Afrikaner nationalist group at the convention, regarded this provision as a guarantee for the preservation of Afrikaner unity and nationality: "'Great victory,' ran his diary entry. '10.27 this morning—20 October 1908—resolution unanimously adopted whereby it is declared that both Dutch and English as the official languages of the Union shall be treated equally and enjoy equal freedom, rights and privileges, etc.' Then he repeated the time and the date, and signed his name." [20] By 1925 Afrikaans had indubitably become the written as well as the spoken language of the Afrikaner people, and in that year it was substituted for Dutch in the constitution. Afrikaans and English remain the official languages of the present Republic.

The interpretation of the language section has given rise to continual controversy between the two white communities in South Africa, especially in the field of education. Afrikaner nationalists of a later generation than Hertzog's determined to corral their own youth into separate public schools and to indoctrinate them with "Christian National Education." Today in the Transvaal all public schools for whites are unilingual, and a white parent is compelled by law to send his children to a school where the medium of instruction is the language spoken at home—English or Afrikaans. The trend is in the same direction in the other three provinces.[21] The other official language is, however, taught as a subject in all white schools, and most white South Africans have now become effectively bilingual.

Afrikaans now possesses an adequate scientific and technical vocabulary. It is the dominant language of politics and administration, and is catching up with English in commerce, industry, and finance. Thus linguistic factors have played a vital part in the rise of the Afrikaner people from their rural and semiliterate nineteenth-century background. It was largely because of skillful and intelligent use of their language that Afrikaners were able to resist assimilation by the British and to move on to a dominating position in a modern industrial state.

While white South Africans have become able to communicate with one another efficiently on the basis of bilingualism, they have remained astonishingly ignorant of the home languages of their African fellow countrymen. No statistics are available concerning the capacity of white South Africans to speak Bantu languages, but there is no doubt that the number who can do so with anything approaching mastery is very small indeed. If a third language is taught at school, it is usually Latin, French, or German, rarely a Bantu language. For communication with Africans, all that most white South Africans aspire to is the capacity to give effective orders to their employees, and for this purpose they use a simplified form of English or Afrikaans, or some terrible hybrid sublanguage they call "kitchen kaffir."

Nearly all Africans continue to speak their traditional languages at home. The census returns ignore the fact that some Africans also use English or Afrikaans at times and that in Johannesburg there is also a hybrid southern Bantu language called "fanigalo," which has developed as a lingua franca among Africans of diverse origins. In addition, many Africans have acquired some competence in either or both of the official languages of the country, by either or both of two processes. First, in the course of their duties in white homes, on white-owned farms, and in white-controlled industries, workers have contrived to pick up an operational knowledge of the language of their white employers. Second, as pupils in schools, children have had literary training in English or Afrikaans.

Until 1954 the main agents of a literary education for Africans were missionaries, most of whom could speak English but not Afrikaans. Missionaries usually used the home language of the African child as the medium of instruction in the first few grades, introduced English as a second language as soon as possible, and switched to English as the medium of instruction in about the fifth grade.[22] In addition, in 1959 about 600 African students attended the English-medium universities of Natal, the Witwatersrand, and Cape Town, and the university college of Fort Hare, while none of the Afrikaans-medium universities admitted Africans. The result was that while Afrikaans more than held its own with English as an operational language of the African manual worker, English became the main literary language of the rising African bourgeoisie, who read English-medium newspapers, listened to the English programs of the South African Broadcasting Corporation, and were receptive to information and ideas from the English-speaking world outside South Africa.

Under the Bantu Education Act of 1953 the government assumed control of virtually all the former mission schools, made the Bantu language of an area the sole medium of instruction up to the end of the eighth grade and the sole medium of examination in all grades except the twelfth, and provided as much time for the teaching of Afrikaans as of English. (In 1963, of a total of 1,770,371 African pupils, 3.4 percent were above the eighth grade and 725 passed the twelfth-grade examination.[23]) Furthermore, under legislation passed in 1959 the government has excluded Africans from the established universities and created separate colleges for Xhosa, Zulu, and Sotho students. African opinion was opposed to these changes; in the Transkei, English is again being substituted for the home language as the medium of instruction in and after the fifth grade, but there has been no reversal in the rest of the country.[24] The net result has been greatly to limit the opportunities of Africans to acquire a training in the English language.

The African inhabitants of the Republic have great linguistic virtuosity. Whereas the whites, with immensely superior educational opportunities, tend to be effectively bilingual in English and Afrikaans, but to have no more than a shallow operational knowledge of "kitchen kaffir," many Africans, besides being masters of their home language, have an adequate knowledge of English or Afrikaans, and can speak "fanigalo" as well as a second Bantu language. In the 1951 census, 29 percent of the Africans aged seven or above were reported to be capable of speaking English or Afrikaans and 71 percent to be unable to speak either of the official languages.[25] The minimum degree of knowledge of English or Afrikaans among the 29 percent was not defined; more recent figures are not available, and sociologists and anthropologists have not added very much relevant information. It is probable that, as a result of the rapid expansion of the modern sector of the economy since 1951, the number of Africans who have acquired some operational knowledge of English or Afrikaans will now have increased considerably; but the number who have mastery of English or Afrikaans is reported to be actually decreasing.[26] If the present educational system continues outside the Transkei, the number may continue to decrease in the future.

One should not ignore the possibility that some members of the South African ruling caste have in mind a model of the linguistic situation that should exist to buttress pluralism in a modern industrial society. In this model, the dominant home language of the ruling caste should be a parochial or national, but not a universal, language, so that its members should not easily identify themselves with Marxist or liberal elements in the outside world; but some members of the ruling caste should have a good command of a universal language for purposes of international trade, diplomacy, and technological progress. The home languages of the subject castes should be several different parochial languages, so that members of the subject castes should be unable to communicate effectively with one another across the "tribal" line, with members of the ruling caste across the color line, or with the outside world across the national line. For purposes of economic exploitation and political subjection, however, there should also be some means of communication between the ruling caste and the subject castes, but such communication should be in parochial sublanguages, to prevent it from transcending the merely operational level.

Several features of this model exist in contemporary South Africa. They originated in the diverse cultural antecedents of the different components of South African society; they are sustained by custom and by all manner of legislative and administrative expedients. Afrikaans has gone a long way toward replacing English as the dominant language of the ruling caste. The different Bantu languages continue to be the home languages of nearly all Africans. Few white people are masters of Bantu languages. Few Africans are masters of English or Afrikaans. Most communication across the color line is in operational sublanguages which cannot promote a sense of common humanity.

But in contemporary South Africa there are features that depart from this model. Many white South Africans are tenacious of their heritage of a universal language. The home language of the majority of the members of the intermediate caste of Colored people is Afrikaans, and that of the minority is English. Many of the Asians also speak English at home. English has great prestige among the African bourgeoisie;[27] and as industrial technology advances, the level of Afrikaans or English required of African industrial workers is rising, diminishing the gap between operational control and mastery of the language. The central contradiction in South African society—between a policy of racial domination and a process of racial integration—is therefore very clearly revealed on the linguistic plane.

Notwithstanding the system of division and suppression, it is possible that the language barriers are breaking down in South Africa. If English were to become the lingua franca, it would provide bridges between the different castes and also between all types of South Africans and the outside world. Or if Afrikaans becomes the lingua franca, as now seems more likely, that, too, will make it more difficult for South Africans to be oblivious of one another's common humanity. In either event, linguistic factors may play a crucial part in the undermining of white supremacy, just as they formerly played a crucial part in the undermining of British supremacy.

TIME, TECHNOLOGY, AND THE GREAT SOCIETY

In conclusion, I wish briefly to raise the question whether we may not be losing the wood for the trees if we create typologies of societies with insufficient regard to the time dimension and the dynamics of change. Pluralism thrives on isolation. A plural society needs to be separated from other societies by a wasteland, an unnavigated ocean, or an iron curtain, for it is threatened by interaction with other societies. The technology associated with the oceanic sailing ship and gunpowder ushered in the modern imperial age, when people from Europe went a long way toward disrupting the structures of all other societies, not only those that they formally subjected, but also those that preserved the forms of autonomy —China as well as India, Ethiopia as well as Ashanti. Is it not possible that the technology associated with the supersonic aircraft and nuclear power is now detracting from the autonomy of all societies to the point where we falsify the picture if we proceed as though the units we have been labeling societies were not themselves associated in a greater society? Already most of the "collectivities" on this planet are more integrally related to one another than were the several "collectivities" in many a colony for several years after their annexation by a European power. Already the United Nations has some structural similarities to the

Swiss Confederation before the Napoleonic invasion, or to the Thirteen Colonies under the Articles of Confederation. Already mankind is intermeshed in an interdependent economy and a network of communications. Instead, therefore, of regarding all societies as being of the same order, it may be more realistic to have in mind a hierarchy or a continuum of societies from those that are small and isolated, through diverse intermediate stages, including the empires and the nation-states, to mankind, the ultimate society. Such a framework would do better justice to the historical record than one that is related to the constitutional norms of a particular era; and it would accommodate those norms in the appropriate place.

It therefore behooves the social scientist to apply the modes of analysis which have been used in this book, not merely to the units that have been labeled societies, but also to the greater society. We need to gauge the cultural diversities among modern man. We need to assess the complex varieties of "structures of accommodation" now existing between the diverse parts of the whole, and between the parts and the whole. And, above all, we need to improve our tools for understanding the diverse forces that are continuously modifying both the cultural diversities and the structures of accommodation.

Insofar as mankind now constitutes a single society, that society is certainly pluralistic. But does its pluralism tend predominantly toward the consensus model or the conflict model? We certainly cannot ignore the many indications that, beneath the forms of the nation-state and the myth of the equality of nations, mankind is drifting toward an unstable pluralism of the conflict type, dominated by the major industrial powers. If this is even partly true, should we not inquire whether the remedies we prescribe to assist the lesser plural societies to move toward consensus may be applicable on the larger scale?

NOTES

[1] Arnold J. Toynbee, *A Study of History* (10 vols.; London: Oxford University Press, 1934–1954); R. G. Collingwood, *The Idea of History* (Oxford: Clarendon Press, 1946), pp. 159–165.

[2] J. S. Furnivall, *Colonial Policy and Practice* (London: Cambridge University Press, 1948); Georges Balandier, "The Colonial Situation," in Pierre L. van den Berghe, ed., *Africa: Social Problems of Change and Conflict* (San Francisco: Chandler Publishing Co., 1965), pp. 36–57.

[3] C. H. Haring, *The Spanish Empire in America* (New York: Oxford University Press, 1947), p. 123.

[4] Isobel E. Edwards, *Towards Emancipation: A Study in South African Slavery* (Cardiff: Gomerian Press, 1942).

[5] A. G. Keller, *Colonization: A Study of the Founding of New Societies* (Boston: Ginn, 1908), chap. 1.

[6] The communes of Senegal contained the nearest approach to a white settler community in sub-Saharan tropical Africa.

[7] M. G. Smith, "Pluralism in Precolonial African Societies," above.

[8] For a review of the literature, see John J. Gumperz, "Language and Communication," *Annals of the American Academy of Political Science* (Sept. 1967), pp. 219–231.

[9] For example, Richard R. Fagen, *Politics and Communication* (Boston: Little, Brown, 1966), does not mention the linguistic dimensions of the subject. Joseph H. Greenberg's 1965 presidential address to the African Studies Association ("Interdisciplinary Perspectives: African Linguistic Research," *African Studies Bulletin*, IX, no. 1 [April 1966]) describes sociolinguistics as a new field, which has so far "been the work almost exclusively of linguists" (p. 15). However, see Gumperz, *op. cit.*, and the works he cites.

[10] Greenberg, *op. cit.*

[11] J. A. Barnes, *Politics in a Changing Society* (Manchester: Manchester University Press, 1954).

[12] Different dialects of the same language are mutually intelligible; different languages are not. The application of this rule does not give a clear-cut answer in every case; even if we had all the data, we would still be unable to say precisely how many languages existed in Africa at any given moment (Greenberg, *op. cit.*, p. 16).

[13] Smith, "Pluralism in Precolonial African Societies."

[14] Margaret Read, "Tradition and Prestige among the Ngoni," *Africa*, 9 (1936), 453–483.

[15] Jan Vansina, *Kingdoms of the Savanna* (Madison: University of Wisconsin Press, 1966), pp. 215–216.

[16] William E. Welmers and Ruth C. Sloan, "A Preliminary Survey of Existing Resources for Training in African Languages and Linguistics," prepared for Georgetown University's Institute of Languages and Linguistics (unpublished MS, Oct. 1957), p. 7.

[17] Lord Hailey, *An African Survey, Revised 1956* (London: Oxford University Press, 1957), chap. ii, is still the most comprehensive statement on the linguistic situation in Africa toward the end of the colonial era. I have also used Welmers and Sloan, *op. cit.*, and Beatrice F. Welmers, "African Languages and Political Administration" (unpublished MS, 1958).

[18] Though Xhosa, Zulu, etc., are commonly regarded as different languages, I treat them as one language, Nguni, because they are mutually intelligible. The same is true of Sotho.

[19] Cited in L. M. Thompson, *The Unification of South Africa, 1902–1910* (Oxford: Clarendon Press, 1960), p. 20.

[20] *Ibid.*, p. 197.

[21] Leonard M. Thompson, *Politics in the Republic of South Africa* (Boston: Little, Brown, 1966), pp. 98–101.

[22] The South African "standards" and "substandards" have been changed into the American grade equivalent.

[23] Muriel Horrell, comp., *A Survey of Race Relations in South Africa, 1965* (Johannesburg: South African Institute of Race Relations, 1966), p. 248.

[24] This has been the most substantial concession obtained by the people of the Transkei in consequence of the introduction of the present system of local government under the Transkei Constitution Act, 1963.

[25] Union of South Africa, *Union Statistics for Fifty Years* (Pretoria: Government Printer, 1960), p. A–19.

[26] Muriel Horrell, comp., *A Survey of Race Relations in South Africa, 1966* (Johannesburg: South African Institute of Race Relations, 1967), p. 237: "The net result of the 1956 syllabus, however, has been that Africans have, increasingly, found difficulty in expressing themselves in either official language. The standard of English is particularly inadequate."

[27] Leo Kuper, *An African Bourgeoisie: Race, Class and Politics in South Africa* (New Haven: Yale University Press, 1965), p. 138.

Chapter 12   The Tribal Area
in South and Central Africa*

Max Gluckman

Every scientific analysis has a specific history, both in the development of its discipline and in the individual development of the research worker. Since this symposium, and my own contribution to it, are on a subject which arouses emotion and moral indignation, I must put my analysis into this double historical perspective.

The approach of a South African like me to the problems of Africa is bound to be colored by his whole background. Two specific events greatly influenced me in my early youth. First, my father was attorney for Clements Kadalie, the founder of the African Industrial and Commercial Union. I heard the affairs of this union discussed many times, and learnt of the difficulties under which African industrial workers lived. Second, my father was attorney for the Ababirwa tribe, which complained that it had been kidnaped by warriors of Chief Kgama of the Ngwato. Again, I heard this case often discussed; I talked with a Bechuana policeman who had come to work for us because he was too terrified to stay in Bechuanaland after giving evidence against Kgama. My father was horrified by what he alleged to be the partial treatment of Kgama, the defendant, as against the callous treatment of the plaintiff, the chief of the Ababirwa, by the British judge who tried the case. He was horrified also that the forum of the case should have been Kgama's capital, where the plaintiffs were surrounded by Kgama's armed warriors. He published his criticisms in articles in the *Rand Daily Mail*, and they were reissued as a pamphlet which is a collector's piece.[1] My father's

* I am grateful to the Nuffield Foundation under their Small Grants Scheme for research assistance, secretarial assistance, and material aids which have greatly facilitated the writing of this essay.

I am also grateful to members of the seminar at the University of California, Los Angeles, particularly Mr. B. Bellman and Mr. J. Mejer, and to members of our seminar at Manchester University, particularly Dr. J. Simons and Dr. M. Southwold, for their helpful discussion of my analysis.

indignation on behalf of his clients and of Africans in general led him to try to found a cooperative to provide funds for the defense of Africans at law, and he was threatened by the government. The cooperative failed because Africans said they could not afford the contributions.

Under my father's influence I inevitably stood on the African side. Later, when I was one of the representatives of the students of Witwatersrand University on the Council of the National Union of South African Students, I was made chairman of a committee to consider the admission of Fort Hare Native [African] College to the National Union, as had been proposed by my university. There I learnt of the intransigence of most of the Afrikaner intellectuals on African questions; eventually I had to resign, because I could not work with the Afrikaner members, and I would not compromise.

I could cite many other accumulative experiences which convinced me that in South Africa ethnic groups on the whole confronted one another in opposition, though many of the white group sided with the Africans who were oppressed and who were refused basic liberties and civil rights. I know little of the tribal areas, but the case of *Ababirwa vs. Kgama* seemed to fit with the doctrine of the late Professor E. Roux [2] that chiefs were reactionary, oppressive agents of the white government, as he and other left-wingers were preaching at the university in the early 1930's. The "poverty" of the tribal areas was emphasized in the 1932 Native Economic Commission's report, on which I wrote an editorial for our university newspaper.

These were some of the opinions I took with me, as background to my training in anthropology, when I began my study of the modern political and social systems of Zululand in 1936. I had believed that chiefs were oppressive and unrepresentative of their people. I soon collected data that corrected this opinion for the Zulu chiefs, whom in my first analysis, written in the field for *African Political Systems* (edited by Fortes and Evans-Pritchard, 1940),[3] I saw as contraposed absolutely as representatives of their people against South African government officials. I saw this situation of chief versus native commissioner as set in the hostility of the color groups, with Africans subordinate, for the discussions I heard among Zulu confirmed the early impressions I had formed in Johannesburg. I did not send this first analysis, written in terms of a series of hatreds and oppositions, to Fortes and Evans-Pritchard, for after reading it through, I asked myself: "How is it that people, Black and White, go about their business so easily, relatively peacefully, and accommodatingly, despite these hatreds and hostilities?" And I remembered that they had done so in Johannesburg, despite clashes and oppression. Therefore I sought for, and found, bases of "cohesion." [4] The South African social system was then, and has become increasingly, a horrible one, morally. But it worked and works, in total and in its parts.

What I learnt then has influenced my whole approach to these problems. A social system may work, despite oppression and hatreds; and it was my professional duty to examine how it worked despite my own dislike—nay, hatred—of its basic premises. I was confirmed in this professional judgment by the publication at that time of Bateson's theory of social schismogenesis.[5] For if ever a system had tendencies to schismogenesis in it, South Africa did. What then countered the drive to deep and increasing schism?

A further experience emphasized my search for "cohesion." At certain levels and in some current situations in the 1930's it was clear that one could see the South Africa polity as composed of "differentially incorporated" (M. G. Smith) color groups or ethnic groups,[6] sharply divided from one another, some dominant, others inferior. And one could reasonably expect that these divisions were likely in a long run of time to increase, while even in the short run, this division would affect all forms of cooperation. Therefore, when I tried to formulate certain processes of social change to cover my data, in terms that would allow them to be applied more widely,[7] I spoke of the principle of the developing dominant cleavage: "In any social system there is a dominant cleavage into groups which runs through all the social relationships in the system. This dominant cleavage is rooted in the fundamental conflict of the system. (In Zululand the dominant cleavage is into White and African groups.) In any part of the system there may be a subsidiary cleavage, operating similarly in that part of the system to the dominant cleavage in the whole system, but the subsidiary cleavage will be affected by the dominant cleavage. . . . It follows that the dominant cleavage of a changing system must produce similar structural developments in all similar parts of the system, even if the cultural form be different." I expounded these principles with illustrations. Here I cite them in order to show that I was, and am, fully aware of the extent to which white and African oppositions dominate the South African system, indeed increasingly so since the 1930's, as shown in the movement from the policy called segregation to that of apartheid. But the experience that influenced, and influences, my presentation of these principles in analysis was hearing Professor W. M. Macmillan, the great historian who first brought Africans and their societies into proper perspective in historical analysis,[8] say: "If people worried about the next ten years, instead of the next fifty years, there would be some hope for South Africa." This taught me that to look into the distant future, or to examine a society at its highest levels of order and oppositions, distracted important attention from immediate, short-run problems. It might well be that at some time in the future differential incorporation of the ethnic groups must produce, under the principle of the developing dominant cleavage, violent disturbance and radical change. In the immediate present my duty as a scientist was to try to understand how the system worked, and was likely to continue working in at least the short run. Thirty years later it still works.

It was then with this personal background that I approached my analyses of Zululand as I found it when I did field research in the mid-1930's. And it is specifically those analyses, reordered in the light of later work, that the organizers of this symposium have asked me to write about. In any symposium, the organizers allot duties to cover a range of problems. I have been asked "to discuss in the perspective of recent developments, factual and analytical, the view of plural societies" which I derived from my Zululand field data. I take it that the first reason behind this request was that the other papers in the symposium are either broad analyses of large-scale plural societies looked at over a long period of time, or comparative discussions of major problems over several such societies. No paper deals with the structure of minor segments, or special groups, or specific sets (Epstein) or domains (Fortes) or relationships within a single society. The historical background to this specific paper is therefore the wish of the organizers to have a paper on some more limited region of social life within an African plural society. I have already indicated that my analysis has to be seen within the kind of wider setting which I have indicated above; and I here gladly express my thanks to members of the seminar in Los Angeles, and particularly Mr. B. Bellman and Mr. J. Mejer, for their comments on the relationship between my analysis and the kinds of analyses of the wider setting put forward by other contributors.

I would myself lay weight on rather different points in the wider analysis. These are summarized below (see pp. 402–404); and when I had read the analyses of my colleagues in this symposium, I wrote out at length for my own satisfaction, my own views on the dominant characteristics and problems of plural societies. These views are to be published in an essay entitled "Tribalism, Ruralism and Urbanism in Plural Societies," in V. W. Turner, editor, *Profiles of Change: The Impact of Colonialism on African Societies* (1969). That essay adds, I hope, to understanding of the full implications of my analysis here. I have also developed part of this present analysis in an essay presented to a Wenner-Gren symposium six weeks after the presentation of this essay itself: it is to be published under the title "Inter-hierarchical Roles: Professional and Party Ethics in the Tribal Areas in South and Central Africa," in M. Swartz, editor, *Local-Level Politics* (1969). It deals at length with problems discussed below (pp. 383–384, 393–395, 397–398, 404). For readers of more than one of these papers, this involves reading recapitulations of facts and summaries of arguments. But the main arguments are variously expanded and added to.

The present essay is thus immediately part of a group of three essays. It has also to be seen in perspective in the development of social anthropology. At the time when I carried out my field research in Zululand, anthropological approaches to the problems of "plural societies" were dominated by concepts of culture, either the idea of "acculturation" of American anthropologists or the "culture contact" of Malinowski's formulation. Fortes and Schapera had begun to advance an approach that regarded personages within African tribal communities, and personages of different kind within the dominant European group, as involved in a series of systematic relations of different type. They were misinterpreted, and then "chastised," by Malinowski (as I have shown in detail) [9] for what was in effect a complete switch of theoretical interest. This switch was to contribute to the breakup of general anthropology into several disciplines, with sociological (sci. social) anthropology becoming distinctive in many respects from culturological (sci. cultural) and psychological (sci. psychical) anthropology. Sociological anthropology began increasingly to find logical associations with sociology, political science, jurisprudence, and economics, as well as maintaining traditional associations with general anthropology.

I believe I was one of the first anthropologists to develop in detail the ideas put forward by Fortes and Schapera when in 1940 I published "Analysis of a Social Situation in Modern Zululand" in *Bantu Studies,* and followed it with an essay on "Some Processes of Social Change Illustrated with Zululand Data" in *African Studies* of 1942.[10] These essays started from detailed records of the observations I made of Zulu and whites interacting among themselves and together. In the first essay I described a series of events recorded by me on a single day. The main event was the ceremonial opening of a bridge built by the Native Affairs Department across the Black Umfolosi River in Northern Zululand. This bridge was a focus of satisfaction for white administrators, missionaries, and traders, and for Zulu of the district. Hence the ceremonial opening of the bridge, which was attended both by whites and Zulu, marked their common interest in a particular enterprise in which they could all rejoice. I examined how the Native Commissioner of the district concerned summoned various white personages, such as the Chief Native Commissioner of Natal, and the Regent of the Zulu Royal House (head of a small tribe but recognized by Zulu as representative of their great past kings), to make much of the occasion at a wider level than the attendance of

Zulu of that district alone would have done. Given that this was an occasion of mutual rejoicing, a striking feature of the ceremony was the spontaneous manner in which whites and Zulu grouped themselves in separate areas around the bridge, so that the effects of the color bar were clearly visible. Despite this division, various whites were able to move into the areas of the Zulu groups and deal with them about other matters of common interest. Zulu, save for whites' servants, could not move into the area of the white group: their subordinate status was clear. Furthermore, there were well-established institutional mechanisms and modes of intercourse for these dealings between whites and Zulu, derived from both white and Zulu cultures, and from the development of a new white-Zulu "community" culture—using "community" to cover a whole domain of shared and adjusted interests and patterns of intercommunication.[11] The Native Commissioner responsible for the organization of the ceremony had drawn on both cultures to set the pattern within which unplanned intercourse between individuals of both ethnic categories proceeded. Dominantly, the ceremony involved prayer by a Swedish missionary, followed by speeches made by the Chief Native Commissioner and other selected whites, official and unofficial, and by the Zulu Royal Regent (from the other side of the road). The Chief Native Commissioner then drove his car across the bridge, breaking a tape stretched over an arch made of branches. This was a ceremony in the white cultural pattern. The Native Commissioner had also stationed a Zulu in traditional warrior's dress to point with an assagai down the side road on which the bridge was built, whenever a car came along the main road, in order to indicate the route. Other men in traditional war dress led the cars across the bridge. Local Zulu women presented beer to the Chief Native Commissioner and he tasted it, and then gave it to the women who carried the beer to give to the Zulu Royal Regent to distribute to the assembled Zulu—here the C.N.C. acted as any Zulu chief would have done. Cattle were also presented to the Regent, both by the Native Commissioner for the government and by the local Zulu chief; and the Chief Native Commissioner told the Zulu to squeeze the gall of one of the government's beasts on the columns of the bridge to bring blessing. The whites departed, after drinking tea. A cup of tea and a piece of cake were carried across the road for the Zulu Royal Regent. He did not join the whites even for this piece of "courtesy." The Zulu Regent organized a feast on slain cattle and on beer for most of the Zulu, while the Swedish missionary organized hymn singing, under soccer goalposts, for some Christian Zulu.

That afternoon I went to a meeting called by the Native Commissioner of the neighboring district for the Mandlakazi section of the Zulu nation, to discuss what was to be done about persistent faction fighting within it. This section of the nation is led by a collateral branch of the Zulu royal House. After the British defeated the Zulu in 1879–80, the Mandlakazi split from the main section in the internecine strife among Zulu, starting in 1881 and ending in 1888 with the establishment of British rule over Zululand. Since then the head of the Mandlakazi has ruled a small tribe, as indeed has the Head of the Royal House itself. The Zulu Royal Regent (who in 1936 was about to be recognized by the South African Government as "Social Head of the Zulu Nation") was at his feast, and came late even though the start of the meeting was delayed for him. The Native Commissioner was speaking when he arrived, and the Mandlakazi, though "enemies" since 1881 of the Royal House, rose and gave the Regent a thunderous royal salute. At the end of the meeting, he upbraided the Mandlakazi councillors for "ruining the house of Uziβeβu," the man who broke the Mandlakazi off from the superior house. He told them they must detect the ringleaders and bring them to the Native Commissioner to be punished, and urged that they must stop the fighting because good money, which should feed, clothe, and educate families, was being wasted in fines. He forbade his own tribesmen to go to weddings in the Mandlakazi area.

I have summarized my records on this ceremony and the meeting from my fuller published accounts. I do so to indicate the kind of observations I made in the field, since these have given me a particular approach to the problems of plural societies. These observations, and many more of similar type, made me realize that in trying to understand social life in Zululand, it was not sufficient to think in terms of groups of whites and blacks, of massed ethnic groups, of overall attitudes of domination and subordination, or of statements in terms of hatred and resentment as against contempt and fear, even to comprehend the system at the highest levels of abstraction. These divisions and associated oppositions were only part of the overall picture at all levels. To understand what was going on in the whole of South Africa, one had to look at that whole as a whole, and also as composed of many different regions, associations, and domains or sets of social relationships directed toward specific purposes. The whole cannot be explained by the parts, but the parts influence the whole. And these social relationships in parts of the total South African state were called into being by a series of variable situations in which personages were mobilized by different goals and values out of a medley of consistent, inconsistent and discrepant, and even contradictory, goals and values.

On the whole at that time I found that Zululand worked as an ongoing social system in which all people could adjust to one another, whatever their race or occupation. Adjustment showed at its roughest in the hectoring attitude of Afrikaner farmers from the neighboring district of white farms driving into the Royal Regent's home to demand, without a tinge of politeness, that he recruit laborers for them, and his parrying politely that demand. Quite otherwise was the courtesy of the Chief Native Commissioner, a courtesy heightened by his knowledge of Zulu culture. Behavior ranged from the subservience of some Zulu toward all whites, to the manner in which others, and particularly traditional chiefs and councillors, would stand and argue to white officials against aspects of government policy.

But overall social life continued peacefully between whites and Zulu under the dominant authority of the whites. I was once at a Mandlakazi wedding when a fight broke out. Two bands of men armed with clubs belabored each other. The Zulu police, sent in force because of the recurrent fighting, fled, save for one mounted constable who tried in vain to control the situation. Then one faction broke and ran. One of its members was struck down. As each of his opponents passed the fallen man, he hit him with a club. I ran and stood beside him; and thereafter, since as a white I was invested with authority, the remainder rushed past without a blow. Police asked me to carry them, and the wounded man, in my car, for they said they feared they would be attacked. They may have been after a lift home. Later, when I described this fight to the Regent, I told him that I had been asked by the white police if I could recognize any of the wounded man's assailants, and truthfully had replied I could not; but I added to the Regent that on the whole I was pleased I could not do so, since I did not want to get involved in being a witness against Zulu in criminal cases. He told me that I was wrong: it was every man's duty to report people who caused such fighting, for it was bad for the Zulu, and the good man must help the government suppress it. On another occasion, at a great gathering of Zulu in the town of Vryheid (in a white farming district) to hear the Regent report on the first deliberations of the newly formed Natives' Representative Council of South Africa, on which he was government nominee, he ordered a drunk man to be flogged with a sjambok for insulting him by saying to him, "You know nothing." When the man had already been badly flogged, I intervened and stopped the flogging. I did so partly because of the pleas of the man in charge of the recruiting organization for the Witwatersrand Gold Mines on whose grounds the Zulu Regent was camped: he feared that if the drunk were seriously injured there would be a scandal involving the organization, which was already unpopular among local farmers who could not get Zulu labor because they could not compete with the wages offered by the gold mines. The recruiter did not speak Zulu while I did;

and he was an old schoolfellow of mine and could exercise pressure on me. Meanwhile I myself found it increasingly difficult to stand by and watch a helpless man flogged: I was caught between the merciful values which some in the white group hold and my professional feeling that if I did not interfere a revealing field situation would develop. Immediately the Regent, who had invited me to the meeting and some of whose attendants I had brought in my car (maybe the reason for the invitation), withdrew such favorable regard as he had displayed for me, and refused to see me. I was living with one of his senior councillors, who now begged me to apologize lest I spoil his standing with the Regent. After a day of this pressure, during which I maintained that the Regent ought to be grateful to me since if the man had been badly flogged there might have been a serious case involving the Regent, I apologized against my better judgment. (I saw later that I should not have apologized.) The Regent appeared to accept my apology, but later I heard from another schoolfellow in the Native Affairs Department that he had complained that I was interfering in his district, and he wished me to be moved out of the district. I went to check this with the Native Commissioner who (since the matter was confidential) only indicated that this report was true. But he did tell me that if I had stood by while a gross assault of this kind was committed, he would have asked me to leave the district.

Here then were the kinds of data that I felt must be subsumed in any analysis of social life in Zululand. As a white anthropologist, I could escape neither from the pressures nor from the contradictions within that field of life. The Regent felt affronted in his position as "king" descended from the great Zulu kings, for his authority, his prestige, and his knowledge (on which he prided himself) were involved in the insult: "You know nothing." He viewed the punishment he ordered by illegal force (as defined by the superior government) as righteous, while Mandlakazi faction fighters were using violence unrighteously. I should have watched the former without interfering, given evidence against the latter. When he was defending his own position vis-à-vis Zulu, my statement that I was trying to save him trouble did not fit his plea, frequently made, for peace, work, and economic development. He had asked me to photograph him ploughing, so that he could show his people that: "I am a chief of the plough, not of the spear."

These incidents also emphasize the extent to which even a white in my exceptional position among the Zulu was acting within sets of personal relationships which brought various types of information to me and exercised pressure on me, on top of my very color which fixed certain patterns of action. I was a member of a set of links through old school and university ties which were of great importance to me during my research, mainly helping, but in some ways hindering, that research. It was impossible to escape from those and other ties with whites, which Zulu tried to operate to their advantage, as they did my presence and my dependence on them. In time I was caught in, and constrained by, the ties I established with Zulu. Most whites to some extent became involved in sets of links with Zulu.

I complete my summary statement of field data with some information on the position of the Native Commissioners. Mr. E. N. Braatvedt, the Native Commissioner of Nongoma District, where I did my main field research, had organized a series of cattle sales which had benefited the Zulu greatly. In the past, Zulu had sold their cattle to traders at prices well below those which the cattle fetched when they reached the main markets. The Native Commissioner persuaded cattle buyers from the cities to come to Zululand on appointed days. Any Zulu wishing to sell a beast brought it to the sale yards where the Veterinary Department sorted all the cattle into small lots of beasts of equivalent value. The cattle buyers then bid, theoretically competitively, against one another for each herd. Even if they made up price rings, the prices were much higher than under earlier arrangements; and the income of the Zulu from the sale of cattle rose. This was in 1937, when the depression was over, and the again expanding mines and industries were short of African labor. Since they offered higher wages than farmers, this meant that farmers were even shorter of labor. The South African Government set up a Commission to enquire into the Shortage of Labour on European Farms, and I listened to its hearings in Nongoma. The Native Commissioner who had established the sales felt he had to defend these sales against statements, appearing in some newspapers, that because more money was coming to the Zulu from the sales, they were not offering themselves for wage labor outside the reserves. He argued that the number of Zulu involved in migrant labor showed no falling off, and hence that the sales were not affecting adversely this flow of labor. (As the market for labor was expanding, it might have been argued against him that more Zulu should have been offering themselves for work.) Only after making that point did he argue further that it was essential to reduce holdings of cattle because of pressure on the soil, and that this was government policy, which his sales were supporting by inducing more Zulu to sell cattle, since prices were higher. The two contentions were to some extent contradictory. He did not argue that it was sound policy to have the Zulu develop an autonomous economic base in the reserves, because seemingly he feared that this might get the farming interests to exert influence on the government to close down the sales—

though I am sure his own view was that the more a Zulu could earn money at home, the better it was for his family and social life. This fear —that those whites who were interested in a large flow of laborers out of the reserves would oppose economic developments in the reserves which might threaten that flow—was held by all government officials. An agricultural officer told me he was trying to keep quiet the success of cooperative creameries he had established among the Zulu who could thus earn money at home, lest these creameries be closed down. And I saw reported in the press that a question was asked in Parliament about the success of economic enterprises in the African reserves, since these might compete with white farmers—a different point from the influence of earnings at home on the flow of Zulu laborers. To which the Minister of Native Affairs replied that they were only teaching tribal Africans to grow crops which it had been proved whites could not grow economically.

Hence my observations showed that at least on the surface white government officers, working in the reserves, moved into positions where they appeared to stand, even if covertly, against the major policies of the white people, if not of the white government, in the interests of the Zulu whom they administered. I have deliberately said "appeared to stand, even if covertly . . . ," because I was not in a position to examine what went on at government headquarters. It may have been the policy of the Native Affairs Department, at that period, to encourage home production in the reserves; and concealment of any success in that effort may have been from the Cabinet as a whole, as well as from parliamentarians representing farming interests lest these maintain that they were threatened both by competition in agricultural products and by the falling off in the flow of laborers when money could be earned by Africans at home. This was a period, we must note, when the government began to prevent Zulu going to the cities unless they had been offered jobs. The answer of the Minister of Native Affairs, quoted above, which looks either as if he were deceived or as if his department was not deeply concerned about African interests, may well have been a skillful equivocation, approved by him, to still fears among, and anticipate attacks from, the whites. In short, in 1936 to 1938—the period of the planned large-scale purchase of Native Trust Land and of Native Development under Hertzog—it may have been possible for government officers to express their professional values in good administration and even development, as well as their undoubted personal interest in the people for whom they were responsible. Later general national pressures prevented the carrying out and implementing of the 1936 Hertzog policies.

I spent much time with government officers, and I was deeply impressed with the extent to which they held to a "professional ethic," if I may phrase it thus. I observed this in formal discussions with Native Commissioners who were much senior to me in age, and it was marked in my much more informal talks with technical officers of around my age with whom I was on the friendliest terms since my entrée to them was through old schoolfellows. In many situations, I saw this professional ethic expressed. In a society where there is a great fear of sexual attacks by black men on white women, this ethic emerged most vividly in a case where the daughter of a poor white, working on the road, alleged that an educated Zulu clerk had proposed in a letter that they have sexual relations. Some of the whites talked of tarring and feathering him, even of lynching [12] him; and the police were sufficiently concerned to have other whites sounded out to ask for support in protecting their prisoner. These other whites were convinced of the Zulu's innocence. The man was charged with *crimen injuria;* and the magistrate trying the case discharged the accused on the grounds that no offense was disclosed, even had he sent the note—and the magistrate doubted its authenticity. The leader of the whites who talked of tarring and feathering was a man prominent in the Nationalist Party; and the magistrate told us that he was sure this man would ruin his career, but he could not bring himself to make a decision against the law. (I have heard that his career was not affected.) Here is an instance of that professional juristic ethic which has so markedly influenced South African judges through a series of treason trials, so that operating within laws which increasingly restrict the expression of any opposition to the policy of apartheid, they have thrown out indictments and discharged accused, even when politically their sympathies lay with the government.

There are, in my judgment, many different ways of analyzing the complexities of social life. At some levels of analysis, it may be profitable to generalize in highly abstract terms about the incorporation of different ethnic groups in a plural society, as M. G. Smith has done,[13] or to extract seven very wide general principles as van den Berghe has done. These abstract formulations may be of different kinds, as shown in several essays in this symposium, and each kind of formulation may be illuminating in giving us understanding in a different way. There is no single best approach to the problem; and each approach covers different relations between the observed phenomena. I myself prefer an approach which attempts to comprehend the complexity of interaction within a social field such as I have sketched by incidents I observed in Zululand, incidents which show how each personage tends to be the focus of pressures of various kinds, and himself by his actions sets in train varied and often contrary processes of further interaction. In these circumstances, when one comes to examine a specific area within the total field of a so-called plural society, I consider that theories of "consensus" and "conflict," as delineated in the introductory essay by Kuper to set the theme of discussion and in the essay by van den Berghe, are not sufficiently refined. In the Zululand field consensus and lack of consensus, within Zulu and white groups and between them, are present at different levels, and at each level in different situations. There is no such thing as overall "consensus" in any social field of interaction. Again, "conflict" is present in varying degrees in different situations. But above all I feel that we need to distinguish "consensus" of various kinds from "conflict" of various kinds by building up a more complicated vocabulary; and I feel I must say that this is something the essays in this book do not attempt to do systematically. Before I proceed with my own analysis, I must essay to develop such a more systematic vocabulary.

In order to present my data and the shaping of my analysis I have written so far in terms of "conflict," "cohesion," and "contradiction," of values and goals and wants, as I did in my early analyses of Zululand. I put forward a more complex vocabulary in the first version of this essay. After the discussion of that vocabulary, both at Los Angeles and with my colleagues at Manchester, I now propose something even more complex. Dr. Martin Southwold has helped me considerably in the following formulations.[*]

We need a series of words to refer both to the observable interactions of persons in their varied roles and of groups, and to refer to ranges and levels of societal interdependence. English has a fair number of words that we can employ thus. I propose to stipulate that I shall specialize different words for different purposes. Immediately, I note that in English there are many more words to describe clashes between persons than to describe collaboration between them. We can therefore use "work with," "help (aid, assist, succor)," "depend on," to describe observable interaction, with "cooperate" as a general word to describe them all; against forms of cooperation stand "argue," "dispute," "quarrel," "fight," "contend," "compete," "riot," "strike," "war," while in noun form we can add "disturbance," all covered by the general word "strife." I shall use these words to cover observable action and presumed associated motivation. On the descriptive level of ideology we can generally speak of "agree" and "disagree." Dr. Southwold has urged on me that when we move to first-order abstractions from observable reality we must distinguish between the ideas that people have about what is occurring in their relationships, and the relations that we as social scientists abstract from

---

[*] My succeeding formulations attempt to take note of the discussions at Los Angeles and Manchester.

our observations. I shall use *consensus* and *dissensus* as polar types to refer to agreement or disagreement between particular persons on a goal or value or closely associated set of goals or values. *Coherence* and the neologism *discoherence* are polar types to cover whether all goals and values, and held views of what the society is like, are considered to be compatible with one another.

When we come to look at the patterns of relations which we as analysts abstract from our observations we need first to distinguish between *motivation* and *social interest*. In my essay, and at the seminar, I spoke of whites and Zulu having common interests in peace and in low maternal and infant mortality rates, and I said too that managers and workers have a common interest in a factory or mine working and producing. At a later seminar, which I did not attend, my argument was further criticized.* One person argued that it was specious to say that workers have this common interest with managers. Workers go to work to earn wages. I consider that to make this criticism is, in sociological or social anthropological analysis, to commit the error of "psychologism." The motives that induce people to do certain things are not the same as the complex of social interests which their actions serve: this is clear from the sociological analysis of ritual or rules of exogamy, for example. Nevertheless, I believe that a common or shared social interest must be demonstrated in the actions of persons. The interest of English workers in factory and mine developed when Luddism ceased, and when striking workers did not damage the machines or plant on which the productive process depended. The manner in which, for example, striking miners keep essential services going expresses their common interest with mine owners and managers in the mine. It is significant that though the Zambian (formerly Northern Rhodesian) Copperbelt mines were opened in the late twenties, and some closed down in the depression of 1931 before reopening in 1933, in 1935 and 1940 the plant and machinery were not attacked by striking African miners who concentrated their assaults on personnel offices.[14] Apparently in 1935 essential services were kept going. In the 1940 strike at three mines on the first day "the smelter staff were called to work to prevent damages to the furnaces through their going out"; but on the next day the smelter shifts were threatened by other workers and they were no longer called out. (Note that in 1926 British steelworkers did not join in the general strike because if the furnaces went out, it would take months to repair them.) Clearly, then, by 1940 African miners at all mines did not appreciate the consequences of not keeping the smelting furnaces working, for, according to the

---

* I was sent the tape recording of this seminar, covering the final discussion of the whole symposium, and found it most useful.

District Commissioner's description [15] of the first day of a strike in 1952 at a mine, "no one came to work except for a handful of essential service workers." Yet though the maintenance of essential services was written into an agreement with the African Mineworkers' Union, when a more militant leadership was elected at one mine in 1954, it called "a strike of all African employees, including essential servicemen, which lasted nearly a week." [16] Recognition of common interest was demonstrated in these events, but not always observed, since miners were aware of these interests in varying degrees. Yet Epstein in his masterly analysis of Copperbelt history in *Politics in an Urban African Community* (1958, pp. 132–133) was able to write that in 1935 and 1940

conceivably, the Africans might have taken to smashing machinery as an expression of resentment against the new system, just as the Luddites had done at a corresponding period of Industrial Revolution of England.

Significantly, they did not do this. By their behavior on these occasions they showed that they were not protesting against an industrial system as such; they were complaining of the position accorded to them within the system.

He then points out that there was, however, an important historical difference. In England production was being moved from cottages into factories; in Central Africa, workers from a traditional subsistence economy were moving into highly developed industry which gave them new wealth.

Acceptance of the industrial system thus involves recognition of an interest in the system. Kuper, in *An African Bourgeoisie* (1965:6), writes in terms similar to mine: "Social relationships extend across racial barriers, weaving complex and varied patterns of interracial contact and creating common interests transcending those of race." The objector at the seminar to the use of "common interests" was prepared to allow "convergent interests": and I would be prepared to accept this, if "common interests" causes confusion. But I feel that one must speak of "common interests" because this emphasizes the high degree of fairly long-term collaboration that establishes systematic interdependence in the economic sphere.[17] "Convergent" seems to me to imply that there is a temporary coming together of interested parties, as among allies like the Soviet Union and the Western powers during the war. African interest in the industrial system of South Africa is not temporary; it is permanent.[18] But out of the common interests between them and whites arise new clashes, as the citation from Epstein above clearly shows.

We therefore need a number of descriptive words for forms of *co-operation,* etc., involving common interest in a system of *collaboration.* At further levels of abstraction we may see collaboration as arising out of *solidarities* and/or the exercise of authority with force at its command.

Against this we need a number of descriptive words for forms of strife leading to clashes within that collaboration. These clashes may arise from straightforward competition between different persons for the same thing. Or they may manifest periodic eruptions of strife out of permanent *struggles* between types of persons, groups, or categories on different sides of a dominant cleavage or subsidiary cleavage in the total system or one of its parts. Struggles may arise out of what I call *conflict* [19] of interest or loyalty or allegiance or value in the system, whenever these conflicts can be resolved by a return to something like the original pattern of social relationships. I am trying here to specialize *struggle* and *conflict* as concepts used as we move more deeply into our analysis of the social system. Both can be used, and have been used, to describe surface interaction; but there are many other words for description, and only struggle and conflict can be given these wider connotations. If the clashes arising out of struggles cannot be resolved by anything like a return to the preceding patterns of social relations, I shall speak of a *contradiction* in interests, values, loyalties, and allegiances.[20] When a cleavage involves a contradiction, it must develop through more forms of struggle.

Despite the development of the dominant cleavage, such as that between whites and Africans in South Africa, the various parts of the polity are linked together in a relatively high interdependence. We may then speak of South Africa as highly articulated. *Articulated* and *unarticulated* are two polar concepts to define the extent to which parts of a system are linked, or not linked, together. (*Unarticulated* is a neologism, since "disarticulated" strictly describes not the state of not being linked together, but "undoing the articulation of," "separating.") If parts of a system are highly articulated, I shall speak of that part as having "cohesion." Some participants at the seminar considered that "cohesion" implies moral approbation. I find no such implication in the dictionary's "tendency to remain united," "force with which molecules cohere"; but "cohesiveness" is a possible substitute.

The crucial purpose of my terminology is to emphasize that it is essential to distinguish between "consensus," as agreement on values and goals, and structural "cohesion," as defining the extent to which the structure of a particular social field is maintained in something like continuous pattern by a variety of factors, such as outright force, and/or economic interdependence, and/or agreement of all the people involved on ultimate goals and their readiness to sacrifice for those goals, and/or the cross-linking of individuals within the total field in terms of a variety of associations and values which prevent most persons from becoming wholeheartedly loyal to one bond and hostile to all other bonds.[21]

Consensus and cohesion are therefore to some extent independent of each other. The distinction can be made most explicitly by emphasizing that one can have, in regard to certain ultimate goals, a very high degree of consensus among the actors in a social field, while the degree of structural cohesion is very low. This seems to be the position in many newly independent African states: the goals of independence, of Pan-Africanism, of some kind of welfare policy, and so on, may be accepted by most of the population and emphasized through a one-party organization. Yet these goals are not realized by consensus: they can be achieved only through industrial and agricultural development leading to what Durkheim called organic interdependence between the segments of new states. This would produce cohesion. On the other hand, there may be in South Africa radical disagreement between various ethnic groups and within them about the goals and values ultimately to be aimed at, so that at *national and provincial, and perhaps city or district, levels,* there is little overall consensus, but structural cohesion may be relatively great, since it emerges at least both from determined use of force by the white government and from the relatively great development of the industrial sector and the farming-for-markets sector. Cohesion arises from high articulation of the parts of a system or subsystem. If cohesion exists in a system where there is also a high degree of consensus, we may speak perhaps of a society with a high degree of *integration.* Integration is lacking where there is cohesion but relatively little consensus, or the consensus exists only within restricted groups.

I am here, I repeat, trying to stipulate that I will use these words in this particular way. I do so because I cannot think of any other suitable words. But I consider that my proposals do not clash with the uses of these words either in other essays in this symposium, or in sociology and social anthropology in general. For example, in his essay ("Pluralism in Precolonial African Societies") M. G. Smith writes: "It is such differences in the modes of corporate organization and articulation within an inclusive collectivity which generate problems of social integration, cohesion, and solidarity, and serve to distinguish pluralities from other societies, whether the latter are institutionally homogeneous or heterogeneous in kind." But he does not define the differences between integration, cohesion, and solidarity, or use them in his analysis; so I feel free to take out "cohesion" and set it, for the purpose of examining degrees of integration, as different from "consensus."

I set these varied terms out in a chart to aid readers. Please note that a spatial representation oversimplifies the complexity of reality. I have to show separately, and apparently opposed, cooperation and strife, when in fact cooperation itself is the source of strife, and certain forms of strife can lead to cooperation. The chart is only a listing of terms, not a substitute for analysis.*

| *Cooperation* (work with, help, etc.) tending to produce *common interests in system of collaboration* which produces either or *solidarities forceful maintenance* (or both) | *Strife* (dispute, fight, etc.) leading to *clashes* based on *struggles* some of which arise out of *conflicts* or *contradictions* present in leading to stable or quantitive shifts slowly in more rapidly changing changing tempo- states rary stasis until of stasis * radical change† (or both) |

These terms are used to describe elements in a system marked (1) *ideologically* by various degrees of participants' agreement or disagreement, including (a) degrees of consensus to dissensus on single or sets of values and goals; and (b) degrees of coherence to discoherence in all values and goals; (2) *analytically* by (a) degrees of cohesion to discohesion in parts of the total system; and (b) degrees of articulation to unarticulation in the relation of parts within the whole system; and (3) *analytically and ideologically* by degrees of consistency and inconsistency in the relation of consensus ↔ dissensus and cohesion ↔ discohesion. High consensus and high articulation produce high consistency and high integration. Low and high consensus with, respectively, high or low cohesion, produce inconsistency and little integration. (I discuss types of equilibrium later.)

I speak therefore of ideological consensus and structural cohesion in parts of the total system. Clearly then consensus and cohesion occur in different areas or in different domains of relationships, and they are present for varying periods of time. We may speak of consensus and cohesion at different levels and for varying runs of time. These remarks apply also to dissensus and lack of cohesion. Above all, consensus between Zulu and whites was mobilized for specific limited purposes in particular situations, while dissensus was manifested in other segregated situations.[22] There were enough, and sufficiently varied, situations of consensus occurring in the articulation of economic and administrative

---

* My thanks here again to Dr. M. Southwold for his help with this vocabulary.

† See Max Gluckman, "The Utility of the Equilibrium Model in the Study of Social Change," *American Anthropologist*, 70 (1968), 219–237. Cf. Godfrey Wilson and Monica Wilson, *The Analysis of Social Change* (Cambridge: The University Press, 1945).

interdependence to produce a fair degree of consistency and integration in Zululand as a whole. Meanwhile, the dominance of the potential force which whites could exercise prevented the Zulu from taking action on the basis of their dissensus from whites. White force was a persistent essential in the cohesiveness of Zululand society.

For example, the relatively few data on Zululand which I have presented in this essay show that there was consensus among the administrative officers and many Zulu on the value of peace within Zulu tribes, and that Zulu and whites were in agreement on the value of the bridge, since it would enable the river to be crossed in flood. Here particularly the bridge led to a hospital noted for its obstetric skill and successes, and both white and Zulu speeches referred to the fact that the bridge would allow expectant mothers to go in safety to the hospital. They were agreed on the importance of reducing maternal and infant mortality, though they might sometimes differ about the means of achieving these ends. I could multiply examples of how Zulu and whites interacted within Zululand, in terms of consensus of several kinds.

It was out of interaction in terms of common interests with related limited consensus that cohesion emerged. Moreover, where migrant labor was important, the office of the government official was essential to the Zulu if communication in many contingencies was to be maintained between Zulu in reserves and their kin in town. Cohesion did not come, in Zululand, solely from the force wielded by whites. Hence my own experience, in Zululand and in three rural areas of Zambia, leads me to disagree profoundly with Davidson's statement in his essay about Zambia: "Nothing appears to have tied these two groupings [of Africans and whites] together except a mutually hateful contiguity from which neither could escape." This is misleading. I agree with him that their interdependence was in "the highest common factor . . . economic," but this is a misleading way of phrasing the high degree of cohesion that emerges from such interdependence. In addition, it leaves out a multiplicity of other factors. By concentrating his analysis on John Chilembwe's rising in Nyasaland in World War I, on the Copperbelt disturbances in 1935 and 1940, and on the rise of the Watchtower sect in the rural areas, Davidson is able with hindsight to look at accumulating resistance to British government rule, and the culmination of the demand for national independence for Malawi and Zambia in protest against the Federation of the Rhodesias and Nyasaland from 1951 onward. But the resistance to the proposed federation began as a demand to remain under the British Colonial Office and as a fight against Southern Rhodesian and settler domination. Only by about 1957 did the aim shift to a demand for independence. This was about seventy years after the British South

Africa Company became established in the region. There were thirty-six years between John Chilembwe's rising and the establishment of the federation. If one is to understand processes of development, one should look also at what prevents immediate disruption of ties and interaction at any period, and not concentrate only on disturbances,[23] let alone telescope these into a continuous clash when they occur many years apart. For from the time in the 1880's to 1890's when British rule was established in "Malawi" and "Zambia," there developed some articulation of the whole, and a fair degree of cohesion in the parts. These constellations were secured partly by the deployment and threat of British force. But there was also mutual accommodation of members of different ethnic groups within the industrial sector, and a linking of this sector to tribal areas which supplied it mostly with labor and to a lesser degree with food. In the rural areas there developed a high degree of consensus between Africans and white officials. Of course, this operates in the total limits of the system. Very few commissioners, if any, have joined the Africans in open rejection of the system, and Africans do not expect them to do so. A few have done so in the British territories.

This statement has been validated by considerable research in Central Africa as well as South Africa. The Barotse cooperated in most situations with the British authorities. Maybe the protection afforded by their treaty underpinned this cooperation. But I found also considerable consensus on certain values, as well as much cohesion, among the Plateau Tonga who complained openly that land had been taken from them for white farmers. They spoke as often, and gratefully, of how the whites had saved them from the constant raids of Barotse and Ndebele. Among the Lamba, where some colleagues and I worked at a time when resettled villagers were bitter about compulsory agricultural regulations, there were also these elements of consensus; they emerged clearly when I described to them the experiments the Agricultural Department was conducting in order to develop a sorghum which would, homesick crop though it is, flourish in their land. Even the descendants of the great conquering Zulu armies only occasionally looked back with regret to the days when as raiding warriors they terrorized other tribes; they recalled as often the terror and uncertainty in their lives and spoke approvingly of the peace and of some types of security brought by the white government.

In the rural areas there may not have been, to paraphrase Davidson, a mutual tying together of the two whole groupings of Africans and whites, on top of mutual contiguity maintained by force, because this kind of tying together of groups occurs in no social field. The tying together consisted of acceptance by tribesmen of many advantages which they saw emerging from the white sector of the society, including material goods, internal peace and protection, education, better medicine, and the like. These gave rise to wants among Africans, and missionaries and administrative officers urged them to satisfy these wants. In addition, in each tribe there were specific groups and persons who turned increasingly to white culture and to relations with white patrons for what they valued. Monica Wilson (née Hunter) in Pondoland (*Reaction to Conquest*, 1936), and Mayer in his study of *Townsmen or Tribesmen* (1961), have shown how decisions, some taken over a century earlier, had largely cut off the schooled people from their pagan neighbors and linked them to whites. I found in Zululand that the division was less marked: Christian and pagan kin still dealt with one another, and Christian kin were the means by which many white influences were introduced to the pagans. Above all, both Hilda Kuper among the Swazi (*The Uniform of Colour*, 1947), and I among the Zulu, found that to understand how the system worked, it was quite inadequate to think in terms of overall attitudes like hatred and rejection: one had to break interaction and separation of whites and tribesmen into several domains or subsystems, in which inconsistent and often contradictory attitudes could be manifested by the same people in different types of situations.[24] By different values and aims the Zulu shifted their allegiances from white officials or missionaries to chiefs and other traditional personages.[25] Attachment in the towns to trade-union organizers was becoming important, and among the Zulu in 1936–1938 these were being called into national councils.

Cohesion can therefore exist in several ways, and so can consensus. We derive these from watching persons collaborate in cooperation by associating, working together, linking themselves together, accepting loyalties to varied persons and goals: these are the terms I am using to describe the course of interaction from which we must extract deeper "solidarities" which may or may not feed into consensus and cohesion. On the other hand, out of collaboration itself come dispute, dissension, argument, disagreement, fights and riots, competition, war—these and other words of similar type describe the actual disturbances in the social field which are presented to our observation. As we try to analyze them we find that they arise from straightforward clashes of interest on occasion. Often they arise from conflicts in terms of varied values, varied goals, and varied types of association. In tribal societies, with their stationary technoeconomies, conflicts of this kind are often established by custom and validated by mystical belief: they break into the hegemony of largely self-subsistent groups which are linked little by the organic interdependence of utilitarian economic ties, to create elaborate cross-links which make societal life possible.[26] Conflicts in modern Zululand arise from attachments through a series of situations to different goals, many of which can be achieved only through collaboration with whites. These conflicts in values and allegiances prevented Zulu manifesting, save in talk and in rare situations of action, wholehearted resentment against the dominant whites. Similar conflicts operated on some whites, as we have seen, so that government officials were moved by their professional ethic [27] to stand against the immediate interests and even values of the major part of the white group, and possibly even against the government they represented.

In commenting on my argument at the seminar, Mr. Bellman and Mr. Meyer argued * searchingly that in acting in this way government officials were in fact pursuing the deeper level and long-term interests of the policy of differential incorporation (M. G. Smith) on which white domination is based. They pointed out that I myself had argued (see below, pp. 397–398) that the tribal land is essential to maintenance of the tribal system and to the manner in which that system is articulated into the South African economy through the movement of Zulu laborers to white-owned mines, industries, and farms. Furthermore, I had argued that the government's policy was to allow only those laborers to move who had jobs in the urban areas. Therefore, to quote Bellman, "the action of the Native Commissioner was based probably on considerations . . . [of] the best interests of the state, for he realized that the breakdown of the traditional system would mean the possible breakdown of the plural society to which he belonged. . . . The colonial administrator is hired to maintain the system of native reserves, a requisite for the plural society, and so he develops a policy by which this can be done. The white farmers and the mining interests, on the other hand, are not directly concerned with these reserves and do not need to be conscious of their implications to the plural structure of the society. These mineowners and farmers demand that their work needs be met, even if it goes against the policy of the colonial administrator." Then the Commissioner who tried to protect his cattle sales, and the Agricultural Officer who tried to protect his creameries, would in fact have been operating to maintain the system as a whole. Meyer's example was that similarly the Assistant Native Commissioner who gave a just decision on the alleged *crimen injuria* assault was maintaining Zulu respect for the law as a whole, including the enforcement of laws which marked the subordinate status of Zulu.

At the seminar I argued that these officials, in their statements and actions, in no way exhibited awareness of these long-term interests for

---

* I have put their arguments summarily in my own words.

the maintenance of the rural areas and of the subordination of Africans within the South African plural society. Later, when I was considering the difference between social interests and individual motivation, discussed above, I realized that I was in danger of committing the error of "psychologism" in sociological analysis to which I have referred. As I say, Bellman's and Meyer's arguments are searching. But I also feel that there is a danger in postulating that policies serve long-term interests in a manner concealed from the actors. In Marxist argument, if the bourgeoisie "exploit" the proletariat, it is in their interests; if they grant concessions in wages and welfare, it is because they see their long-term interests. The British bourgeoisie particularly have been credited with farsightedness here. Yet I feel it is dangerous if we argue that persons serve their own interests, on different runs of time, both when they follow one course of action and when they follow an opposite course of action. Analysis then tends to become a system of political beliefs, defended by secondary elaboration of belief. That is why I have stated that "common interests" exist only if the actors show in statement and action that they are aware of these. I cannot make up my mind on this point, because I lack data on what went on between local officials and the higher echelons of political organization and administration. Hence I can only note Bellman's and Meyer's problems for future research in quite different domains of relationships from those I studied. Clearly, some maintenance of the reserves as productive areas was essential for the South African system, and is increasingly so. But the actors themselves, on my observations, felt that they were acting in defiance of general opinion among the whites of South Africa. This undoubtedly affected their relationships with Zulu, for consensus was established between them and Zulu and this led to a degree of local cohesion within Zululand. However, it seems appropriate here to note, as I have in earlier publications, that some Zulu on some occasions when they were stating their fear of, and opposition to, whites, said that though the cattle sales brought them higher prices, the ultimate effect would be that they would sell most of their cattle and cease to be a nation. Cattle are, of course, of crucial importance for many of their institutions. Zulu ideology in terms of both their traditional culture and their suspicion of whites led them to construe here, as in other matters, actions by the government which appeared to be in their interests, as eventually being against their interests. As one put it: "Whites treat Blacks as they do fish. At first they throw meat into the water and the fish eat it. It is good. The next day there is a hook in it." I saw others hold their hands apart—"A White project is like this and then" (switching their hands round) "we learn what is behind it." [28] On the long-run view, the Zulu agree with Bellman and Meyer.

Here it might be profitable to distinguish between "common interests" and "convergent interests." Clearly in the 1930's it was in the interests of the Chamber of Mines, responsible for the Witwatersrand gold mines and other mines, that the tribal reserves be able to provide some subsistence for the migrant African miners' families. This enabled them to pay lower wages than they would have had to pay if the mining wage had provided the whole support for African miners' families. The mines defended these low wages on the grounds that while high-grade ores could carry higher labor costs, these costs would have made it unprofitable to mine low-grade ores, which were the main ores, and indeed some mines would have been put out of operation. They argued that the whole industrial complex of the Witwatersrand, and the South African economy, depended on the extent of gold mining. It was also argued that if there were to be another depression, it was advisable that the Africans should be able to fall back on their tribal lands. These provided insurance against the insecurities of the world's mining and industrial system. Let me say at once that I do not accept these arguments. But given that the migrant-labor system was seen by the mines as essential to the pattern of the South African economy, it was a necessary part of that essentiality that the tribal areas should be able to provide laborers. Hence in the mid-1930's, when over one-third of recruits for mining in the Transkei were rejected on medical grounds, the Chamber of Mines offered the South African government £10,000,000 for the development of the area. The government rejected the offer, stating this was the government's business! (The discovery of the sulphonimides, enabling the mines to recruit from north of 22 degrees south latitude, eased their labor problem.)

If any system is established, many participants develop varied interests in its working. It was Engels who stressed that slaves had an interest in the system of slavery. I consider therefore that it is not enough to say that the whole policy served only to supply the mines with cheap labor, though I feel strongly that it did that and that this was the basis of mining policy. (But we have to note that in Northern Rhodesia in 1944 a majority of government officials, many deeply concerned for African interests, voted against stabilizing labor on the mines and in towns because they were terrified of what another depression might do, if the one product, copper, fell in value.) Within the South African system, the mines paid more than white farmers did. The Zulu themselves were interested in the system of periodic migration to labor and back, which had become established after their defeat by the British. They wished to reside at home and go out to work: they protested to officials against the new laws which required that they have a job in town before they go there. For they wished to go, earn money (they argued for more money), and then return to their lands which they regarded as their main support. Moreover, they saw in this land the center of their desired way of life, and their hopes; it was the basis of the tribal and family sociocultural systems in which they were involved. I have already argued that the Commissioner and technical officers for various reasons considered that life in the tribal areas, soundly based, was best for Zulu. Hence productivity in the reserves was a convergence of interests between mines, officials, and Zulu; but I suggest there was no development of sense of common interest between Zulu and mine managers in the rural areas, while there was such a development of appreciated common interest, leading to joint action, between officials and at least some Zulu.

Yet even if the Commissioner was serving these long-run interests of the total system, we have to see him as acting by a professional ethic, which is in conflict with the short-run interests of other categories of whites. Therefore, we can see that conflicts within the South African group, like those in the African group, help to maintain cohesion by preventing racial blocks from acting in sharp opposition. Nevertheless, contradictions in the system lead to a slow sharpening of oppositions and solidarities which entail greater and greater potential deployment of force. That force, and the threat of force, are constantly being increased quantitatively in terms of number of police and secret police, number of informers, controlling laws, and so forth, as the dominant cleavage develops. Articulation of all parts of the system is possible only with that force. This original formulation of my principle of the developing dominant cleavage accords with what Bellman and Meyer argued.

Therefore, in terms of the vocabulary I have proposed, I affirm that Zululand in the 1930's exhibited a high degree of cohesion at many levels, and in many situations; and it still does as far as I know. This cohesion arose from the conflicts of allegiance of both Zulu and whites of different types as they pursued often mutually inconsistent goals and lived by discrepant values. I have in this essay shown how this type of conflict of values operated to move the Native Commissioner into a position where his role became an "inter-hierarchical" role as representative of government policy in the larger aspect, and also as representative of the interests of tribesmen. This conflict the Native Commissioner could solve to some extent through the isolation of the areas of administration. There was not a heavy demand at that time for high consensus throughout the administrative system; and the whole Department of Native Affairs was itself involved in conflict over "native policy" since the mere coming of whites to South Africa involved that they bring some of the values of economic and Western "moral" development with them. In my earlier analyses of modern Zululand and political structure, I have examined in even greater detail the interhierarchical role of chiefs.[29] But basic to roles of both these types of officials was the fact that Zululand, as a tribal area, formed a subsystem within the South African state, and that subsystem was a source of considerable satisfaction to most Zulu.

My colleagues and I in Central Africa have here carried out analyses supporting the earlier work of South African anthropologists, including my own work in Zululand.[30] Rural Africans became involved in the developing mining and industrial economy because they had to earn money for taxes, for goods, and for services like education. Most of the tribesmen had to earn this money by migrating for longer or shorter periods to work in white enterprises, mainly in the towns. But they considered that they had little security in their industrial life, and industrial life did not give to many of them the ultimate satisfactions they sought from life. Housing and other difficulties, as well as sentiment, led them to dislike rearing children in the towns, though increasingly many settled in the towns. Houses in towns were often tied to jobs, particularly in Central Africa. There was no provision for unemployment; sickness and accident compensation was very low; and there was inadequate provision of work, or alternatively of pensions, for the old. This insecurity of town and industrial life had been emphasized in the 1930's depression as well as in many other situations. Without security in towns, many, so long as there was land, clung to their tribal affiliation with the security of land to fall back on. In order to operate access to land in rural areas, and to "raid the town for money," as Watson has phrased it for the Mambwe.[31] Zulu maintained their associations within groups of kin, some of whom went out at any one time to earn money, while others remained at home to cultivate the soil and care for cattle as well as wives and children. Some tribes seem to have organized this deployment of men more successfully than others. But all regarded the land as ultimate security and support.

Land here was not an individual item of land which a man owned for himself and by himself. He secured his rights to land in two ways. First, as a citizen of the tribe he was entitled to some arable and building land, and to use of commonage. Second, in all tribes except the widest shifting cultivators, he obtained his rights through membership of a group of kinsmen and/or village. That is, a man's rights to land in his tribal home depended on his accepting membership of a tribe, with all its obligations, as well as its rights. This involved his participating in a working system of social relationships, economic, political, and domestic.

It has to be stressed that the migrant laborer moves not only between two places with different modes of production, consumption, and the like, but also between two distinct types of social system. The tribal system is one which has its own goals and values, even though some of these are radically changed from the traditional past. Here the migrant laborer on his return home can become again, more than in the towns, a man with a variety of roles, with clear affiliations to others, and with culturally approved goals. He can marry, raise children, and acquire satisfaction and prestige there. He can seek prestige within the tribal political system, or in other domains of its total system. All anthropologists must have had something like the following experience. Once, after I had visited Johannesburg from Zululand, I drove back with me two young Zulu ricksha pullers. They came with their bundles, and dressed in rags. One lived in the village that was my base. That night after we arrived, he sat in my hut, with all his father's wives and their children, and other distant kin. He boasted of his adventures in the town, including brushes with the oppressive police. But his proudest moment came when he unpacked his cases and began to distribute his gifts to father, mother, mother's co-wives, full and half siblings. He brought out the money he had earned and discussed its allocation with his father: so much for this purpose and for that, and above all so much toward the marriage payment for the bride he would seek. Next day he dressed in war dress and went dancing over the hills seeking for that bride: he had moved into a system of social relationships full of satisfactions.

That system can offer satisfactions of this kind provided that two sets of circumstances continue. The first clearly is that there should continue to be enough land to support the migrant laborer and his family. The second is that expansion of the industrial sector allows him to migrate there to earn money.

If the land lasts and is sufficient, the tribal system as an organized set of political and social relationships can endure and provide satisfaction; and the white administrators and technical officers, and missionaries, and even traders and recruiters, can be drawn into the several levels of consensus in the social field. The migrant laborers brought money and goods back into the system in return for having their claims to its land, and thereby to a position in its society, preserved. Hence it is not surprising that (according to a survey I made first in 1943), as land became short, the right most emphasized in these societies was the right of every subject to some building and arable land. The right of members within smaller groups to some of the land of those groups was similarly emphasized.[32] As pressure on the land increased with increase of population, following often on restriction of tribal territory as land had been taken for white settlers, chiefs tended to take over unused land already allotted, which was not being worked, after a short period of rest. At this

stage, land was becoming short under the prevailing system of cultivation. The ultimate end of the process was found in Basutoland where
each married man was entitled to only three small fields. Most of these
developments were reported from South Africa and the British Protectorates, but I detected the germs of similar developments in a few scanty
reports in Northern Rhodesia. But I overlooked a statement by Hilda
Kuper in her *Uniform of Colour* (1947:11) about Swaziland that "pressure on land aggravates antagonism within a principality. A chief who
did not distribute his land with any equity, but retained the best plots,
even though they were not used, for his family and favourites, was
publicly censured by his council. Many chiefs endeavour to be fair, and
are guided by the opinion of their advisers."

Moreover, reports from this south central African region which are
now coming in, twenty years later, indicate that wherever possible the
major development is in the same main direction as I outlined, though
there are additional complications. In an article on "Effects on the Xhosa
[of South Africa] and Nyakyusa [of Tanganyika] of Scarcity of Land"
(1963), Professor Monica Wilson concludes that in both these tribes "the
attitude . . . is still that the use of land for cultivation and grazing is a
right to which every man is entitled and in practice they criticize any
individual who lays field to field and leaves his brother landless." In the
Xhosa tribal reserves the area of land for each man is officially restricted,
by village headman and white Native Commissioner. Where some families
had been settled many years ago on freehold and quitrent farms, they or
their descendants have tended to accommodate landless relatives; but
lending and leasing of land, and particularly sharecropping, are widely
practiced. The Xhosa's main source of income is labor migration.[33]

The Nyakyusa have developed cash-cropping on richer land in ancient
craters, but even this land is not yet leased or sold, though Wilson
believes these transactions will soon become common. Wilson says that
the effect of land shortage has been to stop the redistribution of land
periodically as new villages of coevals were established, and to make all
land inheritable in the agnatic line, as the rich crater land always was.
Men are more tied to old villages, there is less movement, and whereas
formerly villages tried to attract new members, they now no longer do so.
Land is not so freely lent. Quarrels can no longer be settled by sections of
villages or individuals moving away. But generally the stress is still on
the rights of all men, and presumably women, to land for their support,
though not necessarily to land that will carry the cash crops. Migration of
men to labor centers keeps the system going.

In Xhosaland in South Africa many married men cannot obtain fields
and are left landless. Mr. Basil Sansom has recently studied a similar

situation in one Pedi chieftaincy in the Northern Transvaal.[34] He has not yet published his analysis, but he has allowed me to summarize his findings of a type of social development not reported from any other tribe. The chief has endeavored to maintain the principle that each married woman is entitled to a tract of land to produce food for her household. But the chief has not been able to ensure that a second category of land, in which title is held by men, is equitably distributed. Technically, title to land cannot be gained or relinquished without the chief's approval. However, wealthy men "borrow" and work the land of poorer tribesmen. A poor man in debt to a wealthy man may virtually surrender his land to his creditor. In this way some men in the chiefdom are able to build up large holdings in "men's land" to the detriment of the holdings of others: they emerge as a set of "land brokers," manipulating debts and land as much for social power and prestige as for monetary gain, since the main source of Pedi income is labor migration. No traditional authorities have entered into these pursuits, and the chief apparently turns a blind eye toward them.

Only one study, by Jaspan of a small tribal reserve in southern Natal in the Republic of South Africa, carried out in the mid-1940's, suggests that a chief in this region of South and Central Africa has tried to gain land at the expense of his subjects. Jaspan states that the chief began to compete with his subjects for land from early on. The chief possesses more livestock than any of his subjects. Eventually some brought a suit against him: they claimed that he had used his official position unlawfully to monopolize the grazing rights in a government-trust farm where grazing is restricted by proclamation. "Part of the reaction of the Chief to this unprecedented act of opposing him at a supratribal level was to accuse the leaders of the 'opposition' and their sympathizers of attempting to destroy him by sorcery and witchcraft. The Chief has for many years steered clear of the district in whch the 'opposition' is centered; he neither eats nor drinks, nor attends any ceremonies or meetings there." Jaspan's implicit contention seems to be that land shortage in this reserve has reached a point where the whole traditional system must break down. The chief cannot even begin to meet his obligations to his subjects. The reserve is so severely denuded of fertility that in many respects it is a reserve residence for men working in white towns, with most of the men absent at any one time. The chief, facing the competition of better-educated men for prestige, maintains his wealth at the expense of his subjects. It is the only report I know of a chief acting thus.[35] In short, so long as there is land, the tribal system can work and give satisfactions, drawing whites in the area into the achievement of those satisfactions. If the land becomes too short, the tribal system will break down, and with it will disappear the satisfactions it grants. An increasingly amorphous mass of peasants, akin to those described for southern Italy by Carlo Levi in *Christ Stopped at Eboli*, will emerge. The peasants will begin to develop new forms of association, either forming political groups pursuing their interests, or entering more chiliastic forms of religious cults.[36]

The second change in circumstances which will alter this type of cohesion, and the articulation of the tribal area with the town, is if the central government forbids tribesmen to move from the relatively impoverished areas into the richer industrial sector to earn money. The rural area alone probably can no longer give adequate satisfactions. I am analyzing elsewhere [37] my own full view of how I would conceive of the sociological problems of plural societies. Here I must say, all too briefly, that I consider that though sociologists recognize as basic the cohesion that arises from economic development, some of them nevertheless tend to lose sight of its implications. I have already said that relatively high economic development in South Africa, compared with the rest of Africa, gives it far more cohesion, and hence what we may call stability of personnel in political offices (even if force is more manifestly repressive), than newer African states seem to have. There is an inherent instability in any society in which vertical divisions between territorial and/or ethnic segments are inadequately crossed by the development of links of organic (in Durkheim's sense), utilitarian, economic interdependence. Without that interdependence, civil war is endemic in the system. In simpler organizations, before the development of the state, civil war may take the form of permanent states of feud between segments; and in segmentary states (Southall) a similar situation, emerging from simple tools of production, simple consumption goods, simple means of communication, and simple weapons, is marked either by the irruptions of segments out of the state or by rebellious war around the kingship. As the economy develops in more highly stratified systems, with the development of more varied standards of living, larger capitals emerge with greater trade and the development of a city aristocracy. Then two other forms of strife are found. First, there may be peasant risings in addition to the struggle of aristocrats for power. Second, some of the peasants are attracted to the cities or proto-cities, and form a city mob, whose support the competing elites have to woo.[38] Not all "riots" start from the city mob, but it is a recruiting ground for rioting and can aggravate protest marches and the like. We know this situation from classical and medieval times. It will tend to develop in modern times wherever there is a numerous, relatively poor, peasantry, and the city economy does not develop rapidly enough to absorb the influx from their ranks. The South African government has prevented this development with draconic measures and ruthless application of the law: since 1938 only those Africans have been allowed in the cities who are necessary for the urban economy. As van den Berghe points out, the employed are committed to the industrial system. In his *Tribalism and the Plural Society* (1960), Mitchell analyzes how the African population in a Central African town is woven into a kind of society by the intricate ties, as well as conflicts of loyalty, between various members. L. Kuper, in *An African Bourgeoisie* (1965),[39] analyzes the similar situation in South Africa. He also brings out, as he emphasizes in his summary introductory statement, that

The races do not confront each other as solid antagonistic blocks. Cooperation and interdependence are more marked than conflict and separation. Social relationships extend across racial barriers, weaving complex and varied patterns of interracial contact and creating common interests transcending those of race. Even the policy of racial segregation, by virtue of its inner contradictions, forges new links and new mechanisms of integration.

Shared privileges and common domination do not guarantee the unity of the rulers. There is an uneven distribution of power among the members of the ruling White group . . . [pp. 5–6 ff.].

The major danger to political stability probably resides in the unemployed and the unemployable. If the cities cannot continue to provide for the migrant laborers from the tribal areas, I believe that here there will be a major cause of political disturbance, and if it is added to increasing land degradation in the tribal areas, these are likely to be the foci of major discontent. Consensus and cohesion within them will weaken, and the articulations linking them into the total system will disappear. Only force will be left. Urban African workers may well form an elite as against the poor peasants of their own ethnic group, even though urban Africans will provide leaders resisting the domination of the whites, as elites everywhere provide some leaders in revolts. But these leaders will be a small proportion of all urban Africans, just as some whites out of the whole white population side with the Africans.

We can now look at the other African states by contrast. Their inadequate industrial development will leave them as unstable polities in terms of personnel in office, even after the withdrawal of the colonial powers. Despite high consensus arising from the struggle for independence, cohesion will be inadequately developed. These governments cannot be as ruthless with their own peasants coming into the cities as is the South African government. There will be city mobs (restricted in numbers in South Africa) who consider themselves underprivileged, and who are likely often to become unemployed. The mob will be an effective force which will have to be cajoled by the military who control the other form of forceful power since weapons are now complex. In South Africa and in colonial regimes military and police were necessarily loyal to their governments; in independent African states they are potential competitors for power with the governments. The rural areas will remain underdeveloped, and be foci of discontent as in South Africa. Because of the demand for high consensus to the state and the party, representatives of the party and the state are less likely to become representatives of the interests of rural areas against the center than was even the South African native commissioner. Their ethic will be that of the party, and not of the profession. Because consensus is high, slight deviations will be regarded as serious issues (as formulated by Durkheim and Simmel). Again, consensus may appear to be high, while cohesion in local areas will not be well developed.

In conclusion, I return to the problem of "equilibrium" which I raised in presenting my chart of analytic terms. Ever since I began to study the course of institutional development in the history of Zululand, from before the rise of Shaka through conquest by the British into the 1930's, I have found it necessary to adopt the view that Zulu history has to be seen in terms of a series of equilibria which, when they change radically, do so fairly rapidly. An original equilibrium of many small tribes lasted for at least four centuries, despite many clashes and divisions of tribes. Over this period I therefore have written, redundantly, but for emphasis, of a "repetitive equilibrium." I argue that increase of population beyond the point of critical density disrupted that equilibrium. A relatively short period followed in which dominant tribes began to conquer their neighbors to set up larger polities than had existed earlier. Suddenly, over a period of eight years or so, the tempo of development accelerated as Shaka established the Zulu kingdom in wars which solved the land crisis. This was over by 1824.[40] The British victory in the war of 1879–80 led to eight years of internecine Zulu fighting, in a new temporary period of equilibrium, with British goodwill and potential support powerful factors. The establishment of British rule in 1887–88 created a new social system. Equilibrium of a kind was rapidly established as common interests between rulers and ruled developed, and new associations emerged.[41] But this was a changing equilibrium with constant alterations in numbers and powers of existent social elements and the emergence of new types of associations and personages. Nevertheless, I feel we have to call it an equilibrium because major elements in the system are constant: control of force by the whites, Zulu seeking work and help from the whites in increasing collaboration, and the continued existence and indeed development of the dominant cleavage. By the 1930's this equilibrium was relatively stable: change was slow. It has persisted, I believe, to the present in its main alignments.

I have argued in a lecture delivered to a plenary session of the American Anthropological Association in November 1966, shortly after the seminar at Los Angeles considered this essay, that the conception of some kind of stasis for periods of different length in at least some domains of relationships is essential if one is to develop an analysis of *institutions*, in terms allowing any kind of generalization. When a state of stasis is seriously disrupted, we move into periods of rapid change, when we may be able to write only narrative history. Then we seek other kinds of generalizations. For a fuller analysis of my view of the utility of equilibrium models I have to refer readers to my early essays and to this more developed lecture.[42] Here I can only conclude by saying that I recognize that in some sense all social situations are marked by change. But changes vary in their nature. Some are repetitive, some are radical. Our dilemma is that the more the detail in which we describe change, the less we grasp the structure of social relations; the more we grasp that structure, the more change and movement elude us. This is the principle of sociological indeterminacy equivalent to Heisenberg's principle of indeterminacy in physics. In this paper I have tried to grasp the structure of one sociogeographic field (Fortes) [43] within the plural society of South Africa. That structure exhibited the characteristics of at least a temporary equilibrium, and it can be analyzed only in terms of an equilibrium model. I have indicated also where change was occurring. On the short run, in terms of the lesson W. M. Macmillan taught me, we must see the equilibrium; and only if we see this equilibrium, in the 1930's, in relation to earlier and later equilibria, can we understand the total process of movement. I consider, as I have argued above, that, for example, Davidson's emphasis mainly on the long-run process has obscured the social alignments and forces, and therefore the complex movements, which characterized the plural society of Northern Rhodesia, and later of Zambia.

Something of the same kind of equilibrium in its main alignments and articulation seems to have persisted in Zululand to the present day. But if there has not been what I call radical change, there have been substantial structural changes. Some of these are measurable in quantitative terms, such as increasing deployment of force. Chiefs seem more divided in how far they support and oppose government, and the type of commissioners and their relations with people may well have altered. I have heard of only two outbreaks that might be called attempts at "revolts," both very small. As one might have expected from the greater land crisis, the situation in the Transkei has been transformed more radically, partly by greater impoverishment of the soil, but mainly by the establishment of industries on the borders close to the reserves, in which workers have been settled on inadequate land. Major land impoverishment seems to have produced there the "Peasants' Revolt," to take the title of Govan Mbeki's book (1964). Chiefs and councillors are there divided more sharply in the extent to which they serve, or oppose, the government than were the chiefs I knew in Zululand in the 1930's. This also reflects their much greater involvement in what is happening in nationwide South African developments. All this is clearly brought out in Mayer's most stimulating article, "The Tribal Elite and the Transkeian Elections of 1963" (1966), which shows the complexities that have to be taken into account. Commissioners, whatever they feel, insist on the imposition of government policy against revolting Africans or even protesting Africans. In other reserves in South Africa, also, there have been revolts. As I say, the movement of revolt is seemingly not so sharply developed in Zululand.

What I have given for Zululand in the 1930's is a type of analysis which I hope brings out the complexities of interaction in an area of a total politico-geographic field where ultimate articulation depends on force, but where there are many other collaborative, and hence cohesive, alignments. I consider that to understand a plural society of the South African type, we must take full account of these complexities of interaction and the complicating articulations which produce them and which they in turn establish. Up to the point of radical adjustment or revolution, it is important to study why such adjustment or revolution does not occur, or why attempts at it fail, as well as to stress the long-term course of deepening cleavage. I consider that my cross section of "equilibrium" in Zululand in the 1930's does bring in, and make sense of, more facts than a straightforward overall view of increasing oppositions, which in some long run of time may produce radical change. Even if force keeps the whole South African system going, other factors of cohesion are significant within smaller domains of relationships.

NOTES

[1] Emmanuel Gluckman, *The Tragedy of the Ababirwas and Some Reflections on Sir Herbert Sloley's Report* (Johannesburg: Central News Agency, 1922).

[2] See E. Roux, *Time Longer Than Rope* (London: Gollancz, 1948).

[3] Max Gluckman, "The Kingdom of the Zulu of South Africa," in M. Fortes and E. E. Evans-Pritchard, eds., *African Political Systems* (London: Oxford University Press, 1940), pp. 25–55.

[4] "Cohesion" is defined above, pp. 388–390.

[5] In extended form in Gregory Bateson, *Naven* (Cambridge: The University Press, 1936), but also in earlier articles.

[6] See my opening to my main work on Zululand in the 1930's: "Analysis of a

Social Situation in Modern Zululand," *Bantu Studies* (1940), and "Some Processes of Social Change Illustrated with Zululand Data," *African Studies* (1942), both republished in my *An Analysis of a Social Situation in Modern Zululand* (Manchester: Manchester University Press, 1958).

[7] *Ibid.* See also the conception of equilibrium and disequilibrium in Godfrey Wilson and Monica Wilson, *The Analysis of Social Change* (Cambridge: The University Press, 1945).

[8] W. M. Macmillan, *Bantu, Boer and Briton* (London: Faber and Gwyer, 1928).

[9] Max Gluckman, "Malinowski's 'Functional' Analysis of Social Change," *Africa* (1947), republished in Max Gluckman, *Order and Rebellion in Tribal Africa: Collected Essays* (London: Cohen and West; New York: The Free Press, 1963), pp. 207–234.

[10] This is not merely my own self-praise. Dr. Hilda Kuper at the Los Angeles seminar referred to the "path-breaking" role of these essays. See also J. C. Mitchell's Foreword to the essays reprinted as Rhodes-Livingstone Paper no. 28 (*Analysis of a Social Situation in Modern Zululand*), and L. Faller's review of this reprint in *American Anthropologist*, 61 (1959).

[11] Phyllis Kaberry criticized this use of the term in her introduction to Bronislaw Malinowski's posthumous essay, *The Dynamics of Culture Contact* (New Haven: Yale University Press, 1946).

[12] In fact, there has never been a lynching in South Africa, as far as I know.

[13] Incidentally, I similarly feel that M. G. Smith's analysis of the Barotse kingdom, of many tribes which I studied, does not take sufficient account of the complexity of intertribal relations within the kingdom. Tribal resentment and revolt, among a few of the subjected tribes, I see as somewhat different from differential incorporation.

[14] See *Report of the Commission Appointed to Enquire into the Disturbances in the Copperbelt, Northern Rhodesia* (Lusaka: Government Printer, 1935), par. 133; *Report of the Commission Appointed to Enquire into the Disturbances in the Copperbelt, Northern Rhodesia* (Lusaka: Government Printer, 1940). These are generally discussed in Arnold L. Epstein, *Politics in an Urban African Community* (Manchester: Manchester University Press, 1958), p. 132 n. 2.

[15] Quoted in Epstein, *op. cit.*, p. 95.

[16] Quoted in *ibid.*, p. 141 n. 1.

[17] This is well illustrated in A. K. Rice's study of how he reorganized an Indian factory and secured the collaboration of the workers (*Productivity and Social Organization: The Ahmedabad Experiment* [London: Tavistock Publications, 1958]).

[18] Therefore Zulu objected strongly to regulations that prevented their moving freely to towns in search of work.

[19] See my discussion of this problem in *Custom and Conflict in Africa* (Oxford: Basil Blackwell, 1963), and *Politics, Law and Ritual in Tribal Society* (Chicago: Aldine Publishing Co., 1965). It is, of course, long established in sociological and anthropological work, but I think I emphasize the role of custom more than most.

[20] In this convention, conflicts can be resolved within the pattern of the system; contradictions cannot, but lead steadily to radical change of pattern (see my *Analysis of a Social Situation in Modern Zululand*, pp. 46 f.).

[21] See my *Custom and Conflict in Africa,* and *Politics, Law and Ritual in Tribal Society.*

[22] This problem is discussed fully in my *Analysis of a Social Situation in Modern Zululand.*

[23] Though a disturbance enables one to examine and exhibit much of the social system which is normally concealed from view.

[24] See articles by Hilda Kuper on Swaziland, and by myself on Zululand, in argument with Taylor, a social psychologist analyzing attitudes, in the Johannesburg magazine, *Trek,* vol. 3 (1945).

[25] See my article, "The Kingdom of the Zulu of South Africa," in Fortes and Evans-Pritchard, *op. cit.,* and my *Analysis of a Social Situation in Modern Zululand.*

[26] An important theme in anthropology and sociology which I have discussed (I repeat as others have) more fully in my *Custom and Conflict in Africa* and *Politics, Law and Ritual in Tribal Society.*

[27] See my "Inter-hierarchical Roles: Professional and Party Ethics in the Tribal Areas of South and Central Africa," in M. Swartz, ed., *Local-Level Politics* (Chicago: Aldine Press, 1969).

[28] Cited in context in my *Analysis of a Social Situation in Modern Zululand,* pp. 59–60.

[29] The position of chiefs is set out in my essay, "The Kingdom of the Zulu of South Africa." This section is reprinted in my *Order and Rebellion in Tribal Africa,* where there is also a discussion of the similar position of the village headman in "The Village Headman in British Central Africa" (first published 1949), by J. A. Barnes, J. C. Mitchell, and myself.

[30] See Max Gluckman, "Tribalism in Modern British Central Africa," in Pierre L. van den Berghe, ed., *Africa: Social Problems of Change and Conflict* (San Francisco: Chandler Publishing Co., 1965), first published in 1960. In this essay I summarize this Central African work, and give references to other work.

[31] W. Watson, *Tribal Cohesion in a Money Economy* (Manchester: Manchester University Press, 1958).

[32] For background material to the following historical analysis see Max Gluckman, *Essays on Lozi Land and Royal Property* (Livingstone, Northern Rhodesia, 1943), and *The Ideas in Barotse Jurisprudence* (New Haven: Yale University Press, 1965), chap. iii.

[33] There is a fuller analysis of the situation among the Xhosa in M. E. E. Mills and Monica Wilson, *Keiskammahoek Rural Survey,* vol. 4, *Land Tenure* (Pietermaritzburg: Shuter and Shooter, 1952).

[34] Research in 1963.

[35] M. A. Jaspan, "A Sociological Case Study: Communal Hostility to Imposed Social Change in South Africa," in P. Ruopp, ed., *Approaches to Community Development* (The Hague: W. van Hoeve, 1953), esp. pp. 105–108.

[36] Peter M. Worsley, *The Third World* (London: Wiedenfeld and Nicolson, 1964), examines this problem generally and gives many references. G. Mbeki, *South Africa: The Peasants' Revolt* (Harmondsworth: Penguin Books, 1964), is a graphic and fine analytic account of recent developments, especially in the Transkei, but somewhat molded by a particular political view so that some of what I have called "cohesion" does not appear.

[37] "Tribalism, Ruralism and Urbanism in Plural Societies," in V. W. Turner, ed., *Profiles of Change: The Impact of Colonialism on African Societies* (London: Cambridge University Press, 1969).

[38] The development is sketched in chapter iv of my *Politics, Law and Ritual in Tribal Societies*. See also E. J. Hobsbawm, *Primitive Rebels* (Manchester: Manchester University Press, 1959).

[39] These studies give references to other works.

[40] There are many books on Zulu history. I present my argument set out here in *Analysis of a Social Situation in Modern Zululand*, and more fully in *The Rise of the Zulu Empire* (in press).

[41] I argue, in *Analysis of a Social Situation in Modern Zululand*, that under British rule equilibrium was quickly established, sketch from archives how the equilibrium developed, and define its structure.

[42] "The Utility of the Equilibrium Model in the Study of Social Change," *American Anthropologist*, 70 (1968), 219–237.

[43] As developed in Meyer Fortes, *The Dynamics of Clanship among the Tallensi* (London: Oxford University Press, 1945).

Part IV Conclusions

Introduction to Part IV

Although Part Four is headed "conclusions," no suggestion is intended that we believe its contents to be in the least definitive. The conclusions consist simply of a system of concepts and of some theoretical suggestions and hypotheses relating to pluralism and plural societies, and derived largely from the papers and discussions in the colloquium. They are presented in the hope that they may be of sufficient interest to social scientists to stimulate further research and analysis. M. G. Smith, in "Some Developments in the Analytic Framework of Pluralism," comments on analytic formulations of pluralism, comparable to that of Furnivall; he reviews critiques of Furnivall's concept; and he presents a general theoretical framework for the analysis of pluralism, in terms of the relationships between three levels of pluralism (structural, social, and cultural). Leo Kuper, in "Ethnic and Racial Pluralism: Some Aspects of Polarization and Depluralization," reviews the contributions as they relate to pluralism and the plural society. He emphasizes racial and ethnic pluralism, with which the case studies themselves are concerned, but at the same time he makes use of general concepts for the analysis, in an attempt to develop a framework of much wider applicability than racial and ethnic pluralism. He defines different dimensions of pluralism, conceiving pluralism as a variable, and comments on social conditions affecting its manifestations. Returning to the original problem of the transformation of "plural societies," he emphasizes that, empirically, societies are characterized by a dualism of tendencies, of cleavage and of integration; and he discusses processes of polarization, by which racial and ethnic divisions are accentuated, and processes of racial and ethnic depluralization, by which integration develops either through individuation or through an intervening stage of sectional aggression.

Chapter 13 Some Developments in the Analytic Framework of Pluralism

M. G. Smith

Social science is a mode of institutionalized cooperation. Its theoretical structures are the work of many hands and take form slowly. No sociological perspective of major importance can be elaborated in an appropriate analytical scheme without undergoing continuous development in the process. Even Marx and Weber, whose early work contains the essence of their developed theoretical systems, died after most productive careers, leaving their expositions unfinished or unsystematized.

This general pattern of slow and indirect growth is nicely illustrated by the theory of social pluralism which J. S. Furnivall advanced nearly thirty years ago.[1] Furnivall died in 1960, having delineated the plural society as a specific type, but without having developed its theoretical basis adequately. After his major study of colonialism, his work remained uncultivated for several years. Neither during the period of waning imperialism nor the hurried decolonization that followed were Western scholars attracted to Furnivall's insights; since then, neither can the new rulers of these plural states, nor can sympathetic observers emphasize their plural features without implicitly questioning their viability, cohesion, and status. However, these are merely some of the factors that account for the limited interest in Furnivall's theory; they are not necessarily the decisive ones. Nevertheless, in the absence of the necessary positive response among sociologists, the rich possibilities of this perspective remain undeveloped. In consequence there does not now exist any agreed or systematic body of concepts and analytic propositions which could pass muster as a theory of pluralism or of the plural society. However, several scholars now share a sense of the problem and a consensus that it merits research and study. The variety of alternative approaches to the study of these phenomena is nicely illustrated by various essays in this volume; and the growing literature on pluralism includes several others.[2] Thus we are here concerned rather with problems of sociological perspective which enter into theory construction than with a single consistent scheme of concepts and propositions. To appreciate the open character of these recent advances, it is useful to review briefly the development of sociological interest in problems of pluralism and in their analytic formulation since Furnivall's day. Further, to illuminate the process and direction of this development, it is necessary to consider those features of the original model which tended to promote new orientations during their necessary revision. To this end it is convenient first to indicate the generality of these phenomena and some of the ways in which some sociologists have attempted to formulate them. After this, we may obliquely consider Furnivall's model by examining the most important criticisms leveled against it; and, finally, with due attention to these criticisms and to the many diverse perspectives in this and other publications, we may try to outline an analytic framework for further studies of pluralism which seems to summarize the present state of this inquiry.

I

As Leo Kuper points out,[3] pluralism has several connotations, some of which are apparently opposed. Here we are concerned only with the denotation that corresponds to Furnivall's usage and its subsequent elaboration. Though Furnivall's notion is only one of several alternatives, it is also quite specific and distinctive; and for reasons a sociologist of knowledge may readily appreciate, it has aroused some quite hostile reactions. Whether the thesis would avoid such hostility under another label may be doubted. But clearly Furnivall was not alone in perceiving the structural distinctness of those social combinations he called "plural societies." In identifying the type, in specifying its properties, and in proposing this designation, Furnivall was merely revising and generalizing ideas formulated by the Dutch economist Boeke,[4] who may himself have been influenced by Spencer and other social Darwinians.[5] Using a variety of differing names, several modern writers have also identified the "plural society" as a distinct structural type, describing its major characteristics.

Preferring the term "composite societies," in 1940 Radcliffe-Brown cited South Africa as an example; and while stressing that "the study of composite societies, the description and analysis of the processes of change in them, is a complex and difficult task," [6] he clearly recognized its importance for sociological theory and practical affairs alike. However, despite his reference to South Africa, Radcliffe-Brown, like Furnivall, identified these "composite societies" with a "colonial situation" such as Balandier and others have described.[7] This equation and typological distinction have been challenged by Raymond Firth among others, and on various grounds.[8] Firth points out that colonial status as such does not establish a distinct societal type, composite or other, which may then be changed by simple decolonization, an observation which receives support from various papers in this volume that describe the plural characteristics of precolonial and postcolonial African societies, as well as colonial ones.[9] Illustrations could be multiplied from other continents and historical periods; for example, after several decades of independence, various countries in Latin America still impress observers with their plural characteristics.[10] Gideon Sjoberg has used the work of Boeke and Furnivall to segregate a special category of "feudal societies" characterized by cultural "bifurcation," though many did not experience colonialism.[11] Names for such institutionally divided societies multiply freely. Besides such terms as "composite" and "feudal," we may cite Manning Nash's "multiple society," [12] Van Lier's "segmental society," [13] the "segmented societies" of Hoetink and Speckman,[14] or Kenneth Little's "social dualism." [15] Such terminology indicates the wide distribution of plural conditions in human societies and their independent recognition by various social scientists.

Recently, stressing the need for systematic comparative study of ex-colonial states, Shils indicates the plural character of their societal base without specific typological designation. "In . . . the new states, the pre-political matrix is in a most rudimentary condition. The constituent societies on which the new states rest are, taken separately, not civil societies, and, taken together, they certainly do not form a single civil society." [16] Such units closely approximate the model of a "non-national state composed of plural cultures" which Manning Nash, following Tax and Wolfe, identifies in modern Guatemala: [17]

As a political type, the non-national state is marked by the presence of two societies within one political network. Although the entire population of the territory is included in a single system of political bonds, only a part of the population is fully aware of the national entity, participates significantly in its politics, and has sentimental and personal bonds of attachment to the entity. This group extends throughout the national territory: it is divided into social classes, and is marked by rural and urban differences. This group is, in fact, the nation and the state. Ranking below this national group in social power and prestige are a series of local societies, the members of which have no, or little, conception of the nation, and no significant participation in its political apparatus. These local societies are of small scale and their customs and way of life are different from the group which constitutes the nation and the state.[18]

Nash also points out that "the political life of a non-national state is conducted in a social system with two levels of social and cultural integration, resulting in different organizations and tasks at each level." [19]

To understand such social systems, he advises us to investigate "in some detailed and systematic analysis how the multiple society operates, the mechanisms of political control, and the social and cultural circumstances which are amenable to, or inimical to, the perpetuation and continuity of such a political structure."[20] On Guatemalan data, he concludes that "a non-national state can only become a nation by winning the adherence of the members of its component local societies."[21]

This conception is equally noteworthy for its analytic boldness and its clarity; yet, though it subsumes Sjoberg's "feudal societies," Little's "dualism," Van Lier's "segmentarism," and Radcliffe-Brown's South African "composite" systems, so far as these are organized in states, it is not sufficiently comprehensive to accommodate the full range and variety of plural societies. Many of the "new states" lack a segregated national elite; and plural or multiple societies may exist without such institutions as the state.[22]

Clearly then, it is neither correct nor instructive to dismiss pluralism as "a cliché of commonsense sociology"[23] or as a general feature of "so-called 'complex' societies."[24] In the opinion of many scholars, it would seem to provide a more objective and incisive analysis of social and political relations in compartmentalized societies like Guatemala than such ill-defined concepts as "primordial attachments"—"the 'givens' or . . . 'assumed givens' of social existence . . . congruities of blood, speech, custom and so on"[25]—or than the yet vaguer postulate of the necessity for societal integration on the basis of common value systems.[26] Indeed, if "primordial" sentiments are derivatives or correlates of "social existence," then their analysis presupposes a thorough study of the specific societal context of this existence, which is precisely what the framework of pluralism seeks to provide. Likewise, to demonstrate that such divided societies as Guatemala owe their "integration" to the prevalence of a common value system within them, it is surely necessary to identify their main components and to determine how their respective valuations order their systems of social relations.

Other writers who have employed conceptions of social or cultural pluralism in analyzing "non-national states composed of plural cultures" include Freedman,[27] Gann,[28] Mitchell,[29] Philip Mayer,[30] Marriott,[31] Sklar and Whitaker,[32] Hoselitz,[33] Benedict,[34] W. A. Lewis,[35] Fallers,[36] and L. A. Despres,[37] all thereby demonstrating the perceived relevance of this approach. Besides Manning Nash, Rex,[38] Hoetink,[39] Despres,[40] Broom,[41] van den Berghe,[42] and Leo Kuper[43] have sought to develop and clarify the theoretical model; and in their independent comparative surveys of legal conditions in the new states, Rheinstein,[44] Schiller,[45] and the Kupers[46] have all found conceptions of pluralism indispensable. Evidently, despite its differing use by different writers, Furnivall's model of the plural society as a distinct type with specific characteristics has considerable analytic relevance. The current wealth of perspectives and hypotheses concerning pluralism, to which this volume bears witness, simply illustrates the intellectual richness of these problems and the recent increase of sociological interest in them.

Besides its standard theories of normative or functional integration in human societies, sociology urgently needs a conceptual framework appropriate for the systematic comparative study of those historical and contemporary societies whose organization and composition positively blocked their functional or normative integration and minimized their internal cohesion. Only by continuous cooperative study of the many dimensions and varieties of these conditions can we eventually construct a single coherent system of analytic concepts and propositions applicable to each specific case and to them all. Until then, our sociological theory remains bound by its basic presuppositions and applicable only to those societies that fulfill its exclusive criteria.[47] It seems, however, that current theories assume substantial uniformity in the institutional bases of the societies with which they deal. Such institutional uniformities simultaneously determine the boundaries of social systems and the levels and modes of normative or functional integration within them. Thus a theoretical framework appropriate for simultaneous comparative and individual analyses of those "multiple," "composite," "segmental," or "bifurcated" societies characterized by a plurality of institutional systems remains to be constructed; and, as Shils suggests, this is surely one of the most important and challenging tasks that confront social scientists today.[48]

II

However exciting or important such exercises in theoretical construction may seem, there are various sociological reservations about the utility of Furnivall's framework which should first be reviewed. These criticisms and reservations may conveniently be grouped in three clusters. Initial reactions to Furnivall's model came from British social anthropologists familiar with colonial Africa and the Far East.[49] A second body of criticism has its roots in recent Caribbean sociology and is addressed to formulations by Furnivall or myself, in equal measure.[50] Finally, there are several criticisms and reservations in the various contributions to the present volume.

I do not propose to discuss this latest body of comment in this essay. Besides their critical elements, the contributions in this volume present new models and perspectives for the analysis of social and cultural pluralism which together illustrate the general awareness that such conditions cannot be adequately handled within a theoretical framework designed specifically for functionally integrated societies of tribal or industrial types. It seems best, then, to regard these differing formulations and perspectives as alternative exploratory strategies and orientations toward common problems of framing concepts and generalizations based on comparative studies of plural structures and their processes of change.

In contrast, the two earlier bodies of criticism both challenge the soundness and relevance of Furnivall's model for the analysis of institutionally mixed societies; and it is therefore necessary to examine these objections. Such a task is simplified by the repetitive character of these criticisms, where they are made explicit. Thus it is hardly profitable to discuss the charges that pluralism is a "sort of sociological reactionary scholasticism" or a "theory of incalculable danger for Caribbean progressivism," [51] whatever that may mean. However, we can and should examine the writer's objection that this approach "overlooks the fundamental unity of the society." "It emphasizes the divisive elements of Caribbean society to the neglect of its emergent unifying elements; it takes racial and religious animosities as given permanent factors instead of seeing them as psycho-sociological accidents flowing from the character of colonial government; and it thereby mistakenly identifies those accidents as central essences of the . . . society." [52] Clearly, such criticism seems more appropriate to analyses based on notions of "primordial attachments" than to the theory of pluralism, whether in Furnivall's or in its present form.

It is neither necessary nor useful to cite and review each of these various objections here. Much of the Caribbean discussion is of a polemic and ideological rather than an analytic, inquiring character. [53] Moreover, almost all the criticisms of major substance were presented by H. S. Morris in two excellent essays published ten years ago. [54] Except for the dogmatic insistence that all societies are normatively integrated, a position which Morris, following Furnivall, apparently rejects, [55] and which I have treated elsewhere, [56] this Caribbean discussion adds little to Morris' critique. I shall therefore restrict this review to Morris' discussion, citing relevant statements from Furnivall's work to indicate the salient features of his model. In this way we can elliptically summarize Furnivall's view and its major sociological criticism. We can then see how recent developments revise Furnivall's scheme to extend its application beyond the colonial Far East. [57] Thus briefly we may trace the development of this analytical framework from its inception.

III

The four most far-reaching and general objections to the perspective of social pluralism developed by Furnivall or others can be listed as follows:

1) This viewpoint "overlooks the fundamental unity" of the societies with which it deals. It minimizes the coherence and integration of their social systems, while emphasizing, perhaps for ulterior purposes, the depth, intensity, and permanence of their internal divisions. To this end, it denies the allegiance of the members to a common set of values and goals.[58]

2) Methodologically, pluralism is said to prescribe the analysis of social systems in a cultural frame of reference, a procedure that is both inappropriate and misleading.[59]

3) This approach misrepresents or distorts social realities by ignoring or minimizing the varied and numerous bonds that link people of different sections in "plural societies," individually, or as categories or groups. Simultaneously, it exaggerates the unity and solidarity of these several sections and diverts attention from their many internal divisions. Pluralism accordingly misrepresents the interrelations of these social sections by overstressing their separateness, integration, internal unities, mutual differences, and conflicts of interest.[60]

4) Plural societies do not constitute a distinct societal class or type; they do not differ significantly, in kind or properties, from "other highly stratified societies" or from those with "minority problems." [61] There is thus no need for any special sociological theory or approach on this score.[62]

It is obvious that these four sets of objections are intimately connected and mutually reinforcing. Each criticism represents an essential feature of the general thesis that societies—or other types of social systems—are functional unities, normatively integrated orders of functionally interdependent parts, and all alike amenable to the same mode and framework of sociological analysis. Though presented with varying explicitness and elaborations or corollaries in more recent critiques by Braithwaite,[63] Rubin,[64] Jayawardena,[65] Benedict,[66] and R. T. Smith,[67] these central objections are all present in Morris' discussion, especially in his second, shorter paper.

Morris based his critique of Furnivall's model on his field studies of Indians in colonial Uganda, having generalized these observations to other Indian communities throughout the former British territories of East Africa.[68] Apparently he chose to regard the populations of these different territories—Zanzibar, Tanganyika, Uganda, and Kenya—as a single "plural society" because all were subject to British domination and contained people of the same "racial" stocks, namely, Britons, "Arabs," Indians, and Africans. Morris did not attempt to analyze the societal structure of any or all of these colonial units, but sought instead to challenge Furnivall's thesis by showing how the Indians of "East Africa" departed from expectations he attributes to Furnivall. In their studies of Indians in Guiana and Mauritius, Jayawardena and Benedict employed a similar procedure.[69]

Briefly, although classified by the prevailing racial legislation and by the colonial administration as a single "Indian Community," Morris found the Kampala Indians sharply segmented by religion, by sect, by caste, by language, and by regional provenience, and also stratified by economic, social, and political criteria. The Indian Muslims were divided by "sect" as Sunni and Shiah; Hindus, by caste, language, and regional origin. To illustrate the Indian organization in Kampala and elsewhere, Morris selects two collectivities, the Khoja Ismailis, a Shiah sect, organized as a corporate group under their absentee "divine ruler," the Aga Khan, and the Patidars who hail from Gujarat, to which they still turn for appropriate brides under a system of intracaste "hypergamous" marriage. At Kampala, both Ismailis and Patidars were organized in 1954 as corporate groups, the former being directed by the Aga Khan to orient themselves to the East African milieu in which they lived, the latter, under their caste-endogamous marriage system, being at least equally oriented to their ancestral villages in India. Following the leads of these "pacemakers," other segments of "Indian communities" at Kampala and elsewhere had also established their own exclusive organizations based on caste or sect, thereby undermining the unity and status of the Central Indian Association, with which the British colonial administrations preferred to deal as a common representative organization. Whereas initially wealthier Indians had pursued influence and power through leadership in the Central Indian Association, by 1954 they first sought office in their respective caste or sectarian body, and then acted as the unit's spokesmen to the British administration. If sufficiently influential, a segmental leader could establish himself as a broker, a political middleman whose prominence within his group and among the local Indians reflected his appointments to official committees, and his relations with Europeans or African leaders. According to Morris, a successful broker would be ascribed an "upper-class status"[70] by other Indians; and at this stage his influence would clearly extend beyond the limits of his own caste or sect.

With these materials, Morris questions Furnivall's model on various grounds, some of which Furnivall seems to have treated specifically. It is convenient at this stage to juxtapose these writers' statements with relevant comments.

Citing Furnivall, Morris first questions an economic interpretation of the foundation of plural societies. "It can perhaps be maintained," he says, "that East Africa, in its present form, 'evolved' in accordance with the free play of economic forces; but examples of plural or ethnically composite societies formed by military conquest in both primitive and civilized conditions are not hard to find." [71] Undoubtedly Furnivall overstressed the strictly economic factor in his analysis of plural societies in the tropical colonies; but the political precondition of this economic order is perfectly evident in his account. "In a plural society . . . the union is not voluntary but is imposed by the colonial power and by the force of economic circumstance." [72] "The plural society is in fact held together only by pressure exerted from outside by the colonial power." [73]

As an economist, Furnivall devoted his attention to those colonial societies that came into existence as products of European commercial and industrial expansion and imperialism. It was in such colonial systems that he thought strictly economic interests were given free reign. To isolate these units for detailed study, he distinguished them from precolonial pluralities as a distinct type, thereby obscuring the theoretical status of either and of his analysis. "Despite certain plural features, tropical society was distinct from the plural society which has been created by modern economic forces." [74] It is clear from the preceding review of precolonial African societies in this volume that Furnivall's distinction is neither self-evident nor sound.

In his eagerness to distinguish tropical colonial societies and those of industrial Europe in the twentieth century, Furnivall made two significant and mutually supporting errors: he strove to identify these colonial societies as a species *sui generis,* when indeed they are only a special subclass of a very widespread societal type, and even in Furnivall's day by no means its only representatives. To validate his distinction, Furnivall treated the normal features of these tropical colonies as essentials of the plural society; prominent among these colonial conditions were multiracialism, dissensus, apathy, and subjugation of the colonized to the interests of the imperial power.

As an economist, Furnivall tended to minimize the significance of political motivations and relations within these colonial systems, except as regards their economic order and the accompanying social malaise. "Ordinarily, control has been established to the economic advantage of the colonial power, [and] the general result has been the domination of tropical society by economic forces." [75] "The plural society arises where economic forces are exempt from control by social will." [76] "Foreign rule in a tropical dependency liberates economic forces, which acting internally produce social disintegration, and acting externally produce economic disintegration, building up a plural society precariously balanced in unstable equilibrium and held in position only by pressure from outside." [77] "The dissolution of the [traditional] political structure is only the first stage in social dissolution, and it is completed by the second, or economic, stage, breaking up the village into individuals." [78] Thus Furnivall's model of colonial society, though insecurely set off as a distinct societal type, clearly presupposes political domination by the imperial power, whether through conquest, negotiation, metropolitan agreements, or by other means; and, while describing these units as the arenas and victims of economic laissez faire, Furnivall also notes that compulsion is often used in furthering the economic interests of the colonizing power. [79]

Morris introduces his central argument by observing that although in East Africa, "the inhabitants . . . conceptualize the structure of their society in a slightly simpler version of the scheme used by Furnivall to describe mixed or composite societies of the Far East"—that is, as a set of occupationally and socially segregated racial sections—this "stereotyped view" merely enables them "to overlook the differentiation into groups and categories within each section, even though these latter divisions may in fact be structurally more significant in the composition of the total society than the broader 'racial' categories. . . . [It] also allows [them] to overlook the actual mingling of members of all sections which occurs, and which is comparable with that found within stratified societies which are not usually classified as plural." [80]

If Morris was merely concerned to show that the stereotyped notions East Africans held about their societies corresponded imperfectly with observable patterns of conduct and interaction, this would be neither new nor relevant to the criticism of Furnivall's model. However, Morris intends to stress that in colonial East Africa the racial sections were neither totally segregated nor united as separate "corporate groups" for internal or external activities. Thus,

in the East African situation . . . members of the society are in their own minds divided into "racial" categories. In fact, the effective structural units are frequently quite other groups. Among the Indians, they are the organized Muslim sects and Hindu castes. Among Africans they are often tribal units or the factional followings of outstanding leaders; and among Europeans—a small minority of the population—it is unusual to find the "community" acting as a whole to defend or further its interests. Questions then arise, how far can Furnivall's conceptual scheme be usefully applied, and how far is East Africa a plural society different from other highly stratified societies? [81]

These questions are surely critical for Furnivall's thesis and its later elaboration. They may be answered at two levels: first, by seeing whether Furnivall did recognize these conditions in formulating his model; and then by comparing plural and "other highly stratified societies."

Writing in 1945, Furnivall described the plural society most succinctly as one "in which two or more groups live side by side but separately, within the same political unit." [82] Continuing, he remarked that "one distinctive feature [of such a society] is the lack of organic unity within each group; each group tends to consist of an aggregate of individuals." [83]

By 1948 Furnivall had perceived the solecism in his description of such "aggregates" as groups, and he accordingly devised a more appropriate terminology. To describe his model, he then wrote as follows: "On looking at a plural society in its political aspect, one can distinguish three characteristics: the society as a whole comprises racial sections; each section is an aggregate of individuals rather than a separate or organic whole; and as individuals, their social life is incomplete." [84] Further, "each section in the plural society is a crowd and not a community." [85] "In each section the sectional common will is feeble, and in the society as a whole there is no common will. There may be apathy, even on such a vital point as defence against aggression." [86] "The plural society is broken up into groups of isolated individuals . . . [and] each section is merely an aggregate of individuals." [87] Thus instead of hypostatizing these social sections as internally unified, solidary "corporate groups," Furnivall tended rather to overstress the "atomization of society"; [88] and he may be more correctly criticized for doing so.

As in Morris' report of colonial East Africa, so likewise in Furnivall's model of the plural society, the constituent "racial" sections are constituted as corporate categories based on social and political distinctions of racial and cultural characteristics; [89] and as corporate categories, such sections are, in some socially significant respects, mutually exclusive aggregates which lack the organizations appropriate to unify them as corporate groups. [90] In an important passage, Morris comes very near to seizing this distinction between corporate categories and corporate groups. Failing to formulate it clearly, he contrasts "unorganized categories" with "corporate groups"; and, finding the racial sections in Kampala unorganized, he concludes that they lack corporate status and are primarily significant as popular stereotypes. [91]

Furnivall frequently asserts that in plural societies "each group holds by its own religion, its own culture and language, its own ideas and ways. As individuals they meet, but only in the market place, in buying and selling." [92] But he also points out that "sometimes a section of the native population is westernized," citing West African and Javanese examples. However, "in all tropical dependencies 'westernized' natives are more or less cut off from the people, and form a separate group or caste." [93] Clearly such differential Westernization presupposes differential exposure of the colonial people to Western influences and models, directly, through interaction, or by other means. Furnivall recognized this explicitly. "In a plural society the sections are not segregated; members of the several units are intermingled and meet as individuals." [94] Morris' observations confirm this for colonial East Africa. There, though Indian leaders may themselves enroll as Freemasons while their wives join an "interracial women's society," "the most active significant relations, then, between Africans, Europeans and Indians, take place at the top of the social system in the larger towns, a fact which might perhaps have been foreseen from the evidence of other plural societies. At the middle and lower levels relatively little interaction occurs." [95] Thus, though Morris interprets them otherwise, his data on intersectional relations and intrasectional organizations illustrate Furnivall's model in detail.

The central question remains: "how far is East Africa . . . (or any other plural society), different from any other highly stratified society?" [96] According to Furnivall, in the colonial plural societies of the Far East, "each group holds by its own religion, its own culture and language, its own ideas and ways. . . . In the economic sphere there is a division of labor along racial lines." [97] Whereas the members of a modern stratified society share a common citizenship and common values and norms, "in a plural society there is a corresponding cleavage along racial lines. . . . There are no common standards of conduct beyond those prescribed by law. . . . All have their own ideas as to what is right and proper, but on this matter they have different ideas." [98] "Even in a matter so vital to the whole community as defence against aggression, the people are reluctant to pay the necessary price." [99] We need merely to compare the various resistance movements against German occupation in Europe after 1941 or the conduct of Britian after Dunkirk with the indifference to Japanese occupation displayed by subject peoples in Malaya, Burma, Indonesia, and New Guinea during the same period to appreciate this difference between plural societies whose "union is not voluntary but . . . imposed" and consensually integrated societies, stratified or other. Almost by definition the latter exclude major popular revolts, while the former provoke and must suppress them to preserve their current structures. From precolonial Africa, we may cite the revolts of Hausa against Fulani in Kano, Katsina, and other territories, and of various conquered people against their Lozi rulers; the Lozi revolt against their Kololo chiefs; the more or less perpetual turmoil of Timbuktu; the Mahdist uprising in the Sudan; Chaka's revolt against the Ndwandwe; and many other instances of violent opposition to rulers of differing ethnic stock.[100] More recent upheavals in Kenya, Cameroon, Algeria, Ruanda-Urundi, Niger, and Zanzibar likewise expressed their plural cleavages. So do the recent collisions in Uganda, Congo, Ghana, and Nigeria, though in these latter cases the conflicts engage ethnic collectivities ranked as coordinates and not hierarchically. Pluralism may prevail among sections of equivalent status and capacities, as for example in the Nigerian Federation, or between "tribes," as in the African category of colonial Uganda. Whether a plurality is stratified or segmental in its form, its normative basis is very insecure, its structure is radically divisive, its cohesion and continuity remain problematic. These are surely not the normal characteristics of modern stratified societies or of stable traditional ones such as China, India, and Rome, or Mongolian or Polynesian societies.[101]

Briefly, the category of stratified societies presupposes communities of citizenship invested with common positive rights and duties, including access to a common law and a common system of political institutions. Plural societies are characterized by the exclusive incorporation of the collectivities that compose them, whether these collectivities are defined by practice or by law, and in racial, ethnic, religious, or other terms. Such a structure may have two quite distinct forms. In one form it ordains sectionally unequal distributions of legal, political, and other rights by the differential incorporation of collectivities within it. In the other, though coordinate and equally autonomous, its component sections constitute mutually exclusive collectivities of primary importance in law, politics, and citizenship alike. In its colonial phase Uganda society was legally established as a structure of differential incorporation. In the period immediately preceding and following its independence, old segmental divisions within the former subject category of Africans increased in depth and intensity without corresponding stratification of these opposing groups.

Evidently, like Furnivall, Morris equates plural with colonial societies which, being explicitly hierarchic, he assimilates to the general category of highly stratified societies. However, by his specific comparisons, Morris illustrates the ambiguity of this category. Though Britain presents an excellent example of a "highly stratified society," [102] the examples he cites are quite extreme, namely, seventeenth-century France and modern South Africa, the latter being Radcliffe-Brown's prototype of the composite or plural society.

Two questions arise: (1) What criteria distinguish "highly stratified

societies" from others that display stratification? (2) Assuming that analytically significant criteria can be found to distinguish "highly stratified
societies," is this category homogeneous? Do all "highly stratified societies" exhibit identical structural and cultural conditions? Or is it analytically useful and necessary to distinguish between them?

In treating these issues Morris is far from clear. Emphasizing that,
however prevalent in colonial societies, social differentiation on the basis
of race is always structurally contingent and may be misleading as an
index of personal alignments, he asserts that a "society such as . . . South
Africa, where the different categories of the population have status and
occupation explicitly and legally defined, has more in common with the
estate system found in 17th-century France than it has with contemporary East Africa. It is true that 'racial' categories which are not unlike
estates exist in East Africa, but within these categories and across their
boundaries, significant structural groups have a freedom and flexibility of
movement more like that seen in present-day France than in South Africa
or other estate systems." [103] Implicitly, then, Morris distinguishes two
broad categories of "highly stratified societies" by the presence or absence within them of specific and explicit legal provisions that differentiate the population by conditions of status and occupation, a system
that, where present, normally entails corresponding differentiation of
civil and political rights among the population. Despite his favorable
accounts of its regime, given "the legal recognition of 'racial' categories
in East Africa," the unequal racial franchise and virtual exclusion of
Africans from the legislature at this date, the racial wage structure and
distributions of occupation, education, income, public burdens, revenues,
and facilities, administrative and legal provisions show that the significant comparisons between South and East Africa in 1954 were rather
different from those Morris chose to stress.[104]

Even so, the comparison still remains critical. Morris is clearly correct
in stressing that racial or ethnic differences are socially significant only
insofar as they are institutionalized to differentiate people within a
society. Under their estate system in the seventeenth century, despite
ethnic homogeneity, Frenchmen were differentiated by law, occupation,
and civil and political status no less severely than are the racial sections
of contemporary South Africa. Hence, if South Africa is a representative
plural society, as everyone except Furnivall agrees,[105] then, given its
similarity to seventeenth-century France, racial or ethnic differences are
not necessary conditions of a plural society. On Morris' view of colonial
Uganda, they are also not sufficient ones; and even if this liberal interpretation of the colonial order by a visiting Briton is rejected, other examples
can be cited to substantiate the point.[106]

Furnivall repeatedly identifies the sectional divisions of plural societies by racial differences, as the preceding quotations show; and Morris makes a real contribution in exposing the contingency of this association by showing that racial or ethnic differences are neither sufficient nor requisite features of social orders based on systematic sectional disjunctions and inequalities. Furnivall's emphasis on the racial basis of social divisions within plural societies almost reduces his model to a scheme for the study of colonial race relations. That the model survives these and other defects that flowed from Furnivall's preoccupation with colonial societies in the Far Eastern tropics is almost entirely owing to his remarkable grasp of the structural essentials that underlay these accidents of time and circumstance.

We can easily appreciate the considerations that led Furnivall to restrict his inquiries to colonial societies created by European industrial expansion. Nevertheless, in attempting to distinguish a societal type in the image of these units, he committed a major methodological error by treating the arbitrary products of historical combinations as necessary and sufficient elements of a distinct societal type. At best, by such procedures Furnivall could only isolate a particular variant of the generic type whose essential structural conditions remained partly hidden beneath the specific forms and substance of these multiracial colonial systems.

Pluralism is confined neither to the tropics, nor to the last four centuries of human history. Where it prevails in a colonial society, as Firth obliquely indicates, decolonization cannot always directly dissolve it.[107] Furnivall himself was disturbed about this.[108] Despite their independence, Latin America and South Africa provide excellent examples of the plural society as Furnivall described it. Evidently Morris perceived this point; and in classifying South Africa with seventeenth-century France as systems of similar structural type, he took a decisive step to free the concept of the plural society from the four arbitrary restrictions by which Furnivall had nearly destroyed it in his desire to segregate colonialism for special study. These four deficiencies of Furnivall's model are (1) its total restriction to and identification with the modern colonial situation; (2) its correlated restriction to tropical latitudes; (3) its restriction to the era of European industrial expansion and laissez-faire capitalism; and (4) its restriction to and identification with multiracial communities.

All these misleading features of Furnivall's model are implicitly repudiated by Morris in classifying contemporary South Africa with seventeenth-century France. It is thus unfortunate that he leaves the status of such societies obscure. The context of his discussion suggests that these are merely variant forms of the highly stratified society.[109] For reasons given above, this interpretation lacks substance. Rather we should recognize that pluralism is restricted neither to colonial societies nor to modern multiracial or multiethnic ones. The plural society in its variant forms is an old and familiar structure. It may even represent, as Spencer and others thought, a particular phase in social evolution. The development of elaborate estate systems among the conquering Franks and Germans in medieval Europe shows clearly how ethnically homogeneous groups may be organized into a series of ranked orders, estates, or closed social sections. Long before the seventeenth-century, these French and German estates were no less sharply distinguished by culture and internal organization than by differences of jural, political, or economic status. Thereafter they were increasingly conceptualized as castes by their members; and even the great French Revolution did not entirely eliminate this.[110]

IV

To analyze the integration of societies characterized by structural pluralism, we must surely examine their structural order in detail to determine the bases of its social divisions, their specific conditions, properties, internal organizations, and interrelations, their conflicting or convergent interests, and the scope, level, and style of individuation which the social structure promotes, accommodates, or excludes within and beween these collective divisions. Structural pluralism consists in the differential incorporation of social aggregates into a common political society. This differential incorporation may be formal and explicit, under the law and constitution, or it may prevail substantively despite them, as, for example, among the American Negroes. The system of differential incorporation may institute total disenfranchisement of a particular section by witholding citizenship from its members, as for example in South Africa or in seventeenth-century France. Alternatively, however variable the system may be in its specific conditions and properties, the collective character, and the scope of its substantive differentiations, must be sufficiently rigorous and pervasive to establish an effective order of corporate inequalities and subordination by the differential distribution of civil and political rights and the economic, social, and other opportunities that these permit or enjoin. The "second-class citizenship" of a social category identified by common disabilities and disqualifications, whether on racial, religious, economic, or other grounds, is merely one common mode of differential incorporation. Communal rolls, restrictive property franchises, and similar arrangements also express and maintain the differential incorporation of specific collectivities within a wider society. Such mechanisms are generally developed to enhance the power of the ruling section or the stability of the social order.

In East and Central Africa, as in many other British colonial territories, racial criteria were employed as bases for differential incorporation. In the French, Belgian, and Portuguese African territories, criteria of "civilization" were employed with like effect under the convenient fictions of assimilationist policy. With the differential access of these social or racial sections to the institutions of the common public domain went differential justice, administrative organization and service, differential allocation of public status, burdens, and benefits. Where, as in colonial East Africa, this differential incorporation consists explicitly in "the legal recognition of racial categories," such racial and structural divisions cannot be regarded as merely incidental or contingent elements of social order, since they constitute its very foundations. It is by reference to such systematic conditions of differential incorporation that plural societies are structurally distinguished from such "highly stratified societies" as modern Britain, France, and Holland, and from such traditional systems as China, India, Zulu, Uganda, Nootka, Yoruba, and Benin.[111] Thus to identify the "underlying structural similarities"[112] of "coherent social systems"[113] based on differential incorporation, for example, in colonial East Africa, we must examine these structural conditions in detail. Failing this, we lack any objective basis for determining the relative "structural significance" of any features observed within them. If a racially diverse population is organized in a single society by differential incorporation on racial grounds, it is perverse to argue that "use of the criterion of race confuses the analysis and may involve the sociologist in irrelevant local political criteria."[114] Likewise, in societies based on conquest or on religious, economic, or other differentiae, analyses that ignored these conditions could scarcely fail to mislead. Indeed, if sociologists exclude as "irrelevant" those structural units and criteria that are institutionalized in a society and perceived as basic by the people concerned, one wonders what underlies their criteria of relevance for sociological analysis.

In practice, Morris does not entirely discount these conditions of differential incorporation. Rather, he seems to take them for granted, much as Geertz regards his "primordial attachments" as "givens—or assumed givens—of social existence." Thus, in evaluating the relative significance of organizational features, Morris simply assumes the social context of differential incorporation in which the "Indian community" of Kampala was placed. "Although associations exist which claim to speak for all Hindus and all Muslims, these entities, like the larger 'Indian community,' are structurally of little importance. The division of the Indian population into Hindu castes and Muslim sects (both Shiah and Sunni) of varying degrees of corporate organization is of greater significance *in the structure of the Indian section* of the society."[115] In short, the system of differential incorporation provides a frame of reference that measures the relative structural significance of alternative elements, among the Indians as well as throughout the whole society. For specific illustrations of such contextualization, we need only look at the essays by Lofchie, Gluckman, Davidson, and Hilda Kuper in this volume. In various ways their papers demonstrate the regulative primacy of the locally specific contexts and conditions of differential incorporation in organizing or restricting individual or collective activities and relations within and across sectional boundaries.

In postulating the "underlying structural uniformities"[116] of Indians, Africans, "Arabs," and Europeans in colonial East Africa, Morris cites Radcliffe-Brown's dictum to the effect that in studying "composite societies" we should examine the "interactions of individuals and groups within an established social structure."[117] Tactfully, he omits the next clause, which questions the quality and degree of the structural establishment by emphasizing that it is "itself in process of change."[118] If the colonial social structure in East Africa had been really "established," the Mau Mau movement and ensuing demands for African independence, the boycott of Indians in Kampala, the revolution in Zanzibar, and other major local upheavals could neither occur nor be understood.

Though Morris omits Radcliffe-Brown's qualifying reference to change, his own ethnographic data illustrate it. However, by confining his discussion to the Indians, he diverts attention from the influence of their structural context, set between British and African social sections, on developments among them. To account for these changes, Morris relies heavily on such culture-historical conditions as Ismaili divine kingship and Patidar intracaste hypergamy, while paying little attention to their selective situational reinforcement by local factors. Describing such procedures as "simply a way of avoiding the reality," Radcliffe-Brown points out: "What is happening in a Transkeian tribe, for example, can only be described by recognizing that this tribe has been incorporated into a wider political and economic structural system."[119] Thus to understand such developments we should specify the conditions of this incorporation and the salient characteristics of the wider structural system. Those "underlying structural similarities" or "uniformities" that express the "wide measure of agreement in many spheres of social life evident in all sections of the population"[120] in colonial East Africa consist simply in the differential incorporation of these sections into "a wider political and economic structural system." No one would seriously argue that in this colonial regime, the racial sections were incorporated on uniform or similar terms; but it is precisely such systematic institutionalized collective disjunctions that constitute plural societies as distinctive systems of differentially articulated sections subject to radically diverse sets of legal, political, economic, and other conditions. To postulate in such conditions any "underlying structural uniformities" or "wide measures of inter-sectional agreement" beyond those inherent in the common system of differential incorporation seems rather odd. That neither of these postulated conditions prevailed in British East or Central Africa during the final years of colonial rule may be seen from the preceding accounts by Davidson, Lofchie, and Hilda Kuper.

Clearly, plural societies are "structural systems" and can only be understood as such. However, by confining attention "mainly to the Indian section of East African society . . . to show how it is internally organized," [121] Morris, and others who adopt this procedure,[122] exclude the data necessary "to understand the composition of the society as a whole and the relationship of Indians to it." [123] This is so because the internal organization of any discrete section in a plural society reflects the context and conditions of its incorporation and presumes their continuity. Structural systems of such diverse constitution and complexity cannot be understood from any single sectionally exclusive standpoint.

Elaborating Radcliffe-Brown's interest in such collective relations "within an established structure, . . . itself in process of change," Shils calls for the "macro-sociological analysis" of their societal integration as follows: "Every constituent institution and stratum of the society or societies of a new state can be studied from the standpoint of the macro-sociological problem. . . . In every instance, the problem is as follows: How does this institution or practice or belief function in the articulation of the society, attaching or detaching or fixing each sector in its relationship to the central institutional and value systems of the society?" [124] Nonetheless, though this problem of social integration remains the central analytic focus, its formulation and pursuit presuppose a structural model of the societal order and its internal articulation, that is, an adequate account of the sectional divisions, their bases, internal organization, and standardized interrelations. Lacking such an account, it is difficult to determine how any given "institution or practice or belief" operates to maintain current articulations within the system, or to change these in either direction.

V

Few would deny the "unity" or boundaries of plural or other societies; but as these differ in their composition, structure, and history, so do they differ in "unity," institutional inclusiveness, consensus, cohesion, and functional coherence. In these regards, two sets of conditions are especially important: (1) the number, variety, and articulation of the institutional systems current among the population in each society; and (2) the ways in which such institutionally differentiated collectivities are incorporated to constitute a common society. These two sets of conditions are closely though variably connected. Institutional differences between collectivities in a common society facilitate and may enjoin their segregation as corporate units, categorical or other. Such sectional disjunctions may take the form of differential incorporation, or they may take the consociational forms discussed below. Always, wherever differential incorporation prevails, one institutionally distinct section dominates the others, normally for its own advantage, and by various means which may include naked force where this seems necessary. Where this dominant section is a numerical minority of the population, as for example in the Far Eastern colonies studied by Furnivall, structural pluralism prevails in its most extreme form.

Alternatively, a number of institutionally diverse collectivities may be united in a single society as corporate units holding equivalent or complementary rights and status in the common public domain, as for instance in Lebanon, Switzerland, and Bwamba, or among the Ga and Terik-Tiriki. This type of structure, a consociation, represents the formal opposite of differential incorporation. It excludes differential distributions of privilege, right, or opportunity in the common public domain between its constituent collectivities, whether or not these share common institutions. Thus, although in such systems citizenship presumes identification with one or the other of these primary collectivities, formally at least no differences of civil status in the common public domain attach to membership in either, since each bears coordinate status. Where substantively effective, this condition of formal equivalence thus ensures that segmental identifications or institutional divergences are treated as optional equivalents in the private domain, with consequent increases in the scope for social mobility, assimilation, and wider allegiances throughout all component groups. The consociations just cited illustrate such tendencies toward increasing cohesion in various forms and degrees.

A third alternative mode of societal incorporation may be illustrated by contemporary Britain, France, Holland, or Denmark. This mode incorporates individuals as citizens directly into the public domain on formally identical conditions of civic and political status, thereby eliminating the requirement of individual membership in some intermediate corporation, segmental or sectional. Under this system, individuals hold their citizenship directly and not through segmental or sectional identifications, irrespective of similar or differing practices in other institutional spheres. Given these characteristics, we may describe this system as one of "universalistic" or "uniform" incorporation. In such an order the institutional observances of individual citizens are equally indifferent except insofar as specific practices are directly or indirectly proscribed. The regime is inherently assimilative in orientation and effect. By assimilating all its members uniformly as citizens, it fosters their assimilation in other spheres also, notably language, connubium, economy, education, and recreation. Under such conditions, within the limits set by law, differences of familial or religious practice are private options of equivalent status and indifference in the determination of individual civic rights. Thus the persistence, modification, and dissolution of such ethnic and religious patterns are all equally consistent with this mode of corporate organization. They are also equally representative of it.

We should therefore distinguish three alternative bases of societal organization and unity, namely, the modes of differential, equivalent, or uniform incorporation. By the first the society is constituted as an order of structurally unequal and exclusive corporate sections, that is, as an explicitly plural regime. By the second, it is constituted as a consociation of complementary or equivalent, but mutually exclusive, corporate divisions, membership in one of which is prerequisite for citizenship in the wider unit. This consociational form is equally appropriate for the union of collectivities having common or differing institutional systems, ethnic origins, language, or religion. The accommodative capacity of this mode of incorporation is shown by the Aztec, Ashanti, Fanti, Egba, Iroquois, and early American confederations, the Delian and Achaean leagues, Malaya and Canada, besides examples already cited.

At best, however, consociations provide an imperfect and conditional basis for union, since they presuppose the structural primacy, internal autonomy, and mutual exclusiveness of the segments that constitute them. Yet, though it prescribes the equivalence of these segments in its inclusive public level, the consociation neither presupposes nor enjoins uniformities of their internal organization or composition, even where, as in Ashanti or the early United States, all shared a common cultural scheme.[125] Within the leagues of ancient Greece formal equality of confederate states was also quite consistent with differences of structure among them; but, for "a more perfect union" than consociation, uniformity in the units and conditions of incorporation is essential, and these can be established only by a radical political individualism that eliminates intermediary collectivities as prerequisite membership units. Where this third mode of incorporation obtains, the sectional organization in which structural pluralism consists is firmly excluded, and citizenship is universalized among individuals. Conversely, where collective relations are institutionalized as differential incorporation, structural pluralism prevails, whatever the ideology or constitutional provisions. This holds equally for the Belgian, French, and Portuguese African territories, for the Negro section of American society today, and for France and Britain from the eleventh to the nineteenth century.

It is evident that differential incorporation is often found in multiracial or multiethnic societies, and on racial bases. Thus in East and South Africa, the colonial Far East, or Latin America, collectivities differentially incorporated into a common society are usually defined in racial or ethnic terms, however misleading such designations may appear to the biological or social scientist. Nonetheless, neither is differential incorporation confined to multiracial or multiethnic aggregates, nor is it always present in them; nor, even where present, is it always prescribed on biological grounds. Even ethnically homogeneous populations constitute plural societies under regimes of pervasive differential incorporation, while ethnically or racially diverse populations may either be unified under structures of uniform incorporation or consociated by incorporation as equal or complementary units. Further, although differential incorporation typically presumes antecedent institutional differences between its collective divisions, it also creates their institutional differentiation within the common public domain; and in consequence of this, even where the differentially incorporated sections initially lacked them, they invariably develop differing institutional practices and organizations in their several collective domains, and in other sectors also. Moreover, since its status and dominion are bound up with the maintenance and scope of this intersectional structure, the dominant section in such societies normally seeks not only to preserve its current control, but to enhance this by promoting further institutional and structural differentiations in other spheres, notably in cult, connubium, economy, education, military organization, and residential segregation. Where, as in Sparta, Ruanda, Ankole, Kano, Ethiopia, Mauritius, medieval Europe, and modern Guatemala, or among the Tuareg, Ndebele, or Efik of Calabar, such sectional differentiations are pursued systematically, then whatever the initial situation, they promote the development of sectionally distinctive institutional systems among the incorporated collectivities by enjoining their structural segregation. To transform such plural orders into unitary social systems, it is therefore necessary to eliminate the bases and units of this sectional organization by incorporating the members of all sections directly and uniformly as citizens within the common public domain, and by making the provisions necessary to ensure that their civic assimilation will be substantively realized in other institutional spheres.

VI

At this point it is useful to specify clearly how institutional practice and social structure are related, and how we may identify culturally significant elements and levels of institutional variation. Both problems appear to puzzle certain writers, who sometimes discount such institutional analysis as "Malinowskian." [126] For clarification, then, we may cite Radcliffe-Brown, to whom "social institutions, in the sense of standardised modes of behaviour, constitute the machinery by which a social structure, a network of social relations, maintains its existence and its continuity." [127]

Institutions refer to a distinguishable type or class of social relationships and interactions. . . . The relation of institutions to social structure is therefore twofold. On the one side, there is the social structure, such as the family in this instance, for the constituent relationships of which the institutions provide the norms; on the other, there is the group, the local society in this instance, in which the norm is established by the general recognition of it as defining proper behaviour. Institutions, if that term is used to refer to the ordering by society of the interactions of persons in social relationships, have this double connection with structure, with a group or class of which it can be said to be an institution, and with those relationships within the structural system to which the norms apply.[128]

In this sense, any mode of collective incorporation is always institutionalized; and being primary for the constitution of the unit and its members, serves to "order . . . the interactions of persons" according to its specific content and form and to their positions within it. Thus, at the comparative or "macro-sociological" level, we should distinguish societal types by basic differences of structure in their institutions of collective incorporation. This is routinely done by anthropologists, for example, when they distinguish societies based on bands from others based on lineages or age-set systems. Despite these typological distinctions, such simple societies all exhibit uniformity in their frameworks of corporate organization. On a wider scale, and by the same criteria, we may also distinguish other types of societies based on consociational or differential corporate structures.

Radcliffe-Brown did not discuss these typological problems formally, but he did try to show how we may determine the limits of structural systems defined as "arrangements of persons in institutionally controlled and defined relationships." [129] He points out that being established as "norms of conduct" and "institutionally controlled," relations of identical type within a single structural system must also be uniform. Thus within a given institutional order, all types of status and role share a common specific form and content; and together, these elements establish the structural uniformity and particulars of the institutional order. Thus, when specific patterns of institutionalized action and social relationships differ in form and content, we should recognize corresponding differences in structural systems; and where such institutional differences are numerous and important in two or more structural systems, these are clearly incompatible in the sense that neither can incorporate essential elements of the other without modifications necessary to avoid the structural dislocations that inevitably follow when different systems of relations and roles are directly juxtaposed as reciprocals. Further, since roles generally cluster in sets, the ramifications of such maladjustments will normally spread beyond the institutional sectors immediately involved, such as the family or work group, to other areas of social action.

Thus, to determine the structural identity or difference of two institutional systems of the same kind, for example, alternative forms of family or cult, we may compare the specific elements that constitute their respective networks of social relations, and the specific connections that link these elements into coherent schemes of social action for collectivities and individuals alike. In this way we can identify and measure the correspondence of two or more institutional systems, or of any particular elements within them; and by the same method, we can specify the precise modifications necessary in either to effect their exact correspondence. To this end we need first to distinguish the elements of each institutionalized system of social relations, and then, by analysis, to determine their internal and external connections as sectors of a wider social system. Thus a uniform procedure enables us to specify and compare the differing levels and types of institutional variation or convergence within specific sectors of a given system, within or between different societies. Such analysis differs from the simple listing and matching of traits by requiring specific determination of the structural connections among the elements of each institutional system, such as kinship or cult, as well as those that hold between them and express their functional integration or discordance.

Now clearly even the highest degree of institutional integration and uniformity does not exclude conflict, as any student of segmentary lineage systems can show.[130] But surely the conflicts that divide a people who share identical institutional organization and orientations differ radically from those that contrapose collectivities differentiated also at the institutional and organizational levels, whether they belong to separate societies or to the same society. Two different types of conflict correspond to these two situations: in one, the antagonists share similar means, norms, goals, procedures, and forms of organization; in the other, they do not. It is characteristic of this second situation that conflicts arising at one level and over specific issues are generalized rapidly and with little institutional restraints to other spheres and to other members of the outgroup.

VII

In the interdisciplinary discussions that form the background to this volume, and also in preparing two papers for these discussions, I had an excellent opportunity to reexamine the notion of pluralism and to try to develop its analytic framework as best I could. Such developments, although implicit in earlier work,[131] seem, looking back, to have arisen here as byproducts of inquiries addressed to other issues. In consequence, they have thus far not been brought into systematic relations; and it seems appropriate to attempt this in closing.

In my first paper, taking up certain questions raised by Leo Kuper in his introductory essay, I tried to determine how the institutional and political aspects and conditions of pluralism were related. This inquiry emphasized the distinction between differential and universalistic modes of incorporation, although I doubt that either term occurs in that essay. Further, it showed that where there were systematic structural differences between constitutional forms of incorporation and the substantive realities of social life, as, for example, in the American incorporation of Negro citizens, then, as Weber said, "it is the actual state of affairs which is decisive for sociological purposes." [132] In short, despite constitutional provisions, differential incorporation may be institutionalized within a universalistic order, and not merely sub rosa. If so, it is seriously misleading to analyze the system solely or primarily in terms of its formal ideology and its inoperative or ineffective laws. Where form and substance diverge structurally, the appropriate evidence for sociological analysis of pluralism or any other condition consists surely in the operational regularities and conditions of social life.

Following this paper, I had the task of reviewing ethnographic materials on precolonial African societies for evidence of pluralism and its correlates. This provided an excellent opportunity to test the hypothesis implicit in my first paper, that differential incorporation was invariably linked with pluralism. The unanticipated result of this test was the isolation of consociations as a specific type or mode of incorporation in which social segments were united as complementary or equivalent, irrespective of the presence or absence of ethnic and institutional differences between them. In concluding that essay, I wondered whether its findings were "illusory or tautological." [133] Having since then considered these questions at length, I doubt that either is the case, for reasons presented at various points in this essay. It remains necessary to consider how these alternative modes of corporate organization are related to differences in the level and scope of pluralism, and to the determination of societal types.

Briefly, we must first distinguish three levels or modes of pluralism: structural, social, and cultural. By itself the last consists solely in institutional differences to which no corporate social differences attach. Social pluralism is the condition in which such institutional differentiations coincide with the corporate division of a given society into a series of sharply demarcated and virtually closed social sections or segments. Structural pluralism consists further in the differential incorporation of specified collectivities within a given society and corresponds with this in its form, scope, and particulars. It institutes or presupposes social and cultural pluralism together, by prescribing sectional differences of access to the common public domain, and by establishing differing contexts and conditions of sectional coexistence, segregation, and subordination. Such conditions preserve or generate corresponding institutional pluralism by fostering diverse sectional adaptations to their distinctive situations and by promoting divergent and sectionally specific collective domains for their internal organization and intersectional relations. Such an order of structural pluralism may be instituted in one of two ways: by the total exclusion of subordinate sections from the inclusive public domain, which is then the formally unqualified monopoly of the dominant group; or alternatively by instituting substantial and sufficient inequalities of sectional participation in and access to this sector of the societal organization.

Insofar as they are substantively enforced, conditions of uniform incorporation exclude structural and social pluralism alike by individualizing citizenship and thereby eliminating sectional or segmental collectivities as representative structures from the common public domain. Thus an effective order of uniform incorporation proscribes social pluralism, though it is equally consistent with cultural uniformities or pluralism among the citizens.

The consociation of social aggregates as equivalent or complementary segments of a wider unit neither presupposes their institutional or ethnic uniformity nor precludes such differences. Consociational modes of incorporation are equally compatible with homogeneity or difference in these respects. On the other hand, wherever it is substantively enforced, such an order formally excludes structural pluralism by prescribing the equivalent status of its component segments instead of their differential incorporation. Thus consociational structures may be found among ethnically and institutionally homogeneous populations, or among peoples of diverse ethnic and institutional background, and even in such extreme cases as Nigeria (1961–1965) or the Terik-Tiriki, in societies characterized by social as well as cultural pluralism and organized as combinations of structurally and culturally distinct coordinate segments.

Consociational systems may operate to preserve or to permit social and institutional differentiation between the segments that compose them. In this respect there are many variations, as may be seen by comparing differentiations among the Terik-Tiriki, Ga, Egba, and Amba. Normally, the social segments that form the consociation are territorially distinct and so form separate local communities, as for instance in Abeokuta or Switzerland. Where these segments also differ institutionally or ethnically, such spatial separation may reinforce or express their social pluralism. Alternatively, as in Lebanon or Buganda under British rule, the segmental constituents of the consociation may be socially and spatially interspersed, in both these cases the boundaries being defined by religion.

In strictly formal terms, given their initial equivalence or complementarity at the consociational level, institutional, social, or spatial differences between the component segments are structurally indifferent to their union. Where such differences prevail, the union should make corresponding provisions to accommodate them. Alternatively, as instanced above, all the segments within a given consociation may be institutionally and ethnically alike. In either case, the consociation as a union of corporate collectivities presupposes their mutual distinctness and complementary equivalence. Thus at the consociational level, individual identification with either of these segments is prerequisite for citizenship, but otherwise indifferent. For its existence and form, the consociation presupposes these segmental divisions.

Formally then, segmental continuities or differences of institutional or ethnic allegiance within consociations should have no wider structural significance, thereby restricting such diversity either to the cultural level or at most to that of the segmental communities. Individual practice and segmental affiliations are thus classified as optional equivalents of the private domain, thereby facilitating social mobility and assimilation unless segmental barriers obstruct this. However, in consociations as elsewhere, social forms and substance often diverge. Formal equivalence may prove impossible to harmonize with the substantive equivalence of the constituent sections; and indeed these features of the consociational order provide fertile fields of dispute wherever the segments whose complementarity or equivalence is presumed differ widely in number, wealth, institutions and social organization, technological and economic capacities, history, ethnicity, and ideological orientations, separately or together. Each of these conditions presents an implicit continuum along which differences may be scaled as greater or less. These continua and degrees of differentiation are often combined in various ways. To illustrate such combinations of segmental differentiations, we need merely cite Nigeria, the federations of British Central Africa and Malaya-Singapore, the defunct West Indies Federation, Uganda, Cameroon, Cyprus, Guiana, Lebanon, the unions of Egypt and Syria, of Senegal and Mali, or the various leagues of ancient Greece. Even when their segmental components share common institutional and ethnic backgrounds as, for example, in the early American confederations, the Ashanti Union, the League of Delos, the Nootka, Kwakiutl, or Iroquois confederacies, in ancient Israel, Switzerland, South Africa, or Canada, the conditions and scope of these unions remain uncertain. This is illustrated by the Swiss civil war of 1846, the American civil war, the war in Lebanon in 1958, the split between Judah and Israel,[134] the military and civil strife of Boer and Briton in South Africa, the unfinished dispute between French- and English-speaking Canadians in Quebec, the numerous secessionist struggles between Kumasi and other Ashanti states,[135] Iroquois division at the outbreak of the American War of Independence,[136] and so on. Notably, as can be seen from the histories of Ashanti, South Africa, the United States, and ancient Israel or Athens, to counteract autarchic tendencies within the segments and to preserve or strengthen these consociations, some central unit endowed with superior authority and resources must emerge or be created, as Rome in Latium, or Kumasi, Athens, Judah, Tenochtitlan, and Washington in their several societies.

The sources and conditions of instability in consociational systems built upon institutionally different segments are reasonably clear. Segmental primacy and equivalence in such unions are recognized by their internal autonomy within the union. It is in such units that citizenship and representation are both explicitly vested. These political conditions facilitate tendencies toward segmental exclusiveness or assimilation equally. As regards probable courses of development, much depends on the number, distribution, and institutional or ethnic identity of the segments, as well as on their absolute and relative size, and common or differing external contexts. Formal equivalence and substantive equivalence are not always easily matched, nor always perceived as such by the interested parties. Segmental equivalence may be taken to mean strict or proportionate equality in representation, office, and in the disbursement of public revenues, or its particulars may be subject to continuous debate. Almost always, the components of a consociation are unequal in numbers, territory, and economic potential, and correspondingly preoccupied with the locally appropriate criteria of their equivalence to avoid differential representation and influence at the center, especially insofar as these central organs are endowed with positive responsibilities and powers over the total society. Under such conditions, real or perceived segmental disparities may evoke segmental protests and policies designed to alter or to maintain current conditions of union and current distributions of power and influence. Autarchic segmental identities are correspondingly reinforced by such intersegmental conflicts; and unless these are effectively restrained or reduced, they may subvert and destroy the consociation by transforming its internal political order into a system of external relations between mutually hostile segments.

Consociations that unite collectivities of differing institutional organization, ethnic provenience, and sectional interest—as, for example, in Uganda, Guiana, Cyprus, or Nigeria—are especially prone to intersegmental strife, given their communal divisions. In such unions, institutionally differentiated segments are also normally unequal in numbers, need, and economic potentials, divided by interests and issues that provoke frequent collisions and segmental demands for secession or dominance. Structurally, although consociations prescribe equivalence or complementarity among their components, they can rarely avoid de facto disparities in distributions of power, influence, and public preference, though such disparities exacerbate segmental fears and tensions among the privileged and unprivileged alike.

Instability inheres in the combination of equally autonomous segments differentiated by structure, size, ethnic and institutional background, interest, need, and power. Lacking any continuous external threat to their joint security, each of these institutionally differentiated segments may seek to preserve or extend its internal autonomy against aggrandizements of others, while stressing its corporate unity and exclusive identity. Beyond a certain level, such intersegmental action reconstitutes the consociation as a system of external political relations between its segments, rather than a condition of social union. Recent events in Malaysia, Uganda, Guiana, Cyprus, the Congo, and Nigeria illustrate this.

Consociations that preserve their initial form and character over several decades without further increase of central regulatory powers simultaneously enhance segmental autonomies and equivalence by severely restricting the scope of central action and joint affairs to the minimum necessary for continuity and coordination of the union. In these cases the central autonomy is weak, and hence subject to that vested in the segments. Viable consociations of this character include the Terik-Tiriki, the union of Ga and Kpesi speakers, and Switzerland, all of which, while differing in organization and institutional content, were greatly strengthened by continuous external threats. Within their union, Terik and Tiriki have maintained their social and cultural distinctness to this day, since "differences of opinion and belief concerning female initiation . . . proved to be an effective deterrent to intermarriage." [137] Among Kpesi and Ga, intermarriage promoted such assimilation in language, institutional practice, and social relations that, although the old consociational units and forms persist, their segments, originally different in language, organization, and culture, are now institutionally alike.

Societies constituted on the uniform incorporation of all members as citizens are universalistic and egalitarian in orientation and form. Such regimes may tolerate wide levels of cultural diversity among their members, but preclude the emergence of corresponding corporate social sections. Where such conditions of uniform incorporation are substantively enforced, being then by law confined to the secondary optional level of private individual conduct, divergent institutional practices cannot segregate sectional collectivities in the public domain. However, where objective social conditions diverge substantially from this framework of universalistic incorporation, as for example among Negroes in the United States, institutional or other differences may coincide with a structure of differential incorporation through which sectional exclusion, opposition, differences of institutional organization and culture are promoted or reinforced. Such differential incorporation may take either of two forms. One social section may be subordinated to the other, or it may be segregated beyond the pale as a dependent collateral like the Transkei or South African Bantustans.[138] Either eventuality establishes structural pluralism with its concomitants, social and cultural pluralism, since even in this second segmentary form, the sections are differentially incorporated into a wider society despite formal disjunction. By contrast, although among the Terik and Tiriki, or among the Muslims and Christians of Lebanon, social and cultural differences persist, structural pluralism is excluded. This is also true of the Swiss and formally, of English- and French-speaking Canadians. Finally, among white Americans, differences of ethnicity and religion prevail without corresponding social exclusions or differential incorporation.

We must thus distinguish three levels of pluralism and three related modes of incorporation. Structural pluralism consists in the differential incorporation of collectivities segregated as social sections and characterized by institutional divergences. Cultural pluralism consists in variable institutional diversity without corresponding collective segregation. Social pluralism involves the organization of institutionally dissimilar collectivities as corporate sections or segments whose boundaries demarcate distinct communities and systems of social action. The differential incorporation that institutes structural pluralism is found only in societies where institutionally diverse collectivities are set apart as corporate social sections of unequal status and resources. In these conditions, if the ruling sections forms a numerical minority of the aggregate, we find the plural society in the classic form described by Furnivall.

It is advisable to clarify the logical status and relations of these typologies before discussing their substantive bases. Despite their differing referents, these two typologies are not entirely independent of each other; nor does either distinguish a set of independent variables. As analytical categories, cultural, social, and structural pluralism refer to three levels of pluralism which differ in their properties, forms, intensity, and range. Though cultural pluralism may prevail without social or structural pluralism, these latter forms of pluralism cannot obtain without commensurate degrees of cultural pluralism. Moreover, while structural pluralism entails social and cultural pluralism, the converse is not necessary. As regards the alternative modes of incorporation, although analytically distinct, they are not necessarily exclusive, and may be combined in various ways to constitute differing types of complex regime. Thus, in South Africa, whites are incorporated differentially from nonwhites, universalistically as citizens of the Republic, and consociationally through the provincial organization. Consociational and universalistic modes of incorporation can be found in societies that lack cultural or social pluralism, but in the latter context they are differentially associated with these different levels of pluralism. While universalistic regimes can accommodate cultural pluralism without substantive change, social pluralism generates a substantively consociational order within them; but neither of these two regimes, if substantively valid, accommodates a state of structural pluralism, which always requires differential incorporation for its constitution and maintenance.

The disjunctions of mutually exclusive collectivities involve differences of social structure which reflect corresponding differences in their basic institutional systems. By contrast, where cultural differences prevail without correlative social divisions, they must be equally consistent with direct individual participation in a common collective life under uniform conditions of incorporation. Whether regionally concentrated or dispersed, such cultural differences will then be individually optional, functional alternatives, restricted to the private domain and to secondary institutional spheres. The resulting combination of cultural diversity and social assimilation is normal in heterogeneous societies.

Societies that contain two or more institutionally dissimilar and mutually exclusive collectivities manifest substantively consociational or differential regimes, even under universalistic constitutions. This arises wherever individual identification with one or other of the associated collectivities is institutionally prescribed and prior, since this ordains individual dependence on representation in and through the collective organizations. Thus, whatever the constitutional form or the spatial distribution of social segments—given a society composed of institutionally distinct and exclusive collectivities—consociational or differential arrangements prevail, formally or informally, separately or together.

Though by no means restricted to contexts of social pluralism, consociation is formally appropriate for the union of institutionally diverse collectivities. However, multiethnic consociational regimes have certain structural weaknesses and face serious problems. In the absence of common external threats and widespread internal assimilations through intermarriage, they rarely endure. Persisting societies that contain institutionally distinct sections are commonly unified under conditions of differential incorporation as plural structures of radically unequal and disparate parts.

Structural pluralism intensifies and enhances the institutional disjunctions that social pluralism involves by prescribing collective differences of status and relation to the common public domain, and by transforming these differences into conditions of inequality and subordination. Whereas consociation assumes intersectional equivalence and encourages social assimilation, structural pluralism is constituted by the differential incorporation of such sections as superior and inferior, and to persist requires their continued disjunction. Where differences of collective organization and institutional practice antedate differential incorporation, pluralism increases and deepens these differences by establishing a new dimension of domination and subordination which imposes radically divergent societal contexts on the collectivities concerned. Moreover, in the absence of such antecedent differences of collective organization and institutional practice, differential incorporation generates them by prescribing distinct societal contexts to which collectivities must accommodate by appropriate socialization and institutional adaptation.

It is necessary, then, to distinguish social pluralism from cultural pluralism, though both assume systemic institutional differences among collectivities within a single society. Under formal or informal consociations, the institutionally distinct segments share identical status and relations with the common public domain, and thus share a common system of government and public law. This political and jural community modifies the institutional segregation of the sections accordingly, and defines their differences as equivalent alternatives. Under differential incorporation, one institutionally distinct collectivity regulates the others, having appropriated societal institutions of government, law, and force. Whereas the manifest equivalence of components—a condition that fosters intersectional association, mobility, and assimilation—is necessary for a stable consociation, the habituation of subordinate social sections to inferior status is equally essential for a stable system of differential incorporation. In short, structural pluralism, the corollary of differential incorporation, involves a special set of arrangements which either generates or extends the collective disjunctions of social pluralism by proscribing intersectional equivalence, mobility, and individuation.

Homogeneous and heterogenous societies may equally well be based on uniform or universalistic conditions of incorporation. Differential incorporation obtains always and only with structural pluralism. Consociations may provide the bases for homogeneous societies, as for example Ashanti, Iroquois, or Nootka. Consociation may also constitute a heterogeneous society as among the Aztec, in Switzerland, or in Lebanon. It may unite two or more structurally distinct homogeneous societies, as in the Terik-Tiriki and Ga-Kpesi cases; or, as in Nigeria, it may unite institutionally heterogeneous collectivities distinguished by culture and social systems as mutually exclusive corporate sections. In the latter case, the consociation exhibits social and cultural pluralism in its sectional basis, while formally excluding structural pluralism by prescribing segmental equivalence. The result, illustrated by Nigeria, Uganda, or Cameroon, is a plural society of differing structure and type from that based on differential incorporation. Whether we apply the same term to both these models, or describe the Nigerian or Ghanaian types as "composite" or as "segmental" societies, following earlier writers, is not of major importance. The internal inconsistencies that threaten consociations of this sort with radical transformations or dissolution have been mentioned above.

Since these alternative modes of incorporation are always institutionalized as formal or substantive conditions of societal structure, their relations with other institutional sectors of the collective life are clearly important, however variable or indirect these may seem. Moreover, given their status as structural alternatives to which different levels and ranges of pluralism correspond, diverse combinations of these types of incorporation are not difficult to find. Perhaps the most complex and obvious example of this is the United States, incorporated constitutionally in explicitly universal terms as a consociation of territorially discrete collectivities, but substantively characterized by the differential incorporation of its Negro citizens. Such a society exhibits heterogeneity and pluralism together, but in differing proportions. In its white sector, cultural pluralism prevails without corresponding social and structural pluralism; across the race line social and cultural pluralism are institutionalized in direct contravention of the constitution. By its consociational form, despite its unreserved universalism, this constitution provides the essential resources for the defense of this system of differential incorporation by guarantees of states' rights.

VIII

However different our formulations may seem, we have not abandoned Furnivall's problem; instead, we have merely attempted to clarify and generalize it. Though he confined his discussion to colonial pluralities, Furnivall identified and formulated the basic issues of social cohesion and development which characterize pluralism in all its many forms and dimensions. Since Furnivall wrote, most of these tropical colonies have attained independence, with greater or less turmoil. As independent states, their vicissitudes and upheavals declare their generic fragility, the product of their plural character and base. To anticipate the smooth development of such societies into nations, or even any rapid, continuous process of modernization within them, is antihistorical and antiempirical in the extreme. We need merely remember Latin America, Belgium, Spain, Portugal, and Germany, all of which have known independence far longer and under far more favorable conditions. For these new "nonnational" states, with their "multiple" societies, internal order and survival are surely the first formidable task; the promotion of internal loyalties and cohesion by the dissolution of sectional divisions, identities, and fears is the second. Though very closely connected, this latter presupposes the first condition.

Furnivall was seriously in error when he wrote "there can be nationalism without a nation." [139] Does communalism exist without a "community," or tribalism without a "tribe"? Surely here Furnivall fell victim to the presuppositions, categories, and symbols of Western culture, which has long invested "nationalism" with a moral supremacy and prevalence it does not always possess. True, leaders of colonial independence movements appealed to sentiments, ideals, and principles of nationalism and self-determination; the public acclaim and support they received was proportionate to popular dissatisfactions and desires to be rid of European rule; but desires for self-determination or independence may prevail without nationalism, and do not presuppose it. It is easier and more common for people to mobilize and unite in opposition to alien rulers than to construct and consolidate new societies under the influence of strictly national sentiments and ideals. It is surely uncommon for people divided by history, language, institutions, habitat, and in many other ways to unite voluntarily and in peace, in the absence of any serious external threat to their common security. The unity of negation is no more satisfactory a basis for assuming the moral solidarity and present or future cohesion of an aggregate in motion than the unity created by their differential incorporation. Even in the simplest situation, such as a lineage feud, this condition is evident. Thus in these new "nonnational" states, it remains necessary to pursue policies that eliminate sectional barriers, identities, and fears among the collectivities that compose them. Ultimately this can be done only through the complementary or equivalent incorporation of these collectivities within the wider unit or by their effective extrusion from the common public domain through the universalistic incorporation of all individuals as citizens.

NOTES

[1] J. S. Furnivall, *Netherlands India: A Study of Plural Economy* (Cambridge: The University Press, 1939); "The Political Economy of the Tropical Far East," *Journal of the Royal Central Asiatic Society*, 29 (1942), 195–210; "Some Problems of Tropical Economy," in Rita Hinden, ed., *Fabian Colonial Essays* (London: Allen and Unwin, 1945), pp. 161–184; *Colonial Policy and Practice: A Comparative Study of Burma and Netherlands India* (London: Cambridge University Press, 1948).

[2] Max Gluckman, *An Analysis of a Social Situation in Modern Zululand* (Manchester: Manchester University Press, 1958); Vera Rubin, ed., *Social and Cultural Pluralism in the Caribbean*, Annals of the New York Academy of Sciences, 83 (Jan. 1960), 761–916; Institut International des Civilisations Différentes, *Ethnic and Cultural Pluralism in Intertropical Countries: Report of the XXXth Meeting Held in Lisbon* (Brussels: INCIDI, 1957); Clifford Geertz, ed., *Old Societies and New States: The Quest for Modernity in Asia and Africa* (New York: Free Press of Glencoe, 1963); Leo A. Despres, "The Implications of Nationalist Policies in British Guiana for the Development of Cultural Theory," *American Anthropologist*, 66 (Oct. 1964), 1051–1077; W. Arthur Lewis, *Politics in West Africa* (London: Allen and Unwin, 1965); Pierre L. van den Berghe, ed., *Africa: Social Problems of Change and Conflict* (San Francisco: Chandler Publishing Co., 1965).

[3] Leo Kuper, "Plural Societies: Perspectives and Problems," above.

[4] J. H. Boeke, *Economics and Economic Policy of Dual Societies* (New York: Institute of Pacific Relations, 1953).

[5] Herbert Spencer, *The Principles of Sociology* (3 vols.; New York: Appleton-Century, 1902), II, pt. 5; Ludwig Gumplowicz, *Outlines of Sociology* (2d English ed.; New York: Paine-Whitman, 1963); Franz Oppenheimer, *The State* (New York: Heubsch, 1922).

[6] A. R. Radcliffe-Brown, "On Social Structure," *Journal of the Royal Anthropological Institute*, LXX (1940), repr. in A. R. Radcliffe-Brown, *Structure and Function in Primitive Society* (London: Cohen and West, 1952), pp. 188–204 (see p. 202).

[7] Georges Balandier, *Sociologie actuelle de l'Afrique Noire* (Paris: Presses Universitaires de France, 1955); Adriano Moreira, "Rapport général: Aspect juridique et politique," in *Ethnic and Cultural Pluralism in Tropical Countries*, pp. 494–498.

[8] Raymond Firth, *Essays on Social Organization and Values* (London: Athlone Press of the University of London, 1964), pp. 177–178; L. Braithwaite, "Social Stratification and Cultural Pluralism," in Rubin, *op. cit.*, pp. 816–831;

Raymond T. Smith, *British Guiana* (London: Oxford University Press, 1962), chap. 5; Raymond T. Smith, "British Guiana," *Sunday Guardian* (Port of Spain, Trinidad), Federation Supplement, April 20, 1958. See also works by Gordon K. Lewis and H. S. Morris cited below.

[9] See papers in this volume by Michael Lofchie, Basil Davidson, Hilda Kuper, Max Gluckman, and myself.

[10] Ralph L. Beals, "Social Stratification in Latin America," *American Journal of Sociology*, 57 (1953), 327–339; Manning Nash, "The Multiple Society in Economic Development: Mexico and Guatemala," *American Anthropologist*, 59, no. 5 (Oct. 1957) 825–838; Manning Nash, "Political Relations in Guatemala," *Social and Economic Studies*, 7, no. 1 (March 1958), 65–75; Benjamin N. Colby and Pierre L. van den Berghe, "Ethnic Relations in South-Eastern Mexico," *American Anthropologist*, 63, no. 4 (Aug. 1961), 772–792.

[11] Gideon Sjoberg, "Folk and 'Feudal' Societies," *American Journal of Sociology*, 58 (Nov. 1952), 231–239.

[12] Nash, "The Multiple Society," and "Political Relations in Guatemala."

[13] R. A. J. van Lier, *The Development and Nature of Society in the West Indies* (Amsterdam: Royal Institute for the Indies, 1950).

[14] H. Hoetink, "Curazao como sociedad segmentada," *Revista de Ciencias Sociales*, 4 (March 1960), 179–192; H. Hoetink, *The Two Variants in Caribbean Race Relations: A Contribution to the Sociology of Segmented Societies* (London: Oxford University Press, 1967); J. D. Speckman, "The Indian Group in the Segmented Society of Surinam," *Caribbean Studies*, 3, no. 1 (April 1963), 3–17.

[15] Kenneth Little, "Structural Change in the Sierra Leone Protectorate," *Africa*, 25, no. 3 (June 1955), 217–234.

[16] Edward A. Shils, "On the Comparative Study of the New States," in Geertz, *op. cit.*, p. 22.

[17] Nash, "Political Relations in Guatemala," p. 65.

[18] *Ibid.*, p. 65.

[19] *Ibid.*, p. 66.

[20] *Ibid.*

[21] *Ibid.*, p. 74.

[22] P. C. Lloyd, ed., *The New Elites of Tropical Africa* (London: Oxford University Press, 1966); Richard L. Sklar and C. S. Whitaker, Jr., "The Federal Republic of Nigeria," in Gwendolen M. Carter, ed., *National Unity and Regionalism in Eight African States* (Ithaca: Cornell University Press, 1966), pp. 7–150; Fredrik Barth, *Political Leadership among the Swat Pathans* (London: Athlone Press of the University of London, 1959); E. R. Leach, *Political Systems of Highland Burma* (London: G. Bell and Sons, 1954). See also references cited in my essay, "Pluralism in Precolonial African Societies," concerning Efik at Calabar, Tuareg, and Bwamba.

[23] Clifford Geertz, "The Integrative Revolution: Primordial Sentiments and Civil Politics in the New States," in Geertz, *op. cit.*, pp. 105–157 (see p. 117).

[24] Raymond T. Smith, review of *Social and Cultural Pluralism in the Caribbean*, in *American Anthropologist*, 63, no. 1 (Feb. 1961), 155.

[25] Geertz, "The Integrative Revolution," p. 109.

[26] Braithwaite, *op. cit.*; Smith, "British Guiana"; Smith, *British Guiana*, pp. 99, 136, 143, 198; V. Rubin, R. A. J. van Lier, and L. Braithwaite, "Pluralism

in the Caribbean," in *Caribbean Studies Special Report 1962*, Caribbean Scholars' Conference, Institute of Caribbean Studies, University of Puerto Rico (1962), pp. 9–18.

[27] Freedman, "The Growth of a Plural Society in Malaya," *Pacific Affairs*, 33, no. 2 (1960), 158–168.

[28] L. H. Gann, *The Birth of a Plural Society* (Manchester: Manchester University Press, 1958); L. H. Gann and Peter Duignan, *White Settlers in Tropical Africa* (Harmondsworth: Penguin Books, 1962).

[29] J. C. Mitchell, *Tribalism and the Plural Society* (London: Oxford University Press, 1960); J. C. Mitchell, *The Kalela Dance* (Manchester: Manchester University Press, 1956); J. C. Mitchell, "Aspects of Occupational Prestige in a Plural Society," in Lloyd, *op. cit.*, pp. 256–271.

[30] Philip Mayer, "The Tribal Elite and the Transkeian Elections of 1963," in Lloyd, *op. cit.*, pp. 286–311.

[31] McKim Marriott, "Cultural Policy in the New States," in Geertz, *Old Societies and New States*, pp. 27–56.

[32] Sklar and Whitaker, *op. cit.*

[33] Bert Hoselitz, "Interaction between Industrial and Pre-industrial Stratification Systems," in Neil J. Smelser and Seymour Martin Lipset, eds., *Social Structure, Social Mobility and Economic Development* (Chicago: Aldine Publishing Co., 1966).

[34] B. Benedict, "Stratification in Plural Societies," *American Anthropologist*, 64, no. 6 (Dec. 1962), 1235–1246; B. Benedict, *Indians in a Plural Society: A Report on Mauritius* (London: H.M.S.O., 1961).

[35] Lewis, *op. cit.*; W. Arthur Lewis, "Beyond African Dictatorship: The Crisis of the One-Party State," *Encounter*, 25, no. 2 (Aug. 1965), 3–18.

[36] Lloyd Fallers, "Equality, Modernity and Democracy in the New States," in Geertz, *Old Societies and New States*, pp. 158–219; Lloyd Fallers, "Ideology and Culture in Uganda Nationalism," *American Anthropologist*, 63, no. 4 (Aug. 1961), 677–686.

[37] Despres, *op. cit.*; Leo A. Despres, *Cultural Pluralism and Nationalist Politics in British Guiana* (Chicago: Rand McNally, 1967); Leo A. Despres, "Anthropological Theory, Cultural Pluralism and the Study of Complex Societies," *Current Anthropology*, 9, no. 1 (Feb. 1968).

[38] John Rex, "The Plural Society in Sociological Theory," *British Journal of Sociology*, 10, no. 2 (June 1959), 114–124.

[39] Hoetink, "Curazao como sociedad segmentada."

[40] Despres, "Implications of Nationalist Policies," and *Cultural Pluralism and Nationalist Politics in British Guiana*.

[41] Leonard Broom, "Urbanization and the Plural Society," in Rubin, *op. cit.*, pp. 880–891.

[42] Pierre L. van den Berghe, "Introduction," and "Toward a Sociology of Africa," in van den Berghe, *op. cit.*, pp. 1–11, 77–88, resp. See also his "Pluralism and the Polity: A Theoretical Exploration," in this volume.

[43] Leo Kuper, "Religion and Urbanization in Africa," in *Religious Pluralism and Social Structure* (Koln: Westdeutscher Verlag, 1965), pp. 213–233; Leo Kuper, "Sociology: Some Aspects of Urban Plural Societies in Africa," in Robert A. Lystad, ed., *The African World: A Survey of Social Research* (New York: Praeger, 1965), pp. 107–130; Leo Kuper, "Structural Discontinuities in African Towns: Some Aspects of Racial Pluralism," in H. Miner, ed., *The City*

in Modern Africa (New York: Praeger, in press). See also his three contributions to the present volume.

[44] Max Rheinstein, "Problems of Law in the New Nations of Africa," in Geertz, *Old Societies and New States,* pp. 220–246.

[45] A. Arthur Schiller, "Law," in Lystad, *op. cit.,* pp. 166–198.

[46] Hilda Kuper and Leo Kuper, "Introduction," in Hilda Kuper and Leo Kuper, eds., *African Law: Adaptation and Development* (Berkeley and Los Angeles: University of California Press, 1965), pp. 3–23.

[47] D. F. Aberle, A. K. Cohen, A. K. Davis, M. J. Levy, Jr., and F. X. Sutton, "The Functional Prerequisites of Society," *Ethics,* 60 (1950), 100–111; Kingsley Davis and Wilbert E. Moore, "Some Principles of Stratification," *American Sociological Review,* 10 (1945), 242–249; Talcott Parsons and Edward A. Shils, eds., *Toward A General Theory of Action* (Cambridge: Harvard University Press, 1951); Talcott Parsons, *The Social System* (London: Tavistock Publications, 1952); Marion J. Levy, *The Structure of Society* (Princeton: Princeton University Press, 1952). For critical evaluation of this thesis, see M. G. Smith, *The Plural Society in the British West Indies* (Berkeley and Los Angeles: University of California Press, 1965), pp. vii–xiii, 50–52, 82–83, 90, and *passim.* For a formal test see M. G. Smith, *Stratification in Grenada* (Berkeley and Los Angeles: University of California Press, 1965.)

[48] Shils, *op. cit.*

[49] H. S. Morris, "Indians in East Africa: A Study in a Plural Society," *British Journal of Sociology,* 7, no. 3 (Oct. 1956), 194–211; H. S. Morris, "The Plural Society," *Man,* 57, no. 8 (Aug. 1957), 124–125; Freedman, *op. cit.;* Benedict, *Indians in a Plural Society,* and "Stratification in Plural Societies"; Gann, *op. cit.;* Mitchell, *Tribalism and the Plural Society.*

[50] L. Braithwaite, "The Present Status of the Social Sciences in the British Caribbean," in Vera Rubin, ed., *Caribbean Studies: A Symposium* (Mona, Jamaica: Institute of Social and Economic Research, 1957), pp. 99–109; Braithwaite, "Social Stratification and Cultural Pluralism"; Rubin, van Lier, and Braithwaite, *op. cit.;* Raymond T. Smith, "British Guiana," and review of *Social and Cultural Pluralism in the Caribbean;* Raymond T. Smith, "Culture and Social Structure in the Caribbean: Some Recent Work on Family and Kinship Studies," *Comparative Studies in Society and History,* 6, no. 1 (Oct. 1963), 24–46; Raymond T. Smith, "People and Change," in *New World: Guyana Independence Issue* (Demerara, Guiana, May 1966), pp. 49–54; Vera Rubin, "Discussion of Social and Cultural Pluralism," in Rubin, *Social and Cultural Pluralism in the Caribbean,* pp. 780–785; Charles Wagley, "Discussion of Social and Cultural Pluralism," in *ibid.,* pp. 777–780; Elena Padilla, "Peasants, Plantations and Pluralism," in *ibid.,* pp. 837–842; Daniel J. Crowley, "Plural and Differential Acculturation in Trinidad," *American Anthropologist,* 59, no. 5 (Oct. 1957), 817–824; Daniel J. Crowley, "Cultural Assimilation in a Multiracial Society," in Rubin, *Social and Cultural Pluralism in the Caribbean,* pp. 850–854; Morton Klass, "East and West Indian: Cultural Complexity in Trinidad," in *ibid.,* pp. 855–886; Elliott P. Skinner, "Group Dynamics and Social Stratification in British Guiana," in *ibid.,* pp. 904–916; Vera Rubin, "Culture, Politics and Race Relations," *Social and Economic Studies,* 11, no. 4 (Dec. 1962), 433–455; George E. Cumper, "Notes on Social Structure in Jamaica," in George E. Cumper, ed., *Social Needs in a Changing Society: Report of the Conference on Social Development in Jamaica, July*

1961 (Kingston, Jamaica: Council of Voluntary Social Services, 1962), pp. 3–11; M. G. Smith, *The Plural Society in British West Indies,* and *Stratification in Grenada;* van Lier, *op. cit.;* Hoetink, "Curazao como sociedad segmentada"; H. Hoetink, "Change in Prejudice: Some Notes on the Minority Problem, with Reference to the West Indies and Latin America," *Bijdragen tot de Taal-, Land- en Volkenkunde,* 119, no. 1 (1963), 56–75; Speckman, *op. cit.;* Despres, "The Implications of Nationalist Policies in British Guiana"; H. I. McKenzie, "The Plural Society Debate: Some Comments on a Recent Contribution," *Social and Economic Studies,* 15, no. 1 (March 1966), 53–60; Rex Nettleford, "National Identity and Attitudes to Race in Jamaica," *Race,* 7, no. 1 (1965) 59–72.

⁵¹ Gordon K. Lewis, review of Eric Williams, *The History of the People of Trinidad and Tobago,* in *Caribbean Studies,* 3, no. 1 (April 1963), 104.

⁵² *Ibid.,* p. 104. See also Braithwaite, "Status of the Social Sciences in the Caribbean," pp. 101–103; Cumper, "Notes on Social Structure in Jamaica," p. 9. For illustrations, see Hoetink, "Change in Prejudice," pp. 66–71, which may be compared with data in Rubin, "Culture, Politics and Race Relations," and with the interpretation in Braithwaite, "Social Stratification and Cultural Pluralism."

⁵³ For examples, see Raymond T. Smith, review of *Social and Cultural Pluralism in the Caribbean,* "Culture and Social Structure in the Caribbean," and "People and Change"; Braithwaite, "Status of the Social Sciences in the Caribbean," and "Social Stratification and Cultural Pluralism"; Rubin, *Social and Cultural Pluralism in the Caribbean,* and "Culture, Politics and Race Relations"; Despres, "The Implications of Nationalist Policies in British Guiana"; Katrin Norris, *Jamaica: The Search for Identity* (London: Institute of Race Relations, 1962); Gordon K. Lewis, *op. cit.*

⁵⁴ Morris, "Indians in East Africa," and "The Plural Society."

⁵⁵ See Braithwaite, "Social Stratification and Cultural Pluralism"; Rubin, *Social and Cultural Pluralism in the Caribbean;* Raymond T. Smith, "British Guiana," and *British Guiana;* Cumper, "Notes on Social Structure in Jamaica"; Gordon K. Lewis, *op. cit.* For Morris' views, see his discussion of "social will" in "The Plural Society," p. 125: "It is not clear what Furnivall intended by the concept of 'social will' or his claim that plural societies do not display it. The presence or absence of this quality is critical in his scheme, and in the context of East Africa would appear to mean that Africans, Arabs, Europeans and Indians do not have a generally agreed set of ideas about right and wrong behaviour for the guidance of social action. The same thing can be said, however, of other societies that are not plural."

⁵⁶ M. G. Smith, *The Plural Society in the British West Indies,* pp. vii–xii and *passim;* M. G. Smith, *Stratification in Grenada.* See also van Lier, *op. cit.,* pp. 16–19.

⁵⁷ M. G. Smith, *The Plural Society in the British West Indies,* pp. 10–175, 304–321.

⁵⁸ Morris, "The Plural Society," p. 125; Morris, "Indians in East Africa," pp. 207–211; Braithwaite, "Social Stratification and Cultural Pluralism"; Gordon K. Lewis, *op. cit.;* Cumper, "Notes on Social Structure in Jamaica," pp. 8–10; Raymond T. Smith, "British Guiana," pp. 25–29; Raymond T. Smith, *British Guiana,* pp. 99–143; Benedict, "Stratification in Plural Societies"; Skinner, *op. cit.;* McKenzie, *op. cit*

[59] Rubin, "Culture, Politics and Race Relations"; Morris, "Indians in East Africa," pp. 208–209; Morris, "The Plural Society," p. 125; Braithwaite, "Status of the Social Sciences in the Caribbean," pp. 101–103; Braithwaite, "Social Stratification and Cultural Pluralism," pp. 823 ff.; Raymond T. Smith, review of *Social and Cultural Pluralism in the Caribbean*, p. 156; Raymond T. Smith, "People and Change"; Ellen Hellman, "Culture Contact and Change in the Union of South Africa," in *Ethnic and Cultural Pluralism in Intertropical Countries*, pp. 363–373; Kenneth Kirkwood, "Ethnic and Cultural Pluralism in British Central Africa," in *ibid.*, pp. 294–324.

[60] Morris, "Indians in East Africa," pp. 207–211; Morris, "The Plural Society," pp. 124–125; Braithwaite, "Social Stratification and Cultural Pluralism"; Skinner, *op. cit.*; Crowley, "Plural and Differential Acculturation in Trinidad," and "Cultural Assimilation in a Multiracial Society"; Raymond T. Smith, *British Guiana*, chap. 5; Benedict, *Indians in a Plural Society*, pp. 32–51; Benedict, "Stratification in Plural Societies"; Cumper, "Notes on Social Structure in Jamaica." But see Broom, *op. cit.*, and M. G. Smith, *Plural Society in the British West Indies*, and *Stratification in Grenada*.

[61] Morris, "Indians in East Africa," pp. 207–211; Morris, "The Plural Society"; Braithwaite, "Social Stratification and Cultural Pluralism"; Rubin, *Social and Cultural Pluralism in the Caribbean*; Raymond T. Smith, *British Guiana*, chap. 5; Raymond T. Smith, "People and Change"; Benedict, "Stratification in Plural Societies."

[62] Morris, "The Plural Society"; Braithwaite, "Social Stratification and Cultural Pluralism"; Raymond T. Smith, review of *Social and Cultural Pluralism in the Caribbean*, and "People and Change."

[63] Braithwaite, "Present Status of the Social Sciences in the Caribbean," and "Social Stratification and Cultural Pluralism."

[64] Rubin, *Social and Cultural Pluralism in the Caribbean*, and "Culture, Politics and Race Relations."

[65] Chandra Jayawardena, *Conflict and Solidarity in a Guianese Plantation* (London: Athlone Press of the University of London, 1963), pp. 9–13.

[66] Benedict, *Indians in a Plural Society*, p. 51; Benedict, "Stratification in Plural Societies."

[67] Raymond T. Smith, "British Guiana," review of *Social and Cultural Pluralism in the Caribbean*, and "People and Change."

[68] Morris, "The Plural Society," and "Indians in East Africa."

[69] Jayawardena, *op. cit.*; Chandra Jayawardena, "Religious Belief and Social Change: Aspects of the Development of Hinduism in British Guiana," *Comparative Studies in Society and History*, 8, no. 2 (Jan. 1966), 211–240; Benedict, *Indians in a Plural Society*, and "Stratification in Plural Societies." For alternative presentations see Sir Hilary Blood, "Ethnic and Cultural Pluralism in Mauritius," in *Ethnic and Cultural Pluralism in Intertropical Countries*, pp. 356–362; K. Hazeersingh, "The Religion and Culture of Indian Immigrants in Mauritius and the Effect of Social Change," *Comparative Studies in Society and History*, 8, no. 2 (Jan. 1966), 241–257; Despres, *Cultural Pluralism and Nationalist Politics in British Guiana*; David DeCaires and Miles Fitzpatrick, "Twenty Years of Politics in Our Land," *New World: Guyana Independence Issue* (Demerara, Guiana, May 1966), pp. 39–45; New World Associates, "Working Notes towards the Unification of Guyana," *New World* (Georgetown, British Guiana), I (March 1963), 1–81.

[70] Morris, "Indians in East Africa," pp. 209–210.

[71] Morris, "The Plural Society," pp. 124–125, citing Furnivall, "Political Economy of the Tropical Far East," pp. 198 ff.

[72] Furnivall, *Colonial Policy and Practice*, p. 307.

[73] Furnivall, "Some Problems of Tropical Economy," p. 168.

[74] Furnivall, *Colonial Policy and Practice*, p. 306.

[75] Furnivall, "Some Problems of Tropical Economy," p. 162.

[76] Furnivall, *Colonial Policy and Practice*, p. 306.

[77] *Ibid.*, p. 506.

[78] *Ibid.*, p. 297.

[79] *Ibid.*, pp. 286–290, 300–303.

[80] Morris, "The Plural Society," p. 124.

[81] *Ibid.*

[82] Furnivall, "Some Problems of Tropical Economy," p. 167.

[83] *Ibid.*, p. 168.

[84] Furnivall, *Colonial Policy and Practice*, p. 306.

[85] *Ibid.*, p. 307.

[86] *Ibid.*, p. 308.

[87] *Ibid.*, p. 310.

[88] *Ibid.*, p. 307.

[89] Morris, "Indians in East Africa," pp. 206–208.

[90] See M. G. Smith, "A Structural Approach to Comparative Politics," in David Easton, ed., *Varieties of Political Theory* (Englewood Cliffs, N.J.: Prentice-Hall, 1966), pp. 113–128; and my earlier papers in this volume.

[91] Morris, "Indians in East Africa," pp. 206–211; Morris, "The Plural Society," pp. 124–125.

[92] Furnivall, *Colonial Policy and Practice*, p. 304; Furnivall, "Some Problems of Tropical Economy," p. 168.

[93] Furnivall, *Colonial Policy and Practice*, p. 305.

[94] *Ibid.*, p. 307.

[95] Morris, "Indians in East Africa," p. 210.

[96] Morris, "The Plural Society," p. 124.

[97] Furnivall, *Colonial Policy and Practice*, p. 304.

[98] *Ibid.*, p. 311.

[99] *Ibid.*, p. 310.

[100] On Timbuktu, see Mahmoud Kati, *Tarikh el-Fettach*, trans O. Houdas and M. Delafosse (2d ed.; Paris: Adrien-Maison veuve, 1964); Horace Miner, *The Primitive City of Timbuctoo* (Princeton: Princeton University Press, 1953), pp. 3–47. On the Lozi and the Kololo, see Jan Vansina, *Kingdoms of the Savanna* (Madison: University of Wisconsin Press, 1966), pp. 209–216; also M. V. Brelsford, *The Tribes of Northern Rhodesia* (Lusaka: Government Printer, 1956), pp. 60–68. On the Zulu, see E. J. Krige, *The Social System of the Zulus* (Pietermaritzburg: Shuter and Shooter, 1936), pp. 3–12; Gluckman, *op. cit.*, pp. 28–31; also Vansina, *op. cit.*, p. 209. On the Mahdist uprising, see P. J. Holt, *The Mahdist State in the Sudan, 1881–1898: A Study of Its Origins, Development and Overthrow* (Oxford: Clarendon Press, 1958).

[101] On Mongol society, see Herbert Harold Vreeland, III, *Mongol Community and Kinship Structure* (3d ed.; New Haven: HRAF Press, 1962); Elizabeth E. Bacon, *Obok: A Study of Social Structure in Eurasia* (New York: Wenner-Gren Foundation, 1958); Lawrence Krader, "Feudalism and the Tartar Polity of the Middle Ages," *Comparative Studies in Society and History*, 1, no. 1 (Oct. 1958), 76–99. On Polynesia, see Marshall D. Sahlins,

Social Stratification in Polynesia (Seattle: University of Washington Press, 1958); also Raymond Firth, *We the Tikopia: A Sociological Study of Kinship in Primitive Polynesia* (London: Allen and Unwin, 1936), pp. 578–598.

[102] G. D. H. Cole, *Studies in Class Structure* (London: Routledge and Kegan Paul, 1955); D. V. Glass, ed., *Social Mobility in Britain* (London: Routledge and Kegan Paul, 1954); Peter Willmott and Michael Young, *Family and Class in a London Suburb* (London: Routledge and Kegan Paul, 1960); W. M. Williams, *Gosforth: The Sociology of an English Village* (London: Routledge and Kegan Paul, 1956).

[103] Morris, "The Plural Society," p. 125.

[104] *Ibid.*, p. 125. For rather different perspectives, see Leo Kuper, *An African Bourgeoisie: Race, Class and Politics in South Africa* (New Haven: Yale University Press, 1965); Philip Mason, "The Plural Society of Kenya," in *Ethnic and Cultural Pluralism in Intertropical Countries*, pp. 325–337; P. C. W. Gutkind, "Some African Attitudes to Multi-Racialism from Uganda, British East Africa," in *ibid.*, pp. 338–355; Fallers, "Ideology and Culture in Uganda Nationalism"; D. A. Low, *Political Parties in Uganda, 1949–1962* (London: Athlone Press of the University of London, 1962); Aidan Southall and P. C. W. Gutkind, *Townsmen in the Making: Kampala and Its Suburbs* (Kampala: East African Institute of Social Research, 1956); A. Bharati, "The Unwanted Elite of East Africa," *Trans-Action*, 3, no. 5 (July 1966), 37–41. A good summary of the political history of the four ex-British East African territories is in A. J. B. Hughes, *East Africa: The Search for Unity* (Harmondsworth: Penguin Books, 1963). For a more interesting case, Canada, see Broom, *op. cit.*, p. 881.

[105] Furnivall, *Colonial Policy and Practice*, p. 305. Compare with Radcliffe-Brown's view (*Structure and Function in Primitive Society*, pp. 201–202), Mayer's (*op. cit.*), Rex's (*op. cit.*), and studies by Leo Kuper and Pierre van den Berghe in this volume.

[106] M. G. Smith, *Plural Society in the British West Indies*, pp. 55, 60–63, 89 f., 111 f., and *passim*. See also data in "Pluralism in Precolonial African Societies," in this volume; also Colby and van den Berghe, *op. cit.*

[107] Firth, *Essays on Social Organization and Values*, pp. 177–178; cf. Sklar and Whitaker, *op. cit.*; Shils, *op. cit.*; Marriott, *op. cit.*; W. Arthur Lewis, *Politics in West Africa.*

[108] Furnivall, "Some Problems of Tropical Economy," pp. 171–184; Furnivall, *Colonial Policy and Practice*, pp. 408–537.

[109] Since this paper was written, two recent restatements by Morris of his objections to pluralism as a framework for sociological analyses confirm this interpretation of his earlier position. See H. S. Morris, review of M. G. Smith, *The Plural Society in the British West Indies*, in *Man*, n.s., 1, no. 2 (June 1966), 270–271; and H. S. Morris, "Some Aspects of the Concept Plural Society," *Man*, n.s., 2, no. 2 (June 1967), 169–184.

[110] Count Arthur de Gobineau, *Essay on the Inequality of Human Races* (Paris, 1853, 1855), trans. A. Collins (New York, 1914); Alexis de Tocqueville, *The Old Regime and the French Revolution*, trans. Stuart Gilbert (Garden City: Doubleday Anchor Books, 1955); Georges Le Febvre, *The Coming of the French Revolution, 1789*, trans. R. R. Palmer (New York: Vintage Books, 1957).

[111] On China, see Maurice Freedman, *Lineage Organization in Southeastern*

China (London: Athlone Press of the University of London, 1958); Ping-Ti Ho, *The Ladder of Success in Imperial China: Aspects of Social Mobility, 1368–1911* (New York: Wiley, 1964); also Bacon, *op. cit.*, pp. 167–176; Hu Hsien Chin, *The Common Descent Group in China and Its Functions* (New York: Viking Fund, 1948). On India, see J. H. Hutton, *Caste in India: Its Nature, Functions and Origins* (London: Cambridge University Press, 1946); Adrian C. Mayer, *Land and Society in Malabar* (London: Oxford University Press, 1952); Adrian C. Mayer, *Caste and Kinship in Central India* (London: Routledge and Kegan Paul, 1955); Oscar Lewis, *Village Life in Northern India* (New York: Vintage Books, 1965); M. N. Srinivas, Y. B. Damie, S. Shahani, and André Beteille, "Caste: A Trend Report and Bibliography," *Current Sociology*, XIII, no. 3 (1959). For the Zulu, see Krige, *op. cit.*, pp. 23–38, 176–183; Max Gluckman, "Kinship and Marriage among the Lozi of Northern Rhodesia and the Zulu of Natal," in A. R. Radcliffe-Brown and Daryll Forde, eds., *African Systems of Kinship and Marriage* (London: Oxford University Press, 1950), pp. 166–206; Max Gluckman, "The Kingdom of the Zulu of South Africa," in M. Fortes and E. E. Evans-Pritchard, eds., *African Political Systems* (London: Oxford University Press, 1940), pp. 25–55. For Uganda, see Audrey I. Richards, ed., *East African Chiefs* (London: Faber and Faber, 1960); Lloyd A. Fallers, ed., *The King's Men: Leadership and Status in Buganda on the Eve of Independence* (London: Oxford University Press, 1964). For the Nootka, see Philip Drucker, *The Northern and Central Nootkan Tribes*, Smithsonian Institution, Bureau of American Ethnology, Bulletin 144 (Washington: G.P.O., 1951). On the Benin and the Yoruba, see William R. Bascom, "The Principle of Seniority in the Social Structure of the Yoruba," *American Anthropologist*, 44 (1942), 36–46; William R. Bascom, "Social Status, Wealth and Individual Differences among the Yoruba," *American Anthropologist*, 53, no. 4 (Oct. 1951), 490–505; William R. Bascom, "Urbanization among the Yoruba," *American Journal of Sociology*, 50, no. 5 (March 1955), 448–454; P. C. Lloyd, "The Traditional Political System of the Yoruba," *Southwestern Journal of Anthropology*, 10, no. 4 (1954), 366–384; P. C. Lloyd, "The Political Structure of African Kingdoms: An Exploratory Model," in Michael P. Banton, ed., *Political Systems and the Distribution of Power* (London: Tavistock Publications, 1965), pp. 62–112; P. C. Lloyd, "Class Consciousness among the Yoruba," in Lloyd, *The New Elites of Tropical Africa*, pp. 328–341; R. E. Bradbury, *The Benin Kingdom and the Edo-Speaking Peoples of South-Western Nigeria* (London: International African Institute, 1957), pp. 13–47.

[112] Morris, "Indians in East Africa," pp. 208–209.

[113] Morris, "The Plural Society," p. 125.

[114] *Ibid.*

[115] *Ibid.*, p. 124; my italics.

[116] *Ibid.*, p. 125.

[117] Morris, "Indians in East Africa," p. 209; see Radcliffe-Brown, "On Social Structure," in his *Structure and Function in Primitive Society*, p. 202.

[118] *Ibid.*

[119] *Ibid.*

[120] Morris, "The Plural Society," p. 125; Morris, "Indians in East Africa," pp. 207–211.

[121] Morris, "Indians in East Africa," p. 194.

122 Jayawardena, *Conflict and Solidarity in a Guianese Plantation;* Benedict, "Stratification in Plural Societies," and *Indians in a Plural Society;* Speckman, *op. cit.*

123 Morris, "Indians in East Africa," p. 194.

124 Shils, *op. cit.,* pp. 23–24.

125 R. S. Rattray, *Ashanti Law and Constitution* (Oxford: Clarendon Press, 1929), pp. 72–284; K. A. Busia, *The Position of the Chief in the Modern Political System of Ashanti* (London: Oxford University Press, 1951), pp. 85–101; John P. Davis, *Corporations* (New York: Capricorn Books, 1961), pp. 156–208.

126 Raymond T. Smith, review of *Cultural and Social Pluralism in the Caribbean,* p. 156; Despres, "Implications of Nationalist Policies in British Guiana," p. 1052; Despres, *Cultural Pluralism and Nationalist Policies in British Guiana,* chap. 1; Morris, review of M. G. Smith, *The Plural Society in the British West Indies,* pp. 270–271; Rubin, *Social and Cultural Pluralism in the Caribbean;* Speckman, *op. cit.,* pp. 4–6; McKenzie, *op. cit.,* pp. 57–58. For my statements on these questions, see *The Plural Society in the British West Indies,* pp. 14–15, 66 ff., 78–86, 112, 157 f., 163–175, and *Stratification in Grenada,* pp. 4–5, 234 ff. For another adaptation of Malinowski's conceptions, see Rex, *op. cit.*

127 Radcliffe-Brown, "On Social Structure," in his *Structure and Function in Primitive Society,* p. 200.

128 Radcliffe-Brown, *Structure and Function in Primitive Society,* pp. 10–11.

129 *Ibid.,* p. 10.

130 Rubin, *Social and Cultural Pluralism in the Caribbean,* claims to find utopianism in this approach. Speckman, *op. cit.,* p. 6, claims that it leads to "trait-counting"; Despres, in his recent work, *Cultural Pluralism and Nationalist Policies in British Guiana,* rejects the distinction between basic and other institutions.

131 M. G. Smith, *The Plural Society in the British West Indies,* pp. 13–16, 40, 66–73, 75–91, 114–115, 157–159, 318–321.

132 Max Weber, *The Theory of Social and Economic Organization,* trans. A. M. Henderson and Talcott Parsons (Edinburgh: William Hodge, 1947), p. 137, chap. 1, sec. 13, par. 2.

133 M. G. Smith, "Pluralism in Precolonial African Societies," above.

134 Roland de Vaux, *Ancient Israel* (2 vols.; New York: McGraw-Hill, 1966), I, 11–13, 92–98.

135 Rattray, *op. cit.,* pp. 127–284; Busia, *op. cit.,* pp. 88, 98–99.

136 Lewis H. Morgan, *League of the Ho-dé-no-sau-nee, or Iroquois* (1851) (New York: Corinth Books, 1962), pp. 27 ff.; John A. Noon, *Law and Government of the Grand River Iroquois* (New York: Viking Fund, 1949), pp. 15–18.

137 Robert A. LeVine and Walter H. Sangree, "The Diffusion of Age-Group Organization in East Africa: A Controlled Comparison," *Africa,* 32, no. 2 (April 1962), 102.

138 Philip Mayer, *op. cit.*

139 Furnivall, "Some Problems of Tropical Economy," p. 171; but see also Furnivall, *Colonial Policy and Practice,* p. 547.

Chapter 14 Ethnic and Racial Pluralism: Some Aspects of Polarizaton and Depluralization

Leo Kuper

In this paper I seek to draw together some of the contributions in this volume, as they relate, first, to concepts of pluralism and the plural society; second, to the dimensions of pluralism and general social conditions affecting its manifestations; and third, to processes of polarization and depluralization of societies characterized by racial and ethnic pluralism. By polarization, in this context, I mean an increasing accentuation of plural division based on race and ethnicity and an intensification of conflict between the plural sections, whereas depluralization here denotes a diminishing salience of ethnic and racial pluralism.

I am deliberately concentrating on racial and ethnic pluralism, since it is with this type of pluralism that our case studies are specifically concerned. Certainly, religious pluralism is significant in many of the societies discussed in this volume, as in Uganda, Algeria, Zanzibar, and South Africa; and the new African states, like the colonial societies that preceded them, are universally characterized by cultural pluralism; but the main emphasis of our contributors is on racial and ethnic division, and this is the primary basis of the pluralism they analyze.

In emphasizing racial and cultural pluralism, I do not mean to imply that this is the very essence of pluralism, and that other expressions of pluralism are merely so conceived by way of analogy. Pluralism is a generic concept which describes a distinctive structure of group relations, and its social basis is varied. It may be constituted by class division, as in Disraeli's description of the structure of English society in the "hungry forties"; or it may be constituted by religious differences, as in Europe during the Reformation; or by differences in culture, race, or ethnic background. These bases of pluralism, which seem remarkably limited, are often found in association within the same society, as when religious and other cultural diversity coincides with racial division.

Clifford Geertz, in his discussion of a similar problem in "The Integrative Revolution," enumerates the following foci of "primordial attachment": assumed blood ties, race, language, region, religion, and custom.[1] By primordial attachment, he means a bond that stems from the assumed "givens" of social existence: "immediate contiguity and kin connection mainly, but beyond them the givenness that stems from being born into a particular religious community, speaking a particular language, or even a dialect of a language, and following particular social practices. These congruities of blood, speech, custom, and so on, are seen to have an ineffable, and at times overpowering, coerciveness in and of themselves."[2] The primordial attachments correspond in part to what I have described as the bases of pluralism, but only in part. Geertz specifically distinguishes primordial bonds from ties to class and party, arguing that groups formed on the basis of such ties are virtually never considered as possible self-standing, maximal social units or as candidates for nationhood, and that conflicts between them do not as a rule put into question the political integrity of the society. By contrast, disaffection based on race, language, or culture threatens partition, irredentism, or merger, a redrawing of the very limits of the state, a new definition of its domain.[3]

This is a valid argument for distinguishing the different bases of pluralism. Where pluralism rests on race and ethnicity, it seems to possess somewhat distinctive features, certainly as compared with even rigid and pervasive class distinctions. There is a greater likelihood of what Geertz describes as "primordial sentiment"; or, as Ali Mazrui comments in his contribution, tribes and races are more "total identities" than economic classes. But an important qualification is necessary. The plural structure of a society arises from the interaction of the plural sections. This is common to all forms of pluralism, whether of race, ethnicity, or class. There may be little that corresponds to an ethnic unit in the intermittent and detached relations, and the separate coexistence, of numerous and small local communities, and there may be little consciousness of a common ethnic identity. The reality of ethnic grouping and the awareness of ethnic identity, and similarly of racial organization and racial consciousness, may arise only in the process of incorporation and participation in the plural society. It is the interaction within this context of the plural society which affects the significance attached to race and ethnicity, the ideological emphases on these identities and their structural implications.

At the same time, though this may not be universally true, racial and ethnic sections have an origin, a basis of existence, external to, and preceding, the societies in which they are now incorporated, in contrast with classes that emerge only in societal interaction. In consequence, they are likely to have more enduring, comprehensive, and unique histories, a greater affinity perhaps for sentimental elaboration of identity, and a larger capacity for reasserting exclusive loyalties, after long periods of increasing commitment to broader, more inclusive, civic loyalties. It is because of such distinctive qualities, and because the case studies in this volume are primarily concerned with the pluralism of race and ethnicity, that I think it appropriate to develop the argument from this basis.

THE PLURAL SOCIETY

The concept of the plural society proved controversial throughout the colloquium. An initial problem was whether plural societies as defined in the Furnivall tradition, and by M. G. Smith, could really be described as societies. Was there sufficient interaction, and of such a nature, as to justify the use of the word "society"?

Davidson raises this issue in his analysis of pluralism in Northern Rhodesia/Zambia. He is concerned with the applicability of the concept "plural society" to Northern Rhodesia at different periods in its history, but his argument implies the need to redefine the concept. He asserts that in the early stages of white domination "Africans were no more members of Northern Rhodesian society, as recognized and constituted by duly enshrined authority, than the cattle and the game for whom 'reserves' were also soon marked out." When the Colonial Office took over, "nothing so organic even as a society of 'conflict pluralism' now appeared. . . . What the settlers had in mind was to impose a fully integrated but entirely separate European society upon a congeries of African societies. . . . there was in practice an utter domination and an unbounded subordination with no bonds or rights or obligations established between the two except those of the settlers' convenience. Nothing appears to have tied these two groupings together except a mutually hateful contiguity from which neither could escape." I take Davidson's meaning to be that the relationships between whites and Africans so lacked reciprocity, being unilaterally determined and imposed as upon objects rather than subjects of action, that they could hardly be described as social relationships, and that the mere incorporation of these diverse groups into a single political unit could hardly be conceived as constituting a society. He therefore prefers to draw a distinction between "a *system* of differential incorporation and a *society*, supposing the latter to have the organic characteristics of common values, or of evolving common values which the former does not have."

For Ali Mazrui, it is this very discontinuity, this extreme segmentation of groups, which characterizes the plural society. He writes that the "extreme case of a plural society is a society of total identities, of self-contained cultural systems or exclusive racial groups. . . . Relationships between the groups are at the level of either bare coexistence or minimal contact. This is perhaps the 'pure type' of a plural society." And he draws attention to the contradiction between plurality and unity in the conception of a plural society, quoting J. C. Mitchell's comment that the problem of plural societies lies in this contradiction: In what way can these societies be both plural and societies? Indeed, if they are plural, can they be societies?

A second problem raised in regard to the concept of the plural society relates to the level of analysis. There may be quite varied manifestations of pluralism at different levels of observation, or there may be pluralism at some levels and not at others. Alexandre makes the point that the plural society looks very different according to the level of observation, whether it be the Republic as a whole, la Métropole, A.O.F., a single colony, or a district, and he comments that even at the level of the district, there are so many variables that it is well-nigh impossible to draw a general picture. There may be a homogeneous African population in the district, with a French commandant, or the district may comprise several tribes or factions of tribes, with traditional chiefs or with nontraditional chiefs from other tribes.

A cognate problem is that of defining the boundaries of the system of interaction which constitutes the plural society. For both Furnivall and M. G. Smith, the plural society is a politically constituted territorial unit. But the boundaries of the system of interaction constituting the pluralism may not only extend beyond the territorial limits of the political unit, but they may vary in extension in different historical periods or in different situations. Thus Thompson emphasizes the distinction between tropical and temperate colonies: whites in the tropical colonies are a population of transients closely linked to the metropolis, whereas white settlers in the temperate colonies become an integral part of the colonial society. Presumably, then, the pluralism of the tropical colony would more firmly include the metropolis. Moreover, the socially meaningful units for the analysis of pluralism change over time, and Thompson therefore argues that the concept of society should be elastic enough to take cognizance of the realities of the social order in different eras and different areas from those in which we live or specialize. As nation-states are increasingly related to one another in the contemporary world by an interdependent economy and a network of communications, the boundaries of pluralism increasingly extend to the greater society.

Hilda Kuper raises the same question. She comments on the danger of translating the fluidity of changing relationships into rigidly formulated "analytic units" of autonomous political arrangements, which are then used as "real units" of comparison. Her paper offers a wealth of material, illustrating the varied dimensions of pluralism in different situations, as, for example, the repercussions of the partition between India and Pakistan on the relations among Indians in South Africa, or the contrast between Lohanas and Ismailis among the Asian communities of Uganda, with a greater commitment by the latter to the local Ugandan society, and a continuing participation by the former in the social relationships of their ancestral Indian society.

By way of further questioning of the concept of the plural society, there is Alexandre's criticism that it is ambiguous; he suggests that by "dropping the phrase 'plural society' altogether one can avoid the risk of nominalism which is in most cases a consequence of equivocal terminology in the social sciences." And van den Berghe rejects the concept, as formulated by M. G. Smith, on the two grounds that there may be pluralism, even though the constituent groups share the same general culture, and that the demographic ratio, whether the dominant group is a majority or a minority, does not so profoundly affect the structure of society as to justify the use of a typology that implies important qualitative discontinuities.

Some of the controversy over the concept of plural society stems from differences in political perspective between a radical revolutionary view and a liberal evolutionary view of the possibility of restructuring sectional relations in a plural society. It is the issue raised in my own paper, "Political Change in White Settler Societies," in which I explore the significance of individuation, and of social relationships across sectional divisions, for the restructuring of the plural society, though my conclusions in relation to South Africa rather support radical interpretations. It is the issue raised by Max Gluckman when he disagrees profoundly with Davidson's statement about Northern Rhodesia, prior to the late 1940's, that nothing appears to have tied these two groupings of Africans and whites together except mutually hateful contiguity from which neither could escape. It is an issue raised in different forms by various contributors and discussants, and it was expressed also in the assertion that M. G. Smith's papers in the colloquium formulated a theory of structural determinism. This is an interpretation which Smith explicitly rejects, and which his papers do not support. At the same time, he assigns a primary significance to structural pluralism, emphasizing the tendency for perpetuation of social cleavage, of cultural diversity, and of political and economic inequality, and the resistance to evolutionary change or erosion by cultural uniformities or associational continuities. It is these views that give a radical cast to his conception, even if structural pluralism is not assigned a role analogous to that of the relationship to the means of production in Marxist class theory.

This conflict of political perspectives is especially relevant to processes of change in plural societies, and I shall return to it in the discussion of polarization and depluralization. As to some of the more specific controversies over the concept of the plural society, I think they are easily resolved. Definitions seem to be in part a matter of taste. I would say that it is of the very essence of a plural society that it should be both plural and unitary, both discontinuous and continuous in its pattern of relations between the diverse groups. Indeed, I would regard this dualism as characteristic both of pluralism and of the plural society. The problem of the social boundaries within which the phenomena of pluralism should be analyzed seems to me to relate more to the requirements of analysis than to problems of conceptualization. The plural society may be conceived as a territorially defined unit, but this in no way implies that analysis be confined to these territorial limits. On the contrary, analysis should be pursued as extensively as necessary to interpret the plural relations. The position is the same as in the study of a factory, for example, where the internal system of the factory may be taken as the unit of analysis, and relationships may be followed to their extensions in the external system. Certainly under contemporary conditions, and in the context of the cold war and of racial tensions, the boundaries of plural relationships tend to be worldwide. Van den Berghe's objection to the concept of the plural society relates to aspects of a specific model and does not provide general grounds for its rejection. The dangers of nominalism are very real, and argument moves continuously from models of the plural society to actual societies which are assumed to exemplify the plural society, in such a way as to cause great confusion. But with an awareness of this tendency, it should be possible to guard against confounding the model with empirical reality, and against the consequent distortion of both.

In contrast with the objections raised against the use of the concept of the plural society, the idea of pluralism itself seems to have found acceptance, though in varied formulations. Since the plural society is simply a particular form of pluralism, it is best to proceed to a discussion of pluralism and of the relationship between different conceptions of pluralism and of plural societies.

PLURALISM AND THE PLURAL SOCIETY

There appears to be considerable agreement among contributors to this volume that pluralism is characteristic of all societies, or certainly of all complex societies; there is less agreement on what constitutes pluralism.

Mazrui, in "Pluralism and National Integration," offers the most eclectic approach. He writes that his definition of pluralism is comprehensive:

In its diversity of tribal and racial groups, we would regard Uganda as a case of ethnic pluralism. In its variety of systems of life, we would regard it as an instance of cultural pluralism. In the competitive relationship between Catholicism, Protestantism, and Islam in the life of the country, we would attribute religious pluralism to the total society. In its multiparty system, however unstable, the country had for a while maintained competitive pluralistic institutions —a framework for power contests in the polity. In its quasi-federal structure, while it lasted, the country had *constrictive* pluralistic institutions—an attempt to narrow the field of contest in advance by entrenching a certain division of powers prior to the scramble for other areas of political or social control. Pluralism is, in short, a complex of relationships between groups in a wider society.

Pluralism in a society refers then quite simply to a diversity of groups which sustain social relationships with one another. There is seemingly no limitation of pluralism to a specific type of relationship. Thus Mazrui comments that when Laski substituted for the notion of "Man *versus* the State" a view of society which thought of political life in terms of relations between groups, he was putting forward a theory of pluralism. Pluralism would seem to include both competitive and noncompetitive relationships between groups, though I think this is not certain. An earlier statement, that "there is pluralism in every society" since "pluralism is often a competitive complex of diverse groups—and virtually every society has its rival groups," can be interpreted as excluding noncompetitive relationships. As to the plural society, it is distinguished by the kind of pluralism involved, that is to say, in the "pure type," a pluralism of "total identities" or approximating total identities.

The eclectism is in some ways attractive, since it permits the accommodation of diverse approaches to pluralism, and particularly the antithetical conceptions of pluralism I discussed in the opening paper. I refer to conceptions of pluralism in terms of a competitive balance between groups conducive to democratic government, or in terms of conflict, of cultural incompatibility and sectional domination. Moreover, Mazrui's approach to the depluralization of plural societies as a process by which total identities become partialized presents, in a different perspective, the problem of social change from segmented to functionally differentiated societies, or from primordial attachments to civil politics.

Van den Berghe defines pluralism in strictly structural terms as "(1) segmentation into corporate groups that frequently, though not necessarily, have different cultures or subcultures; and (2) a social structure compartmentalized into analogous, parallel, noncomplementary but distinguishable sets of institutions." To this core definition, he adds a number of characteristics frequently associated with pluralism, such as relative absence of value consensus, cultural heterogeneity, conflict, and sectional domination.

Of the two aspects of structure described by van den Berghe, the reference to "segmentation into corporate groups" is clear enough, though it should perhaps be amplified by the inclusion of corporate *categories* to read "segmentation into corporate groups and categories," since subordinate plural sections may not have that measure of inclusive organization which is implied in the concept of corporate group. As to the reference to "sets of institutions" into which the social structure is compartmentalized, the problem is more complex. I understand him to mean that there may be pluralism even when members of different groups engage in the same institutional practices, of worship, marriage, inheritance, and so on, since he makes the specific point that cultural difference is not necessary to pluralism. The distinguishable sets of institutions must therefore refer to the participation of members of different groups in separate institutional structures, regardless of uniformity or difference in institutional practice. Pluralism, then, connotes segmentation, and institutional segregation, of corporate groups and categories. I cannot be certain of this interpretation, however, since van den Berghe specifically excludes from his definition of pluralism corporate group segmentation into institutionally identical units. In regard to the plural society, though van den Berghe conceives of pluralism as a variable, he does not develop a concept of a type of pluralism which would constitute the plural society, and as already mentioned, he rejects M. G. Smith's concept of the plural society.

I have commented that there has been a movement in M. G. Smith's ideas from an emphasis on cultural pluralism to an emphasis on structural pluralism. But pluralism in all his earlier formulations is essentially a structural category, defining the relations between groups of different culture. In his first paper on "Social and Cultural Pluralism," [4] he is concerned with cultural pluralism as an attribute of groups bound together by the distinctive pattern of group relations which he describes as pluralism or the plural society, and which he identifies in this volume by the characteristic of differential incorporation. He is not dealing with cultural pluralism as a disembodied phenomenon. In any event, he conceives of structure and culture as related through institutions. Since institutions combine social and cultural aspects, the culturally differentiated sections will also differ in their internal social organization. [5] The movement of ideas to which I refer concerns the processes, rather than the concept, of pluralism. Smith's first paper ascribes a primary role to cultural incompatibilities in molding the plural structure of the society. His present contribution emphasizes rather the primary significance of differential incorporation, but conceptually the differentially incorporated groups are still distinguished by cultural differences, whether antecedent to or consequent upon the differential incorporation.

Smith's final formulation of the concept of pluralism is given in the preceding paper, "Some Developments in the Analytic Framework of Pluralism." In differentiating three levels of pluralism—cultural, social, and structural—he constitutes cultural pluralism as an analytically distinct category consisting in institutional diversity without corresponding collective segregation. Since he views institutions as combining social and cultural aspects, I take his meaning to be either that cultural pluralism refers to institutional diversity regarded in detachment from the structure of groups within the society, or that the term is to be applied to situations where institutional diversity is not associated with structures of collective segregation. Where it is so associated (that is to say, where there is "organization of institutionally dissimilar collectivities as corporate sections or segments whose boundaries demarcate distinct communities and systems of social action"[6]), we have social pluralism; where there is also differential incorporation into hierarchies with sectional inequality in status and resources, then social pluralism becomes structural pluralism.

Both social and structural pluralism relate to the structural level of analysis. The plural society is simply a society characterized by structural pluralism in which the dominant group is a numerical minority. Under these conditions, Smith believes that structural pluralism attains its most extreme form. Whether minority domination is so highly correlated with extreme pluralism as to justify its inclusion as a special characteristic of the plural society, and whether the difference between majority and minority domination so profoundly affects the structure of pluralism as to justify the use of a typology that implies important qualitative discontinuities, are matters for empirical determination. Meanwhile it seems useful to distinguish plural structures with dominant minorities as a special category for research.

By way of concluding this review of concepts of pluralism, I should mention Alexandre's use of the word "plurality," as the work of all complex societies, and his preference for a consensual conception of pluralism, that is, one in which plurality is accepted as a basis for social relations. Max Gluckman has not concerned himself specifically with the concept of pluralism or of the plural society; he is presenting his own views on plural societies in an essay entitled "Tribalism, Ruralism and

Urbanism in Plural Societies," to be published in V. W. Turner, editor, *Profiles of Change: The Impact of Colonialism on African Societies* (in press). However, he writes in his paper for our colloquium that "there is an inherent instability in any society in which vertical divisions between territorial and/or ethnic segments are inadequately crossed by the development of links of organic (in Durkheim's sense), utilitarian, economic interdependence. Without that interdependence, civil war is endemic in the system." This is similar to the approach of J. C. Mitchell, who chooses the relative lack of counterbalancing cleavages across the component ethnic groups as one of the significant features of the plural society, in contrast with the cultural and ethnic differences which he views as, in themselves, of no account.[7] Perhaps pluralism, in Gluckman's conception, can be defined as vertical division between territorial or ethnic segments, without reference to the extent of crosscutting relationships between members of different segments.

These definitions of pluralism and the plural society seem almost as diverse as the phenomena themselves. Conceptions of pluralism vary both in the range and in the type of phenomena encompassed by the term. Mazrui offers the broadest definition: pluralism is a complex of relationships between groups in a wider society. There is reference to the social bases of pluralism in his distinction between ethnic, cultural, and religious pluralism, and to some political expressions of pluralism, in which case he uses the term "pluralistic institutions," but there is apparently no limitation to the nature of the group relationships constituting pluralism. Pluralism in this sense is characteristic of all societies. Van den Berghe narrows the concept of pluralism to a type of cleavage between groups, expressed generally in segmentation of the society, and more specifically in distinctive institutional practices. Pluralism, in his usage, may perhaps still be regarded as characteristic of most complex societies; but it excludes functional differentiation, such as the division of powers among the executive, administrative, legislative, and judicial branches of the government, and conceptions of a competitive balance between interest groups based on differentiated functions. M. G. Smith defines cultural pluralism broadly in his last paper as institutional diversity: his conception of social and structural pluralism is, however, highly restricted in its application. The terms refer to a sharp and pervasive cleavage in the form of systematic disassociation between the members of institutionally distinct collectivities. This is certainly not a general characteristic of societies, nor can his conception of pluralism accommodate the pluralism of competitive balance of interest and veto and pressure groups.

As to the plural society, reactions vary from total rejection of the concept to a conception of the plural society as an extreme form of pluralism, either the pluralism of total identity or the pluralism of extreme systematic, pervasive disassociation. Intermediate between these conceptions is an approach to the plural society as a society characterized by both divisive and integrative structures, or by both vertical and horizontal cleavages, in such manner that the vertical and divisive cleavages threaten to prevail.

Faced with this embarrassing riches of choice, I am reluctant merely to indicate an arbitrary preference. I propose then to proceed with a discussion of conditions and dimensions of pluralism and of processes of polarization and of depluralization, primarily as they emerge from the case studies in this volume, in the hope that this further analysis may be of value in developing an approach to concepts of pluralism and the plural society.

CONDITIONS OF PLURALISM

By conditions of pluralism, I refer to those general characteristics of societies which may be expected to influence significantly the expression of pluralism within them. Almost all our case studies deal with the *historical background and context* of relations between the plural sections, as significant conditions of pluralism. The poetic insight that "history never dies, at any rate in Ireland," seems appropriate also for the history of plural relations in many other societies. The historical dimension would include such aspects as the nature of colonial policy and of direct or indirect rule, the past conflicts and other contacts between the plural sections, and the historiography, myth, and stereotype in which these experiences are given contemporary expression and significance.

The discussion of the appropriate analytic unit for the study of pluralism stressed the relevance of *relations between societies*, or of relations established by plural sections across societal boundaries, and of international relations, as further significant conditions. Clearly in an era of decolonization, and under conditions in which the plural sections were racially differentiated as in colonial Africa, and under conditions of the cold war, United Nations involvement, extensive international investment, and an increasingly operative world value system repudiating racial discrimination, the boundaries of African pluralism are worldwide. The internal relations of the plural sections may be quite transformed by the possibility, and reality, of foreign support and international intervention.

M. G. Smith, in "Pluralism in Precolonial African Societies," analyzes, as a main theme, the influence of the *structure and culture of the plural sections* on the types of interethnic accommodation resulting from their interaction. In many of the remaining case studies, there is similar concern with conditions of cultural and structural diversity, though less explicit. These conditions are particularly significant in the constitution of "stranger" groups. They are significant also for the analysis of the different ideologies of the colonizing powers, and of the relationship between ideological mission and actual practice, or between the formal and substantive aspects of colonial (and white settler) rule.

The scale of the society is likely to influence the manifestations of pluralism. By *scale* of the society I mean the extent of functional differentiation, elaboration of political and economic institutions, level of technological skills and material equipment, and size of population. In such a small-scale society as that of Zanzibar, revolutionary change in the structure of power was a relatively minor operation, and could be carried through by a few revolutionary leaders with modest armed support. There may be little relationship between the revolutionary assumption of power and the plural structure of the society. Revolutionary change may take the form of a sudden coup without any thoroughgoing polarization of the society into hostile armed camps. In a society that is more complex and of larger scale, revolutionary change in power would call for a massive operation, directly related to the plural structure and preceded by substantial polarization. Variation in scale is likely to affect many other aspects of pluralism, quite apart from the possibilities and character of revolutionary change. Functional differentiation may provide a basis for intersectional relations cutting across the plural cleavages, and in this way promote a depluralization of the society. Conversely, the organizational and technical resources of more complex and larger-scale societies may more readily permit elaboration of effective formal structures of political control, and thus perpetuate sectional domination.

The consequences for pluralism of variations in the *demographic basis* are discussed by both van den Berghe and Smith. Two aspects should be distinguished: first, the number of persons in each of the plural sections, both their absolute numbers and their numbers relative to one another; and second, the numbers of the plural sections themselves, whether biplural or multiplural.

As to the influence of *relative numbers,* or demographic ratio, Smith concludes, in "Pluralism in Precolonial African Societies," that there is no invariant relationship between the forms of interethnic accommodation established by different groups and the demographic ratio of their numbers. Presumably, however, there are certain probabilities of relationship under specified conditions of culture and structure. Thus I assume a higher probability of domination resulting from the contact between ethnic units of roughly similar technologies and organizational resources, where there is a substantial disparity in numbers. Conversely, where the dominant ethnic, or racial, section is a small numerical minority, its domination should generally presuppose a more advanced technology and greater organizational capacity; and there may be qualitative differences in the structure of the society, under conditions of minority domination, as suggested by Smith's concept of the plural society. Once the plural structure of the society is established, the demographic ratio is naturally affected by this structure, and it may become the basis of specific political action, influencing immigration policies, communal and qualified franchise arrangements, and the forms and processes of decolonization.

As to *absolute numbers,* there is some suggestion in these papers, with reference to the white settler situation, that plural divisions are accentuated with an increase in the number of white settlers. Alexandre writes that the French commandants, if they were to be effective, were obliged to Africanize, to go native to a certain extent, to rely on African assistants since they were short of European personnel, to integrate. Germaine Tillion, in her book *France and Algeria,* makes a somewhat similar comment on the integrative effects of aloneness, when she writes that the first colons "steeped themselves in Algeria; it penetrated them to the marrow—because a man alone can resist a crowd no longer than a sponge resists the sea." [8] With increasing numbers, Alexandre suggests, integration is slowed down, particularly in the towns and main outstations, the white settlers turning in on themselves and away from Africans. Mercier makes the same observation in regard to increasing social distance between Europeans and Africans in Dakar, referring to a numerical threshold beyond which, as competition mounts, there is an increasing probability of interethnic violence. [9] I would suppose the effect of small numbers to be quite variable, and influenced by cultural differences. English settlers may consistently maintain great social distance, regardless of their numbers. Where there are larger numbers, there is certain to be increasing penetration of indigenous societies, and growth of intersectional, as also no doubt of competitive, relationships. White settler numbers, in the English colonial situation, were of course, significant for the possibility of maintaining realistic claims for independence.

The consequences of variation in the *numbers of plural sections* are mentioned in van den Berghe's paper, and they are a specific focus of Hilda Kuper's analysis in " 'Strangers' in Plural Societies." A general exploration of the relevance of variation in numbers of groups may be found in a paper by Jean-Louis Quermonne, "Le Problème de la Cohabitation dans les Sociétés Multi-Communautaires," [10] the latter term corresponding to "plural societies." Quermonne distinguishes two categories *sociétés bi-communautaires* and *sociétés pluri-communautaires,* in the sense of "un nombre élevé de communautés au point de donner l'impression d'une mosaïque." [11] As to *sociétés tri-communautaires,* he believes that if they do exist, their situation is generally precarious, and that, upon decolonization, the third community tends to disperse or to identify with one of the two predominating communities.

The presence of a third section seems quite characteristic of European colonization in Africa. Perhaps extreme cultural and social distance between dominant and subordinate groups imposes the need for an intervening third group. The separation of this third group from both whites and Africans is certainly very marked in the case of Indians in South Africa and East Africa, and I suppose that at certain periods of their history, or in certain provinces, there was a situation approximating that of *sociétés tri-communautaires.* What the fate of these communities will be in such decolonized societies as those of Kenya or Uganda, it is still too early to discern.

The significance of numbers of plural sections is naturally variable. Quermonne shows how it is affected, *inter alia,* by demographic ratios, such as numerical parity or inequality of the populations of plural sections in biplural situations, and the command of an absolute majority by a single plural section in the multiplural situation. This is related, in turn, to patterns of localization, whether plural sections are localized, and if so whether they constitute a numerical majority in their areas. I think that the situation in which plural sections are localized and do constitute local majorities, and in which there is nevertheless some dispersion of their members in the localities of other sections, may be a circumstance contributing to crosscutting loyalties and national integration where conditions are stable, but to violence and conflict where there is tension between the sections.

I have already commented on the *social bases* of pluralism. The contributors to this volume, proceeding in fact from varied concepts, refer to a variety of bases of pluralism, including race and ethnicity, as socially defined, religion, culture and language, regional and territorial organization, ecology and economy, caste, estate and class. These bases may be compared with the foci of "primordial sentiment" enumerated by Geertz, or with Quermonne's list of particularisms which constitute the individuality of the communities (*particularismes géographiques, ethniques, religieux, culturels et linguistiques, économiques et sociaux*).[12]

Pluralism is likely to vary in some relationship to its different social bases. Presumably discontinuity and cleavage will tend to be more extreme where pluralism incorporates such "maximal social units" as territorially organized ethnic units, or where many different bases of pluralism coincide, as in colonial societies in which indigenous peoples and European rulers were distinguished by race, ethnicity, religion, culture and language, regional and territorial organization, ecology and economy. There may also be differences in persistence, related to the accessibility of the distinguishing characteristics, as, for example, ease of conversion to the religion of the dominant group where the basis of pluralism is religious difference, as compared with acquisition of the race of the dominant group in situations of racial pluralism. I turn now to consider some of these variations in the dimensions of pluralism.

DIMENSIONS OF PLURALISM

I have selected for comment the more important dimensions of variation in the manifestations of pluralism. The dimension of *particularism-universalism* relates to the mode of incorporation. M. G. Smith, in his third paper, distinguishes between structures in which individuals are incorporated directly, on identical conditions, as citizens, and structures in which they are incorporated indirectly, through their segmental or sectional identification, such as membership in an ethnic unit. The first mode of incorporation he describes as *universalistic* or *uniform;* the second may take one of two forms, either *equivalent* incorporation, where the society is constituted as an order of structurally equivalent but exclusive corporate sections, and *differential* incorporation, where it is constituted as an order of structurally unequal, exclusive, corporate sections. *Differential* incorporation he identifies as structural pluralism.

I shall use the terms *universalistic* or *uniform,* as above, to describe direct incorporation of individuals, and the term *particularist* for structures in which the primary units are corporate sections or divisions, and in which individuals are incorporated through their membership in these units. In this sense particularism would be constituted by both *equivalent incorporation* and *differential incorporation,* that is, to say in the case of ethnic units, by both ethnic consociation and ethnic domination.

Differential incorporation is the structural form of many of the systems of domination familiar to students of stratification theory, and exemplified, in their wide variety, in our case studies of African societies. It includes all the different styles of colonial rule—French, British, Portuguese, and Belgian—and also mandated territories and protectorates. It may be conceived as a variable, measured by a range of constitutional forms from those in which there is extreme differentiation of the plural sections to those approximating equivalent incorporation. There may be variability in the mode of subordination of different ethnic units; or there may be uniform incorporation, at the formal level, but differential incorporation at the substantive level; or there may be a combination of uniform and differential incorporation, as for example in uniform franchise arrangements which have the effect of enfranchising small numbers of a subordinate ethnic section, while disenfranchising the great majority.

Equivalent incorporation appears in its most characteristic form as a federation of autonomous, territorially based divisions. There may also be equivalent incorporation of ethnic or religious or other sections which are neither autonomous nor territorially based. Thus, equivalent incorporation may be found in structures that loosely federate relatively distinct societies, as well as in centralized political structures. Some of the diversity of these types of incorporation is examined by Quermonne, though under different terminology.[13] He distinguishes procedures for national integration of the different communities from institutional devices guaranteeing their cohabitation. National integration, a process of *"uniformisation progressive"* in the way of life and legal status of members of the different communities, corresponds to "uniform incorporation." Guarantees for cohabitation of the communities, corresponding in many ways to equivalent incorporation, he treats under the two headings of federal and pluralist systems.

Pluralist systems, for Quermonne, have somewhat the same connotation as in the pluralist theories of competitive balance, the basis of the pluralism, however, being the racial, ethnic, regional, religious, or other communities, and not functionally differentiated structures. Quermonne describes the philosophy of pluralism as resting on the conception that political societies are not simply composed of individuals, but are constituted equally by intermediate communities whose political existence ought to be recognized independently of the citizenship of the members who compose them. Pluralism consists then in conferring juridical personality on these communities and recognizing them as corporations intermediate between the individual and the state, with political participation proportional to their numerical importance and constituting at the same time a real representation.[14] There may be a single electoral college, or plural colleges; proportional representation in a lower house and equal representation in an upper house; and apportionment of different executive positions among the communities.

Federal systems vary in the extent to which the populations of the federated units are interspersed. These differences in concentration or dispersion may be expected to influence the stability of intersectional relations.[15] Federations readily dissolve into separate societies, or they may be transformed into systems of differential incorporation. The reverse movement from differential incorporation to equivalent incorporation is unlikely, save under guarantee or control by an outside power.

Here I have in mind the British policy of decolonization in such territories as Kenya and Northern Rhodesia/Zambia, which progressed from differential incorporation of the plural sections to an increasing equivalence, preparatory to independence and constitutional depluralization.[16]

The distinction M. G. Smith makes between modes of incorporation is a valuable contribution and basic to any concept of pluralism. He applies these categories to the general political structure of the society, but they are equally applicable to institutional structures, such as churches, schools, universities, or industrial establishments. A typology of institutional structures would include the following:

1) *Separate* structures, corresponding to separate societies, as in the separation between independent Ethiopian churches and parent mission churches.

2) *Federated* types of structure, corresponding to equivalent incorporation, such as federations of African, Colored, and Indian political associations, each maintaining its separate organization and autonomy. Where there is political domination of the society by one of the plural sections, the federated structures are likely to be confined to subordinate plural sections.

3) *Parallel* structures,[17] where there are divisions into different sections, such as racial divisions, separated at the local level, for example, but brought together at other levels by district or regional committees, or shared national presidents and executives.

4) *Colonial-type* structures, corresponding to differential incorporation, with separation and direct, or indirect, rule. These would include *intercalary* structures, functioning between dominant and subordinate sections, and serving both to maintain separation and to provide contact and control. Parallel, colonial-type, and intercalary structures were commonly used in the mission churches in Africa.

5) *Unitary* structures, corresponding to uniform incorporation of individuals without reference to racial or ethnic identity. In the movement toward integration, there is often an intermediate type of structure, with substantial integration at the level of ordinary members, but with the de facto reservation of most positions of executive and financial control for members of the politically dominant group.

Measures of particularism and universalism may thus be sought at both the societal and institutional levels. There may, of course, be variation between institutional structures of the same society, in the reliance on particularist or uniform modes of incorporation, thus adding to the complexity of analysis at the institutional level.

The dimension of *segregation-assimilation* is independent of the mode of incorporation, though closely related to it. Uniform modes of incorporation may encourage assimilation, and differential modes of incorporation may enjoin segregation, but they do not fully determine either. Even in the extreme case of apartheid in South Africa, where the principle of differential incorporation of the racial groups is systematically applied under penal sanctions with the object, *inter alia*, of imposing segregation, there are many relationships across corporate boundaries, deviating from the prescribed patterns.

Van den Berghe discusses this dimension under the concept of social pluralism. He distinguishes three levels of social pluralism: group (or sectional), institutional, and individual. "At the group level," he writes, "social pluralism is a direct function of the extent to which mechanisms of social or spatial distance or avoidance exist between corporate groups, or an inverse function of the density of the network of intergroup ties, or, to use a different measure yet, a direct function of the ratio of *intra*group ties to *inter*group ties." To these measures, he adds the further measure of differences in quality of intergroup and intragroup relations, constituting role polarization. Social pluralism at the institutional level refers to the range in the number and types of institutions shared by members of different sections, and at the individual level to the ease of movement from one section and one institutional structure to another.[18] I think his discussion provides a useful framework for specifying some of the variable dimensions of segregation-assimilation.

Cultural diversity-homogeneity has been very closely analyzed by M. G. Smith, both in his paper, "Social and Cultural Pluralism," and in his contributions to this volume. His papers offer a system of basic concepts, distinguishing between cultural homogeneity, heterogeneity, and pluralism, between the private and the public domains, between sacred and secular orientations, and between modes of institutional articulation. He refers also to institutional capacity to absorb other groups, or institutional exclusiveness, as in the observation that the "Nyasa Ngoni evidently made no attempt to incorporate captive or conquered peoples in their age-regiments; and, having no alternative structures capable of accommodating and socializing large numbers of non-Ngoni to their society, these Ngoni slaughtered or sold defeated groups into slavery, without even seeking to occupy their lands" ("Pluralism in Precolonial African Societies"). Van den Berghe organizes this dimension of cultural diversity along a range from *maximally pluralistic,* as between European colonizers and African pastoralists, to *minimally pluralistic,* where there are only subcultural differences. Gluckman selects for emphasis the polar concepts of *consensus-dissensus,* to refer to agreement or disagreement between particular persons on a goal or value or closely associated set of goals or values, and *coherence-discoherence* to describe the compatibility or incompatibility of "all goals and values, and held views of what the society is like."

Two further aspects should be emphasized: first, values regarding cultural diversity, whether tolerant and approving, or intolerant and oriented to cultural uniformity; and second, values affecting attitudes to "strangers" and members of other racial or ethnic groups, whether predisposing to receive and assimilate, or hostile and exclusive. There is often an ideological component in the expression of these values, which are responsive to the economic and political relations between the plural sections.

The dimension of *inequality-equality* is expressed in the differential access to, and distribution of, power, status, and material resources.

The final dimensions to which I refer, *discontinuity-continuity* and *superimposition-dissociation*, are to an appreciable extent summarizing measures. The dimension of *discontinuity-continuity* may be viewed from two different aspects. The first relates to the structure of the society, and the substructures of its institutions. Extreme discontinuity may be expressed in the differential incorporation of plural sections, as in a sharp discontinuity of political rights, where the franchise is reserved for all adult members of the dominant group, and subordinate sections are totally disenfranchised. It may be expressed in ecological pattern, as in the extreme segregation of residential areas in many of the African colonies, and the profound qualitative differences between them; or in wide cultural differences between groups, including differences in language, or in extreme inequality in their possession of material resources. Discontinuity does not necessarily imply separate structures. There may be great discontinuity within a single structure, as in the discontinuity in earnings of unskilled and skilled workers in industrial organizations; and there may be almost as much discontinuity in the church of a single denomination, such as the Anglican church in South Africa, as in the separate structures of the South African government's apartheid policy.

The second aspect of *discontinuity-continuity* relates to the distribution of members of the plural sections in the various structures. The range is from substantial continuity in distribution, where recruitment is relatively open for members of all the plural sections, to substantial discontinuity, as when different levels and structures are reserved for different sections. In some cases, the mode of differential incorporation may establish an absolute correspondence between discontinuity in structure and discontinuity in distribution, as in a discriminatory franchise which excludes subordinate groups from parliamentary participation. In others, there may be a varying relationship between the structural and distributive aspects of discontinuity. Thus, in South Africa, discontinuity in wage structures coincides with the concentration of Africans at the level of unskilled wages; but this concentration is not absolute. There is some recruitment of Africans to semiskilled and skilled manual employment, as well as to clerical and professional posts, so that the actual distribution of personnel from different plural sections is less discontinuous than the structures themselves. On the whole, however, I would anticipate that the greater the discontinuity in structure, the greater the probability of differential recruitment. The presence of an intermediate third section, such as Indians in colonial East Africa, may be associated with greater continuity both in structure and in recruitment, when the system is viewed as a whole, but with greater discontinuity as between some of the plural sections, as for example Africans and Europeans, precisely because of the intervening position of Indians.

There are naturally variant patterns of continuity and discontinuity in different structures, and variant patterns of recruitment. Conflicting patterns, as for example of increasing continuity in economic structure and recruitment, and of persistent or even increasing discontinuity in political structure, are likely to stimulate revolutionary action. It is inevitable that there should be appreciable continuities, both in structure and culture, between groups that have lived together for long periods, though many of these continuities may have little significance for constitutional change.

The dimension of *superimposition-dissociation* is derived from Dahrendorf's discussion in *Class and Class Conflict in Industrial Society*.[19] There is superimposition to the extent that lines of cleavage coincide throughout the structures of the society, and dissociation to the extent that these lines of cleavage diverge (or are orthogonal, to use van den Berghe's phrasing of this point).[20] In the present context, extreme superimposition would connote that the plural sections are differentiated by culture (including language), mode of incorporation, segregation, and access to power, status, and resources; that there is discontinuity in group membership and level of participation, both at the institutional and societal levels; and that unresolved issues of conflict between the plural sections increasingly cumulate. Extreme superimposition corresponds to Mazrui's concept of total identity, and, where there is domination also by a culturally distinct minority, to M. G. Smith's concept of the plural society.

Gluckman offers the polar concepts of *articulation-disarticulation* and *cohesion-discohesion* to describe the extent to which parts of a system, or subsystem, are linked, or not linked, together. Cohesion refers to the maintenance of the structure of a particular social field in something like continuous pattern by such factors as outright force, economic interdependence, agreement on ultimate goals, and/or crosscutting loyalties. It is a dimension that is clearly related to *discontinuity-continuity* of structures and to *superimposition-dissociation*, but it is concerned with a different aspect. A third summarizing measure of the extent of cohesion would certainly be valuable.

POLARIZATION AND DEPLURALIZATION

Superimposition of cleavages in a wide variety of structures, and under conditions of systematic domination, is likely to be associated with processes of polarization into hostile camps. But this is not necessarily the case. The dominant group may command the resources to maintain cohesion and compel compliance, so that there is little manifestation of conflict, and subordinate sections are, or seem, quiescent under this powerful domination. Indeed, there may be a measure of acquiescence, and not merely quiescence. Conversely, sections may become polarized in their relationships even under conditions of increasing dissociation between sectional membership and societal participation. Clearly the subjective reactions are an integral part of polarization, and it is these aspects that Lofchie stresses in his discussion of the character of plural societies in the developing areas. He finds a source of extreme conflict in the dissonance between pervasive ideas of human equality, and prevailing social and political arrangements which deny this equality.

Subjectively, polarization is marked by the heightened salience of sectional identity, and the increasing perception of social relationships in terms of racial, ethnic, or other sectional conflict. Political reactions become polarized, as shown by antithetical interpretations of the same event (as, for example, the disturbances at Sétif, Algeria, in May, 1945, assumed on the Moslem side to be a provocation organized by the colons, and, on the side of the colons, to have been premeditated by the Moslems),[21] or by antithetical emotional responses to the same event (jubilation by the dominant group, despondency by the subordinate, as in the celebration of heroes' days by the conquerors, transmuted by the conquered into days of mourning). These political reactions are often made explicit in ideologies, which both express and promote polarization. In my paper, "Conflict and the Plural Society: Ideologies of Violence among Subordinate Groups," I sketched one such ideology, its main tenets being that the society is divided into reciprocally exclusive sections, between which there is absolute opposition of interest and irreconcilable conflict; that only violence can be effective for change, and that it is both necessary and inevitable; and that the life chances of the subordinated sections are governed by a collective destiny from which there is no escape through mediating structures and individuating processes. Naturally ideologies of violence among dominant and subordinate sections crystallize in some reciprocal relationship to each other.

At the objective level of polarization in social interaction, there is contraction of the middle ground of optional intersectional relationships, and sharpening of the qualitative contrasts between intersectional and intrasectional relationships. Lines and issues of cleavage are superimposed, and this is expressed in the rapid escalation of the most varied, and sometimes most minor local and specific disturbances to the level of general nationwide intersectional conflict. There is increasing violence, mounting by a dialectic of violence and counterviolence; and probably there are broad dialectical processes within the society, arising out of the distribution of land and of power, and driving toward more extreme polarization.

Depluralization, by contrast, indicates subjectively the diminishing salience of racial, ethnic, or other secional ties. There may be explicit ideologies which assume the common interests of members of different sections, assert the efficacy of compromise and intersectional cooperation, and affirm the social ideal of assimilation (as in ideologies of the common society, or of the "melting pot"). Objectively, there is increasing continuity in the structures of the society, and in the distribution of population in these structures. Other bases of association, horizontal linkages arising from common interests and functional differentiations, cut across the initial clevages. Segregated, parallel, and intercalary structures dissolve, and there is increasing integration in institutional structures. Qualitative differences in intrasectional and intersectional relationships diminish. With the increasing significance of many diverse bonds between people of different sections, lines of cleavage and issues of conflict become dissociated, thus reducing the probability of escalation from minor disturbances. There is a commitment to compromise, and the cumulative experience of compromise and conflict resolution may be expected to encourage further depluralization.

Now I assume that, empirically, societies are very rarely polarized. They may appear so when ideal type models are transposed into descriptions of actual societies, or in revolutionary ideology, or in academic discourse with its partiality for dichotomized concepts. Perhaps there may be some approximation to a polarized state in times of revolutionary struggle, though even in the extreme case of the Algerian revolution, lines of cleavage by no means precisely coincided with the divisions between the plural sections. Fanon, in "Algeria's European Minority," [22] describes the collaboration of European and other non-Arab Algerians with the revolutionary forces. Germaine Tillion observes that during the actual period of revolutionary struggle, even among the most fanatic, the most committed, the most compromised ultras, there are almost always curious ambivalences which explain certain incredibly rapid reversals; [23] and she records that as she listens to Moslem Algerians of any faction, there is "not one among them, in the cities or in the country, who doesn't number in his immediate family at least one victim of our [French] repression. And none who hasn't some relative engaged in the rebellion and at least one seriously compromised in the eyes of the F.L.N. May fate spare them a purge from either side, for not one family will escape without losses." [24] Dualism, ambiguity, ambivalence—I am not sure what terms to use—generally characterize the relations of the plural sections, even in revolutionary situations. Outside of absolute genocide, there are always elements of both convergence and divergence, of cleavage and integration, between the plural sections. [25]

The *dualism* of tendency seems quite explicit in many of the contributions to this volume. It is expressed in *conceptual approaches:* the conception of pluralism as a continuum varying along certain dimensions (van den Berghe); the characterization of depluralization as a movement from the extreme of separate coexistence to coalescence, through a process by which identity becomes increasingly partialized (Mazrui); the approach to plurality (pluralism) as the work of all complex societies, which can generate either a conflictual or consensual situation (Alexandre); the insistence that there must be some measure of organic interrelatedness, before the term "plural society" can be used to describe a system of plural relationships (Davidson); and the analysis in terms of the relations between consensus and dissensus, cohesion and lack of cohesion, cooperation and strife, and so on (Gluckman).

Dualism is quite characteristic of many of the *statuses* described in these case studies. Alexandre shows the most varied dualism in the statuses of colonizers (missionaries, colons, traders, and administrators) and in the new statuses of ruling African elite, participating simultaneously in one totally non-African culture and several variegated indigenous ones; and Hilda Kuper probes the variations in dualism within the Asian populations of East Africa.

Dualism inheres also in the *personality;* it is particularly marked among westernized African intellectual elites, who combine plural opposition within their own personalities. Malek Haddad, an Algerian writer *d'expression française,* in his phrase "la langue française est mon exil," captures some of the pathos of ambivalence in cultural identification with both France and Algeria; and in his description of his own generation as one of transition, a generation of curios in the museum of colonialism, beset with contradiction, nonsense, and paradox,[26] he expresses a condition of ambiguity and confusion in the process of emancipation from colonial domination. Tillion observes that "all the elite groups of the Maghreb nations have engaged, since adolescence, in a double participation: first, in the structures dreaming of independence and consequently steeped in love, pride, and concern for their country; subsequently (or rather, at the same time), in a complete absorption of French culture, imbibed at the very heart of our universities." [27] The westernized intellectual, leading the movement for independence from colonial rule, in a sense strikes also against himself. But the dualism persists: it is not resolved by independence. Gordon writes of a progressivist-Islamic dichotomy in the ideological consciousness of independent Algeria,[28] and quotes Mustapha Mohammedi on the *déchirement* in Algerian thought: "Pulled at by a Cartesian rationalism learnt at European universities, tugged at by an absurd and atavistic logic, drawn to an exquisite and elegant poetry, it can only find rest and salvation in the religious principles of Islam." [29]

At the societal level, my own paper, "Political Change in White Settler Societies," analyzes the dualism in processes of cleavage and integration, and seeks to estimate the significance of individuating processes in providing new bases for the restructuring of racially divided societies. Thompson's analysis of the language situation in South Africa shows the dualism between policies of racial separation and domination on the one hand, and processes of racial integration on the other. Lofchie's paper on Zanzibar, as I interpret it, demonstrates the varied potentialities for change which may inhere in plural structures by reason of dualisms in relationships and processes. From a transcontinental perspective, the revolutionary change in Zanzibar may appear simply as an inevitable consequence of a situation in which Arabs so oppressed Africans that the latter were forced to rise up and strike down their oppressors in bloody slaughter. On closer analysis, however, it appears that there was diversity among both Arabs and Africans, the patterns of Arab-African pluralism varying with different African ethnic groups and histories of contact and of land settlement, and that there were ties of loyalty and identity and of common religion between sections of these populations. It would seem also that the bloody revolution was by no means predetermined and inevitable, that it was led by a small group of mainland Africans with much support from Hadimu and mainland Africans, and that the existing provisions of the constitution might well have provided effective means for peaceful evolutionary change.

This dualism has important consequences for processes of structural change. In the first place, processes are reversible, so that as depluralization proceeds and horizontal linkages multiply and circumstances seem to favor the homogenization of the society, the old cleavages may be reasserted with great vigor. There is no automatic process of evolutionary change by progressive increase in intersectional relationships. Second, and closely related to reversibility in process, the dualism provides in certain situations the possibility of effective choice between strategies of polarization and strategies of depluralization. There are of course other situations, which are so highly structured by political regulation and deployment of force that they leave almost no room for maneuver and virtually restrict choice to violent revolution or submission. But this is not the usual situation: there are often significant alternatives in choice of political action.

Various processes are described in this volume as contributing to depluralization. They include conflict and conflict resolution: an evolutionary process of increasing functional differentiation, providing new bases for association between members of different sections, and the progressive extension of social relationships across the original sectional divisions; conversely, a dialectical process in which sectional identities are emphasized and sectional divisions sharpened in the movement to depluralization; and regulated processes of change toward a system of uniform incorporation under the control of an outside power. There is almost no discussion in these papers of the role of charismatic leaders, political parties, nationalist movements, and the one-party state as agents of depluralization, creating broad loyalties which transcend the plural divisions, and establishing a political framework within which members of different sections may come together in new relationships. The reader is referred for these perspectives to the analyses, among others, of Coleman and Rosberg in *Political Parties and National Integration in Tropical Africa*.[30]

Conflict as conflict resolution is one of those paradoxes in the work of Georg Simmel which has intrigued scholars. Some of the validity of this paradox seems to derive from fleeting and changing concepts of conflict. My own reaction to theories that accomplish a metamorphosis of conflict into conflict resolution is somewhat guarded, since I am acutely conscious of, and perhaps overemphasize, the potentially destructive consequences of conflict in the context of racial and ethnic pluralism. In "Conflict and the Plural Society: Ideologies of Violence," I describe violence of conflict as contributing to polarization; and it is, of course, a common observation that racial or ethnic groups often polarize in situations of intersectional violence. Danger may indeed be a fearful amalgamator, relegating ideas and theories to the background and creating an impassioned solidarity.[31] But violence between sections does not necessarily polarize the society. The demand for "black power" by some Negro groups in the United States, and an increasing readiness to respond to traditional white violence with Negro counterviolence, have certainly stimulated movements toward racial polarization among certain strata, but they have also encouraged intersectional cooperation among other strata. Clearly, the conditions under which violence polarizes need to be specified. Even when this is the obvious trend, the violence also turns inward as the warring sections liquidate or neutralize those among their members who would seek intersectional solutions, indicating a situation somewhat short of polarization.

For Mazrui, it is conflict resolution, not conflict, which is a necessary condition for integration in plural societies. Conflict is simply the occasion for conflict resolution. But since there can be no resolution without conflict, both conflict and its resolution are necessary conditions of depluralization. Conflict is apparently conceived as including a very wide variety of forms. Conflict resolution seems to be more narrowly conceived in terms of adjustment, since Mazrui writes that "it is the latter conception of conflict resolution which might perhaps offer the best insights into the process of integrating total identities." He sees the process of depluralization, then, as a process of increasing contact and interaction, with gradual multiplication of areas of conflict in consequence of the increasing interaction, and cumulative experience of conflict resolution by compromise or adjustment. It is this experience of conflict resolution which in his view deepens the degree of integration. He does not assume, however, that the cumulative experience of conflict resolution automatically flows from the extension of areas of conflict. He is careful to specify as conditions contributing to the possibility of conflict resolution, first, the cumulative power of precedent in resolving conflict, and at the subjective level, the awareness of reciprocal dependence and a shared ideology. Presumably, where these conditions are absent, and particularly in the absence of extensive interdependence, conflict is more likely to polarize the society.

The basis for interdependence is laid by such processes as differentiate the social participation of members of different sections and promote intersectional relations between them. The most generally accepted theory, that of Durkheim, finds the source of transformation from segmented to organically interdependent societies in the progressive division of labor and increasing functional differentiation. In contemporary African societies, this process would take the form of industrial and urban development, providing the occasion and necessity for association across sectional boundaries. But the presence of racial and ethnic pluralism distinguishes many of these societies from the segmented societies of Durkheim's theory, and the assumption that the progressive division of labor promotes depluralization must be qualified. I have already commented that depluralization may be a reversible process even in situations of considerable interdependence; politicians readily find in racial and ethnic cleavages a resource for political exploitation. Moreover, there may be so massive a superstructure of institutional devices for maintaining the pluralism that the progressive division of labor is insulated from the structure of power. There may be increasing continuity and fluidity in the economic structure, and in religious and other structures, and, at the same time, increasing discontinuity and rigidity in the political structure, as in South Africa. Differential political incorporation may raise formidable barriers to evolutionary change, even with increasing integration in other spheres. Hence, when M. G. Smith specifies as necessary conditions for depluralization a uniform mode of incorporation, provision of equal opportunity, and public enforcement of fundamental freedoms, the immediate problem is how these conditions are to be established. Perhaps the situation is such that political change can be effected only if subordinate groups mobilize their sectional power—a dialectical process of depluralization by means of polarization.

There are thus two antithetical possibilities in the process of change. In one, depluralization proceeds by individuation, or homogenization, or by *gleichschaltung* or *uniformization* (to borrow the terms used by van den Berghe in this connection). Depluralization is often conceived in these terms, as a reduction of the plural sections to individuals, who are absolutely interchangeable and randomly distributed throughout the structures of the society; in Mazrui's phrase, there is coalescence of identity. With increasing experience of policies of assimilation, optimistic assumptions as to the assimilative capacities and aspirations of groups, are beginning to be modified by the conception that the essential sphere of depluralization is the public domain, while pluralism may readily persist in the private domain without raising issues of discrimination and prejudice.

The second process of depluralization through an intermediate phase of sectional aggression seems paradoxical. It appears, however, to be the process that is operating in English-Afrikaner relations in South Africa, though this is by no means certain. Raymond Smith affirms the necessity for a similar intervening phase in Creole society, arguing that before ethnic identity can be transcended, it must be *asserted* in order to ensure the stature, participation, and self-respect of everyone in the local community, not because race is a necessary basis of social identity, but because it has been made so in Creole society.[32] The difficulty is, however, that racial and ethnic sentiments are not easily controlled, and deflected from one goal to another; they seem to be autonomous, subject to their own laws, gathering their own momentum, and releasing fiercely destructive impulses under the guise of altruistic dedication. A less hazardous basis for depluralization may be found in some combination of sectional organization and aggression with individuation and interdependence.

It is clear that depluralization is charged with a high potential for destruction and violence; and yet in the British African colonies, the first stage, that of decolonization, was accomplished with relatively little violence. Control of the process of change by an outside power may afford protection against the excesses of racial and ethnic particularisms. International guarantees of minority and individual human rights have been relatively ineffective in the past, and under the conditions of the cold war, which casts small nations in a role instrumental to the policies of the Great Powers. But there is no intrinsic reason why they should not prove effective in the future. The peaceful resolution of internal conflict between racial and ethnic sections may very well be contingent on the reduction of international tensions and the movement toward a world community of nations.

NOTES

[1] Clifford Geertz, "The Integrative Revolution," in Clifford Geertz, ed., *Old Societies and New States* (New York: Free Press of Glencoe, 1963), pp. 112–113.

[2] *Ibid.*, p. 109.

[3] *Ibid.*, p. 111.

[4] M. G. Smith, *The Plural Society in the British West Indies* (Berkeley and Los Angeles: University of California Press, 1965), pp. 75–91.

[5] *Ibid.*, p. 14.

[6] "Some Developments in the Analytic Framework of Pluralism."

[7] J. C. Mitchell, *Tribalism and the Plural Society* (London: Oxford University Press, 1960), p. 28.

[8] Germaine Tillion, *France and Algeria* (New York: Knopf, 1961), p. 121.

[9] Pierre L. van den Berghe, *Africa: Social Problems of Change and Conflict* (San Francisco: Chandler Publishing Co., 1965), p. 291.

[10] Jean-Louis Quermonne, "Le Problème de la Cohabitation dans les Sociétés Multi-Communautaires," *Revue Française de Science Politique*, 11, no. 1 (March 1961), 29–59.

[11] *Ibid.*, p. 36.

[12] *Ibid.*, pp. 31–32.

[13] *Ibid.*, pp. 42 ff.

[14] In Ali Mazrui's conception of the processes of national integration, the pluralism described by Quermonne would be a phenomenon occurring in the third stage of the movement from pluralism to integration—the stage of compromise.

[15] See Quermonne's discussion (*op. cit.*, pp. 37–38) of the relationship between localization and "cohabitation équilibrée."

[16] See Leo Kuper, *An African Bourgeoisie* (New Haven: Yale University

Press, 1965), chapter 23, for a discussion of differences among African leaders in South Africa over policies to be followed after liberation. Competition between the African National Congress and the Pan-Africanist Congress in South Africa took the form of an ideological controversy over policies of multiracialism or of nonracialism, the former referring to equivalent incorporation of racial sections, the latter to uniform incorporation of individuals, regardless of racial identity.

[17] See Leo Kuper, "Structural Discontinuities in African Towns: Some Aspects of Racial Pluralism," in H. Miner, ed., *The City in Modern Africa* (New York: Praeger, 1967).

[18] Pierre L. van den Berghe, "Pluralism and the Polity: A Theoretical Exploration."

[19] R. Dahrendorf, *Class and Class Conflict in Industrial Society* (London: Routledge and Kegan Paul, 1959), pp. 213 ff., 316–317. Dahrendorf uses the term "pluralism" as synonymous with "dissociation." His conception of pluralism corresponds to the model of crosscutting loyalties and structurally varied affiliations. As this usage is antithetical to my own as expressed in this paper, I am retaining the alternative form "dissociation" to avoid confusion.

[20] "Pluralism and the Polity: A Theoretical Exploration."

[21] Tillion, *op. cit.*, p. 131. See n. 31, below.

[22] Frantz Fanon, "Algeria's European Minority," in his *Studies in a Dying Colonialism*, trans. Haakon Chevalier (New York: Monthly Review Press, 1965), pp. 147–178.

[23] Tillion, *op. cit.*, p. 177.

[24] *Ibid.*, p. 173. But Tillion also refers to the impassioned solidarity of Moslem Algerians under danger, and in an earlier passage (see n. 31, below) to the Moslem unanimity which had taken shape by 1956. Evidently there is flux and ambiguity.

[25] See the analysis of dualisms and of divergent and convergent currents in social relationships in Georg Simmel, *Conflict and the Web of Group-Affiliations* (New York: Free Press of Glencoe, 1964), chap. 1.

[26] See G. E. von Grunebaum, *French African Literature: Some Cultural Implications* (The Hague: Mouton, 1964), p. 39.

[27] Tillion, *op. cit.*, p. 176.

[28] David C. Gordon, *The Passing of French Algeria* (London: Oxford University Press, 1966), p. 111 *et seq.*

[29] *Ibid.*, p. 114.

[30] James S. Coleman and Carl G. Rosberg, Jr., eds., *Political Parties and National Integration in Tropical Africa* (Berkeley and Los Angeles: University of California Press, 1964).

[31] Tillion, *op. cit.*, p. 174. Tillion also draws attention to a factor that may be highly significant in polarizing sections, that is, when violence is exercised in circumstances that establish sectional responsibility: "In the political circumstances of 1956, and in view of a Moslem unanimity that had taken shape by then, the executions were, moreover, affronts which compromise not an irresponsible subordinate (like the tortures), but the entire institutional body. And this is what a certain stratum of 'colonial' public opinion insisted on, the definitive compromise of the only possible arbiter of the conflict, in order to render that conflict insoluble" (pp. 144–145).

[32] Raymond T. Smith, "People and Change," in *New World: Guyana Independence Issue* (Demerara, Guiana, May 1966), p. 54.

Bibliography

Bibliography

PLURALISM

AGUIRRE BELTRÁN, GONZALO. *El Proceso de Aculturación.* México: Universidad Nacional Autónoma de México, Direccion General de Publicaciones, 1957.

ANDRAIN, CHARLES F. "Democracy and Socialism: Ideologies of African Leaders," in David E. Apter, ed., *Ideology and Discontent* (New York: Free Press of Glencoe, 1964), pp. 155–205.

ARON, R. "Social Structure and the Ruling Class," *British Journal of Sociology,* I (March 1950), 1–16.

BALANDIER, GEORGES. "The Colonial Situation," in Pierre L. van den Berghe, ed., *Africa: Social Problems of Change and Conflict* (San Francisco: Chandler Publishing Co., 1965), pp. 36–57.

———. *Sociologie actuelle de l'Afrique Noire: Dynamique des Changements sociaux en Afrique Centrale.* Paris: Presses Universitaires de France, 1955.

BANTON, MICHAEL. *Race Relations.* New York: Basic Books, 1967.

BEALS, RALPH L. "Social Stratification in Latin America," *American Journal of Sociology,* 57 (1953), 327–339.

BENEDICT, B. *Indians in a Plural Society: A Report on Mauritius.* London: H.M.S.O., 1961.

———. "Stratification in Plural Societies," *American Anthropologist,* 64, no. 6 (Dec. 1962), 1235–1246.

BERRY, BREWTON. *Race Relations: The Interaction of Ethnic and Racial Groups.* New York: Houghton Mifflin, 1951.

BLOOD, SIR HILARY. "Ethnic and Cultural Pluralism in Mauritius," in *Ethnic and Cultural Pluralism in Intertropical Countries* (Brussels: INCIDI, 1957), pp. 356–362.

BOEKE, J. H. *Economics and Economic Policy of Dual Societies, as Exemplified by Indonesia.* New York: Institute of Pacific Relations, 1953.

BRAITHWAITE, L. "The Present Status of the Social Sciences in the

British Caribbean," in Vera Rubin, ed., *Caribbean Studies: A Symposium* (Mona, Jamaica: Institute of Social and Economic Research, University College of the West Indies, 1957), pp. 99–109.

———. "Social Stratification and Cultural Pluralism," in Vera Rubin, ed., *Social and Cultural Pluralism in the Caribbean*. Annals of the New York Academy of Sciences, 83 (Jan. 1960), 816–831.

BROOM, LEONARD. "Discussion," in *ibid.*, p. 889.

———. "Urbanization and the Plural Society," in *ibid.*, pp. 880–891.

Caribbean Studies Special Report 1962. Caribbean Scholars' Conference. Institute of Caribbean Studies, University of Puerto Rico.

CARR, E. H. *The Twenty Years' Crisis, 1919–1939: An Introduction to the Study of International Relations*. 2d ed. London: Macmillan, 1949.

COLBY, BENJAMIN N., and PIERRE L. VAN DEN BERGHE. "Ethnic Relations in South-Eastern Mexico," *American Anthropologist*, 63, no. 4 (Aug. 1961), 772–792.

CROWLEY, DANIEL J. "Cultural Assimilation in a Multiracial Society," in Vera Rubin, ed., *Social and Cultural Pluralism in the Caribbean*. Annals of the New York Academy of Sciences, 83 (Jan. 1960), 850–854.

———. "Plural and Differential Acculturation in Trinidad," *American Anthropologist*, 59, no. 5 (Oct. 1957), 817–824.

———. "Urbanization and the Plural Society," *ibid.*, pp. 880–891.

CUMPER, GEORGE E. "Notes on Social Structure in Jamaica," in George E. Cumper, ed., *Social Needs in a Changing Society: Report of the Conference on Social Development in Jamaica, July 1961* (Kingston, Jamaica: Council of Voluntary Social Services, 1962), pp. 3–11.

DAHL, ROBERT A. *Pluralist Democracy in the United States: Conflict and Consent*. Chicago: Rand McNally, 1967.

DAHRENDORF, R. *Class and Class Conflict in Industrial Society*. London: Routledge and Kegan Paul, 1959.

DALTON, PETER. "Broome, a Multi-Racial Community: A Study of Social and Cultural Relationships in a Town in the West Kimberleys, Western Australia." Unpublished M.A. thesis, University of Western Australia, Perth, 1964.

DESPRES, LEO A. "Anthropological Theory, Cultural Pluralism and the Study of Complex Societies," *Current Anthropology*, 9, no. 1 (Feb. 1968), 3–26.

———. *Cultural Pluralism and Nationalist Politics in British Guiana*. Chicago: Rand McNally, 1967.

———. "The Implications of Nationalist Policies in British Guiana for the Development of Cultural Theory," *American Anthropologist,* 66 (Oct. 1964), 1051–1077.

DOBBY, E. H. G. "Resettlement Transforms Malaya. A Case-History of Relocating the Population of an Asian Plural Society," *Economic Development and Cultural Change,* 1, no. 3 (1952), 163–189.

FALLERS, LLOYD. "Equality, Modernity and Democracy in the New States," in Clifford Geertz, ed., *Old Societies and New States: The Quest for Modernity in Asia and Africa* (New York: Free Press of Glencoe, 1963), pp. 158–219.

———. "Ideology and Culture in Uganda Nationalism," *American Anthropologist,* 63, no. 4 (Aug. 1961), 677–686.

FRANKEL, CHARLES. *The Democratic Prospect.* New York and Evanston: Harper and Row, 1962.

FREEDMAN, M. "The Growth of a Plural Society in Malaya," *Pacific Affairs,* 33, no. 2 (1960), 158–168. Repr. in I. M. Wallerstein, ed., *Social Change: The Colonial Situation* (New York: Wiley, 1966), pp. 278–289.

FURNIVALL, J. S. *Colonial Policy and Practice: A Comparative Study of Burma and Netherlands India.* London: Cambridge University Press, 1948.

———. *Netherlands India: A Study of Plural Economy.* Cambridge: The University Press, 1939.

———. "The Political Economy of the Tropical Far East," *Journal of the Royal Central Asiatic Society,* 29 (1942), 195–210.

———. "Some Problems of Tropical Economy," in Rita Hinden, ed., *Fabian Colonial Essays* (London: Allen and Unwin, 1945), pp. 161–184.

GANN, L. H. *The Birth of a Plural Society: The Development of Northern Rhodesia under the British South Africa Company, 1894–1914.* Manchester: Manchester University Press, 1958.

GANN, L. H., and PETER DUIGNAN. *White Settlers in Tropical Africa.* Harmondsworth: Penguin Books, 1962.

GEERTZ, CLIFFORD. "The Integrative Revolution: Primordial Sentiments and Civil Politics in the New States," in Clifford Geertz, ed., *Old Societies and New States: The Quest for Modernity in Asia and Africa* (New York: Free Press of Glencoe, 1963), pp. 105–157.

GEERTZ, CLIFFORD, ed. *Old Societies and New States: The Quest for Modernity in Asia and Africa.* New York: Free Press of Glencoe, 1963.

GITLIN, TODD. "Local Pluralism as Theory and Ideology," *Studies on the Left*, 5, no. 3 (1965), 21–45.

GLUCKMAN, MAX. *An Analysis of a Social Situation in Modern Zululand*. Manchester: Manchester University Press, 1958.

———. "Tribalism, Ruralism and Urbanism in Plural Societies," in V. W. Turner, ed., *Profiles of Change: The Impact of Colonialism on African Societies*. London: Cambridge University Press, 1969.

GORDON, MILTON. "Assimilation in America: Theory and Reality," *Daedalus*, 90 (Spring 1961), 263–285.

———. "Social Structure in Group Relations," in M. Berger, T. Abel, and C. H. Page, eds., *Freedom and Control in Modern Society* (New York: Van Nostrand, 1954), pp. 141–157.

GREEN, THOMAS F. *Education and Pluralism: Ideal and Reality*. Syracuse: Syracuse University Press, 1966.

GUSFIELD, JOSEPH R. "Mass Society and Extremist Politics," *American Sociological Review*, 27 (Feb. 1962), 19–30.

GUTKIND, P. C. W. "Some African Attitudes to Multi-Racialism from Uganda, British East Africa," in *Ethnic and Cultural Pluralism in Intertropical Countries* (Brussels: INCIDI, 1957), pp. 338–355.

HAUG, M. R. "Social and Cultural Pluralism as a Concept in Social System Analysis," *American Journal of Sociology*, 73, no. 3 (Nov. 1967), 294–304.

HAZEERSINGH, K. "The Religion and Culture of Indian Immigrants in Mauritius and the Effect of Social Change," *Comparative Studies in Society and History*, 8, no. 2 (Jan. 1966), 241–257.

HEARD, KENNETH A. *Political Systems in Multiracial Societies*. Johannesburg: South African Institute of Race Relations, 1961.

HELLMAN, ELLEN. "Culture Contact and Change in the Union of South Africa," in *Ethnic and Cultural Pluralism in Intertropical Countries* (Brussels: INCIDI, 1957), pp. 363–373.

HOETINK, H. "Change in Prejudice: Some Notes on the Minority Problem, with Reference to the West Indies and Latin America," *Bijdragen tot de Taal-, Land- en Volkenkunde*, 119, no. 1 (1963), 56–75.

———. "The Concept of Pluralism as Envisaged by M. G. Smith," *Caribbean Studies*, VII, no. 1 (April 1967), 36–43.

———. "Curazao como sociedad segmentade," *Revista de Ciencias Sociales*, 4 (March 1960), 179–192.

———. *De gespleten samenleving in het Carabisch gebied: Bijdrage tot de sociologie der rasrelaties in gesegmenteerde maatschappijen*. Assen, 1962.

———. *Het patroon van de oude Curacaose samenleving: Een socio-logische studie.* Assen, 1958.

———. *The Two Variants in Caribbean Race Relations: A Contribution to the Sociology of Segmented Societies.* London: Oxford University Press, 1967.

HOSELITZ, BERT. "Interaction between Industrial and Pre-industrial Stratification Systems," in Neil J. Smelser and Seymour Martin Lipset, eds., *Social Structure, Social Mobility and Economic Development* (Chicago: Aldine Publishing Co., 1966).

HSIAO, KUNG-CHUAN. *Political Pluralism: A Study in Contemporary Political Theory.* London: Kegan Paul, Trench, Trubner, 1927.

HUTTON, J. H. *Caste in India: Its Nature, Function, and Origins.* London: Cambridge University Press, 1946.

INSTITUT INTERNATIONAL DES CIVILISATIONS DIFFÉRENTES (INCIDI). *Ethnic and Cultural Pluralism in Intertropical Countries: Report of the XXXth Meeting Held in Lisbon on the 15th, 16th, 17th and 18th April, 1957.* Brussels: INCIDI, 1957.

JAYAWARDENA, CHANDRA. *Conflict and Solidarity in a Guianese Plantation.* London: Athlone Press of the University of London, 1963.

———. "Religious Belief and Social Change: Aspects of the Development of Hinduism in British Guiana," *Comparative Studies in Society and History,* 8, no. 2 (Jan. 1966), 211–240.

KAGAME, ALEXIS. "Le Pluralisme ethnique et culturel dans le Rwanda-Urundi," in *Ethnic and Cultural Pluralism in Intertropical Countries* (Brussels: INCIDI, 1957), pp. 268–293.

KALLEN, HORACE M. *Cultural Pluralism and the American Idea: An Essay in Social Philosophy.* Philadelphia: University of Pennsylvania Press, 1956.

———. "Democracy versus the Melting Pot," *The Nation,* Feb. 18, 1915, pp. 190–194; Feb. 25, 1915, pp. 217–220.

KIRKWOOD, KENNETH. "Ethnic and Cultural Pluralism in British Central Africa," in *Ethnic and Cultural Pluralism in Intertropical Countries* (Brussels: INCIDI, 1957), pp. 294–324.

KLASS, MORTON. "East and West Indian: Cultural Complexity in Trinidad," in Vera Rubin, ed., *Social and Cultural Pluralism in the Caribbean.* Annals of the New York Academy of Sciences, 83 (Jan. 1960), 855–886.

KORNHAUSER, W. *The Politics of Mass Society.* London: Routledge and Kegan Paul, 1960.

———. "'Power Elite' or 'Veto Groups,'" in S. M. Lipset and Leo Lowenthal, eds., *Culture and Social Character: The Work of*

David Riesman Reviewed (New York: Free Press of Glencoe, 1961), pp. 252–267.

KUPER, HILDA, and LEO KUPER, eds. *African Law: Adaptation and Development.* Berkeley and Los Angeles, University of California Press, 1965.

KUPER, LEO. *An African Bourgeoisie: Race, Class and Politics in South Africa.* New Haven: Yale University Press, 1965.

——. "Religion and Urbanization in Africa," in *Religious Pluralism and Social Structure,* International Yearbook of Religion (Koln: Westdeutscher Verlag, 1965), pp. 213–233.

——. "Sociology: Some Aspects of Urban Plural Societies in Africa," in Robert A. Lystad, ed., *The African World: A Survey of Social Research* (New York: Praeger, 1965), pp. 107–130.

——. "Structural Discontinuities in African Towns: Some Aspects of Racial Pluralism," in H. Miner, ed., *The City in Modern Africa* (New York: Praeger, 1967).

LEWIS, GORDON K. Review of Eric Williams, *The History of the People of Trinidad and Tobago,* in *Caribbean Studies,* 3, no. 1 (April 1963), 104.

LEWIS, W. ARTHUR. "Beyond African Dictatorship: The Crisis of the One-Party State," *Encounter,* 25, no. 2 (Aug. 1965), 3–18.

——. *Politics in West Africa.* London: Allen and Unwin, 1965.

LIPSET, S. M. *The First New Nation: The United States in Historical and Comparative Perspective.* New York: Basic Books, 1963.

LITTLE, KENNETH. "Structural Change in the Sierra Leone Protectorate," *Africa,* 25, no. 3 (June 1955), 217–234.

LLOYD, P. C., ed. *The New Elites of Tropical Africa.* London: Oxford University Press, 1966.

McCORD, WILLIAM. *The Springtime of Freedom: Evolution of Developing Societies.* New York: Oxford University Press, 1965.

McKENZIE, H. I. "The Plural Society Debate: Some Comments on a Recent Contribution," *Social and Economic Studies,* 15, no. 1 (March 1966), 53–60.

MARRIOTT, McKIM. "Cultural Policy in the New States," in Clifford Geertz, ed., *Old Societies and New States: The Quest for Modernity in Asia and Africa* (New York: Free Press of Glencoe, 1963), pp. 27–56.

MASON, PHILIP. "The Plural Society of Kenya," in *Ethnic and Cultural Pluralism in Intertropical Countries* (Brussels: INCIDI, 1957), pp. 325–337.

MAYER, PHILIP. "The Tribal Elite and the Transkeian Elections of

1963," in P. C. Lloyd, ed., *The New Elites of Tropical Africa* (London: Oxford University Press, 1966), pp. 286–311.

MILLS, C. WRIGHT. *The Power Elite*. New York: Oxford University Press, 1956.

MITCHELL, J. C. "Aspects of Occupational Prestige in a Plural Society," in P. C. Lloyd, ed., *The New Elites of Tropical Africa* (London: Oxford University Press, 1966), pp. 256–271.

———. *The Kalela Dance: Aspects of Social Relationships among Urban Africans in Northern Rhodesia*. Manchester: Manchester University Press, 1956.

———. *Tribalism and the Plural Society: An Inaugural Lecture Given in the University College of Rhodesia and Nyasaland on 2 Oct., 1959*. London: Oxford University Press, 1960.

MOREIRA, ADRIANO. "Rapport général: Aspect juridique et politique," in *Ethnic and Cultural Pluralism in Intertropical Countries* (Brussels: INCIDI, 1957), pp. 494–498.

MORRIS, H. S. "Indians in East Africa: A Study in a Plural Society," *British Journal of Sociology*, 7, no. 3 (Oct. 1956), 194–211.

———. "The Plural Society," *Man*, 57, no. 8 (Aug. 1957), 124–125.

———. Review of M. G. Smith, *The Plural Society in the British West Indies*, in *Man*, n.s., 1, no. 2 (June 1966), 270–271.

———. "Some Aspects of the Concept Plural Society," *Man*, n.s., 2, no. 2 (June 1967), 169–184.

NASH, MANNING. "The Multiple Society in Economic Development: Mexico and Guatemala," *American Anthropologist*, 59, no. 5 (Oct. 1957), 825–838.

———. "Political Relations in Guatemala," *Social and Economic Studies*, 7, no. 1 (March 1958), 65–75.

———. "Some Social and Cultural Aspects of Economic Development," *Economic Development and Cultural Change*, VII (1959), 137–149.

———. "Southeast Asian Society: Dual or Multiple," *Journal of Asian Studies*, 23 (1964), 417–431.

NETTLEFORD, REX. "National Identity and Attitudes to Race in Jamaica," *Race*, 7, no. 1 (1965), 59–72.

NEW WORLD ASSOCIATES. "Working Notes towards the Unification of Guyana," *New World* (Georgetown, British Guiana), I (March 1963), 1–81.

NORRIS, KATRIN. *Jamaica: The Search for Identity*. London: Institute of Race Relations, 1962.

ONO SHIN'YA. "The Limits of Bourgeois Pluralism," *Studies on the Left*, 5, no. 3 (1965), 46–72.

PADILLA, ELENA. "Peasants, Plantation and Pluralism," in Vera Rubin, ed., *Social and Cultural Pluralism in the Caribbean*. Annals of the New York Academy of Sciences, 83 (Jan. 1960), 837–842.

PERROW, CHARLES. "The Sociological Perspective and Political Pluralism," *Social Research*, 31 (Winter 1964), 411–422.

POLSBY, N. W. "The Pluralist Alternative: How To Study Community Power," *Journal of Politics*, 22 (1960), 474–484.

QUERMONNE, JEAN-LOUIS. "Le Problème de la Cohabitation dans les Sociétés Multi-Communautaires," *Revue Française de Science Politique*, 11, no. 1 (March 1961), 29–59.

RADCLIFFE-BROWN, A. R. "On Social Structure," *Journal of the Royal Anthropological Institute*, LXX (1940). Repr. in A. R. Radcliffe-Brown, *Structure and Function in Primitive Society: Essays and Addresses* (London: Cohen and West, 1952), pp. 188–204.

RATNAM, K. J. "Constitutional Government and the 'Plural Society,'" *Journal of South-East Asian History*, 2, no. 3 (1961), 1–10.

REX, JOHN. "The Plural Society in Sociological Theory," *British Journal of Sociology*, 10, no. 2 (June 1959), 114–124.

RHEINSTEIN, MAX. "Problems of Law in the New Nations of Africa," in Clifford Geertz, ed., *Old Societies and New States: The Quest for Modernity in Asia and Africa* (New York: Free Press of Glencoe, 1963), pp. 220–246.

RIESMAN, DAVID, REVEL DENNEY, and NATHAN GLAZER. *The Lonely Crowd: A Study of the Changing American Character*. New Haven: Yale University Press, 1950.

ROSE, PETER I. *They and We: Racial and Ethnic Relations in the United States*. New York: Random House, 1964.

RUBIN, VERA. "Culture, Politics and Race Relations," *Social and Economic Studies*, 11, no. 4 (Dec. 1962), 433–455.

RUBIN, VERA, ed. *Social and Cultural Pluralism in the Caribbean*. Annals of the New York Academy of Sciences, 83 (Jan. 1960), 761–916.

RUBIN, V., R. A. J. van LIER, and L. BRAITHWAITE. "Pluralism in the Caribbean," in *Caribbean Studies Special Report 1962*, Caribbean Scholars' Conference, Institute of Caribbean Studies, University of Puerto Rico (1962), pp. 9–18.

SCHILLER, A. ARTHUR. "Law," in R. A. Lystad, ed., *The African World: A Survey of Social Research* (New York: Praeger, 1965), pp. 166–198.

SHILS, EDWARD A. "On the Comparative Study of the New States," in Clifford Geertz, ed., *Old Societies and New States: The Quest for Modernity in Asia and Africa* (New York: Free Press of Glencoe, 1963), pp. 1–26.

————. *The Torment of Secrecy: The Background and Consequences of American Security Policies*. London: Heinemann, 1956.

SIMPSON, GEORGE E., and J. MILTON YINGER. *Racial and Cultural Minorities: An Analysis of Prejudice and Discrimination*. New York: Harper, 1953.

SJOBERG, GIDEON. "Folk and 'Feudal' Societies," *American Journal of Sociology*, 58 (Nov. 1952), 231–239.

SKINNER, ELLIOTT P. "Group Dynamics and Social Stratification in British Guiana," in Vera Rubin, ed., *Social and Cultural Pluralism in the Caribbean*. Annals of the New York Academy of Sciences, 83 (Jan. 1960), 904–916.

SKLAR, RICHARD L., and C. S. WHITAKER, JR. "The Federal Republic of Nigeria," in Gwendolen M. Carter, ed., *National Unity and Regionalism in Eight African States* (Ithaca: Cornell University Press, 1966), pp. 7–150.

SMITH, M. G. *Dark Puritan*. Kingston, Jamaica: University of the West Indies, 1963.

————. "Ethnic and Cultural Pluralism in the British Caribbean," in *Ethnic and Cultural Pluralism in Intertropical Countries* (Brussels: INCIDI, 1957), pp. 439–447.

————. "A Framework for Caribbean Studies," *Caribbean Affairs* (University College of the West Indies, 1955).

————. "The Plural Framework of Jamaican Society," *British Journal of Sociology*, 12, no. 3 (1961), 249–262.

————. *The Plural Society in the British West Indies*. Berkeley and Los Angeles: University of California Press, 1965.

————. "Social and Cultural Pluralism," in Vera Rubin, ed., *Social and Cultural Pluralism in the Caribbean*. Annals of the New York Academy of Sciences, 83 (Jan. 1960), 763–777.

————. *Stratification in Grenada*. Berkeley and Los Angeles: University of California Press, 1965.

SMITH, RAYMOND T. *British Guiana*. London: Oxford University Press, 1962.

————. "British Guiana," *Sunday Guardian* (Port of Spain, Trinidad), Federation Supplement, April 20, 1958.

————. "Culture and Social Structure in the Caribbean: Some Recent Work on Family and Kinship Studies," *Comparative Studies in Society and History*, 6, no. 1 (Oct. 1963), 24–46.

SMITH, RAYMOND T. *The Negro Family in British Guiana: Family Structure and Social Status in the Villages.* London: Routledge and Kegan Paul, 1956.

──────. "People and Change," in *New World: Guyana Independence Issue* (Demerara, Guiana, May 1966), pp. 49–54.

──────. Review of *Social and Cultural Pluralism in the Caribbean,* in *American Anthropologist,* 63, no. 1 (Feb. 1961), 155–157.

SPECKMANN, J. D. "Die Houding van de Hindostaanse Bevolkungsgroep in Suriname ten Opzichte van de Creolen," *Bijdragen tot de Taal-, Land- en Volkenkunde,* 119, no. 1 (1963), 76–92.

──────. "The Indian Group in the Segmented Society of Surinam," *Caribbean Studies,* 3, no. 1 (April 1963), 3–17.

TOCQUEVILLE, ALEXIS DE. *Democracy in America.* Trans. Henry Reeve. London: Saunders and Otley, 1835–1840. 4 vols.

VAN DEN BERGHE, PIERRE L. *Caneville: The Social Structure of a South African Town.* Middletown: Wesleyan University Press, 1964.

──────. "Introduction," in Pierre L. van den Berghe, ed., *Africa: Social Problems of Change and Conflict* (San Francisco: Chandler Publishing Co., 1965), pp. 1–11.

──────. *South Africa: A Study in Conflict.* Middletown: Wesleyan University Press, 1965.

──────. "Toward a Sociology of Africa," *Social Forces,* 43 (Oct. 1964), 11–18.

VAN LIER, R. A. J. "Culture Conflict in de Heterogene Samenleving," *Sociologish Jaarboek,* Deel VIII (1953–54), 36–56.

──────. *The Development and Nature of Society in the West Indies.* Amsterdam: Royal Institute for the Indies, 1950.

──────. *Ontwikkelung en Karakter van de West-Indische Maatschappij.* The Hague, 1950.

──────. "Samenleving in een Grensgebied: Een Sociaal-Historische Studie van de Maatschappij in Suriname." Unpublished Ph.D. thesis, Leiden University, The Hague, 1949.

VAN RENSELAAR, H. C. "Die Houding van de Creoolse Bevolkingsgroep in Suriname ten Opzichte van de Andere Bevolkingsgroepen (in het Bizonder ten Opzichte van de Hindostanen)," *Bijdragen tot de Taal-, Land- en Volkenkunde,* 119, no. 1 (1963), 93–105.

WAGLEY, CHARLES. "Discussion of Social and Cultural Pluralism," in Vera Rubin, ed., *Social and Cultural Pluralism in the Caribbean.* Annals of the New York Academy of Sciences, 83 (Jan. 1960), 777–780.

WAGLEY, CHARLES, and MARVIN HARRIS. *Minorities in the New World:* Six Case Studies. Pp. 285–295. New York: Columbia University Press, 1958.

WERTHEIM, W. F. *East-West Parallels: Sociological Approaches to Modern Asia.* The Hague: W. van Hoeve, 1964.

————. *Indonesian Society in Transition: A Study of Social Change.* 2d rev. ed. The Hague/Bandung: W. van Hoeve, 1959.

————. "Society as a Composite of Conflicting Value Systems." Paper read at the IVth World Congress of Sociology at Stresa-Milan. 1959. Stencil copy.

WITTERMANS, ELIZABETH. *Inter-ethnic Relations in a Plural Society.* Groningen: J. B. Wolters, 1964.

YINGER, J. M. "Integration and Pluralism Viewed from Hawaii," *Antioch Review,* 22 (Winter 1962–63), 397–410.

ZINKIN, M. *Asia and the West.* Chap. 12, "The Plural Society." London: Chatto and Windus, 1951.

GENERAL

ABERLE, D. F., A. K. COHEN, A. K. DAVIS, M. J. LEVY, JR., and F. X. SUTTON. "The Functional Prerequisites of Society," *Ethics,* 60 (1950), 100–111.

ALMOND, GABRIEL A. "Introduction," in Gabriel A. Almond and James S. Coleman, eds., *The Politics of the Developing Areas* (Princeton: Princeton University Press, 1960), pp. 3–64.

ARISTOTLE. *Politics.* Trans. Benjamin Jowett. New York: Modern Library, 1943.

ARNETT, E. J. *The Rise of the Sokoto Fulani, Being a Paraphrase and in Some Parts a Translation of the Infaqi'l Maisuri of Sultan Mohammed Bello.* Lagos: C.M.S. Bookshop, 1922.

AUSTIN, D. *Politics in Ghana, 1946–1960.* London: Oxford University Press, 1964.

AXELSON, ERIC V., ed. *South African Explorers.* London: Oxford University Press, 1954.

AZIKIWE, NNAMDI. "Essentials of Nigerian Survival," *Foreign Affairs,* XLIII, no. 3 (April 1965), 447–461.

BACON, ELIZABETH E. *Obok: A Study of Social Structure in Eurasia.* New York: Wenner-Gren Foundation, 1958.

BARBOUR, NEVILL, ed. *A Survey of North West Africa (The Maghrib).* London: Oxford University Press, 1959.

BARNES, J. A. *Politics in a Changing Society.* Manchester: Manchester University Press, 1954.

BARTH, FREDRIK. *Political Leadership among the Swat Pathans*. London: Athlone Press of the University of London, 1959.

BARTH, HEINRICH. *Travels and Discoveries in North and Central Africa*. London: Ward, Lock, 1902. 2 vols.

BASCOM, WILLIAM R. "The Principle of Seniority in the Social Structure of the Yoruba," *American Anthropologist*, 44 (1942), 36–46.

———. "Social Status, Wealth and Individual Differences among the Yoruba," *American Anthropologist*, 53, no. 4 (Oct. 1951), 490–505.

———. "Urbanization among the Yoruba," *American Journal of Sociology*, 50, no. 5 (March 1955), 448–454.

BATESON, GREGORY. *Naven: A Survey of the Problems Suggested by a Composite Picture of the Culture of a New Guinea Tribe Drawn from Three Points of View*. Cambridge: The University Press, 1936.

BATSON, EDWARD. *Report on Proposals for a Social Survey of Zanzibar*. Zanzibar: Government Printer, 1948.

———. "Social Survey of Zanzibar." Verifax.

BAXTER, P. T. W., and AUDREY BUTT. *The Azande and Related Peoples of the Anglo-Egyptian Sudan and Belgian Congo*. London: International African Institute, 1953.

BEATTIE, JOHN. *Bunyoro: An African Kingdom*. New York: Holt, Rinehart and Winston, 1960.

BEIDELMAN, THOMAS O. *A Comparative Analysis of the Jajmani System*. Locust Valley, N.Y.: J. J. Augustin, 1959.

BERNARDI, B. "The Age-Set System of the Nilo-Hamites," *Africa*, 22 (1952), 316–322.

———. *The Mugwe: A Failing Prophet—A Study of a Religious and Public Dignitary of the Meru of Kenya*. London: Oxford University Press, 1959.

BHARATI, A. "A Social Survey," in D. P. Ghai, ed., *Portrait of a Minority: Asians in East Africa* (London: Oxford University Press, 1965), pp. 13–63.

———. "The Unwanted Elite of East Africa," *Trans-Action*, 3, no. 5 (July 1966), 37–41.

BIOBAKU, SABURI O. *The Egba and Their Neighbours, 1842–1872*. Oxford: Clarendon Press, 1957.

BLOCH, MARC L. B. *Feudal Society*. Trans. L. A. Manyon. London: Routledge and Kegan Paul, 1961.

BLUMER, HERBERT. "Industrialisation and Race Relations," in Guy Hunter, ed., *Industrialisation and Race Relations: A Sym-*

posium (London: Oxford University Press, 1965), pp. 220–253.

BOURDIEU, PIERRE. *The Algerians.* Trans. Alan C. M. Ross. Boston: Beacon Press, 1962.

BRADBURY, R. E. *The Benin Kingdom and the Edo-Speaking Peoples of South-Western Nigeria.* London: International African Institute, 1957.

BRELSFORD, M. V. *The Tribes of Northern Rhodesia.* Lusaka: Government Printer, 1956.

BRIGGS, LLOYD CABOT. *Tribes of the Sahara.* Cambridge: Harvard University Press, 1960.

BROCKELMANN, CARL. *History of the Islamic Peoples.* Trans. Joel Carmichael and Moshe Perlmann. New York: Capricorn Books, 1962.

BROWN, PAULA. "Patterns of Authority in West Africa," *Africa,* 27 (1957), 261–278.

BURROWS, R. *Indian Life and Labour in Natal.* Pamphlet no. 23. Pietermaritzburg: South African Institute of Race Relations, 1952.

BUSIA, K. A. *The Position of the Chief in the Modern Political System of Ashanti: A Study of the Influence of Contemporary Social Changes on Ashanti Political Institutions.* London: Oxford University Press, 1951.

BUXTON, JEAN. *Chiefs and Strangers: A Study of Political Assimilation among the Mandari.* Oxford: Clarendon Press, 1963.

————. "The Mandari of the Southern Sudan," in John Middleton and David Tait, eds., *Tribes without Rulers: Studies in African Segmentary Systems* (London: Routledge and Kegan Paul, 1958), pp. 67–96.

CALPIN, G. H. *Indians in South Africa.* Pietermaritzburg: Shuter and Shooter, 1949.

CARY, M. *A History of Rome Down to the Reign of Constantine.* London: Macmillan, 1945.

CERULLI, ERNESTA V. *Peoples of South-West Ethiopia and Its Borderland.* London: International African Institute, 1956.

CHAILLEY, M., *et al. Notes et études sur l'Islam en Afrique Noire.* Recherches et Documents du CHEAM. Paris: J. Peyronnet, 1962.

CHEVALIER, FRANÇOIS. *Land and Society in Colonial Mexico: The Great Hacienda.* Trans. Alvin Eustis. Berkeley and Los Angeles: University of California Press, 1963.

CHILVER, E. M., and P. M. KABERRY. "Traditional Government in

Bafut, West Cameroon," *Nigerian Field,* 28, no. 1 (1963), 4–30.

CHIN, HU HSIEN. *The Common Descent Group in China and Its Functions.* New York: Viking Fund, 1948.

CHINOY, ELY. "Society," in Julius Gould and William L. Kolb, eds., *A Dictionary of the Social Sciences* (London: Tavistock Publishers, 1954), pp. 674–675.

CODERE, HELEN. "Power in Ruanda," *Anthropologica,* n.s., 4, no. 1 (1962), 45–85.

COHN, NORMAN R. C. *The Pursuit of the Millennium.* London: Secker and Warburg, 1957.

COLE, G. D. H. *Studies in Class Structure.* London: Routledge and Kegan Paul, 1955.

COLE, G. D. H., and RAYMOND POSTGATE. *The Common People, 1746–1946.* London: Methuen, 1946.

COLEMAN, JAMES S. *Nigeria: Background to Nationalism.* Berkeley and Los Angeles: University of California Press, 1958.

COLEMAN, JAMES S., and CARL G. ROSBERG, JR., eds. *Political Parties and National Integration in Tropical Africa.* Berkeley and Los Angeles: University of California Press, 1964.

COLLINGWOOD, R. G. *The Idea of History.* Oxford: Clarendon Press, 1946.

COLSON, ELIZABETH. "The Plateau Tonga of Northern Rhodesia," in Elizabeth Colson and Max Gluckman, eds., *Seven Tribes of British Central Africa* (Manchester: Manchester University Press, 1951), pp. 94–162.

COOPPAN, SOMARSUNDARUM. "The Indian Outlook," in Prudence Smith, ed., *Africa in Transition: Some BBC Talks on Changing Conditions in the Union and the Rhodesias* (London: Max Reinhardt, 1958), pp. 159–168.

CORNÈVIN, ROBERT. *Histoire du Dahomey.* Paris: Editions Berger-Levrault, 1962.

CORY, HANS. *The Indigenous Political System of the Sukuma and Proposals for Political Reform.* Pp. 63–91. Dar es Salaam: Eagle Press, 1954.

COSER, LEWIS A. *The Functions of Social Conflict.* Glencoe, Ill.: Free Press, 1956.

CROWDER, MICHAEL. *Senegal: A Study in French Assimilation Policy.* London: Oxford University Press, 1962.

CUNNISON, IAN G. *History of the Luapula: An Essay on the Historical Notions of a Central African Tribe.* Cape Town: Oxford University Press, 1951.

————. "Perpetual Kinship: A Political Institution of the Luapula,"

Human Problems in British Central Africa, no. 20 (1956).

DAHL, ROBERT A. *Who Governs? Democracy and Power in an American City.* New Haven and London: Yale University Press, 1961.

DAVIDSON, B. *The African Awakening.* London: Cape, 1955.

————. *Report on Southern Africa.* London: Cape, 1952.

————. *Which Way Africa?* Baltimore: Penguin Books, 1964.

DAVIDSON, J. W. *The Northern Rhodesian Legislative Council.* London: Faber and Faber, 1948.

DAVIS, ALLISON, BURLEIGH B. GARDNER, and MARY R. GARDNER. *Deep South: A Social Anthropological Study of Caste and Class.* Chicago: University of Chicago Press, 1941.

DAVIS, JOHN P. *Corporations: A Study of the Origin and Development of Great Business Combinations and Their Relation to the Authority of the State.* New York: Capricorn Books, 1961.

DAVIS, KINGSLEY, and WILBERT E. MOORE. "Some Principles of Stratification," *American Sociological Review,* 10 (1945), 242–249.

DELAROZIÈRE, R. *Les Institutions politiques et sociales des Populations dites Bamileke.* Institut Français d'Afrique Noire, Centre du Kameroon, Memo 3 (1950), pp. 66–98.

DE KIEWIET, C. W. *A History of South Africa, Social and Economic.* London: Oxford University Press, 1942.

DE ST. CROIX, F. W. *The Fulani of Northern Nigeria.* Lagos: Government Printer, 1944.

DE VAUX, ROLAND. *Ancient Israel.* New York: McGraw-Hill, 1966. 2 vols.

D'HERTEFELT, MARCEL. "Développements Recents," in M. d'Hertefelt, A. Troubworst, and J. Scherer, *Les anciens royaumes de la Zone Interlacustre Meridionale* (London: International African Institute, 1962), pp. 227–236.

————. "Les Elections communales et le consensus politique au Rwanda," *Zaïre,* XIV, no. 5–6 (1960), 403–438.

————. "Mythes et idéologies dans le Rwanda ancient et contemporain," in Jan Vansina, Raymond Mauny, and L. V. Thomas, eds., *The Historian in Tropical Africa* (London: Oxford University Press, 1964), pp. 219–238.

————. "The Rwanda of Rwanda," in James L. Gibbs, Jr., ed., *Peoples of Africa* (New York: Holt, Rinehart and Winston, 1965), pp. 403–440.

————. "Stratification sociale et structure politique au Rwanda," *Revue Nouvelle,* XXI (1960), 449–462.

D'HERTEFELT, MARCEL, A. TROUBWORST, and J. SCHERER.

Les anciens royaumes de la Zone Interlacustre Meridionale.
London: International African Institute, 1962.

DICKENS, CHARLES. *Bleak House.* London: Oxford University Press,
1948.

DIKE, K. ONWUKA. *Trade and Politics in the Niger Delta, 1830–1885:
An Introduction to the Economic and Political History of
Nigeria.* Oxford: Clarendon Press, 1956.

DOLLARD, JOHN. *Caste and Class in a Southern Town.* Garden City:
Doubleday Anchor Books, 1957.

DORJAHN, V. R. "The Organization and Functions of the Ragbenle
Society among the Temne," *Africa,* 29 (1959), 156–170.

DOS SANTOS, J. *Ethiopia Oriental.* Convento de S. Domingos de Evora,
1609.

DOUGLAS, MARY. *The Lele of the Kasai.* London: Oxford University
Press, 1963.

———. "Matriliny and Pawnship in Central Africa," *Africa,* 34, no. 4
(1964), 301–313.

DRUCKER, PHILIP. *The Northern and Central Nootkan Tribes.*
Smithsonian Institution, Bureau of American Ethnology,
Bulletin 144. Washington: G.P.O., 1951.

DUFFY, JAMES. *Portugal in Africa.* Baltimore: Penguin Books, 1963.

DUPIRE, MARGUERITE. *Peuls Nomades: Etude descriptive des
Wobaabe du Sahel Nigérien.* Paris: Institut d'Ethnologie,
1962.

———. "The Place of Markets in the Economy of the Bororo (Fulbe),"
in Paul Bohannan and George Dalton, eds., *Markets in Africa*
(Evanston: Northwestern University Press, 1962), pp. 335–
362.

DU PLESSIS, ISAK D. *The Cape Malays.* 2d ed. Cape Town: Maskew
Miller, 1947.

DURKHEIM, EMILE. *The Division of Labor in Society.* Trans. George
Simpson. Glencoe, Ill.: Free Press, 1947.

EASTON, DAVID. *The Political System: An Inquiry into the State of
Political Science.* New York: Knopf, 1953.

EDEL, MAY M. *The Chiga of Western Uganda.* London: Oxford University Press, 1957.

EDWARDS, ISOBEL E. *Towards Emancipation: A Study in South
African Slavery.* Cardiff: Gomerian Press, 1942.

EHRENBERG, VICTOR. *The Greek State.* New York: Norton, 1964.

EHRLICH, CYRIL. "The Uganda Economy, 1903–1945," in V. Harlow,
E. M. Chilver, and A. Smith, eds., *History of East Africa,* II
(Oxford: Clarendon Press, 1965), 395–475.

ELKINS, STANLEY M. *Slavery: A Problem in American Institutional and Intellectual Life.* New York: Grosset and Dunlap, 1963.

EMERSON, RUPERT. *From Empire to Nation: The Rise to Self-Assertion of Asian and African Peoples.* Boston: Beacon Press, 1960.

ENGELS, F. *Socialism, Utopian and Scientific.* Trans. E. Aveling. Chicago: Kerr, 1914.

EPSTEIN, ARNOLD L. *Politics in an Urban African Community.* Manchester: Manchester University Press, 1958.

EVANS-PRITCHARD, E. E. "Kinship and Local Community among the Nuer," in A. R. Radcliffe-Brown and Daryll Forde, eds., *African Systems of Kinship and Marriage* (London: Oxford University Press, 1950), pp. 360–391.

————. *The Nuer: A Description of the Modes of Livelihood and Political Institutions of a Nilotic People.* London: Oxford University Press, 1949.

————. "Zande Blood-Brotherhood," *Africa,* 6 (1933), 369–401. Repr. in E. E. Evans-Pritchard, *Essays in Social Anthropology* (London: Faber and Faber, 1962), pp. 131–161.

————. "The Zande State," *Journal of the Royal Anthropological Institute,* 93, pt. 1 (June 1963), 134–154.

FAGAN, B. M. *Southern Africa during the Iron Age.* London: Thames and Hudson, 1965.

FAGEN, RICHARD R. *Politics and Communication.* Boston: Little, Brown, 1966.

FALLERS, LLOYD A., ed. *The King's Men: Leadership and Status in Buganda on the Eve of Independence.* London: Oxford University Press, 1964.

FALLERS, MARGARET CHAVE. *The Eastern Lacustrine Bantu (Ganda and Soga).* London: International African Institute, 1960.

FANON, FRANTZ. "Algeria's European Minority," in F. Fanon, *Studies in a Dying Colonialism,* trans. Haakon Chevalier (New York: Monthly Review Press, 1965), pp. 147–178.

————. *Pour la révolution africaine.* Paris: François Maspero, 1964.

————. *Studies in a Dying Colonialism.* Trans. Haakon Chevalier. New York: Monthly Review Press, 1965.

————. *The Wretched of the Earth.* Trans. Constance Farrington. New York: Grove Press, 1963.

FICHTER, J. H. *Sociology.* Chicago: University of Chicago Press, 1957.

FIELD, M. J. *Social Organization of the Ga People.* London: Crown Agent for the Colonies, 1940.

FIRTH, RAYMOND. *Essays on Social Organization and Values*. London: Athlone Press of the University of London, 1964.

──────. *We the Tikopia: A Sociological Study of Kinship in Primitive Polynesia*. London: Allen and Unwin, 1936.

FORDE, DARYLL. "Death and Succession: An Analysis of Yakö Mortuary Ritual," in Max Gluckman, ed., *Essays on the Ritual of Social Relations* (Manchester: Manchester University Press, 1962), pp. 89–123.

──────. "Governmental Roles of Associations among the Yakö," *Africa*, 31 (1961), 309–323.

──────. "Unilineal Fact or Fiction: An Analysis of the Composition of Kinship Groups among the Yakö," in Isaac Schapera, ed., *Studies in Kinship and Marriage* (London: Royal Anthropological Institute, 1963), pp. 38–57.

──────. *Yakö Studies*. London: Oxford University Press, 1964.

──────. *The Yoruba-Speaking Peoples of South-Western Nigeria*. London: International African Institute, 1951.

FORDE, DARYLL, ed. *Efik Traders of Old Calabar*. London: Oxford University Press, 1956. 2d ed., 1963.

FORDE, DARYLL, and G. I. JONES. *The Ibo and Ibibio-Speaking Peoples of South-Eastern Nigeria*. London: International African Institute, 1950.

FORTES, MEYER. "Descent, Filiation and Affinity: A Rejoinder to Dr. Leach," *Man*, LIX (Nov. 1959), 193–197; (Dec. 1959), 206–212.

──────. *The Dynamics of Clanship among the Tallensi*. London: Oxford University Press, 1945.

──────. "The Political System of the Tallensi of the Northern Territories of the Gold Coast," in M. Fortes and E. E. Evans-Pritchard, eds., *African Political Systems* (London: Oxford University Press, 1940), pp. 238–271.

──────. "Ritual and Office in Tribal Society," in Max Gluckman, ed., *Essays on the Rituals of Social Relations* (Manchester: Manchester University Press, 1962), pp. 53–88.

──────. "The Structure of Unilineal Descent Groups," *American Anthropologist*, 55, no. 1 (Jan.–March 1953), 17–41.

FORTES, MEYER, and E. E. EVANS-PRITCHARD. "Introduction," in M. Fortes and E. E. Evans-Pritchard, eds., *African Political Systems* (London: Oxford University Press, 1940), pp. 1–23.

FOSBROOKE, H. A. "An Administrative Survey of Masai Social System," *Tanganyika Notes and Records*, no. 26 (1948), 1–50.

FOWLER, H. WARD. *The City State of the Greeks and Romans*. London: Macmillan, 1952.

FRAENKEL, MERRAN. *Tribe and Class in Monrovia*. London: Oxford University Press, 1964.

FRANKENBERG, R. *Village on the Border: A Social Study of Religion, Politics and Football in a North Wales Community*. London: Cohen and West, 1957.

FRAZIER, E. FRANKLIN. *Black Bourgeoisie: The Rise of a New Middle Class in the United States*. New York: Collier Books, 1962.

————. *The Negro Family in the United States*. Chicago: University of Chicago Press, 1940.

————. *The Negro in the United States*. New York: Macmillan, 1949.

FREEDMAN, MAURICE. *Lineage Organization in Southeastern China*. London: Athlone Press of the University of London, 1958.

FRIEDRICH, CARL J. "Political Pathology," *Political Quarterly*, 37 (Jan.–March 1966), 70–85.

FROEHLICH, J. C. "Les problèmes posés par les réfugiés montagnards de culture paleonigritique," *Cahiers d'Etudes Africaines*, 4, no. 15 (1964), 383–399.

GAMBLE, G. P. *The Wolof of Senegambia*. London: International African Institute, 1957.

GANN, L. H. *A History of Northern Rhodesia: Early Days to 1953*. London: Chatto and Windus, 1964.

GANSHOF, F. L. *Feudalism*. Trans. Philip Grierson. London: Longmans, Green, 1952.

GELFAND, M. *Northern Rhodesia in the Days of the Charter: A Medical and Social Study, 1878–1924*. Oxford: Basil Blackwell, 1961.

GERTH, H. H., and C. WRIGHT MILLS, eds. *From Max Weber: Essays in Sociology*. New York: Oxford University Press, 1946.

GHAI, D. P. "An Economic Survey," in D. P. Ghai, ed., *Portrait of a Minority: Asians in East Africa* (London: Oxford University Press, 1965), pp. 91–109.

GHAI, YASH. "The Future Prospects," in *ibid.*, pp. 129–152.

GIBBS, JAMES L., JR. "The Kpelle of Liberia," in James L. Gibbs, Jr., ed., *Peoples of Africa* (New York: Holt, Rinehart and Winston, 1965), pp. 197–240.

GIBSON, GORDON D. "Double Descent and Its Correlates among the Herrero of Ngamiland," *American Anthropologist*, 58 (1956), 109–139.

GIDE, ANDRÉ. *Voyage au Congo*. Paris: Editions de la Nouvelle Revue Française, 1928.

GLASS, D. V., ed. *Social Mobility in Britain*. London: Routledge and Kegan Paul, 1954.

GLUCKMAN, EMMANUEL. *The Tragedy of the Ababirwas and Some Reflections on Sir Herbert Sloley's Report*. Johannesburg: Central News Agency, 1922.

GLUCKMAN, MAX. *Custom and Conflict in Africa*. Oxford: Basil Blackwell, 1963.

————. *Economy of the Central Barotse Plain*. Livingstone, Northern Rhodesia: Rhodes-Livingstone Institute, 1941.

————. *Essays on Lozi Land and Royal Property*. Livingstone, Northern Rhodesia: Rhodes-Livingstone Institute, 1943.

————. *The Ideas in Barotse Jurisprudence*. New Haven: Yale University Press, 1965.

————. "Inter-hierarchical Roles: Professional and Party Ethics in the Tribal Areas in South and Central Africa," in M. Swartz, ed., *Local-Level Politics* (Chicago: Aldine Press, 1969).

————. "The Kingdom of the Zulu of South Africa," in M. Fortes and E. E. Evans-Pritchard, eds., *African Political Systems* (London: Oxford University Press, 1940), pp. 25–55.

————. "Kinship and Marriage among the Lozi of Northern Rhodesia and the Zulu of Natal," in A. R. Radcliffe-Brown and Daryll Forde, eds., *African Systems of Kinship and Marriage* (London: Oxford University Press, 1950), pp. 166–206.

————. "The Lozi of Barotseland in North-Western Rhodesia," in Elizabeth Colson and Max Gluckman, eds., *Seven Tribes of British Central Africa* (Manchester: Manchester University Press, 1951), pp. 1–93.

————. "Malinowski's 'Functional' Analysis of Social Change," in Max Gluckman, *Order and Rebellion in Tribal Africa: Collected Essays* (London: Cohen and West; New York: The Free Press, 1963), pp. 207–234.

————. *Politics, Law and Ritual in Tribal Society*. Chicago: Aldine Publishing Co., 1965.

————. *The Rise of the Zulu Empire*. In press.

————. "Tribalism in Modern British Central Africa," *Cahiers d'Etudes Africaines*, 1, no. 1 (1960), 55–70. Repr. in Pierre L. van den Berghe, ed., *Africa: Social Problems of Change and Conflict* (San Francisco: Chandler Publishing Co., 1965), pp. 346–360.

————. "The Utility of the Equilibrium Model in the Study of Social Change," *American Anthropologist*, 70 (1968), 219–237.

GOBINEAU, COUNT ARTHUR DE. *Essay on the Inequality of Human Races.* Paris, 1853, 1855. Trans. A. Collins. New York, 1914.

GOODY, JOHN R. *Death, Property and the Ancestors: A Study of the Mortuary Customs of the LoDagaa of West Africa.* London: Tavistock Publications, 1962.

———. "Fields of Social Control among the Lodagaba," *Journal of the Royal Anthropological Institute,* 87, pt. 1 (June 1957), 75–104.

———. *The Social Organization of the LoWiili.* London: H.M.S.O., 1956.

GORDON, DAVID C. *The Passing of French Algeria.* London: Oxford University Press, 1966.

GRAY, RICHARD. *The Two Nations: Aspects of the Development of Race Relations in the Rhodesias and Nyasaland.* London: Oxford University Press, 1960.

GRAY, ROBERT F. *The Sonjo of Tanganyika: An Anthropological Study of an Irrigation-based Society.* London: Oxford University Press, 1963.

GREEN, A. W. *Sociology: An Analysis of Life in Modern Society.* 2d ed. New York: McGraw-Hill, 1956.

GREEN, M. M. *Ibo Village Affairs.* London: Sidgwick and Jackson, 1947.

GREENBERG, JOSEPH H. "Interdisciplinary Perspectives: African Linguistic Research," *African Studies Bulletin,* IX, no. 1 (April 1966).

GREENSTONE, J. DAVID. "Corruption and Self-Interest in Kampala and Nairobi," *Comparative Studies in Society and History,* 8 (Jan. 1966), 199–210.

GROUSSET, RENÉ. *The Rise and Splendour of the Chinese Empire.* Trans. Anthony Watson-Gandy and Terence Gordon. London: Geoffrey Bles, 1952.

GULLIVER, P. H. *The Family Herds: A Study of Two Pastoral Peoples in East Africa, the Jie and Turkana.* London: Routledge and Kegan Paul, 1955.

———. "The Karamajong Cluster," *Africa,* 22, no. 1 (1952), 1–21.

———. *Social Control in an African Society: A Study of the Arusha, Agricultural Masai of Northern Tanganyika.* London: Routledge and Kegan Paul, 1963.

GUMPLOWICZ, LUDWIG. *Outlines of Sociology.* 2d English ed. New York: Paine-Whitman, 1963.

HAILEY, LORD. *An African Survey, Revised 1956.* London: Oxford University Press, 1957.

HALL, R. S. *Zambia.* London: Pall Mall, 1965.

HAMMETT, IAN. "Koena Chieftainship in Basutoland," *Africa*, 35, no. 3 (July 1965), 241–250.

HANNA, A. J. *The Story of the Rhodesias and Nyasaland*. London: Faber and Faber, 1960.

HARING, C. H. *The Spanish Empire in America*. New York: Oxford University Press, 1947.

HARLEY, G. W. "Notes on the Poro of Liberia," *Peabody Museum Papers* (Cambridge, Mass.), 19, no. 2 (1941).

HARRIS, ROSEMARY L. *The Political Organization of Mbembe, Nigeria*. London: H.M.S.O., 1965.

———. "The Political Significance of Double Unilineal Descent," *Journal of the Royal Anthropological Institute*, 92, pt. 1 (Jan.–June 1962), 86–101.

HAYES, CARLTON J. H. *Nationalism: A Religion*. New York: Macmillan, 1960.

HO, PING-TI. *The Ladder of Success in Imperial China: Aspects of Social Mobility, 1368–1911*. New York: Wiley, 1964.

HOBSBAWM, E. J. *Primitive Rebels*. Manchester: Manchester University Press, 1959.

HOCART, A. M. *Kingship*. London: Watts, 1941.

HODGKIN, THOMAS L. *African Political Parties: An Introductory Guide*. Harmondsworth: Penguin Books, 1961.

HOGBEN, S. J. *The Muhammedan Emirates of Northern Nigeria*. Oxford: Clarendon Press, 1930.

HOLMBERG, ALLAN R. "Changing Community Attitudes and Values in Peru: A Case Study in Guided Change," in Richard N. Adams, John P. Gillin, Allan R. Holmberg, Oscar Lewis, Richard Patch, and Charles Wagley, *Social Change in Latin America Today: Its Implication for United States Policy* (New York: Vintage Books, 1960), pp. 67–84.

HOLT, P. J. *The Mahdist State in the Sudan, 1881–1898: A Study of Its Origins, Development and Overthrow*. Oxford: Clarendon Press, 1958.

HOPEN, C. E. *The Pastoral Fulbe Family in Gwandu*. London: Oxford University Press, 1958.

HORRELL, MURIEL, comp. *A Survey of Race Relations in South Africa, 1965*. Johannesburg: South African Institute of Race Relations, 1966.

———. *A Survey of Race Relations in South Africa, 1966*. Johannesburg: South African Institute of Race Relations, 1967.

HORTON, ROBIN. "The Kalabari Ekine Society: A Borderland of Religion and Art," *Africa*, 33, no. 2 (1963), 94–114.

HORTON, W. R. G. "The *Ohu* System of Slavery in a Northern Ibo Village Group," *Africa*, 24, no. 4 (1954), 311–336.

HUGHES, A. J. *East Africa: The Search for Unity; Kenya, Tanganyika, Uganda and Zanzibar*. Harmondsworth: Penguin Books, 1963.

HUGHES, A. J. B. *Kin, Caste and Nation among the Rhodesian Ndebele*. Manchester: Manchester University Press, 1956.

HUNTINGFORD, G. W. B. *The Galla of Ethiopia: The Kingdoms of Kafa and Janjero*. London: International African Institute, 1955.

———. *The Nandi of Kenya: Tribal Control in a Pastoral Society*. London: Routledge and Kegan Paul, 1953.

———. *Nandi Work and Culture*. London: H.M.S.O., 1950.

———. *The Southern Nilo-Hamites*. London: International African Institute, 1953.

INGHAM, K. *The Making of Modern Uganda*. London: Allen and Unwin, 1958.

JAMES, C. L. R. *The Black Jacobins: Toussaint L'Ouverture and the San Domingo Revolution*. New York: Random House, 1963.

JASPAN, M. A. *The Ila-Tonga Peoples of North-Western Rhodesia*. London: International African Institute, 1953.

———. "A Sociological Case Study: Communal Hostility to Imposed Social Change in South Africa," in P. Ruopp, ed., *Approaches to Community Development: A Symposium Introductory to Problems and Methods of Village Welfare in Underdeveloped Areas* (The Hague: W. van Hoeve, 1953), pp. 97–120.

JEFFRIES, M. D. W. "The Batwa: Who Are They?" *Africa*, 23, no. 1 (1953), 45–54.

JOHNSON, CHARLES S. *Shadow of the Plantation*. Chicago: University of Chicago Press, 1934.

JONES, G. I. "Ibo Age Organization," *Journal of the Royal Anthropological Institute*, 92 (1962), 191–211.

———. "The Political Organization of Old Calabar," in Daryll Forde, ed., *Efik Traders of Old Calabar* (2d ed.; London: Oxford University Press, 1963), pp. 116–160.

———. *The Trading States of the Oil Rivers: A Study of Political Development in Eastern Nigeria*. London: Oxford University Press, 1963.

JOSHI, P. S. *The Tyranny of Colour: A Study of the Indian Problem in South Africa*. Durban: E. P. and Commercial Printer, 1942.

KABERRY, PHYLLIS M. "Traditional Politics in Nsaw," *Africa*, 29 (1959), 366–383.

KABERRY, P. M., and E. M. CHILVER. "An Outline of the Traditional Political Systems of Bali-Nyanga, Southern Cameroons," *Africa*, 31, no. 4 (1961), 355–371.

KALENDA, PAULINE MAHAR. "Toward a Model of the Hindu Jajmani System," *Human Organization*, 22, no. 1 (March 1963), 11–31.

KAMINSKY, HOWARD. "The Free Spirit in the Hussite Revolution," in Sylvia L. Thrupp, ed., *Millennial Dreams in Action: Essays in Comparative Study* (The Hague: Mouton, 1962), pp. 166–186.

KARIS, T. "South Africa," in Gwendolen M. Carter, ed., *Five African States: Responses to Diversity* (Ithaca: Cornell University Press, 1963), pp. 471–616.

KATI, MAHMOUD. *Tarikh el-Fettach*. Trans. O. Houdas and M. Delafosse. Paris: E. Leroux, 1913. 2d ed. Paris: Adrien-Maison veuve, 1964.

KAUNDA, KENNETH D. *Zambia Shall Be Free: An Autobiography*. London: Heinemann, 1962.

KEALEY, PATRICK. *The Politics of Partnership*. Baltimore: Penguin Books, 1963.

KELLER, A. G. *Colonization: A Study of the Founding of New Societies*. Boston: Ginn, 1908.

KIRK-GREENE, A. H. M. *Adamawa Past and Present: An Historical Approach to the Development of a Northern Cameroons Province*. London: Oxford University Press, 1958.

KOHN, HANS. *The Idea of Nationalism: A Study of Its Origins and Background*. New York: Macmillan, 1944.

———. *Prophets and Peoples: Studies in Nineteenth Century Nationalism*. New York: Macmillan, 1957.

KOPYTOFF, IGOR. "The Suku of Southwestern Congo," in James L. Gibbs, Jr., ed., *Peoples of Africa* (New York: Holt, Rinehart and Winston, 1965), pp. 441–477.

KRADER, LAWRENCE. "Feudalism and the Tartar Policy of the Middle Ages," *Comparative Studies in Society and History*, 1, no. 1 (Oct. 1958), 76–99.

KRIGE, E. J. *The Social System of the Zulus*. Pietermaritzburg: Shuter and Shooter, 1936.

KUPER, HILDA. *An African Aristocracy: Rank among the Swazi*. London: Oxford University Press, 1947.

———. "The Colonial Situation in Southern Africa," *Journal of Modern African Studies*, 2 (July 1964), 149–150.

———. *Indian People in Natal*. Pietermaritzburg: Natal University Press, 1960.

———. "The Indians of Natal," in Prudence Smith, ed., *Africa in Transi-*

tion: Some BBC Talks on Changing Conditions in the Union and the Rhodesias (London: Max Reinhardt, 1958), pp. 115–124.

———. *The Swazi.* London: International African Institute, 1952.

———. *The Uniform of Colour: A Study of White-Black Relationships in Swaziland.* Johannesburg: University of Witwatersrand Press, 1947.

KUPER, HILDA, A. J. B. HUGHES, and J. VAN VELSEN. *The Shona and Ndebele of Southern Rhodesia.* London: International African Institute, 1954.

KUPER, LEO. "The Heightening of Racial Tension," in Pierre L. van den Berghe, ed., *Africa: Social Problems of Change and Conflict* (San Francisco: Chandler Publishing Co., 1965), pp. 237–247.

———. *Passive Resistance in South Africa.* New Haven: Yale University Press, 1960.

KUPER, L., H. WATTS, and R. DAVIES. *Durban: A Study in Racial Ecology.* New York: Columbia University Press, 1958.

LAMBERT, H. E. *Kikuyu Social and Political Institutions.* London: Oxford University Press, 1956.

LEACH, E. R. *Political Systems of Highland Burma.* London: G. Bell and Sons, 1954.

LEACH, E. R., ed. *Aspects of Caste in South India, Ceylon and North-West Pakistan.* Cambridge: The University Press, 1960.

LEAKEY, L. S. B. *Mau Mau and the Kikuyu.* London: Methuen, 1952.

LEFEBVRE, GEORGES. *The Coming of the French Revolution, 1789.* Trans. R. R. Palmer. New York: Vintage Books, 1957.

LENIN, V. I. *State and Revolution.* New York: International Publishers, 1932.

LEVI, CARLO. *Christ Stopped at Eboli: The Story of a Year.* Trans. Frances Frenaya. New York: Farrar, Straus, 1947.

LEVINE, ROBERT A., and WALTER H. SANGREE. "The Diffusion of Age-Group Organization in East Africa: A Controlled Comparison," *Africa,* 32, no. 2 (April 1962), 97–110.

LEVY, MARION J. *The Structure of Society.* Princeton: Princeton University Press, 1952.

LEWIN, J. *The Colour Bar in the Copper Belt.* Johannesburg: South African Institute of Race Relations, 1941.

LEWIS, I. M. *A Pastoral Democracy: A Study of Pastoralism and Politics among the Northern Somali of the Horn of Africa.* London: Oxford University Press, 1961.

———. Review of *Notes et études sur l'Islam en Afrique Noire,* in *Africa,* 35, no. 4 (Oct. 1965), 444–445.

516   Bibliography

LEWIS, OSCAR. *Village Life in Northern India: Studies in a Delhi Village.* New York: Vintage Books, 1965.

LEYBURN, JAMES G. *The Haitian People.* New Haven: Yale University Press, 1941.

LEYS, COLIN. "What Is the Problem about Corruption?" *Journal of Modern African Studies,* 3, no. 2 (1965), 215–230.

LHOTE, HENRI. *Les Touaregs du Hoggar.* Paris: Payot, 1955.

LIEBENOW, J. GUS. "Liberia," in James S. Coleman and Carl G. Rosberg, Jr., eds., *Political Parties and National Integration in Tropical Africa* (Berkeley and Los Angeles: University of California Press, 1964), pp. 448–481.

LIENHARDT, GODFREY. "The Western Dinka," in John Middleton and David Tait, eds., *Tribes without Rulers: Studies in African Segmentary Systems* (London: Routledge and Kegan Paul, 1958), pp. 97–135.

LIPSET, S. M. *Political Man: The Social Bases of Politics.* Garden City: Doubleday, 1960.

LITTLE, KENNETH L. *The Mende of Sierra Leone: A West African People in Transition.* London: Routledge and Kegan Paul, 1951.

———. "The Political Function of the Poro," *Africa,* 35, no. 4 (1965), 349–365; 36, no. 1 (1966), 62–72.

———. "The Role of the Secret Society in Cultural Specialization," *American Anthropologist,* 51 (1949), 199–212.

LLOYD, P. C. "Class Consciousness among the Yoruba," in P. C. Lloyd, ed., *The New Elites of Tropical Africa* (London: Oxford University Press, 1966), pp. 328–341.

———. "The Political Structure of African Kingdoms: An Exploratory Model," in Michael P. Banton, ed., *Political Systems and the Distribution of Power* (London: Tavistock Publications, 1965), pp. 62–112.

———. "Sacred Kingship and Government among the Yoruba," *Africa,* 30 (1960), 221–223.

———. "The Traditional Political System of the Yoruba," *Southwestern Journal of Anthropology,* 10, no. 4 (1954), 366–384.

———. *Yoruba Land Law.* London: Oxford University Press, 1962.

LOFCHIE, MICHAEL F. *Zanzibar: Background to Revolution.* Princeton: Princeton University Press, 1965.

LONDRES, A. *Terre d'ébène (la Trait des Moirs).* Paris: A. Michel, 1929.

LOW, D. A. *Political Parties in Uganda, 1949–1962.* London: Athlone Press of the University of London, 1962.

LUWEL, M. "Développements recents: Burundi," in M. d'Hertefelt, A. Troubworst, and J. Scherer, *Les anciens royaumes de la Zone Interlacustre Meridionale* (London: International African Institute, 1962), pp. 237–246.

McHENRY, J. PATRICK. *A Short History of Mexico.* New York: Doubleday, 1962.

MACKINTOSH, JOHN P. "Electoral Trends and the Tendency to a One Party System in Nigeria," *Journal of Commonwealth Political Studies,* I (Nov. 1962), 194–210.

MACMILLAN, W. M. *Bantu, Boer and Briton: The Making of the South African Native Problem.* London: Faber and Gwyer, 1928.

———. *Warning from the West Indies: A Tract for Africa and the Empire.* Harmondsworth: Penguin Books, 1938.

McMULLAN, M. "A Theory of Corruption," *Sociological Review* (Keele), 9, no. 2 (July 1961), 181–201.

MALCOLM, D. W. *Sukumaland: An African People and Their Country; A Study of Land Use in Tanganyika.* London: Oxford University Press, 1953.

MALINOWSKI, BRONISLAW. *The Dynamics of Culture Contact: An Enquiry into Race Relations in Africa.* New Haven: Yale University Press, 1946.

———. *A Scientific Theory of Culture and Other Essays.* Chapel Hill: University of North Carolina Press, 1944.

MAQUET, J. J. *The Premise of Inequality in Ruanda.* London: Oxford University Press, 1961.

MAUNIER, RENÉ. *The Sociology of Colonies.* Trans. E. O. Lorimer. London: Routledge and Kegan Paul, 1949.

MAYER, ADRIAN C. *Caste and Kinship in Central India: A Village and Its Region.* London: Routledge and Kegan Paul, 1955.

———. *Land and Society in Malabar.* London: Oxford University Press, 1952.

MAYER, PHILIP. "Migrancy and the Study of Africans in Towns," *American Anthropologist,* 64 (June 1962), 576–592.

———. *The Lineage Principle in Gusii Society.* London: Oxford University Press, 1949.

———. *Townsmen or Tribesmen: Conservatism and the Process of Urbanization in a South African City.* Cape Town: Oxford University Press, 1961.

MBEKI, G. *South Africa: The Peasants' Revolt.* Harmondsworth: Penguin Books, 1964.

MEAD, MARGARET, and RHODA MÉTRAUX, eds. *The Study of Culture at a Distance.* Chicago: University of Chicago Press, 1953.

MEAD, MARGARET, and RHODA MÉTRAUX, eds. *Themes in French Culture: A Preface to a Study of French Community.* Stanford: Stanford University Press, 1954.

MEEK, C. K. *Law and Authority in a Nigerian Tribe: A Study in Indirect Rule.* London: Oxford University Press, 1937.

———. *Tribal Studies in Northern Nigeria.* London: Kegan Paul, Trench, Trubner, 1931. 2 vols.

MEINERTZHAGEN, R. *Kenya Diary, 1902–1906.* Edinburgh: Oliver and Boyd, 1957.

MERCIER, PAUL. "The European Community of Dakar," in Pierre L. van den Berghe, ed., *Africa: Social Problems of Change and Conflict* (San Francisco: Chandler Publishing Co., 1965), pp. 283–300.

———. "Evolution of Senegales Elites," in *ibid.,* pp. 163–178.

MICHELS, ROBERT. *Political Parties: A Sociological Study of the Oligarchical Tendencies of Modern Democracy.* Trans. Eden and Cedar Paul. New York: Collier Books, 1962.

MILLS, M. E. E., and MONICA WILSON. *Keiskammahoek Rural Survey.* Vol. 4: *Land Tenure.* Pietermaritzburg: Shuter and Shooter, 1952.

MINER, HORACE. *The Primitive City of Timbuctoo.* Princeton: Princeton University Press, 1953.

MINISTÈRE DES COLONIES. *Documents scientifiques de la Mission Tilho (1906–1909).* Vol. II, pp. 461–468, 510–537. Paris: Imprimerie Nationale, 1911.

MOORE, SALLY FALK. *Power and Property in Inca Peru.* New York: Columbia University Press, 1954.

MORGAN, LEWIS H. *League of the Ho-dé-no-sau-nee, or Iroquois* (1851). New York: Corinth Books, 1962.

MORRIS, H. S. "Communal Rivalry among Indians in Uganda," *British Journal of Sociology,* VIII, no. 4 (Dec. 1957), 306–317.

MORTON-WILLIAMS, P. "An Outline of the Cosmology and Cult Organization of the Oyo Yoruba," *Africa,* 36, no. 3 (1966), 243–261.

———. "The Yoruba Ogboni Cult in Oyo," *Africa,* 30 (1960), 363–374.

MOTTOULLE, L. *Politique Sociale de l'Union Minière du Haut-Katanga pour sa Main-d'Œuvre indigène et ses résultats au cours de vingt années d'application.* Brussels: Van Campenhout, 1946.

MURDOCK, G. P. *Africa: Its Peoples and Their Culture History.* New York: McGraw-Hill, 1959.

MYRDAL, GUNNAR. *An American Dilemma: The Negro Problem and Modern Democracy.* New York: Harper, 1944.

NADEL, S. F. *A Black Byzantium: The Kingdom of Nupe in Nigeria.* London: Oxford University Press, 1942.

———. "Dual Descent in the Nuba Hills," in A. R. Radcliffe-Brown and Daryll Forde, eds., *African Systems of Kinship and Marriage* (London: Oxford University Press, 1950), pp. 333–359.

———. *The Foundations of Social Anthropology.* London: Cohen and West, 1951.

———. *The Nuba: An Anthropological Study of the Hill Tribes of Kordofan.* London: Oxford University Press, 1947.

———. *Nupe Religion.* London: Routledge and Kegan Paul, 1954.

———. "Nupe State and Community," *Africa,* 8, no. 3 (1935), 257–303.

———. "Social Symbiosis and Tribal Organization," *Man,* 38 (1938), 85–90.

NEWBURY, C. W. *The Western Slave Coast and Its Rulers: European Trade and Administration among the Yoruba and Adja-speaking Peoples of South-Western Nigeria, Southern Dahomey and Togo.* Oxford: Clarendon Press, 1961.

NICOLAISEN, JOHANNES. *Ecology and Culture of the Pastoral Tuareg with Particular Reference to the Tuareg of Ahaggar and Ayr.* Copenhagen: National Museum, 1963.

———. "Political Systems of Pastoral Tuareg in Ayr and Ahaggar," *Folk,* 1 (1959), 95–104.

NOON, JOHN A. *Law and Government of the Grand River Iroquois.* New York: Viking Fund, 1949.

NYERERE, J. K. *Democracy and the Party System.* Dar es Salaam, 1963.

OBERG, K. "The Kingdom of Ankole in Uganda," in M. Fortes and E. E. Evans-Pritchard, eds., *African Political Systems* (London: Oxford University Press, 1940), pp. 121–162.

Observer (London), May 9, 1965.

OLIVER, ROLAND A. *The Missionary Factor in East Africa.* 2d ed. London: Longmans, Green, 1965.

OLIVER, ROLAND, and J. D. FAGE. *A Short History of Africa.* Baltimore: Penguin Books, 1962.

OLIVER, R., and G. MATHEW, eds. *History of East Africa.* Vol. I. Oxford: Clarendon Press, 1963.

OLMSTED, FREDERICK LAW. *The Slave States before the Civil War.* New York: Capricorn Books, 1959.

OMER-COOPER, JOHN D. *The Zulu Aftermath.* London: Longmans, Green, 1966.

OPPENHEIMER, FRANZ. *The State: Its History and Development Viewed Sociologically.* Trans. John M. Gitterman. New York: Huebsch, 1922.

PALMER, H. R. *Gazetteer of Bornu Province.* Lagos: Government Printer, 1929.

PALMER, MABEL. *The History of Indians in Natal.* London: Oxford University Press, 1957.

PARSONS, TALCOTT. *The Social System.* London: Tavistock Publications, 1952.

PARSONS, TALCOTT, and EDWARD A. SHILS, *Toward a General Theory of Action.* Cambridge: Harvard University Press, 1951.

PATTERSON, J. R. "Report on Borsari District, Bornu." Provincial Office, Bornu. Unpublished MS, 1918.

PEDROSO GAMITTO, A. C. *King Kazembe and the Marave, Cheva, Bisa, Bembe, Lunda, and Other Peoples of Southern Africa; Being the Diary of the Portuguese Expedition to That Potentate in the Years 1831 and 1832.* Trans. Ian Cunnison. Lisbon: Junta de Investigacöes do Ultramar, 1960.

PERISTIANY, J. G. *The Social Institutions of the Kipsigis.* London: Routledge and Kegan Paul, 1939.

PHILLIPS, ULRICH B. *Life and Labor in the Old South.* Boston: Little, Brown, 1963.

POST, K. W. J. *The Nigerian Federal Election of 1959: Politics and Administration in a Developing Political System.* London: Oxford University Press, 1963.

POWDERMAKER, HORTENSE. *After Freedom: A Cultural Study of the Deep South.* New York: Viking Press, 1939.

PRINS, A. H. J. *East African Age-Class Systems: An Inquiry into the Social Order of Galla, Kipsigis and Kikuyu.* Groningen: J. B. Wolters, 1953.

RADCLIFFE-BROWN, A. R. *Structure and Function in Primitive Society.* London: Cohen and West, 1952.

RAMCHANDI, R. R. "Racial Conflict in East Africa with Implications for the People of Indian Origin: A Case Study of Uganda." University of Delhi, 1965. Mimeographed.

RATTRAY, R. S. *Ashanti Law and Constitution.* Oxford: Clarendon Press, 1929.

READ, MARGARET. *The Ngoni of Nyasaland.* London: Oxford University Press, 1956.

———. "Tradition and Prestige among the Ngoni," *Africa,* 9 (1936), 453–483.

REHFISCH, F. "The Dynamics of Multilineality on the Mambila Plateau," *Africa,* 30, no. 3 (1960), 246–261.

Report of the Commission Appointed to Enquire into the Disturbances in the Copperbelt, Northern Rhodesia. Lusaka: Government Printer, 1940.

Report of the Commission Appointed to Enquire into the Disturbances in the Copperbelt, Northern Rhodesia, Together with the Governor's Despatch to the Secretary of State on the Report. Lusaka: Government Printer, 1935.

RICE, A. K. *Productivity and Social Organization: The Ahmedabad Experiment.* London: Tavistock Publications, 1958.

RICHARDS, AUDREY I. *Economic Development and Tribal Change: A Study of Immigrant Labour in Buganda.* Cambridge: Heffer, 1952.

———. "The Political System of the Bemba Tribe," in M. Fortes and E. E. Evans-Pritchard, eds., *African Political Systems* (London: Oxford University Press, 1940), pp. 83–120.

RICHARDS, AUDREY I. ed. *East African Chiefs: A Study of Political Development in Some Uganda and Tanganyika Tribes.* London: Faber and Faber, 1960.

ROTBERG, R. I. *Christian Missionaries and the Creation of Northern Rhodesia, 1880–1924.* Princeton: Princeton University Press, 1965.

ROUX, E. *Time Longer Than Rope: A History of the Black Man's Struggle for Freedom in South Africa.* London: Gollancz, 1948.

ROYAL INSTITUTE OF INTERNATIONAL AFFAIRS. *Nationalism: A Report by a Study Group of Members of the Royal Institute of International Affairs.* London: Oxford University Press, 1939.

RUDÉ, GEORGE F. E. *The Crowd in History: A Study of Popular Disturbances in France and England.* New York: Wiley, 1964.

RUNCIMAN, STEPHEN. *Byzantine Civilization.* New York: Meridian Books, 1961.

SAHLINS, MARSHALL D. *Social Stratification in Polynesia.* Seattle: University of Washington Press, 1958.

SANGREE, WALTER H. "The Bantu Tiriki of Western Kenya," in James L. Gibbs, Jr., ed., *Peoples of Africa* (New York: Holt, Rinehart and Winston, 1965), pp. 43–79.

SANSOM, G. B. *Japan: A Short Cultural History.* Rev. ed. New York: Appleton-Century-Crofts, 1962.

SCHAPERA, ISAAC. *Government and Politics in Tribal Societies.* London: Watts, 1956.

———. *A Handbook of Tswana Law and Custom.* 2d ed. London: Oxford University Press, 1955.

———. "Kinship and Politics in Tswana History," *Journal of the Royal Anthropological Institute,* 93, pt. 1 (June 1963), 134–154; 93, pt. 2 (Dec. 1963), 159–173.

———. "The Political Organization of the Ngwato of Bechuanaland

Protectorate," in M. Fortes and E. E. Evans-Pritchard, eds., *African Political Systems* (London: Oxford University Press, 1940), pp. 56–82.

———. *The Tswana.* London: International African Institute, 1953.

SCHULTZE, A. *The Sultanate of Bornu.* Trans. P. A. Benton. London: Oxford University Press, 1913.

SCHUTZ, A. "The Stranger," *American Journal of Sociology,* XLIX, no. 6 (1944), 449–507.

SCHWARZ, WALTER. "Nigerians Want More Than Bribery Trials," *Observer* (London), May 8, 1966.

SHEDDICK, Y. G. J. *The Southern Sotho.* London: International African Institute, 1953.

SHEPPERSON, GEORGE, and THOMAS PRICE. *Independent African: John Chilembwe and the Origins, Setting, and Significance of the Nyasaland Native Rising of 1915.* Edinburgh: University Press, 1958.

SIMMEL, GEORG. *Conflict and the Web of Group-Affiliations.* Trans. Kurt H. Wolff and Reinhard Bendix. New York: Free Press of Glencoe, 1964.

———. "On the Significance of Numbers for Social Life," in Kurt H. Wolff, trans. and ed., *The Sociology of Georg Simmel* (Glencoe, Ill.: Free Press, 1950), pp. 97–98.

———. "Strangers," in G. Simmel, *Introduction to the Science of Society,* trans. R. Park and E. W. Burgess (Chicago: University of Chicago Press, 1924), pp. 322–327.

SIMMONS, D. "An Ethnographic Sketch of the Efik People," in Daryll Forde, ed., *Efik Traders of Old Calabar* (2d ed.; London: Oxford University Press, 1963), pp. 1–26.

SKINNER, ELLIOTT P. *The Mossi of the Upper Volta: The Political Development of a Sudanese People.* Stanford: Stanford University Press, 1964.

SKLAR, RICHARD L. *Nigerian Political Parties: Power in an Emergent African Nation.* Princeton: Princeton University Press, 1963.

SMITH, M. G. *Government in Zazzau, 1800–1950.* London: Oxford University Press, 1960.

———. "The Hausa of Northern Nigeria," in James L. Gibbs, Jr., ed., *Peoples of Africa* (New York: Holt, Rinehart and Winston, 1965), pp. 119–155.

———. "Historical and Cultural Conditions of Political Corruption among the Hausa," *Comparative Studies in Society and History,* 6, no. 2 (Jan. 1964), 164–194.

———. "The Jihad of Shehu dan Fodio: Some problems," in I. M. Lewis, ed., *Islam in Tropical Africa* (London: Oxford University Press, 1966), pp. 408–424.

———. "Kagoro Political Development," *Human Organization,* 19, no. 3 (1960), 137–149.

———. "Political Anthropology," in *International Encyclopedia of the Social Sciences* (New York: Macmillan, forthcoming).

———. "Secondary Marriage in Northern Nigeria," *Africa,* 23, no. 4 (1953), 304–312.

———. "The Social Organization and Economy of Kagoro." Unpublished MS, 1951.

———. "A Structural Approach to Comparative Politics," in David Easton, ed., *Varieties of Political Theory* (Englewood Cliffs, N.J.: Prentice-Hall, 1966), pp. 113–128.

———. "The Two Katsinas." Unpublished MS.

SMITH, PRUDENCE, ed. *Africa in Transition: Some BBC Talks on Changing Conditions in the Union and the Rhodesias.* London: Max Reinhardt, 1958.

SOUTHALL, AIDAN W. *Alur Society: A Study in Processes and Types of Domination.* Cambridge: Heffer, n.d. [1956].

SOUTHALL, AIDAN W., and P. C. W. GUTKIND. *Townsmen in the Making: Kampala and Its Suburbs.* Kampala: East African Institute of Social Research, 1956.

SOUTHWOLD, MARTIN. *Bureaucracy and Chiefship in Buganda: The Development of Appointive Office in the History of Buganda.* Kampala: East African Institute of Social Research, 1960.

SPENCER, HERBERT. *The Principles of Sociology.* New York: Appleton-Century, 1902. 3 vols.

SPENCER, PAUL. *The Samburu: A Study of Gerontocracy in a Nomadic Tribe.* London: Routledge and Kegan Paul, 1965.

SPIRO, HERBERT J. "The Rhodesias and Nyasaland," in Gwendolen M. Carter, ed., *Five African States: Responses to Diversity* (Ithaca: Cornell University Press, 1963), pp. 361–470.

SRINIVAS, M. N., Y. B. DAMIE, S. SHAHANI, and ANDRÉ BETEILLE. "Caste: A Trend Report and Bibliography," *Current Sociology,* XIII, no. 3 (1959).

STALIN, J. *Foundations of Leninism.* Rev. trans. New York: International Publishers, 1932.

STAMPP, KENNETH M. *The Peculiar Institution: Slavery in the Ante-Bellum South.* New York: Vintage Books, 1964.

STENNING, DERRICK J. "The Pastoral Fulani of Northern Nigeria," in James L. Gibbs, Jr., ed., *Peoples of Africa* (New York: Holt, Rinehart and Winston, 1965), pp. 361–402.

STENNING, DERRICK J. *Savannah Nomads: A Study of the Wodaabe Pastoral Fulani of Western Bornu Province, Northern Region, Nigeria.* London: Oxford University Press, 1959.

TANDON, YASH. "A Political Survey," in D. P. Ghai, ed., *Portrait of a Minority: Asians in East Africa* (London: Oxford University Press, 1965), pp. 65–88.

TAYLOR, BRIAN K. *The Western Lacustrine Bantu (Nyoro, Toro, Nyankore, Kiga, Haya and Zinza, with Sections on the Amba and Konjo).* London: International African Institute, 1962.

THOMPSON, C. H., and H. W. WOODRUFF. *Economic Development in Rhodesia and Nyasaland.* London: Dobson, 1954.

THOMPSON, LEONARD M. *Politics in the Republic of South Africa.* Boston: Little, Brown, 1966.

———. *The Republic of South Africa.* Boston: Little, Brown, 1966.

———. "The South African Dilemma," in Louis Hartz, ed., *The Founding of New Societies: Studies in the History of the United States, Latin America, South Africa, Canada, and Australia* (New York: Harcourt, Brace and World, 1964), pp. 178–218.

———. *The Unification of South Africa, 1902–1910.* Oxford: Clarendon Press, 1960.

TILLION, GERMAINE. *France and Algeria.* New York: Knopf, 1961.

TOCQUEVILLE, ALEXIS DE. *The Old Regime and the French Revolution.* Trans. Stuart Gilbert. Garden City: Doubleday Anchor Books, 1955.

TORDOFF, WILLIAM. "The Ashanti Confederacy," *Journal of African History*, 3, no. 3 (1962), 399–417.

TOYNBEE, ARNOLD J. *A Study of History.* London: Oxford University Press, 1934–1954. 10 vols.

TROUBWORST, ALBERT. "L'Accord de cliente et l'Organisation politique au Burundi," *Anthropologica*, n.s., 4, no. 1 (1962), 9–44.

———. "Le Burundi," in M. d'Hertefelt, A. Troubworst, and J. Scherer, *Les anciens royaumes de la Zone Interlacustrie Meridionale* (London: International African Institute, 1962), pp. 113–169.

TRUMAN, DAVID B. *The Governmental Process: Political Interests and Public Opinion.* New York: Knopf, 1962.

TURNBULL, COLIN M. *The Forest People.* New York: Simon and Schuster, 1961.

———. "The Mbuti Pygmies of the Congo," in James L. Gibbs, Jr., ed., *Peoples of Africa* (Holt, Rinehart and Winston, 1965), pp. 281–317.

ULLENDORFF, EDWARD. *The Ethiopians: An Introduction to Country and People.* London: Oxford University Press, 1965.

UNION OF SOUTH AFRICA. *Union Statistics for Fifty Years.* Pretoria: Government Printer, 1960.

VAN DEN BERGHE, PIERRE L. "Dialectic and Functionalism: Toward a Theoretical Synthesis," *American Sociological Review,* 28, no. 5 (Oct. 1963), 695–705.

VAN DER SPRENKEL, SYBILLE. *Legal Institutions in Manchu China: A Sociological Analysis.* London: Athlone Press of the University of London, 1962.

VANSINA, JAN. "A Comparison of African Kingdoms," *Africa,* 32, no. 4 (Oct. 1962), 324–335.

———. *Kingdoms of the Savanna.* Madison: University of Wisconsin Press, 1966.

VASILIEV, A. A. *History of the Byzantine Empire, 324–1453.* 2d English ed., rev. Madison: University of Wisconsin Press, 1958. 2 vols.

VON GRUNEBAUM, G. E. *French African Literature: Some Cultural Implications.* The Hague: Mouton, 1964.

VREELAND, HERBERT HAROLD, III. *Mongol Community and Kinship Structure.* 3d ed. New Haven: HRAF Press, 1962.

WAGNER, GUNTER. *The Bantu of North Kavirondo.* London: Oxford University Press, 1949–1956. 2 vols.

———. "The Political Organization of the Bantu of North Kavirondo," in M. Fortes and E. E. Evans-Pritchard, eds., *African Political Systems* (London: Oxford University Press, 1940), pp. 197–236.

WATSON, W. *Tribal Cohesion in a Money Economy.* Manchester: Manchester University Press, 1958.

WEBB, MAURICE, and KENNETH KIRKWOOD. *The Durban Riots and After.* Johannesburg: South African Institute of Race Relations, 1949.

WEBER, MAX. *The Sociology of Religion.* Trans. E. Fischoff. Boston: Beacon Press, 1963.

———. *The Theory of Social and Economic Organisation.* Trans. A. M. Henderson and Talcott Parsons. Edinburgh: William Hodge, 1947.

WELMERS, BEATRICE F. "African Languages and Political Administration." Unpublished MS, 1958.

WELMERS, WILLIAM E., and RUTH C. SLOAN. "A Preliminary Survey of Existing Resources for Training in African Languages and Linguistics." Prepared for Georgetown University's Institute of Language and Linguistics. Unpublished MS, Oct. 1957.

WHITAKER, C. S., JR. "Three Perspectives on Hierarchy: Political

Thought and Leadership in Northern Nigeria," *Journal of Commonwealth Political Studies,* III, no. 1 (March 1965), 1–19.

WHITE, C. N. M. "Clan, Chieftainship and Slavery in Luvale Political Organization," *Africa,* 27, no. 1 (1957), 59–74.

WHITELY, WILFRED. *Bemba and Related Peoples of Northern Rhodesia.* London: International African Institute, 1951.

WILLIAMS, R. M., JR. *Strangers Next Door: Ethnic Relations in American Communities.* Englewood Cliffs, N.J.: Prentice-Hall, 1964.

WILLIAMS, W. M. *Gosforth: The Sociology of an English Village.* London: Routledge and Kegan Paul, 1956.

WILLMOTT, PETER, and MICHAEL YOUNG. *Family and Class in a London Suburb.* London: Routledge and Kegan Paul, 1960.

WILLS, A. J. *An Introduction to the History of Central Africa.* London: Oxford University Press, 1964.

WILSON, GODFREY. *The Constitution of Ngonde.* Livingstone. Northern Rhodesia: Rhodes-Livingstone Institute, 1939.

———. "The Nyakyusa of South-Western Tanganyika," in Elizabeth Colson and Max Gluckman, ed., *Seven Tribes of British Central Africa* (Manchester: Manchester University Press, 1951), pp. 251–291.

WILSON, GODFREY, and MONICA WILSON. *The Analysis of Social Change.* Cambridge: The University Press, 1945.

WILSON, MONICA. "Effects on the Xhosa and Nyakyusa of Scarcity of Land," in D. Biebuyck, ed., *African Agrarian Systems* (London: Oxford University Press, 1963), pp. 374–391.

———. *Good Company: A Study of Nyakyusa Age-Villages.* London: Oxford University Press, 1951.

———. *Reaction to Conquest: Effects of Contact with Europeans on the Pondo of South Africa.* London: Oxford University Press, 1936.

WINANS, EDGAR V. *Shambala: The Constitution of a Traditional State.* Berkeley and Los Angeles: University of California Press, 1962.

WINTER, E. H. "The Aboriginal Political Structure of Bwamba," in John Middleton and David Tait, eds., *Tribes without Rulers: Studies in African Segmentary Societies* (London: Routledge and Kegan Paul, 1958), pp. 136–166.

———. *Bwamba: A Structural-Functional Analysis of a Patrilineal Society.* Cambridge: Heffer, 1956.

WIRTH, LOUIS. *The Ghetto.* Boston: Beacon Press, 1964.

WITTFOGEL, KARL A. *Oriental Despotism: A Comparative Study of Total Power.* New Haven: Yale University Press, 1957.

WITTFOGEL, KARL A., and FENG CHIA-SHENG. *History of Chinese Society: Liao (907–1125).* Transactions of the American Philosophical Society, n.s., vol. 36. Philadelphia, 1949.

WOLFF, KURT H., ed., and trans. *The Sociology of Georg Simmel.* Glencoe, Ill.: Free Press, 1950.

WOOD, MARGARET M. *The Stranger: A Study in Social Relationships.* New York: Columbia University Press, 1943.

WORSLEY, PETER M. *The Third World.* London: Wiedenfeld and Nicolson, 1964.

———. *The Trumpet Shall Sound: A Study of "Cargo" Cults in Melanesia.* London: MacGibbon and Kee, 1957.

WRAITH, RONALD E., and EDGAR SIMPKINS. *Corruption in Developing Countries.* London: Allen and Unwin, 1963.

WRIGLEY, C. C. "The Changing Economic Structure of Buganda," in L. A. Fallers, ed., *The King's Men: Leadership and Status in Buganda on the Eve of Independence* (London: Oxford University Press, 1964), pp. 16–63.

ZANZIBAR PROTECTORATE. *Notes on the Census of the Zanzibar Protectorate, 1948.* Zanzibar: Government Printer, 1953.

ZOLBERG, A. and V. "The Americanization of Frantz Fanon," *Public Interest* (Fall 1967), pp. 49–63.

Index

Index